CENTENNIAL SOUVENIR HISTORY

GOUVERNEUR MORRIS.

CENTENNIAL
SOUVENIR HISTORY

OF

GOUVERNEUR

ROSSIE, FOWLER, HAMMOND, EDWARDS,
DeKALB

———

COMMEMORATING

"OLD HOME WEEK"

AUGUST 24-30

1905

,f

WATERTOWN, NEW YORK
THE HUNGERFORD-HOLBROOK CO
1905

Aq 4379

HUNGERFORD HOLBROOK CO
PRINTERS
WATERTOWN N Y

FOREWORD.

THE history of Gouverneur has been written four times with greater or lesser detail   In that portion of this book written by myself, there has been no attempt to improve upon what has been done by those who have preceded me   Dr Hough who first wrote of the town in 1853 had the advantage of personal acquaintance with many of the pioneers   Durant, of Ogdensburg, and Pierce, of Canton, in collaboration, (L H Evarts, publisher) followed in 1878, using all the material gathered by Hough and extending it with the official records of towns, churches, business and other organizations, and personal histories of some of the more wealthy citizens   In 1870 Mrs C A Parker, of Gouverneur, made the first complete history of the town, for which she had unusual facilities in acquaintance with the immediate successors of the pioneers, as well as a few of the pioneers themselves   The land-office records of Judge Dodge were valuable aids to her also   She began collecting data nearly half a century prior to the publishing of her excellent work   In 1894 Gates Curtis, of Ogdensburg, followed, using Hough's and Mrs Parker's histories freely in his recital, but adding little to them, though presenting the record in more consecutive order and in different phraseology, and enlarging upon the later-day industries

For any historical event there can be but one correct history   Repetitions may have merit in literary style or accuracy of statement, but these advantages are of trifling import to the public   What I have set forth is largely new matter   It has been gathered and committed to paper within the space of three weeks   Its abrupt termination is chargeable to the exigencies of "Old Home Week" in which interest it is published   There is a mass of material never gathered awaiting the competent hand   It has just begun to pour in upon me when the call of the publisher for "copy" came   Most of it was too late to be used There is a general lack of appreciation of the historical value of written records of all kinds   It is not too much to say that any written paper, be it a simple receipt or book account, or letter, if fifty or more years in age, has a value   It may not seem relevant to the owner, or even to the historian now, but the future writer may be able to fix dates or facts by means of it, that may prove of great importance

I am indebted to many persons for data, old memoranda, scrap-books, legal and other documents, for which I am grateful   Many having priceless records have withheld them   For the former praise is inadequate, for the latter silence

FOREWORD

is none too profound To Mrs Erwin Barnes, Mrs Col Spencer, Mrs H L.
Smith Mrs Maria Lansing, Mrs Robert Dodge, Mrs E H Neary, Miss Emeline VanBuren, Mr B G Parker, Mr James Thrall, and many others, my
thanks are due To my co-editors who have prepared special papers on subjects pertaining to their several callings or interests, I can only express the
obligations of those who will read the book Their contributions make the volume of lasting value so that it is believed that, as a whole, no equally good presentation of the interests of Gouverneur has been published

To write of the town satisfactorily, at least two years time are needed
Records at Canton and Albany should be exhausted Every aged citizen should
be consulted Every written line with half a century between it and the historian should be scanned Time for deduction, and especially elimination, must
be taken Thus only can the most enduring work be done

It was a question how the book could be profusely illustrated and still leave
a margin for Old Home Week festivities It was solved by allowing no full page
or large portraits to appear, and by making every engraving of the same size
(about twenty per cent larger than were shown on the sample pages) thus giving no preferences The only departure from this is the frontispiece portrait
of Gouverneur Morris In the case of groups the cost was covered by large
subscriptions to the book, amounting in one case to $100 It was possible by
using one size of single portraits to make advantageous rates with engravers
and the reduced size also lent itself to grouping in a few instances as in the
Presidents of the Agricultural Society

Old Home Week has awakened great interest in local history It should
culminate in the formation of a Historical Society There will be relics and
memorabilia at the coming gathering that ought afterward to have a permanent
home, accessible to all A nucleus once formed will enlarge with the passing
years It will be the shrine to which every new find or resurrected manuscript
or legend will come The result will be of value to the public and the future
historian

Never since 1861 has any movement enlisted such unanimity in sentiment
and action as Old Home Week and the Memorial Arch The "knocker" has
been inconspicuous in numbers and personality His isolation was marked and
his tenacity of purse and purpose pitiful

Gouverneur, June 1, 1905   J S C

GOUVERNEUR—A MONOGRAPH.

By J. S. Corbin.

GOUVERNEUR was settled in 1805. In that year a party of four hardy pioneers from Hartford, Washington County, N. Y., started on foot from their homes and, with only a pocket compass to guide them, entered the trackless wilderness in search of "Cambray," the most westerly of the famous "Ten Towns." They passed around the southerly end of Lake George, and from that point followed, as well as intervening mountains and water-

courses permitted, the direction indicated by their compass, which must have been, singularly, almost if not exactly, the course of the southwesterly boundary of St. Lawrence County. These pioneers came at the solicitation of Dr. Richard Townsend, who was the land agent of Gouverneur Morris, the owner of a large territory in the county, the settlement of which, as was customary in those days, was promoted by special effort.

Jay S. Corbin.

The boundaries of the various counties in the state had before 1805 been determined, and the records were easily accessible to Dr. Townsend at Albany, so it is no stretch of credulity to infer that the course chosen was the same as laid by the surveyor of the southwestern boundary of the county, or S. 54 W. in technical language. This is the more probable as some histories assert that Dr. Townsend accompanied the first party through the wilderness. An extension of this line passes directly through Caldwell at the head of Lake George.

The names of the four pioneers mentoned were Isaac Austin, Eleazer Nichols, Willard Smith and Pardon Babcock.[1] Another list gives the names as Willard Smith, Isaac Austin, Pardon Babcock, John Alden, Ambi Higby and Morris Mead.[2] The little band was under the leadership of Dr. Townsend.[3] Still another history, distinguished for careful research and a trustworthy sifting of authorities, names the first four as above, and places the planning and direction of the expedition under the leadership of Isaac Austin.[4] This last account was obtained from the immediate descendants of Mr. Austin, and the acquaintanceship of the author with the Austin family was such as to entitle her record to the fullest confidence.

The statement with which this account begins, namely, the date of settlement of the town, is not made without the best authority. The first pioneers while intending to reach "Cambray" in fact emerged from the wilderness at what is now known as East Dekalb, but then as "Smith Settlement," or about twelve miles from the location they finally selected. After a brief stop near

---

(1) Gazeteer of New York, 1860.   (2) Hough's History of St. Lawrence and Franklin Counties, 1853.   (3) History of St. Lawrence County by Gates Curtis, 1894   (4) History of Gouverneur by Mrs. C. A. Parker.

the present site of Gouverneur village, they returned to their Washington county homes, to prepare for a more lengthy stay, the selection of land, and the preparation for moving their families to the new country. Equipped with provisions and the few tools necessary for building the primitive log cabin needed for protection, they again started in the fall of the same year, 1805, this time with horses, and by way of the Black River Country, reaching the spot they had before camped upon, in early October. They left their horses at Boon's Upper Settlement, now known as Boonville in Oneida County, as the trail from there was impassable save to men on foot. The record is that they obtained a surveyor, Col. Barton Edsall of Madrid, (afterward Waddington) and began clearing the forest away. Necessarily this involved the location of definite boundaries and this was the first work of the surveyor. These acts constituted a settlement, in fact and in law, albeit the first deed issued was early in the following year. With the then slow methods of travel, and the necessity for making transfers through Morris, the distant owner, it is not probable that any deeds could have been received by Dr. Townsend for delivery and record earlier than 1806.

Early in the last named year, the pioneers brought their families and the more extended and successful efforts for the clearing of the lands and the growing of crops for sustenance began.

It is not the purpose of this account to repeat the historical researches made by others, nor to paraphrase them under a new, verbal dress. Only such salient points will be touched upon as are necessary to give a running glance at the general trend of events during the early years, in order to connect them with later history. The field up to about 1870 has been well gleaned and nothing of supreme interest can be added to this date. The time to write history is while history is in the making. Many pens have done this for Gouverneur so well that nothing of remote happening is left to be recorded. That remarkable

Dr. Franklin B. Hough.

historian, Dr. Franklin B. Hough, has recited the earlier history of much of this northern country with infinite detail and painstaking accuracy and subsequent historians, who have extended his record on to later times, have drawn from his exhaustless researches liberally. It is one of the cherished memories of the writer of these lines that Dr. Hough while living at Somerville, N. Y., took enough interest in his boyish enthusiasms to take him upon his knee and show him his large collection of curiosities, a cabinet of minerals of great rarity and Indian relics gathered from the various tribes then in the state under the direction of the state authorities. And the parting gift was some duplicate sheets of the state report upon the Indian tribes, sent him for revision by the state printer before binding, and filled with pictures of pipes, tomahawks and wampum.

Cambray as originally mapped by the surveyor-general of the state, contained 64,000 acres and was ten miles square. It embraced all of the present town of Gouverneur and nearly one-half of the present town of Macomb In 1841 by act of legislature, the portion of Macomb named was detached and since that date the boundaries of Gouverneur have remained intact until 1904 when the Board of Supervisors of the county detached from Macomb a small portion from its southerly corner, containing about two square miles, and attached the same to Gouverneur Future maps of both towns will hereafter have less regular outlines as this change substitutes a zigzag line about two miles long, having many angles and windings, for the old boundary which was the northerly leg of the famous "Oxbow" Of the original "Ten Towns" only Canton, Potsdam and Lisbon have retained their first boundaries Probably this is due to the location of the principal place of business, mills, markets and town meetings, which in the towns named were near the center of the ten-mile square

Early in 1807 the population of Gouverneur was increased by the coming of eight more families, namely Dr John Spencer, Stephen and Benjamin Smith, Israel Porter, Stephen Patterson, Daniel Austin, Isaac Morgan, and Dr Townsend, the land agent of Gouverneur Morris, removed his family to the new settlement from their Washington county home All these took up lands within two or three miles of the present site of the village, Mr Morgan's log cabin is remembered as being located near where the farm house of A L Freeman now stands There are still some evergreen trees standing that mark the site of the primitive rooftree A local authority gives the site of this cabin as nearly opposite the brick house of Mrs I W Stacey The first bridge spanning the Oswegatchie in town was built in the summer of this year by Isaac Kendall, costing $500, and some of the more elderly of our citizens will remember that the only pier required was midway between the eastern shore and the first island Nature provided the other supports in the two islands and the four spans were thus happily within the measure of the great stringers cut from the nearby forest "The bridge had no railing save the heavy beams pinned to the sides for protection"[1] The original pier was replaced by one of sandstone, laid without mortar, when James Parker built another bridge twelve years later, and this stood intact with one replacement, (the one having a railing of turned balusters), until twenty-eight years ago when the present iron bridge was built spanning the entire reach and rendering a pier unnecessary The pier foundation of flattened logs, when removed, was found to be as sound as when first placed in the river bed During the present Centennial year, a new plate girder bridge will be erected at a cost of about $18,000, the present abutments being so well preserved as to need no change save a relaying of the top courses or a substitution of concrete caps of one to two feet in thickness This bridge will be the fifth crossing the Oswegatchie at Main street The first three bridges were located a trifle farther down stream than now and their floors were about three feet lower than at present Later, in 1807, came Colburn Barrel and Roswell Wilder and in 1808 Joel Wilder, James Parker, John Parker, Ephraim Case, Jonathan S Colton (locally known as "Strong" Colton) Wm Cleghorn,

_____
[1] Mrs Parker

Henry Welch, Jeremiah Merithew, Jesse Dewey, Stephen Patterson, James Thompson, James Haile and Jonathan Payne. The names of many of these pioneers are still found in this and adjoining towns and probably the major part of them are perpetuated by descendants under other names. The blood of sturdy old Isaac Austin's family still courses in the veins of the Holbrooks, Cushmans, Waids, Nortons, Corbins and other families, while those who bear relationship to the Smiths number several hundred. The pioneers came here to settle and they staid after coming. There are wandering pioneers who continue the business of pioneering all their lives and some of them by successive removals have traversed the entire span of the continent. Our ancestry was not of this class.

In 1808 also came Timothy Sheldon from Pawtucket, Rhode Island, the first from that state, Reuben Noble, Wm. W. Rhodes, Richard Kimball, and the

Capt. Rockwell Barnes.

famous builder and millwright, Capt. Rockwell Barnes. From the oldest carpenter in town who knew Capt. Barnes while in his activities, it is learned that he was famous at "pushing" the work in hand, enjoyed taking large and difficult jobs and that he was, as usual with that class of workmen, not a master at fine carpentry. He was a man of tremendous activity and enterprise.

"From this time forward settlements increased rapidly and farms were cleared from year to year from the original forest."[1] How rapidly the town grew from this time until the present is shown by the following table taken from the U. S. and state census returns:

1810......227	1845......2600	1875......3830
1820......765	1850......2738	1880......4165
1825.....1267	1855......2856	1885......no census.
1830.....1552	1860......3201	1890......3851
1835.....1796	1865......2915	1895......no census.
1840.....2538	1870......3539	1900......3915

The table is instructive. The growth was rapid, as will be seen, during the first forty years. The panic of 1837, famous in financial annals, checked the growth so that the increase in the five years from 1840 to 1845 was less than one hundred, or less than one-half the increase due to births alone. There could have been no accessions from 1840 to 1855, inclusive, by immigration. The division of the town in 1841 took away a small number, probably not many as "for many years the settlements were limited to small neighborhoods on the state road and no schools were opened until 1818."[2] Even as late as 1850, the population of Macomb was only about 1400.

The student of economics of a later day, well understands how this condition, amounting practically to a retrogression, might have easily been ameliorated by the national government and much distress, not only in the town but

---

(1) Curtis.   (2) Curtis' History.

in the nation at large, have been averted Being a question of volume of currency, it was only necessary to increase that volume Any circulating medium endowed with the supreme power to pay debts and taxes, would have met the emergency fully, whether such medium were made of metal, or paper or both materials The material used is nothing, the law that is put in it is the omnipotent factor

About seventy years anterior to this period of sore distress among the early settlers of the town, Gouverneur Morris, for whom the town was named graduated at "King's College," now Columbia He was seventeen years of age and a little later we find he was engaged in public matters by way of discussions and political contentions "He had been admitted to the bar and had a restless craving for excitement."[1] It is recorded that at this period of young Morris' life there was also a dearth of money The people called loudly for more as was natural, and he answered them in almost exactly the terms that Wall Street and the controllers of money answered a similar call at a later day He told them that it would bring bankruptcy, that it was a putting-off of the date of payment that must be made anyhow, that "artificial credit" (whatever that is) would cause farmers and speculators to go deeper into debt, and indeed, all the stock arguments so familiar to us who passed through a similar experience after 1879 Morris was the scion of a landed aristocracy He imbibed the prejudices of that class and had little sympathy with those who aspired to better their material condition He was thoroughly in accord with that spirit later personified in Alexander Hamilton—the rights of special privilege, and the rule of wealth

At this time we find him writing, before taking a trip abroad, giving as his reason for going that it was "to form my manners and address by the example of the truly polite, to rub off in the gay circle a few of the many barbarisms which characterize a provincial education, and to curb the vain self-sufficiency which arises from comparing ourselves with companions who are inferior to us "[2] That discloses the home atmosphere in which he was bred and, incidentally, it is of interest to remember that England governed the territory in which he was nurtured and England, therefore, inspired the sentiments quoted, as well as those he uttered against an increase of money when it was needed We had the same influence at work after our Civil War, for it is unfortunately true that the Republic has never been free from those in high governmental places who toady to English opinion, and English opinion as it reaches us is but the reflex of a decadent and aristocratic dogmatism Lombard and Wall streets are always in sympathy and interest One is no farther removed from true Americanism than the other The adolescent Morris during the years between his graduation and his majority, must be written down as an insufferable prig It is distinctly a happiness to find him awakened at the age of 23, by the reverberations from Concord and Lexington and Bunker Hill!

It has occasionally been claimed by newspaper correspondents that Gouverneur furnished a thousand men during the civil war A glance at the table

(1) Gouverneur Morris by Theodore Roosevelt, 1888   (2) Roosevelt

discloses that the whole population of the town in 1860 was but 3201, less than
one-sixth of which could have been eligible for military service   The census record of 1865 tells the story of those gloomy days much more truthfully   The
population had fallen off some three hundred in the previous five years   The
natural increase was probably not less than 300 more, so those who went to the
front must have numbered considerably less than one-third the newspaper state
ments   The writer's remembrance is that there was some movement toward
the "Genesee country" around the forties, and this disturbs any definite conclusions as to variation of population

The growth of the town since 1860 has been reasonably rapid considering
the large number of removals to the west   The "prairie schooner" with its
white sheet covering over bows bent from green saplings, freighted with the
family and the lighter household goods, was a not unfamiliar sight fifty or sixty
years ago, even in this region adjacent to the great lakes, by which route the
greater number journeyed   Then followed the railways and the western pil-
grimage was accomplished thereafter by their use, and it has continued unin-
terruptedly until the present

Gouverneur was first known under its present name in 1810   April 5th
of that year the original ten mile square which had borne the name of "Cambray" was named after its owner, Gouverneur Morris   The boundaries remained intact until 1841, when about one-third of the area lying north of Beaver
Creek was detached as has been mentioned   Undoubtedly this change in outline
came about from the fact that the village of Gouverneur was located so near the
southern boundary that travel from the opposite side of the township for town-
meetings, courts and other purposes, was something of an undertaking with the
roads as they must have existed at that time   Had the four pioneers, unhin-
dered by the tortuous Oswegatchie at Little Bow, chanced upon the water-power
at Elmdale as they left "Smith Settlement" in search for "Cambray," it is not
an illogical inference that the boundaries of Gouverneur would today stand
"four-square to every wind that blows "

About the year 1806, the stone "mansion" of Gouverneur Morris must have
been built near the "natural dam" nearly two miles down the river from the
village   The conception of the rigors of a northern winter by Mr Morris is
shown by its being built in a hillside with one-half of its walls buried and the rear
portion facing the north, wholly devoid of windows   So far as the writer is
aware there is no other example of this style of architecture in the town save
that of Benjamin Smith of the Bow   His ancient brick dwelling was pat-
terned somewhat after the type of the Morris erection and is still in fine
preservation   The second land agent of the proprietor, lived in the Morris
building some years   Its primary purpose, however, was as a summer home for
Mr Morris during his annual visits to his domains   Roger Maddock was the
second agent   The date of his occupancy of the place was about 1816, the
year of Mr Morris' death [1]   The solid character of the walls is attested by

---

[1] History of St Lawrence County   L H Evarts   1878

their standing intact today after almost a century, save a crack in the wall caused by earthquake shock Dec. 18, 1867.

It has been occupied for nearly a century as a farm residence, but occasionally has done duty as a storehouse of odds and ends. It is one of the quaint curiosities of the town. It is not known that Mr. Morris occupied it more than

twice on his annual visits to his northern lands. One of these visits was in 1809, and it is remembered that he then boarded ten or twelve workmen while they were building the first grist and saw mills in the town. These were not his first visits, however, to northern New York, as he was a guest of Nathan Ford, at

The Morris " Mansion "

Ogdensburg, several years earlier. It was his intention to found a village there and to this end he laid off a mile square adjoining the "natural dam" (a rock crossing the river and forming a complete dam giving a fall of seventeen feet without artificial addition) but his plans were frustrated by the building of the bridge at the present village in the previous year, to opening of the first store by John Brown in 1809 near the easterly end of the bridge, and finally in 1816 by the grist and saw mills of Israel Porter and others at the westerly end of the bridge. These improvements seem to have determined the site of the village and as the death of Mr. Morris followed in 1816, "Morris Mills" as Natural Dam was then called, ceased to attract residents and the mile square was cut up into farms and sold soon afterward. About this latter date occurred the difficulty between Dr. Townsend and Mr. Morris, the tradition of which is well preserved, and it resulted in Mr. Townsend's discharge and the employment of Roger Maddock mentioned above.

A sketch of Dr. Townsend's life is not without interest on account of the part he played in the first history of the town from 1805 to 1816. He was born in Hebron, Washington County, a few miles from Hartford, from which place the first settlers and himself set out in their journey through the trackless wilderness in 1805. He removed to Delhi, Delaware County, after studying medicine, engaged in the lumber business and as this took him to the city of New York occasionally, he became acquainted with Gouverneur Morris. This resulted in his appointment as agent for the sale of the lands in this section of the county. After his quarrel with his principal, he remained in Gouverneur many years, and it is recorded of him that he took up the practice of his profession during the epidemic of typhus fever in 1813, of which no published account is accessible, but finally removed to Philadelphia, Jefferson County, then known as Quaker Settlement, and died there in 1826, the year that marked the close of the lives of two presidents, Adams and Jefferson. He was buried at the latter place. In 1900 his son, Robert Wilson Townsend, came to visit the scenes of his birth and childhood and received the warmest welcome from the citizens. He was one of the students at the Seminary in 1834, his name appearing in the second catalogue of that institution, erroneously given, probably as "Henry" though Benjamin M. Townsend lived in town that year and had "five male persons" in his household, two of whom were not subject to military duty. His

Lean A. Townsend

death occurred in August, 1904, in Southern Illinois. His son, Lean A. Townsend, grandson of Dr. Townsend, is at this writing cashier in a bank at Galesburg, Ill. The Doctor took up land where the farm of Wallace McKean now is, built a portion of the house now occupied by McKean, used it as a hotel for some years and afterward built the house in Gouverneur village now occupied by Fred Fuller, which is generally known as the "Townsend House." The creek flowing into the Oswegatchie just below the bridge of the Aldrich Paper Co., is known as the Townsend Creek.

Several historians recite that Dr. Townsend owned the only slave, a negress, ever brought into the town, but this is probably an error as the tradition exists that Dr. John Spencer, an 1807 settler, and Benjamin Leavitt, who came about 1808, both brought men slaves, a not unusual event in the annals of the county, as Nathan Ford, of Ogdensburg, land agent for Samuel Ogden, had a slave and Major John Borlund, of DeKalb, also brought one, a woman, when he came here from Massachusetts. Slavery was lawful at that date in New York State, a repeal of the act not becoming operative until July 4, 1827, so no reflections can be cast upon those who retained ownership of the labor of negroes, and this is all the slavery that ever existed in this nation, or in the colonies, under the protection of law, namely, the right to the labor, not to the persons, of men of color. It was much like the right of a master to the service of an indentured apprentice. "It existed in every state that adopted the Constitution in 1788."[1] The author quoted declares that when the Northern states passed anti-slavery laws, those owning this species of property, made haste to sell their holdings to the South before the laws became operative. There is neither history nor tradition connecting any person with such traffic in this town or county. "In 1810 St. Lawrence County had five slaves. The state then contained 14,638."[2] The two instances in

---

[1] Alexander H. Stephens, War Between the States. 1870.   [2] Hough.

Gouverneur were nothing more than the provision of homes for dependent people from motives of obligation or charity

The fact of the intimate business and personal relations of Gouverneur Morris with the land agent for this section, Dr Townsend, and the further fact of the ownership of a colored woman by the latter, makes the attitude of Morris of much interest on the subject of slavery It was Morris who was entrusted with the final draft of the Constitution, and it was he who wrote therein, "No person held to service or labor in one state under the laws thereof, escaping into another, shall, in consequence of any law or regulation therein be discharged from such service or labor, but shall be delivered up on claim of the party to whom such service or labor may be due" We may regard Morris' work, however, as but a clerical one and that he simply embalmed in words the sentiment of the convention as set forth in long-continued debate, sometimes accompanied with acrimony and resistance

"Slavery, however, aroused his enmity on much broader grounds than those of political power He had already striven for abolition in the New York convention, and he renewed the struggle on the National field On moving to insert the word 'free' before 'inhabitants' he made a speech of great force and eloquence, beginning

" 'Much will depend on this point I will never concur in upholding domestic slavery It is a nefarious institution It is the curse of heaven on the states where it prevails' "[1] Morris, as has already been adverted to, was in much sympathy with English opinion at this period of his life He was but thirty-six years of age and England had been for some time in the throes of an anti-slavery movement Not that Morris was a servile copyist of any one's opinion, but he was conversant with all great issues and must, perforce, have agreed or disagreed with each

The personality of Gouverneur Morris must always remain a matter of great interest to the town to which he gave his name He was born in 1752 at the feudal residence in Morrisiana, ten miles north of the City Hall in New York His birthplace had been in the family for three generations, the Morris family being holders of a considerable tract of land under colonial patent in the southern portion of Westchester county, this patent running back to the year 1697 The Morris family were among the aristocrats of the time when English customs prevailed in the colonies, then under jurisdiction of the mother country Large landed estates were the foundation of the privileged classes in England, and the social system there prevalent was fast becoming engrafted upon the colonies when the Revolution checked the spread of monarchical ideas, and the diffusion of democratic equality became the watchword thenceforth

In a considerable sense, Morris wrote his own biography Not in a formal way, but he was an industrious correspondent, a voluminous writer on national and other public topics and he preserved copies of whatever he wrote It is mostly from these sources that we derive whatever information in a personal way we have of the man Roosevelt says that Morris was unfortunate in having

---

[1] Henry Cabot Lodge in Atlantic Monthly for April, 1886

so turgid a biographer as Jared Sparks, a contemporary, who filled three goodly sized volumes with selections, and omitted the original matter that might have been had first hand, at the time he wrote   Whatever the cause, Gouverneur Morris has never had justice done to his memory in popular estimation

"He was a man of the world and of society, a wit, a philosopher, and a fine gentleman, he was also a bold and ardent patriot, an able and most practical statesman, a distinguished lawyer, and a successful manager of large business affairs "[1]   Most of his letters contain some satirical sentence or allusion, for he was famous as a keen and incisive wit   In 1815 he wrote, "The people must feel before they can think   Expect heroism from a sheep, charity from a wolf, and music from a crow, and perhaps you may not be disappointed, but do not expect, or even hope for reason from the populace "   To one who sympathized with him on the loss of his leg, he said, "Oh sir the loss is much less than you imagine, I shall doubtless be a steadier man with one leg than with two " The accident he suffered occurred in 1785 in Philadelphia   "In his capacity of young man of fashion, he used to drive about town in a phaeton with a pair of small, spirited horses, and because of some whim, he would not allow the groom to stand at their heads   So one day they took flight, ran, threw him out and broke his leg   The leg had to be amputated and he was ever afterwards forced to wear a wooden one."[2]   So, when Morris visited Gouverneur in 1808-9 he must have stumped about "Morris Mills" while building his grist and saw mills, and while planning the future village that was to occupy the mile square he laid out for the purpose

Whatever whimsicalities Morris exhibited during his life, and they were many, he undoubtedly came honestly by them   His father in 1760 inserted this clause in his will

"My son, Gouverneur, shall have the best education obtainable, but never be sent for that purpose to the Connecticut Colony, lest he imbibe in his youth the corruption and cunning so inherent in the character of the people of that colony, which is so interwoven in their constitutions, that they cannot conceal it, although by means of the sanctified garb of religion, they labor to impose themselves upon the world for honest men "

In view of the fact that Yale and Harvard were both in the vigorous years of their formative period, and though in different colonies with similar curriculums, this admoniton was undoubtedly intended to guard the youthful Gouverneur from the insidious teachings prevalent in both institutions   Some enterprising Connecticut Yankee must have sold him a wooden ham!

Morris' claim to historic remembrance will rest chiefly upon these things he first suggested the Erie canal, he made the final draft of the Constitution of the United States he invented the coinage system adopted by the National government, he wrote the Constitution of the State of New York, as a member of the Continental Congress he was foremost in every effort to shake off the tyranny of England, he was Minister to France, as a statesman, he was intent upon the good of his country though sometimes mistaken as to policy, as

(1) Henry Cabot Lodge (2) Roosevelt

a lawyer he was original, forceful, pugnacious, and brilliant. He opposed the doubling of the tariff in 1816 at a time when it was about one-fourth as burdensome as now; he advocated "hard money" taking his initiative from Adam Smith and the school he engendered; he opposed Jefferson in the latter's advocacy of entrusting the people fully with the people's affairs; he maintained all his life a singular inclination toward aristocratic customs, privileged classes and a landed gentry, and he championed the cause of the disunionists at the Hartford Convention. In 1812-14 he opposed the war with England although he had been the foremost champion of the Revolution against her aggressions. These are blots upon an otherwise fair escutcheon and we may well overlook them in view of his great services to his country.

Gouverneur Morris 4th.

This brief and necessarily imperfect recital of the salient points in the career of Gouverneur Morris, may well be brought to a close by the prediction he made in 1801, which has been closely fulfilled.

"The proudest empire in Europe is but a bauble compared to what America will be, must be, in the course of two centuries, perhaps of one! If with a calm retrospect to the progress made within forty years, we stand on the firm ground of calculation, warranted by experience, and look forward to the end of a similar period, imagination shrinks from the magnitude of rational deduction."

The first death among the settlers was that of Emily Porter, two years old, daughter of Israel Porter. This was in August, 1808, and it brought to the minds of the pioneers that they had made no provision for the burial of the dead. In fact, they could not have acted officially in securing such a spot for the town was without officers as yet, the first election occurring almost three years later. The town still carried the name of Cambray and this continued until 1810 when it was changed to Gouverneur. In the month following the death referred to, however, the citizens appealed to Mr. Morris for the donation of a burying-ground, and the deed illustrated was prepared and sent to the settlers immediately. It is drawn in the stately hand of Mr. Morris, and we are indebted to the fact of its irregular character for its being wholly written instead of a half printed document. It recites that: "Whereas the inhabitants of Cambray, have requested the grant of a piece of two acres of land for a burial ground, and have solicited a part of lot No. 85, beginning at a post standing due east from the Island Falls forty links above the pitch of water, and 7 chains 32 links from the high water mark, and running thence south five chains and fifty links, thence east three chains and sixty-four links, and thence north five chains and fifty links, and thence west three chains and sixty-four links. I do hereby devote the above place to the burial of the dead and will execute a grant therefor to the town, when incorporated. In witness thereof I have hereunto set my hand and seal the tenth day of September, in the year of our Lord, 1808.

Sealed and Delivered   GOUVERNEUR MORRIS

in the presence of

Deed from Gouverneur Morris of two acres for a burying ground.

Whether an actual deed was ever given in the place of this promise to give one, is unknown. The "two acres" became overcrowded by 1860, and the growth of the village had brought the tract well within the built-up portions. In the year named the Riverside Cemetery was laid out, containing thirty-six acres, which have been twice extended by additional purchases. The removal of bodies from the gift of Mr. Morris began April 28, 1860. Thomas M. Thayer was in charge of the removal and his account book of the work has been preserved. The entire two acres was dug over and many burials were found of which there was neither record or headstone. These unknown were buried in a plot by themselves in the new cemetery. The record is explicit in details of all such, giving the location as well as possible in relation to surrounding buildings, or other graves which were well marked and known. The total removals were 637 and the time occupied in the work, which appears to have been continuous, was two weeks. The well known accuracy of Mr Thayer, and the account from which this record is drawn, made by his own hand, is reliable and the statement in other histories placing the number of removals at "over 700" is erroneous. "No trace of the remains of the first occupant, the little child of Israel Porter, were discovered."[1]

The inevitable missionary made his appearance early. Two came in 1806 and Isaac Austin, who seems to have been a devout sectarian, gave them the use of his house in which to hold services. It would seem from the account as recorded in one history, that they alternated with a Methodist preacher from the "Rich Settlement" now Richville, in holding Sabbath exercises, both using Mr Austin's hospitable roof, though the latter was of the Baptist persuasion. The record of all religious movements in the town is well preserved in the various histories published, and no repetition will be made here. The latest accession to the already numerous churches as yet unrecorded, is the Unitarian, having a handsome building on Trinity Avenue, unique in architecture, well adapted to its purpose and devoid of exterior suggestion as to its intended use. When it is realized that Christian righteousness is simply personal rightness, dividing dogmas will depart and unification will take the place of division. It is the unessentials that engender theological strife. It is a happiness to read that the first settlers all joined in worship. We have yet to learn again the lesson that conduct is the vital essence, and creed but the imperfect expression of it, with all the crude mistakes incident to human fallibility. The "Church Universal" is not a dream!

The memory of a good woman who came with the pioneers of 1807 deserves mention as other writers have passed her praiseworthy deeds by. "Aunt Fanny Dewey," wife of Jesse Dewey, mother of Warren, Maria, Lucy and Noah Dewey, is remembered as one who gave her best care to every sick and sorrowing neighbor and whose log cabin door carried a latchstring in easy reach of every one in want. She was of sweet and womanly nature and her children, (the writer names only those he remembers) were worthy of her. Maria, was a school teacher for many years and as such had no superiors in the town. Her penmanship was, to youthful eyes at least, a model, and her dominion in the school room was characterized by that obedience due only to superior excellence. Warren has only recently passed into the unknown hereafter, at the ripe age of ninety. Noah early went to the then far west, settling in Napoleon, Ohio, and became wealthy as a merchant. Lucy, wife of Harvey Smith, mother of Brayton and Burton Smith, long since ceased her earthly journey. There

(1) Evarts History 1878

still survives of the children of Aunt Fanny one daughter in Carthage, Missouri.

This recital recalls that Aunt Fanny's place was taken later by another Dewey, not related or at least only remotely, to the excellent woman mentioned. She was the wife of Eleazer Dewey, living near the Dekalb line on the Richville road. In 1840 or thereabout, the Thompsonian system of treatment for the sick had a considerable following in the town. Mrs. Dewey became a convert and it is remembered how she carried the youthful of the neighborhood through the mumps, measles, chicken-pox and scarlet fever, with herbal medicines gathered by herself, assisted by wet-sheet packs and hydropathic treatment generally as the disease seemed to her to warrant. And while memory lasts, the smile with which she greeted her patients every morning as she came to their bedside, will remain vivid and this poor and belated tribute is all one of them can offer to prove his gratitude.

It is interesting to trace the history of the Thompson family. James Thompson was born in 1783 at Hartford, Washington County, N. Y., from which place came the first four settlers of Gouverneur.

The Thompson Family—Four Generations.

He was early married to Betsy Downs, daughter of "Squire Downs" of Hartford, and in 1808 came to Gouverneur, bought fifty acres of land of the "Morris tract" from Dr. Richard Townsend, paying four dollars an acre for it.

He was more fortunate than some of the early settlers as he was able to pay at once for his purchase. Here he began clearing land upon which to erect some rude buildings and also for a place for small crops, then returned to Hartford, and in 1810, removed all his earthly possessions to his newly purchased land.

He hired a man to transfer his household goods in a wagon and on top of these treasures was placed a feather bed whereon there rode in state for these long, weary two hundred miles, his young wife and infant son. Mr. Thompson himself drove the oxen, cows, sheep and pigs. This family endured many of the hardships common to pioneer life.

A small log house sheltered them for a time but later on the rapidly increasing family demanded more spacious quarters, and a second log house was built, larger and containing many additional conveniences. Here a large family was housed for many years until the house now standing was built. The fifth child, James Harvey, has always remained upon the farm his father chose and cleared, and in the house he assisted to erect in 1835.

Eleven children came to this wilderness home Two died in early infancy, while eight stalwart sons and one daughter grew up to bless the home.

Mr. Thompson died in 1845 and his wife twenty years later

When the Baptist Church was organized, we find the name of Mrs Betsy Thompson among the constituent members Mr Thompson subsequently joined the church and for many years led the choir, in fact his family often constituted the choir An old near neighbor enjoys telling of the days when two of the boys "carried the soprano," the older ones taking the other parts It was a proud day for the lads, Oscar and Harvey, when they rose to sing God's praises in the sanctuary arrayed in some new red vests made from their mother's broadcloth cloak This family was especially musical, and many of the next generation still consider no harmonies sweeter than the singing heard when a number of these brothers met and sang their old anthems, hymns and "select pieces "

The oldest son, Abram Downs, followed his father as choir leader and was also not unfrequently "lay reader" in the absence of the pastor

He married Deborah Columbia, daughter of Dr Wolcott Griffin, long a practicing physician of those earlier days

These eight brothers soon scattered far and wide, going east and west and now but three survive, James Harvey who still walks among us bearing well his eighty-five years, surrounded by his children to the fourth generation, and enjoying the well-earned rest which has come to him in the sunset of life Beside him there remain Judson Morris, the tenth child, who for over forty years has been a resident of St. Louis, and Joseph Sawyer, the youngest of the family

It would appear from data relating to the families resident in the town in 1809, that the following settlers came during that year William Colton, Elkanah Partridge, Joseph Bolton, Ahohab (misnamed "Holeab" in some histories) Smith, Caleb Drake, Benjamin Clark, James Barnes, Calvin Bullock, Ephraim Gates, Colburn Barrell, Reuben Nobles, Richard Kemble, (who may have been Richard Kimball who came the previous year), John Hovt, Daniel Austin and Medad Cole "Besides these, William Canning, Sela Coleman, Alfred Cole, Harvey Black, Charles McLane, James and John Parker, Josiah Ward, and a few others being mostly single men, were living in town or came in soon after "[1] Josiah Ward subsequently married Patty Austin, daughter of the pioneer of 1805, while another daughter, Rebecca, married Henry B Holbrook, a later accession to the early settlers who came in 1813 and took up land four miles from the village on the Richville Road, building a log cabin and making a considerable clearing He was succeeded by Gilbert Rundell well remembered as a barn builder and expert in the use of the broad-axe Rundell subsequently went to Wisconsin, and the only letter the writer remembers to have seen that was arranged in the style current in revolutionary and colonial days, namely, on a very large sheet of paper, exceeding our foolscap size, folded and tucked in and sealed with a red wafer, in place of the modern envelope, was written by Gilbert Rundell after he reached Wisconsin in a "prairie schooner." Sixty years and more ago, the art of correctly indicting, folding,

(1) Hough's History

sealing and addressing a letter was taught by every schoolmaster, and the excellent penmanship of the early days attests the thoroughness of the instruction. The postage indicated by the sending office, was one shilling, written in the English style.

Rundell was in turn succeeded by Amasa Corbin, Sr., the Henry B. Holbrook tract thus becoming a part of the Corbin farm of about four hundred acres, being the part lying westerly of the road. The plow has not yet obliterated the site of the cabin cellar, the cabin being occupied by Corbin several years after his purchase in 1830 until his frame residence, copied after a prevalent New England style, (himself and wife coming from Berkshire County, Mass.), was built, after which the cabin was taken down.

Josiah Waid was sheriff of the county from 1847 to 1849. He built the large frame house still standing in fine preservation, in North Main Street on the highest rise of ground within the corporation limits. The character of the owner for thoroughness is shown by the present condition of the building, which after more than seventy-five years stands true to plumb and level from sill to ridge-tree.

Josiah Waid.

Alfred Cole first settled on the farm owned by the late Henry Noble, near the Creek on the "Scotch Settlement" road, but becoming involved in some contention with Gouverneur Morris, abandoned that place for another location three miles easterly on the Ford tract, where he settled on a farm now owned by J. Frank Cole in the easterly part of the town. Probably he owned about 1855, the oldest team of horses the town has boasted, one being 28 and the other 29 at the date named, neither having ever been shod or broken to the saddle.

Colburn Barrell settled on land opposite the present residence of Gray B. Sheldon, built a frame house thereon which stood until recently, but, being unoccupied many years, fell into decay. The spring nearby was doubtless a determining factor with Mr. Barrell in selecting this location instead of the more sightly one on the hill nearby.

Medad Cole was a shoemaker and pursued his calling among the older population up to about 1845, moving his bench and tools wherever work offered. It is remembered that for several years he did the boot and shoe making in the family of the writer's father, staying usually about ten days each year. It was customary then for farmers to have their hides and skins tanned "at the halves," the portion coming to themselves being manufactured into footwear by the most accessible cobbler. Medad Cole was the first to marry in the town, his wife being a Miss Patterson of whom the histories give no more than her name.

Ephriam Case settled on a farm in the southeastern corner of the town, lived there many years and reclaimed a goodly sized area from the wilderness. He purchased the "service or labor" of the colored woman brought from Washington county by Dr. Townsend, but subsequently returned her, as failing health on the part of the woman made the transaction of doubtful value to him A part of his original farm is now owned by Fred B Hill He was a strict Sabbatarian, this being of interest as showing the change in sentiment that rapidly occurred in the third of a century preceding the advent of George Thompson, the English anti-slavery agitator in Boston, in 1840

Willard Smith, one of the four pioneers who came through the wilderness in 1805 in search of "Cambray," settled on the farm now occupied by George M Dodds He was one of four brothers, two of whom, Benjamin and Stephen, accompanied by their father Aholiab, came probably in 1806, and were followed in 1807 by the fourth brother, Rufus The excellent judgment of these men was shown by the lands they selected which are among the best in the town It was not so easy to judge of the character of the soil when every foot of it was covered by the virgin forest, as now The three first named took lands at the Little Bow, Benjamin the farm now occupied by Samuel Smith, his grand-son, Stephen the Henry B Holbrook farm, and Rufus the Levi N Smith farm Willard's name is perpetuated in that of Willard Thayer, a grand-nephew now resident in the village Aholiab died at the age of 92 in 1840 The cellar of the house he lived in is still unfilled A little knoll on the farm whereon stands the brick house built by Benjamin, marks the spot and is still known in the family as Gran'ther's Hill His grave is in the family cemetery at Little Bow as is that of his wife, Lydia It is a fair inference that Allen Smith, son of Willard, and the first white child born in town, first saw the light May 8, 1806, at the Dodds farm Buel A Smith, son of Allen, is remembered with love as one of the capable teachers in the early fifties

To the more elderly of those now living who were born around the thirties and forties, how remote seemed the incidents of the war of 1812 in their younger days, as they listened to the oft told tales of terror ! Yet only as many years had passed as have swiftly fled since the Civil War of 1861 We count that a recent event, however But to our children and grandchildren, the "Great Rebellion" is as remote as the Revolution Thus quickly is obliterated the vividness of scenes that stirred the blood of those nearer the active participants

Looking back over the century and a quarter that elapsed between the signal defeat of England's power in the colonies, after seven weary years of war, we are at a loss to understand how, so soon after measuring the valor of American troops, she was ready to engage in another trial at arms with those who had less than thirty years before humbled the arrogant cross of St George and driven it across the seas to the place of its origin Undoubtedly the old animosities engendered on both sides by a struggle for liberty on one hand and a settled purpose of subjugation on the other, still lingered and needed but a trifling motive to fan it again into a blaze. There was the desperate fear on the part of those living near the border of Canada, and it is with these that we are more immediately concerned, that the roaming, unsettled tribes of Indians could again be marshaled under British direction, for the massacre of Wyoming had not been forgotten England had declined to abide by her treaty of peace after the Revolution, and refused to vacate several American posts she

had captured during that war She even built a fort on American soil and re-
jected our demand to evacuate and dismantle it   In diplomacy she attempted
to coerce us into acknowledging the independence of the Indian tribes in the
great Northwest, thus putting it within her power to negotiate treaties with
them and thereby again secure a foothold upon the vast territory she foresaw
was ultimately to become a part of the United States   These were the moving
causes of the war of 1812   It seems to have come without preparation on our
part   We had neglected to make allies of the French Canadians, though the
time was opportune because of the signal assistance France had rendered us in
the Revolution   Fealty to the mother land has ever characterized the French
Canadian   It blazed up in the Papineau insurrection   Never has the antagonism between "Upper and Lower" Canada been stilled until Laurier, a citizen
of Quebec became premier   The French and English inherited prejudices have
never been welded, today they are only quieted by a composite antagonism to
our stupid tariff exclusion, and the more stupid political cry at home of "protection," "smoking factory chimneys" and "Canada for Canadians"   The
bond is a slight one

There was another incitement to the war of 1812, remote, not immediate
Europe had begun to look with wondering eyes on the progress of the new Republic, and the dissensions among a free people so often predicted did not ma-
terialize   We were united and were making astonishing progress in wealth, invention, agriculture and all the arts of peace   France emerging from the
Reign of Terror was in the throes of a struggle for liberty, and all monarchial
Europe had as by common impulse, sought her destruction   Napoleon arose
from the chaos of internecine strife and soon all Europe was confounded and
overwhelmed by the brilliancy of his career   Republicanism not only at home,
but abroad, must be destroyed   Hence arose the conflict we are to consider

The Canadian border from Plattsburg to Sackett's Harbor soon bristled
with block houses in every town as protection from the Indians   It was expected that England would invoke the aid of her ancient allies once more.   In
Gouverneur, a block house was built near the intersection of Main and Clinton
streets, and if the exact spot is known, it should be marked by a block of our
native marble before forgotten   It was surrounded by a stockade containing
an acre of ground   The histories locate this block house in Clinton street near
the present store of W A Henderson, but local authority declares that it occupied the site of Fred B Fuller's residence and forms a part of the walls
thereof

A second block house was also built, tradition says, near the house of Isaac
Austin   This is the more probable as that indomitable pioneer enlisted and
went to the front with the first volunteers, and it is quite natural that he would
provide whatever protection he could for his family before going   There is no
record obtainable of the names of those who enlisted or were drafted into the
service in 1812 from Gouverneur   It is probable that in proportion to population, those who went equalled in percentage, the hundreds who, in 1860 took
part in the Civil War either voluntarily or by compulsion   The population of

the town was about 300 in 1812. In this war the foe was at every man's door, wary, silent, treacherous and easily seduced by British gold as had been proved years before. Every man became a volunteer in effect, performing home duty to give his neighbor opportunity to guard the frontier. The alliance of the red-coat with the red-skin, gave special terror to he situation. Grim as is the memory of the 60's, that of 1812-14 must have been far more terrifying to those then upon the stage of action. The St. Lawrence was at their doors—the Potomac, to their descendants, was six hundred miles away.

The embargo declared against Great Britain and her colonies, five years before the actual hostilities, had also a potent effect in fomenting strife. Merchants were interrupted in their business ventures; commerce was palsied; farms depreciated in value; future prospects were blighted and a general feeling of insecurity was engendered. Military forces were stationed at Ogdensburg to prevent any intercourse between the peoples of the adjacent shores. The effect of the embargo of 1807 might well be studied by our later day politicians. Tariff rates can easily be increased until the resultant effect is practically an embargo. The declaration of war was made in June, 1812. It was official notice that hostile incursions from Canada and predatory warfare with the Indians was at hand. The alarm seems to have been mutual on both shores of the St. Lawrence.

So far as the campaign in this war relates to the northern frontier, it had an inglorious termination. Ogdensburg was captured and looted by the British forces, and no counter victory was achieved by American arms. Washington was invested and burned by the enemy and this division of forces undoubtedly saved the invasion and retention of this section from Britain. General Wilkinson, who had command of the men in Northern New York, was court-martialed for inefficiency, tried at Troy on several charges, but after a protracted defence was finally acquitted.

In 1813 Simeon Hazelton came to Gouverneur in search of a new home. He had been a farmer of influence and means in Sandgate, Vt., and on his ar-

rival selected lands on the Scotch Settlement road, about two miles from the present village. He remained here only three years, however, finally settling in the town of Fowler. With him came from Vermont three children, the eldest being Asa Lyman, who subsequently became a surveyor of skill. He made many surveys of the town and possibly served in that capacity in laying out the incipient village. He was a man of influence in Fowler to which town he went when nine years of age, became supervisor in 1842-43 after having held

Simeon Hazelton

minor town offices. His father, Simeon, was the first town clerk of Fowler. Soon after serving as supervisor, Asa L. removed to Washington, D. C., where he still lives, being at this writing ninety-eight years of age. The Hazelton family was a notable one, and although more intimately identified with the growth of Fowler, is entitled to recognition here from the facts above set forth.

The year 1817 brought, among others, two brothers, Harmon and Thomas Harvey VanBuren, the latter a soldier in the war of 1812. They settled on

the Johnstown road, named from Johnstown, N. Y., from which place other settlers came. The VanBurens were from Montgomery county and three years later were joined by Peter, a younger brother, who in 1831 became a hotel keeper and whose memory is still fresh. The trees in the park are standing monuments to his care for he was most insistent for their preservation, planting many with his own hand and watering others continually until their growth was assured. A familiar sight forty years ago was "Uncle Peter" with team

Thomas H. Van Buren.

and driver, water-tub and wagon, carrying pails of water during the heated seasons, to refresh the growing trees.

Looking back over the century the student of social movements is struck with the trials, the discomforts, the privations, the dangers even, men will endure in order to obtain what should be a free offering of the Giver of all good, a spot of ground upon which to build a home. We are slavish followers in the matter of land tenure, of English customs, even as our common law is a direct heritage from that source. All wealth, all sustenance, all life, must come from the soil. To deny every child of Adam a right of access to the bosom of Nature, that Mother so kind, so generous, so careful of the welfare of all, is to deny the right of existence. Whoever is willing to champion the pri-

Main Street and Park about 1860.

vate ownership of a square foot of soil, must be equally ready to defend the private ownership of water, air, and the gentle dew from heaven. These are nature's bounties. They were not given to a few but to all. Man has made legal barriers to their universal use, but man, after four thousand years of up-growth, has not yet found a better way to avenge the taking of life than by the taking of another life. So long as one person can say to his neighbor, you shall not grow the food you require for the preservation of your life from this land because I have a title deed, so long will poverty reign, social inequality exist, and the line of demarkation between those who have and those who have not, will become more insurmountable. The privations endured by the pioneers of Gouverneur, rightly interpreted, prove, if proof were needed, how tense is the struggle for a small strip of land, from whose bounty the wants can be assured. For hundreds of years, Ireland has been in ferment because the humble cotter could not obtain his share of that which the rich landholder withheld from him. Land monopoly is as odious as any monopoly. Men will always oppose monopoly in the abstract, though we, educated to the land system formulated by the English feudalist, have not yet emerged from the veil sufficiently to see the truth plainly. If every human being is entitled to life, he is entitled to the means of preserving life.

Stephen B. VanDuzee came in 1813, with his parents, being four years old at the time. Hartford, Washington county, that center from which came so many of Gouverneur's earliest settlers, was his birthplace, and to it he returned when thirteen years old, going from there to Scranton, Vt., when eighteen and there learning the trade of wheelwright. In 1831 he again came to Gouverneur and soon after began manufacturing furniture, which business he followed with success for more than sixty years. His death occurred April 24, 1893.

Stephen B. Van Duzee.

Stained with age yet perfectly legible, is the receipt of Dr. Spencer, then trustee of the Presbyterian church:

Rec'd Gov'r the 7th Nov'r 1822 of Hezekiah H. Smith by the hand of Wm. Kemp ten Dollars for his assignment for the Meetinghouse & for the support of Mr. Murdock.   JOHN SPENCER."

A search of the histories does not disclose the name of Hezekiah H. Smith, but he must have been a man of character as were all of that name at the period of which we write. He evidently did not subscribe "ten dollars" for the "meetinghouse" or the excellent and careful Dr. Spencer would have used the word "subscription" instead of "assignment." The chirography and spelling of this document are of that exact and painstaking sort so many of the men of his period followed, for it was counted something of a disgrace for any boy having school privileges, not to acquire a correct, albeit somewhat stately handwriting. The signers of the Declaration almost to a man, left their names in ink as clearly decipherable as if in print. With the exception of that of "Step. Hopkins," the oldest member of that patriotic gathering, who was in his sixty-ninth year, there is no tremor either in signature or flourish, to indicate that the signers had an overshadowing consciousness that, as one of them said, "if we do not hang together we will all hang separately."

An old account book bound in vellum, with column rulings adapted to the English money system, well preserved and the ink as fresh as if written yesterday, yields many items of interest. The first is dated Nov. 29, 1825, at which time the owner lived in Scotland, and the values are extended in pounds, shil-

lings and pence   He was a baker by trade and there are charges for "biscuits,"
"loaves," "small rolls," etc , in profusion with an occasional sale of bran which
shows that Graham was still an unknown factor in breadmaking   A "4-qr
loaf" meaning one weighing three and a half pounds, is charged 10d   The ex-
cessive land rentals paid to the titled gentry of the realm, evidently appears
in the price of the loaf   "One stone Fine Flour" is entered at 2 shillings 10
pence, which would be at the rate of 70 cents for fourteen pounds reduced to our
reckoning   A memorandum reads "In the year 1832 I commenced farming on
my own book   The land had been partly cleared before it came into my hand
and there was half an acre that had not been plowed and I had no team " Oct 26,
1832, is the item "For expense in bringing Clapboards from Rossie to his (Mr
Duey s) house 1s 6d " These two items were made the year of the coming
of the owner of the book to Gouverneur   "Paid for Crane Irons, 3s " "Paid
for Oven Mantletree Irons, 1s 10d " The newly arrived immigrant had not
yet acquired the mysteries of $'s and cents   "Paid Mr Maddock for 27 Glass
Lights $1 08 " "Paid Mr Dodge for a letter 10 cents," "For Shoeing Oxen
and Mending Ring 11 shillings—I pay half, ' are charges made in 1833   In
1836, "Paid Raymond Austin for sawing 180 boards 36 cents " indicates that
the custom was to charge by the cut instead of by the board measure   May
20, 1836, "Sold Mr Rockwell Barnes 12 bush of Oats at 4s ," and later, "Paid
Mr Barnes for Framing my barn $16 72 " The total income from the farm
in 1836 appears to have been $357 58   Pork brought 4 cts , eggs of which "79
dozen were sent to the village" and sold for $7 10 or 9 cents per dozen, wool
48 cents, wood ashes 12 cents, corn 75 cents, butter 14 cents, oats 31 cents,
wheat $1 13, barley $1, potatoes 25 cents   There are many erasures and al-
terations in the figures showing that the new citizen was struggling with the
reduction of pounds to dollars, English to "York" shillings and pence to cents
In 1833 he paid "Mr Townsend of Gouverneur" for 2 bushels of Hair, 37½
cents   As Dr Richard Townsend had gone to Philadelphia several years before, this "Townsend" must have been some other than he, probably the "Francis D Townsend ' of the census of 1835   There is an item not readily understood, reading, "Dec 13, 1833, James paid for me one-half of Cotton at 3s
to weave into cloth—what the weaver will charge neither he nor I know " In
this year he paid 84 cents for a newspaper   Did the early editor deduct postage from his subscription price?   Aug 10, 1845, "Charles Johnson charges
me for framing on House $3," followed by another charge of $3 25 for a like
service   In Dec of the same year he bought of 'Mr Parsons a Stove at $8,
one elbow and pipe $1 00 " A few days later he paid "Mr Vanduzee for my
seat in the Meetinghouse in two installments $25 00 " In the ten years follow-
ing 1844 are thirty-one entries of money "Paid B B Beckwith Cash," usually
$5 each time   The last four of these were paid to "Mr Charles Anthony "
Probably these were in lieu of the usual "donation" to the minister, as there are
other entries for "seat in meetinghouse" scattered through the fifty years of
continuous record   The book is full of the names of the old builders of the town
with whom the accountant had dealings   It is difficult to desist from further ex-

tracts, albeit, they naturally decrease in interest the nearer we come to the present generation

The present day plan of leasing farms "at the halves," or by an agreed price "per cow," seems not to have prevailed in the earlier history   Here is a copy of an old lease dated 1824 in good preservation   "This Agreement made and completed this first day of November, 1824, between John Hoyt of the first part of Gouverneur, County of St Lawrence, State of New York, and Daniel Grout and Randall D Price of the town and county aforesaid, of the second part" etc in which 100 acres "on the Morris Tract, being the first lot north of James Hales' is leased for one year for this rental   Hoyt is to furnish "one good plow and harrer," one third of the seed for sowing and planting, and Grout & Price are "to cut the grass and divide in the field, putting one half in Hoyt's barn" and to divide the english grain in the half-bushel, the corn in the basket, the flax in the bundle and deliver to the said Hoyt one-third of the grain, corn and flax," and Hoyt is "to be to one-half of the expense of carting manure and to have one-third part of the straw and corn fodder and punkins" and the whole is signed by the three parties in interest, and witnessed by James Haile and Stephen Johnson   The seals are crude, diamond shaped bits of paper, cut from another sheet of same sort as that written on, and attached with red wafers which last have faded to a "crushed strawberry" tint   There is an endorsed addendum in which Hoyt agrees to pay one-half the taxes   The whole, excepting signatures, is in the handwriting of Daniel Grout and marks him as an amateur lawyer of good enough skill to be able to draw a contract that would 'stand law" undoubtedly   The land covered by this lease is included in the farm of John R Hill on the "Scotch Settlement" road

The social current did not always flow without an occasional ripple   Our forefathers while men of peace were also men of opinions   Read this document that has been rescued from the past

'The petition of your devoted friends whose names are hereunto subscribed humbly sheweth That we are now considered as residing in School District No   in the town of Gouverneur, County of St Lawrence, State of New York, being very remote from the central part of s^d District so that our children can in no wise be Benefited by the School in s^d District pray that you will take our case into your wise consideration and Set us off from s^d District & annex us to District No 1 in the town of Rossie in the county aforesaid as we your petitioners in Duty bound shall ever pray   Dated Gouverneur Apr 27th 1819   To the Commissioners of Common Schools in the Town of Gouverneur

BENJAMIN PAYNE,

WILLIAM FREEMAN,

AMBROSE STAMAN "

There was a counter petition apparently, though the absence of the number of the School District in the foregoing document makes it impossible to identify that movement with the following

"To the Commissioners of Common Schools of the Town of Gouverneur We your humble petitioners pray that as you have Divided the District No 4 that you would discontinue your Doings and let the Same be set back and in so doing you will very much oblige your humble petitioners

Gouverneur, July 4th, 1823

SAMUEL MERRIAM	DAVID MILLER
ANSEL JOHNSON	J S COLTON
DANIEL KEYS	BELA HOUGH
WILLIAM CLAGHORN	ALANSON HOUGH
JULIAN PERRY	ISAAC SMITH
CALEB S JOHNSON	DANIEL SEARS
MARTIN EASTERLY	NATHANIEL MARTIN
IRA PERRY	SIMEON JOHNSON
JESSE MARTIN	ELIJAH HOUGH J¹
I W PORTER	ELIJAH HOUGH
ALANSON TOWNSEND	WALTER S HYER
ELISHA BASS	ALBY SMITH
	JAMES MURDOCK "

If this was a counter petition, the signatures although numbering twenty-five as against three, was insufficient to move the "Commissioners" After due deliberation of the latter, for they did not do things without much weighing of the pros and cons in those days, the following official document was issued

NOTICE

is hereby given to the Trustees of School District No 4 Gouverneur that a division of said District was made by the Commissioners of Common Schools in said Town on the 16th day of the present month Bounded as follows beginning at the southeasterly side of John Putmans house thence on the road running to the road that leads from Kenneys to Streeters Containing half the land laying between the two districts N° 4 and N° 7

JAMES HAILL
Commissioner of Common
Schools of Gouverneur

Gouverneur Feb 16th 1824

There is an almost utter absence of punctuation marks in the foregoing documents Alby Smith remembered to end his name with a period Daniel Keyes always spelled his last name with two e's but the petition shows only one This does not invalidate the document—its genuineness is unmistakable—but it shows that the brother of the man who made the first axes in Gouverneur on the site now occupied by the Van Duzee Mfg Co 's shop, probably told the canvasser for signatures to "put him down "

Here is a memorandum of interest to those faithful sons of Scotia wherever found, showing how soon after making their homes in the new land, they made plans for upholding the cause ever nearest to their hearts

Gouverneur, June 21 1837

We the undersigned form ourselves into a Body to support the Bible Society according as God shall prosper us and a box shall be kept by the treasurer where all donations shall be deposited and shall be deivered to the Treasurer or agent of St. Lawrence Bibe Society every six months commencing on the first of January next.

John Thomson,	David Hill,
James Hill,	Catherine Hill,
James Rutherford, Junr	Helen Patton,
George Rodger,	Altha Shead,
James Hill, Junr	James Rutherford."

How thoroughly characteristic of the nationality of the signers, this document is? They did not wait until the crops were garnered before pledging themselves to give "as they were prospered." Of no people save one, could that deathless lyric, The Cotter's Saturday Night, been written. So none other than the sons and daughters of those whose simple faith and fealty were celebrated in that poem could have conceived and executed this document at a time when they were struggling for the bare necessities of life. It was a reproduction in the new land, thousands of miles removed from hearthstones their infancy knew, of the scene that Robert Burns immortalized.

About 1837 the first agitation for a railroad from Ogdensburg to Albany began. Six years previously the Mohawk & Schenectady road, 17 miles in length, and the first in the state, had been finished and was in successful operation. The citizens of this town were not unobservant of the new method of travel and transportation, and though feeble in resources, never ceased to cherish the determination to secure an outlet at the first opportunity. These aspirations took shape in 1852, a meeting being held in Gouverneur Jan. 8th of that year to receive the report of the survey and form a company. It is not the purpose to here recite the history of the Potsdam & Watertown R. R. which has several times been written. In Gouverneur Edwin Dodge and Wm. E. Sterling were made directors of the new line among a board of thirteen and the first named was made president. Daniel Lee of Watertown was elected treasurer.

Col. H. B. Keene was an important factor in the promotion of the old Potsdam & Watertown R. R. subsequently merged into the R. W. & O. R .R.

He was a large landed proprietor as farming possessions were then counted, and he gave time, money and pecuniary endorsement to the undertaking, going to the verge in the latter particular so that, had the effort failed, it must have involved him in ruin. He was a man of indomitable energy and determination, self-educated in the school of practical experience, and the want of some method of reaching outside markets with the products of this and Jefferson counties, justified him in taking hazards to secure that result. He canvassed his immediate territory assiduously for stock

Col. H. B. Keene.

subscriptions and it is a surprise not to find his name among the first officers of the company. Probably the division of official honors was made by locality largely as is usual. Later he received due reward for the risks and labors he made, in the enhancement of the value of his lands. He was the first station

agent at Keenes, named for himself, for the new road on its completion   It is
interesting to notice that, as first surveyed, the line was 75¼ miles long and
Hermon was named as a station between Richville and Dekalb   The diversion to
include Hermon added about six miles, the present distance from Watertown
to Potsdam being 69 miles

Here is an interesting little paper relating to the early history of this
railroad

Treasurer's Office Potsdam and Watertown R. R Co ,
Watertown, Dec 8th, 1854

Received of J R Absalon of the Town of Fowler, 45-100 of a Dollar being
bal of int on ten Shares of Stock standing in his name on the Books of the
Potsdam and Watertown R R Co

45-100 of a Dollar   D Lee.
ten Shares   Treasurer

Every dollar of that ten shares was lost as an investment   It was the price
the citizens along the line paid for the new improvement   Everybody who took
stock in the enterprise suffered in like manner   Currently with the writing of
these words, all the metropolitan magazines of large circulation, are publishing
astonishing disclosures of corporate rapacity and legalized robbery   It is no
new thing with the railroad corporation   The history of the Potsdam and Watertown R R brings this home to us when we recall it   There was no intention
on the part of the capitalists in New York City who financed this road, to permit the stock to remain in force, nor eventually, be of the slightest value to
those who invested in it   Enough was collected of the innocent residents along
the line to grade the road and this amounted in Oct , 1852, to $750,000 [1] The
Absalom family were French refugees from the province of Lorraine, robbed of
their ancient estates in France by the revolutionists of 1789 and driven to America, where by thrift they became again possessed of comfortable fortunes   Did
the one named in the receipt above who represented three other families descended from the original settler and then accumulated money savings, become
painfully aware that the taking by force of the landed possessions of his father
in his native country was fairly offset by the taking by finesse in this?   In the
sweep of territory a score of miles in breadth, and reaching from Watertown to
Potsdam, no person having a hundred dollars at command, escaped the stock-
solicitor   That they did not revolt and seek justice when their certificates became worthless paper, was due probably to the appreciation of their properties
by the advent of the new road   This appreciation, however, was no justifica-
tion for the sacrifice of their cash accumulations

Fifteen years after the events recorded above, the writer, then a teacher in
Springfield, Mass , became acquainted with a wealthy bondholder of this road,
then merged into the R W & O system   Remembering how his father had been
victimized, he sought an explanation of the methods used in its accomplishment.
The process was simple enough   The capitalist invested in the bonds of the
road , the victim in the stock   The bond was a first mortgage   A failure to pay

(1) Hough

its interest resulted in foreclosure and sale of the road and the bondholder bid it in There was nobody else interested in buying so he bought at his own price, usually but a fraction of the cost of the road Scarcely a road is now built into new territory but that this fraud is perpetrated upon its stockholders

Today the old Potsdam and Watertown railway is a part of a gigantic system covering many states From being a large factor in the growth and prosperity of the town, it has become an engine of oppression It makes the price of every article of large natural production shipped over its lines There was a time when the dealer in butter and cheese for instance could conduct his business at a profit, but the railway has taken that from him. The price of every head of live stock is fixed before the animals leave the station and no skill of the dealer can avert a loss if it is so determined by the offshoots and co-sharers of the railway at the point of destination Arbitrary and exorbitant freight rates are charged, wholly independent of service performed and the rule is to exact all the traffic will bear The result of these oppressive measures is shown in the fact that no farmer in the town, not possessed of some special line, as the raising of blooded stock, running a milk route or similar specially profitable business, can earn as owner and manager of a farm, more than the commonest day wages of the laborer His investment in land and buildings nets him nothing more than if he sold his time to any employer The wife and the larger boys and girls of the family work for nothing It is idle to gloss over these things They are true And they are as true of every other rural locality as of Gouverneur We are not specially marked for exploitation The man who produces wealth should be the master of his product The corporation that transports it for him should be his servant But the positions are reversed through the granting of special privileges, and the servant has become the master

David Hill

The forerunner of the Gouverneur Agricultural and Mechanical Society is sketched with graphic interest by one of the farmers of the town, David Hill, long since gathered to his fathers He left a record dated Oct. 22, 1858, which is of sufficient interest to warrant reproduction here He writes

"I often ask myself why our farmers plow their lands so miserably I thought can there nothing be done to improve this condition? So I started out one day to try what could be done among my acquaintances on the west side of the village, about holding a plowing match. I found them all willing if some one would take the lead So, I posted notices all over calling upon the farmers to meet and appoint judges, name date and place of trial and provide means to pay the prizes At the meeting we raised $24, and named the farm of Samuel Smith on the Rock Island road for the place of trial, on Thursday, Oct. 22 The day proved a fine one and there were upwards of three hundred present Eleven plows started and the work was done in a manner those present never saw before James Brown, a Scotch-

man, took the first prize along with a Welshman, David Lewis, who was given
the same amount, as the work was equal We judges distributed the remainder
of the money among them as it was the first trial of the kind"

The success of the plowing match led to a call for the formation of a fair
organization and the account proceeds

"January 16, 1859, I was in Gouverneur and found that mostly every
farmer I talked with would like to have a Town Fair   So I and George Parker
posted up notices all over the town calling a meeting in the Town Hall on the
22nd day of January to appoint a Committee, and draft a constitution according to law   Chas Anthony, Esq was made president of the meeting and a
name was chosen—The Gouverneur Agricultural and Mechanical Fair   We
invited all the neighboring towns to take a part in it   One of the days was to
be a Sale Day, an entirely new thing in this part of the Country   The Fair
took place Sept 14, 15 & 16 and we got the Canton tent by paying charges
both ways on it   But the wind rose to a hurricane, and blew it down in the
morning of the 14th   The secretary told me he sold two thousand tickets at
the gate and over and above two hundred family tickets. We saved $200 and
I was glad of it as we directors had bound ourselves to foot the Bill, if we fell
short   We had an address from Thomas Clark of Jefferson county   The
plowing match came off on the 16th, and was keenly contested by the Welsh
and Scotch as none of the Yankees cared to enter the list   We had an old Bull
Plow there that was made in 1812   They got two blind horses and two men to
match to lead them and they walked backwards   Gouverneur has beat both
county and state fairs on squashes and cheese this year"

The "bull-plow" was tried on the site of the present residence of Amasa Corbin at the corner of Main and Rock Island Streets in a dry gravelly loam, and
it was impossible to make it stay in the ground   The most modern plow could
not have been made to turn a furrow in that soil however   It belonged to
Milton G Norton and is still in existence

The tickets for the first fair were printed by two lads having type enough
to set the words "Admit One" in a mortise, the "press" being a pine lever about
thirty inches long and the ink being applied with the finger   Bristol board was
supplied for the fair association and cut into ticket size with a jack-knife There
was no printing office in town and as the youths had the only type securely
locked in their "form" with a wooden wedge, the possibility of counterfeiting
was not considered   The names of the members of this amateur printing firm
were Alonzo J VanDuzee and J S Corbin

By courtesy of the Daughters of the American Revolution, the writer is
placed in possession of a document of great interest of which this is the title
page

STATE OF NEW YORK
Census of the State for the year 1835
Town of GOUVERNEUR, County of ST LAWRENCE
BOOK No ONE

Who was the census taker does not appear but the document is unquestionably an official copy It was rescued from the fire in 1877 which destroyed other town records by happening to be at the time in the possession of A Z Madison and at his death went into the hands of Mrs Sarah Madison of Buffalo from whom Judge E H Neary received it Under the column headed "The Name of the Head of Each Family," are the following names, comprising every one in town in the year 1834 The list is so valuable that it is repeated here, lengthy as it is, in order to ensure its preservation for future historians

Ayers, Eli
Ayres, Ebenezer
Ayers, William
Adams, Lyman
Austin, Elwell E
Atwood, Joel
Austin, Raymond
Aldous, Stephen
Bolton, Joseph
Boutwell, Martin
Breese, Harvey
Buck, Roger
Beardslee, Chas H
Baxter, James
Beardslee, Ezekiel
Beardslee, Elias S
Ball, Elisha
Babcock, James
Blandin, Samuel
Barber, Moses
Bosworth, Jabez
Barker, Nathan
Billings, Amasa
Brooks, Joseph
Brooks, William
Barrel, Almon
Ballou, Jirah
Bowen, William
Barney, James K
Barney, Milton
Bowne, James
Barnes, Norman
Barnes, Rockwell
Bolton, John
Barrel, Colburn, Jr
Bowhall, Demarkis
Beck, Christopher
Bolster, Jared L
Beebe, Smith
Babcock, John
Cross, Solomon
Cross, Joel

Crawford, James
Culbertson, William
Campbell, George W
Colton, Jonathan S
Clark, James
Cunningham, James
Cole, Alpha
Carrington, Aaron
Corbin, Amasa
Crawford, David
Collins, Benjamin
Case, Samuel
Cone, Sylvanus
Conklin, James
Curtis, Charles
Cooper, Aaron
Case, Ephraim
Cunningham, Joseph
Clark, Charles
Culbertson, John
Dodds, Alexander
Dewey, Eleazer
Dodge, Henry
Dodge, Lyman
Dodds, Andrew
Dodge, Edwin
Dodge, William H
Davis, Nathaniel
Drake, Caleb
Drake, Luther
Drake, Hiram
Dewey, Fanny
Drovenor, Joseph
DeWitt, Moses
Dickinson, Braddock
Davis, Roswell
Darling, Robert
Eager, Emery
Ells, Lewis
Fosgate, John
Freeman, William
Fredenburgh, Abraham Jr

Foster, William
Fradenburgh, Peter
Frasier, Theodore
Fairbanks, Joel
Fairbanks, Samuel
Fradenburgh, Alexander
Frasier, Benjamin
Fuller, James
Guernsey, Willard
Guernsey, Wilder
Grout, Daniel
Goodenough, Abel
Griffin, Wolcott
Goodrich, Charles
Goodrich, Thomas
Greene, Allen
Green, John
Gillman, Mary
Hough, Bela
Hawley, Percival
Hudson, Henry
Hopkins, Joseph
Hyer, Walter S
Hunt, Asa Jr
Hamblin, Hiram
Heath, Morrison
Harris, Luther
Hills, Nathan
Hunt, Richard
Holbrook, Henry B
Hulbert, Augustus
Haile, James
Hering, William
Hill, James
Haile, Nathan
Hill, David
Heath, Joshua
High, Samuel
Haven, Clement
Haywood, Levi
Helmer, J E
Johnson, Stephen

Johnson, John

Johnson, Ansel

Jones, Jacob

Kneeland, Sally B

Kentfield, Elias

Keyes, Joel

Kenyon, Moses C

Kimball, Richard

Kelsey, Samuel

Keyes, Daniel

Keyes, Calvin F

Kelsey, Frederick W

Kinney, Amos

Kinney, Barnet B

Kimber, William

Keith, Barnabas

Kinney, John

Killmer, William

Leavitt, Benjamin

Livingston, Wm A

Lanphaer, Freeman

Lake, James

Lashbrooks, Nathan

Lashbrooks, Charles

Lashbrooks, Orin

Lashbrooks, Runa

Lake, John I

Livingstone, Alexander

Lashbrooks, Hiram

Lashbrooks, James

Lashbrooks, William

Maddock, James

Murdock, Hiram

McKay, Alby

Marble, Jonathan

Miller, David

Mix, Eli

Merriman, Ora

Merithew, John

Merithew, Jeremiah

Morgan, Isaac

Morse, Horace D

Martin, Harvey

Murdock, Jonathan

Mitchell, Hiram

Moran, Francis

Moltonner, George

    (Malterner?)

Nichols, William

Nichols, Geo W.

Northup, Levi

Nobles, Reuben

Nobles, Lyman

Nelson, VanRensselaer

Nelson, Isaac

Northum, Eli R

Nichols, Eleazer

Norton, Milton G

Osborn, Olonzo

Orvis, Charles

Peden, James

Phillips, David

Parmeter, Suell

Porter, Israel

Peck, Josep

Parsons, Lewis B

Parker, James

Parsons, Myron

Parsons, Israel R

Prentice, John

Phelps, Benjamin W

Patton, Thomas

Phelps, Alfred

Prentice, Willard

Peters, Alfonzo

Parsons, Oliver

Parker, William

Peck, David

Peck, Nelson

Perrigo, Isaac H

Rice, James

Robertson, John

Rhodes, William W

Rhodes, John

Rhodes, William

Reed, William C

Rice, Randall D

Rhoades, Ebenezer

Rhoades, Asa

Rutherford, James

Rundell, Gilbert D

Richardson, William

Russell, Jesse M

Risley, Jeremiah

Stone, Joseph

Smith, Benjamin

Smith, Harvey D

    ("inc. A Z M")

Smith, Benjamin H.

Smith, Joseph, 2nd

Smith, Nathan W

Smith, Joseph

Smith, Samuel

Smith, Rufus

Smith, Isaac

Smith, William

Smith, Amon

Smith, Jonathan L.

Smith, Isaac P.

Smith, Jason

Smith, Calvin

Smith, David

Smith, Silas

Smith, Willard

Smith, Abida

Smith, Laura

Smith, Stephen

Smith Zebina

Smith, Benj. 2nd

Smith, Allen

Skinner, Joel

Schofield, Noah

Shipman, Rowland

Sheldon, Timothy

Swan, Abel

Seaman, Ambrose

Stiles, Sanford

Stoddard, Elisha G

Spencer, John

Streeter, Erasmus E.

Streeter, Dianthyn

Sherwin, Isaac C

Sabin, William Jr

Slyter, Jonathan

Sears, Daniel

Sheldon, Martha

Secker, Peter

Thrall, Isaac

Tuttle, Chandler

Townsend, Benjamin M.

Thrall, John

Townson, Alanson

Townson, Levi

Townsend, Francis B.

Thompson, James

Thayer, Asahel

Thayer, Horace

Thayer, Enoch
Thayer, Willard
Turner, Miles
Thompson, John
Tanner, Fitch
Thompson, Thomas
VanDuzee, James
VanDuzee, Stephen B
VanBuren, Samuel
VanBuren, Thomas H
VanBuren, Harman
VanBuren, Peter
VanDuzee, David

Vary, Richard H
VanNamee, Stephen
VanNamee, John
Walling, William
Walling, Almond
Walling, Joshua
Woodward, Amasa
Winchell, Morris S
Wade, Josiah
Wilcox, David
Welch, Thomas
Walling, Samuel
Want, Lynde

Wright, Enos
Williams, Thomas W
Wilson, William
Wilson, Robert
Wilson, William Sweys
Washburn, Nehemiah
Washburn, Patience
Walker, David
Wilson, Samuel B
Wilson, Amos
Woodruff, Geo C

Benedict, N T
Clark, Harvey
Conklin, John
Dunlap, Joseph
Gittel, Charles

Gray, A N
Gray, I W
Goodale, George D
Hopkins, Gustavus
Heald, John

Jewett, B N
Lawton, Daniel B
Mills, Willard C
Poste, Alson C
Smith, James H

The names beginning with "Benedict, N T" are in a separate list following the main schedule Though each was set down as the "head of family" there were no "female persons" nor other "male persons" than themselves in the "family" They were the bachelors of 1834 All save two were eligible to military duty and all save one was of voting age Were they living alone in some humble cabin, clearing a spot in the wilderness to which they might bring some future mistress of the home when fortune had smiled upon them? The census shows a total of 923 males and 873 females in Gouverneur, a total of 1796, which corresponds exactly with the number given in the census returns on page 10 which were obtained from another source There were 178 "male persons subject to military duty," 353 "male persons entitled by the constitution of this state to vote," 42 "male persons not naturalized," which shows that foreigners were not pursued so industriously and made to "swear in," as now, no "paupers," which item may profitably be contrasted with the thousands of dollars now annually expended by the town poormaster, no "persons of color not taxed", no "persons of color who are taxed", and these two records will be found still persisting in the census being taken as these words are penned, the "number of married female persons unmarried under the age of sixteen years" was 427, the "number of marriages occurring where the female resided" was 14, the "number of births" was male 39, female 44, or about one to every four families, indicating that "race suicide" was not a peril, the "number of deaths" was male 15, female 16, a fair indication of splendid constitutions and steady habits, the "number of acres of improved land occupied" was 7,249¼, a record of painstaking accuracy when that fraction of an acre is remembered, the "number of neat cattle owned" was 3,390; the "number of horses owned" was 451; the "number of sheep owned" was 4,071 the "number of hogs owned" was 1,130, the "number of yards of fulled cloth manufactured in the domestic way in the fam-

ily" was 2,926, the "number of yards of flannel and other woolen cloths manufactured in the domestic way" was 4,250 the "number of yards of linen, cotton or other thin cloths manufactured in the domestic way," was 2,716, in
which was included by the "marshal" as the census taker was officially termed,
the "tow" cloth so manufactured   There were two "idiots' in town, one of
each sex, which were supported by a "son" in one case and by "property left
by father" in the other   In manufacturing the town was in its infancy   Of
"grist mills" there was one (Israel Porter's) in the construction of which $4,500
worth of raw materials were used and $4,950 of manufactured articles, which
seems a large cost for the size and capacity of the mill Mr Porter owned   Had
the head of the bureau at Albany called for the number of runs of stone instead
of the cost of the mill, the information conveyed would have been much more
lucid, as the capacity of the mill would have been indicated thereby as well as
its cost   The "saw-mills" numbered three, Barnes' costing $1,500, Austin's
costing $2,025 and Hunt's costing $3,000   Of "oil mills" there were none   Of
"fulling mills" one, belonging to S Cone, costing $4,685   Of "carding ma-
chines" one, belonging also to Mr Cone, costing $3,750   Of "cotton factories"
none   Of "woolen factories" none   Of "iron works' none   Of "trip hammers' one belonging to Joel Keyes and costing $2,000   Of "distilleries" none.
The one built by John Brown about 1814 had evidently failed to pay   Of "asheries" there were three. W L Sterling & Co had two costing together $6,050
which seems a large estimate, and one owned by Lewis B Parsons costing $452
The days of "black salts" had passed or nearly so but house ashes were in demand and were sought for diligently, large wagons carrying 100 bushels being
sent out by the owners of the asheries for them   The price of "a shilling a
bushel" remained without fluctuation for probably fifty years   Of "tan-
neries" there were also two, Benjamin Howard Smith's costing $3,000 and
Benj M Townsend's (?) costing one-half as much   This concludes the entire
list of manufactories in the town   Altogether there were just twelve of them

There are puzzling annotations in the original handwriting of whoever
compiled this census for the town, some of which are not comprehended, others
are   W E Sterling is set down as boarding with Peter Van Buren, an "aside"
not intended probably for record at Albany   "A Z M", probably A Z
Madison, is counted in with the family of Harvey D Smith   The 207 head of
"neat cattle" belonging to John Spencer is explained by the word "drover"
Joshua Heath's record of owning no land is explained by his holdings being
included with "Mr Wait's in company " Wait has the credit of owning 120
acres of improved land, which is the largest acreage ascribed to any citizen save
Milton G Norton, who has an equal amount and James Parker who has 5 acres
more.   Amasa Corbin is credited with 30 "neat cattle" which comports well
with the fact that he was the first cheesemaker of the town   He came from near
the famous region in Massachusetts (Cheshire) which made the 1,450 pound
cheese for Thomas Jefferson, then just inaugurated president, and Elder John
Leland a Baptist divine of National celebrity, (born 1754, died 1841), presented it to the president, hauling it on a sleigh in the early part of the winter

of 1801 Gouverneur's first cheese product, later destined to expand to a large industry, was marketed in Montreal, to which place it was drawn on a sleigh, via Chateaugay, the St Lawrence crossed on the ice, and the cheese was sold for three cents per pound Later Ogdensburg bought the output of this dairy, and a lasting friendship was created between the buyer, Amasa Woolley and the seller Still later, this maker sent his cheese to Boston in "casks" holding six to nine cheese, the casks being made by "Si ' Morgan in a cooper shop near the John Richardson farm on Rock Island road Alanson Townson had 90 acres of improved land, Morris S Winchell the same, which is curious as Winchell was a harness-maker by trade, Francis Moran had 100, Lynde Wait and M G Norton each 120 Jas Parker 125, and Elwell E Austin and Jason Smith each 150 acres which two last show the advantage of having an ancestry among the first settlers who came through the wilderness in 1805, hunting for "Cambray" with the aid of a pocket compass The ancient copy of the official returns of the "marshal" is of such exceeding interest that the writer is loth to abandon further deductions from it A memorandum in pencil on the last page shows that it took the "marshal" eight and one-quarter days to make his canvass, his various routes, and the time spent on each are specified and the statutes then in force provided that he should be paid whatever amount the supervisors of the county allowed There was no stated compensation in the law

The matrons of those days now distant almost three-quarters of a century must not be forgotten What a splendid body of women they were! Were other records destroyed, written history obliterated, memories paralyzed and tradition silent, there is enough in the census of 1835 to prove her position in the making and building of the town Seven women are classed as heads of families, very one of whom had children numbering from two to seven All lived on farms seemingly, except one, as she has no "improved" acreage credited to her All save one had live stock to care for which confirms the last statement Her tireless industry is embalmed in the record of 2,926 yards of fulled cloth, 4,250 of flannels 2,716 of tow cloth and linen and 703 pounds of linen thread, not to mention 569 pounds of flax seed which may have been threshed out by the masculine element of the family, albeit the "threshing" was done by drawing the matured stalks through a set of iron teeth which stripped the seed off, and this process was called "rippling" It was followed by "breaking" to separate the woody portion, "scutching" or beating it with a broad blade of wood about 30 inches long, and "combing" which was not unlike the process of rippling the seed What a lovely sight one of those old flax-fields must have been when the plant, about three feet high, was in bloom and the field presented a waving mass of blue blossoms of delicate hue! The spinning and weaving of the wool and flax was the winter work of the household The family of William Ayres produced in the winter of 1834-5 24 yards fulled cloth, 70 of flannel and 36 of tow cloth or coarse linen The mother of the writer has to her credit 20, 66, and 15 yards respectively Caleb Drake in whose family were three "females," has the prodigious amount of 20, 52 and 77 yards This is

WIVES OF PIONEERS
and Early Settlers
IN GOUVERNEUR

1. Patty Austin—wife of Josiah Wald, came when nine years old with her parents and the first four families in 1806. Her father came twice in the previous year *2. Lucy Garrett*—wife of Willard Smith, pioneer settler in 1806 *3. Betsy Downs*—wife of James L. Thompson, pioneer settler in 1808. *4. Nancy Nichols*—wife of Rufus Smith, daughter of Eleazer Nichols, came with first four families in 1806. *5. Almira Streeter*—wife of Elwell Austin (son of Isaac Austin and brother of Patty Austin) came from Brattleboro, Vt. *6. Sophronia Adams*—wife of John Fosgate, 1814-1873, came with four children in a lumber wagon to this settlement *7. Nancy Bowen*—wife of Timothy Sheldon, 1785-1856, pioneer in 1810. *8. Betsy Ayers*—wife of Thomas H. Van Buren, 1796-1882, pioneer about 1817. *9. Caroline Jackson*—wife of Benj Howard Smith, 1806-1898, came from Randolph, Vt., in 1724 *10. Eliza Blish*—wife of Judge Jas. Skinner, 1811-1900, came to Wegatchie in 1847, to Gouverneur village 1852 *11. Mrs. Roduy Smith*, has distinction of living to the age of 101 years, died in Sept., 1895. *12. Lucretia Allen*—wife of Erwin Barnes, 1823-, came from Waitesfield, Vt, 1835. *13. Cassandana Bullard*—wife of James M. Spencer, 1815—, came from Massachusetts, 1821. *14 L. Maria Hosmer*—wife of Rich. Parsons, 1814-1905, came from Johnstown, N. Y., 1839.

the largest amount in the schedule, though Rufus Smith's family came within two yards of it Consider the spinning involved in these figures! It may be taken as within the truth that each yard required at least 150 yards of yarn to weave it One gets dizzy in further multiplying But the mothers of 1834 doubtless accepted the task as one of the ordinary duties incident to the locality and the youthfulness of the town,, which was not yet thirty years old

"What became of the flax seed?" was asked of the oldest lady in town as these deductions were being prepared "It was put in tow bags and sent away, I don't know where' In Carthage at this time was an oil mill It had a trundle stone of granite, was driven by water and undoubtedly consumed all the seed produced here Transportation was too difficult yet to permit long hauls. Mr Allen Wight who saw this mill a few years later, confirms this view, and names $2 to $3 as the price per bushel

The production of linen thread was another part of women's work at this time A "hank" or skein contained 40 turns of the reel or 100 yards It was sold by the pound to local merchants, such as was not needed in making the clothing at home It seems somewhat anomalous that the State of New York should order its "marshals" to secure statistics of the flax seed product and omit all reference to hay and grain in a community where there were 9,042 animals and 1196 in population to feed

The ancient census record is not by any means exhausted Inferences and deductions come to one

"Thick as the leaves in Vallambiosa,"

us the yellow pages are turned It is a surprise to find ' Strong" (Jonathan S) Colton reported as having no improved land, only three head of cattle and one horse, when it is remembered that the sturdy old sectarian was among the early ones to come (1808) and that he took up a large tract west of the village on his arrival The expanation is found in turning to the name of Milton G Norton who came in 1835 and bought Mr Colton's holdings early in that year Accordingly we find Mr Norton credited with 120 acres of improved land which represents the industry of the first owner during the time he occupied it, which was probably more than a quarter of a century

1834' Seventy-one years have passed since the record here preserved was made by our fathers. Every human being in the town in 1834 is named or represented here. Two generations have been born and come to maturity, and have largely passed onward Not one single soul of the 327 named is left They did their share in making the history of the town Not all of them suffered the extreme hardships of the pioneers, for the way had been blazed for some, the clearings made, the humble dwellings had been built, the earth had been subdued in part, and there was comfort and smiling plenty throughout the town We inherit the thrift of their hands We enjoy the benefits of the schools, the churches, the splendid examples of their lives. We shall not forget.

On a sheet of letter paper without ruling, 7 1-2 x 12 inches in size, stained with the progress of seventy-two years, in a hand of faultless style, not a misspelled word save "Gouverneur," which is entirely pardonable in anybody save a Frenchman, letter-perfect otherwise except the small "p" in the closing sentence, is the following interesting letter

Putney (Vt) Jan 30, 1823

Dr Spencer

    Dear Sir

    I take the liberty to introduce to you the bearer Doctor Hiram Murdock who has been induced to visit Gouverneur with a view to settle there, should circumstances (after trial) appear sufficiently favorable I most cheerfully recommend him as a worthy young Man and am enabled from information, to be relied on, to state that he is well read & has a thorough knowledge of his profession—he is studious and Doctor Chamberlain (my friend and neighbor) gives me his opinion that Doct' M will, (with fair opportunity) become eminent in Physic & Surgery He has attended Lectures at the Med. Ins at Caselton in this State & Pittsfield Mass As I expect soon to become an Inhabitant of G I feel a greater interest in the success of Doctor M than I otherwise should

      please to remember Mrs S & myself to Mrs Spencer

Very Respectfully Yours,

Benjn Smith

    The letter was folded, tucked in and sealed with a green wafer and being delivered by "the bearer" was not postmarked nor charged with the York "shilling" which was the postage rate then current Dr Spencer evidently responded favorably and without professional jealousy for we find "Dr Hiram Murdock" in the census of 1834 settled as a substantial citizen, having seven children apparently in his family, 12 acres of improved land, 35 head of neat cattle, 4 horses which denotes an extensive "ride," and 68 sheep with which to clothe his numerous progeny Mrs M was a worthy helpmate doubtless for there were woven 28 yards of full cloth, 17 of flannel and 4 pounds of linen thread spun in the family Dr Murdock is remembered as an able practitioner and he followed his profession many years in town, coming here soon after the writing of the above letter of introduction If those having ancient documents like this would freely give them to the writers of history, much valuable information could be preserved which, though seemingly unimportant now, may be of priceless value to those coming after us He who wantonly destroys a written document venerable with the passage of the years, robs his successors of that which is rightfully theirs

    What may be called the Plank Road Epidemic, reached Gouverneur in 1848 It seems to have quickly followed the adoption of a new State Constitution in 1846, under which special legislation was forbidden to joint stock corporations or at least greatly abridged Hundreds of companies were formed all over the State to build Plank Roads and thousands of miles were laid in the four years, 1848-52 In the more central part of the State oak planking was usually used but in the evergreen sections like our own hemlock was universally employed Isaac Sherwin is remembered as a contractor for several miles in this town ard Dekalb and his outfit of teams and men was a novelty as such operations had not theretofore been done in the town, being before the days of railroad grading The Gouverneur, Somerville and Antwerp Co, with Chas Anthony as treasurer, built twelve miles connecting the towns named It was finished in 1850 In the opposite direction the Gouverneur, Richville and Canton Co built 16 miles in 1849-50, and had Wm E Sterling as its treasurer Toll gates were erected at distances of about four miles and loud were the anathemas at having to pay for what had up to that time, been free—the right to travel The thrifty citizen from the Scotch Settlement complained at the cost of driving over only one mile of hemlock plank when coming to mill and to meeting, and a reduction of rates was made in his behalf These roads cost about $1,000 per mile and were mostly failures as investments That from Ogdensburg to Heuvelton was successful however The hemlock planking soon decayed The surface became ridgy like a corduroy construction, and complaints were continuous "Running the Toll Gate" became common, the law was occasionally invoked, and many companies either "turnpiked" their routes or graveled the surface in order to allay popular objection and maintain the existence of their toll-collecting privilege Ultimately the roads were freed from corporate control and travel resumed its immemorial right to freedom It was simply one lesson in the school of experience, pointing to future public ownership of all the roads by which men travel whether of plank or macadam or steel The whole scheme was not unlike the "Tulip Mania" in Holland centuries earlier, in its intensity and magnitude Like all "fitful fevers" it soon exhausted itself It left as a legacy, however, a better roadbed and hills whose steepness is in no case over 1 foot in 16

  · The heading of a well preserved paper reads "Order of Exercises at the Semi-Annual Exhibition of Gouverneur Wesleyan Seminary Tuesday Evening January 26, 1841" The exercises continued the following evening and in all there were 23 numbers Of these only seven are labeled 'original," the rest being declamations and none of the sex were accorded a public appearance "Upper Canada furnished two of the forensic aspirants, Norwich, Conn, another, Syracuse a fourth, while the remainder were from local neighborhoods Among the list the writer recognizes but two familiar names, Louis J Haile and Avery J Smith The former became a stalwart son of the soil whose word was as good as his bond and both were unquestionable The latter became a patent attorney in Springfield, Mass, acquiring an extensive and lucrative practice Chas T Pooler was of the family that built the two-story stone mansion near Richville, long remarked by every traveler and now owned by Mary (Griffith) Roland George R Brown of Richville, went to Ohio after which he seems to have been forgotten here Noyes S Wentworth had a brother who held a professorship in the Seminary from 1837 to 1842 and who died at Sandy Hill in 1886 Amasa M Barbur died soon after the "Exercises" catalogued in the document we are quoting from Jas M Madison was the son of A Z Madison, prominent in the early annals of the town, who removed to Fredonia, N Y, living there to an advanced age The exhibition was the first of the Seminary under Methodist management The program was printed in Ogdensburg at the Republican office which received the greater part of the job work of this section at the time The remaining names of whom no trace has been attempted from lack of time, are James A Stacey. DeKalb, Dixon Alexander. DeKalb, John S Marvin. Watertown, Lewis Cameron, Elizabethtown, U C, Morenus Thrasher, Rutland, Wm D Cummings, Merrickville. U C, John Thompson, Somerville; Samuel Philips. Hammond Daniel O Goodrich, Gouverneur, Henry McGonegal, Syracuse, Charles Parsons, Perry, and James A Dean, Ogdensburg

Rescued from an outhouse in which it was fast going to decay, is a bulky volume weighing fifteen pounds, bound in sheep and boards and bearing the title of "Census of New York—1845 " The forms used by the "marshals" had been expanded so that the statistics cover about double the items named in the 1835 census heretofore examined A rapid survey of this bulky volume reveals the following regarding our town, the figures being for 1834

Oats (acres)	1278	Breweries	none
Oats (bush)	32985	Raw Silk Mfrs	none
Neat Cattle	4276	Reef & Dumb (female)	1
Cows	1859	Blind	none
Butter (lbs)	127361	Idiots (male)	2
Cheese (lbs)	57785	" (female)	2
Horses	605	Lunatics	none
Sheep	7455	Indians	none
Fleeces	4995	Churches	
Wool (lbs)	14619	Baptist (1) cost	$550
Hogs	1366	Episcopal	none
Grist M (1) prod	$7000	Presbyterian (1)	$850
Saw M (4) prod	$4800	Congregational (1)	$1150
Fulling M (1) prod	$4810	Methodist	none
Carding M (1) prod	$3400	Roman Cath	none
Cotton Fac	none	Dutch Ref	none
Woolen Fac	none	Universalist	none
Iron Works	none	Unitarian	none
Trip Ham (1) prod	$1500	Jewish	none
Distilleries	none	Quaker	none
Asheries (4) prod	$17500	Colleges	none
Glass Fac	none	Universities	none
Rope Fac	none	Academies (1) cost	$4000
Chain Fac	none	Female Seminaries	none
Oil Mills	none	Normal Schools	none
Oil Cloth Fac	none	Other Inc Schools	none
Dyeing & Printing	none	Common Schools (20) cost	$2912
Clover Mills	none	Select & Private Schools	none
Paper Mills	none	Pupils	535
Tanneries (2) prod	$3800	Average Attendance	341

Inns & Taverns	3	Manufacturers	none
Wholesale Stores	none	Mechanics	30
Retail Stores	6	Lawyers	4
Groceries	2	Ministers	8
Farmers & Agl'ists	231	Ministers' Salaries	$1450
Merchants	8	Doctors	3

The butter and cheese industries not reported in the previous census ten years earlier, had reached large figures in 1845   Oats was the only small grain worth naming apparently for none other is mentioned   The manufacturing industries do not seem to have grown materially and the faulty manner of taking the census is shown in their being no "manufacturers" reported at all   The churches not included in the census of 1835, are known to have increased by one.   For some reason the ordinary mind cannot comprehend, the number of acres of improved land is omitted so that we cannot ascertain how much was added to the 7294¼ acres existing ten years before   "Neat cattle" increased only from 3390 to 4276, showing that the great dairying industry had not yet been foreseen   St. Lawrence county was discriminated against in a number of details which were compiled in other counties   The volume is curiously constructed, every leaf being pasted in, and is a good example of official wastefulness.

It was common enough in old English legal practice to specify a ridiculous consideration in transferring real estate by deed   It may surprise the present generation in Gouverneur to know that at least two transfers contain similar provisions   In 1823 Israel Porter conveyed to (Dr) John Spencer, Rockwell Barnes and Josiah Waid, "three-fourths of a certain piece of land whereon now stands a saw-mill," "containing one acre of ground as surveyed by Moses Rowley"   The consideration for this land was "one hundred dollars by me received, and the further sum of one barley corn to be paid annually hereafter"   There can be little doubt that eighty-two barley corns must be due the heirs and assigns of Israel Porter at this time.   If the interest were payable also in barley-corns, there might be enough of it all to measure a full pint by this time, especially if a struck measure were insisted upon as was the rule with small grains and is still.   Eight years later the "barley-corn" appears again, this time Mr Israel Porter is the party of the first part again, and as such stipulates for a further replenishment of his granary   This time he conveys the "two-eighths part" he had reserved in the aforementioned one acre, to John Spencer, Raymond Austin, Abby Smith and Joel Keyes, and in this transfer he is joined by "Lucy, his wife," who seems before this to have forgotten to sign with her lawful spouse and thus divest herself of her dower rights in 1823.   The histories are clear in stating that eight "families" came to settle in 1807, among which was that of Mr Porter   The only consideration mentioned in this deed is this·   "To have and to hold the above mentioned shares of said premises to the said parties of the second part forever   Yielding paying therefor unto said parties of the first part forever hereafter the yearly rent of one barley corn " If this consideration was never paid, what right exists today that may be enforced by the successors of "the parties of the first part?"

Some Potsdam experience may assist in answering this question A water power on the dam in the village of Potsdam was early conveyed by deed, a part of the consideration being one peppercorn annually forever

A few years since the heirs of the grantor made demand for the "peppercorns" due and not receiving them, began suit for recovery of title, and were successful

This sketch of the life of John Garrett, a Revolutionary soldier whose remains repose in Riverside Cemetery, is interesting, and has not before appeared in the local histories

John Garrett was born in England about 1757 He came to America as a British soldier during the Revolutionary war While he was fighting with the British, his sympathies began to turn, finally he deserted and joined the Continental army in Connecticut According to the records in the Adj General's office (Connecticut) he served as a private in Capt Hinsman's Co Discharged Aug 25, 1775 Also a private in Capt Pettibone's Co Engaged March 26, 1777 Discharged May 5, 1777 His name also appears as a pensioner and private residing in New York, under act of 1818 He was married twice and had three or more children,—his daughter Lucy being the wife of Willard Smith, one of our first settlers Another daughter was the grandmother of Dr Geo B Barnes and wife of James Barnes He died at the house of his granddaughter, Mrs Willam Rutherford in 1853, was buried in the old burying ground, but the headstone may now be found in the G A R plot in Riverside

At the time he deserted the British, he was for several days in the woods without food, finally he was so nearly starved he went into a log house and asked for food As the woman set a large bowl of bread and milk before him, he heard the British soldiers, who were trying to capture him, say "Here is Garret now" He dashed out of a door on the opposite side and succeeded in hiding in a nearby cornfield

Elisha Barrell, of Hartford, Washington Co, left an interesting account of his journey from Gouverneur where he had evidently been on a visiting tour, probably to see Deacon Colburn Barrell's people, as they came from that county It was probably in the year 1826 as that date is written on the back page of the little folded sheet, having 12 pages 2½ x 3¼ inches in size and bound with an ancient brass pin The writing is faded and the paper yellowed with age Here is his account

"Left Gouverneur on Thursday the 19th day of Sept . (1826), traveled through Somerville, Antwerp, Philadelphia, stopt at Leray, spent 3 cts for beer, then to Watertown, spent 6 cts for beer, it is very rainy I traveled 2 miles and put up at Browns' spent 1 shilling 2nd day, traveled to Adams, spent 4 cents for milk, then through Ellisburg, Mexico, and then to Huntingtons in Richland and staid all night, bill 18 cts 3rd day, stopt in the morning at Daniel Chapels and gave 1 shilling for a bowl of bread and milk, then traveled through Constantia, Cicero, spent 18 cents for cider and dinner, then went on to Salt Point into Onondago and Marcellus and got to Mr Perrys in the evening and put up till Monday   Monday morning started for Conquest, went to Elbridge, down to Cato, crossed the bridge at Lysander, spent 6 cts for toll and cider and then went on and arrived at Uncle Josephs about the middle of the afternoon   Wednesday went to Auburn, spent 5 cts   Thursday 20th started from Conquest for home, come down to Buckville (Bouckville?) spent 8 cts for rum, then took the toe path and came down to Weeds Basin and got on board of a boat to go to Syracuse   Boat fare 25 cts and 9 cts for lodging and bitters   At nine mile creek then took the turnpike, took breakfast in Salina, then went on for 8 or 10 miles and got on board of a wagon and rode to Oneida Creek, paid 17 cts, staid at Verona till Monday   Then traveled into Westmoreland and took dinner with Mr Lee, then come into Schuyler and put up at Hecocks for night, spent 18 cts   Stopt at Utica spent 6 cts   Then spent 25 cts for bitters and cider then 18 cts for my bill at Hitts tavern in Broadalbin   Then traveled on to Galway, spent 25 cts for breakfast, then 6 cts for a ride, and got to Saratoga springs spent 6 cts to Chavrun (Sharon?) put up at night at Emersons, bill 18 cts   Then come into Grisswolds and got breakfast 12 cts   then 3 cts for crossing the bridge to Sandy Hill and 3 cts for beer   At Nottrups grocery and then took dinner at home "

The journey was evidently made on foot and must have covered in its devious course at least 300 miles   The time taken, including the various stops, was 16 days, and the expense, eliminating "beer," "cider" "rum" and "bitters" was $2 42   All this casts a sidelight on the methods of the early days   Compare this journey with one today in a Pullman !

Gouverneur had its canal spasm in the early days   Here is a petition which was passed out for signatures probably in 1840 although it is dateless, the Ogd & Lake Champlain R R to which it alludes, having been surveyed that year

"To the Honorable the Legislature of the State of New York

The undersigned inhabitants of the County of   would respectfully represent, that the country bordering upon the Oswegatchie and Grass Rivers and Black Lake abounds in ores of Iron and Lead and other minerals of a quality and to an extent unsurpassed by any portion of this, or any other State in the Union, added to which there are extensive forests of valuable timber, and an unlimited amount of Water Power—all of which are nearly valueless from the want of a cheap and easy mode of transportation to market   That it appears from a recent report of the commissioners and Engineer appointed by the State, to survey the route of a Rail Road from Ogdensburg to Lake Champlain, that the navigation of those Rivers and Lake can be opened for Steam Boats to an extent of about 100 miles, at a cost of about $2,700 per mile   That in the opinion of the undersigned the interests of the State generally, and of the northern portion thereof particularly, call for an immediate construction of this work

Your petitioners would therefore solicit, that a law be passed at your present session for the improvement of the navigation of the Oswegatchie River from Oxbow to Ogdensburg—the Natural Canal—the Grass River and Black Lake, in a manner and to the extent mentioned in the Report above referred to."

Hough says The Oswegatchie Navigation Co formed some years earlier than the date of this petition, was to improve the water ways to the town of Gouverneur and along Natural Canal up to Canton village   If this scheme had carried, we should today be able to buy coal, for instance, one dollar a ton cheaper than now, as Carthage, having the protecting aegis of the Black River canal, is enabled to do

The Erie Canal attracted nation-wide attention from its magnitude and necessity   Gouverneur was not a silent observer of the improvement as this document shows   Long before the advent of the "promoter" of the railway, the town was fully alive to the importance of overcoming its isolated position There was the great water-way to the north, and the denser populated region to the south, with the new artificial water-way, and no means of reaching either. Harvey D Smith had represented this district in the Assembly in 1829, Edwin Dodge in 1832, Preston King in 1835-7, but these forceful men were too early to benefit this petition, while Geo Redington, 1842-4, John Leslie Russell, 1845, and Asa L Hazelton, 1846, were too late to be of service in its behalf.   What might have been its fate had we been represented by men like these, it is idle to speculate   But perhaps, it is well that the movement did not succeed so far as Gouverneur is concerned   A river whose tortuous course from Gouverneur to Richville, for instance, covered forty-nine miles while the direct roadway measured but seven, could hardly have been an ideal means for reaching the outer world

As these closing lines are being written, the work of erecting the Memorial Arch in the village park, is being carried out   It was at first proposed to build a copy of the monument to the Father of his Country at Washington, reduced to one-tenth size, which would have comported well with surrounding architecture and have afforded large surfaces for inscriptions hereafter   Gradually, the arch came to be preferred by the public and plans were accordingly made for that

Within the arch on a polished slab built into one leg of the structure, will be engraved the names of the pioneers who came in 1805 and 1806   On the opposite slab similarly built the veterans of the Civil War will place an inscription not yet decided upon   In a copper box, mortised into the corner stone, (laid June 14, 1905) are the names of hundreds of children and others who have contributed toward the monument fund   No movement in the town of any character, ever met with so universal a response and support as the Monumental Arch   As soon as the drawings were completed and publicly shown, the contributions began pouring in   The structure is to be built of Gouverneur marble, and it is to be completed before the Old Home Week Festival, Aug 24-30, 1905

(Sketches of about fifty of the men who were most active in building the town, were prepared in the interval between the first announcement of Old Home Week and its assured success, in order to save every moment of time possible

These were to be used in the History wherever relevant as the latter progressed. The abrupt termination of the narrative on account of demands of the publishers, required that, if used, these sketches (for which portraits had been engraved) should appear here in a body instead of being scattered through the work. Those personally known are drawn as they appear to the writer, with studious avoidance of fulsome praise. A few were contributed by those most

competent to speak. The pioneer, so far as time permitted and data and portraits could be had, has been accorded space here though he may not have had honors given him in life. No attempt to arrange these sketches has been made as to merit or prominence. The number could easily be doubled, and would have been with time. All save five have laid aside the cares, these being the oldest men living in town. These are the men whom our fathers and ourselves, knew in the daily walks of life.)

Hon. Edwin Dodge was born in Kent, Connecticut, Dec. 13, 1801. Early in life his father removed to Northern New York and Mr. Dodge entered the office of Hon. Micah Sterling at Watertown as a law student. Having been admitted to the bar he was in 1829 engaged by Gouverneur Morris as his agent in charge of large tracts of land in St. Lawrence County, and removed to Gouverneur with his wife, a niece of Mr. Sterling.

In 1830 he was appointed postmaster and held that office for nineteen years. In 1832 Mr. Dodge was elected a member of Assembly and in 1845 was appointed a side judge of the court of common pleas for a term of two years. Under the new state constitution of 1846 he was elected the first county judge of

St. Lawrence County, holding the office from June, 1847, to December, 1855,
Mr. Dodge was also one of the first board of trustees of Gouverneur upon its incorporation as a village in 1850, for a number of years a trustee of the Gouver-

neur Seminary, and one of the incorporators of the Water Works Company. He was largely instrumental in
the organizing and financiering of the Potsdam and
Watertown Railroad, of which he became the first president. Confident in the future of St. Lawrence County and of its great mineral wealth, he did much toward
investigating and exploiting the mining industries and
the present has given ample proof of his sagacity and
foresight.

Judge Dodge was a man of keen business ability,
progressive and energetic, who by his efforts did
much to benefit the community in which he lived.

Judge Edwin Dodge.

With charitable impulses and a high sense of public duty he gave freely of his
time and money to the improvement of Gouverneur along educational, charitable
and religious lines. Throughout his life he was a consistent and earnest Democrat, and his political and personal acquaintance extended to many states of
the Union. He died Nov. 15, 1877, leaving his widow and three children, William Robert Dodge, Edwin Gardiner Dodge and Mrs. John Lansing.

In the early years of Gouverneur's history, the life and labors of Joseph
Hopkins in the cause of advanced education and character building, left a pos-

itive and lasting impress. His methods were peculiar to
himself. He did not follow the routine of text books.
He was a graduate of Hamilton College. Hamilton's
curriculum in 1825 was not the University course of
1905. But the influence of Mr. Hopkins' teaching
tended to individual research by his students that was a
forerunner of better schools. He sought to develop
thought and character rather than to load the memory
with facts. There were strong men and women who
went out from that school to battle with life, duty and
opportunity. Some were teachers, citizens, bearers of

Prof. Joseph Hopkins.

high trust and responsibility. His students uniformly bore tribute to his worthy character and kind personalty. Mr. Hopkins was of early New England
ancestry, born in Bridgeport, Ct., Oct. 26, 1796. While a young lad his parents settled in Rutland, Jefferson Co. He shared with them the usual pioneer
life until his majority. He worked his way through Hamilton College. He
was a good scholar, particularly in Latin and English. After teaching elsewhere he became principal at Gouverneur from 1834 until the school came into
care of the M. E. Church in 1840 as Gouverneur Wesleyan Seminary. He married Permelia Picket of Fowler, Aug. 27, 1835. Six of their nine children are
yet alive, scattered from Minnesota to the Pacific. For about thirty years his
home was on his Gouverneur farm, now the home of Mr. S. F. Hartley. His
last few years were with his sons in Minnesota where he died Dec. 13, 1875.

His body was buried in the Cemetery at Gouverneur. In early life he was a whig, later a Republican. In religion a Presbyterian.

It is interesting to notice the tendency of the early settlers to come from one locality, and how this hegira soon spends itself so that, after a few years

Oliver Parsons.

there is no further exodus. Oliver Parsons, then thirty-one years of age, came from Johnstown, in 1820, and was soon followed by Richard and Myron, his sons. Like all the early fathers of the town, these sturdy pioneers went through the usual period of paying for their several landed properties by making and selling "black salts," which was about the only article exchangeable for money. Johnstown Street was a forest then with but the semblance of a roadway cut through. They found their abiding places about three miles from the incipient village on that street. Scan the features of Oliver and the character of man he was is apparent. The square mouth and set lips, the expansive forehead, the solid jaw all betoken a man of action and determin-

Myron Parsons

ation. Myron lived upon the farm he took up until his span was reached. Richard became a merchant, and the one-story, red-painted building where the Egert Block now stands will be remembered by a few who still recall the tall, courteous man with spectacles who sold hardware, stoves and tinware there. His wife saw Lafayette on his

Richard Parsons.

visit to America in 1824 and retained to an extremely old age a lively recollection of his courtly manner and dignified presence. Richard Parsons was a gentleman of the old school. Like so many of the pioneers he seems to have had much humor in his composition. The "Northern Farmer" cook stove which supplanted the brick oven in the farmhouse of the writer's father, came from his stock and did duty for many a long year. Another is still doing daily duty in Richville after a continuous service of sixty years.

Col. James M. Spencer was born in Gouverneur May 26, 1811, the son of Dr. John Spencer and Elizabeth Burnett, who came to this town from Windsor, Conn., in 1807. On October 8th, 1833, he married Cassendana, daughter of Ezekiel Bullard and Eunice Boyden, who were among the early settlers of the town. Col. Spencer died March 15, 1884. The greater part of his life was passed in the house which was built by his father about 1829 or 1830 and was known all through this section by his name (Spencer House), and which was burned November 23, 1889. He was prom-

Col. James Spencer.

mently connected with the State militia 248 Regt., N. Y., in earlier days and obtained his title from that connection. He was a man who figured largely in the affairs of the village and must occupy a prominent position in the annals of St. Lawrence county. Col. Spencer was a public spirited man. He was a large property owner and the land on which the depot and buildings now stand was given to the R. W. & O. railroad company by him for that purpose. He was a man of sterling merit, one who gives character and solidity to the community in which he lives. At this date his widow, a remarkably bright lady of ninety, and three children, Mrs. Adele E. VanNamee, Dr. James M. Spencer, a practicing dental surgeon of this village, who rendered gallant and efficient service as a cavalry officer during the rebellion, and L. M. Spencer, now of Rochester, survive him.

Benjamin F. Leavitt came in 1808-9. He was a mason by trade, and laid the wall under the first frame barn in town built by Isaac Austin on the lot

Benjamin F. Leavitt.

where the well-known house of the Austin family still stands. He was a man of push and persistence, and bought and paid for a large tract on the Richville road, at the same time raising a large family which he educated in a manner according with the times. He was a man of set opinions, and once having formed a judgment, was slow to change it. An ardent partisan in the early days when partizanship was much more rancorous than now, he brought down to the day of many now living, a stern, impetuous style of political argument, in which the conspicuous feature was that it was based on conviction. He was the sort of settler the town needed in its infancy and he did his part in building it. Always an earnest churchman, he brought his family up in "the nurture and admonition" as was customary in those days. Gouverneur at that time was not unlike the days of the Pilgrim fathers in its religious austerity. It was a condition which found ready support from Mr. Leavitt. He built a sawmill and thus showed his enterprise, and the product of his mill was used in buildings nearby to the exclusion of remoter lumber. He made brick from the clay in the creek bank opposiite the dwelling of Geo. M. Dodds, in the early forties. He died in 1875.

Alexander Dodds was born in Scotland 1770, married Jane Wilson 1804, together came to Gouverneur 1833, settled on the Scotch Settlement road opposite the present school-house three miles from the village and there lived to the years 1864 and 1857 respectively. The history of this venerable couple is interesting. Mr. Dodds, like so many of his countrymen in the first third of the last century, became determined to move to America. To earn money to cover the voyage, he engaged at farming in his native town, Kelso, at an agreed price of five pounds or $25 for six months labor. The sailing vessel, being buffeted with adverse winds, was six weeks on the voyage. Five children had come to them before leaving Scotland, Katherine, Margaret, Andrew, John and Alexander. The three sons were during life among the most excellent and progressive citizens of the town, all living to an old age and acquiring comfortable properties. Surviving representatives of all three families are still to be found in our town.

Timothy Sheldon, coming from Rhode Island at an early day, (1810), took up a farm three miles from the village on the Richville road. He built the house

now occupied by his son, Gray B. Sheldon in 1823, moving to the village later as advancing years came on. An original character, quaint, humorous, incisive in speech; he could condense in a word the salient characteristics of those he knew by a change in their names, or a title, or prefix derived from some peculiarity. He had opinions and expressed them; he was latterly, much interested in reading for information, and he could remember and repeat in new words what attracted him most. Once he became a convert to O. S. Fowler's system of concrete building and always wanted to construct an

Timothy Sheldon.

octagon house of cement and gravel. Probably he was the only farmer in town who bought a complete set of Appleton's Cyclopedia, at the current price of $80, and he became familiar with much of the information it contained. His younger manhood was marked by a trip to Alabama with a relative after coming to Gouverneur. They went to Olean, N. Y., built a flat-boat, and with their belongings reached their destination by way of the Allegheny, Ohio, and Tennessee rivers. He was not attracted by what he found in Alabama and he came back to Gouverneur on horseback, riding the entire distance, swimming and fording rivers, the first bridge on the journey home being one near Buffalo. This journey was characteristic of the spirit which actuated the man. He enlisted in the war of 1812 and went to the frontier.

John VanNamee came to Gouverneur when at the age of 13, from Fairfield, N. Y., and followed the occupation of farmer for some years on Johnstown

Street across the road from the present cheese factory where the VanNamee farmhouse is still in fair preservation. He subsequently became a tinner by trade, working for Richard Parsons and several others following him in that line of business. He was a man of genial temperament, small and spare in build, and it is said of him that

John Van Namee.

Gilbert L. Van Namee.

he never had a sick day until the final close of his life. His son Gilbert L. became a druggist, built one of the finest stores in town for that particular trade and conducted the business several years with success. The writer well remembers him when a clerk in the general store of Sterling & Cone with which firm he became conversant with the retail trade of the town in almost every

branch save drugs, as the firm named had but one competitor, and each carried everything the community needed as was the custom sixty years ago. Gilbert was a great lover of good horses and for many years kept one or more of
fine breeding.

James Bowne came to Gouverneur in 1814 as agent for the father of
Gen. Philip Kearney, a soldier of both the Mexican and Civil wars, in the former of which he lost an arm at the assault on the City of Mexico, and
in the latter was killed at Chantilly in 1862. The Kearney Tract was ori-

ginally nearly three-fourths of a mile wide, containing
10,000 acres, and extended from the St. Lawrence river
to the southerly boundary of Gouverneur. Mr. Bowne
settled near Kearney Bridge, where he followed the avocation of farmer and land agent. The property he then
acquired is still in the Bowne family. The Kearney
tract was reduced by sales to Parish and Nicholas Low
so that it finally was about one-fourth of a mile wide,
and from its narrowness and length, the latter being
about twenty miles, it probably became known as the
"Sheepwalk." James Bowne appears to have been a man

James Bowne.

of much force of character and left an honorable record that is prized by his
descendants. The Bowne name frequently appears in the records of Flushing,
L. I. They were non-conformists, coming from England because of religious
persecutions, and it is of record that John Bowne entertained the celebrated
English preacher Geo. Fox, (born 1624, died 1690), the services being held under a venerable oak which was standing in 1860. "The Bowne House stands in
Parsons & Co.'s Commercial Garden and Nursery and is in a fine state of preservation."[1] There is some evidence that the celebrated Barbara Heck in whose
house in John street, New York city, the first Methodist church was organized,
was a member of the Bowne family. She is buried at Blue Church, Canada,
between Prescott and Brockville on the shores of the St. Lawrence.

John Fosgate, born in Essex, N. Y., in 1800, came to Gouverneur in 1832,
died in 1874. Such is the epitome of a long life of activity, probity, gentle demeanor and open hand. He was among the earliest if
not the first, brickmaker in town; he kept a hotel at
the junction of Johnstown and Main streets many years,
until the location of the depot in 1856 transferred the
traveling trade to the east side; he engaged in lumber
and milling at the same time and had all the business of
those lines for more than a quarter of a century; he
speedily rebuilt these mills when they were burned in
1853 and continued the grist mill until 1874, selling
the saw mill some ten years previously to Bidwell &
Baldwin. Mr. Fosgate was a business man of honesty,

John Fosgate.

and as he came at an early date, played an important part in the town's progress.

(1) Gazetteer of New York

He married Sophronia Adams in 1823, and fifteen children were born to them. Of these five remain, Lucy, Paige, George, Jane and Susan. Mrs. Fosgate died in 1873 aged 67 years. She is spoken of as a wife of rare excellence and a mother of wise discretion.

Harvey Douglas Smith, born 1789 in Pawlet, Vt., at sixteen clerk in a store at Sudbury, filling like position in Poultney two years later, and finally in

Harvey D. Smith.

business for himself at the latter place; this was the early career of Mr. Smith before coming to Gouverneur. He arrived here in 1824, opened the first "apothecary" store in the place, continued in business twenty-five years, latterly occupying a part of the stone building since fitted up by the late J. B. Preston as a law office. He held many positions of public trust; was justice of the peace thirty-seven years; member of the state assembly in 1829, surrogate in 1859 and special county judge a year earlier. "Harvey D." as he was familiarly called, was one of those rare men whose presence is a blessing to the community. He was a peacemaker in every contention; an adviser in every perplexity, a friend whose counsel was at command of all who asked and when given was followed with confidence; a man so gifted with the graces of self-abnegation, lofty aspirations, and sterling common sense, that his word was law and his deportment a model. He discouraged litigation and sent disputants from his court with the injunction of settle their dispute privately; he was a leader in the church of his choice and his fellow-members of all ages looked to him as the embodiment of wisdom. A sensitive nature withal, a man of culture and broad enlightenment; a citizen who met every public duty without seeking position; liberal in purse to the needy; a ready wit and bubbling over with humor; such was Harvey D. Smith and he died in 1864 mourned by every one who knew him. We shall not look upon his like again.

Myron Cushman was born in Rupert, Bennington County, Vt., July 27, 1812, and died in Gouverneur Jan. 22, 1880. When twelve years of age with his parents, John Cushman and Annie Fuller, settled in Ellisburg, Jefferson Co. At the age of sixteen he learned the tailor's trade, which was ever after the chief occupation of his life. In 1840 he came to Gouverneur, where he afterward resided. He possessed in a great degree the characteristics of his New England ancestors. He is entitled to the honor of casting the first and only abolition vote in this town, at the first election when that ticket was in the field. He was one of the old directors and conductors of the Underground Railroad, the dividends of which were the keeping of a free table for all runaway slaves and Abolition lecturers, for many years. In 1861 he took arms for the defence of the country and was made Lieutenant in the 92nd Regiment. He married Susan Waid, daughter of Josiah Waid and grand-

Myron Cushman.

daughter of Isaac Austin. Children now living are Mrs. Wm. Whitney, Mrs. G. B. Barnes and Miss Christialania E. Cushman.

Milton Barney was born May 1, 1808 in Adams, N. Y. He was the son of Sylvanus Barney and Miriam Kingsley Barney. His ancestors were of Welch

Milton Barney.

descent, emigrating to this country at an early period and settling in Vermont. His father with a colony of relatives went from Vermont to Adams, N. Y., some time before the year 1800, where they built homes and established themselves in various business enterprises. When Milton was seven years old his father was drowned in the Black river at Watertown, leaving his mother with a large family of children. At nine years he commenced working for farmers for support. He attended the district school in winter for two or three years. When older he went into a chair factory in Watertown as apprentice. After serving his time there, at 21 years he removed to Gouverneur and opened a shop for chair-making and painting. For many years it was the only business of the kind in the town. Nov. 6, 1833, he was married to Katherine Starr VanBuren, daughter of Barent VanBuren and Grace Denison VanBuren. Six children were born, three dying at an early age. His eldest son, Albert M., died in 1886, Bradley L. is living in Hanford, California, and Mrs. Sarah G. B. Winslow in Washington, D. C. Early in Mr. Barney's career in Gouverneur he erected a building for his business which was destroyed by fire a few years later at a great financial loss to him. With a strong nerve and unflagging energy he put his shoulder to the wheel to re-establish his business by building a much larger factory. His health failing, he disposed of this property to get a well earned rest. Soon after he built the house at the corner of Barney and Clinton streets (now owned by A. J. McDonald) in which he died July 3, 1885, aged 97 years. He was one of the solid business men of Gouverneur. His word was sacred, his integrity unquestioned, and he was the soul of honor.

Milton G. Norton came in 1835, being preceded some five years by a brother-in-law, and when each had prospered sufficiently they built themselves houses alike in design and after the then prevalent style in Massachusetts, from which state both came. These houses were among the finest in town when built. Mr. N. became known as a progressive farmer, a student of all the current literature relating to his calling, and was usually the first to adopt labor-saving machinery. He brought the first subsoil plow into town; he built a revolving rake for himself when that implement was unknown save through the farm papers; he was certainly the first (with the relative mentioned) to bring in combined reapers and mowers, both driving to Utica for them, a round trip of 160 miles. Timothy Sheldon had bought a single

Milton G. Norton.

mower the year previously, but it was not a success. Mr. Norton became interested in blooded stock and his famous four yokes of Devon oxen, so perfectly matched for age, size, color and training that any pair might be yoked together, caused much interest at the early town and county fairs. He drove them alone with an enormous whip long enough to reach every "off" animal. As a farmer he was successful: as a citizen he was awake to public interests: as a breeder the first to import fine-wooled Merino sheep; as a business man careful, sagacious and honest.

Peter VanBuren, Gouverneur's venerable hotel-keeper of forty-five years ago, and earlier, began business in a brick building which stood where the brick residence of his daughter, Emeline, now stands. From

1831 until this building burned in the spring of 1848, he entertained the traveling public, a period of seventeen years. In 1848 he built the well-remembered, two-story, white, frame building on Main street now the site of the St. Lawrence Inn, continuing here until 1869, or thirty-eight years in all, counting both hotels. This last named house became noted among the hostelries of the period. "Uncle Peter" as every one called him with much more of real friendliness than is now usual in the use of the term, was a favorite with the traveling public, and his house was specially known for its good table, cleanly appointments and the general air of home comfort that pervaded it. The ancient wood fireplace was always piled high with cord-wood as the chill season came on and became an attraction often spoken of after its cheerful glow had departed. His beefsteak, always broiled by himself, for he would trust no professional cook

Peter Van Buren.

with this important detail, was the special delight of the connoisseur in cookery. The solid men of the town often came in to spend the evening with him for he was well read in current happenings and discussed them with intelligence. He was

Van Buren Hotel 1860. Burned 1881.

the ideal old-time gentleman, and the familiarities usual in hotels were never allowed to degenerate into license. No ribaldry or profanity were heard when the proprietor was near, nor could any patron indulge his appetite too freely. Tradition has preserved many incidents of his life and all are to his credit. He was a "boniface" of the best sort and his memory will long survive. He died in 1870.

James Hill, the eldest son of James and Janet Sheill Hill, was born in the town of Hammond, Dec. 18, 1821. When seven years of age he came with his parents to the town of Gouverneur to reside; locating in what is called the

Scotch Settlement; and their family being the first Scotch to settle in this town. As he grew to young manhood he assisted in cutting down the forest and clearing the land. When twenty-one years of age he apprenticed himself to Deacon Thomas Thayer of this town, to learn cabinet making and worked with him three years in a building which stood where now stands the Masonic Temple. After this he worked for a number of years as a carpenter in summer and a cabinet maker in winter. In January, 1854, he was married to Jane Storie of Rossie, and settled on a farm which he

James Hill.

bought in the Scotch Settlement. In April, 1864, his wife died, and in March, 1866, he was married again to Miss Jane Markwick of Rossie, who died in 1894. In 1866 he bought the farm on the Rock Island Road where he still continues to reside.

James, Willett, William Henry and Charles Hicks Bowne, four brothers, sons of James Bowne who came in 1814, were all identified with the growth of

William H. Bowne.

Charles H. Bowne.

Gouverneur during the last sixty years. The first remained on the homestead farm all his life, the other three engaging more actively in business as merchants in the village at various periods of their lives. William Henry was many years in the dry goods trade and was esteemed highly for his strict probity. Willett and Charles H. were in partnership in the hardware trade several years. They built the portion of the Union Hall block occupied by themselves. The Bowne family including James Bowne the elder, played an important part in the building of the town. They were descendants of a prominent family of the same name in Flushing, L. I., who held positions of prominence there.

Edward Hall came upon his farm in January, 1844, when he was confronted by the labor of clearing it from its timber and putting it into a state of cultivation. Having no knowledge of forest-clearing he secured the services of an experienced woodsman with whose aid he made much progress toward desired results, but while improving the land, debts accumulated which by economy, industry and perseverance he succeeded in discharging and in bringing the farm to its present condition. As a dairyman his judgment has been good in the selection of dairy cattle and he has given them the most efficient care, never during his sixty years as dairyman having lost an ailing animal save two that died of that fatal disease, milk-fever. In the year 1854 he succeeded

Edward Hall.

in producing 190 lbs. of butter from each of 15 cows by the more crude methods of dairy appliances of that time. Cautious to a fault, conservative and slow to adopt labor-saving machinery until convinced of its merits, yet withal a good salesman and constant reader of the best agricultural papers, and fairly successful, he might not be called one of the most progressive of farmers, being "slow but sure" in his methods, honest dealing his purpose, industrious in his habits and he is still an early riser and active at the age of 84 years.

Newton Martin Curtis was born in Depeyster, May 21, 1835. He was educated in the common schools and in 1854 entered Gouverneur Wesleyan Seminary where he remained two years.

General N. M. Curtis.

His military bent showed itself at this time by his choice of subjects for essays. In the program of the "Annual Exhibition of the Students of Gouverneur Wesleyan Seminary, Morning Session, June 28, 1854," Mr. N. Martin Curtis had the first number which was "Anniversary of the Battle of Monmouth, June 29, 1778," and again in 1855, June 26th, he read another essay on the "Benefits of War." While the accident of birth gave him to another town, Gouverneur claims him as her own because she fitted him for a place among the bravest and best.

March 3rd, 1857, he was appointed postmaster at Depeyster, as a Democrat. This position he held until July, 1861. Mr. Curtis was a Democrat from his majority through the presidential campaign of 1860, when he voted for Douglas, and was on the Democratic ticket for Member of Assembly from the first St. Lawrence District. At the first call for volunteers after the capture of Fort Sumter, in April, 1861, he enlisted, enrolling April 14th, and was commissioned Captain of Company H, 16th N. Y. Volunteer Infantry, May 7, 1861. The 16th, including Capt. Curtis' Company, was at the first Battle of Bull Run though not actively engaged. May 7, 1862, he was seriously wounded at West

Point, Va October 4, 1862, he returned to the field He was then transferred to the 142nd N Y Volunteers with a commission as Lieutenant Colonel On January 21, 1863, he was again promoted, getting a Colonel's commission, and was placed in command of the 2nd Brigade, 2nd Division of the 10th Corps, stationed at Cold Harbor. June 10, 1864, in place of Colonel Drake, who was killed in action June 25, 1864, he was assigned to command of the 1st Brigade, 2nd Division 10th Corps "For distinguished service upon the field" he was given the brevet rank of Brig General, and assigned to duty under this brevet rank, January 4, 1865, and was appointed Major General of U S. Volunteers by brevet "for gallant and meritous services" at the capture of Fort Fisher, the rank to date from March 13, 1865 April 15, 1865, he was assigned to duty as Chief of Staff to Gen E O C Ord, commanding the army of the James, and on July 1, 1865, he was assigned to command of Southwestern Virginia This command he held until mustered out January 15, 1866.

Through the war he was looked upon by his superior officers as a cool headed daring officer and a man to be depended upon in an emergency. but the world knew little of him until nearly the close of the war, when his brilliant capture of Fort Fisher made him famous And the country knows him today as the "Hero of Fort Fisher" At Fort Fisher he was wounded four times, once in the face, twice in the arm, and had a rib broken, but continued to direct the attack until a fragment of a shell struck him in the eye The battle was nearly over, and Gen Abbott continued the battle as planned by Gen Curtis For five hours he was unconscious and was reported dead, one of the war correspondents writing an obituary After the Capture of Fort Fisher, the N Y State Legislature passed a resolution thanking him and his command for services rendered in that engagement After his discharge he returned to his home in Depeyster On the 14th of August following, he was appointed Collector of Customs for the District of Oswegatchie, holding the office until appointed Special Agent U S Treasury Department, March 4, 1867, resigning the latter office in 1880 Gen Curtis was always interested in agriculture, owning a farm to which he devoted all his leisure time This together with his executive ability, lead to his election as President of the St Lawrence County Agricultural Society in 1874, and continuous re-election until 1878 In 1880 he was President of N Y State Agricultural Society, and from its organization in 1880 he was Secretary of the Board of Control of the N Y Agricultural Experiment Station In 1887 he was elected its President

About 1875 he joined Dahlgren Post 113 G A R of New York, which he left to organize Ransom Post 354 of Ogdensburg, being the latter Post's first commander February 23, 1888, he was elected Department Commander Grand Army of the Republic of the Department of New York State, receiving 476 votes, the three other candidates only getting 300 In 1883 Gen Curtis was elected to the Assembly by the Republicans of the 1st St Lawrence district and re-elected in 1884 In 1885 there was a rupture in the Republican ranks in the 1st district and Gen Curtis run on an "Independent" Republican ticket, defeating the regular nominee by a substantial majority He continued in the

Assembly until 1891 when he was elected to Congress to fill a vacancy. In 1892 he was elected for the full term and again in 1894. March 4, 1897, he retired from Congress by expiration of his term and has taken but little part in the political affairs of his county since. In July, 1897, he was appointed Inspector of Soldiers Homes, which position he still holds. For several years he has been working on a History of the 16th N. Y. Volunteer Infantry. The work is nearly completed now and is to be published the coming fall. Gen. Curtis is a man of strong character and among the people who know him best, he is thoroughly liked. No veteran of the 16th or 142nd Infantry will hear a word against ...d ... re as ready today to fight for him as they were in the trying days of the Rebellion.

Daniel Peck came to Gouverneur in 1876 as proprietor of the Fuller House, then newly completed. He had been an inn-keeper at Little York for twelve years.

Daniel Peck.

Prior to that he enlisted in the 106th N. Y. Inf. at Ogdensburg as 2nd Lieut. July, 1862, serving until 1864, when he was honorably discharged. He was promoted captain while at the front. He came to Fowler from Clarendon, Vt., engaged with the four Fuller brothers, who had built a blast furnace at Fullerville five years before. In 1846 he became a partner, the furnace was rebuilt, changed to hot-blast, and the making of bar iron which the Fullers had begun in 1835, was continued. The writer remembers that his father exchanged a quantity of cheese with this firm a little before the 50's, turning over the iron received to his blacksmith in exchange for smithing. Iron constituted a sort of currency then. What a commentary on the laxity of the National government in not providing its citizens with sufficient money to make exchanges with! Surrounded as this furnace was with fuel and mines of the best ore, a gigantic industry might have resulted had there been an adequate money supply. Daniel Peck was in some respects an extraordinary man. As a partisan he was implacable and invincible to argument. As a statesman, for he served the state three terms in the assembly, he voted for what was right as he saw the right. He was quick at repartee in argument, strong in invective, extremely popular as a hotel-keeper, and many a traveler has journeyed miles out of his course in order to partake of his hospitable board. In the army he did excellent service for his country. He was an uncompromising patriot, an honest man, and whoever assailed his integrity did so either from ignorance or malice. He was missed when old age debarred him from the activities; he was mourned when the final parting came.

The memory of a good man does not die with him. Melville H. Thrall came to Gouverneur from Johnstown, N. Y., in 1819, when five years old, lived on his farm on Johnstown street sixty-five years, dying in 1884. Hs life was devoted to good deeds. Wherever a sick or suffering fellow creature was to be found there was Mr. Thrall to comfort and sustain. He was a devoted churchman, and as such was ready and anxious to bear his share of the public burden

Melville H. Thrall.

necessary for its welfare. He lived the life he professed, and no better judgment than his can be accorded any man. Such public positions as he occupied were never sought by him. He accepted them as his duty and filled them with scrupulous fidelity. None better than he deserved the title of Nature's nobleman.

In 1818 came George Lockie with his father, he being eight years old. They came by way of Montreal and the St. Lawrence River, coming up the latter in a Durham boat. They were sixteen weeks on the sea. The elder Lockie settled in Rossie near the Indian River opposite the subsequently discovered lead mines. At twenty-four our subject took up a farm near Elmdale and three years later had a comfortable frame house built (which still forms a part of old family home) and to this he took his newly made bride, Catherine McLaren of Scottish parentage like himself. The marriage was in 1840. The trail between his father's house and his land, about six miles in length, was covered by a dense woods, there being but two small clearings in the whole distance. Mr. L. became an expert with the rifle in his lusty young man-

George Lockie.

hood, and at the annual fortnight devoted to hunting, averaged two deer daily, the saddles and skins of which were sold. He was a leading citizen in the town, held various positions of trust and died at a ripe old age respected by all who knew him. He could tell a story with infinite humor, and the annual Burns festival usually found him at the head of the board with some new contribution to the jollity of the evening.

Dr. Grosvenor Swan was born in the town of Heath, Mass., March 27, 1819. His parents moved from there to the town of Gouverneur when he was seven years of age. He received his education in the common schools and Gouverneur Seminary, then entering the ministry (Universalist) preaching for several years, being engaged at the same time in the study of medicine. Prior to

Dr. Grosvenor Swan.

his entering the Eclectic Medical College of Cincinnati, O., where he graduated in 1853, he practiced his profession in Gouverneur till 1869 when he removed to Chicago and two years later was one of the victims of the great fire which decided him to locate in Hartford, Conn., where he resided until his death in 1891. He was a man eminent in his profession, with an intellect which threw light, learning and love across the path of human advancement. No estimate of Dr. Swan is complete without a reference to his irrepressible sense of humor. He was an inimitable raconteur, a natural actor, and there was an aptness and point to his wit that left a sense of pleasure with the listener. His humor was never rasping, acrid or wounding, but it came bubbling spontaneously from a heart having no guile. His stories became famous in his immediate neighborhood and were often retold but without the delicious savor he gave them.

Dr. James B. Carpenter came to Gouverneur after the Civil war. He was a son of Jonathan and Lucy Carpenter, of Fowler, being one of a family of ten children. The Carpenter family were from New England originally, going from Connecticut to Johnstown, N. Y., and from there the subject of our sketch came to Northern New York. He was educated in the old Gouverneur Wesleyan Seminary, subsequently graduating at Cassleton Medical College in Vermont. Twenty years practice in Theresa, Jefferson Co., fortified him with a fund of experience which the National government utilized in the army as surgeon of the 25th Regiment N. Y. S. Vols. The Flower family from which came Roswell P., later governor of the state in 1892-4. were residents of Theresa and Dr. Carpenter in 1849 married Roxaline, a sister of the future governor, who was one of the few who could think in millions as easily as the ordinary man can in single dollars. The terrific battles of Gettysburg, the Wilderness and Fredericksburg, found Dr. Carpenter at his post as at all minor engagements in which his regiment was involved, and he retired from the arduous service with honor. He was a steadfast but not an aggressive partisan in politics and always affiliated with the democratic party. He was a man who is remembered as being held in high esteem as a practitioner by the citizens of the town as well as by the members of his profession.

Dr. J. B. Carpenter.

John Bower Preston, familiarly known by the last two names written, was a well-known figure in town almost his entire life. At the age of eighteen he entered the family of his adopted brother, Judge James M. Smith, of Buffalo, and was fitted for the profession of the law, and at the age of twenty-two was admitted to the bar. After two years he removed to Hastings, Minn. On the breaking out of the Civil war he soon enlisted receiving a commission as Captain in the 3rd Minnesota regiment, which was at once ordered to Tennessee. On June 1, 1862, his regiment was obliged to surrender for lack of ammunition. The officers were offered their liberty on parole, but thought it not honorable to leave their men to endure a Southern prison.

Maj. J. B. Preston.

Thereupon the whole number were imprisoned in an old cotton factory. There they suffered great privations. Upon an exchange of prisoners in September, Mr. Preston returned to his old home in Gouverneur. In the following summer when, in conjunction with other patriotic young men, having raised principally in St. Lawrence and Jefferson counties the 20th N. Y. Cavalry, he was commissioned as Major of that regiment which was sent to join the Army of the Potomac. Major Preston continued in the service a brave and able soldier until Lee's surrender. Soon after he received an honorable discharge and returned to Gouverneur where he spent the remainder of his life. He resumed the practice of his profession proving a thorough lawyer and good citizen, always active to pomote the best interests of the town. He died suddenly in Gouverneur Dec. 26, 1898.

Emory W. Abbott came to Fowler in 1836, a boy of seventeen, as clerk in the store of Justus Picket, his future father-in-law. He became a partner of

Emory W. Abbott.

Mr. Picket in 1840 and for thirty years carried on a general business, including farming, merchandise, shoemaking, blacksmithing and an ashery. In those early days supplies were drawn by oxen and horses from Utica: purchases being made in New York, and transportation from New York to Utica being made by canal. Mr. Abbott was for many years Supervisor of Fowler: (also Justice of the Peace); and was chairman of the County Board during the Civil War, in which capacity he contributed largely to providing men and means which gave to St. Lawrence County its glorious record during that trying period. He represented his district in the Legislature during the years 1856-57 and while there assisted in procuring the necessary legislation for the creation of St. Lawrence University from which institution one son and three grand-sons have since been graduated. Mr. Abbott came to Gouverneur in 1871, since which time he has lived easily on a modest competence, allowing full scope to his literary tastes and keeping abreast of the times in all matters pertaining to National progress. He is now enjoying the "ease and dignity" of a ripe old age, yet continues always alert to the interests of the County, State and Nation.

Orison Dean was one of those quiet, unassuming men whom it was a pleasure to meet in business or a more intimate social way. He came to Gouverneur in 1866 as partner in the firm of Weston, Dean and Aldrich, and with them conducted the most extensive business for over forty years the town had then or has since known. The firm soon became a synonym for square dealing and exact treatment of its customers and to this reputation Mr. Dean contributed a full share. He was well-informed upon all the current topics usually uppermost in men's minds, and could converse with intelligence concerning them. He was broad-minded in his judgments toward his fellow men, charitable in his opinions and slow to censure. Skilled in the wood-craft

Orison Dean.

pertaining to his business, he was ready with pikepole and peevey and in his younger days never sent a man into danger that he was not ready to share himself. One of the sights always noticeable to strangers was the figure of Mr. Dean, then in his seventies, actively guiding the "drive" over the runway in this village. It was his habit to add a little to every load of lumber he personally sold so that the buyer would have scripture measure. His fund of experience in business was large and his memory accurate, so that a conversation with him was a delightful remembrance. The general judgment of his townsmen is that he was a solid unassertive, trustworthy man, successful in business, genial to everybody, and one who never forgot a favor nor remembered a wrong done himself.

George Bigelow Winslow was born June 23, 1832, in Adams, Jefferson Co., N. Y. His ancestors were of good old Puritan stock, having come over in the

Mayflower. At the early age of sixteen, he began the battle of life unaided and alone, as his parents had died. When seventeen years old he apprenticed himself to learn the tinner's trade at Watertown, N. Y. When his time of service expired, he went to Gouverneur, N. Y., and was employed by Messrs. Sterling & Cone to work at his trade. He continued with them until about the year 1860 when he and Mr. Gilbert L. VanNamee formed a partnership in the hardware business, which they carried on until the outbreak of the Civil war. Mr.

Capt. Geo. B. Winslow.

Winslow enlisted in the month of August, 1861, to serve in "Battery D." 1st N. Y. Light Artillery. He was commissioned first Lieutenant and was later made Captain in the same Battery, known as "Winslow's Battery." History had honored this Battery by calling it "The Banner Battery" and says of it that it was in more engagements than any similar organization in the "Army of the Potomac." May 5, 1863, he was wounded during the first day's fight in "The Battle of the Wilderness," which compelled him to resign a few months later. In 1865, the townspeople of Gouverneur honored him by helping to give him the Postmastership of that village, which office he held for eighteen years. Mr. Winslow was school trustee for twenty years, the greater part of that time the sole trustee of District No. 1, and gave much of his time to advance education in Gouverneur. He was Secretary of the Gouverneur Agricultural Society nine years, and was a public spirited, zealous worker in all good enterprises. He died Sept. 30, 1883, aged 51 years.

Robert Ormiston was born in Jedboro, Scotland, in 1807. Coming with his parents to America in 1818, they settled with many other Scotch families in Rossie upon land purchased from David Parish. After his father's death, he continued to carry on the farm until about his 30th year, selling it to John Dickson and moving to Oxbow where he began as a merchant. In 1861 he moved to Gouverneur buying the store and stock of Wm. E. Sterling then in hands of executors. He built a commodious residence at corner of Main and Gordon streets after moving the Sterling store to Main street to the lot now occupied by William Draper as a drug store. Here he successfully continued the drygoods trade, dying April 10, 1871, the tenth anniver-

Robert Ormiston.

sary of his coming to Gouverneur. He was a staunch Presbyterian, a Republican in politics, and served the town four years as Supervisor, being elected for a fifth term one month prior to his death. To know him was to esteem him. He was one of the few who could carry the strenuous activities of life without effort and no untoward event could ruffle him. He is remembered for his quiet dignity, and gentle address toward those having business or official relations with him.

Henry Rushton was born 1815 and removed from England to Edwards, N. Y., and died 1892 at Gouverneur. In 1833 or 4 he engaged in the mill business,

first purchasing a small grist mill which afterwards burned, built another and a saw-mill on the east of the river, following these with the large grist-mill on the Island. When travel began to the South Woods, he built the Rushton House, which was burned July 4, 1894. He owned several stores and other buildings in the village and a large tract of timber land. He belonged to no religious sect or secret society, but liberally aided all who asked. He was always doing something useful for the village where he spent the larger part of his long life. He was a contributor to the Union Church,

Henry Rushton.

erected in 1886, where services could be held free to all on Sunday and other occasions. He had something to do with public affairs, but he was never a politician. He sought no office but held several of trust. In the days of "general training" he held for several years a captain's commission and was highway commissioner, town clerk and supervisor until he declined to serve longer. Some of his friends unknown to him, during the Civil War, obtained from Gov. Fenton a Captain's commission for him in the army but he was obliged to decline it from ill-health.

George M. Gleason was born in the town of Pitcairn, St. Lawrence County, September 16, 1829, and spent his boyhood and early manhood there. On his 32nd birthday, September 16, 1861, he entered as a private in Company I, 60th N. Y. Vol. Infty. When the first indications of war developed Mr. Gleason's voice was heard on the side of the Union and he was instrumental in getting men to enlist from his part of the county without delay. The company which he joined went to the front shortly after he enlisted. He was soon promoted to the position of second Lieutenant and later to Assistant Quartermaster of his regiment. He served in that capacity until August, 1862, when he suffered a severe attack of typhoid fever which com-

George M. Gleason.

pelled his return to his home. He went to the war a stalwart man and during the weeks of his sickness was reduced in weight to about one hundred pounds. Mr. Gleason began his political career when he was made a member of the Board of Supervisors from his native town, shortly after the close of the war, which he held for three years. In 1866 he was elected to the lower branch of the New

York State Legislature where he served six consecutive terms, and became one of the leaders in the Assembly. In 1869 Mr. Gleason moved to the town of Gouverneur which town he represented for several terms on the Board of Supervisors. Soon after this he began the study of the law and was admitted to the bar in 1879, at that time a law partnership being formed with G. S. Conger under the name of Conger & Gleason, which continued until January, 1883. Mr. Gleason then practiced law alone until 1886, when a partnership was formed with Arthur T. Johnson, under the name of Gleason & Johnson, which continued until July, 1900, when Mr. Gleason retired on account of poor health. In the political world he was one of the most prominent men from Northern New York for many years and had a large influence in the Republican party of this section of the state. He was a delegate to the National Republican Convention at Chicago in 1888, in 1890 was appointed Collector of Customs for the District of Oswegatchie and held that position for two years.

When the First National Bank of Gouverneur was organized in 1881 Mr. Gleason was made its President which position he held until a few months before his death. He served several terms as President of Gouverneur Village and held many other local positions and was always foremost in every movement for the benefit of the community in which he lived. He died from apoplexy at his home on the 29th day of September, 1901, leaving him surviving his widow Sally, and four daughters, Mrs. Arthur T. Johnson, Mrs. James F. Brodie of Nashville, Tenn., Mrs. T. O. Bogert of Ithaca, N. Y., and Mrs. N. J. Conklin of Rochester, N. Y., and one son George H. Gleason of Springfield, Mass.

Mr. Gleason was married in 1855 to Sally Harris of Pitcairn, who died at Gouverneur June 30, 1902.

Albert Milton Barney born in Gouverneur, N. Y., Nov. 18, 1837. Died in New York, August 24, 1886. Was the eldest son of Milton Barney and Katherine Van Buren Barney. He was educated at Gouverneur Wesleyan Seminary and subsequently took a special course in higher mathematics and civil engineering, to which he added a course in law and was prepared to take his examination for admittance to the bar, when the firing on Fort Sumter changed the course of his life. On the receipt of the intelligence, April 15, 1861, that the National flag had been struck, he wrote in conspicuous letters and posted on the door of the village postoffice, the words: "Fort Sumter has been fired upon; all patriots and lovers of their country are re-

Gen. A. M Barney.

quested to take action in this crisis." At the meeting convened upon this notice he was the first to volunteer in the company sent out from his native town. He was commissioned 1st Lieutenant and mustered into the U. S. service in the 16th N. Y. Vol. Infantry May 15, 1861. Promoted to be Captain in same regiment June 26, 1862. Lieutenant Colonel 142nd N. Y. Volunteer Infantry, January 21, 1863; Colonel same regiment Jan. 15, 1865 and Brevet Brigadier General U. S. Volunteers March 28, 1865; and mustered out with his regiment June 7,

1865; closing a term of over four years of active military service, present and ready for duty at all times and in every engagement and battle in which his regiment participated; performing his duty with so much ability and distinguished bravery that his several promotions were made on the official recommendations of his superior officers, without the solicitation or interference of political or personal friends. In February 1869, he was appointed Special Agent U. S. Treasury. A few months later Collector of Customs at the Port of Brownsville, Texas. Two years later appointed Special Agent of the Treasury, which position he held at the time of his death. He was an officer (military and civil) of the Federal Government twenty-one years, charged with great responsibilities, important trusts, delicate transactions, involving the custody and disbursement of a large sum of public money, each of which he discharged with high courage, great ability and sound discretion, and with such scrupulous exactness in financial transactions that no auditing officer discovered an error in his accounts.

He was twice married. His first wife was Leonora Chamberlain, daughter of Peleg Chamberlain of Gouverneur. His second wife was Lutie M. Smith of Rochester, N. Y.

He was a member of the Military Order of the Loyal Legion of the United States.

Amasa Corbin came here in 1830. He had been a farmer in Berkshire county, Mass., and continued in that calling all his life. He came from Revo-

lutionary stock, having no less than four ancestors of his name, officers and soldiers, in the war for independence. His father was killed just prior to the war of 1812 while drilling a military company at Plattsburg, of which he was captain. Our subject was a man of extensive reading and marvelous memory and could reason and argue political, religious and historical questions with much force. Notwithstanding his ancestry, he was a man of peace and as such opposed the Civil war from its inception to its close. To him the war pre-

Amasa Corbin, Sr.

sented itself in two aspects: Is it to save the Union? Then let those who say so obey the Constitution and the laws. Is it to "cast the shackles from four million slaves?" The negro is worth nothing to himself, his neighborhood or the nation except under direction of a superior race. That was his reasoning and it was not to him a matter of majorities or popular clamor. He cared little whether others agreed with him or not. Whether he answered the first question correctly must always remain a problem for it is not demonstrable. It clarifies the inquiry, however, to ask "If our present knowledge of the South and the negro, the conditions of 1860 again prevailed, would civil war result?" As for his second answer, let the present condition of the black man as contrasted with his status in slavery, speak. The only human being, white or black, this nation ever knew, who was absolutely care-free so far as food, clothing, shelter and indeed all the necessities were concerned was the negro in slavery. He claimed that war never settled a principle. It only settled the preponderance of gun-powder and strategy. It may sometimes be necessary but it was not in 1861. In this conclusion he exercised the traditional rights of an American freeman and he insisted on those rights. The story is told that he received a soldier's vote in 1864 with instructions to cast it for Abraham Lincoln and that he did so, driving 25 miles to an adjoining town after himself voting for another candidate, thus canceling his own ballot, in effect. The story is probably true for it illustrates his manhood perfectly. Amasa Corbin was in some respects an original character, sometimes visionary, sometimes mistaken but never irresolute. He arrived at an opinion quickly and held to it afterward. He was never acrimonious in argument with his neighbors, and delighted in the family visits so common in the earlier days. He could sell an animal of his own raising at its full value for he first settled in his own mind what it was worth and then adhered to it until the buyer acquiesced. He was progressive in his calling, and with Milton G. Norton brought the first two reapers and mowers into town. It was on a "Manny" that he sat, singing to the rhythm of its rattling cutter-bar,

"This is the way I long have sought,
But until now I found it not,"

and this story, told wherever he was known and persisting until the present, is a true one. Could he have been asked his preference as to how this sketch should be written he would have said, like one of old, "Paint me as I am."

George Parker, prominent in the life and progress of Gouverneur for more than thirty years, was born in Watertown, N. Y., June 7, 1826, and died

Capt. George Parker.

in Gouverneur, May 11, 1883. He was reared on a farm, educated in the common schools, and when a young man entered the employ of an elder brother in the mercantile line at Theresa, N. Y. In 1852 he came to Gouverneur and established a grocery business, also dealing largely in furs, mink, otter and other fur hearing animals, being at that time numerously trapped by the St. Regis Indians and woodmen in this section. Mr. Parker's first active labors for promoting the welfare of the community were in the line of founding the Gouverneur Agricultural and Mechanical Society of which he was the first Secretary and to which he gave liberally of his time and abilities. He served the Society as Secretary from 1857 until entering the army, and in later years again filled that office and also served as President.

Among the foremost to respond to the call for defenders of the Union he enlisted at the first call for troops and was elected Captain of the Infantry Company, raised in Gouverneur. The departure on May 5, 1861, of the company which became Co. D 16th N. Y. Volunteer Infantry, forms a prominent incident in the town's history. Captain Parker commanded his company from the first Bull Run to Charles City Cross-Roads, in which battle he was severely wounded, both limbs being torn by a piece of bursting shell. He was appointed corps commissary on the staff of General Franklin, a position for which he proved to be especially adapted. At the expiration of the two years' term of service, the regiment was mustered out. The home coming of Co. D forms another notable event in Gouverneur's history, and its captain as well as many of its members returned to find others in the places they had left when they went to their country's defence.

At the general election in 1863, Capt. Parker was elected on the Republican ticket Member of Assembly from the First District of St. Lawrence county and re-elected the following year. One result of his labors in the Assembly has since been and still remains a great benefit not only to Gouverneur but to all the country along the Oswegatchie River and this was the passage of the bill creating Cranberry Lake reservoir by which the flow of water is regulated to a degree that prevents both floods and low water, enabling mills and other industries to have reliable water-power.

In 1876, Capt. Parker was appointed Collector of Customs of the port of Oswegatchie, filling the position for three years. Returning to Gouverneur in 1870, he engaged in various enterprises, but principally followed the occupation of land surveying. In 1880 he was Supervisor of United States census, having the territory of six counties. At the time of his death, he represented Gouverneur on the Board of Supervisors. Few men in this community had so wide a circle of friends, including all classes and all ages and few were so willing at all times to befriend whoever needed a friend.

George Parker was united in marriage June 19, 1856, with Mrs. Helen R. Inman at Cincinnati, Ohio. Three children were born, one daughter dying in infancy. His widow, his son, Barnard G. Parker, and daughter Helen I. Parker are now residents of our village.

Christopher Brown, now in his 86th year, is of Scotch parentage, though American born. He recounts many incidents of his early life, and it will per-

haps be a surprise to many that he and the late Willett Bowne were fellow-carpenters, and it is remembered to the latter's good credit that Mr. Bowne testifies to his genial companionship and unfailing good humor. "I always found him as square a man as I ever knew" are his words. They worked together several years. Mr. Brown was a builder and counts to his credit eleven school-houses in this town and Macomb. The first four-lighted windows, those still in the Baptist parsonage, were put in by him after the architect's drawings were

Christopher Brown.

made calling for "five-lighted sash, meaning five lights high and three wide." It was at his solicitation that the sash were changed, he guaranteeing that they would be satisfactory after completion. He worked on the Second Baptist church during its entire building, in the 50's, and during his long life, while not employed on a farm, has been connected as builder with many farm buildings in the town. A quiet, non-assertive man, he was always worthy of trust in his calling and in his sunset years he holds the respect of those who know him best.

Henry Sheldon, second son of Timothy Sheldon, was born in Gouverneur, in 1814. After obtaining such education as local conditions permitted, Mr.

Sheldon at the age of 21, anticipated Horace Greeley's advice and went west. He remained in Michigan about ten years, and in 1846, owing to ill-health, returned to Gouverneur.

Mr. Sheldon was an industrious and painstaking man, and any work in which he engaged received his best efforts. He took life seriously. To faithfully perform all the duties of a Christian citizen was his highest ambition. At an early age he became a member of the Baptist Church, and was one of its leading and most devoted members, serving as deacon for many years.

Henry Sheldon.

Mr. Sheldon possessed a fondness for books. This fact possibly led him to take up the business of keeping a bookstore, in which he was engaged for several years, selling out to G. G. Dains in 1869 or thereabouts. The custom of keeping a journal which was so much in vogue in the earlier years was followed by him from 1835 till 1873. This journal contains many facts and items of particular interest to his children. He held decided opinions on all questions of religion and politics. He was an ardent republican and strongly opposed to masonry and other secret societies. Mr. Sheldon died in 1873.

Amos S. Egert, long time a merchant in Gouverneur, was one of those sterling men who honor the town of their adoption. He conducted in connection with his brother Chas. P. Egert, a dry goods and general business, finally buying out his brother and conducting the business alone. This store and Sterling & Cone's were the only ones in town then. He built the large brick, three-story block at the corner of Main and Clinton streets, the first of that height in town, and filled it with the usual large variety of goods common to a country store of the time. The first floor was then the entire size of the block and was not divided into two stores until he and his successors, Killmer & Jepson, had discontinued business. He is remembered for his

Amos S Egert.

always pleasant smile and greeting. He was typically honest in his deal and drew trade from many miles outside the usual territory that traded in town when his stock was enlarged on occupying his new block. After quitting business here he went to Prescott, Ont., began in the distilling business with John Wiser, his former bookkeeper and clerk many years, but the firm as a firm were not harmonious and soon dissolved. Mr. Egert then moved to Ogdensburg and began the business of produce, forwarding and commission, which he continued until his death in 1887. He was born in Trenton, Oneida Co., in 1826, Oct. 2nd.

He acquired a large property by habits of fair-dealing and prudent investments.

Levi N. Smith was one of the progressive farmers of the town. He married a daughter of Henry B. Holbrook, a pioneer, bought the farm that anoth-

er pioneer, Rufus Smith, cleared, and began the business of dairying. He built fine farm buildings that were at one time the model of the town, and acquired a competence at the business of farming. Retiring from his farm, he moved to the village, engaged in business as dealer in cheese and butter, which he continued for about twenty years. He built the large dwelling on South street, now owned and occupied by W. H. Hall. He is remembered as a man of reliable character, quick to avail himself of new improvements in farming utensils, and untiring in industry.

Levi N. Smith.

Benj. Howard Smith was one of the pioneers who bore the heat and burden of the day when the town was new. Coming in 1824 from Williamstown, Vt., at the age of twenty-four, with little capital save a healthy body, willing hands and a good trade, he labored two years to found a home. He then went back to the vicinity of his old home, and married the daughter of a farmer, who had been a pupil of his when he taught the village school two years before. Together they braved the hardships of a journey to this town, crossing Lake Champlain on the ice, and finding their way through the forest which covered much of the territory between Plattsburg and their destination. His trade was that of a tanner and currier and they found

B. Howard Smith.

their first home in the tan-house. One wintry morning they found their store of vegetables frozen. They made the clothes they wore from cloth the thrifty housewife spun the yarn for and then wove; even the thread was spun by her. Those were the days of no railroads, no telegraphs, no cookstoves, no matches; not even the postage-stamp had appeared. Many a time the kind-hearted postmaster read the letter to the early settler which had come to his office, then restored to his own official care to await the time when its proper owner could earn the postage due. By industry and frugality Mr. Smith was able in a few years to build a substantial frame house on the site later occupied by the VanBuren Hotel, and later still by the present St. Lawrence Inn. In time he gave up his trade of tanner, bought a farm of two hundred acres on the north-east side of the village, a considerable part of which is now within the corporation boundary. The fair grounds, East Side school and many residences are on his original farm. In 1867 he built the handsome home where he spent his last days, at the corner of Rock Island and Barney streets. Mr. Smith was well educated for the time. He taught school several terms and was Justice of the Peace several years also, was a reader and thinker, and a consistent member of the Presbyterian church for more than seventy years. His descendants are proud of his piety, his perseverance and his honorable name. He died Jan. 17, 1899, and his wife Nov. 19, 1898.

Erwin S. Barnes, son of Rockwell Barnes, a pioneer, was born in Gouverneur Dec. 24, 1814. He was educated in the old Gouverneur Academy and

taught school twenty-five terms thereafter, these being divided between district, graded and academic schools. He spent about fifteen years in mercantile lines, meeting with the usual success which in those times was never large. He married Lucretia Allen in 1842 who still survives, a woman remarkable for her retentive memory of old events and her lively interest in present day progress. She was among the first of the aged persons to express a keen desire for the success of Old Home Week and she furnished data of value to those in charge

Erwin S. Barnes

of the more immediate direction of that effort. Mr. Barnes was School Commissioner and Superintendent of Schools a number of years. He is remembered by one country boy as having visited the school where the boy was being drilled into the mysteries of the three R's and leaving such a lively sense of his kindness, humor and good nature that even the story he told to illustrate "Doing one thing at a time," could almost be repeated after the lapse of fifty years. He died March 27, 1895.

Deacon Thomas M. Thayer was one of those sturdy, always to be depended upon citizens who honor the community they live in. He came here from Burke, Franklin county, in the latter part of the 30's, and began business as a cabinet-maker. Those were the days before machinery played such a part in this trade as now. His shop stood on what is now the westerly portion of the Anthony residence lot and his dwelling directly across the street where the Masonic Temple now stands. He was a mainstay of the Baptist church during all the active years of his life and held such official positions as it could offer. He was Justice of the Peace though not bred to the law, his sense of justice being better in administering justice than any trifling

Dea. Thomas M. Thayer.

with legal and quibbling technicalities. He was a man in some sense like the revered Harvey D. Smith, and many went to him for advice in time of trouble and he was helpful to such. The Bible was to him a rule and guide and he never stopped to question its entire truth from cover to cover. His special gift in prayer is well remembered. Whenever a tactful and reliable service was called for by the public, he was first to be thought of. Two of his sons went to the front during the Civil war, but his antipathy toward strife and bloodshed was not changed. In his dealings with his fellow men he was always honest to the verge of honesty; his handiwork was substantial and there must be much of it still in use for he built not for a day. There was no other man just like Deacon

Thayer in the community; there was none other more trusted and the memory of his probity, sincerity and unselfish spirit have survived him. He died in 1885, July 3d.

John Killmer, son of William and Esther (Porter) Killmer, was born Aug. 5, 1824, at the family homestead in Essex county, N. Y., and when six years old

(his father learning of the cheap and fertile lands in the St. Lawrence valley) came with the family to Gouverneur, located on the Little Bow road on what was known for three-quarters of a century as the Killmer Farm. It is now owned by W. Baker. Here John grew to manhood, sharing with his father in the labors of the farm, attending the district school in the village and two terms at the Seminary. At twenty he was apprenticed to Milton Barney to learn the painter's trade, continuing with Mr. Barney until 1850, when with a brother-in-law, Ahio S. Wood, they purchased the inter-

John Killmer.

est of Mr. B., this being the beginning of the well-remembered firm of Killmer & Wood, which continued until 1868. They manufactured wagons, carriages and sleighs, and their work was reputable for its thoroughness. Subsequently the firm went into the grocery trade and after the retirement of Wood, Mr. Killmer had as partners successively, Ezekiel Beardslee and M. D. Morris. He built the marble front store on Main street which still bears his name. About 1890 he retired from business on account of failing health and his remaining years were spent in quietness, cared for by his faithful wife, Sarah (McKean) Killmer to whom he was married in 1852. He died May 18, 1902. John Killmer was a man of good business ability, industrious, popular as a merchant and one it was a pleasure to deal with. He had a large number of friends who will bear witness to this saying "John Killmer was an honest man." His store was the gathering place of many who were attracted by the genial smile of the proprietor, being in its day the club-room of the older citizens. He had much confidence in human nature and this often resulted in losses, his good nature being sometimes taken advantage of. A regular attendant at the Presbyterian church, a member of Gouverneur Masonic Lodge, for upwards of forty years he was a public spirited citizen and served his town in various offices. He was Excise Commissioner two terms, or six years, trustee of the village several years, being elected by votes of both parties. No jobber in franchises was able to impose upon the people whom he represented. In national politics he was a republican but not hotly partisan, and politics played no part in his duties as a public servant. Such unselfish citizens are none too common and it were well had we more like him today.

Benjamin F. Skinner came into this section from Washington county (in 1847) from which section came the earliest pioneers of the town. He had been a farmer but was influenced in coming by the possibilities in iron production. In connection with a partner named Blish, whose daughter he subsequently married, he built an iron furnace at Wegatchie, in 1848, capable of making five tons of pig iron daily. It was conducted five years, during which time about 2,000 tons of pig were produced and sold. The ore used came from Caledonia ore-bed which was well known as a producer of ore of a good grade, having been worked at intervals for more than a third of a century previously. About 1852 Mr. Skinner abandoned the furnace, moved to Gouverneur village, bought the dwelling then standing on the southerly side of the present High School lot, living there a number of years but moved to

Benjamin F. Skinner.

the farm now owned by the heirs of Isaac W. Stacey, which he bought and put the buildings into repair. He lived here during the remainder of his life dying at the ripe old age of 84. He held various official positions in town, acquiring the title of "judge" by which he was universally addressed by his townsmen, was one of the incorporators of the Episcopal church in 1866 and was a man who was esteemed by all who knew him. Never aggressive in his opinions, he was singularly free from prejudices and in business affairs was trusted, and in his church, honored. He was always a democrat, and in the early 60's was cool and deliberate in his judgments when so many were convulsed with passion or hatred. A just man; a worthy citizen; a model in deportment; a gentleman in dignity; such is the memory of him by one who knew him in his later years.

A record of Caleb Johnson, a Revolutionary soldier, came too late to have place alongside that of John Garrett whose history has had attention. These two are the only Revolutionary veterans buried in our cemetery. Caleb Johnson was born in Middletown, Ct., Nov. 20, 1745. One of his ancestors who spelled his name "Jnoson" signed the Dedham compact Apr. 1, 1775. He enlisted in Capt. Sumner's company, was at the battle of Saratoga when Burgoyne was defeated. He served in the Continental army two years. In August, 1785, he married Naomi Sutliff at Haddam, Ct. She was his second wife. Shortly after he moved to Johnstown, Fulton Co., N. Y., living there until 1821 then moving to Gouverneur and living with his son John, until his death Jan. 17, 1835. His sons Ansel, Caleb and Amasa had preceded him a year or two and his two daughters, Mrs. John Robinson and Mrs. Jonathan Carpenter, came about the same time. He was granted a pension by the U. S. government in 1832 for two years' service. After his death the pension was continued to his widow. His living descendants so far as known are:

Miss Josie Carpenter,
Mrs. Nina Carpenter Irving,
Mrs. Leta Hazelton Morehouse,
Mrs. Cecil Hazelton Margner,
Henry Carpenter,
Clarence M. Johnson,
John B. Johnson,
Herbert O. Johnson,
Charles Carpenter,
Caleb Carpenter,
    (of Gouverneur),
Mrs. Catherine Carpenter Mowatt,
    (of Hailesboro),
Mrs. Leta Carpenter King,
    (of Fine),
William Carpenter,
    (Soldier's Home, Mich.),
Charles Johnson,   (of Fowler),

James E Johnson.
  (of Canton),
Mrs Lottie Johnson Stevens,
  (of DeKalb),
Mrs Lucy Carpenter Horton,
  (of Chaumont),
Earl Hazleton.
  (of Watertown),

Archie Johnson.
  (in Ohio),
Everett Hazleton.
  (of Charles City, Ia),
Mrs Stephen Rolph.
  (in Minnesota).
Mrs Cora Johnson Laidlaw.
  (of Portland, Ore)

Edward Hartley. the subject of this sketch was the second child and oldest son of John and Abigal White Hartley, born June 15, 1807

John S Hartley was of a roving disposition, residing for short intervals in Massachusetts, Maine, Canada and New York State   Always in the new and sparcely settled sections of the localities where he made his residence, his children had poor opportunity for schooling

Edward attended school but three months before he came of age   In the winters of 1828 and '29, he attended the district school at Heuvelton where his father's family resided   At the close of the winter's school in 1829, he shouldered his axe, his only capital and started out to do for himself   For the next few years we find him devoting his time during the winter months to the chopping of cord wood, at which he was quite expert, often cutting and piling twenty-four cords a week, and the making of square timber, and the summer seasons were spent in the manufacture of salt at Salina, a suburb of Syracuse   Public conveyances were not always accessible in those days, and the trip to Syracuse was frequently made on foot

In the fall of 1833, he hired to D Austin to go to the south side of Beaver Creek and hunt deer for one month, the price to be paid was fifteen dollars if he got twenty deer. and eighteen dollars if he got twenty-five   Report says that the first nineteen shots made. he killed eighteen deer

Attracted to the northern part of Gouverneur by the abundance of white oak and elm timber, Mr Hartley came to Gouverneur accompanied by Uriah Waters the next fall, and entered into a contract with Benj Smith for certain of the oak timber north of the Oswegatchie River on mile square lots Nos 29, 32, 33, 34, 47, 48, 49, 52, 53 and 54   Contract was dated Nov 13, 1834, signed Gouverneur Morris, by his attorney Benj Smith   This was the 3d Gouverneur Morris—the 2nd who was the owner of the town. having died in 1816   The oak was made into staves, which were hauled to the bank of the Oswegatchie by ox teams and then rafted by Hartley and Waters and floated down the Oswegatchie and St Lawrence rivers to Quebec

He spent the winter of 1836-7 in the manufacture of oak staves and elm timber on the same tract of land, but the staves and timber were sold on the bank   He took a contract of his first fifty acres in 1837, cleared a few acres of land and erected a comfortable log house that summer   Married Miss Jennett Sophia Thomas of Augusta, Canada, February, 1838, and immediately moved to their new home in the woods, bringing with them a yoke of oxen. one cow, a dog and the trusty rifle

Three children were born to them; Sylvester F. Dec. 4, 1838; Laura S. Jan. 22, 1840, and Edward T. Aug. 16, 1841.

In politics Mr. Hartley was a consistent democrat to the time of the Compromise Act of 1850 and its legitimate results, the passage of the fugitive slave law, the barbarous cruelties of which caused such a wave of indignation to sweep over St. Lawrence County that his democracy was lost sight of, and in his desire for a more humane and equitable treatment of the colored race, he became not only a "Black Republican" but a member of the so-called underground railroad, the object of which was to assist the man fleeing from bondage to breathe the free air of Canada. Though silence left no records of those who were passed over the trail, the land marks of the old route are still with us and the motives of those silent workers in the interest of humanity, are no longer questioned.

While his home bore the marks of a thrifty farmer, he experienced the joys and sorrows that came to all. The long illness and death of his youngest son, Edward T., in 1862 was deeply mourned, and the death of his only daughter, Mrs. Leslie Parlin in 1871, seemed to have a restraining influence on his afterlife. His wife and faithful co-worker passed away in 1882 and he followed her eight years later in the fullness of a ripe old age of 83 years, and a work well done as he understood it.

Sylvanus Cone, a grandson of Barzilla Beckwith who served in the Revolutionary war, came to Gouverneur in 1832 and purchased that tract of land

Sylvanus Cone.

known now as John Street, extending on either side to the river. He also bought the water-power now called the Graves mill power and here he carded wool into rolls which were given out to the farmers' wives to spin and weave into cloth, the latter being returned to him to dye and dress. Some cloths so produced were surprising in texture, finish and fineness and there are perhaps a few living who remember them. Mr. Cone was an active member of the First Presbyterian church for many years, often reading sermons in the absence of the pastor. He was a man of correct habits and ready wit and was often found at his place of business with pen in hand composing verses or records of various happenings that came within his purview. He was called upon at times to speak at public gatherings, and a Fourth of July speech made by him is one of the traditions. He had good facility of language and could relate incidents either with pen or tongue picturesquely. Retiring from active business early in life on account of bodily infirmities, he still maintained a lively interest in public affairs. He was a Mason for years, and in politics was first a Whig and later a Democrat, on the dissolution of the former party.

Sylvanus Cone is remembered by the writer of these lines as a delightful story-teller and he was always listened to with interest and close attention. He could round out a political argument with some ludicrous story with which his mind was plentifully stored. The gathering of the aged cronies about

"Peter's" hospitable fire was an event that once witnessed was not easily forgotten. Mr. Cone on such occasions, had opinions, and expressed them clearly but with becoming modesty, however, and he could and did discuss all public measures and men in this forum for years. He was of that "dependable" quality so common among the early settlers, and no man questioned his integrity, though in the days preceding the Civil war there were those who differed with him in opinion. This proved his independence of mind and was creditable to him. As a manufacturer he did much in building the town. He used the same water-power granted by Gouverneur Morris to William Downs in 1814, conditioned upon his building and operating a carding and fulling mill "timely in the ensuing season to card the fleeces which may be taken from the sheep at that time, and the mill to dress the cloth." Such literary matter as has survived him, is of peculiar quality and has now and then a tinge of the quaint humor that characterized him. He died in 1877 in his 85th year.

Charles S. Cone, son of the preceding, now aged 85, is still in active business as a banker in the city of St. Louis, Mo. Many who hark back to the

Charles S. Cone.

years around the fifties, will remember him as a partner of William E. Sterling in one of the only two general stores in town at that time. There was no grocery then. Whitfield M. Goodrich, with a single counter a dozen feet in length, did not start in the grocery line until about 1856. Mr. Cone was born in Lee, Mass., now a manufacturing town of some distinction, in 1821. How he came to this section is shown by his parents having moved to Washington county from which so many of the pioneers started for the northern wilds, and coming with them on their removal here in 1832. He was then a boy of eleven and his education was acquired mainly in the old High School and the Seminary which succeeded it. When of age William E. Sterling hired him at $25 per month as clerk, but this was after he had acquired a five years experience, for he began clerking at sixteen. Shortly after his majority he became a partner with Mr. Sterling, continuing until 1857, when he went west, first to Keokuk, Iowa, then to Cincinnati, where he became treasurer of the old Ohio & Mississippi railroad, and this position he held for thirty years. Then in 1888 he went to St. Louis where he now resides, and daily takes up his task as second assistant cashier of the State National Bank. He appears, from a newspaper account, to possess his father's sense of humor. He is remembered as a tall, genial smiling young man, pleasant to buy of and courteous to the humblest or youngest patron of his counter. Those who knew him well in the long ago will be glad to look upon his face again.

John Johnson was born in Johnstown, N. Y., in 1801. His parents were Caleb Johnson a veteran of the Revolution, born near Middletown, Conn., in 1745, and Naomi Sutliff born at Haddon, Conn. Both father and mother were descended from families who came to New England within two years after the Mayflower as shown by the list of those sailing from London within that time.

He moved into the town of Gouverneur when twenty years of age, settling upon

a farm on the Somerville road which he proceeded to clear up. The census of 1835 for the year of 1834 shows that he then had fourteen cows, a horse, and a sheep, and that he had thirty acres of land cleared. A few years later he exchanged this farm for a larger one and in the early fifties his herd of cattle had increased to forty. The "Black Salts" period had passed. June 16th, 1846, he was married to Sally Freeman, daughter of David and Marie Freeman. In 1846, he with Orin Freeman, Freedom Freeman, Augustus Preston and A.

John Johnson.

C. VanDyck, as trustees, erected at Somerville the first Methodist Church in St. Lawrence County south of East DeKalb.

John Johnson inherited many of the characteristics of his Puritan ancestors, and whatever may at this date be said of the righteousness of the cause that led them to leave homes of comparative luxury, for the trials and hardships of an untamed wilderness, there must be credited to them a courage and tenacity to principle worthy of any cause. We call them today Puritans, and speak of the sturdy adherence to their convictions as bigotry, but we are, however, compelled to admit that their descendants have girdled the continent marking a trail from ocean to ocean, of uprightness and steadfastness that are admirable. In the fifties the Kansas troubles, together with the passage of the fugitive slave law, served to solidify and extend the abolition movement. Garrison, Smith, Phillips and the New England continent of Puritans, said slavery in a land of the free was a disease worthy of drastic treatment, to the extent of extirpation if necessary. John Johnson became identified with that party at the expense of many a taunt and sneer. One of his sons recalls hearing a brother-in-law, an intense constitutionalist, call him a "Nigger stealer." His reply was "C—— I have no doubt of your honesty, but you are allowing your loyalty to the constitution to over-ride your humanity. The Constitution is of men, humanity of God." From then on he made a night's drive always returning before the household was up in the morning, and but for an accident, none but the faithful mother would have had knowledge either of the fact or cause of his absence. On a winter's night one of the children arose from bed and went to the kitchen for a drink of water, and found lying stretched out about the old fire place, three black men, the first he had ever seen. Filled with terror, he fled to the bedside of the father and mother to be told there was nothing to fear, but as he loved the father to never divulge what he had witnessed. For several years the boy kept the knowledge thus gained with the silence that only a boy is capable of maintaining, and only when blood and gold had settled forever in this country the question of slavery, was the story of the underground railroad, of which the old homestead was a station, told. The brothers-in-law, although taking so radically different views, remained friends to the end, each respecting the honesty of the other's convictions. John Johnson died at what had been his home for more than a half century, December 15th, 1878.

Newton Aldrich was born in Luzerne, Warren County, New York, June 6, 1830. His ancestry is English. His father, Seth Aldrich, was a successful

farmer and a prominent citizen of Warren County. Mr. Aldrich was reared to farm life and was educated in the public and private schools of Luzerne and Glens Falls Academy. Inclined to mercantile pursuits in 1852 he began as a merchant in his native town and became one of its leading business men. His ability and worth were recognized by his fellow-townsmen, and at the age of 21, he was chosen supervisor. He was re-elected the following year and again in 1856. In 1862 he was elected a Member of Assembly from Warren County. He refused a renomination the next year.

Newton Aldrich.

In 1866 Mr. Aldrich became identified with the business interests of Gouverneur. In that year the firm of Weston, Dean & Aldrich was formed and in 1867 he became a resident of Gouverneur, and the erection of the saw-mill at Natural Dam, subsequently operated by that firm, was begun. He was a member of Aldrich, Dean & Aldrich, successors to the original firm, until the latter co-partnership was superseded by the Aldrich Paper Co. in 1900, and the saw-mill property was converted into a paper manufacturing plant. Mr. Aldrich has large and varied business interests in Gouverneur and vicinity. He is a stockholder in and director of the Aldrich Paper Co., is vice-president of the United States Talc Co., is a stockholder in the International Lace Manufacturing Co. and is President of the Bank of Gouverneur.

Parallel with his business career, he has attained prominence in public affairs. In 1872, he was elected supervisor of the town of Gouverneur and represented his town continuously in that capacity until 1902, with exception of a period of four years, 1879 to 1882 inclusive. His poise of mind, his comprehensive grasp of affairs, soon placed him among the leaders of that very able body of county legislators. For years he served as Chairman of the most important committees, being at the head of the committee which had charge of the erection of the county court-house. He was three times chairman of the board. For upwards of twenty-five years he was a trustee of the Gouverneur Wesleyan Seminary. He was many years a trustee of Gouverneur Village, and in 1883 was elected its President. In 1886 he was appointed a member of the State Board of Charities by Governor Morton, a trust which he today discharges with fidelity.

Always a generous friend and public-spirited citizen, in 1900 his philanthropic impulses found expression in the beautiful library building given the Gouverneur Reading Room Association. In politics Mr. Aldrich is a Republican and for over a quarter of a century has been prominent in the councils of his party. A man of rare executive ability, of sterling integrity, of proverbial modesty, Mr. Aldrich today at the ripe age of seventy-five, enjoys in an exceptional degree the confidence and esteem of all who know him.

In 1858 he was married to Kate Griffing of Washington County   They have one son, Herbert G. Aldrich.

Dr Elijah Morton of Richville, was born in Hatfield, Mass, in 1802 In his youth he came to Herkimer county, N Y, was educated in Fairfield Academy, a noted institution of learning in the earlier days   He followed his academic work with a course of study in medicine and became well-versed in pathology and pharmacy   During this period he supported himself by teaching   He gained an enduring reputation as a practitioner after coming to Richville in 1833, and long after he had passed the meridian of success, his counsel was sought by his former patrons who would brook no empiricism in their family doctor   Dr M was eminently a safe adviser in his profession   He was cautious to a degree in naming an ailment and encouraged no false hopes of quick recovery by flattering promises   His black, leathern saddle-bags, adapted to bestride the withers of his dapple-gray horse, at a period anterior to the modern roads, when his visits had to be made on horseback, are still a memory with a few   His keen, deep-set eye, the affable smile, the cheery word, the courtly salutation to the "madam" of the household   the treatment in small doses with all nausea removed by deft and aromatic mixtures, (and this at a time long before homeopathy had gained a footing in the region where he practiced)   the sense of perfect trust his patients had in his skill, these things come back to one who knew him well during all his practice after the first twenty years   He had a love for the natural sciences and was well read in them   He was deferential to the opinions of others, even of a boy when discussing matters in this attractive field, and would listen and argue his side of a moot question in mechanics or philosophy with such sweetness of disposition that his opponent always had a new sense of the weakness of his own position   He was tenacious in argument withal, but never dogmatic, and after having formulated an opinion as to the merits of any contention, he stood manfully by it against whoever came   This quality led him to firm positions on national or political affairs and in the days preceding the Civil war, he held to one judgment regarding it and its finality   His calling taught him that no process of education, civilization or equality could remove the kink from a curly hair or shorten the reach of a projecting heel   His neighbors who have survived now know what he knew a half-century ahead of his time   He was never assertive of his conclusions but he sturdily, though silently, resented any attempt to manufacture opinions for himself   He was a genial companion with those who had tastes similar to his own whether their years numbered more or less than his   He had a strong sense of humor and could imitate and mimic the colored brother with exactness when in congenial company   A negro melody had a charm for him and he usually was an appreciative listener to such when opportunity offered   His judgment upon the feasibility of navigating the air, brought out by the experiences of LaMountain and Haddock, stand today as true as when he uttered them and the charlatanry apparent in every fresh experiment attests the accuracy of his views   Men will fly when in the process of evolution they become birds, (if ever), and not until then.   One thing always marked his practice, he was as assiduous in the care of the poor as of the well-to-do and he never pressed the collection of a bill where it would prove burdensome to the debtor. A good man passed when he laid down the cares. A just man; a man devoid of prejudices; lenient toward the follies and failures of his neighbors though not unobservant of their errors; a gentleman of the old school; a knight in his calling; a man of whom the world could justly ask, "When shall we look upon his like again?" Such was Dr. Morton in the zenith of his powers and as such his memory is cherished by those who knew him best. And this is the judgment of one who knew him intimately, was proud to call him friend and who had unusual facilities for forming a correct judgment of the man. He died in 1888.

John Cheeney Rich of Richville, came to this place from Cooperstown, Otsego Co., with his father, Salmon Rich, (from whom the town takes its name), in March, 1804, and though but a lad of fourteen, did his share of the work in clearing up what was then a solid forest and in building the log house, the first on the town site, and which stood a little back of the present residence of E. A. Rich. Not many years later he was engaged to teach the first school in the first schoolhouse ever built in the town of Gouverneur, which stood near the site of the old Fosgate Hotel. In 1819 John C. Rich in company with his brother, Christopher C. Rich, carried on the hotel at Richville. He was the first Postmaster, having been appointed in 1824, and served in that capacity for twenty-five years. He was also justice of the peace for several terms.

John C. Rich.

He possessed an even disposition, affable manners and good judgment, with a wit that was keen but never unkind. His death occurred at the home of his son, the late Wm. B. Rich, in September, 1869.

Augustus E. Norton was born in Lanesboro, Mass., in 1817, eleven years after the birth of his oldest brother, Milton G. Norton. He came to Gouverneur in 1835 with the latter, living with him on the present Norton farm on the Somerville road four years or until he was twenty-one. He was a student of the old High School, acquired a good education, taught four years in Amsterdam, N. Y., came back to Gouverneur and bought a farm, married Mary Ann Read whose parents, William C. and Lydia Read, came from Putney, Vt., in which place Mrs. Norton was born in 1818. Her coming to Gouverneur ante-dated that of Mr. Norton by about eight years.

He did not remain at farming long, but selling his place after working it five years, he came to the village and began the business of fire and life insurance, being the first to make a distinctive calling of that business. His genial manner, and careful methods soon brought him a goodly income which he husbanded with care. He lived at this

A. E. Norton.

time in the house subsequently built into the Grove Hotel in West Main street. He was especially popular among farmers, and probably at one time had substantially all the insurance on farm property in town. He was one of the first Masons and held offices in that organization many years. After accumulating a handsome property, he bought a property on East Main street, that now owned and occupied by Edward Barry, built the house thereon in substantially the shape it is now in, and continued the insurance business there until his death. He was one of the first officers in the Agricultural Society, and took great interest in its advancement giving his time freely toward it. His policy holders were looked after carefully and one of the remembrances of him is his constant travel about the region covered by his business in a covered buggy, attending to renewals. He was an excellent citizen, devoted to the upbuilding of his town, never a member of any church but always contributing to the support of one. When one recalls the old worthies of the town, those whose word could be relied upon and whose lives were marked by a wholesome regard for the rights of others, the name of Augustus E. Norton comes to mind naturally.

Artemas Barnard Lynde, late of Richville, was born in Springfield, Vt., Dec. 26th, 1803. Coming to Richville from Antwerp about the year 1839, he

A. B. Lynde.

purchased the hotel from John and Christopher C. Rich and christened it the Lynde House. A great hostelry was this hotel during the days of the plank road and the stage coach when the sound of the coach horn, at the top of the Pooler Hill gave notice to the people in general and the postmaster in particular that the United States mail was close at hand. He was proprietor of this hotel about 15 years. He retired from active business in 1856 and built the commodious residence on Main street, where his daughter, Mrs. Wm. Walker, now resides. The Congregational society were indebted to his generosity and public spirit for their first real start toward a church edifice in the gift of the large church lot together with the building that stood thereon, which when sold netted the society $300. His death occurred in 1876. The firing upon Sumter fired the heart of Mr. Lynde and he gave money and time to promoting enlistments among his younger townsmen. A memory of him is still fresh in which his appearance, at a "war meeting" offering a ten dollar bill to the first young man to volunteer, remains as a picture.

Willard Smith, the pioneer of 1805, was born Feb. 27, 1784, in Connecticut. Under leadership of Isaac Austin and accompanied by Eleazer Nichols and Pardon Babcock, and possibly also by Dr. Richard Townsend, the land agent of Gouverneur Morris, he came through the wilderness from the southerly end of Lake George, arriving at the site of the present village of Gouverneur

Allen Smith.

in the spring of the year above named. His life up to that time had been passed
at Hartford, Washington county, N. Y. He took up the lands now included in
the farm of George M. Dodds and his son Allen Smith, the first born of the
the early settlers was born here. He married Lucy Garret in March, 1805, according to the record furnished by one of his descendants, but it is more probable that the date should be some years later as John Garrett, her father, had not
then come to the new settlement in Cambray. John Garrett was a revolutionary
soldier, who died in Gouverneur Feb. 16, 1853, in his 98th year. Lucy Smith
died Oct. 26, 1876, in her 93rd year. A daughter, Lucy, born July 16th, 1817,
became the wife of William Rutherford. A daughter of the last named pair,
also named Lucy, is the wife of Proctor Jewett and is living in North Main
street. No portrait of Willard Smth is in existence. He died March, 1844.

Among the early settlers of Richville whose interests were closely identified
with the welfare of the little town, none was more honored than James Steward

J. S. Lake.

Lake. Born March 15th, 1797, he came to this town
from New England when still a young man and settled
on the broad acres that he thereafter called home. He
was a staunch follower of the Silas Wright democracy
and died in that faith. He was a man of industrious,
frugal habits. When making the final payments on his
land, he at one time walked to Ogdensburg and back, as
he expressed it, "between sun and sun" that he might
apply the money saved on his indebtedness. He was an
intelligent, public-spirited man and the only man in
town to subscribe anything toward the building of the
Potsdam & Watertown R. R., taking several shares of
stock. He died in 1871 at his home on the Gouverneur road, tenderly cared for
by his foster daughter, Mrs. Horace White, Jr.

Benjamin Smith, usually spoken of as "Benjamin of the Bow," was an important factor in the early history of Gouverneur.

Samuel Smith, who now resides on the Old Homestead farm at Little Bow,
is the grandson of Benjamin Smith, the first settler at Little Bow. Benjamin
Smith, with his brothers, Stephen and Willard (who was the pioneer of 1805),
with their families, and Aholiab and Lydia, their parents, came from Hartford,
Washington Co., N. Y., in the winter of 1807. Benjamin Smith settled at Little Bow on land now making up the farms of Samuel Smith, Mrs. Catherine
Smith and O. W. Bailey. His plan was to build a canal from the Oswegatchie
river at Natural Dam to the bend in the river at Little Bow and thus secure an
extensive water power that should furnish the nucleus for a village. His plan was
frustrated by the growth of the settlement at Gouverneur.

Benjamin Smith built the old brick house at Little Bow, (for a hotel),
about 1822. Both the brick and the timber were obtained on the farm. He
fell from the building while constructing it and died from the injury in 1826.

After his death the main part of the farm, now known as the Old Homestead, became the property of his son Jason Smith. He was one of seven chil-

dren, was born in 1802, and died in 1884. During his later days he was a prominent resident of Gouverneur village. By his first wife, Jane Crawford, he had a large family. Of the three surviving, Samuel Smith now owns and occupies the old Homestead. He was born in 1834; married Eliabeth Markwick in 1854; served in the Civil war from 1861 to 1864. Of his children the first daughter, Mary, died in infancy; the second daughter, Maud Elizabeth, died in 1896; the eldest son, Albert Eugene, died in 1899. The surviving son, Elmer William, is a teacher in Colgate Academy, Hamilton, N. Y.

Horace White, Sr., of Richville, was born in Heath, Mass., in October, 1794. He was a grandson of that Josiah White who with his nine sons fought

throughout the Revolutionary war, and a direct lineal descendant of Capt. John White who came to the rugged shores of New England on the Mayflower. He married Lucy Hall, of Ashfield, Mass., in 1825, and they settled on White creek, Richville, shortly after, where Mr. White lived and died a useful and respected citizen. By his careful management and economy he acquired considerable valuable real estate. In his early life he was an Episcopalian, but later became a Universalist. He had a retentive memory and was ever able to quote passages from any part of the Bible. He was noted for his strict honesty, integrity and strength of character, qualities inherited from his Puritan ancestors. His word could always be relied upon. He hated deceit and was never known to say other than he really meant. He died at the advanced age of 83 years.

Horace White, Sr

"Uncle Moses" as Moses Barber of Richville was familiarly called, was among the early settlers who came to this town from Massachusetts. He located on a tract of land in Gouverneur, some two miles from Richville, cleared the land, built house and barns and the broad fertile fields, bearing testimony to his industry, were owned by him at the time of his death. Soon after coming to this section he built a store, the second that was built in Richville, and occupied it as long as he lived. Somewhat eccentric in all his ways, he was true to his friends and his integrity was never questioned. His business methods were rigid and unchangeable; he marked his goods when received and never varied from his price no matter who the customer was. Fashion could not depreciate his goods nor did the corner in cotton disturb him, he always adhered to his price. He was a life long whig and republican. His death occurred at his home in this village in 1875.

It must have been about 1835 that he took up the farm named, for a settler who came in five years before, often told of hearing the resounding blows of Mr. Barber's axe, sometimes by moonlight. He was then a bachelor, lived in a small shack about ten feet square built of rough hemlock and standing about twenty rods east of the present red farmhouse. After about six or eight years of this life, he married a lady from Vermont, who is well remembered for her quiet demeanor, scholarly ways and cordial sympathies, but she was ill fitted for the rough duties of pioneering and seemed never to accept them save as a duty. Mr. Barber was the last large farmer in town to buy a mowing machine. The writer well remembers his following a "Manny" driven slowly that he might see how it worked, and finally denouncing it as "a cow-starver". It was certainly twelve years after that "a cow-starver" appeared upon his fertile creek flats, for one of his agreements with tenants was never to mow a crop except by hand. These were typical characteristics of the man but they never affected his neighbors for he was most considerate of others rights.

Gorham Cross of Richville, was born Oct. 4th, 1808, at Goffstown, N. H., and was the youngest of ten children. From the age of two and a half years until he was past twelve, he lived at Weare, N. H., attending a common school. In 1818, his father went to the west even to the wilderness of Northern New

York and took up land in Philadelphia. It took fourteen days to make the journey during which Gorham for the first time saw a stove, and in trying to find out what it was burned his fingers. When twenty years old he taught in a log school house near Sterlingville for ten dollars a month and "boarded round." The next winter he taught in LeRay. He was married in Utica in September, 1831, by Rev. Dr. Lansing, his bride being Miss Sophia Murdock. Three weeks later Mr. Cross was converted under the preaching of Rev. Lewis

Rev. Gorham Cross.

Wicks, and feeling that he must preach, delivered his first sermon in December, 1831. In Burrville, in 1839, the Congregational Association gave him a license to "improve his talents in preaching". Being ordered to St. Lawrence County to work he made the journey on horse-back and came to Richville, a stranger. Inquiring at Steward Lake's for the deacons, he was sent to Josiah Walker and Orson White. This commenced what, with the exception of a few years spent in Rensselaer Falls, was a continuous service of fifty years in the Congregational Church at Richville. Probably no one in Northern New York knew more of the history of families in St. Lawrence and Jefferson Counties than he. His knowledge and memory of people and places was wonderful. He was deeply interested in the temperance and anti-slavery movements and warmly supported both. He was a man of strong personality, and was greatly beloved and honored by all who came in contact with this grand old man. His death occurred in 1894.

James Brodie, born June 4, 1815, at Yetholm, Scotland, was a merchant tailor in Gouverneur from about 1860 till his death which occurred about 1898, the date of the latter not yet appearing upon his headstone in Riverside cemetery. He came to this country in 1834 having acquired the trade of tailor, which he followed two years in Kingston, Canada, then settling in Rossie. He married Helen McGregor of Hammond in 1841, and fifteen years later, Eliza Niblock. Mr. Brodie was one of those old-time, old-fashioned, reliable men, whose word nobody thought to question. He never knew the meaning of the current phrase "tricks of the trade". His work was always the best and whatever the quality of the goods selected by his customer, the workmanship on it was reliable. As one of the merchants of the town he did his part in maintaining the reputation of those in trade who preceded him by half a century or less, and whose names and features have been preserved in this volume as far as possible in the limited time at command. His photograph was not obtainable from those having it, for reproduction here along with the other worthies who have given name and lustre to the town's progress.

William E. Sterling was born in Lyme, Conn., June 9, 1801. He died March 5, 1861. These are the only facts connected with his life obtainable from records. He conducted a dry goods and general store in the brick block which was demolished to make room for the present Union Hall block, the site of his store being that now occupied by the Van Duzee furniture store. Later he formed a partnership with Charles S. Cone which continued until 1857 when Mr. Cone went west, Mr. Sterling moving to a new store which he had built on the corner of Main and Gordon streets. He continued trade here, adding a considerable line of hardware, until his death. Appeals to his descendants for a photograph for reproduction were, as in the case of James Brodie, unavailing. He was a man of solid character and held a central place in the town's records for many years. He built the brick residence now occupied by D. J. Whitney. Dying as Mr. Sterling did, before the days of an established local press, there is no obtainable record of his life.

HISTORY OF ROSSIE.

By Herbert O. Johnson.

In 1792 Alexander Macomb purchased of the state of New York, all of the town of Rossie and several hundred thousand acres more for 8 pence an

H. O. Johnson.

acre. He failed to make good, however, and did not get a title. The first title was given to Daniel McCormick Mch. 3, 1795, and for four months he was the owner of the town, when he sold an undivided fifteenth. Between July 10, 1795, and July 24, 1804, Richard Harrison, Abijah Hammond, Wm. S. Smith, Wm. Constable, Robert Gilchrist, Theodosius Fowler, Francis Childs, Jonathan H. Lawrence and Jonathan Dayton were all interested in the lands of the town.

On July 24, 1804, all the heirs of Wm. Constable and the executors of his will signed a deed conveying to James Donatiaous Le Ray de Chaumont "A citizen of the United States" the town No. 2 in great tract No. 3 also called Somerville. Dec. 2, 1808, James Donatiaous Le Ray de Chaumont and Grace, his wife, gave a warranty deed to David Parish, covering the whole town of Rossie; the description in the deed was based on a map and survey made by Benjamin Wright.

In 1796, the state bought the land of the Indians and agreed to pay "at the mouth of the river Chazy" on Lake Champlain on the third Monday in August, 2230 pounds, 6 shillings and 8 pence, with an annual payment on the third Monday in August each year "forever thereafter" the sum of 213 pounds, 6 shillings and eight pence. For value received, the "Seven Nations or tribes of Indians" did "cede, release and quit claim to the people of the state of New York forever, all claim, right or title of them, the said Seven Nations or tribes of Indians to lands within said State" thereby making good the title of the state.

In 1806, Ambrose Simmons, Oliver Malterner, Amos Kinney, Jr., Samuel Bonfy, Silvins Waters, Josua Stevens, Jerome Waldo, Geo. W. Pike, Benjamin Pike, Jr., Ebenezer Bemis and David Shepard made contracts for land in the town of Rossie, near the present village of Somerville. A part if not all of the men making a personal visit and locating their land that year, returning to their homes in Herkimer County late in the fall.

In 1807, Joseph Teall and Reuben Streeter purchased or rather contracted for all the eastern end of the town from where the Oswegatchie River crosses the town at Wegatchie. According to Hough's History of St. Lawrence Co., the contract was made through George Morris a nephew of Gouverneur Morris, though the county records do not show that Gouverneur Morris owned any land in the town of Rossie. In 1810 they were given deeds to over 1600 acres, by David Parish. They came from Herkimer County, to Somerville in 1807 and Mr. Streeter made the first clearing the same year. It was about half a mile east of Wegatchie on the farm now owned by Mr. Henry Force.

The usual trials of pioneer settlers fell to the lot of those hardy men It was no easy task to hew a farm from the forest and the first year there was little to live on except game and such provisions as they brought with them which could not have been very much Through the first winter they all made small clearings and in the spring of 1808 crops were planted, most of the seed having been carefully saved from the little store brought with them from Herkimer County

By 1809 the little community began to find life somewhat easier, roads had been built, one to Gouverneur, another from Somerville to Wegatchie and from there to Natural Dam, where there was a grist mill Mr Streeter built a saw-mill at Wegatchie that year, and boards could be secured for doors and floors

In 1810, David Freeman, James Streeter, Joseph Teall, Diamond Wheeler, Eli Winchell, Simeon Stevens, John Wilcox and Daniel Wilcox, the latter un-married, moved to the new country, several of them had been up the summer be-fore and built log houses for themselves, so that all that was necessary to set-tle was a fire on the hearth and their few household goods in place To start a fire on his hearth, one of the men, Mr Freeman, walked half a mile to borrow a burning brand

Because of the easier access probably no settlement had been started west of the Oswegatchie River previous to 1810, in that year, however, Mr Parish de-cided to open up the western end of the town

It was, of course, known that Black Lake extended from the settlement near Ogdensburg to the boundary of Mr Parish's possessions in Rossie, and of-fered an easy route to the St Lawrence River Early in the spring of 1810, he sent Mr Daniel W. Church, who had superintended the erection of a stone store for Mr Parish in Ogdensburg, to the head of Black Lake to look for a water power He found a very promising power on the Indian River about one-half mile above its junction with the Lake

In the early summer of 1810 Mr Church with seven men, one of whom took his wife as cook, boarded a Canadian bateau for the head of navigation on Indian River where a water power had been located They landed just at sunset Fastening their sail to poles, they made a tent for the married pair, while the rest of the party rolled themselves in their blankets and slept on the rocks by a fire they had built The next day, a two room shanty was put up with material they had brought with them That was the first house in what is now Rossie village It was on the island near where the old furnace now stands

Some previous attempt to establish a settlement, or station at Rossie had been made, for the early settlers found a boat loaded with stone and sunk in Indian river, that had evidently lain there for many years, and at a point where the stone store was later built, an excavation had been made, as though some building was to be erected Why, or by whom, no one knows A theory plausible at least, is that it was done by the French Missionaries

The Sulpitians erected a mission building on the point where the Oswe-gatchie River flows into the St Lawrence at Ogdensburg in 1749 Many years ago the corner stone was found in removing the walls On it was a Latin inscription which translated reads   "Francis Picquet laid the foundations of this habitation in the name of the Almighty God in 1749."

There are many evidences that the Indians were numerous around Black Lake   Old Indian hearths, rude pottery and earthworks, implements of the chase and of warfare have been found all along its shores   It is quite probable that the Sulpitians desired to establish a mission station in the midst of the Indian homes

No one will ever know for there is no known record French or English, regarding the boat load of stone in the bottom of Indian River, or the hole in the ground on its shore, nor can any one tell why it was abandoned   It may have been an unrecorded frontier tragedy   There were many such, whatever the cause   It no doubt delayed the beginning of Rossie's history for many years

The work on the saw-mill was begun the day following their arrival   Mr Church says in an autobiography "The first work we did was a saw pit and set the whip saws going and by night had a log hut of two rooms covered with the plank cut for the dam and flume "

By hard and well directed effort the mill was completed and ready to operate before winter

It was quite essential to the prosperity of Mr Parish's tenants, and the improvement of his lands that some means of closer communication between the different sections he established   With this end in view, he engaged Mr Crary, a surveyor of Antwerp, to run a line from OxBow through Rossie to Ogdensburg, to determine the feasibility of building a road between those points.   Mr Crary reported such a road impossible   Mr Parish at once wrote to Mr Church, asking him to examine the ground and give his opinion   Mr Church says, "I started one afternon with one man and went through to Vrooman's Chanity (shanty) where we stopped that night, and as soon as daylight in the morning, Vrooman with us, to show us the county line, we started and began our line as soon as we could see   We ran over a point on the ridge and down into the cedar swamp where the long crossway now is "   After a breakfast of raw pork and bread, they continued their line reaching a point near the Helmer farm at night and the next morning finished their survey   Mr Church reported that the road could be built but at "considerable expense "

During the winter of 1810 and 1811 Mr Church built a bridge across the Indian River at the foot of "big hill" just above the present bridge   At the same time lumber was sawing at the new mill for contemplated buildings in Rossie, and also for a boat the "Genesee Packet" that was to be built in Ogdensburg.   The next summer, 1811, a road was constructed on the line run by Mr Church between Rossie and OxBow   This road connected with a road previously built from OxBow through Wegatchie to Somerville and completed a road from end to end of Mr Parish's possessions

Rossie was made to feel the effects of the war of 1812 in various ways. While it was out of the path of soldiers, sent north both by the U S Government and by the State, and was far enough from the Canadian border to be free from the annoyance of foraging parties, it was nevertheless so near the seat of war on the northern frontier that it experienced the excitement and some of the hardships of actual war On one occasion the able bodied men or a part of them at least, were ordered to pack two weeks rations, shoulder their muskets and march to Ogdensburg. It was a "hurry call' and the trip was made in one fatigueing day's march, arriving late in the evening. The men camped that night and the next day were ordered to shoulder their muskets and march home again They left their rations with the half starved soldiers camped there, some of whom were living on flour and water mixed and roasted over the campfire

To the settlers from the Mohawk country who had experienced the horrors of Indian warfare during the Revolutionary war, a means of defence was a great and pressing necessity Most of the able bodied men in the eastern end of the town gathered on a point in the road from Somerville to Wegatchie about three-fourths of a mile from the latter place, on what is now a part of the Teal farm to erect a block house They worked frantically cutting and hewing timber, for the block house must be substantial and safe So the timber was all squared that entered into its construction It was finished in a very short time and the community breathed easier

A small block house was started at Somerville, near the little creek that flows by the town, on the land now owned by John Salmon This was of round logs and was never completed

It is not surprising that the war with its probable British and Indian alliance should send a thrill of fear through the inhabitants of that part of the town for most of them came from Herkimer County where the Indian allies of the British had committed the most villainous atrocities during the Revolutionary war The older settlers had passed through these horrors Grandmother Malterner, the mother of Oliver and Geo Malterner, and Mrs David Freeman had fled to a swamp with her little brood, during that awful period, and from there had seen night illuminated, the torches being her own home and the houses of her neighbors, by their light had seen women and children carried off to captivity or torture or their heads split with a tomahawk, had seen the brains of infants dashed out on rocks She had come within a second of death at the hand of an Indian warrior whose uplifted tomahawk was caught by another Indian as its sharp blade was about to descend upon her head Her husband was a captive at Quebec, carried off by these same Indians.

Something like a panic prevailed upon the declaration of war. The sight of an Indian, no matter how innocent he might be, would send the people to cover Before the blockhouse was finished, and while the men were at work on it, a young man by the name of Keeney came rushing through the settlement at Somerville saying, there was a party of Indians on the war path Seizing a gun from its pegs in one of the houses he swore a magnificent oath that he would protect the settlers if he had to exterminate the whole tribe Women ran screaming from their homes, some guarding their children, others leaving them in their fright, one woman dropped a child she was carrying and ran on Grandmother Malterner cautioned silence, but silence was an impossibility in the frenzied state prevailing She gathered some most valued possessions in a bundle, saw that the children were all together and started for the blockhouse collecting sons and daughters, including the infant that was dropped in the cornfield The men hearing of the peril, started for their homes, meeting the fugitives on their way At night all were safely gathered at the blockhouse where they remained for several days It was the belief of the settlers, when the excitement was over, that Keeney saw no Indians, but was seeking a reputation for valor

The same summer, 1812, Mr Streeter's saw mill at Wegatchie burned and its destruction was attributed to the Indians The incident came near causing another panic Later it was found that the mill had been fired by a man living near who left the country the same night, never to return

In 1813, Rossie village was captured by the British and was in possession of the enemy for about 24 hours

A gang of horse thieves and all-around toughs, deserters from both armies and vagabonds from both sides of the St Lawrence, made then headquarters at Rossie, making raids in various directions, but chiefly into Canada, stealing horses and running them to the rocky ravines around Rossie where they were kept until there was a chance to sell them These raids became so frequent and so bold that the Canadian authorities determined to put a stop to them With that end in view, Col Frazier with a company of British regulars, came over by way of Morristown The "invading army" surrounded Rossie village and captured it, but as no resistance was offered the battle was both bloodless and powderless The force was divided, a part being left to guard the town, the balance were sent to hunt up the thieves No captures were made, however, and the next day the soldiers marched back to Brockville This ended the war so far as the town of Rossie was concerned

The excitement of new business enterprises, the work of building mills, houses and roads, and the toil and moil of making productive homes in the wilderness, drove all thoughts of war from the people's minds, and the routine of life was resumed as though there had been no interruption

Until Jan 1, 1811, Rossie was a part of the great unwieldly town of Russell which then embraced the present towns of Russell, Fowler, Pierpont, Pitcairn, Rossie and parts of the towns of Hammond and Fine

In 1810, Benjamin Pike in behalf of the inhabitants of the section of the town bordering on Jefferson County, requested of the free holders that they might be set off from Russell, the intention being to annex themselves to Gouverneur There seemed to be no objection to letting them go, as the following from the records of the town of Russell shows "At a special meeting of the free-holders and other inhabitants of the town of Russell assembled on Tuesday, the first day of January, 1811, at the dwelling house of Moses A Bunnell, in said Russell, voted to grant the request of Benjamin Pike, in behalf of the inhabitants of that part of Russell called Somerville that they be set off from Russell and annexed to Gouverneur" The part so set off embraced the townships numbered 1, 2 and 7 Hammond, Killarney and Somerville of tract number 3 That is the present towns of Fowler, Rossie and part of Hammond

After the separation, it was decided to form a separate town instead of becoming a part of Gouverneur. On January 27, 1813, a special act of the Legislature was passed incorporating the town of Rossie. In the act a day was named for holding the first town meeting. The day passed and no meeting was held. The following extracts from the records of the town gives the reason. "The proceedings of a town meeting held by the Justice of the Peace for the town of Rossie at the house of Reuben Streeter on Thursday the 16th day of September in the year of our Lord one thousand eight hundred and thirteen, agreeable to the statutes made and provided, In the case of neglect of the town in not choosing town officers at the legal time of holding town meeting, they not having been informed of their incorporation in time, we, the subscribers, Justices of the Peace in and for the County of Saint Lawrence, having met for the purpose above mentioned, have chosen and appointed the following persons as town officers for this year." The following list of officers were named. Supervisor, Reuben Streeter; Town Clerk, Geo W Pike; Assessors, H G Berthrong, Jedediah Kingsley, Benjamin Pike; Commissioners of Highways, Simeon Stevens, Diamond Wheeler, Alvin Wight; Constable and Collector, Elias Teall. Overseer of the Poor, Samuel Bonfy and Silvius Waters, and "seventhly chose Reuben Streeter, Benjamin Pike, Silvius Waters and Ebenezer Parker overseers of the highways in the several districts in which they respectively live, and lastly do agree and appoint the next annual town meeting to be held at the house of Reuben Streeter, in said town."

Signed   Isaac Austin, Pardon Babcock and Diamond Wheeler, Justices of the Peace.   Attested by Geo W Pike, Town Clerk. There follows a record of receiving and placing on file the oaths of office for all the chosen officials.

Diamond Wheeler was evidently the only justice in the new town. Pardon Babcock and Isaac Austin were residents of Gouverneur and were of the first party of four men to visit Gouverneur with the intention of settling there. This was in 1805. Mr Berthrong named as assessor was the first "inn keeper" at Rossie.

Mr Streeter had moved to the block house shortly after its completion, it being the only house of any size in town. For many years the town meetings were held there.

The new town was named by Mr Parish, Rossie, being the name of a castle in Scotland owned by his brother-in-law. His sister's name was Rosa. Somerville was named from Somerville, N J, which was familiar ground to some of the land holders of that time. Hammond was named from Abijah Hammond, who, with W S Smith, owned large tracts of Macombs land, the other township forming the new town of Rossie. Killarney was doubtless named by McCormick, who was a native of Ireland.

When the town was formed, the settlers had made a good showing for that time, and their number on the first assessment roll showed a list of thirty-seven taxpayers, not all residents of the town, however, there were 499¾ acres of land cleared and 90,575 acres wild, the total valuation being at $183,754 00

The buildings did not show up very well, they were only valued at $2,990 00 which certainly could not be considered extravagant in the way of house building

The assessment roll was for the present towns of Rossie, Fowler and Hammond   The greater part of the land cleared was in the vicinity of the present village of Somerville.   There was a small settlement at Hailesboro in Fowler though not very much land was cleared   In Hammond, one man had established himself at Chippewa Bay and a hermit lived somewhere in the woods   At Rossie village a small clearing had been made around the mill   Of the 499 acres cleared, less than 100 lay outside the Teall and Streeter tract

Throughout Northern New York, the first industry started was the sawmill, after which came the flour mill, then followed any thing that the proprietors looked upon as likely to enhance the value of their lands or help their tenants in their struggles with adverse nature   The pioneer found certain aspects of nature an enemy to be conquered   It was a far cry from a dense forest to waving fields of grain, yet the waving fields of grain were necessary to their prosperity, almost their existence   The one implement that he must have was the ax   a gun came next   He moulded his own bullets, made his own powder, with these implements and an iron kettle for his wife he was ready to face the forest   He had the hardihood, energy and good health that were sure winners   His first move was the erection of a log house with one or two rooms below and a loft above   The saw mills sometimes furnished boards for floors and partitions and sometimes they were split from pine logs   This is a description of the home of David Freeman, built in the summer of 1810, that has been handed down from generation to generation   It was built of square logs and contained two rooms on the ground floor about seven feet high   Above was one room at first, though later partitioned, about three feet high on the sides and seven or eight at the peak   At one end the chimney and fireplace was built   It was of stone and formed a part of the end of the house   It was rough and irregular   and the children amused themselves by climbing up its sides. It was very much like climbing stairs and from it they crawled through the little window into the loft   Inside there was more of an attempt at symmetrical lines   The stones were more smoothly laid and it was rudely plastered in places   The fireplace was wide and deep, almost large enough to set up a bed   From its capacious throat hung a pot-hook   a hook hung at the end of a chain just over the fire, the other or top end of the chain being fastened at the top or part way up the chimney   At the side of the fireplace was attached a crane   The boards in the floor were loose   Tradition says that the cracks in the walls were stopped with lime mortar, though more often clay was used

All the houses were very much alike, except that some, most in fact, were made of round logs, instead of hewn timber   Baking was done in the kettles until the dignity of a brick oven was reached   This oven was built out of doors, so that baking day depended somewhat on the weather   Baking was quite an elaborate process   In the first place they must have "oven wood," dry wood cut short and split fine   The fire was built several hours before the baking was to be done to get the oven hot Once hot, the baking could be done without further fire. The result was far better bread than can be made in the modern stove or range, at least the old people used to say so

The farmer must be a mechanic as well, for most of his farm tools and furniture he made with his axe, jack-knife and sometimes if especially fore-handed, a draw shave. He made his drag, table, chairs, bedstead, put up shelves and made chests for the storage of linen The only wagons were those in which they moved from Herkimer or wherever they came from Those who had no wagons, used sleds The runners hewed out of a "natural crook" selected with great care from some tree Nevertheless, these hardy pioneers enjoyed life, enjoyed work, they liked to see the little clearing around the house grow larger acre by acre, the little patch of wheat, not enough for the year's consumption, expand until there was a surplus, enjoyed telling how many acres of rye they had sown, and the corn, how luxuriantly it grew

They read nature, not books, aside from bibles, there were not a hundred books in the town and only now and then a newspaper They were up early enough to hear the birds in the morning, every bird's voice was familiar to them They were strong, healthy, hearty and could sleep, and the homely fare was enjoyed to the uttermost The children were strong of limb, tanned and freckled by being always out of doors Healthy from simple food and constant exercise It was a pleasure to live.

The education of the children of the community commenced in 1811 when a Mr Maynard opened a school in a little log house on the farm now owned by Wallace Emonds, about one mile west of Somerville There were no school districts, in fact no school provided for except as the people subscribed for the purpose The pioneers paid a certain amount for tuition and boarded the teacher a certain length of time, while he with a good birch rod and an English reader directed the young idea The method of teaching was peculiar to the time, many things of a religious character were taught The alphabet was memorized before any attention was given to the appearance of the letters When the children reached the proper age, the multiplication table was committed to memory and then the youth learned to sing it During the boy's entire education until he got big enough to "lick the teacher" he was given frequent lessons in dancing to the tune whistled by the birch rod, as it cut the air in its descent on the home made woolen that clothed his sturdy form

Not until 1815 was the matter of education taken up officially On March 30th of that year, the town was divided into three school districts, number one, comprising the present town of Fowler, number two, all of Rossie from No 1 to the Indian River, while No 3 reached from the Indian River to the St Lawrence The little log school house of district number two was standing not a great many years ago, though all trace of it is gone now It was near where the first school was taught by Mr Maynard On Mar 31, 1814, a feeble cry was heard at the home of Mr and Mrs Williams It was the first cry of just that kind that had been heard in the town and was a little baby boy's protest against uncongenial surroundings. Because he was the first baby in the new town he was named "Rossie'—William Rossie Williams His advent may have hurried the people of the town in their efforts to establish a better school system, for at the town meeting that year Reuben Streeter, James Howard and Noah Holcomb were named "commissioners of common schools" No school meeting was held—all the school business being transacted by the above board and at regular town meetings In 1816, it was voted, that three times the money shall be raised for the support of common schools that is allowed by the state The records do not show the amount

A wolf bounty of $5 00 was offered in 1855, there was also a fox bounty of 55 cents It was ordered at town meeting that "hogs should not run at large" and that ' cows should not run at large near any tavern or mill in the winter season "

Until April 15, 1815, the town of Rossie extended from the present village of Fullerville to the St Lawrence River On that date, the town of Fowler was organized and with it went school district No 1 The division took a goodly lot of territory but comparatively few inhabitants Of the industries a saw-mill and grist mill at Hailesboro were all the new town possessed

It was a fortunate thing for the town of Rossie that David Parish was induced to invest in its real estate for he, and the others who followed, took a personal interest in their tenants, knew them all and were always looking after their welfare

David Parish was the second son of John Parish, an English gentleman who was a resident of Hamburg where he was interested in a Rothschild bank David was educated with the expectation that he would continue his father's business, but instead, he was employed by European capitalists to transfer certain credits from the Spanish colonies in Mexico to Europe Mr Parish located in Philadelphia where he met Robert and Gouverneur Morris, the Ogden families, so prominent in the history of Ogdensburg, LeRay de Chaumont and others interested in northern lands, and through them was induced to make large purchases He never became a citizen of the United States, and the State Legislature on Nov 8, 1808, passed an "enabling act" giving him permission to ' purchase or take by descent any real estate within this state, and to hold and dispose of the same in like manner as a natural born citizen " He built a fine place at Ogdensburg where he made his home most of the time until 1816 when he returned to Europe, where by investment in a concern that proved to be a corrupt institution, he lost heavily and died in 1826 possessed of but little property outside of his American holdings He died intestate and without issue His heirs were his father, John Parish, and his brothers, George, Charles, Richard and John Being aliens they could not hold real estate in New York, except by special act of Legislature Such an act had been passed, however, in 1817 allowing David's brother, George, who had acted as his agent since his return to Europe, to hold real estate, thus he inherited The remaining heirs brought suit through the court of Chancery and obtained a judgment The property was sold to the highest bidder by Peter Seton Henry, master in Chancery, and was purchased by Joseph Rossell, the confidential agent of the Parishes The deed to Rossell was dated June 26, 1827, and on July 2, 1827, Joseph Rossell and Louisa, his wife, gave a deed of all the property to George Parish For six days Mr. Rossell owned the property. Mr. Rossell came to this country to escape conscription in Napoleon Bonaparte's army and was often the only representative of the Parishes in this country Until his disastrous speculation in Europe, David Parish was very wealthy. He with Steven Girard of Philadelphia, put up seven millions—almost half of a sixteen million dollar loan negotiated by the government in anticipation of the war of 1812-15 with England He was generous, but practical in his generosity, aristocratic in the best sense of the word, energetic, painstaking and not discouraged by apparent failures His brother George, who succeeded him in management and finally in possession of the property in Northern New York, was a man with many of his characteristics He, too, was educated for a commercial life, in addition to a finished literary course He had traveled extensively and continued his trips to many lands while owner of Rossie George Parish was born in 1781 and was about 35 years old when he came to America

The difficulty experienced in settling the estate of his brother David, made George more careful That there might be no trouble in case of his death, he executed a "Last Will and Testament" in which he bequeathed his property in the state of New York to Joseph Rosseel of Ogdensburg in trust for his brother Richard, his heirs, etc. Mr. Rosseel was further directed to "Devise and bequeath the estate aforesaid to competent trustees He died very suddenly in Paris, Apr. 22, 1839, while preparing for an extensive journey in Asia, leaving as heirs, Richard Parish of Hamburg, John Parish of Bohemia, Charles Parish of Hamburg and Elizabeth Hamilton of Glasgow His will was proved July 12, 1839, before Horace Allen, Surrogate of St Lawrence County

For the second time Mr. Rosseel was in possession of all the Parish property in New York State On Dec 6, 1841, Mr. Rosseel sold to George Parish all the land in Rossie The deed recites the will of George Parish and further says "the said Richard Parish has authorized and directed the said Joseph Rosseel to grant, sell, and convey to his son, George Parish, all lands etc and in consideration of $228,000 00 conveys with other lands in the town of Rossie township of Somerville, the unsold residue of various lots amounting to about 1700 acres This deed also covered all personal property, machinery, mines and minerals On Dec 31, 1859, another deed was given by Mr. Rosseel wherein he conveyed "all real and personal estate of what nature and kind, whatsoever Whereof, the said George Parish, deceased, died seized or possessed or was in any way or manner entitled or interested. not otherwise conveyed."

George Parish 2nd, a nephew of David Parish, was the last of the name to live in this country He possessed the extensive ability of his uncles, managed the property in a way to keep values increasing, but was less inclined to make improvements that were not of direct benefit to his property His pace was rather more swift than that of the previous owner He kept quite extensive stables, maintained his house in great style, evidently was rather fond of display, though always easily approached He gave himself no air of superiority in his contact with other men   There are four old lithographs in the Laidlaw house at Rossie that Mr Parish had executed in Germany shortly after taking possession of the property in 1841,—one is of Victoria lead mine, one of the iron works at Rossie   He spent a great deal of his time in Europe and gave powers of attorney to different people to transact any business including the transfer of real estate   Joseph Rosseel and his son, John Francis, Charles R Westbrook, Royal Phelps, Robert Gordon, Benjamin F. Butler (Maitland Phelps & Co) were among those to whom such power was granted About 1866 he was given the title of Baron VonSettonburg by Austria and at once removed to that country, and so far as is known, no member of the Parish family has visited the United States since   He died in 1883   About 1899, a deed was given by Oscar Parish through his attorney, closing out the last little end of the Parish interests in this country

For sixty years the Parish family took a personal interest in Rossie, spending their money freely for its betterment, entering into its history when it was a wilderness, watching and directing its growth until it became a prosperous highly cultivated and well developed town, then leaving   They are as much a part of its history as its mines, mills or farms

In 1812, iron ore was discovered at about a mile east of Somerville   Mr Parish sent samples to Albany for assay   The assay proving satisfactory, enough ore was sent to give it a trial in a furnace   The furnace trial showed the ore to be of good quality, making a superior grade of iron   Mr Parish in 1813, began the erection of a furnace at Rossie Village   Mr James Howard, a brother-in-law of D. W Church, and who had worked with Mr Church in Ogdensburg, was placed in charge of the building operation   A Mr Bempo, an English furnace man was made the first manager and conducted the first blast in 1815 which was a complete failure   Then began a series of costly experiments, lasting until about 1819, when Mr Bembo gave it up and returned to England, no further work being done there for a number of years   Meanwhile Mr David Parish had returned to Europe, 1816, and his brother George had assumed the management of the Parish property   In 1817 James Monroe, President of the United States, visited Rossie as a guest of Mr Parish   The same year, the recorded vote in the town, for Governor, was Daniel D Tompkins 14 and Preston King 5, making 19, the total number of votes cast in the town for Governor of the great state of New York

Some time in the 20's, Mr Parish opened correspondence with a Mr Call of New Jersey who was familiar with furnace work as practiced in Germany He came to Rossie in 1822 or 23   Under his management a successful blast was made for Messrs Keith, Marvin & Sykes, to whom Mr. Parish had leased the furnace for experimental purposes   Having demonstrated that the furnace was a success, they gave it up and it was leased to S Fuller & Co   After three years, Mr Parish bought the contract of Messrs Fuller and made a long lease with Robert R Burr of New Jersey   Mr Burr gave up his lease in 1827 after having run the furnace for only two or three years   For ten years the furnace was idle

In 1837, Mr Parish built a new stack and in other ways enlarged and improved the property and May 12th the furnace was again blown in In 1844, the furnace was again enlarged Between 1837 and 1852, something over 17000 tons of iron was made

In 1848-9 a foundry and machine shop was built in connection with the furnace. The shop was devoted largely to material for railroad construction

In 1844, George Parish, 2nd, a nephew of David Parish, became owner of the Parish interests in St Lawrence County He kept the furnace property until 1864 when he sold it and the iron mines at Keenes and Caledonia to Samuel W Torrey, who in turn sold the property to the Rossie Iron Works, a corporation of which Mr Torrey was made President The furnace was blown out for the last time in 1867 and is now a somewhat picturesque ruin owned by Mr John P Clary of Rossie

The furnace at Rossie was built to smelt the ores found at the Caledonia mine, which had been opened in 1812 For many years all the ore mined was hauled to Rossie usually by the tenants of Mr Parish, he paying them from $1 00 to $3 00 per ton for hauling Mr Parish and his attorneys managed the mines until the property was sold in 1864, when Mr. Chas R Westbrook of Ogdensburg was given the management by the Rossie Iron Works Mr Westbrook was of an old Ulster County family, his ancestors having settled there in 1640 In 1883 his son, Charles S succeeded him in the management which he retained until 1890, when Mr Gregory P Hart succeeded him and continued until the mine was closed in 1893

The history of the mine would furnish a good ground work for the financial history of our country, its periods of activity and of depression being almost the same as the periods of financial prosperity and gloom Until the 40's all the ore mined was hauled to Rossie Between that time and the building of the railroad in 1856, other furnaces had been built near by and used Caledonia ore From 1868 to 1873, the mines reached high tide, at times 400 men were employed After 1873, there was but little ore shipped until 1879, when another wave of prosperity struck the iron interests In 1881-2, the hand drilling was mostly abandoned and the work was done with compressed air A machine shop was built and a company store started under the management of Mr Addison Cummings, a native of the town of Rossie In 1887, shipments of ore stopped, and from then no work was done except to keep the mine free from water In 1890, shipping was resumed in a small way, lasting until 1893, when everything, pumps, tracks and all machinery was taken from the mines and they were allowed to fill with water The property was placed in charge of Mr. Victor Boulet, who had been in the employ of the company since 1868 coming from the "Grand Banks" where he had been a fisherman.

The Rossie Iron Works made application for a voluntary dissolution and Mr. Joseph P Curtis was appointed receiver to sell the property On Sept 26 1898, the property was sold, Mr Chas S Westbrook and Mr James M Wells buying the mines and mineral rights

In 1900 Mr Westbrook pumped out the Caledonia mine and sold to the

Rossie Iron Ore Co., who have continued its operation since, first under the management of Mr. Rodie until 1904, when the present manager, Mr. Brimsmead assumed charge. He is a native of New York, a technical graduate with a wide practical experience, having been connected with mines in Missouri, Montana, British Columbia and South America. At present about 100 men are employed at the Caledonia Mine and they are raising about 200 tons of ore per day.

The first postoffice established in the town of Rossie was at Rossie village, May 16, 1816. It was the eleventh office in the county, the first having been established in DeKalb in 1806. Mr. Roswell Ryon was the first postmaster and was one of the supervisors of the town.

In 1828 a postoffice was established at Somerville, Solomon Pratt was the first postmaster being succeeded by Martin Thatcher, Ward P. Lewis, H. R. Albro, Chauncey B. Fell, Lyman Merriman, Gilbert Wait, Hiram Hall, Chas. Witt, J. B. Johnson, (whose portrait is given), P. M. Crowley, A. A. Scott, John Brickley, and Geo. VanOrnum. In January, 1905, the postoffice was discontinued.

The postoffice at Spragueville was first established at the house of Alexander Wright on Shingle Creek, some distance from its present location. Later it was moved to Steels Corners, then to Spragues Corners. It was first named Shingle Creek then Keensville and finally Spragueville, its present name. Mr. Wright was the first postmaster, followed by Daniel Wilcox, Geo. F.

J. B. Johnson

Steele, Eben Gillett, A. M. Vedder, L. G. Draper, D. W. Sprague, Geo.Steele, D. W Sprague, A. H. Johnson, (whose portrait appears), and Frank Johnson, the present encumbent.

A good roads movement started June 8, 1812, when a company composed of David Parish, L. Hasbrouck, N. Lord, J. Rosseel and others was incorpor-

ated with a capital of $50,000 and was known as the Ogdensburg Turnpike Co., for the purpose of making a turnpike road from Ogdensburg to Wilna. They turned the road over to the town in 1826. This road extended from OxBow to the Morristown line. The town maintained its own roads from 1826 to 1848, when the Gouverneur, Somerville and Antwerp Co. was formed to build a plank road from Antwerp through to Gouverneur. This road crossed the town of Rossie at Somerville, being only about 1½ miles in the town. The company was incorporated Dec. 30, 1848. The road was

A. H. Johnson.

finished in September, 1850. The directors were C. P. Egbert, S. B. VanDuzee, (portrait shown), Gilbert Wait, N. L. Gill, Chas. Anthony and Martin Thatcher. Gilbert Wait and Martin Thatcher, the latter being treasurer, were both residents of Somerville. Jan. 23, 1850, the Hammond, Rossie and Antwerp Plank Road Co. was incorporated to build

a plank road from Antwerp via Ox Bow and Hammond to Ogdensburg. From OxBow to the Morristown line it was in Rossie. Its directors were Ira Hinsdale, E. Brainard, Z. Gates, A. P. Morse and D. W. Baldwin. Mr. Baldwin was a resident of Rossie and manager of the Parish industries of the town.

The construction of the plank road through the town presented two difficult problems; one was crossing the long swamp about a mile out of OxBow and the other

S. B. VanDuzee.

was the approach to Indian River. The swamp was soft and gave no secure foundation for a road bed. At Indian River, there was an almost perpendicular descent of over 50 feet. There was a standard grade established for plank roads, which must not be exceeded. This made it necessary to cut down the hill which was rock and fill from there to the river, a distance of about one-eighth of a mile and a fill of over forty feet at its greatest depth. Messrs. Frazier & Co. took the contract to build the road from OxBow to Rossie for $7,000. The approach to the Indian River cost all they had got for the whole road. The road was completed in December, 1850. After the plank was worn out, the company was permitted to gravel the road and maintain it as a turnpike, collecting the toll the same as before. In 1880 the company's charter expired and the road was turned over to the town. Previous to 1854, when the railroad was completed from Watertown to Potsdam, crossing the town at Keenes, where a station was established, there had been two lines of stage coaches, running via Antwerp, Somerville and Gouverneur north, the other from Antwerp to Ogdensburg by OxBow, Hammond, Rossie and Morristown. Before the advent of the railroad, all produce was hauled to Albany or Troy.

In 1818 an element entered the town, destined to have a great influence in shaping its moral and industrial growth. In that year, came Robert Ormiston, (portrait accompanying). William Faichney, James Dixon, James Fairbairn, Thomas Elliott, Donald McCarvie, James Henderson, Colon McLaren, James Douglass and Andrew Dodds, with their families. They sailed from Scotland for Quebec. From Quebec they sailed up the St. Lawrence as far as Prescott, where they met one of Mr. Parish's agents who induced them to visit Rossie. They finally settled in the town between the Oswegatchie and Indian Rivers, now known as Scotch Settlement, Mr. Parish agreeing to clear three acres of land and build a log house for each family, and furnish a yoke of oxen for each two families, and give each

Robert Ormiston.

a cow, provision and seed wheat for a year. In 1819 Robert Clark, Andrew Culbertson, John Henderson, Andrew Fleming, John Dodds, James Hobkirk, John Tait, James Ormiston, David Storie, Wm. Laidlaw and James Lockie, joined the little colony   John McRobbie, Thos Turnbull, and his brothers Michael, Adam, Andrew and William, came in 1820

In 1829 or 30 Joel Jepson who had moved to Rossie from Vermont, was planting corn   His little daughter, nine years old, was dropping it for him, she saw a peculiar looking stone, white and covered with cubes   She hit it breaking it into numberless cubes, and squares of a dark gray color   She had discovered the Victoria Lead Mine   No real effort was made to work the rich deposit until 1835, when on Dec 11 Mr Parish made a contract with Mr Bliss T Nash, to prospect for minerals in the town of Rossie, one of the conditions being that Mr Parish was to get fifty cents a ton for all iron ore mined and seventy-five cents for all lead   Any lead mined was to be smelted at Rossie The contract was for ten years   On May 12, 1837, two lead mining companies were incorporated, one was named the Rossie Lead Mining Co , and the other the Rossie Galena Co   Both were to be capitalized at $24,000   The two companies worked on the Coal Hill vein   Some work was done by the Rossie Galena Co in 1836 but no extensive operations were commenced until 1837, when both companies put an immense number of laborers at work   The smelting was done under a contract with Messrs Moss and Knapp, whose furnace was on Indian River, something over a mile from the mine   They got $25 a ton, and all over 68 per cent that the ore might yield in lead, giving them over $28 a ton for smelting   Work was discontinued by both companies in 1840   The Victoria and Union veins had been worked by Mr Parish   He also opened a mine on what was called the Robinson or Indian River vein, out of which he took 1,100 pounds of lead at a cost of $1,600   The two companies operating Coal Hill vein took out 3,250,690 pounds of metalic lead, the ore yielding 67 per cent on an average   After remaining idle for more than ten years, Mr Parish, to whom the leased mine had reverted, made another lease to R P Remington, for ten years, with a privilege of ten years more   Mr Remington was to pay a royalty of 1-12 of all lead mined   A stock company was formed Sept 8, 1852, called the Great Northern Lead Co , capitalized at $500,000   The best machinery that could be procured was installed   They ran the mine about three years, with miners from Cornwall, England, when they were forced to close   The low price of lead and high royalty made it a losing venture

In 1854 J B Morgan leased the mines running them with varying fortunes until 1868, when they were again closed   About this time the Parish interests in the town of Rossie were nearly all closed out, A Pardee buying the mineral rights in the western end of the town and also buying about 365 acres of land at the Victoria and Union Mines   The mines were opened for the last time in 1875 under the management of Mr John Webb, Mr Pardee's agent   The work only lasted about one year when the mines were finally closed   The mines and mineral rights still remain the property of the Pardee estate   Mr Ara J. Moore of Dekalb being the present agent

The advent of railroads, the invention of automatic machinery, and the concentration of manufacturing in large centers were all factors in ruin of the small interior towns, even though they had water powers of great value. No town in St. Lawrence county was harder hit than Rossie. At one time the villages of Somerville and Rossie were the leading places in the county and Wegatchie had promise of being a manufacturing center of great importance. Rossie had its furnace, foundry and machine shop, saw mill, grist mill, oat-meal mill, though the latter was never much of a success. Now, there is a saw mill doing purely local work, a grist mill, grinding feed mostly, four stores, two hotels and two blacksmith shops.

Wegatchie had a furnace, saw mills, grist mill, spoke factory, woolen mill, and stone mill. Now there is the woolen mill owned and operated by H. K. Wright; one saw mill, a store, hotel, cheese factory and blacksmith shop. Somerville possessed in its days of prosperity two furniture factories, one carriage factory, two blacksmith shops, stores and two hotels. Now there is a blacksmith and carriage repair shop, one store and a hotel. The postoffice has yielded to the mail carrier and been abandoned.

There are five religious societies in town, one Catholic, one Presbyterian, and three Methodist. The Catholic society begins officially in 1846 when an attempt was made to build a church. The frame was raised but never enclosed. Previous to that, priests from Ogdensburg had visited the community with more or less regularity. By 1861 a church was completed. St. Patricks society was incorporated in 1872 with Thomas Kane and Thomas Spratt as the first trustees. The pastors have been Father Clark from Carthage, Fathers Harvey, Sherry, De Shannbac, McDonald, Rossiter, and Brown from Redwood, and Fathers Kelly, who built the present stone church, Fitzgerald, O'Neil, who died at Rossie in 1899, and the present pastor, the Rev. Father Crowley of Rossie.

The Presbyterian Society was organized in 1855. Andrew Laidlaw, William Allen, James Brodie, George Lockie, (whose portrait appears), and David McFalls, (portrait shown), were the first trustees. The pastors have been John McGregor, James Gardiner, Alex. Adair, Wm. H. Robinson, Daniel A. Ferguson, John E. Beecher, Elias B. Fisher, John A. Pollock, Albro Green and Chas. G. Mitchell. They have a handsome church overlooking the Indian River. The Methodists at Rossie village have never built a church. Their first pastor was the Rev. Samuel Orvis appointed in 1844. He was followed by Henry Woodruff, J. Francis, G. W. Plank, Samuel Griffin and P. M. Crowley. These pastors serving until 1854, when the church apparently ceased to exist until 1868, when it reorganized with A. T. Nichols as the first pastor.

George Lockie.

Wegatchie has a small Methodist organization served by the preachers located at OxBow.

On Aug. 16, 1845, the Methodist Episcopal Society of Somerville was organized with Hiram Hale, Orin Freeman, John Johnson (portrait) Freedom Free-

John Johnson.

man, Augustus Preston and A. C. VanDyke as trustees. In 1846 a church was built. Silas Slater was the first pastor, followed by P. M. Crowley, C. C. Symes, J. Zimmerman, C. E. Beebe, J. Austin, L. Whitcomb, M. O. Kinney, S. Ball, D. Simmons, G.P. Kinney, S. Blackburn, C. W. Brooks, S. Boyd, H. Hesselgraves (1871), A. L. Smith, A. T. Nichols, J. G. Price, A. G. Woodard, (whose portrait is given), W. P. Hall, B. M. Phelps, John Bragg, G. S. Hastings, A. Warren, T. H. McClanthan, and the present pastor, H. Hesselgrave.

The first Universalist Society of Somerville was incorporated in 1842 with Lyman Merriman, Alva Weeks and Wm. Ayres as the first trustees. For many years services were held with more or less regularity, being supplied from the St. Lawrence University at Canton much of the time. A church was built in 1846. The society has gone out of existence and a few years ago the church was sold.

The town of Rossie has good reason to be proud of her record in the war of 1861 to 1865. But few towns in this or any other state, furnished more volunteers for the same population than Rossie, while the village of Wegatchie sent nearly one man to every six of her total population, to the front. Anoth-

Rev. A. G. Woodard.

er direction in which the town takes great pride, is the character of the men sent to the county Legislature. Her supervisors have always been strong men, deeply interested in the town's welfare. Mr. Reuben Streeter, the first supervisor, was a man of exceptionally strong character, wielding a greater influence during the town's infancy than any other one man. He served as supervisor in 1813-14-16-17-18 and 29. Theodocius O. Fowler was elected in 1815. He was a resident of what was later the town of Fowler and was the first supervisor of that town. In 1819 and 1825, Ebenezer Martin was elected, and in 1820 Russell Ryan. Lewis Franklin followed Mr. Ryan holding the office until 1824. James Howard was elected first in 1826 and again in 1827. William Brown served one year, 1828. In 1830 Solomon Pratt was elected holding the office until 1832. He was again elected in 1835 and in 1845-6 and in 1852 he was appointed to fill vacancy, holding the office until 1854. Wm. Skinner was supervisor in 1833-4 and in 1836-7-8 Robert Clark held the office. Martin Thatcher was elected in 1839 and 1840; William B. Bostwick was elected in 1843; reelected in 1844 and again in 1858. H. V. R. Wilmot held the office in 1847-8. Zacheus Gates followed Mr. Wilmot in 1849 and in 1851 and 52, dying the latter year. R. R. Sherman served one year, 1855, followed by D. S. Baldwin, in 1856-7. From 1859 to 1863 James H. Church was supervisor. Thomas A. Turnbull served in 1864-65 and 66; again in 1870 he was elected, holding the office until 1874 and finally in 1878 he served one year. In 1867-68 and 69

Dr. David McFalls (portrait) was the executive officer of the town. Abial E. Helmer followed Mr. Turnbull, holding the office during the years

1875-76-77-79-80-83-84-85 and 86. George McLear, a democrat, was elected in 1881 and again in 1882. John Barry was elected in 1887 and re-elected in 1888. In 1889, D. W. Church held the office for one year. From 1890 to 1894, James W. Marshall (portrait) was supervisor. Dr. Fuller was elected in 1895, serving during the years 1896-7-8-9 and was re-elected in 1901. The May following he died. Mr. Marshall was appointed to fill the vacancy, and at the next town meeting he was elected for the full term, holding the office until 1905, when John Barry was again elected and is now supervisor.

Dr. David McFalls.

There are many of Rossie's citizens who are deserving of more than passing notice. Such men as Reuben Streeter, James Howard, the Churches and Turnbulls, James Marshall and many others who have identified themselves with all that meant progress, improvement, and honesty in the town's affairs. The influence of such men will last as long as time and Rossie owes to them more than can be realized.

Mr. Streeter was of New England parentage, possessing all the traits that make a leader in pioneer life. His wealth was freely expended for the benefit of the community in which he lived. He gave the new town of Rossie its start in the direction of honest growth.

James W. Marshall.

His old age was clouded by the loss of property brought about by an unfortunate lawsuit. In the 40's he left Rossie for Vermont, where he died.

Mr. Marshall was a native of the town. He was born at Spragueville, where his boyhood was spent. After his marriage he moved to Somerville, where the remainder of his life was spent. He had many things to hamper him, yet by force of character and the will to go ahead, he succeeded in becoming a man of influence in his town and a man looked upon by the Board of Supervisors, as one of the few men worthy of leadership. Of him, it can safely be said that he never knowingly did a mean thing or wronged any man.

The Churches were always identified with the town's best interests. Daniel Church, son of Daniel Whipple Church and Dorothy (Wheeler) Church, was born in the town of Canton, Sept. 17, 1809. His father was one of the first pioneers who settled St. Lawrence County and who in 1810 surveyed and laid out the road through the long swamp between OxBow and Rossie, a thing that had been considered impracticable.

Daniel came from Morristown to Wegatchie in the town of Rossie in the year 1855, and engaged with his brothers, Louis and Howard, in the woolen business. In 1867, the factory was burned and rebuilt by Daniel the same year   This mill is still in operation and the little village is yet often called Church's Mills, after the men who so long ago were active there

Mr Church was of New England descent, his ancestor, Richard Church, being one of the first settlers of Hartford, Conn   The pioneer life which he had lived strengthened his sterling qualities and though he had very few advantages except of the most primitive sort, his natural desire for knowledge was so strong that he mastered many branches of science, without the aid of school or teacher and his ever widening range of useful information was a source of surprise even to his intimate friends

Modest, retiring, and unobtrusive by nature he was a fearless thinker and dared to investigate thoroughly the great questions of life and stood by his convictions sometimes almost alone

He hated sham and hypocrisy and inculcated honesty, charity, temperance, economy and love of humanity, both by precept and example

In 1848 he married Harriet Law Wheeler of Groton, Mass   Then four children are Martha Adams now Mrs G S Conger, whose portrait will be seen in the group of Daughters of the American Revolution, Mary Hayward, who was lost at sea November 22, 1873, Daniel Whipple, a civil engineer in Chicago, Ill, and Harriet, now Mrs A W Orvis

His wife died October 22, 1878, and five years later, the cares, toils and disappointments of life came to an end and Daniel Church entered into rest July 13, 1883

Mary Hayward Church, second daughter of Daniel and Harriet Church, was born in Morristown, N Y, July 20, 1851   Her childhood days were spent at Wegatchie, where the beauties of nature surrounding her helped to develop her innate artistic qualities and at an early age her fondness for drawing was displayed, her pet animals being always her patient models

Ella Turnbull, a natural artist, of Wegatchie, guided her first efforts and later she studied at the Gouverneur Wesleyan Seminary   In 1870 she entered Cooper Union in New York City, where she spent two years in honest, patient work, earning besides a diploma and two silver medals, the love and admiration of her co-workers and teachers   So much encouragement was given her that she decided to go to Europe to study in the great art galleries there   Her whole soul was filled with love for her chosen art, and her parents, with remarkable unselfishness and love, gave her the opportunity which in those days was quite uncommon

November 15, 1873, the steamer Ville du Havre left New York harbor with nearly three hundred passengers on board   None with brighter prospects, purer and higher aims than Mary H Church, then only 22 years old   In mid-ocean and at midnight, a sailing vessel, the Loch Earn, came gliding through the waters   There was a collision and this large steamer, the finest, strongest and most elegantly equipped on the ocean, in ten minutes sank out of sight, 226 people were lost, Mary H Church being one of the number

James H Church, a brother of Daniel, was born in Canton   He learned the clothiers' trade in Antwerp and with his brother started the woolen mills at Wegatchie, one of that village's industries that still survives

The Churches trace their ancestors back to the 17th century, Samuel being born in Massachusetts some time in that century His son, Nathaniel, was born at Hadley, in that state in 1704

It is impossible to do justice to the men who made Rossie Messrs Pratt and Thatcher of Somerville, were two who deserve more than passing mention. Mr Gilbert Wait for many years one of the town's assessors, and so on, for Rossie has been fortunate in having more than her share of strong men, such as give to communities a name that stands in history, not so much for great deeds as for sterling honesty

HISTORY OF FOWLER.

By Allen Wight (aged 81).

Fowler was formed from Rossie and Russell, embracing Killarney No. 7 (of the subdivision of No. 2 of Macomb's purchase) and Portaferry No. 11, April 15, 1816. The first town meeting was held at the house of Noah Holcomb.

Allen Wight.

At the time of its erection, No. 7 constituted school district No. 3 of Rossie. On the 10th of April, the townships of Edwards (No. 8) and Fitz William (Hermon) previously in Russell, were attached to Fowler, but afterwards taken off in the formation of those towns.

In forming Pitcairn in 1836, a triangular portion of No. 11, beginning in the County line at the most westerly corner of No. 11 and run thence southeast along the county line three miles, thence at right angles until it intersected the line between No. 7 and No. 11 (2 1-6 miles), was retained by Fowler. It contained 2,087 acres. On the division of the Great Tract into townships, No. 7 fell to Gilchrist and Fowler. On the 3rd of August, 1810, the former conveyed his share to the latter. Theodosius Fowler on the 15th of May, 1821, conveyed to his son, T. O. Fowler, under whom most of the town was settled.

Theodosius O. Fowler was a captain in the Continental Army of the Revolution. He received his commission as ensign in 1776, was promoted to Lieutenant and in 1778 to Captain in the N. Y. 1st Regiment, but in 1780 was transferred to the 2nd Regiment, in which he served until the close of the war. He was present and took part in the battles of Long Island, Saratoga, Monmouth and White Plains, and shared in the hardships of the camp at Valley Forge and Morristown. The first set of town officers were Theodosius O. Fowler, Supervisor; Simeon Hazelton, Clerk; Noah Holcomb, Eben Cole, Benjamin Brown, Assessors; John Parker, Noah Holcomb, Commissioners of Highways; Benjamin Brown, Noah Holcomb, Overseers of the Poor; Simeon Hazelton, Samuel B. Sprague, Overseers of Highways; Alvin Wright, Constable and Collector; Alvin Wright, Simeon Hazelton, Eben Cole, Commissioners of Common Schools; Theodosius O. Fowler, Jedediah Kingsley, Richard Merrill, Inspectors of Common Schools. Names of Supervisors with years of service:

Theodosius O. Fowler, 1817.

Benjamin Brown (to fill vacancy) 1818.

Eben Cole, 1818 to 1821.

Justus Picket, 1825 to 1829, 1831-32, 1837-38.

Stillman Fuller, 1830, 1833-34.

William Hurlbut, 1835-36.

Henry H. Haile, 1839-40-41.

Asa L Hazelton, 1842-43.
Alfred Burt, 1844-45
Herman Fuller, 1846-47
Adison Giles, 1848-49, 1855-56-57-58
Thomas J Hazelton, 1850-51, 1853-54, 1859, 1865
Emery W Abbott, 1852 and 1860 to 1864 inclusive
Daniel Peck, 1866 to 1875 inclusive
Abner H Johnson, 1876-77
George W Kelley, 1878-82.
Simeon H Austin, 1883
Henry W. Johnson, 1884-87
Wm T Clark, 1888-90
Simeon H Austin, 1891
Wm T Clark, 1892-94 to 1899
G M Holmes, 1900 to 1905.

The first settlement in the town of Fowler was made by Brigadier General James Haile from Fairfield, Herkimer Co, who came into the town to explore and who purchased of Richard Townsend, agent for Gilchrist and Fowler, in the month of June, 1807, a tract one mile square on the ground where the village of Hailesboro now stands, under obligation to build mills within a year. In the fall of the same year, General Haile came with several men to commence the erection of the mills, with Captain Ward, as millwright, and Captain Jason Robinson as carpenter. A saw-mill was built the same fall and a small grist mill with one run of stones was put in operation in 1808, which was swept away by a freshet in 1809, and was rebuilt the following year, with one run of stones A second run of stones was added the following year, 1810 A superior mill was built in 1844, with Wm Robinson as millwright and Jason Robinson and Rockwell Barnes as carpenters Elijah Sackett from Hartford, N Y, came to town in 1808 and was employed as miller, until his death in the spring of 1812 He was the first white person who was known to have died in town

Lemuel Arnold, John P Ryon, Charles Ryon, Smith Cleveland, Ebenezer Parker and others came and settled soon after In 1811 Samuel B Sprague made the first stand on the Lake Road, about a mile west of Little York in a log shanty, but afterwards built on the hill north of Little York where Byron Wight now lives

During the war of 1812 several families left the town from fear of the Indians. The town did not begin to settle rapidly until 1820 The Wight family came in the winters of 1820 and 1822 with ox teams from Herkimer County Abner, Reuben, Jason, John, Alvin, Harvey and a sister, Abigail Green, following their uncle, Jason Robinson John and his mother stopped the first night in town at Hezekiah Hodgkins' a few rods from the present house on the Balmat farm in December, 1820, where he met Laura Hodgkins, whom he afterwards married in November, 1821 (Hezekiah Hodgkins was a brother to Pardon Babcock's wife) John Wight settled on the farm where the first tale was

dug and ground   Abner settled in the west part of the town   Reuben married
Susannah VanBuren, cousin to President Martin VanBuren, and removed to
Ohio in 1834, near Cleveland, and died of cholera twenty days after he reached
there, leaving a family of twelve children   Alvin married Eunice, a sister
of George Diaper in 1823   Diaper held the office of Justice of Peace in West
Fowler for several years   John Parker purchased the land where the village of
Fullerville now is and built for a hotel down the river on the old Turnpike, the
house now owned by E Austin

The earliest religious organizations in Fowler appear to have been by the
regular Baptists and Methodists   The Baptists' first organization in Fowler
was made Jan 30, 1822, under Elder Jonathan Payne, the original members
being thirteen in number, viz Benjamin Brown and wife, Ephraim Gates and
wife, Josiah T Lawton and wife, Asa Wade and wife, Noah Barrell and wife,
James Baines, Martin Rowley and Hannah Johnson   Elder Noah Barrel became then pastor in November, 1822   The duration of his pastorate is not
known   Elder Wm Gorrey came in 1828 and remained three years   Next came
Elder Guernsey and in June, 1833, he was succeeded by Elder M Wilkie   In
1835 they built a house of worship at Fullerville at a cost of about $1,200,
mainly through the influence and assistance of the Fuller brothers who were all
Baptists   Prior to this they had worshipped in the school house   In May
1836, Elder Brand became their minister and served them for two years   Elder
John Peck then preached to them for two years, from the fall of 1838   Then
for five years, they appear to have had no regular preacher, but Elder David
Deland came in 1843 and remained for about one year   The last three resided
at Fullerville   In 1851, Elder Nichols was engaged to preach part of the time
The church went in a decline and from 1855 to 1870 continued very low   In
1876, but seven members remained and worship was discontinued   Their last
minister was the Rev H C Dike

The Baptist Society of Antwerp and Fowler was incorporated Dec 31
1825, with Moses Birge, James M Graves and Peter Smourney, trustees They
built a church at Steels Corners, but this is all gone , all dead   The Methodists
held worship here at a very early day, but we have no account of their organization or earliest teachers   They had a strong society in Fullerville and vicinity before 1837 at which time N R Peck was the pastor   About 1845 they
purchased the unfinished church of the Presbyterians and completed it   They
also owned a parsonage in Fullerville   Their organization was kept up until
about 1865   The church edifice is still standing   The Universalist appears to
have always been the strongest of the churches in Fowler   The first Universalist
Society in the town of Fowler and Gouverneur, was organized January 26,
1832, Simeon Hazelton and twenty-five others being the original subscribers to
the constitution In June the number had reached seventy-two   Their earliest
preachers were Elders Longworthy, Wilcox and Wood   The Little York Universalist Society was formed March 22, 1841, Jabez Glazier, Leman Fuller
Simeon Hazelton, Albert A Vedder and John P Ryon being the first trustees
A church was built at Little York by Simeon Hazelton at a cost of $1,200 about

the year 1840. A sum of money had been placed in the hands of a committee some years before by T. O. Fowler for the purpose of building a church and the members of the committee had either died or moved away and it devolved upon Mr. Hazelton to build the church. The church was afterward sold to the Free Baptists, dressed over and furnished and is now used by them.

Simeon Hazelton

The first Universalist Society of Gouverneur and Hailesboro was formed Jan. 27, 1849, Addison Giles heading the list of trustees. The original members numbered eighteen. In 1851 the Rev. C. Dodge was their pastor, preaching every fourth Sabbath in the school house.

The Union Church edifice at Hailesboro was erected in 1860 on land donated by H. H. Haile and on Jan. 3, 1861, a meeting was held for the sale of pews. The record gives a list of fifteen pews sold at that time, aggregating $905. On the same day, the Universalist Union Society of Hailesboro was organized in the new meeting house, with Francis Farmer, Wm. T. Burt and Daniel Z. Sartwell as trustees.

The West Fowler Free-will Baptist Church was organized in 1826 by Elders Dodge and Waite. Their first pastor was Rev. Amasa Chandler. A church edifice was built in 1852. Their last regular pastor was B. F. Jefferson.

Maj. Henry H. Haile.

The Free Baptist Church of Fowler was organized on March 17, 1877, at Little York and Albert E. Smith, Allen Wight, and Justus Barnes elected as trustees. B. F. Jefferson, pastor.

The Baptist Society soon after purchased the old church from Simeon Hazelton and re-seated it, and dressed it over and continued their meetings under the direction of C. A. Morehouse and have continued under the leadership of different ministers since.

The town was covered with a heavy growth of timber. On the extreme north and south sides was considerable spruce, mixed with hemlock and some pine, which was devastated with fires at an early date. A wide strip crossing the town nearly north and south, contained a strong, heavy soil, covered with a heavy growth of timber, especially hemlock. One Wm. Newton purchased 73 acres of what is now the farm owned by L. L. Austin and let the job of felling 40 acres to Daniel Woodcock, John Woodcock and Hiram Bates, which was burned over and afterwards cleared by Samuel A. Austin. About the same time, 1835, John Wight on the opposite side of the road, slashed about nine acres from which years after, 120 large hemlock stumps were removed, varying in size from two to upwards of four feet in diameter. Notwithstanding the immense growth of timber, but little use could be made of it, although there has been built and operated not less than twenty-two saw-mills in the town   They were slow, crude affairs, compared with a modern mill

The life of mills and bridges built of the best of timber, insufficiently covered, has been only about 8 to 12 years   The old saw-mill was a crude, slow affair.   No matter what the size of the log, it would take from ten to fifteen minutes to cut a board twelve feet long   The up and down saw hung in a gate that only made one stroke to a turn of the water-wheel   About 1850, the saw was taken out of the gate and geared so as to make four or five strokes to one turn of the wheel, but not until about 1860 was the large circular saw used on the Oswegatchie River, consequently a thousand feet of lumber must have been a large day's work for an old saw mill depending much upon the size of the logs   The old mills were run with wooden wheels made on the spot by the ordinary mechanic, requiring a large quantity of water to operate them and a large bulkhead to make a cut through the length of the log   For example, a man by the name of Asa Barker was working the mill on the outlet of Sylvia Lake and in making a cut the length of a log, emptied the bulkhead   Some obstruction prevented him shutting the gate properly, so he set the log at the head, next went under the saw gate to set the tail end of the log and enough water had gathered in the bulkhead to start the wheel and down came the gate that held the saw and knocked him down and his left arm fell across the log in front of the saw and cut or broke it, cutting all but the artery in the front part of the arm, and he was able to travel over a half mile to get help, and no doctor within reach had nerve enough to amputate the arm and good luck was his   It was done up the best it could be and he had a fairly good arm afterward

In 1825 works were erected by Jasper Clark at Haileboro for the sawing and working of veined limestone, which abounds in the vicinity   The business was continued by him and his successor, Addison Giles, for a number of years, and then abandoned   About the same time, a carding and fulling mill was put in operation by Raymond Austin   After him, it was owned and carried on by Addison Giles, and later by James and Edwin McIntosh, who about 1865, transformed it into a manufactory of woolen cloths   An interest with them was purchased by J H Abbott and they afterwards sold the remainder to E W Abbott, and it was then operated by J H Abbott & Co , employing about twenty hands and making about 30,000 yards of cloth annually   The cloth making was abandoned a few years ago, and the power used in talc manufacture for about seven years   The establishment is now idle

About 1850, Jesse Bannister commenced the business of chair making   His establishment was afterward owned by Seymour Sweet, who used it as a Cooper's shop   It was then owned by E W Abbott and used by Cyrus Barnes for making axe-helves   From him, it passed to Carpenter and Tupper, who used it as a wood-working shop until it was destroyed by fire about 1871, after which it was rebuilt by J H Carpenter, the present owner by whom it is carried on as a planing-mill, sash, blind and door factory

George W Carpenter ran a tannery for a few years just above J H Carpenter's shop on the same flume now used as a grist mill by Charles A Clark.

The first store opened in Hailesboro was by Wm Hurlbut in 1825 He was succeeded by Justus Picket, who continued it until his death in 1842, since which time it has been kept by Horace Baines, John R Stewart, Farmer & Stewart, Theodore Clark, Mathias Fithian, S D Rich and J T McCombs Another store has been kept on the opposite corner of the street by Edwin Noble

The first hotel in Hailesboro was opened about 1835 by Wm Hurlbut It has since been kept by Geo P Holmes, Apollas Leggett, S D Rich, and now by Mrs S D Rich

The principal business at Hailesboro is preparing talc for market The talc mining and manufacturing is the largest and most extensive business of any in the town There are at present eight large mills operating night and day, all run by water power, except one, grinding and bolting from 25 to 100 tons a day each, for the past ten to twenty years, all these are in the towns of Fowler and Edwards

There were many years ago, three distilleries in the town for the manufacture of whiskey from rye, corn and potatoes One on the Francis Hilts farm, one on the E. Johnson farm above Little York and one at Fullerville The writer of this well remembers having assisted in raising two crops of corn on new cleared land, threshing it out, having a little of it ground and a pint basin of the meal fed to each cow, the balance being taken to the distillery, exchanged for double whiskey, a bushel for a gallon, and what was not drank was sold for fifty cents per gallon, when butter sold by the tub for eight cents cash per pound to Wm E Sterling in Gouverneur.

Jabez Glazier with Ransom H Gillett and Asa Woodcock, came into the town on foot in 1819 from Hadley, Saratoga County, made selection of lots and went back and moved in with their ox-teams Glazier located upon the turnpike, Gillett went and taught school in Edwards, finally going to Ogdensburg and studying law, receiving an appointment to an office in the Treasury Department at Washington, where he assisted Asa L Hazelton to a clerkship, where he reached the same position Gillett held, and is living there now at the age of ninety-eight years

Jason Wight acted as agent for Fowler for several years while keeping hotel at Little York, afterward Jabez Glazier was his agent until Fowler sold to T D. Carpenter and left the town when Judge Dodge took the agency

The large majority of the early settlers came with ox-teams and a cow and spent most of their time the first winter with their cattle in the woods, felling timber and helping them to get a scanty living from the browse of buds and twigs among the brush, thereby preparing for clearing the land for the next season's crops, and burning the timber and making potash from the ashes, which was about the only thing that brought them any money

Richard Merrill divided the town into big lots when in a square form, one half mile square, but made many subdivisions in all sorts of shapes to suit pur-

Asa L. Hazelton.

chasers, and he died in the woods about the year 1835 or 36. Then Asa L. Hazelton made the surveys until he sold his instruments to Allen Wight in 1853.

The first birth in town was in the family of Richard Merrill. The first marriage was John Parker to Elizabeth Sackett, who taught the first school in Gouverneur.

For many years the mail was carried by a boy or light man on horseback from Antwerp to Canton by way of Edwards and Russell. Then changed and carried in wagons or sleighs from Gouverneur to Fine by way of Edwards.

The largest purchaser of lands from Fowler was Thaddeus Hildreth from Herkimer County. He bought over a thousand acres in this vicinity of Chub Lake and gave his nephew Thaddeus Willard fifty acres and leased the remainder to him, which upon Willard's failure to pay for it, was divided into two farms, one to A. H. Payne and the other to Wm. McKean. Hildreth purchased several thousand acres besides from time to time as his means accumulated, and resold farms to different individuals. Settlers came in from Herkimer, Saratoga and Montgomery Counties soon after the advent of General Haile. The Burt family, Alfred Sawyer and Daniel with their sisters: Chauncey and Robert Conant, William and Joseph Farmer, Wm. Hurlbut, Caleb O. Root, the Baxters, the Wights and numerous others, with but little means, generally taking contracts of land and consequently, as they mostly raised quite large families, took several years to pay for their lands and support themselves.

The inhabitants of Fowler were not possessed of any peculiar personal characteristics, were generally industrious, honest in their dealings, frugal, temperate, religiously liberal in their views, and in their early days generally Democratic, but upon the great breaking up of the parties about the years 1856 to 1860, the great majority entered the Republican party.

The Fowler Library was incorporated April 12, 1831, with Simeon Hazelton as Librarian, and Justus Picket, Albert Vedder and Reuben Wight, as trustees. It contained Rollins Ancient History, Josephus' works, Lewis and Clark's expedition to Oregon, Arabian Nights, Volney's Ruins, Comstocks Chemistry and Philosophy, Noah Webster's History of Diseases and other works, all of which the writer of this read and studied with much interest. The books all disappeared years ago except Webster on Diseases.

There have been built in the town twenty-two saw mills at different times on the Oswegatchie River and its tributaries. All have served their purpose and disappeared.

In 1853 Allen Wight bought good hemlock lumber for $4 a thousand; spruce for $6; pine mostly clear stuff for $10; shingles $1.25 or a thousand for a day's work at carpentering, showing but little, if any, difference between the comparative prices of labor and materials then and now.

About 1840, some Mormon missionaries came into the town and made several converts. One Silsbury in the west part of the town engaged in preaching the doctrine in school-houses, and one Rogers near Little York preached for a few years, and a third one at Fullerville, Heath, preached the Joseph Smith doctrine of polygamy for a time. Several of their converts left and joined the Mormons in the west.

At the time of Addison Giles' first election to the office of Supervisor, a whig, there were only seven whigs in town, and previous to that time there were over forty abolitionists in the town led by Martin Mitchel, while at the same time there was only about forty-three in the rest of the county.

The town probably furnished its full share of volunteers in putting down the Rebellion, but we have no means of knowing how many enlisted from the fact that other states offered large bounties and a class of speculators induced men to go with them and join a regiment in Connecticut. The writer of this was threatened with personal violence for making a statement in a public meeting that the town's quota called for would have been filled had it not been for the fact that a class of knaves and scoundrels had taken the men out of town and sold them to other places.

There is not known to have been but one murder committed in town. One Samuel Kirkham, living on the old turnpike between the Balmat farm and the John Parker place, shot his wife in the woods on the back part of the John Wight farm, using lumps of cast iron picked out of the sand at the furnace at Fullerville for shot. He was an object of curiosity to the children in 1835 because he wore his beard about a foot long. He was sent to Auburn and died chained to the pump for refusing to work.

Soon after the settlement of Little York, a small store was opened by Wm. Lawrence who had come from New York to take charge of the erection of the Fowler Mansion. He was succeeded by Martin Mitchell, after whom came

Emory W. Abbott.

Abner H. Johnson.

Justus Picket, after whose death in 1842 the store was kept many years by Emory W. Abbott and an establishment run for many years for manufacturing pot and pearl ashes, calling for 400 or 500 or more cords of wood every year. Afterwards the store was occupied by A. H. Johnson and S. H. Austin, then sold to G. W. Kelley, finally to L. L. Austin, when later it burned with other buildings. One Aaron Rowley for a short time kept a store in Little York and then removed to Gouverneur.

Simeon Hazelton & Sons also built a store in Little York and ran it in connection with a large ashery until about 1851, when Ward Glazier kept the store for two or three years, and Thomas J. Hazelton continued it several years more, when it was sold and the old building converted into a blacksmith shop for which it is still used.

The first school house in Little York was of logs within a few feet of where M. V. B. Hazelton's house now stands and in which a Universalist minister by

the name of Wood lived some time, and was occupied as late as 1850 by a shoemaker. A frame schoolhouse was built on the ground where Varnum Green now lives and a school house was built in 1840 on the site where the present school house stands, veneered with brick, built by Benjamin Brown who moved to Fine subsequently. Little York, having no water power to invite manufacturing, has not grown beyond a mere huddle. Chester H. Sprague employed from a half dozen to a dozen men for several years making boots and shoes, supplying the town and surrounding towns.

M. V. B. Hazelton.

Between 1840 and 45 the writer of this with one John Green, made friction matches, splitting them with a small hand machine and keeping Edwin A. Carpenter on the road wholesaling them to merchants in the different towns at prices but a little higher than they are sold at the present day.

Chauncy Goodrich carried on the business of tanning hides and skins on shares and for pay, with shoe-making for several years.

In July, 1895, Little York was swept by fire, taking the old hotel and barns with the stores and the next year a movement was begun to build a town hall on the site of the old hotel, and a fine structure was erected for a hall with a store in the lower story, and a clerk's office and store were built on the opposite side of the street, the store being kept by A. C. Johnson & Son, with the postoffice as an adjunct.

The building that was built for a wagon-shop is now used as a hotel.

The village of Fullerville is in the southeastern part of the town. Here John Parker built his early saw-mill in 1813 on the west branch of the Oswegatchie. This mill was burned in 1822 and was rebuilt the next year. It was about the only improvement there until the coming of four brothers from Vermont named Fuller, Sheldon, Stillman, Heman and Ashbel. They formed a business firm under the name of S. Fuller & Co. They had experience in iron working in the town of Rossie, and at once began the erection of a blast-furnace. It was finished in 1833 and put in operation on ores from Edwards and Pitcairn and the magnetic ores from Jayville and Clifton. The admission not long afterwards of a Mr. Maddock, changed the firm to Fullers and Maddock, but the latter soon retired.

The furnace finished its last blast in October, 1837, having produced about 3,500 tons of iron.

In 1846 the firm of Fullers & Peck composed of Sheldon and Leman Fuller and Daniel Peck, rebuilt the old furnace and put in the hot blast. They operated the works until 1861 when they were closed. Ten years later, Daniel Sterling and brothers took up the industry but closed down in two years. In 1875 the property was purchased by Bixley, Clark & Co., who put in a new tuyere and other improvements. A little later George H. Clark became the proprietor and continued operations to about 1882 when business was again given up for good. For a few years, Fullers & Peck operated a forge making bar iron from scrap and ores, also making blooms which were taken to Carthage for making cut nails.

Daniel Peck.

The Fullers built a grist mill on the east side of the river, which with fifteen acres of land adjoining, was sold to Rockwell Bullard & Co. (Edwin Rockwell, Luther Bullard, Chester H. Benton and Oliver Benton) in 1838. Two years later this firm finished a forge for making blooms from ore. James R. Bignall made the blooms under a trip hammer.

In 1861, Frank Fithian built a shingle mill as an addition to the saw mill, tore down the old grist mill, but sold out soon after to Balmat & Brayton. They after a few years sold to the Oswegatchie Pulp Co. composed of F. H. Haile, S. H. Austin, Charles Clark and Geo. H. Clark. This mill was burned in 1892.

A short time previous to 1863, Heman Fuller had built a saw mill on the east side of the river above the old furnace dam, which Chester H. Sprague purchased and put in a muley saw and two shingle mills and had just commenced to run it the next winter when it was burned, and the next year he put up the building which he afterwards sold to the Keller Brothers into which they put machinery for the manufacture of wood pulp and afterwards for manufacturing talc, for which it is still used.

About the same time Mr. Sprague purchased the water-power below the bridge and on which the Ontario Talc Co. erected recently a large mill that is now (1905) in successful operation by Messrs. Gardner & Potter.

The first mercantile business at Fullerville was by Fuller & Co. in connection with other interests. Rockwell Bullard & Co. kept a store and another was opened about 1865 by F. H. Davidson on the west side. Then by C. D. Carr on the east side. He sold out to Balmat, the present proprietor.

The first hotel was kept by C. G. Edgerton on the east side of the river.

About 1839 a hotel was opened on the west side which was kept by several different ones. The Franklin House, now owned and kept by Sidney Brown, was built by Hezekiah Hodgkins about 1830 and has changed hands as to title twenty-four times. The postoffice was established in 1832 with Heman Fuller as postmaster.

The first cut nails made in Northern New York were cut from plates rolled from blooms made at Fullerville about 1835. The cut nail was a Massachusetts invention, devised in 1810 but it made slow progress, owing probably to the inferior strength and liability to split in driving. The early rolled iron was very impure, the plates being "laminated" with scoria or slag which in the early processes was not eliminated from the iron when it was in a spongy state in the process of puddling   Hiram McCollum carried on the business at Carthage, employing a man named Thomas Dunlevey whose principal characteristics were great expertness in feeding the plate to the cutting machine, and his fondness for whiskey   He was able to cut 500 pounds of 4d or "shingle" size nails per day   Nails were made by machinery as early as 1810 at Auburn, N Y, but whether cut nails or not, the record does not show, but they were probably a sort of clinch nail, cut and subsequently headed by a second process as was customary with the early makers

One of the blooms forged at Fullerville weighing about 50 lbs is now doing duty as a land-mark at the corner of a seven-acre lot bought by the Gouverneur Wood Pulp Co   It is in the center of the road nearly in front of the house occupied by Cephas Leonard   It was about 4 inches square and 12 inches long when first set but in the process of years, has probably been reduced in size and weight by oxidation   The early irons were more porous than the finer grades afterward made, owing to the presence of slag which admitted moisture so that they were more subject to "rusting" than now

There are no records to show the time of settlement of many of the inhabitants of the town for several years after the organization of the town   It is known that about a mile west of Fullerville, Alvin Wright, Oliver Wright and Ephriam Stockwell settled and took part in the town's organization, but left the town, removing to Ohio in 1833, with two of the Wights, Reuben and Alvin   There were three Coles, Ira, Eli en and Medad, in town at the time of its organization, Benjamin Brown, who married a VanDuzee, Ira Kingsley, Stephen Mosher, Chauncey Conant, Robert Conant and Andrew Baxter   Noah Holcomb bought ten acres on which the Balmat family are buried, now owned by David H Balmat, and sold it to Joseph Smith, Smith sold it to John D Balmat, where Balmat lived and died   John D Balmat with his brother, Peter, came over from Paris where they had been an eye-witness of the bloody scenes of the French Revolution and settled first in the town of Champion, Jefferson County, afterwards removing to Fowler

John D was educated for a Catholic priest, but became a convert to the teachings of Voltaire, Tom Payne and Volney and consequently became a liberal critic after the style of Dr Lyman Abbott   The writer heard the latter a few years ago compare Christ's sermon on the Mount with the 109th Psalm!

Mr Balmat married Miss Nancy Gooder, whose father came over as an officer with Lafayette in the Revolution   They reared a family of eight boys and six girls and although I lived within a mile of them from early childhood to manhood I have no recollection of ever hearing one of them indulge in any profane language

On the Balmat farm is located one of the large talc mills of the town, belonging to the Union Talc Co   The farm is noted for the variety of valuable ores it contains, zinc, lead, silver and gold being found, and a large number of cabinet minerals of no commercial value are also found here   The zinc appears to occur in quantity but has not been worked except to sink a shaft 80 feet, but it contains a large percentage of sulphurets which depreciate its value

The following list of names are sons and daughters of the first settlers who are living at the date of this record (June, 1905)

Fred H Haile,	Mrs G G Johnson,	Albert Pike,
David H Balmat,	Dexter Leggett,	G M Hodgkin,
John Sprague,	M V B Hazelton,	D W Fuller,
Andrew Wight,	Mrs Mary Merchand,	Joseph Bigarel,
A S Davis,	Mrs John Day,	Asa L Hazelton, (98)
Asa Davis,	Mrs John Sprague,	Mrs Alvin Harris,
Mrs C P Holmes,	Allen Wight,	Marinas Edgerton,
John B Absalom,	Edwin Davis,	Warren B Pike,
Hiram Baxter,	H P Legate,	Ward Glazier,
D P Woodcock,	G D Hazelton,	Alvin Harris
Asa B Woodcock,	Jacob Merchand,	

Theodosius O Fowler came to Killarney in 1814   He insisted that his father should give him almost the entire township   He married Amelia DePau, whose father built him a stately mansion on the shore of Sylvia Lake, then known as Lake Killarney, but rechristened Sylvia Lake from Miss Sylvia Fowler, a daughter of Theodosius   The account in one history stating that Mr Fowler's father built the mansion is an error   Mrs Theodosius Fowler's mother was one of three daughters of Count DeGrasse, who came from France and who commanded the fleet at the mouth of the James River at the seige of Yorktown in 1781   He prevented the escape of Cornwallis by sea   The British fleet in the harbor surrendered to him   The mansion spoken of was begun in 1820 and was finished three years later at a cost of $17,000   The interior was finished, in some rooms, in mahogany and polished marble brought from France in one of DePau's ships   A mahogany table from this elegant home is now owned by H Wight

Here the Fowlers lived in summer, often entertaining their friends from New York City   During the winter they resided in the city themselves, but latterly lived during the whole year in the mansion   The mansion was burned in 1872 and the hewn stones were removed to Gouverneur village and relaid in the fronts of the Killmer & Morris blocks and the Fuller House where they may still be seen

Fowler sold to Thomas D Carpenter in 1838 from whom the land passed to John L Parker and after his death to his son, D L Parker

Ward Glazier was born in Oakham, Mass , Sept. 22, 1818   His father Jabez, came to the wilderness township of Fowler the following year and became a leading business man consequent on his employment by Theodosius O Fowler the owner of the township, as his land-agent and general manager of his business affairs   His grandfather was a Revolutionary soldier and pensioner, dying at West Boylston, Mass , aged 97   He was postmaster a number of years, acted as Justice of Peace besides holding various other town offices   Ward's

Ward Glazier.

minority was spent in clearing land, running a saw-mill
built by his father, and the usual work falling upon the
young man of that day. His education was acquired at
the common schools of his town, and in Gouverneur Wesleyan Seminary.

When 22 years old, with his father he went to
Boston with a drove of 400 cattle, taking along several
fine horses as a speculative venture. During this trip
while stopping at his grandfather's house, he met Me-
hitable C. Bolton, whom he afterward married. She
died in Fowler in 1890. Returning with his young wife
they settled on a farm now known as the Glazier homestead or Maple Grove. Here he managed his land and conducted a general
store until a California enterprise induced him to sell his interests and start for
the land of gold. It was a hazardous journey and was abandoned on the death
of the projector. The Civil war found him ready to cast aside peaceful pursuits and respond to the call for volunteers.

In August, 1861, with others, he recruited Co. I 92nd N. Y. Inft. then being raised by Jonah Sandford, and while not achieving distinction by deeds of
daring, went through the Peninsular campaign, won the esteem of his officers
and the love of the corps by his efficient treatment of wounds in the Medical Department, being called thereto by Surgeons Hewitt and Mansfield, who knew
of his skill. At Fair Oaks he was prostrated by the concussion of a solid twelve
pound shot which passed close to his head, shattering a nearby tree. Notwithstanding his enfeebled condition afterward, he remained at his post for six
succeeding days without removing his clothing. At the end of that time, paralyzed and exhausted, he was obliged to go to the hospitals at Harrison's Landing, Va., David's Island, N. Y., and the Thrall Home Cure in New York City,
at last leaving for home on crutches.

Remaining on his farm until 1885 he opened a pension office in Gouverneur
and for twenty years has followed that calling. When 80 years old he married
Mrs. Eliza S. Fuller. Mr. Glazier has the distinction of having shipped the first
car of freight, consisting of butter, venison, grass-seed and poultry over the
Boston & Albany R. R. as well as urging the introduction of refrigerator cars
on the Ogdensburg & Champlain R. R.

When five years old he started for school one day through the woods, the
school being about one mile away, happy in the possession of a new straw hat
and trudging along with dinner-basket on his arm, when he was startled at
seeing a large "dog" peering at him through the bushes. Thinking the dog
belonged to a neighbor he at first made efforts to call him, but every advance
was met with a low growl and a display of teeth. Finally his eye caught sight
of a bushy tail and at once knew his visitor was a wolf. Remembering what
had been told him about running from wild animals, he cautiously backed away
and was soon relieved of his fears. The next morning his father shot a large wolf
where he had been waylaid.

In the army he recalls administering a thrashing to a Dr. O'Leary, who had kicked a wounded soldier whose leg had just been amputated. In the subsequent years this gave him more satisfaction even than the discharge of the doctor from the service which quickly followed. At this writing Mr. Glazier carries his 88 years with vigor, dimmed but undaunted, and is seen at his office every working day.

Peter Absalom was born in Lorraine, France, June 20, 1815, two days succeeding the battle of Waterloo. At a sacrifice for the benefit of her children,

Peter Absalom.

his mother disposed of her home, sailed in 1831 in one of Mr. DePau's ships for America, lived in New York City during the winter and came to Fowler May 25, 1832. He took up a tract of land, cleared it of the forest growth, and began a prosperous career as a farmer. He was a natural mechanic, and built, with his father, a loom which is still in existence, hewing the timbers for it from timber taken from the forest. The French settlers were an honest, industrious class and Peter Absalom was of like disposition. He died Aug. 26, 1890.

His father, Sebastian Absalom, (originally spelled "Absalon" of noble ancestry, was born Nov. 27, 1778. He was a blacksmith and weaver in France and on coming to this country occasionally followed these trades. His mother was Margaret A. Tiseraud, born 1788. The children coming from France with him were Catherine, Peter, Nicholas, Margaret, Guerard, Marchande (now living in Jefferson County, aged 87), the latter having a daughter grand-daughter, great-grand-daughter and great-great-grandson. The family had relatives at Cape Vincent and in the early days often walked the distance between Fowler and that place in eighteen hours.

Other French pioneer settlers were M. Brunelle, a cabinet-maker; Louis Bigarel, master at arms in his native country, where every young man had to serve at least four years in the army; M. Filbert, who was wounded at Waterloo; M. Pelcheur in the battle of Waterloo also and taken prisoner by the English; Louis Bazille an expert swordsman from Paris and a soldier under Napoleon, who lived to an age of 100 years; Hurelle, a carpenter; Christopher Le-Maitre, a tanner; Sherwin, a cabinet-maker, who was taken prisoner by the Prussians at Waterloo; Augustus Rederick, a mechanic, who deserted the Austrian army to serve under Napoleon, and was also at Waterloo; Gaudin family from Switzerland, who came separately at various times. These names are well remembered by the older citizens of Fowler who survive at this writing.

David H. Balmat.

David H. Balmat was born in Champion May 16, 1822, and has lived the most of his life in Fowler. He married Sophronia Wight, and four children born to them are living. John

D , father of David was born in Paris, France. Jan 3, 1785, his mother being
a "lady" by birth and consequently obnoxious to the common classes, was obliged
to flee to America to escape the mob during the Reign of Terror He was
Joseph Bonaparte's land agent for years before settling in Fowler June 10,
1812, he married Nancy Gooder, who was born near Utica and lived to nearly
one hundred years Major Gooder, her father, was one of eleven officers who
came with Lafayette and Baron DeKalb during the American Revolution He
was wounded at the battle of Brandywine and was in the service at Bunker Hill
and the siege of Yorktown Jacques Balmat is said to have been the first to
ascend Mont Blanc His relationship to the Balmat family of Fowler is known
but not traceable

HISTORY OF HAMMOND.

By Alexander Allen.

THE EARLY DAYS.

When the Revolutionary war closed in 1783 and for thirteen years afterwards, the British held possession of the only little settlements and fortifications located in the extreme northern part of New York, namely: Carlton Island in the St. Lawrence River and Oswegatchie at the mouth of the Oswegatchie river. These places were held principally as a rendezvous for their soldiers coming to Northern New York by the way of the St. Lawrence river. Although according to a treaty made at the close of the war, these fortifications were dismantled, yet they still remained in possession.

Alexander Allen.

Very little was known about this locality except along the south side of the river; back of that for hundreds of miles was one vast wilderness. All this part of the country had not been conveyed to any one by the British government; therefore it belonged to the United States and was a part of the state of New York. The Mohawk Indians, who claimed title to all this land, surrendered that title to the United States at a treaty held with them at Albany, but not until March 29th, 1795. But previous to this, and as early as in 1785 by legislative enactment, the state of New York had made provision to dispose of the unappropriated lands of the state to individuals, and accordingly the surveyor-general was directed to survey off and make a map of two ranges of townships on the south side of the St. Lawrence River for sale. These were afterwards known as "The Ten Towns."

These towns were to be as near as possible ten miles square, therefore would contain 64,000 acres each, and were to be subdivided into square mile lots for convenience in selling to individuals of limited means..

The front towns included Louisville, Madrid, Lisbon, Oswegatchie and Hague, now called Morristown, but have since been divided and subdivided. Two years later they were conditionally offered for sale at Albany and bid in by individuals, the principal buyer being Alex. Macomb, hence the term so often used in your deeds: "Part of Macomb's purchase." Several transfers were made during the preceding years and many actual settlers took up lands, and the ten towns had petitioned to be made a part of Clinton county, but that would make a great inconvenience in transacting county business, therefore a further petition was presented to the legislature on Feb. 8th, 1802, and signed by nearly every actual settler, asking for the erection of a new county, which petition was speedily granted, and the act passed March 3rd, 1802, whereby St. Lawrence became the largest county of the State, almost an empire of itself, more than twice as large as the state of Rhode Island, and larger also than the state of

Delaware, with the town of Hammond and 5,000 acres added, it having an area of 2,880 square miles

When the county was surveyed and laid out, there was a long, narrow (and uneven on one side) strip of land on the western side of the county not named, and which was placed under the jurisdiction of the town of Oswegatchie, and later, in 1807, when the town of Russell was organized, it was included in that town

By a vote of the freeholders of that town it was released Jan 1st, 1811, with the intention of being annexed to the town of Gouverneur, but resulted in the formation of a new town named Rossie which was organized in 1813

A settlement was made in the part of the town which is still Rossie in 1805, but not at Rossie village until 1810, and the blast furnace was started in 1813, and put in blast in 1815   Some histories claim this furnace to be the first one in Northern New York, but I have been informed that the first furnace built and operated in New York State was built at Alpine in the town of Diana, at the outlet of Lake Bonaparte, and was erected by Joseph Bonaparte, but operated by his son-in-law, Mr Zebulon Hoel Benton   The Gazetteer of New York State (1860) gives the date of the "Alpine" furnace as 1847, and the builders Suchard & Farvager   A furnace was built in 1833 at Sterlingbush (then Louisburg) on the outlet of Lake Bonaparte   These are the only furnaces on record in Lewis county   The building of the iron works at Rossie led to the opening of an outlet to the St Lawrence River, which was done by the construction of a road over the hills and across Black Creek, through that part of the town which is now Hammond, there intersecting the military road which led to Ogdensburg and later on by a shorter route to the river by going to Chippewa Bay, where Mr Parish, the owner of the iron works, had built a wharf and erected a large warehouse in 1817

We have referred to land being sold in large quantities to Alex Macomb, a merchant of Detroit, Mich, who had passed up and down the river several times and was enchanted with the beautiful scenery, which led him to purchase so extensively, nor do we wonder at it   He had sold quite a large tract to David Ogden and Ogden in turn sold it, or a part of it, to his brother-in-law named Abijah Hammond, a merchant prince of New York City, but, poor man, he never knew what he possessed, for without ever feasting his eyes on the sight of his northern possession, he sold 28,871 acres to David Parish in 1814 for a paltry profit of a few dollars   perhaps never realizing what he had lost

The nominal price of land sold by the state in those days was twelve and one-half cents per acre   The middle man made a profit and Mr Parish's established price was five dollars per acre, but on unusually favorable terms

The first actual resident in Hammond is said to have been William McNiel, who resided in a cave in the sandstone ledge at Chippewa Bay, quite near to where the warehouse was built   He is said to have come there previous to 1812   A few settlements had been made at various places, but the first land contract was made by Wm Wiley in 1818 for a piece of land where Hammond village now stands   Mr Wiley and McNiel, as well as some others, came from Vermont, but it is not stated whether they "abandoned" their farms to emigrate here. Isaiah Wiley, son of Wm Wiley, was the first white child born in the town. We know but little of his history save that he spent nearly all of his life here and died at a good old age

As no one resided here at the time of the war commencing in 1812, it was not the scene of any strife, but the British built a block house and a small fortification on Chimney Island directly opposite to Chippewa Bay and about eighty rods from the Canadian shore. The chimney still remains standing as a monument of that struggle. The creeks and bays along the shore afforded a hiding place for a gang of thieves who made incursions into the country and appropriated to their own use cattle and horses. Nor were their raids confined to one side of the river, for what they stole on one side they took to the other side and sold or hid away. Various stories are related of how they even seized the British army's paymaster, and captured the money chest and secreted the same on Chippewa Point or sunk it in the waters of Chippewa creek. But all these have been thoroughly ventilated in previous histories

The boom to develop and open up this part of the country, which was planted immediately after the close of the Revolutionary war, now began to bear fruit at the close of the 1812 war. Mr Parish opened a land office at Chippewa and installed Loren Bailey as his agent, who came to the place July 31st, 1818. During that same year, several Scotch families whose destination was upper Canada, and who came by the way of Montreal in sailing vessels and up the river in Durham boats, had stopped at Prescott to obtain other means of transportation. There they were intercepted by Mr Parish's agent, Joseph Rosseel, who offered them strong inducements to cross the river and go up to Rossie to visit the Scotch settlement, which they did, but being far more favorably impressed with his possessions near the river, they accordingly decided to take up land and form a settlement about one mile west of Hammond village. Of those who settled there during that year were Peter Allen, John and David Gregor, John Baird, Wm Cowan, John and James Hill, all of these had families except the two latter. For a temporary residence, until they could build shanties for their families, they took up their abode in the large warehouse built by Mr. Parish the year previous

Peter Allen selected the farm where John Nicol now resides, John Gregor the farm directly opposite, and the Hills immediately adjoining them. David Gregor engaged with Mr Parish as overseer in some of his work at Rossie, where he removed his family. During the following year there were large additions to this settlement, as well as other settlements being made. Andrew Nicol, with a large family, James Rodger, Robert Morris, Robert and Andrew Shiell, and Thomas Dodds, all of the above located on the Bay Road; also Samuel Webster and Wm Tappan, from New Hampshire, located at South Hammond. In 1820 Jonathan King built a tavern at the Military Road, where his son and later his grandson lived, and where now lives his great-grandson, Myron King. In the same year (1820) quite a few families came from Rome, N. Y., to the southwestern part of the town (Calahogia); of these were Joseph R Denner,

Ira Taplin, Hazen Taplin, George Martin, and later Robert Taplin, Henry Smith, Ephriam Wilson, and Abraham, Reuben and Jonathan Reynolds   The former party came through the wilderness in carts drawn by oxen, the time consumed in coming being about six days   It may be interesting to the reader to know how others came to Hammond

The emigrants from Britain crossed the ocean in sailing crafts by way of Montreal, where they were transferred to Durham boats to navigate the river   The Durham boats were rudely constructed, having neither sail or spar, but had an enclosed cabin in which the emigrant might eat and sleep   They were sometimes drawn by horses, and sometimes were rowed or poled along   Sometimes the men took a pull at the hawser   As they did not travel by night, the time usually consumed in making the trip to Ogdensburg, a distance of 140 miles, was seven days   Thomas Phillips, who came from Trenton, N Y, in 1819, came on foot   Christopher Phillips came also from Trenton in 1820 with his wife and one child on horseback   He was the first blacksmith in town, and his shop stood where Mr Stiles' store now stands, and his log house where the American Hotel was located   There was a small store and a tavern and three or four houses comprised the whole   About this time a few settlements were made across Chippewa Creek at and near Oak Point, and a bridge was made across the creek   We have no knowledge of when or by whom this bridge was built   The settlers were Samuel Morse, Ira Allen, Reuben Allen, and George Eliott   The latter sold his improvements to a Mr Cowin, who opened a store in 1824   There also lived at Oak Point at that time a Mr Jones who opened a liquor store   Frederick Thatcher had a grocery store   Mr Marvin a general store   Mr Battel and Mr Atwood also came prior to this   In the same year came Abram Schermerhorn, Mr Garret and Mr Hicks, who came from Trenton, Oneida Co, and drove their own teams, the three teams bringing all their household effects   Mr Schermerhorn opened a hotel and also built a tannery and a shoe shop, also a distillery

About this time came also Daniel Schermerhorn, who built and operated a tannery at Chippewa Bay

In the spring of 1826 there moved into North Hammond, and was perhaps the only one living there who came in that decade, Ethan R Hammond, who, with his wife, drove from Plattsburg, N Y, leaving there late in the winter, when there was four feet of snow on the ground, they came to Malone, when there came the spring break up   They exchanged the sleigh for a wagon, and were nine days making the trip   Mr Hammond at once took up a farm and began clearing   The first winter was spent in a pioneer shanty   They had no glass in the windows and hung up blankets to keep out the cold and the storms   Mr Hammond was born Oct 5th, 1805, and is therefore in his one hundredth year   He voted at fifteen presidential elections, including the last one, at the age of ninety-nine years   Otis Gardner, who is a native born resident of the town, is seventy-seven years of age and is living on the same farm where he was born

By an act of the State Legislature passed March 30, 1827, the town of

Hammond was erected and became the twenty-first in number in the county, ranking the twentieth in population and twenty-second in area, and containing 35,815 acres   There are also about 160 islands and shoals lying opposite to and under the jurisdiction of the town

THE CANDLELIGHT PERIOD

The illumination of the pioneer's home began in many places long before the moulded candle had an existence there   The most primitive light in use was the pine knot, or the light from the fire of the burning logs on the fire place grate   Many a favorite book has been read, many a hard lesson learned, knitting and even sewing done, and if a few neighbors called in, a friendly chat was had around the old fire place, lighted only by the blazing light upon the hearth

Then came the dip light—a fat deer has been killed and from it a hard, white tallow, not unlike mutton tallow, but harder even, perhaps there is more than is required for cooking purposes, so a portion of it is melted in a small basin, and into it a strip of cotton cloth which has been dipped into the melted tallow, is placed over the edge of the dish, and is then ignited   Then by capillarity it continues to feed itself until the tallow is exhausted

But mankind is a progressive being, so the dipped candle takes its place   The wick is dipped into the melted tallow and allowed to cool, then redipped again and again, until a candle has been formed   For a candlestick a piece of board or a block is procured, an augur hole is bored into one side, the candle is inserted and is ready for use   But man is an inventive creature also, and a candle mould has been invented, and the neighborhood, perhaps five or six in number, join together and buy a candle mould, which will mould three, six or twelve candles at once

Beef tallow is now quite plentiful, or even the family can afford to kill a sheep, and from it procure a quantity of tallow, so a quantity of candles are moulded and the moulds are then passed to some other joint owner in the settlement, and the same process is there gone through

The family can now afford metal candlesticks, and with many, fancy brass ones were brought from the old country and are now brought into use   Another essential article is a pair of snuffers, and the candle light period is now at its zenith

With the best regulated families the whale oil lamp is brought into use, in which wick is used but no chimney or globe is necessary

Later came the camphene lamp, in which the article used is nothing more or less than a rectified spirits of turpentine and it was used more in stores and public places

Petroleum was discovered and first used for lighting in 1859, but was not brought into general use in our town until about 1863, when a common, tin, one gallon can, filled with refined petroleum or kerosene oil, could be obtained for one dollar and fifty cents

The same outfit today can be procured at a country store for from twenty-five to thirty-five cents   An improvement on the above now used in our homes is acetylene gas

THE SETTLEMENT OF THE TOWN

The year 1830 began a new era in the history of the town The first census being taken showed a population of 767 and in the following five years no other town in the county showed such a gain   The state census for 1835 reported a population of 1327 or a gain of seventy-three per cent Some towns decreased, Gouverneur increased 16 per cent and Rossie gained five in number only It was during those five years that so many Scotch emigrants came, besides more from Vermont and a great many more from Trenton, though Isaac Forester, Benjamin Soper and Sidney Soper with their families all came from Canada From Scotland there came William Rodger and a family of eight sons, four daughters and one son-in-law The Brodie family, James W Hoag and brothers, Mr Cuthbert, Sr , and family, William Smith, wife, three daughters and three sons-in-law, three sons and their wives and children also came The sons were William, Robert and John The Smith family settled in the northern part of the town and each son had three sons named respectively William, Robert and John Robert, however, had five sons, and they afterwards removed to Morristown The three sons of the elder Smith, as well as himself, were all tradesmen of no mean order, having served their apprenticeship in Scotland

The old people took up a home and lived in a log house standing midway between John A Taylor's and James Leadingham's farm houses, where he did undertaking, furniture and other carpenter work, and perhaps no man ever came into town who added so much to the material comfort of the early settler as he Scarcely a house in the whole town was without either chairs, tables, beds, a wooden clock, spinning-wheel, flax-wheel or a reel, or farming implements for out-of-door use and to this day many of these may be found and in use, although Mr Smith has been dead for upward of sixty-five years

During this decade came the Canadian Rebellion in 1836, but none of our town's people took any part The loyal people of Canada were worked up to a high pitch against the American people and made many threats At one time during a religious service in the Bay Road schoolhouse, a man rushed in to the house and reported that an armed band were crossing the river to attack our people and burn their homes, the result was the meeting was broken up and the people dispersed to their homes by the false report

One young man who was sent on an errand to Hammond was accosted by a couple of recruiting officers for the Patriot Army and induced to enlist Without consulting his parents he decided to go at once lest they should object The officers left him by the fireside at the hotel while they went to dinner, and he being hungry this angered him so much that, on serious reflection, he concluded to arise and go to his father which he accordingly did During the Civil war the same "boy" served nearly three years in the Union Army It was during this decade that so many stone houses were erected, yet Thomas Dodds built the first one in 1820 It has since been remodelled but it stands today and is occupied by his great-grandson, four generations occupy it

During the period alluded to forty dwellings, one church and seven school houses were constructed of sandstone, some of them have served their day and are replaced by wooden structures

In 1840 the census report showed a population of 1845, or a gain of over 240 per cent in ten years, and during the next ten years each had been quietly attending to his own affairs, clearing the forests to make more fields and clearing the older fields of decaying hard wood stumps, to be ready for the coming mowing machine During all that period all the farm work was done by hand It was no uncommon sight to see eight or ten men in the hay field, in tandem, keeping stroke as they swung their scythes through the heavy grass

The grain was cut with cradles and one good man could rake and bind and keep up with a cradler

The Mormon excitement occurred during this period, when a few of our people were proselyted to that faith and joined the others on their journey to Nauvoo, Ill One old man and his wife, also one young man and his sister were among the converts The old gentleman died there, and later the widow returned to her home and kindred The young man and sister went on to Salt Lake City where he became a latter-day saint and apostle, and married eleven wives The sister secured a one-sixth interest in a husband and they both spent their remaining days in Utah

With 1850 came the mowing machine A P Morse brought the first one into town, the "Ketchum," a one wheel, side-draft, combined so as to reap by affixing a large wooden rim around the driving wheel, thus raising the cutter-bar high enough to cut the grain The following year two "Manny" combined mowers and reapers and in 1852 there was added fifty-seven more of the same Later came the two-wheeled mower and the old Manny was dubbed the "Horse Killer," although it served its day well and saved a great deal of labor in cutting the immense fields of wheat produced during the fifties

It would be impossible to give the acreage, but forty bushels per acre was accounted a fair yield, and in one instance eighty bushels were produced from an acre

From 1850 to 1860 there was added to the population of the town 149 when it reached high tide mark and began to wane The Civil war coming on a good many enlisted, some began to move away because new and improved farming tools did not require so much farm help

The self rake attachment where by an automatic attachment the bunch of grain sufficient for a bundle ready for the man to bind was thrown off was a saving of one man for every reaper in town Then later came the binder, the improved horse rake, the hay fork, all of these silently warned the laborer that his services were no longer required About one man out of twelve inhabitants enlisted in the "war for the Union," or 162 men Of these about twenty gave up their lives for the cause, one died in Andersonville rebel prison, two were killed in battle, some died of their wounds, and perhaps one-half died of disease

At home, the people although busy with avocations, were not indifferent to the calls for men and money to prosecute the war Rather than allow more

drafts to be made on our people, money was freely subscribed and one thousand
dollars bounty offered to her volunteers

Two drafts had already been made, some were allowed to enlist and many
who could not be spared commuted, others sent substitutes   At the close of the
war the census returns showed a population of 1819, or a loss of 149 in five
years, and in 1870 it fell to 1757, or nearly one hundred less than there was in
1840, but the people took on new energy and went on with their work   Then
the prospects were good for a railroad to run through the town to Ogdensburg
and an effort was made to bond the town to aid in its construction   It required
a majority of the free holders   The effort was made and barely succeeded, but
strong resistance was offered by the "anti-bonders" who did not want to mortgage their farms to benefit a corporation and they also declared that the railroad was a foregone conclusion and would be completed without the town's aid
The bonding party held the fort and commissioners were appointed who were
authorized to execute bonds for sixty thousand dollars payable in thirty
years with interest payable semi-annually at seven per cent for which the town
was to receive a like amount of stock in the railroad   The anti-bonders secured
an injunction on the proceedings of the commissioners, proving that they had
proceeded illegally, when the other party went before the legislature and
secured an act legalizing the illegal acts of the R R commissioners of the town,
thus carrying the day   and at the first meeting of the board of supervisors a
tax of four thousand two hundred dollars for interest on the bonds and one thousand dollars as a sinking fund were levied on the town   It seemed like a great
burden on the people for about that time or soon afterwards the legal rate of
interest was reduced to six per cent

At the first collection of taxes some even refused to pay their tax until
their chattels were levied upon   And at the first annual town meeting, like one
or two former ones, town politics ran up to fever heat   two candidates for supervisor were in the field, after a hard day's fight the board announced that
there was no choice, the vote being a tie, therefore, another town meeting was
called and it is said that every man over twenty-one years of age and a few
under that age residing in town voted that day   The vote resulted in sustaining the present incumbent, who had allowed the tax to be made against the town,
by a very small majority, thus settling the question for all time

After the road was completed to Ogdensburg the railroad bonds were
placed on the market and found ready sale at par, and with the money received,
the bonds were redeemed, the great burden of tax was thrown off and the people
were again happy, new life was instilled and a market for all our produce was
brought to our doors

Shortly after this debt was discharged the people by a vote of the taxpayers incurred a debt of $3,500 to erect a Town Hall which is quite an ornament
to the town   The debt for the above has since been liquidated

POSTOFFICES AND MAIL SERVICE

The first postoffice established in town was at Hammond village in 1824,
and Arnold Smith was postmaster   His salary the first year was $15 90   Prior

to that date, letters were usually directed to Ogdensburg in the care of Joseph Rosseel, or to Morristown, and from thence were forwarded by chance or a messenger dispatched for the purpose The old time letter was written on a large, unruled sheet of paper, very much like the old foolscap, or school-cap paper, and written on three pages, then neatly folded so that the writing was all enclosed and the address placed on the back or unwritten page, hence the use of the term or request "Will you back my letter " The letter was then sealed with a wafer or with colored sealing wax   A box of colored wafers was an indispensable article beside the old gray goose quill pen and the bottle of home-made ink   No envelopes were used until about 1837, nor postage stamps until 1847 to 1850   And so late as the 50's ink made from soft maple bark with a small piece of copperas, was used in the common schools, and to that date it was a part of the teacher's duty to sharpen the quill pen and set the copy, and sometimes to rule the unlined paper in the copy-book

The postage on early letters to foreign countries was fifty cents, and on domestic letters as high as twenty-five cents, but the cost was regulated by the distance sent   Within my recollection, ten cents was charged on a letter to California or the Pacific coast, and twenty-five cents to Britain or other foreign countries, and ten cents to Canada   A letter coming from Canada was often paid in part and postage due collected on delivery from six to ten cents

The records of mail carrying prior to 1836 are incomplete on account of being destroyed by fire   But the first route we know of was from Jan 1, 1829, to Jan 1, 1833, from Denmark, Lewis Co, by Carthage, Wilna, Antwerp, Rossie, Hammond to Ogdensburg, 62 50 miles, contractors Parker and Sherwood of Utica, paying $4,748 60 per annum

Later than this the mail was carried by Theresa and South Hammond, Hammond to Ogdensburg, three times a week   In 1837 the mail service required only one round trip a week from Theresa to Hammond

Back in the 50's the old four horse coach was used and the line was owned by Mr Reuben Nott of Somerville, sheriff of the county in 1853-5

When the stage came within one-fourth of a mile from the postoffice a horn was blown to announce its coming, the mail bag was hurriedly carried in and the contents of the pouch were emptied on the floor, and the Hammond mail sorted out, then the balance together with the outgoing mail were replaced in the bag without delay and carried to the stage

Usually a good many passengers and some freight was carried, sometimes crowded; but like all stages there was always room for one more

A postoffice was established at South Hammond in 1833 with Jonathan King P. M, and one at Oak Point in 1840   Both of these were afterwards discontinued   At North Hammond in 1861 by Asa T Barber P M —these offices were supplied by a carrier from Hammond who usually made the trip on foot twice a week

The postoffice at Chippewa Bay was established in 1880 with Alex Allen P M, with three mails per week

Soon afterwards the Oak Point, No Hammond and Chippewa route was consolidated into one, and still later it became a daily mail route   Mr Allen held the office for 18 years, when W Backus the present incumbent took the office   The office at Hammond has been held by Henry Buttick, Abel P Morse, Peter McCrady, Orange G Waldo, David Moyer Ahda Sherman Palmer, E S. Ketchum, Benjamin Franklin and Daniel D Moyer

For several years two daily stages were placed on the Ogdensburg and Antwerp line, running alternately in opposite directions, but not until 1876 was the office supplied by railroad, and then only one mail from the east and one from the west each day.

The stage route was then changed to run between Hammond and Gouverneur, supplying the intermediate villages

In 1899 a rural free delivery route from the Hammond office was established, supplying the Bay Road, Chippewa Bay and triangular road, each morning, and in the afternoon to Pleasant valley River road, Oak Point and North Hammond, the office at Oak Point and No Hammond being discontinued, but the office at Chippewa was retained on account of a large mail to the islanders and cottagers at the river.   There is a postoffice at South Hammond. Mrs Anna F Billings is P M

ROADS AND BRIDGES

Compared with adjoining towns the expense for bridge construction and maintenance has been very light there being but two bridges of any size, one across Black creek leading to Rossie, and one over Chippewa creek to North Hammond   The latter bridge was first built in 1851 by James S More and Robert Welsh   It was since rebuilt above water, and later an iron structure, built about 1890, has taken its place   Several years ago the bridge across Black creek was rebuilt and a long bridge, which ran across the marsh bordering the creek was removed, and an attempt made to fill in with stone and refuse from the quarries.   The town sunk a large quantity of stone (and also of money) and every spring for a few years found an excellent place for a ferry from the end of the bridge to the high land   It was finally remedied by laying down trees and long logs crosswise of the road and placing the stone thereon About twelve years ago the town procured a stone crusher, and that being brought into use freely, backed by a large quantity of stone which had accumulated at the numerous quarries and in fence corners, together with a liberal town appropriation, and the commutation of the highway tax instead of statute labor, very great improvement has been made on the highways of the town

A special town meeting was very recently held at the polling place, to vote on an appropriation of $1,300 to procure a new stone crusher and outfit   The appropriation was carried by a majority of 34 votes   So that new and much needed improvements will soon be the order of the day

FINANCIAL CONDITION OF THE TOWN

The assessed valuation of the town is $832 900 and the town is practically out of debt

Considering the fact that the town, only a few years ago, built a fine town hall at an expense of $3,500, and also later appropriated quite a large sum for highway purposes, all of which have since been liquidated, goes to show that Hammond is in a prosperous condition

THE PRESS

Our town can boast that we have a newspaper published within our borders, the Hammond Advertiser, which was first printed in 1886 on a job press, one page at a time. It has four pages, 11 by 16 inches

David Moyer was the founder and the editor, and Wm B Burton was the foreman   At the end of the second year Mr Burton purchased the outfit and became the editor, manager, foreman, devil and mailing clerk   He discarded the job press and purchased a Washington Hand Press and enlarged the paper to a six column folio   The hand press did service for five years, when he purchased an up-to-date cylinder press and engine   The paper is now being printed on the same press, but has been reduced to a four page paper, and the press is driven by the latest make of gasoline engine   The plant is valued at about $5,000

The circulation is rated in Rowell's Newspaper Directory as less than one thousand, but it extends into nearly every state in the Union and many Canadian points.

Although the paper has been in existence for upwards of nineteen years, Mr Burton and some member of his family have done the entire work and have never missed an issue, except during the winter of 1902, when he suffered from a severe illness and the office was closed   The "Advertiser" has outgrown its quarters four times   The paper is republican in politics, but quite independent, and is the organ of any party or creed who wish to express their views on any subject in a reasonable manner   Its size often makes it a subject of ridicule compared with the immense sheets now offered at the same price, but it is the home paper and is gladly welcomed as a friendly visitor by those who have removed to distant places, and its discontinuance would be a severe loss to the village and the town   But the little village paper is a success and not an experiment

HAMMOND VILLAGE,

The Village of Hammond was incorporated Aug 29, 1901, (the date the election was held)   The officers were W T Stiles, President, W D Evans and Fred Mayer, Trustees; Byron A Evans, Treasurer, C C Forester, Clerk   The present offices, C C Forrester, President, Fred Mayer and D E Eustis, Trustees; W. T Stiles, Treasurer, A M Stiles, Clerk   The census in 1901 was 339   Present census, 400   The valuation, $110,000   The Evans Mfg Co and the Wm Soper Mfg Co have small dynamos which they light their plants with.   Mr Soper lights two stores with his electric machine, W T Stiles and J T Rodger   The other stores and hotel are lighted with acetylene gas

The following are the merchants of the village in 1905

W T Stiles, Brown Bros, hardware, C C Forrester, dry goods, J T Rodger, clothing, W R Wilson, I Franklin, W. J Ireton & Co, grocers, W D Evans, harnesses, carriages, furniture and farm implements, A E Woodside, boots, shoes and harnesses, E J Murphy, boots and shoes, Geo H

Wylhe, druggist and jeweler, Lena Dygert, Mrs Woodworth, milliners; Fred Mayer, Wm Gibson, blacksmiths, James Scanlon and D G Bacon, barbers, Guy Taylor, meat market, R Evans, flour and feed, Donald Bros, undertakers, D D Moyer, postmaster, H K Kern and Geo. H Rodger physicians, W B Burton, editor Hammond Advertiser Secret societies Independent Order of Foresters, established in 1890, Court Hammond, No 545, membership now 137, Comp Court Rhesa No 80, membership 45, Modern Woodmen of America, established 1903, Camp Hammond, No 11156, membership 52, Knights of Maccabees, established 1904, Tent No —, Independent Order of Odd Fellows, established 1904, Hammond Lodge, No 9, membership 100 Rebekahs have been granted a charter and organize this month. Eastern Star has been organized (1904) and prospects are that we will soon have a Masonic Lodge

Mr. Stiles has established a telephone line in village and town Many of the farms have taken advantage of it and some of our merchants can talk with the farms five miles out

We also have the Central New York Telephone and Telegraph Co line, Great North Western Telegraph Co, New England Telegraph Co., Citizen's Telegraph Co, American Telegraph and Telephone Co The Citizens Line Telegraph was organized and put up from Chippewa Bay to Hammond, three miles, in 1890, at an expense of $400 which was subscribed for at five dollars per share A good share of the amount was taken by laboring men who worked out their interest in the same Although a small affair it paid a good dividend to its owners and is the same line mentioned above

SCHOOLS AND EDUCATION

The first school house erected in town was during the year 1819 on the Bay road, and in the following winter a school was taught by Dr James Scott of Lisbon Later, several log school houses were built in various sections of the town. And during the stone-house period seven substantial and commodious ones were built, two of which after serving their day and generation, were torn down and replaced by modern wooden structures The old "Block school house" a small structure which stood on the Silas Robinson farm very near where the cheese factory is now located, was used for school purposes until 1852 It remained there for a long time afterwards, as if all were loath to destroy the "Alma Mater" of so many of our towns people

The town now has thirteen districts, the Hammond Union Free School (Number 1) being under the management of the State Regents, and has four departments taught by four teachers of whom Mr Lewis is principal

The town received $2,000 this year from the State and has a surplus of $500 on hand from the School and Gospel fund

THE CHURCHES

Although the Methodists had held services at an early date, no church was organized until 1832 In 1835 a church was built near Hammond village which served their use until 1873 when the present church was erected at a cost of $7,000 Their present pastor is Rev Mr Andrews

The Universalist church was organized in 1870 and a church edifice erected the same year. The first pastor was Rev D L R Libby. At present only occasional services are held

An effort is being made to establish a Roman Catholic church Mrs Kate Donald has presented the society with a church site

The First Presbyterian church of Hammond was organized April 1st. 1821, and was named The First Union Pres Society of Rossie Rev James Sanford of OxBow was pastor The first members were Peter Allen, James Rodger, John Hill, Thomas Dodds, John Mercer, David Gregor, James Hill, Robert Sheill, John Gregor, Alpheus Talcott, John Baird, Agnes Baird, Janet Stewart Allen, Margaret Rodger, Janet Dodds, Helen Sheill, Janett Allen Gregor, Patty Talcott, Mary Gregor, 19 in number The elders were James Rodger, David Gregor, John Hill There was added also James Hill, Alpheus Talcott The trustees were Loren Bailey, Thomas Dodds, Nathaniel Ives Rev James Rodgers, who was also one of the elders, was the first pastor. He was licensed by the Presbytery of Ogdensburg March 6th. 1823, and served as pastor for six years

Rev John M McGregor, who came from Scotland in 1830, was soon afterwards licensed as pastor and served as such until 1852 During the same year Rev James Gardner, D D , who was a teacher in the St Lawrence Academy of Potsdam, succeeded him and served as pastor until 1869

Rev James Rodger, now of Farmington, Minn , who had recently graduated from a Theological Seminary, supplied the church for two years He had been a teacher in an American college at Constantinople, Turkey, for two years and was a grandson of the first pastor.

Rev Harry B Swift, of Indiana, and Rev Andrew Milne, formerly of Canada, each served the church for one year

Rev Daniel A Ferguson, D D , the present pastor, was installed June 16th, 1875, and his thirtieth anniversary has just been celebrated by the church

Church service was first held in the barn of Thos Dodds, afterwards in the school house at Chippewa Bay and at private houses around town In 1833 a movement was made to build what was afterwards known as the Stone Church, which was completed and dedicated in 1838 and during the pastorate of Rev J M McGregor In 1871 the church building was torn down and the present structure built, and was dedicated Jan. 17, 1872 It has since been refitted inside and a handsome organ worth $1,800 placed in it With the parsonage built in 1876, the entire property is valued at $14 000

There was added to the church membership during the pastorates of Rev James Rodger 20 members, John M McGregor, 128; James Gardner, 166. D A. Ferguson, 392 The church now reports 276 members with 45 on her Absentee and Inactive Roll

All the pastors who have served the church are now deceased with the exception of the Rev James Rodger, Farmington, Minn , and the present pastor When Mr. Ferguson preached his anniversary sermon lately he said that he had baptised on an average of six infants a year, and that on an average eleven persons had been received on confession of faith each year. Of the 392 persons received into the church only 55 were received from other churches. Of the 312 persons on the active and inactive list only 44 were members thirty years ago. He has officiated at 214 weddings and 311 funerals and has preached upwards of 3,500 sermons.

The church has sent out into the ministry Rev. James G. Rodger, Ph. D., Ocean Beach, Cal., Rev. James F. Brodie, D. D., Fisk Univ., Nashville, Tenn., John Leadingham, Theological School at Honolulu, Sandwich Islands, Rev. Thomas C. Miller of New York City, Rev. Alex. Wouters, Memorial Church, Syracuse, N. Y., Albert L. Evans in Auburn Theological Seminary. The church has also been a large contributor to the working force of churches in different portions of our land. The Ladies Foreign Missionary Society connected with the church has contributed over $2,000 in 28 years. The Ladies Home Missionary Society $1,300 in 24 years. The Ladies Improvement Society $1,300 in 13 years.

The growth of the church has been continuous and healthful. The number of families represented in it has nearly doubled in twenty years, thus showing its growing influence. Mr. Ferguson is Stated Clerk of the Presbytery of St. Lawrence, and Permanent Clerk of the Synod of New York, both responsible positions which require a mailing list of correspondents of from six to seven hundred letters per year besides printed circulars. He has not been absent a single Sabbath on account of illness in all those thirty years and but few on vacation except in 1895 he took an extended trip to the British Isles. Thirty years ago the church gave for benevolent objects $101. Last year it gave $659. During the thirty years it gave $11,350 for benevolence and $34,967 for local support.

THE CEMETERIES

There are several burying places in the town, the oldest perhaps, being the Hammond church ground located by custom near the Presbyterian church. This ground is filled, however, and not used, but is kept up and neatly fenced at the expense of the town. The Rarick ground was opened in 1829 and contains upwards of eight hundred graves. It is located at South Hammond. The Butrick ground is near the railroad track and Hammond village on the farm once owned by Sylvester Butrick, and is beautifully located. A little cemetery and church lot was given to the village of Oak Point years ago by George Eliott, a merchant of that place. There are several graves in that ground, but when it failed to be kept in proper order, the remains of many were removed to other grounds. The Pleasant Valley cemetery was opened in 1839. Previous to that date a man named Ripley took up a piece of land that is now a part of Robert R. Wilson's farm, and began a clearing on top of the hill. One day when he had gone to the woods his wife took her little son and climbed the hill to where the father was at work, guided by the sound of the blows made by the ax. She went through the woods until within sight of him when the little lad in great glee ran from his mother toward his father, just as a tree was toppling to fall. The mother called to the child but he being ignorant of the danger, rushed on   And there the parents stood as if riveted to the spot, compelled to witness the life crushed out of their little one midway between them   They having no burial lot it was arranged to make his grave on a gravelly piece of land near the roadside not far from their home. This was the first grave made at what is now Pleasant Valley   In the early fifties the writer knew every grave in the lot   Today there are upwards of three hundred graves   There are several private grounds and many are buried outside of the town

ACCIDENTS

The first fatal accident recorded in the history of the town was the falling of a tree that killed Wm Cowin, one of the early pioneers   Mr Parish with his usual generosity, paid the fare of his widow to the old country

A little son of Andrew Nicol was drowned in Chippewa creek, while on an errand up the creek where his father was at work   He was not missed until his father returned at night

Robert Jepson was drowned while crossing Crooked creek on the ice in 1857.

In the winter of 1854 Joseph, son of Robert Riddell, while cutting down a tree with his father, was struck by a small piece of the dead top of the tree and instantly killed   The accident occurred just over the line, and only a few feet from where the Ripley child was killed.

In 1863 Boone Hicks, a stranger who was visiting in town, was drowned while crossing Chippewa creek on the ice

A boat load of people while crossing the river from Oak island to Canada, in attempting to change seats, capsized the boat and two or three were drowned   One woman clung to the boat several hours until insensible, and was finally rescued

The steamer Buckeye while passing up the river and not far from the American shore, struck a rock or shoal during the night of September 16, 1865, and sunk in a few moments   The boat had on board 20 passengers besides a crew of about thirty   Three women passengers were drowned.   The remaining passengers and crew all safely got into three or four life boats and went ashore   The boat was afterward raised and repaired

Along this line it is worthy of mentioning the absence of drowning accidents and collisions among the many pleasure boats on the St Lawrence River   There have been several accidents on the railroad to town's people employed in railroad service   Robert Jepson, William Bowen and Henry Delong, all young men and acting as freight brakemen, were instantly killed at different times, and a Mr Grant had the misfortune to lose both arms by falling under a train in motion

TRANSPORTATION.

The facilities for shipping produce out of town and bringing merchandise in, before the railroad entered our town, were not of the best   Several commodious steamers stopped at Oak Point and conveyed passengers to and fro, during the summer months, but this manner of transporting hay, grain and lumber was too expensive   About 1850 Robert Allen constructed at his own

Tome, now Allen's Park, the sloop Industry, which ran in connection with the new railroad just built to Ogdensburg, carrying freight to the upper ports of the river. Large quantities of lumber were made and hauled to Chippewa Bay for shipment. James Denner purchased two small schooners for freighting purposes. The "Mary" of 130 tons burden, was built at Sackets Harbor, and the S. P. Johnson of 150 tons. They plied between Lake Ontario ports and Ogdensburg in the lumber, grain and salt trade, for several years. The Johnson finally went ashore near Big Sodus, the owner sold the wreck which was rebuilt and taken to Lake Erie. The schooner Mary sailed out of Oswego during the fall of 1861 with a cargo of coal, crossing the lake and while at anchor in Picton Bay, Ont., during the night was run into and sunk and all on board were drowned, or at least never heard from. Her topmast can still be seen in a clear day near the surface of the water.

Mr Denner later purchased two larger sailing craft, the schooners Volunteer and Billow, which sailed the lake and river during and later than "war time," and were profitable property but proved unfortunate to the owner. The Volunteer went ashore in Mexico Bay in 1869 laden with fruit and all on board were drowned.

During the seventies this class of vessels was superceded by steam barges which carried larger cargoes and were not hindered by adverse winds, and the railroad then running into our town took large quantities of freight formerly carried by water. Some smaller steamers were put on both as freight and passenger carriers. The steamer John Harris, a new boat built for Morristown parties, was put on the river in 1874, and the same year the Stranger from Alexandria Bay to Ogdensburg, made daily trips touching both at Chippewa Bay and Oak Point, and were both successful. Later the Cygnet owned by parties in town, and the Guide owned and run by Capt. Frank Dana, were put on the line, but both proved "too slow" for this age and were sold. Capt. Dana purchased the Massena, which proved to be a staunch craft and profitable to the owner.

Capt. Dana was a resident of the town but removed to Alexandria Bay, the terminus of his route. The Massena was burned at the dock at Ogdensburg in 1903, after which he purchased the Riverside, which is still on the old route. Capt. Dana died during the present year, but the boat is still owned by his family.

Most of the exports of the town now find a way to market by rail, except cheese, which finds a ready market at Brockville, Ontario, from thence by boat to Montreal, where it is shipped to England after being branded as Canadian goods. Not that the brand is superior but that the English markets discriminate in favor of our neighbor's product.

POLITICAL ASPIRATIONS

If any of our town's people ever had any political aspirations their ambitions have certainly never been gratified farther than to represent their own town at the county seat, except that Sylvester Butrick represented the Assembly district as a member of that body at Albany in 1833 and 1834

Our aged townsman M L. Laughlin was elected School Commissioner for the First Commissioner District in 1860 and held the office for four terms of three years each While he held the position he brought the condition of the schools up to a high standard of perfection Previous to 1856 each town had charge of its own schools and worked independently of others Teachers' associations were not known so there was a lack of system Mr. Laughlin with his colleagues did much to establish a needed uniformity in school books, and to bring the teachers together to discuss methods of teaching

MANUFACTURERS

The first machine shop or manufactory of any kind in town was carried on by John Taplin who came to town in 1830 and resided where W S Cuthbert now lives He was the inventor and maker of a sweep horse power for threshing and sawing purposes.

Later than this Robert Sheill, one of the pioneers of 1818, at his farm began the manufacture of "The Highland Mary" plow, wheel horse rakes, butter workers, and other farm implements, which met with ready sale

But no castings were ever made in town until the Evans Manufacturing Co was incorporated Jan. 1st, 1903, with a capital of $25,000 for the purpose of manufacturing disc harrows, plows, castings They also made elm veneering. Mr Fred Mayer is President, B A Evans is General Manager and Treasurer, and Albert Mason, Secretary, and the company are all workers and have a daily increasing business which will compel them to enlarge their plant at an early date

There are five cheese factories engaged during the summer months making English cheese which finds a ready sale in Brockville and also in New York markets

The Wm. Soper Manufacturing Co are engaged in the manufacture of all kinds of lumber, shingles, sash, doors and planing and custom grinding of provender They also have an electric light plant by which they generate light for their own establishment and light several stores in the village

EXPORTS AND OTHER RESOURCES

When the pioneers first found their way to town and had provided themselves with houses to shelter themselves, they found an abundance of fish and game for subsistence, but the surplus if any did not find a market whereby they could procure money with which to meet incidental and necessary expenses such as taxes, postage, doctor bills, &c The first commodity that brought the ready cash was Black Salts, which was simply a concentrated lye, and found ready sale at from three and one-half to four cents a pound at the stores in town, but more often was sent to Brockville But finally there was a glut in the market and other means had to be resorted to Then came a demand for oak pipe staves which were riven out of red oak logs cut five feet in length These had a cash value on the river shore and were shipped by boat down the river to Montreal thence to the West Indies At nearly every hamlet or village where there was a store, an ashery was erected for the manufacture of potash, which differed from black salts in being prepared by leaching lime and ashes The ashes were bought by the merchant who generally owned the ashery and paid for in "store pay." They were formerly delivered at the ashery but later the merchant sent a team around to gather the article which then had a cash and a trade price ten and twelve cents per bushel

Fall wheat found a ready market later and steers and other young cattle two and three years of age were bought by dealers and taken away in droves, the wintering of which would require twice the sum today that the seller procured at the time for the stock sold

In certain portions of the town especially in the valley of Chippewa creek and a narrow strip of about forty rods on the ledge on the north side of the creek was an immense pine forest of large sized trees, also through all the broken and hilly portions of the town   The most of the lumber was sawed up at home, but a quantity of it was shipped or rafted whole to be used as spars of vessels which required the soundest and straightest trees   Many of these trees were of immense size as the old stumps standing today will testify, measuring five and six feet across   Some of these stumps have stood the test of time for seventy-five years

And yet these trees sold at a very low price and the manufactured lumber at home sold for five and six dollars per thousand   During the 1830-1840 period cord wood began to be a salable article commanding seventy-five cents per cord on the bank, then rising in price step by step until during the Civil war it brought in 1864 $5 00 per cord   At nearly every available place on the river shore wood docks were erected where steamers could 'wood up," taking on from twenty to seventy-five cords at one loading   The old time tugs of Calvin and Breck, which towed the great rafts of logs covering acres of the river, would often clean out a dock and the surrounding yard until they resembled a floating island   •

In later years the N T boats used immense quantities of wood from our town until bituminous coal came into use   Charles Lyon owned nearly all the land lying between Chippewa Bay and the county line a tract of twelve hundred acres   At one time he lost one thousand cords of steamboat wood by a forest fire

Later, dairying began to be one of the chief industries, the farmer packed away the summer make of butter in large tubs or firkins, then usually buyers came around and bought it up   In the fall of 1861 it brought from nine to twelve and one-half cents per pound

Prior to the war wheat was one of the staples, afterwards barley was a salable commodity   Not until about 1870 was any cheese made in factories although several farmers made dairy cheese which commanded a fair price when properly made   Since 1870 the dairy interests have received greater attention and the greater quantity of milk is manufactured into cheese   For a few years past the winter milk is sold at the milk station and finds a market in New York city   So that winter dairying is receiving more attention than formerly   And from the above date hay is one of the chief exports   The same attention is not given to the sale of dressed hogs as formerly, but the farmer finds it less labor to sell by live weight   Other staple products of the farm are veal calves and fat cattle and lambs   Poultry receives its share of attention   All of these articles find ready buyers at home or he may ship it to the cities and take his chances of securing a better price

Immense quantities of hay are also shipped out of town each year, being bought up principally by local dealers

CONTRIBUTED PAPERS.

THE SETTLER'S TRIALS.

By Francis M. Holbrook.

MY grandfather, Isaac Austin, one of the four original settlers of the town who came through the wilderness in 1805, from Washington County, N. Y., was born in Williamstown, Mass., about thirty miles from Hartford, in the county named, where he waited to hear from Gouverneur Morris in answer to his inquiry as to the inducements Morris would make to settlers on his lands in Northern N. Y. The reply was, substantially, that 160 acres of land would be given him. It was this inducement that brought the pioneer here early in 1805, and which resulted in his settling here later on in the fall of the same year.

Francis M Holbrook.

When they left Washington county in 1806 they came up the Mohawk valley to Utica where they stopped over night. Land was being sold there on the Mohawk flats, (now said to be worth several hundred dollars an acre), for $3 per acre. My grandmother (who was Tabitha Foster before her marriage in Williamstown, Mass.), wished to stop there and buy land and begin work at once. But grandfather reminded her that he was under obligations to Gouverneur Morris to go to this town and settle on the 160 acres offered him as a gift. Grandmother thought that the land about Utica was as fine land as they could wish, in which opinion every one acquainted with that splendid section will agree.

Land was being sold in Cambray, as this town was then called, at $1.25 per acre. Leaving Utica they started northward, being guided by marked trees, the road such as it was extending only as far as Boon's Upper Settlement, now Boonville, though there was a little travel along paths or trails as far as The Long Falls, now Carthage. The river here was not bridged until 1813, or eight years later.

The journey I am writing about occurred in the spring of 1806. Grandfather had been here twice in the previous year. The family that came in 1806 consisted of Rebecca, Elwell, Patty and Joshua and their parents, Isaac and Tabitha Austin. I do not have any remembrance of their story of the rest of the journey from Utica, but when they reached here, they stopped at a hotel on the hill on the west side of the river, there being no bridge, the tavern-keeper's name being Israel Porter. The present two-story house owned by Judge Neary was afterward built by Porter and kept as a hotel, the log portion in which my grandparents stayed and which was all the hotel there was, formed a wing to the frame building at first.

They made a raft and took the oxen, wagon and children across below the falls or rapids, to where the house, started the year before, was being built. This was on the sight of the house now well known as the Austin house between Clinton and Austin streets. The floor was made of hemlock boughs and my mother used to tell me that the first meeting held in Gouverneur was at this house, the minister being on his way from Ogdensburg to Utica, and stopping over for the purpose on Sunday. They called in a few of the neighbors who wore straw hats and linen shirts of home-make, although it was in the dead of winter, and there in the primitive cabin, destitute of everything we now class as necessaries, offered up their allegiance to the Most High.

My father, Henry B. Holbrook, lived four years in Gouverneur before he was married. He cleared most of the land on which the main or central part of the village now stands. It was then a bushy, hemlock grove and he received $4 per acre for clearing it. He boarded with the man who then kept the hotel across the river, but I do not know whether it was Israel Porter or not. There were four including himself, who boarded there at the time. They used to amuse themselves Sunday mornings trying to throw stones across the river at a point a little above what is now known as the "Goose Bend," the river being about twenty rods wide there. My father was a Benjamite. He could throw stones with tremendous force and was the only man who could plant one on the steep hill on the farther shore. The axeman of those days who could cut the cleanest "calf" and the youth who could throw the most of his fellows "square hold," was accounted the best man and was looked up to with considerable awe.

After boarding four years Henry B. Holbrook married Rebecca Austin, eldest daughter of Isaac Austin. Isaac Bolton, brother of John Bolton, was present and gave the bride away. After this marriage, my father contracted for a piece of land 80 acres in extent, on what is now the Richville road, four miles east of the village, subsequently owned by Amasa Corbin, Sr. Gilbert Rundell succeeded him on this land, taking it under contract also, and Rundell sold to Amasa Corbin who, unlike most of the settlers, brought enough money with him in 1830 to pay for it, his wife who was a Foster from near Williamstown, Mass., from which place my grandfather had come, having $500 as her dower while Amasa had saved up $200 from his earnings before coming. On this 80-acre tract my father built a log house, and probably cleared 50 acres of it as that is the number reported in the 1835

Amasa Corbin, Sr.

state census as being "improved" at that time. Seven children were born in this cabin, Lydia, Emeline, Isaac, Betsey, Daniel, Frank and Henry, the latter dying in 1825.

While clearing he built a large barn, of the standard "thirty by forty" size, Rockwell Barnes hewing the timbers and my father doing the "scoring." This frame, with sills only renewed, is still in the finest preservation and in daily use. The hewing is wonderfully smooth for the scorer evidently understood his business, and each timber, is without a "wany" corner. The frame timbers are large, all of rock-elm, and the bracing was sawed and pinned. The pine lumber in this barn, flooring and all, was cut on Pine Hill, Macomb, (then a portion of Cambray), by Aaron Carrington, sawn at Elmdale in Carrington's mill, rafted to "Rich's Landing" at the mouth of Borland Creek one mile below Richville, and drawn from thence to the frame which stood about sixty rods northeast of its present site, having been moved twice in the more than three-quarters of a century since it was built.

Rockwell Barnes.

It stood at first near the steep bank of the brook where plaster sand was afterward found and dug. The frame was put up in four weeks time from the felling of the trees in the forest nearby.

Many incidents occurred to the new settler on this tract but I will mention only two or three. My father had a patch of corn near the house and when it began to ripen, a black bear quietly took possession. His visits were made at night and "Jack", the dog, was soon cognizant of the presence of the intruder. This dog is remembered as one of the best of his kind. He kept the bear at bay, finally driving him up a tree where the bear seated himself upon a limb about thirty feet from the ground. Help was summoned while the dog stood guard, and two neighbors came with guns. A third took his post near by, counted "one, two, three—fire" and both guns spoke together and the bear tumbled to the ground. As this adventure occurred at twelve o'clock at night, it was of a sufficiently exciting character to be long remembered

My father also experienced a "hold-up" by wolves shortly after the incident mentioned He had three horses, two of which he customarily drove in the team while the third was yet a colt Returning one day from the village he found the colt had disappeared My mother told him the colt had gone toward the road now called the Welsh road running from the corners near Rock Island bridge to Richville It was almost sunset but my father started for the colt through the woods, emerging near the present Rock Island cheese factory There he was held up by five wolves, sitting on their haunches in the middle of the road, defying him to pass He gathered a handful of stones, and opened the battle His skill with his strong left arm stood him in good stead As each missile whistled through the air, there came an answering howl from the pack At last they gave way leaving him master of the immediate field Knowing the treacherous nature of the animals, he did not cease to guard against a rear attack and walked backward the entire distance to the house where Addison Hall now lives, about half a mile, the wolves following and growling viciously The shanty then standing at this place was owned by Cecil Rhodes Elder Barnabas Hall, a spiritualist and Universalist, afterward owned the place Meantime, my mother becoming frightened at the long absence of her husband, started at 12 o'clock midnight to find him She had a long tin horn, a usual household necessity of those days, blowing it vigorously but getting no answering call Two neighbors persuaded her to wait till daylight and about eight o'clock next morning the colt and its owner appeared in good order

This is one of the events in the life of my father while living on the tract now known as the Corbin farm There were many others of interest, enough to fill a book, but I will leave them to others to supply

I was born on this farm and in the log-house spoken of, July 10, 1823 At twenty I took a school in Edwards for the winter The school-house was built of stone by a Scotchman whose name I do not recall I had 108 scholars through the winter, which was that of 1842-43 The next fall Laban Skinner and myself took a job of driving 300 head of cattle to Boston for John Rhodes, then a merchant of Gouverneur We left Gouverneur in the last days of August, 1843, driving the cattle to Antwerp where we put up for the night We sat up all night watching the drove to keep them from a grain field adjoining Election time was just then approaching and Clay and Frelinghuysen were the Whig candidates and Polk and Dallas the Democratic nominees The campaign following was an exciting and strenuous one

Laban Skinner, my partner was a great singer, having been in the Presbyterian choir many years About midnight he struck up a campaign song then current Some of it I can remember and it ran thus

> Now Polk and choke will always rhyme,
>   And Dallas and gallus are quite sublime,
> We'll dose the tox on poke-root pizen,
>   Harrah for Clay and Frelinghuysen
> At Linden Hall the foxes hold,
>   The coons all laugh to hear it told,
> Ha! ha! ha! such a nominee
>   As James K. Po'k of Tennessee!

Our own Silas Wright was nominated for vice-president with Polk but refused saying that he did not propose to ride behind on the black pony (slavery) at the funeral of his slaughtered friend Martin Van Buren '

We arrived at Boston with the cattle in due time I remained there with relatives who were the ancestors of A J Holbrook, who will be remembered as cashier of Godard's Bank early in the 70's He is now in the Boston post office

The year 1843 was one of salvation for the Millerite persuasion, or was expected to be at least. Sixteen miles from Boston where Wellesley College now stands, Skinner and I busked corn on our way home. We lost no opportunity to earn a dollar. The place was in a state of excitement over the expected ascension which had been predicted to occur from that hill. The trumpet was to sound, and the robes of white had been donned for entrance into glory. We waited for the trumpet but it wasn't blown while we were there. It is one of the curious circumstances that my daughter was sent to this spot years after for education at the college. My two oldest daughters were educated at Vassar.

As I write this I am 82 years old. How long I shall be spared I know not, but I believe what I have here written will prove of interest to all who enjoy Old Home Week or read the History in which this will appear.

THE SCOTTISH ELEMENT.

By George H. Robinson.

George H. Robinson.

In the earlier days of the 19th century, when this part of St. Lawrence County was sectionally settled by such Scotch families as the Lockies, Dodds, Browns, Robinsons, Rodgers, McClarens, Brodies, Taitts, Dicksons, Clarks, Pringles, Flemings, Hills, Nobles, Watsons, Clelands, Todds, Grants, Laidlaws, Darlings, Ormistons, Faichneys, Stories, Hardies, and McDoualds, it was all a dense, howling wilderness, with only an occasional clearing, generally where a roving squatter had found temporary quarters for the time being, with only a blazed trail running through the timber here and there to mark the line or road, this being all that furnished a guide to the settlers in traveling from place to place. There was the prowling wolf, the migratory bear, the screaming panther or the almost domestic deer as it grazed on the succulent grasses, which furnished a rare treat to these beauties that roamed the wilderness almost undisturbed. There under these conditions, the Scotchman found a home, and from the dense forest sturdily and unflinchingly hewed out productive fields, and in time gained a competence that, when death came, found them in position to render invaluable assistance to those who were in line to take up the work of their fathers and continue the chain of ancestry transmitted to their care.

In earlier years, here the Scotch planted their settlements, erected their homes, cleared the land, cultivated the soil and thus made the pre-historic home of the Indian, an Eden of thrift and a garden of civilization. Too much cannot be said of the industry of these first settlers from the ancestral home of a Wallace, a Bruce and of Burns, the Bard of "Bonnie Scotland," who in the inspiration of the hour sought to found and build up homes in the "land of the free," severed the ties that held them by the tender necessities of childhood and those most dear to them, and with that unselfish pre-eminent attribute that constitutes the man, became the instrument inspired by nature to help revolutionize and bring into use, and develop, an old-created but newly discovered world in the hemisphere of the west. They have added much to the prosperity, wealth and thrift of their adopted town. As a factor of enterprise, their perseverance, invulnerable push and indomitable grit, have passed down through the several generations, which becoming instilled into the minds of their posterity here, accomplished much and will continue to be felt long after the commingling of the races and nationalities have absorbed, or nearly so, all lineal traces. In some cases the line has almost become obliterated, and can only be pointed out through certain families, by reference to some great grandparent, whose memory is more of the present than the past, and whose family ties are so remote, it would be hard to prove that any relationship ever existed. This may in the future be the outcome, but the past examples will never be erased from history's page and will prove an incentive for future generations to emulate. There is not a town covered by this history but has felt the impetus imparted to it by the iron nerve of the early Scotch settler and after giving timly deserved credit to other nationalities represented here, a great vacuum would still exist had not the Scotch emigrants created their "Scotch settlements" throughout this section No scheme of deception was ever tolerated in their ranks, while the Holy writ was found in every home The sacred family altar was erected at every hearthstone The Bible and church obligations were first and all other things second The fruits of their church-living example has permeated the entire commonwealth, and has done much toward holding down all insubordination that might have gained a footing here on our shores, and proved disastrous to our free institutions, our country, our homes, and our land They have brightened the page of history by their unswerving allegiance to their Christian faith and their devoted sense of duty to their friends, their high appreciation of the rights of American citizenship The sanctity of the Sabbath they revered, and their fidelity to Christian principles was the sacred pledge of their intense loyalty The latch string to their homes always hung on the outside of their doors, and needed no gilt edged, printed label of invitation, for in the benevolence of their hearts, none ever left their humble dwellings without aid

---

MUSICAL REMINISCENCES.

By Grace H Corbin

I am indebted to the aged and highly respected Harvey Thompson for the peg upon which I shall hang these reminiscences of the musical past

That the early toilers in a new country found time for musical recreation I have been assured

Chorus music found expression in the singing-schools and church choirs at a time when the violin and organ in the meeting-house were regarded as "instruments of the devil"

Jas I Thompson, the father of Harvey Thompson, led the choir in the old Baptist church away back in the twenties and, it is said, he sang a fine tenor His daughter Sophroma led the soprano with her small brothers, Oscar on the one side and Harvey on the other, and the voices of the entire choir rang out with clarion distinctness guided only by the key-note from Jas Thompson's pitch-pipe

The Thompsons were all musically inclined, of whom nine brothers at one time practically comprised the choir

Early in the thirties David Wilcox, the itinerant singing-school master introduced the "fiddle," Isaac King, the flute, and Deacon Willard Guernsey the bass viol Brother Wilder Guernsey sang a good bass and was at one time the organizer and leader of a singing-school

Miss Emeline Smith, (now Mrs E H Drake), and her sister Elizabeth were sopranos, Louis Loomis, tenor, John Leavitt, bass, Lydia Austin and Olive Barrell were among the choir singers of a later date

Joel Keyes conducted the Presbyterian choir for twenty years about the same time Among the choir members was Thomas Goodrich who possessed a rare tenor voice Mr Goodrich had a large family of children, who as soon as they could read music were given places in the choir, their names were Selina (the eldest), a soprano, John, Daniel, Mary, Julia, Ann, Robert, Charles, and Fidelia, also soprano The latter, now Mrs F E Burt, is a successful vocal teacher in Brooklyn, her daughters, Mary T Burt and Julia A Burt, have large classes in vocal and piano respectively in New York City

The late Mr Howard Smith played the bass viol and John Goodrich the violin with the choir, during the ministry of Rev B B Beckwith

Capt Geo B Winslow will also be remembered as choir-master in the Presbyterian church with Maria Dodge, Sarah Barney, William Roger and Jas S Black, Dr Parmelee, Orville Van Buren, Delia and Julia Cone and others in the choir

Glancing down the line to more recent times, we are reminded of a number of musical people active in the business and social life of the present day. The following "poetic" extract found in a scrap-book, though in a humorous vein gives merited praise and reference to several always cordially welcomed on concert programs, in solo and chorus.

OUR CHOIR.

Now, Freddie (1) and Eddie (2) the kids of our Choir,
  Well known to our musical people,
The whole congregation their voices admire
  Resounding well up tow'rd the steeple.

Gay Eddie's a basso both valiant and bold,
  With voice that comes clear from his shoes,
And Freddie's a tenor whose style we are told,
  Is what you'd expect him to choose.

Sweet Alice, (3) soprano, the gem of the Choir,
  For lucre doth warble they say,
But is not the laborer worthy her hire
  Who charmingly warbles high A?

Our mezzo-soprano, (4) that good-looking dame,
  With voice low and sweet in its compass,
Is not to be sneezed at by us, all the same,
  (We don't want to kick up a rumpus.)

Now gaze on our alto (5) so gifted and mild,
  To solo she never aspires,
Perhaps for this reason is never much riled
  As usual in other church choirs.

And now comes the baritone, (6) here you get style,
  To paint him we cannot now tarry,
He's firm and so faithful, but once in a while
  Gets mad as the very old Harry.

At last comes our organist (7) pretty well known,
  Outside of our town—we admit it,
He's too independent and somewhat high-flown,
  By Judas, I've just about hit it!

A most pleasant duty it is to relate,
  What a blind man could almost see clearly,
They (8) sing well together it's fair for to state,
  In harmony perfect—or nearly.

(1) Fred. Hall.   (2) Ed. Van Duzee.   (3) Alice Lawrence.   (4) Mrs. H. Sudds.   (5) Mrs. W. F. Sudds.
(6) Henry Sudds.   (7) W. F. Sudds.   (8) The choir.

W. F. Sudds.

Although the days of the old-fashioned singing-school have passed, its good work in sight-reading and chorus will not be forgotten. With a broader scope and greater aspirations the Choral Union was organized and ably conducted for over ten years by Prof. W. F. Sudds. Their first concert program, April 23, 1878, contained such numbers as "Festival Hymn," by D. Buck; "He watcheth over Israel" from "Elijah;" "Hallelujah" chorus from the Messiah.

Soloists from away were several times secured for the Choral Union and other concerts of this period; Miss J. Etta Crane, Miss Howe, and Miss Lillian Bacon will be most pleasantly remembered on these occasions.

A few extract numbers from these concerts may recall several pleasing musical affairs.

Chorus.—"Song of the Vikings."

Violin Solo.—Fantaise Melodique,   -   -   -   -   - *Singelee*
Miss Edith Norton.

Song.—"Sing, Smile, Slumber,"   -   -   -   -   - *Gounod*
Miss Julia Hotchkiss.

Song.—"Thou Art Not Near Me,"   -   -   -   - *W. F. Sudds*
Mrs. Henry Sudds.

Recitative and Bass Solo.—"The Heathen Raged,"   -   -   -   -
Prof. Donaldson Bodine.

Duet.—"Spring Flowers,"   -   -   -   -   - *Reinecke*
Miss Lillian Bacon and Miss Edith Norton.

Solo with Violin Obligato.—"Angel's Serenade,"   -   -   - *Braga*
Miss Alice Lawrence.

In these pleasant reflections over the highly creditable work done in song, our thoughts turn to many who have successfully followed other lines of musical culture.

In the year 1869 a music department was established in the Gouverneur Wesleyan Seminary under Prof. Dains' principalship by Mrs. Jessie E. Paul, who during the six years of her work there, graduated a number of successful pupils. Miss Julia Hotchkiss, a pupil of Mrs. Paul has won recognition as a church soloist and teacher of music in New York City and in the South and West.

Another was Miss Harriet B. Cutting, whose cherished name recalls not only a delightful artist of the piano but also a beautiful character, whose untimely death came in the beginning of a promising career. Miss Cutting studied in New York under Hoffman and Dr. Mason, followed by a two years course in Berlin under Dr. Raif, where unremitting practice eight hours a day undermined her health. Returning to America, she accepted

THE CITIZENS' BAND.

Chas. M. Taitt (Director,) Solo Bb Cornet; W. R. Crossman, Bb; Edward James, Bb; Louis Seff, 1st Bb cornet; Harry Hinton, 2nd Bb cornet; Claude Gates, Eb cornet; Pearley Lytle, Piccolo; Howard Peck, Eb Clarinet; Wm. R. Jones, Bb Clarinet; George Seaman, 1st Alto; Alex. Laidlaw, Sr., 2nd Alto; Lawrence Lewis, 3rd Alto; Frank Livingston, 1st Tenor; Grant Kalev, 1st Trombone; Elmer Lytle, 2nd Trombone; Herbert Clapp, Baritone; Guy Rebyor, Bb Bass; Frank Turnbull, Eb Bass; Earl Kenyon, Eb Bass; Al. Clapp, Snare Drum; Carl Clapp, Bass Drum. Louis Boulet, Propertyman.

COLONIAL MINUET.

Upper Row—Read left to right—Kate Henderson,   Florence Earl,   Cassie Salsbury
                             Verne Wight,   Glen Severance,   Glen Farmer.
Lower Row—Hazel Jenne,   Vera Hurlbut,   Jessie Lee,   Helen Kelly,   Irma Sackett,
             Bert Hurlbut,   Lawrence Lewis.   Harold Starbuck,   Ernest Hartley,   Philip Spencer.

a responsible position as teacher of piano in a school of music in Springfield, Mass. A few months later her health gave way; she returned to her home and friends where after a short illness she died.

The following extract from a bill-poster dated June 30th, 1881, may revive pleasant recollections.

"GRAND BAND CONCERT by the Gouverneur Cornet Band for the benefit of Prof. Frank Thompson, Cornetist! Union Hall. Miss J. Etta Crane of Potsdam and Miss Harriet B. Cutting. A Fine Duet (the only copy) by the Misses Drake and Smith! Union Hall."

One of the established musical necessities of our village is the Citizen's Cornet Band, at present under their popular leader, Mr. Chas. M. Tait. Its inspiration is essential to every patriotic demonstration and popular movement.

Speaking of music and patriotism recalls a great celebration July 4th, 1903, when fifteen thousand citizens were assembled in our town to celebrate the nation's birthday. It was on this memorable occasion that sixteen leading society young people in the quaint and picturesque ball gowns of a century ago danced to the strains of Mozart's Minuet from Don Juan discoursed by the Citizens' Band; and Miss Von Goodnough won distinction by singing "The Star Spangled Banner" before the same large assembly.

To Prof. Marsh is due the credit of establishing the present system of music instruction in the public schools of our village.

There is one singer whom Gouverneur is proud to claim and who is a universal favorite wherever her rich contralto is heard. Mrs. Edith Norton-Reusswig is now singing in concert in New York and conducts the singing in the First Baptist Church in Somerville, N. J. The many friends of Mrs. Reusswig gladly accord to her the first place among the vocalists of Northern New York.

There are others from our former towns-people who are truly missed in musical circles. Miss Anna Tumpson, now pianist and instructor in Connellsville, Pa.; Alfred Mackay, an organist of much promise in Pittsburg, Pa.; Mrs. Bertha Huyette-Sudds, and Miss Helen Keefer, formerly in the Presbyterian choir as solo sopranos are among them.

Edith Norton Reusswig.

In closing, this sketch would seem incomplete without general reference to those of musical culture who still remain with us, most kindly contributing their aid and talents to the success of musical affairs.

We have good choirs in all the churches, among whose conscientious leaders may be mentioned Mrs. H. C. Rogers of the Methodist, Mrs. Jennie Phelps-Corby of the Baptist, and Mr. Tait of the Presbyterian churches, whose organist Mrs. Lillian Tait-Sheldon is a favorite song composer.

There are also the music teachers, cultivating true musical taste among the young people under their instruction.

Mr. Clarence M. Johnson and Miss Helen Markwick, teachers and musicians of taste, together with several others form a group of music lovers proficient in their several lines of musical art.

Mrs. H. C. Rogers.

Clarence M. Johnson.

Whatever else might be said of their good work will find sufficient record in the commendation of their many friends.

GOUVERNEUR IN SONG AND STORY.

By Florence Earle Payne

Undoubtedly the virgin literary sod, in this locality was turned by the hand of Mrs Cornelius Parker, when she began in the year 1850 the preparation of the History of Gouverneur, afterward published in pamphlet form With her husband, who was then a land agent, she made numerous excursions into the surrounding country and while he attended to his business she gathered material for future use from the older inhabitants Each succeeding year makes this work of greater value and although she has written and published continuously since that period, "The History of Gouverneur" is, and always will be the Alpha of local literary interest

Nelson Bruet of the firm of Bruet & Co who purchased the "Northern New Yorker" the first paper published in Gouverneur, was a man possessed of a highly poetical nature During his residence in the towns of Edwards and Gouverneur he mingled literary pursuits with his ordinary calling The paper was discontinued in 1851 and he removed to Jefferson, Wisconsin, where he practiced law until his death The following is the only available quotation It is from an unpublished poem

LINES ON THE PRESENTATION OF A ROSE

" I take the rose kind brother
Which thou hast offered me
For thou mayst pick another
From off the parent tree'
* * * * * *
"It came in the early morn,
And midday saw its bloom
That ere another was born,
To smile upon its tomb"

Miss M M Smith was a native of Dekalb She was the pioneer among her sex in journalism in the town of Gouverneur In those days adverse criticism followed the footsteps of women who walked in new and diverging paths, but she was prepared to
"———publish right or wrong
Fools are my theme
Let satire be my song"
By her fearless example she helped to emancipate her sex from the slavery of custom and blazed a trail for genius to follow when she published "The Rising Sun" She also published a novel entitled "Kick Him Down Hill" An artist of no mean ability, she painted and dreamed until the light of her weird intellect became clouded and finally went out forever She was removed to the hospital for the insane at Ogdensburg

Mrs Cornelia McFalls is well known in this vicinity In the heart of this village which loves and appreciates her warm honest natured and versatile talent she has sung her sweet songs always Although no literary "blue-stocking", for quoting from her own words, she can "work with one hand and write poetry with the other," the very spirit of poesy breathes in every line of her dainty verses The little gems "Forget-me-nots" from the pen of this author ought to have a place in this volume, but
' We have a sprig of forget-me-not
We are wearing for thee in our hearts'
Mrs Mary S Gillette whose maiden name was Van Ness, was born on a farm in the town of Rossie so near to the border of Jefferson County that she might easily have drawn inspiration from its magnetic soil Much of her life was spent in Watertown and among the "Thousand Isles," where she has a summer home In the year 1878, she published a book entitled "Facts and Fancies," and in the year 1888 "The Pleasures of Memory" ap-

peared in book form. Her rare talent and genial sunny disposition make her a welcome visitor in the homes of her relatives and friends since the death of her husband. The following lines are from "Facts and Fancies."

THE SEA SHELL

"Opal, and ruby, and amethyst,
Their glories show by the moonbeams kissed
Shimmering down through the quivering wave,
To light the halls of the sea queen's cave,
Arabesques of quaint device,
Of jewels rare of countless price,
Hadst thou a voice how well thou could'st tell
Of old ocean's wonders! O beautiful shell!

Miss Helen J. Parker of Gouverneur is a marvel of literary activity. She is the Editor of the Grand Army Journal, a paper devoted to the interests of the Grand Army of the Republic, and its auxiliary, the Woman's Relief Corps. The Sons of Veterans, Ladies of the G. A. R. and other kindred societies all find space in its columns. While thus occupied she finds time to lend a helping hand to every enterprise of any degree of merit that is projected in the town. She is a member of the New York Press Association and is a familiar figure at their annual gatherings. Although her business qualifications make her an important factor in the outside world, her greatest enjoyment is found in the home where she resides with her widowed mother.

Macomb has furnished us an author of more than ordinary ability in James F. Sayre, but Gouverneur now claims him as her own. He was born in England, came to Macomb at the age of five years and resided there until manhood. He is a veteran of the Civil War and an inventor of some merit—having been granted several patents. He has been a contributor to the leading journals of New York, Albany and other cities for many years. His book 'Lenore and I,' a love story in verse, was favorably reviewed by the Saturday Review, Times, of New York, and other journals. He has quite a number of unpublished poems of equal merit that will eventually be published in book form.

"That man is father of his fate
Is the conclusion of the sages.
His destiny he doth create,
'Tis fruitage of his deeds, the wages
Of his own wisdom, or his folly
One harvests mirth, one melancholy — *Lenore and I*"

Miss Sarah F. Sprague, of Chicago, occupies a place as unique as it is lofty in the literary firmament. She was born in Fowler and educated at the Gouverneur Wesleyan Seminary, St. Lawrence University, and Oswego Normal School. She was at one time part owner of an educational journal in Rochester, is the author of "Methods for Teachers" and has recently completed a series of Readers for a firm in Boston. Although her work lies mainly along educational lines, she has been a contributor to some of the leading journals of the day. While visiting a friend in Seattle, Washington, she wrote the words of the college song adopted by the "University of Washington." This poem was copied into the New York Sun in choice selections of verse.

CUBAN RALLY SONG

From the Rochester Democrat and Chronicle

Sound, ye trumpets! Sound on high!
Let your echoes fill the sky,
Make a loud, triumphant noise,
Sound the rally for the boys,
March from Maine and Tennessee,
Sail for Cuba! Set her free!

March from Western hill and plain,
Wake the echoes once again,
Spain no more at us shall scoff,
Spanish chains we'll help throw off
Every man from sea to sea,
Fight for Cuba, Cuba free!

Let it never more be said
Babes and women cry for bread,
Homes in flames and honor lost,
While we stand and count the cost!
Shall these human vampires be?
Wait no more! Set Cuba free!

Rouse, Columbia! Lend a hand!
Drive the dastards from the land!
Spanish rule denies a crust,
Spanish soldiers glut their lust,
Force them from the land and sea!
Rally, men! Set Cuba free!

Helen Townsley Knox was born in Dekalb. She was educated at Houghton Seminary, married J Earle Knox of New York City and resided there up to the time of her death, two years ago. She was for years a regular and valued contributor to the columns of the "New York Sunday Sun." With literary excellence she combined rare graces of character that greatly endeared her to every one with whom she came in contact.

Mrs Laura Stevens Allen won fame and money contributing to the columns of the New York Sun. Left an orphan at an early age, she made her home with her aunt, Mrs E G Seymour, of Hermon. She married Ernest L Allen of Chicago, and during her residence in that city was a leading spirit of its most exclusive literary circle. She removed with her husband from Chicago to New York, where his death occurred.

Cornelius Carter, called the "Poet of the Adirondacks," lived in the town of Edwards. Three years ago his poems were collected and published in book form. He was an ardent lover of nature and his verses are replete with descriptions of her beauties. He built for himself a cabin on the "Plains," where he lived summers and many a weary sportsman has sought shelter under its hospitable roof. He served his town as Justice of the Peace and Supervisor. His death occurred recently at his home in South Edwards. One of his most popular poems was

"FAREWELL TO THE ADIRONDACKS"

Farewell, thou lovely region,
  Long time I've been with you,
Have slept upon thy bosom
  And viewed thy peaks so blue

Have heard the scream of panther
  And hoarser growl of bear,
Where game are wont to wander,
  On mountains bleak and bare

Where songs birds, at the dawning,
  Awake me from repose,
And zephyrs soft and sighing
  Kiss petals of the rose

Where the cool, rushing river
Controlled by laws that be,
Goes wandering on forever
To the mysterious sea

Where God, the mighty Maker,
Wrought mountains bold and grim,
Made the bright sparkling water
And valleys broad and dim

Oh! I could dwell supernal
Amid Thy spruce and pine
Until the God Eternal
Shall fold the wings of time

Farewell, then, lofty mountains,
And you, ye valleys fair,
For I must cross the waters,
I'm summoned to be there

Miss Emma Paul of Gouverneur is a young lady whose articles have occupied prominent places in the Cosmopolitan, Munsey, and other magazines She was born in Quincy, Florida, and during the war was with her mother in a small town in Georgia, near Andersonville prison, some times in the midst of hostile troops Her father attended school at the Gouverneur Wesleyan Seminary and her mother was at one time a teacher in the same institution She is a graduate of Ives Seminary

Miss Cora Loomis of Gouverneur is a writer of verse and her early productions gave great literary promise

J S Corbin is a prolific writer on Political Economy Those who have read his published articles can not fail to appreciate his terse arguments and forceful manner of sustaining them and those that treat of local events have great influence in moulding popular opinion The stupendous task of preparing the "Souvenir History of Gouverneur," in such a short space of time, fell into his hands and it will always stand as a fitting monument to both his executive and literary powers He was almost three score when the activities of a business life were laid aside, and a more frequent use of the pen permitted

Jesse T Reynolds, who was a resident of this town at the time of his death and lived here the greater portion of his life, was the author of a book entitled "Conflict of Reason and Theology " History also shows that he figured conspicuously in the literary growth of this town

Chas Winslow, son of Capt Geo B Winslow, a native of Gouverneur, was up to the time of his tragic death a writer on the staff of the New York Tribune

Thomas Downing of Rochester, formerly of Macomb, has written several poems of greater or less merit

Harvey Ormiston who went West from this town and died there was one of the verse writers of his time

To the town of Fowler belongs the honor of giving birth to that most talented son of the soil, Willard Glazier He reached the pinnacle of fame at one bound when he published the thrilling story, "The Capture, The Prison Pen and Escape,' of which 100,000 copies were sold This book was followed by "Three Years in the Federal Cavalry," 1870, "Sword and Pen," "Battles of the Union," 1874, "Across the Continent," 1876, "Heroes of Three Wars," 1878, 'Peculiarities of American Cities," 1883, "Down the Great River,' 1887 In this latter book he made the claim of discovering the headwaters of the Mississippi In the controversy that followed he ably defended himself in a series of articles published in the 'Albany Sunday Press " He was a most indefatigable worker and traversed hundreds of miles of territory and endured countless hardships to gain the necessary information for the preparation of his books Author, soldier, lecturer, explorer, gentleman, and neighbor, it is not the privilege of Gouverneur to crown him Our Hero, for his laurels have been won from a grateful nation Alas! "Taps" have sounded "Put out the lights, a life is done"

The veteran author, Edward Everett Hale once took a journey through this section of country and in one of his early stories, "The Children of the Public," the scenes are laid in Gouverneur and Rossie, proving that even at that early date genius was stimulated by this bracing atmosphere Literary greed almost induces one to reach out and lay claim to the Sun of the North country, Irving Bacheller, but surely this town is to be forgiven for feeling that it has a mortgage on its idol and namesake, Gouverneur Morris As he carries the name of Gouverneur higher and higher up the ladder of fame, the heart of this people will go with him always

This article is not designed as a complete and authentic history Some there may be who scattered seed in hidden places Unknown, modest flowers are these—

> So they bloom on, and breathe their incense up to Him
> Who made them, that they might perfume these hidden nooks,
> And scatter petals in the limpid purling brooks,
> That spots remote might catch the scent of violets

GOUVERNEUR—A CENTENNIAL POEM.

By James F Sayer

Fair Gouverneur, my heart's delight,
Would that I could thy charms recite
In fitting strains, and render due
Acknowledgements for all that you
Have been to me since, when a boy,
I felt the overflowing joy,
That did my buoyant bosom fill,
When first from brow of Thompson's hill
Thy presence on my vision burst
My mission then to slake my thirst
For knowledge at the loved old Sem
That student's Mecca, 'twas no gem
Of architecture, by the side
Of what is now our city's pride
'Twas small and mean, but O, its walls,
To us who met within its halls,
Are ever sacred, and will stand
In memory as something grand

As luminary of the North,
As pioneer who first held forth
The torch of science, that did pour,
From out the founts of classic lore,
The rare enchantment of the past
Into our lives Too sweet to last
Those halcyon days The chapel bell
In memory rings, but who can tell
Where are the youths and maidens fair
Who met with us for song and prayer,
And sly exchange of glances fraught
With meanings books have never taught?
A few of them may yet be found

Near the old enchanted ground,
But most have gone, some east, some west,
And many, whom we loved the best,
Who of us were the flower and pride,
Have passed beyond the grand divide
And those of us, who yet remain
On earthly shores, may as we drain
The cup of life find it divine
As 'twas within this early shrine

The Oswegatchie winds between
Enchanting shores where e'er it goes,
But most inspiring 'tis I ween
Where it so picturesquely flows
Through Gouverneur Its long grand sweep
Above the Town, its graceful curve
Around the sacred soil where sleep
Our loved and lost And then the swerve
To northward of its beauteous shores
To where it musically pours
Apparently into a lake
Land-locked, northbound by Easton's range
Of hills, and here its features take
Of such a transformation strange,
Such swan's neck semblance, that the bend,
The quiet graceful beauteous trend
Out from the hill, leaves margin wide
Upon the warm the sunny side
Of rare poetic ground, with room
For gardens fair below the home
Of him who bountifully fills
Our marts with grapes from native hills

One hundred rare eventful years,
Have passed since hardy pioneers,
Of toil and hardships unafraid,
The crude but sure beginnings made
Of thy fair self O Gouverneur!
Tell me O Muse what was the lure
That led thy founders from a home
Of peace and plenty on to roam
To Northern wilds, where hillocks wear
Their cloaks of snow through half the year,
Its very wildness had its charms
The air was bracing, strange alarms
Were tonics, aye the panther's yell,
And howl of wolves, that nightly fell
Upon the lonely settlers ears,
The unavowed, the fitful fears
Of Indian raids, did send a thrill
Through manly breasts, a sturdy will
To do and dare they fostered Men
Of mettle were determined then
To win in face of dangers new
And so as soon as came to view
The present site of this fair town,
The new homeseekers here laid down
Their household goods, their penates,
And fell to slaughtering the trees,
And of their corses shelters made
For man and beast, and still they laid
On sturdy blows, till ax and brand
Had cleared a virgin spot of land
For cornfields, while from forests round
The clearing, that did then resound
With rifle shots, delicious meat
Came forth, rare venison and neat
Rare furs for mats and clothing Farms
Were soon created, with the charms
Of tingling cowbells, dinner horns,
The low of cattle, and the morns
Made vocal by proud chanticleer,
The cackling from his harem near,
The happy grunts from pigs in sty,
The turkey's gobble and the cry
Of hungry calves for absent dams,
The bleating of the sportive lambs,
The filly's whinney, while at play
In pastures green, the stallion's neigh,
The kitten's mew, and Rover's bark,
Who with the children loved to lark

But Gouverneur although thy morn
Of life was passed in fields of corn,
And wheat, and pasturage for kine,
The charms of nature did combine
To change thy course Thy very site

Was beauty's self, it did invite
New emigrations Side by side
Were built their dwellings, satisfied
With small allotments, if so be
The lovely river they might see
But not on loveliness alone
Could people live, so the millstone
Was started, a sure toll to win
From gusts of grangers, and within
The settlement rose shop and store
More trade to draw, and, as the more
Home seekers came, more houses new,
And church, and schoolhouse rose to view,
The streets extended, bridges spanned
The witching stream On every hand
Was sound of hammers Blocks arose
To airy heights, and no one knows
To what extent had gone the same
Had not hissed forth from tongues of flame
The word, "hath never city stood
For long that's built alone of wood "
Time after time the fire fiend raged
Upon our streets, was not assuaged
His fury, till were one by one
The blocks rebuilt of wood and stone

Serene between her guardian hills
Lies Gouverneur The wind that chills
Is broken by kind Natures wall,
The Babcock hill, and Bald Face tall
Always delays awhile the beams
Of morn while we round out our dreams
O pleasant vale, did ever dream
The early settlers by thy stream
Fair Oswegatchie what a change
The years would bring? Did fancy s range
E'er picture how the oxcart slow
By the barouche and the auto
Would be displaced? How monthly mail
Would change to hourly one by rail,
How cabins rude would be displaced
By mansions, and cowpaths that laced
The fields be changed to boulevards?
And how unsightly stumpy yards
Would change to parks and velvet lawns,
Fresh at the noons as at the dawns,
All pearled and freshened by the showers,
Born of the tall twin water towers
On Crown of Bald Face? Shielders grand
From dust and fire for us they stand
How full-cloth mill would yield its place
To large palatial halls where lace
Is deftly woven, being fair
As snow falls hanging in the air,

Or frost work on the window panes,
Or drifting showers of apple bloom
Within the dandelion's home,
In the sweet-scented Mayday lanes?
How, as time passed, the people good
Would raze their temples built of wood,
And meet for worship where divines
Break bread of life in marble shrines?
How that unsightly rocks, that marred
The landscape, would be mined and carved,
As costly marble, o'er our land
To every part, to make more grand
The architecture of our time,
And monuments make more sublime?

Our quarries, factories and mills
To Gouverneur must give renown,
But that which most the bosom thrills
With pride, in this our queenly town,
Is memory of the noble ones,
And their succeeding stalwart sons,
Who founded, prospered us, and saved
Us when secession's banner waved.
The household names of just a few
To whom are ever honors due
Are Austin, Babcock, Spencer, Smith
And Porter, Patterson, and with
The later ones are Walling bold,
And Parker, Barney, Barnes who sold
His life for freedom, our first one

To lay his earthly all upon
Our Country's altar; Winslow's band
Of heroes, known as "Battery D,"
And scores of others, who our land
From slavery did help to free.

Now all who erstwhile breathed the air
Of Gouverneur, come home, and share
With us, on this centenial year,
Our celebration, our good cheer.
Come home from where is ever drouth
Of glistening snow, the sunny South.
Come to us from the Golden Gate
From mountains grand, and prairies free,
Come from the puritanic state,
Come from the islands of the sea,
Come from Alaska's fields of gold,
Come from wherever is unrolled
Our starry flag, in east, or west,
Or north, or south, come to the best,
The dearest spot beneath the sun,
To all who here their lives begun.
Come from the cities, ships, and mines,
Come lawyers, doctors and divines,
Come teachers, authors, singers all,
And by your presence, help to call
Up pleasant memories of the past,
And help a future to forecast
Of wonderous growth, and large increase
Of products of the arts of peace.

PICTURESQUE GOUVERNEUR.

By Alice Corbin Livingston.

Look at the grim, rocky fortress known as Gray's Hill; let your mind revert to the pioneer settlers in the boldly-outlined forest who gave a kitchen corner and the penny of privation for a neighborhood library; dream of oriental splendors where the setting sun turns its diminishing lights on the rolling hills o'ertopping the Sheldon Creek; lose yourself in rugged reveries in the northern portion of the town where hills "rock-ribbed and ancient as the sun" pervade, or follow the Oswegatchie, caressingly winding its course in picturesque abandonment and you can readily see how this normal, healthy child, Gouverneur, nestling in the foothills of the Adirondacks, owes its first charm to natural environment.

Within the mind strong fancies work,
    A deep delight the bosom fills,
Oft as I pass along the bank
    Of these fraternal hills.

Alice Corbin Livingston.

Since the days when the roving schoolboy let down the bars of Waid's Pasture, to revel in the wintergreen lot beyond, or the local and prosaic drain-pipe emptied its slimy but growth-reviving waters at the roots of the maple whose foliage took on the shape of a

sphere, the goddess of peace has waved her olive-branch and the barriers of isolated selfish-
ness called fences, are removed, leaving the verdant lawns as emerald carpets whereon the
common family of mankind may walk.

The beauty of the homes of Gouverneur is not in the lavish expenditure of wealth, for
it has no palaces, but in the care for the little details which make home attractive. The carefully trimmed lawns are sufficiently large to give tasteful settings to the homes. In the old
world the pavement takes the place of the sod here. As a consequence, there is a grey approach, repellant, cold and austere. There is infinite detail and difference in the dwellings,
for the distant architect has invaded the place, and so, no two are cut to the same pattern.
In many the touch of personal fancy and conceit in landscape decoration, given perspective
by broad streets and artistically arched elms and maples, separated by the smooth, white
macadam of the streets, make Gouverneur a city set on a hill and the most beautiful town
in this or any state.

"Beauty is truth," and truth manifested herself like a green bay tree and lo! old
Gouverneur Wesleyan Seminary is replaced by the modern high school, symmetrical and
severe, but expressing in its architectural lines good substantial thought for good substantial
people. It is an advance upon the old grey sandstone wall to which never an ivy clung.
"The drooping flower of knowledge changed to the fruit of wisdom" and as nature lavished
her wealth in mottled marble veins, the churches, outgrowing the sombre and ultra orthodoxy
of the past, took on new and splendid garments. Truly, Gouverneur is a city of churches
and one feels the silent influence of these stately edifices, the homes of thought and aspiration
suggestively realized.

> "Ever the Rock of Ages melts,
>   Into the mineral air,
> To be the quarry whence to build
>   Thought, and its mansions fair."

Nor is the commercial world lacking in the artistic. Devastating fires have resulted only
in fine brick and marble buildings, whose sky-lines do not bespeak the "overreach" but rather
a dignified concept for a practical people.

As the inner, true life needs not the blare of trumpet to make it known, so the modest
but elegant library strikes the keynote.

> "If thou indeed derive thy light from heaven,
>   Then to the measure of that heaven-born light
> Shine, Poet in thy place and be content."

Main Street and the Park 1860.

One of the few remain-
ing landmarks, the con-
fidant of every child
while in the joys and
sorrows of school-life, is
the bit of woodland,
Dodge's Grove, a pleasure
land which Nature fram-
ed for her delight, resting
in the very heart of the
busy town. This, too,
now bears the guinea
stamp. Homes are claim-
ing the right of way and
to the shame of Gouver-
neur, the only native forest remaining is nearing
the mournful condition of
"something remembered,
something lost."

Riverside, gently sloping in undulating waves toward the scarce-moving Oswegatchie, gives the beholder a glimpse of quiet stream and green meadow, where each bright blossom mingles its perfume with that of flowers which never bloomed on earth. Reverent care of an unconsciously conceived idea, aided by nature's kindly thought, has converted God's Acre into a fitting place in which to dream of the Sabbath of Eternity.

The most pardonable pride a Gouverneurian has in his beautiful town is the natural fall of water and its crescent rapid below, at Natural Dam. The steep and lofty marginal cliffs join the landscape with the quiet of the sky. The little lines of sportive wood run wild, impress one with thoughts of deep seclusion, made quiet by the harmony of the water's ceaseless song so that one forgets the rumbling mill-wheels near.

As the mind's eye rests upon this beautiful city in a bower of interarching foliage, the focal point is the simple, symmetrical Park, located in the center of the mart, surrounded by stores, banks, churches and educational halls, it seems silently to speak "Thou art troubled about many things—rest."

Many castles in Spain had been built ere all this wholesome taste manifested itself. The inner and outer eye had become so adjusted as to recognize beauty as a commodity, because when utility becomes artistic, it is re-created and in turn gives a higher grade of usefulness. Possibly because of its location, Gouverneur was first artistic, then utilitarian, and these in turn gave this blending of the practical and the beautiful, an expression of the One Mind Universal.

> "Beauty through my senses stole,
> I yielded to the perfect whole."

THE ANTIQUITIES OF THE HOUSEHOLD.

By Nettie Sternberg Whitney

Household Antiquities—The very words carry our thoughts back to our grandmother's attic! How we spun an imaginary thread on the great wheel or, perchance, brought from their corner, the candle-moulds or cherished foot-stove.

We little thought, then, the old spinning-wheel, relegated to the attic when not in actual use, would today hold a place of honor among our cherished treasures. It was only an article of service. On it was spun the yarn which was later made into all manner of woolen materials for the household.

The blankets were woven at home, the "full-cloth" for men's garments was woven and colored by the same hands, the stockings and mittens were knitted by the kitchen firelight, and if there still remained a few spare hours, the daughter of the house might be found busily engaged upon a piece of homespun cloth, fashioning her one garment of luxury,—a quilt, i. e., a woven petticoat, quilted by hand.

The little flax-wheel, with its distaff so enticing to the novice, was another busy article of the household machinery.

The flax was gathered from the fields and spread upon the ground to cure. When decomposed so the chaff or straw would break from the flax, it was taken up and threshed, the coarser or tow part removed, and the finer part or flax, twisted into hanks for the distaff of the flax-wheel. The tow was spun into coarse yarn, which in its turn was woven into heavy linen cloth suitable for men's working clothes, overalls, and grain bags. The flax made a finer grade of linen which was converted into tablecloths, sheets, towels, etc. The very finest grade was reserved for the Sunday shirt, with its collar attached, the white vest and linen trousers, the embroidered petticoat, collars and cuffs, and the valances for the spare bed.

From the products of these two wheels, the famous coverlids of our grandmother's days, were made. After spinning, the woolen yarn was doubled, twisted, and reeled into hanks or skeins. It was then colored and when dry, put upon the swift from which it was wound, by a quill-wheel, upon quills or spools for the shuttle of the loom.

The bleaching of the linen yarns required an equal amount of labor, so the making of a coverlid was no small undertaking The designs were quite elaborate, though usually of a conventional form while the colors were blue and white, occasionally changed for red or green and white While designs and colors might vary, one principle remained fixed—each coverlid contained white yarn and that was always linen The art of coverlid weaving was not confined to the women Many men were adepts in this work

Another treasured possession was the down bed, often used as a covering Imagine sleeping upon a feather bed with a down bed over you' Yet, how many boys, whose later years were made famous by deeds of valor, have finished the days labor and sought repose on a bed whose mattress was a husk tick, whose springs were supplied by the old rope bedstead, and whose covering was a down bed

The warming-pan was a newer device for the comfort of the guest It consisted of a large, round, shallow dish, usually of brass or copper, with a hinged cover and a handle about four feet long Burning embers were put into this pan, the cover securely fastened, and it was then moved about the bed between the sheets Its warmth must have been very welcome when one considers that many a house had no stove and but one fire place The foot-stove was an invention which partially filled a long felt want, because of its portability These little stoves, usually from eight to twelve inches square and six or eight inches high, were of perforated tin or sheet iron Their fuel was a charcoal of domestic manufacture In winter the stove was carried by its bail-like handle to church or in sleighs on the journey to town

The great clock, its face painted so white, its weights of iron and whose interior mechanism was made entirely of wood and whittled by hand, came as a much needed piece of housefurnishing Previous to the invention of the clock and sun-dial, the house-wife reckoned the flight of time by a certain shadow and a crack in the floor or some such stationary mark History records several instances where the grandfather's clock with its roomy case, has safely sheltered some member of the family from the attack of Indians

The introduction of candle-molds lessened the housewife's labor not a little The original method of doubling the wicks and then coating them with tallow, by dipping them into the hot liquid, suspending from a slender wooden rod between two chairs until dry and then repeating this process until the wicks attained the size of a candle, was long and tedious The moulds were easily threaded with the wicking and is easily filled with the hot tallow The absolutely necessary accompaniments of these tallow candles—the snuffers and tray—were always within reaching distance Occasionally the candle-sticks, snuffers and tray would be of brass or pewter but generally speaking, the candle-sticks, because of their required numbers, were of tin or wood In the humblest homes, sometimes a turnip was whittled into shape and made to do service as a candle-stick Then the fingers of the master or mistress of the house did the work of the snuffers The candle was followed by the fluid lamp The first of these were of pewter, about three or four inches across, either round or oval in shape, and having at one side, a projection about two inches long In them were burned tallow, bear's grease, or oil by means of a bit of rag or candle wicking which lay on the little projection and extended into the fluid Each lamp was supplied with a chain and hook or spike, by which it could be hung from a nail or fastened into the back of a chair if the light was needed lower These were called Betty Lamps

The old brass and iron knockers were not as utilitarian as ornamental The first door fastenings were wooden latches worked by a latch string which hung through a small hole, outside the door To lock the door, was simply to pull the string within the hole, thus cutting off all means of lifting the latch from without Small wonder is it that a more ornate decoration for the main entrance of the home was soon devised, and found its expression in these knockers which were the ancestors of our present day door bells

The kitchens were always cheerful with the glow from the huge fireplaces On hooks against the chimney, hung the cherished musket, which in Colonial days was often called the "Queen's-arm" Nearby hung the mould which shaped the musket bullets Think of the necessary labor' One at a time, they were run from the molten mass, cooled and extracted

The chief furnishing of every fireplace was the andirons—simple or elaborate, as the means of their possessor might allow. For the kitchen fireplace, iron was usually chosen, while for the best room they might be of brass or even steel.

In some homes the very costliest possessions—the pots and kettles—hung by pot-hook, crane or trammel, within the chimney place. The great brass or copper kettle often held twelve gallons. The iron pot might weigh thirty pounds and lasted in daily use for several generations. The iron skillets, gridirons, bake-kettles, and Dutch ovens were all made to stand on legs. Sometimes in the fireplace corner stood several three-legged iron stools, of different heights, called trivets. By their use, the desired proximity to the fire might be obtained. The need for this stilting up of cooking utensils is evident. If the bed of coals was too deep for the pots or skillets legs, then it must stand on a trivet or be suspended from above. From its swinging crane hung the iron teakettle with abbreviated spout and bulging sides. How clear the voice of its song, yet I have heard remarked of it,—"grandmother used to boil eggs in her iron teakettle".

Even toasting-forks and frying-pans were fitted with long, adjustable, wooden handles, which helped to make more endurable the heat from the blazing logs. Occasionally the fire did not crackle and blaze. Then the bellows was brought from its corner and the family cook proceeded to blow up the refractory flames.

In some kitchens the rotary paring machine had been installed and the product of the orchard and field thus finished, might be seen hanging from the ceiling, in long festoons of dried apples and circles of golden pumpkin.

The rare old china, so much sought after today, occupied a place on the kitchen dresser, dining rooms being chiefly in the great or town houses. The "flowing blue" mulberry and willow pieces were most in evidence, and proud indeed was the wife who could boast a set of dishes and a toilet set of the same pattern. The shapes of the dishes appear very quaint to us. Tea pots, sugar bowls, and cream pitchers often had legs while cups rarely had handles. The huge tureen and the platters of corresponding size were the cherished members of the set. Wooden plates, two-tined forks, and steel knives with bone handles, and pewter spoons were the usual accompaniments of the snowy homemade tablecloths. This last named article was sometimes entirely lacking, the neatly scoured boards being without cover.

Among the more elegant labors of the busy housewife, the arts of embroidery and lace making were paramount.

Who can describe the hours of patient industry beside the glowing hearth or flickering tallow candle? Who knows the hopes or fears that were woven into her silent stitchery? We only know that from her inherent love of things beautiful and her equal devotion to her self-imposed tasks, there were wrought for us those rare old treasures. Treasures of a time long passed away and whose memories fade with each succeeding generation. As we touch the filmy 'Tulip under-sleeves,' literally covered by its pattern of eyelet embroidery or gaze at the quaint cap of hand-run bobbinet lace, we often wonder how so much time could have been devoted to such tasks. Each piece represents so many hours, taken from a sturdy life, but not purloined from the necessary drudgery of every pioneer woman.

CONTRIBUTED PAPERS.

"OLD HOME WEEK."

Its Conception, Development and Consummation.

By F. H. Lamon.

The idea of attempting to interest the people of Gouverneur in an "Old Home Week" gathering, in commemoration of the one hundreth anniversary of the settlement of the town of Gouverneur, was suggested to me in February last, by the effort then being made by the people of Jefferson County in a similar enterprise.

F. H. Lamon.

A personal canvass was made by me, among influential citizens, who without exception gave words of approval and promises of support when the scheme was briefly outlined before them. This gave the needed encouragement and on February 21 the Northern Tribune published the first story on the subject. Indications of interest immediately cropped out on all sides, enabling the Tribune the following week to tell of the sentiment that had been aroused and to publish several letters of commendation from prominent citizens. A week later, the time seeming right, another personal canvass was made with the result that a public meeting was called by J. S. Corbin, G. S. Conger, S. F. Hartley, E. D. Barry, J. B. Johnson, Amasa Corbin, W. R. Perrin, J. G. Clutterbuck, and F. W. Sprague, as a temporary committee, for Thursday evening, March 9, at the village board room in Masonic Temple, with the following citizens present: J. V. Baker, A. E. Cushman, H. O. Johnson, Charles M. Taitt, E. W. Abbott, B. F. Brown, F. M. Holbrook, Fred Norton, E. H. Neary, J. B. Johnson, G. S. Conger, F. W. Sprague, H. C. Rogers, S. F. Hartley, George L. Tait, and F. H. Lamon.

Judge Conger was chosen chairman and F. H. Lamon secretary. The purpose of the meeting, namely, to consider the advisability of holding an "Old Home Week" gathering, was explained, and the plan being approved by all present, it was unanimously voted that it was the sense of the meeting to hold an "Old Home Week". A committee for selecting a date and providing a place for holding a second public meeting, was appointed, consisting of J. V. Baker, S. F. Hartley, B. G. Parker, J. B. Johnson, and B. F. Brown.

The second meeting was held in Masonic Temple Hall, Thursday evening, March 16, Judge E. H. Neary, presiding. The business session was preceded by a short entertainment, consisting of a solo by Orvis Hesselgrave, readings by Misses Blanche Hodgkin and Blanch Van Derzee, followed by an address by Col. Martin R. Sackett, United States Consul at Prescott, Ont., and remarks by J. S. Corbin, Allen Wight, F. M. Holbrook, Fred H. Norton and others. The scheme was heartily approved by the 200 or more persons present. A permanent executive committee consisting of Amasa Corbin, J. B. Johnson, B. F. Brown, A. T. Johnson, Walter W. Hall, and H. G. Aldrich was named, Amasa Corbin being elected president, F. H. Lamon, secretary, and Henry Sudds, treasurer. This executive committee was empowered to create sub-committees and to have entire charge of the undertaking. Mr. Corbin was out of town at the time of his election, but on his return, accepted the office as did all the others. At a meeting shortly succeeding Mr. Corbin's return, August 24-30 was the time selected for holding the "Old Home Week" gathering and Centennial celebration.

The problem of financing the enterprise was solved by the decision to publish an illustrated souvenir history of the towns of Gouverneur, DeKalb, DePeyster, Macomb, Rossie, Hammond, Fowler, and Hermon. To raise the money required on a legitimate basis, by giving the public a work of value, instead of attempting to solicit donations proved to be the keynote of success. J. S. Corbin was selected as historian-in-chief, to be assisted by half-a-hundred persons, each selected with a view to his peculiar fitness for handling the subject assigned. How well their work was done is shown by the volume of which this article is a part.

Subscriptions for the history were solicited by the members of the executive committee,

the secretary and a few others who were anxious to have the undertaking a success. The first $800 was quickly raised. Increased effort brought it to the $1000 mark. Buyers soon became scarce and by the time $1200 had been received, the committee was about to abandon the undertaking. In the meantime, there had been considerable talk of erecting a monument to the memory of the pioneer settlers and the soldiers and sailors of the town of Gouverneur, in connection with the celebration. In place of the monument, D. G. Scholton, village president, suggested a memorial arch for which he submitted a design, upon which, President Corbin at once declared himself in favor of the arch. With the "Old Home Week" and the history to finance, however, Mr. Corbin, felt that to take on the burden of erecting the arch would require more time than he could afford to give. It was a case of "live or die" for "Old Home Week." A meeting of the executive committee was held, consequently, on Thurs-

day, May 4, at which it was found that but $1200 worth of histories had been sold. "Boys, if you will show me $2000 in subscriptions for the history by Saturday night, I will agree to finance the arch," was the statement made by Mr. Corbin. This inspired renewed courage but when Saturday night arrived, several hundred of the $2,000 were still lacking. It was a dramatic moment, when J. B. Johnson slowly arose and impressively offered a document containing the signatures of the following citizens: W. W. Hall, H. C. Rogers, B. F. Brown, W. R. Perrin, B. G. Parker, J. B. Johnson, F. H. Lamon, J. B. Thompson, E. W. Duffie, D. G. Scholton and J. V. Baker, each of whom agreed to pay for enough copies of the history at the standard price of $5 per volume to make up the deficiency. The smile of appreciation which radiated from the president's face was worth all the chances the "boys" were taking. Turning to Mr. Scholton, he said: "Prepare the working drawings of the arch according to the design you have submitted and give me a perspective view drawing at the earliest date possible." "Old Home Week" was thus saved from a humiliating death, and the illustrated history and the memorial arch were assured.

The work of compiling historic data, pictures and biographical sketches, and of securing subscriptions for the history was now taken up with greater enthusiasm. Business men left their desks and went out among the people in the interests of "Old Home Week." By main force, the idea was lifted, boosted and carried to a triumphant success.

A distinctive part of this success was owing to the idea of the memorial arch which immediately became popular. Bids for furnishing the stone and erecting the arch were asked for from producers of Gouverneur marble, the contract being awarded to the Extra Dark Marble Company for $1650 Permission to erect the arch over the walk crossing the park in East Main Street was unanimously voted by the Board of Village Trustees, after which it was decided that the first ceremonies would take place most appropriately on Memorial Day

At 11 45 on the morning of Memorial Day ground was broken for the arch The ceremony was a simple, yet impressive one Following the rendition of "Home, Sweet Home," by the Gouverneur Citizens Band, President Corbin made a few remarks appropriate to the occasion and invited Christopher Brown as one of the oldest natives of the town, to remove a spadeful of earth from the site of one leg of the arch, and Osmon Welch as one of the oldest veterans to perform a similar service on the site of the other leg Others of Gouverneur's elderly and honored citizens followed, among them being E W Abbott, J D Easton, Allen Wight, Ward Glazier, Elijah Bailey, Harvey D Thompson, Frank M Holbrook, P P Clark and George S Parsons

A contribution of $150 from E H Barnes Post G A R formed the nucleus of a fund for financing the arch The balance of the money is being raised by popular subscription, hundreds of men, women and children giving according to their means The corner stone of the arch was laid on Flag Day, the name of every contributor to the fund being deposited in the stone The U S Government will, it is expected, donate a Dalgren gun to be mounted upon the arch, which is to be completed and dedicated "Old Home Week"

The plans for "Old Home Week" include a series of high class entertainments, morning, afternoon and evening for seven full days Re-unions of Gouverneur Wesleyan Seminary students, of the veterans, churches, Masons, Odd Fellows, Foresters, Maccabees, and all fraternal organizations, band concerts in the park afternoons and evenings, triumphal arches erected at several points in the village, prominent personages of state and nation to be present and royally entertained, a day set apart for the opening of Gouverneur's industries, the lace mill, paper mill, marble quarries, and talc mills and mines, an industrial parade, and military and civic demonstrations, public buildings decorated, electric fountains and illuminations making the business section spectacular at night Among the entertainments offered will be festival choruses, an opera, Ball of the Silver Greys, banquet to distinguished visitors, parades, serious and comique, a tournament of knights with a crowning of the Queen of Beauty A log cabin is to be erected at headquarters for a historic loan association, and as a bureau of information

---

THE BANK OF GOUVERNEUR.

By H Sudds

Previous to 1860, Gouverneur was without Banking facilities, the few residents of the town who found it necessary to borrow from Banks, being obliged to go to Watertown or Ogdensburg, and as the good old custom then prevailed of requiring all notes to be absolutely paid at maturity, borrowers would "skirmish round" and borrow or pick up enough of the bills of other banks to pay their notes, and could then get a new note discounted and receive the proceeds in the bills of the lending bank, it being a great object with the banks in those days, to keep their bills in circulation

In the year 1860, however, shrewdly foreseeing the future growth and needs of the village, and with due regard to their own interests, Charles Anthony of Gouverneur and James G Averill and William J Averill of Ogdensburg became the pioneer bankers of Gouverneur and on the first day of October of that year, began the banking business under the firm name of Charles Anthony & Co, in the small, white, one-story wooden building previously used by Mr Anthony as a law office, standing on the site of the store now owned by Mrs Helen Draper and occupied by G P Tait & Son as a dry goods store Mr Anthony already had a small brick vault in the office, an old safe was borrowed from Ogdensburg and a cheap desk and counter provided, although for a few weeks, Mr Anthony personally did all the work and received the deposits on his law table

The paid in capital was only $10,000, one-half contributed by Mr Anthony and the remainder by the Averills, but owing to the known financial strength of the partners, the firm enjoyed unlimited credit, and if, as was sometimes the case, the cashier had to "skin round" on the street to pick up currency to meet checks, no one was in the least disturbed, but if they could not get their money that day, they would wait till the next.

The business increasing, Mr. Robert P. Wilson was employed to do the clerical work, which he continued to do, till on the breaking out of the Civil War in 1861, he enlisted and

the position was offered to Henry Sudds, who for the next four or five years did all the bank work and also a good deal of law copying, until the increasing business of the bank required all his time. He was then appointed Cashier and continued to fill that position, with various assistants, till early in 1871, when he resigned to engage in the banking business in Ogdensburg and Andrew J. Holbrook was appointed in his place.

In 1873, the prosperity of the concern warranted and required better accommodations and it was removed to a new and commodious building at the corner of Main and Park streets, where the business is still carried on, although the interior has recently been entirely remodelled, resulting in the elegant and up-to-date banking room now in use.

Early in 1874, Mr. Holbrook's management not being entirely satisfactory, Mr. Sudds, whose new business had not been very successful, was offered and accepted his old position, continuing on without change until 1879, when the partners being well advanced in years, decided to incorporate, and the business was merged into a State Bank, called the Bank of Gouverneur

Of the members of the firm of Charles Anthony & Co, Charles Anthony, afterwards President of the Bank of Gouverneur, died in 1892 and was succeeded by Newton Aldrich William J Averill, afterwards Vice-President of the Bank of Gouverneur, died in 1897 and was succeeded by Henry Sudds James G Averill died in 1896

The business of Charles Anthony & Co had always been fairly successful and although the partners had regularly drawn dividends at seven per cent, besides two or three large extra dividends, one of them equalling the entire capital, the remaining capital and accumulated earnings were sufficient to provide the entire $50,000 capital of the new bank, and to divide up about $25,000 more on the final closing up of its affairs

On the seventh day of July, 1879, the Bank of Gouverneur began business with Charles Anthony as President, William J Averill, Vice-President, and Henry Sudds, Cashier, one-half the stock being owned by Charles Anthony and the other half by the Averill family

In 1882, Henry Sudds became a stockholder and director and in 1883 it being thought best to take in a few other prominent business men as stockholders, the capital was increased to $80,000 It was further increased to $100,000 in 1891, this time by a Stock Dividend from the accumulated earnings, and Mr Newton Aldrich and his son became stockholders at that time In the year 1900, James O Sheldon, who had filled the position of Teller for several years, was appointed Assistant Cashier and now acts in both capacities The Bookkeepers of the bank have been successively, C J Cushman, H H Noble Frank B Hoover George W Smith and Leon B Murray

After a continuous experience of almost forty-five years, and passing through the many periods of panic and depression occurring during that time the managers feel an honest pride in the fact that all obligations have been met on demand, that no customer has ever lost a dollar by them and that the institution is at the present time, larger, safer and in better condition than ever, and while their earnings and profits have been by no means phenomenal, they have been considerably better than the average, the records showing that while the amount of capital actually paid in has been only $10,000 and $30,000 of that no longer ago than 1883, there has actually been paid in dividends

By Charles Anthony & Co	$ 55,000
By Bank of Gouverneur	180,200
Add to this the present Capital and Surplus	154,000
Making a total of	$389,200

And showing a profit of $349,200 on the $40,000 paid in

The increase in business is well shown by the fact that while in June 1880, the

Capital and Surplus was	$ 60,000
And the Deposits	135,000

The respective amounts are now

Capital and Surplus	$154,000
Deposits	440,000

The list of former Directors, now deceased, includes the well known names of Charles Anthony, James G Averill, William J Averill, William H Averill, Edwin G Dodge and William R Dodge, the present Directors are, Henry Sudds, Newton Aldrich, Charles H Anthony, Edward D Barry, James H Rutherford and Herbert G Aldrich, and the officers are Newton Aldrich, President, Henry Sudds, Vice-President and Cashier, and James O Sheldon, Assistant Cashier

The Bank has for some years paid its stockholders ten per cent per annum, besides paying all taxes

THE FIRST NATIONAL BANK.

By Leslie Burdick.

The First National Bank of Gouverneur, N. Y., was organized February 19th, 1881, by Hon. George M. Gleason, Hon. Henry R. James, Hon. Dolphus S. Lynde, Abel Godard, Lawson M. Gardner, A. L. Woodworth, Hon. Leslie W. Russell and Hon. Newton Aldrich. The above named constituted the first Board of Directors and, with Mr. Gleason as President, Mr.

Aldrich as Vice President and Mr. Woodworth as Cashier, the bank opened for business April 2nd, 1881, with a paid up capital of $55,000.00.

In 1891, F. M. Burdick succeeded Newton Aldrich as Vice-President and in 1901 was elected to succeed G. M. Gleason as President, who retired on account of ill health but retained his place as Director until his death later in the same year.

Fred H. Haile was elected Vice-President in 1901, and A. L. Woodworth has been Cashier since the bank was organized.

The present Board of Directors consists of F. M. Burdick, President; Fred H. Haile, Vice-President; A. L. Woodworth, Cashier; Arthur T. Johnson and Lorenzo Smith. The bank now has the same amount of capital, $55,000 00, an earned surplus fund of $19,900 00, and undivided profits of $10,000 00 The deposits amount to about $400,000 00

During its existence the institution has enjoyed uninterrupted prosperity as may be best shown by the fact that it has paid in dividends to its stockholders the sum of $116,600 00

After a period of nearly twenty-five years the constantly increasing business necessitated the enlargement of the banking rooms which was done during the past year New steel ceiling and wall coverings have beautified the interior, while modern office devices, new desks and a copper bronze railing on the counter facilitate the handling of business

The books, papers and records of the bank are all contained in a separate modern fire proof book vault, fitted with metal filing cabinets and appliances for their proper care and preservation

In these improvements the greatest stress was laid upon safety and security and to this end was constructed a modern fire and burglar proof steel safe deposit vault This structure is in full view of the street both day and night and is built entirely of massive plates of armor plate and chrome steel welded and bolted together into one mass The outer door to this vault weighs over four tons and is locked by twenty-four bolts held in place by two combination locks and a triple movement time lock The inner door is locked by eighteen bolts held by a double combination lock The whole mass weighs about twenty tons and is as impregnable to the attack of burglars and fire as human ingenuity can make it In this vault are kept the funds of the bank together with private safe deposit boxes for rent to individuals for the safe keeping of valuable papers, jewelry, mementoes, etc

GOUVERNEUR SAVINGS AND LOAN ASSOCIATION
By Benj F Brown

It was in December, 1891, that a paper was circulated by B F Brown, securing the names of all persons who were favorable to organizing a local savings and loan association The first meeting was called on January 6th, 1892, at which time M R Sackett was elected chairman and B F Brown Secretary, at whose office the meetings were held After discussing the matter at some length a committee of three, consisting of A W Orvis, B F Brown and B G Parker, were appointed to draft articles for a constitution in order to perfect a permanent organization A committee was also appointed consisting of M R Sackett, J B Johnson and B G Parker, to advertise a general meeting to be held on January 19th At this meeting the report of the committee on a constitution was adopted and it was further decided to incorporate under the law of New York State, provided by an Act passed April 10, 1851

On January 14th, 1892, the following officers and trustees were elected for one year B G Parker, President, M R Sackett, Vice-President, B F Brown. Secretary, Frank Starbuck, Treasurer, A W Orvis, Attorney, Trustees, S W Payne, A L Woodworth, Henry Sudds, W W Hall, and J F Hodgkin Of these Parker, Brown, Orvis and Payne have continued to hold the same office

The first stock of the Gouverneur Savings and Loan Association (as it was so christened), was issued February 13th, 1892 There were no less than ninety-six original stockholders subscribing for 393 shares of $250 each The general plan originally was for each subscriber to pay, or deposit, with the Association, 25 cents per week on each share until the sum of said payments plus the dividends earned and credited to each account was equal to $250 Nine of these accounts, or 27 shares, were paid regularly until Dec 1904, when the Directors declared the shares matured In maturing these shares there had been paid in $168 and $82, credited as dividends A few years after organizing, two other methods of savings were devised where large amounts could be deposited at any time One was to issue a certificate of not less than $50, or multiples of $50, but not to exceed $2500 Our third and last method was to receive deposits of $1, or multiples of same not to exceed $2500, on a book account, the same to be withdrawn at pleasure and not unlike a regular Savings Bank Book This has been our most popular stock and has induced many to lay by for future contingencies a snug little sum that will prove of great good.

It was the belief of the promoters that a local institution that encourages and fosters the savings of its people is of untold benefit to that community. The men that have put their personal efforts into building up this savings association has not been for personal gain, as they have not profited beyond any other citizen; but the spirit has largely been to help and

encourage those to ways of saving and thrift who need such help and to assist others in building and owning their own homes. Our motto has been, "The American Home the Safeguard of American Liberties." This broad and philanthropic view has not been confined to those who have had the personal oversight, but many other citizens who have spoken a good word and expressed confidence in the men and methods who were in active charge.

The Association has grown steadily and rapidly being the largest local association in the State north of the large cities of Syracuse and Utica. The assets have increased from $7,314.77 at the close of the first year to nearly $400,000 at the present time.

As this Association is purely mutual with a minimum expense, it has been able to credit 7 to 8 per cent per annum on its Installment Stock and 3½ to 4 per cent per annum on

Savings and Prepaid Stock, beside accumulating a surplus of about $5,000. These dividends are all credited or paid semi-annually.

The present officers have served for several years and are as follows: B. G. Parker, President; T. J. Whitney, Vice President; B. F. Brown, Secretary; H. C. Rogers, Treasurer; A. W. Orvis, Attorney. Trustees—E. H. Neary, S. W. Payne, G. S. Conger, Geo. E. Pike and J. O. Sheldon.

THE FIRST BAPTIST CHURCH.

By Mrs. E. H. Neary.

The pioneers of this town brought with them, in addition to the goods and chattels that have been mentioned, Christian principles, which they practiced from the first settlement of the town.

The Sabbath was strictly observed, meetings being held for religious purposes in the various homes. Meetings for prayer were also held in addition to the Sabbath observance. Most of the people were members of Baptist Churches in their former homes.

As time passed their numbers increased and they felt the need of a church home.

They formed articles of Faith and Practice and a Church Covenant and presented these to a council consisting of three persons, Rev. Amasa Brown, Timothy Attwood, and Eli Carrington of the First Baptist Church of Hartford, Washington County, who met to consider the petition of these people for the organization of a church. On the eighteenth day of February, 1811, the committee accepted the articles of faith and they were constituted a church of Christ with 18 members. The name chosen was the First Baptist Church of Gouverneur.

The members of this early church were as follows: Jonathan Payne, Stephen Patterson, Eleazer Nichols, John Brown, Hezekiah Nichols, Isaac Austin, Benjamin Drake, Aaron Att-

The First Baptist Church.

wood, Joel Attwood, Tabitha Austin, Zilpha Gates, Patty Payne, Betsey Thompson, Nancy Nichols, Lovicie Smith, Polly Brown, Alice Payne, and Hannah Attwood.

Jonathan Payne, one of their number, was their first pastor and served five years. The church joined the St. Lawrence Baptist Association at its first session in Stockholm, in 1812.

From 1816 to 1825 the church was without a settled pastor but the pulpit was supplied the greater part of the time and 163 were added to the membership.

In 1822, a number were dismissed to form a church in Fowler and in this year also the church completed its first house of worship so far at least as to occupy it.

During the pastorate of Rev. J. W. Sawyer, who was called in May 1828, there was much disturbance in the church growing out of the Morgan excitement in the Masonic order. The church voted to exclude all members who refused to withdraw from that order. Most of them refused and were accordingly excluded. This continued for a little over a year when they returned to the church on terms that were acceptable.

In 1834, sixteen of their members were dismissed to form a church in Richville.

In 1841, during the pastorate of Samuel Pomeroy, the first parsonage was built, the house now owned by James H. Rutherford on Grove Street.

Again members were dismissed to form a church in North Gouverneur, but in 1847 the church disbanded and they resumed their membership.

In 1838, the church reports 199 members, 115 scholars in the Sunday School, 13 teachers, a Woman's Benevolent Society, and a promising Woman's Missionary Society. For missions, education, and Bible translation, they contributed $176.65.

The pastors following Mr. Payne were Noah Barrel, J. W. Sawyer, Clement Havens, E. W. Locke, N. Broughton, Samuel Pomeroy, J. N. Webb, Conant Sawyer, H. A. Morgan, O. W. Babcock, George A. Ames, J. W. Daniels, J. B. Child, J. W. Putnam, E. P. Weed, H. C. Townley, M. L. Rugg, H. S. Swartz, F. A. Marsh, D. D. Monroe, A. W. Rogers and J. G. Clutterbuck.

Under J. W. Putnam's pastorate the present parsonage was built. While Rev. H. C. Townley was pastor, during the winter of 1878 and 1879, $2,500 were spent in repairs, organ and stained glass windows.

Under the pastorate of Rev. D. D. Monroe, it was resolved to build a new edifice. Accordingly the corner stone of the present building composed of Gouverneur marble was laid June 5, 1894, and it was dedicated November 5, 1895, the forty-fifth anniversary of the dedication of the former edifice. The new one cost about $25,000.00.

Rev. A. W. Rogers.

Mr. Munroe was succeeded by Rev. A. W. Rogers, a young man of marked spiritual attainments as well as financial ability, who began his labors April 1, 1897. His work was greatly impeded by the heavy burden of a church debt of about $12,000, as a result of the erection of the new edifice. The pastor realized that the prosperity of the church largely depended on the removal of that debt. He labored earnestly and efficiently to remove this heavy financial burden and succeeded in doing so before the close of his pastorate, November 1, 1903.

Soon after, the church extended a call to Rev. J. G. Clutterbuck, the present pastor, who was then a student in Hamilton Theological Seminary. He accepted the call, continued his studies in the Seminary and preached for the church most of the time up to his graduation in June 1904. His portrait appears in the clergymen's group.

According to the church record, the present membership is 213. A Sabbath School has been maintained since the beginning and numbers at present 320.

In conclusion, the church can appropriately say, surely, goodness and mercy hath followed us all our days.

THE PRESBYTERIAN CHURCH.
By Mrs. Harvey L. Smith.

On May 24, 1817, seven years after the organization of the Baptist Church, and eleven years after the arrival of the first settlers, the Presbyterian Church had its birth. Hence it has a history lacking but twelve years of a century.

The Presbyterian Church.

The church was founded with six names upon her roll: William Cleghorn, Jonathan Colton, Elijah Hough, William Colton, Mrs. Betsey Colton and Mrs. Hannah Colton.

These names deserve to be perpetuated, as they are the beginning of a church life, whose influence for good in this community is beyond the computation of any man.

The church was formed under the supervision of Rev. Nathaniel Dutton, of Champion.

Two months after the church's inception the first sacrament was administered to twenty-two members.

Nearly three years elapsed before the church was legally constituted a society with corporate power, which was accomplished April 29, 1820.

During these three years, they had neither pastor nor stated preaching.

Reading meetings were held nearly every Sabbath, and even printed sermons were so scarce that "Burder's Village Sermons" were read and re-read to the congregation, but it is recorded that religious privileges were highly appreciated and thankfully enjoyed.

So far they had no house of worship. In 1820, the first meetinghouse was erected. It is thus described: "It was enclosed, a floor was laid, seats were constructed of slabs with the flat side upwards, and stool legs."

Here, with unplastered walls, without a stove in winter, the congregation worshiped for five years.

In carts and sleds drawn by oxen, these people came to this tabernacle punctually and regularly, some of them from a distance of five miles.

Thus they struggled on until their hearts were made glad by the settlement of Rev. James Murdock as their first pastor. He served the church faithfully for four years, and it grew and prospered.

In 1824, the first rude structure was replaced by a more comfortable building. Up to this time the membership did not exceed seventy-five. In 1825, the church experienced a work of grace, which is historic through the labors of the noted evangelist, Rev. Chas. G. Finney, with the result of eighty persons added to its number.

Mr. Murdock was succeeded by Rev. Richard C. Hand, who continued in the church six years. He was greatly beloved by the people and richly blessed in his labors. Following his pastorate, the church was without a pastor for five years.

Among those who served as stated supply during this trying experience, were Rev's. Jonathan Hovey, Bucknell and Robert F. Lawrence. On October 10, 1838, Rev. Simeon Bicknell was installed as pastor. He remained only two years, and was succeeded by Rev. John Orr, who supplied the pulpit for two years.

Rev. B. B. Beckwith.

In 1843, Rev. B. B. Beckwith was called to be the pastor. "Here seemed to have ended the troubles of the church and it now entered upon a career of steady and useful habits, growing and strengthening from year to year.

The same year in which Mr. Beckwith became the pastor of the church, the building of a new house of worship was begun, and completed in 1844. After a long and fruitful pastorate of twenty-three years, Mr. Beckwith was compelled to resign by failing health. He was succeeded by Rev. N. J. Conklin, March 13, 1866. The ministry of Mr. Conklin is fresh to a large number of the present membership, and precious to all who were associated with him. Of rare executive ability, strong in faith and love for Christ, a genial friend and faithful pastor, the church during his ministry enjoyed great prosperity. A new parsonage was built and the church enlarged and the membership grew from 179 to 297.

Mr. Conklin preached his farewell sermon in 1879. A call was then tendered Rev. Tryon Edwards, who entered upon his labors February 1880, and closed them in 1886. A scholar of exceptional learning, a writer of no mean ability, a gracious and godly man, his memory is cherished here with esteem.

The present pastor, Rev. William F. Skinner, received from the church a unanimous call and was installed in June 1887. He came to us in the ardor of his youth. He remains with us in the strength and vigor of maturity. It behooves us not to speak too much here of his warm heart, his thorough culture and his true piety. Suffice it to say, that we hope he may long be the last pastor. Through his faithful labors, the church has nearly doubled its membership since his ministry began—numbering now 445—and more than doubled its benef-icences. Through his influence the people were inspired to build and pay for the spacious and costly edifice it now occupies.

Of the Sunday School with upwards of 300 members, its missionary work and its Christian Endeavor Society, there is not space to speak here.

The beautiful parsonage just east of the church, is a recent gift to the Presbyterian Society from Mrs. Myra A. Dean and her daughters.

THE METHODIST EPISCOPAL CHURCH.

By Mrs. F. M. Barber.

The Methodist Episcopal Church

The early history of Methodism in Gouver-neur is unique, and peculiarly interesting. But few persons now living are aware of the almost insurmountable difficulties which the "early fathers" had to overcome in the for-mation of their so-ciety here because of the bigotry, ridicule, prejudice and opposi-tion current at that period everywhere. Or-iginally they were part of a circuit embracing Spragueville and sev-eral other surrounding villages, but as early as

1828 they were strong enough to have a regular pastor, Benjamin Dighton, by name, but as they had no church their meeting place is unknown.

In 1830, Dr. Townsend who lived in the house now occupied by Wallace McKean, opened his dwelling as a temporary church-home to this struggling but determined people, where they remained until the Brick School House was rented for the modest sum of $13 per year. Here, in the building now occupied by the Steam Laundry, the standard of the M. E. Church was first raised by the Rev. Lyndon King in 1832, and a "village class" was formed con-sisting of Isaac Smith and wife, Joseph Smith and wife, Moses Kenyon and wife, and a few others. Later they were greatly reinforced by the coming of Dr. E. L. Beardslee and wife. These sturdy men and women were the *pioneers* of the early church in this locality. With brave hearts and willing hands they laid the foundation stones of their own peculiar faith *deep* and *strong*. Their heroic courage is well represented by an old favorite hymn they often sang:

"We want no cowards in our band
Who will our colors fly,
Our army calls for *valiant* men
Who're not afraid to die."

After using the Brick School House for three years they found more desirable quarters in the chapel of the Gouverneur High School. When this building was destroyed by fire January 1, 1839, they were compelled to return to their former place, remaining until the completion of the Gouverneur Wesleyan Seminary. This property being under the control and patronage of the Black River Conference, became their permanent home from 1839 until 1863. The chapel and other rooms were used for places of worship. At this period they were greatly strengthened by the helpful presence of Rev. Jesse D. Peck, who was Principal of the High School at the time it was burned, and it was through his ceaseless efforts and energy that the Seminary was erected. In 1862, under the pastorate of Rev. Francis A. O'Farrel, the society were able to purchase the Congregational Church which stood on the site of the present church edifice for $1,000. It was a "red letter day" for this people when the full amount was secured by subscription, and they were privileged to occupy their *own* property free of debt. Little did they dream that in seven years the old shell would be outgrown, and in its place would rise a new and modern structure as if by magic, capable as was supposed at that time, of accommodating their congregation for a generation to come. Not only temporal but great spiritual prosperity attended their efforts at this time, which resulted in a large increase of membership. In 1897, this building became inadequate to their needs and the old structure was replaced by the commodious one of marble now occupied. During the pastorate of S. T. Dibble, the present church edifice was erected and a modern parsonage was built, also churches at Natural Dam and Hailsboro. Although now a separate charge, they were originally branches of Gouverneur Church.

Owing to the itinerant system the list of pastors is long. The older ones have long since entered "the silent bourne."

Very precious memories cluster around the names of those who have served in later years, the most of whom are now engaged in active service in other fields. They are C. W. Parsons, A. J. Cowles, (now deceased), W. D. Chase, M. W. Chase, S. T. Dibble, S. W. Greenfield, E. B. Topping, C. L. Peck. M. G. Seymour is the present pastor. His portrait appears in the group of clergymen.

No genuine sacrifice is ever wasted. The early seed of Methodism scattered in virgin soil in weakness, has been raised by God in mighty power. With a membership now numbering over 400, with a flourishing Sunday School of 900 pupils, including the "Home Department," the "Cradle Roll," and the "Cosy Branch," with a church property valued at $25,000, who can tell of the marvelous results which may be achieved in the future? One by one the workmen fall but the work goes on. The living links which bind the present with the past are few, but whatever of change may come the church will stand and throughout all ages the watchword for her worshipers shall be,

> "Build thee more stately mansions, O my soul,
> As the swift seasons roll!
> Leave thy low vaulted past!
> Let each new temple, nobler than the last
> Shut thee from Heaven, with a dome more vast
> 'Til thou at length art free
> Leaving thine outgrown shell by life's unresting sea."

THE PROTESTANT EPISCOPAL CHURCH.

By Mrs. Jessie A. Paul.

The Protestant Episcopal Church.

In the year 1866, many residents of the village, desiring the worship of the Protestant Episcopal Church, had quietly assembled with other denominations, until an opportunity offered to resolve themselves into a corporate body.

Rev. J. Winslow of Watertown, N. Y., being the Missionary in charge at that time held the first services, February 1866, in the chapel of the Wesleyan Seminary, which was kindly tendered them by the Trustees of the school. Within two months, April 16th, 1866, parish organization was effected, and Trinity Church was incorporated. The first Wardens were B. F. Skinner and A. B. Cutting; Vestrymen chosen, Wm. H. Bowne, J. S. Honeycomb, J. D. Easton, A. E. Norton, A. M. Barney, A. S. Egert, G. E. Burt and Thomas Jones.

Judge Benjamin F. Skinner.

Aaron B. Cutting.

Rev. J. Winslow, as a minister, established many Parishes in Northern New York, and will be remembered as a genial, courteous man, having a merry joke for everyone. No public meeting was complete without him, and underneath his merry speech there was always a sober thought, a serious view, to be impressed. He died in 1893, aged 74, and his memory will be cherished by all who knew him.

Within another two months, an eligible lot of land was offered, on which to build a church, by Messrs. Jas. G. and Wm. Averill, of Ogdensburg, N. Y. The vestry resolved to build, a subscription was started for raising funds, and never was a paper more industriously circulated. The ladies, too, united their efforts for the advancement of their beloved object. Festivals, weekly sociables, sewing societies, suppers, were held to raise funds for furnishing the new church, and they worked joyously and unitedly. The Ladies Aid Society was organized in 1866 and elected the following officers: Pres., Mrs. A. Egert; Treas., Mrs. J. B. Preston; Sec., Mrs. L. Barney; Directresses, Mrs. S. Beebee, Mrs. Hoover and Mrs. Conklin. There were thirty members. As a result of the year's work $900 was added to the church fund.

The corner stone was laid on the 10th of September, 1866; the clergy present were: Acting Rector, Rev. J. Winslow; Rev. Kiding, of Potsdam; Rev. Linn, Theresa; Rev. Brewer, Carthage, (now Bishop of Montana); Dr. T. Babcock, Watertown; Rev. Biret, Canton; and Rev. Foster Ely, Rondout, N. Y. Early in the fall of 1867 the present unique church was completed, at a cost of about $7,000. The basement being fitted up for a Parish school, and used for that purpose.

July 8th, 1867, Rev. E. Dolloway was called to the Rectorate and remained three years; a Sunday School was established and an efficient choir aided the young Rector in making the services impressive and devotional.

May 1869, a house and spacious lot at the northwest corner of John and South Streets was given for a Parish Rectory, by Judge James Smith, of Buffalo, N. Y. The church was dedicated free from debt July 29th, 1869, with appropriate ceremonies and it was provided in the original subscriptions for the building of the church, that the pews or sittings should be assessed yearly for the contingent revenue of the Parish. In 1870, Trinity Church was admitted into the Diocese of Albany. Rev. J. H. Babcock served as Rector for one year, when Rev. Wm. M. Ogden succeeded him and remained four years, from 1875 until 1880. The following clergymen have served as Rectors of Trinity Church: Rev. T. Barry, Rev. H. C. Miller, Rev. J. Thornlowe. Rev. B. K. Kirkbride. When the Rev. S. B. Bostwick of Sandy Hill, N. Y., accepted the Parish and died while in charge, March 16th, 1881, he was succeeded by Rev. J. D. Skeene, who was Rector for a year and six months, during which time a pipe organ was purchased, and an organ chamber was built.

The old Rectory was sold and the proceeds put into a larger and more convenient house, at the rear of the church lot, which was completed in 1882. Feb. 1883, Rev. B. K. Phelps succeeded Rev. Skeene. From April 1885, Rev. Sommerville served as Rector until 1889.

Since that date Rev. Jas. A. Dickson has very efficiently continued the work of the Parish. The heavy debt on the church at that time, was paid, $5,000 being given to the church by Mrs. S. Beebee. The group of clergymen also contains his portrait.

In 1893, the old organ was exchanged for a new one at an additional expense of $1,100. The money was raised within the year by the Ladies Aid Society, Mrs. J. B. Preston, President, and this was her crowning work in the church, where she had labored devotedly from the first. The Ladies Aid Society are still helping to defray the expenses of the church, and since 1900 have paid into the treasury, $1,150.

Rev. J. A. Dickson.

A branch of the Woman's Auxiliary to the Board of Missions is doing considerable Mission work.

The young ladies of the Parish formed the Guild of St. Agnes to assist in the expenses of the church. Music and the congregation will bear testimony to their continued success in furnishing fine music.

THE CATHOLIC CHURCH.

By Katherine Leahy.

In 1850, it is said, there were only two Catholic families in Gouverneur. But its business, at that time increasing, a number of Irish and French Catholics settled in the village and its vicinity and services were occasionally held for them by Rev. James Mackey of Ogdensburg, and by other priests. These services were held in private houses. But the erection of a church being contemplated, in 1856 a lot located on South Street was purchased of Judge Dodge. However, as the number of Catholics was yet small and their means limited, nothing was done about building and the lot was afterwards sold.

Gouverneur was then attached to the parish of Canton and was attended regularly from that place. During the ministry of Rev. James O'Driscoll a lot and building located on Park Street was purchased as a place of worship. This building, formerly the Methodist

Church, was dedicated December 22, 1874, but was destroyed by the great fire of January 15, 1875. An insurance of $1,000 was collected and a new church, their present house of worship on Gordon Street, was erected in 1875 and dedicated by Bishop Wadhams on Nov. 25th, in that year. Its whole cost was four thousand dollars.

The Catholic Church

In 1877, Gouverneur was detached from the parish of Canton and Rev. Thomas Kelleher was appointed its first resident pastor. He remained in charge of the parish only about one year.

Gouverneur was then made a part of the parish of Rossie and was attended from that place until 1882, when Rev. D. Guilbault was appointed its resident pastor and remained until the appointment of Rev. E. C. Laramee in 1883. Rev. Father Laramee remained in charge of the parish until October, 1896, when he was succeeded by its present pastor, Rev. M. F. Gallivan. The parish at present consists of about one hundred and forty families.

THE FIRST UNITARIAN CHURCH.

By Mrs. G. S. Conger.

For many years a growing number of people in Gouverneur and vicinity while recognizing the value of religious sentiment and the importance of incentives to the highest aims in life, yet felt unable to subscribe to the creeds of the so called orthodox churches and were unwilling even by a nominal connection with them to be considered as believers in the forms and dogmas which seemed inseparable from those churches. No movement was made toward the formation of a separate society until in April, 1895, when Rev. Ure Mitchell of Edwards began holding meetings in Masonic Temple. Unitarian literature was distributed and interest was aroused, and in May, 1895, a preliminary organization was formed, which declared that its "object in addition to charitable work, moral teaching and correct living should be the searching after and dissemination of religious truth." A board of trustees was elected May 26, 1895, consisting of Moreton P. Abbott, Miss Loie Austin, Charles S. Bodman, Gerrit S. Conger, Miss Ella Hall, Miss Nora Herring, G. Murray Holmes, Eddis N. Miller, Harvey H. Noble, Miss M. M. Smith, James F. Sayer, and Mrs. Barbara E. Waldo, and Rev. Mitchell was engaged and regular meetings were held.

In November 1895, platform meetings were held in Union Hall, at which Rev. D. W. Morehouse, Secretary of the Middle States Conference, Rev. Samuel R. Calthrop, Rev.

Thomas R. Slicer and Rev. Wm. M. Brundage, all prominent ministers of the Unitarian faith, took part. Shortly afterward a branch of the Woman's Alliance was organized among the ladies, and it has ever since been of great service to the cause.

In March 1896, Mr. Mitchell resigned as pastor, and from that time until November 1896, occasional services were held partly conducted by candidates, partly by lay members, but largely by friendly ministers of our sister denomination, the Universalist church.

June 9, 1896, a meeting was held, 29 members being present at which it was voted to incorporate under the name of "The First Unitarian Church of Gouverneur." The following nine trustees were elected by ballot: G. S. Conger, A. T. Johnson, Dr. C. B. Hawley, J. F. Sayer, H. H. Noble, Charles Bodman, George G. Royce, M. P. Abbott, and A. W. Orvis.

Articles of incorporation were prepared and filed June 12, 1896.

The First Unitarian Church.

In November, 1896, Rev. Hasket D. Catlin accepted a call from the church and immediately entered upon his duties as pastor.

The society had from the beginning held its meetings in Masonic Temple Hall, but it now began to consider the feasibility of building a church. In November 1897, a committee was appointed to look up a site and the next spring a building lot on Trinity Avenue was purchased and a building committee appointed.

Mrs. Minerva P. Nichols, an architect of Brooklyn, very kindly made and presented the plans for the church, and in July 1898, work on the new church was begun. The first service in the church was held December 4, 1898, and the dedication services were held January, 1899, at which Revs. D. W. Morehouse, S. R. Calthrop, W. M. Brundage, H. P. Forbes and H. D. Catlin took part.

In January 1900, Mr. Catlin tendered his resignation as pastor. Mr. Catlin had served the society most acceptably for nearly four years. He was a gentleman of rare attainments and his ripe scholarship was nowhere more agreeably shown than in his Wednesday evening bible study class, which to those who attended was most instructive and helpful. Mrs. Catlin was held in high esteem as a most agreeable lady and very active in all that pertained to the social life of the church.

Rev. Charles A. Livingston accepted a call and began his pastorate in November 1900. Installation services were held in January following. In June 1901, Mr. Livingston married Miss Alice Corbin, daughter of J. S. Corbin of Gouverneur. Mrs. Livingston became a most efficient worker and aided her husband in all the activities of the church. Mr. Livingston was a man of great literary ability, and a brilliant preacher. Many of his sermons were masterpieces and it was a matter of deep regret to the congregation when he tendered his resignation to take effect January 1, 1904.

In June 1904, Rev. Wayland L. Beers became the fourth pastor of this church. Mr. Beers is a man of scholarly attainments and deep religious feeling, a fine sermonizer and heartily interested in his work, in all of which Mrs. Beers is an able and efficient helper. Under his pastorate renewed encouragement is manifested and an effort is now being made with excellent prospects of success to pay off the remaining indebtedness of the church. Mr. Beers' portrait appears in the group of clergymen.

THE GOUVERNEUR SCHOOLS.
By Prof. F. R. Darling.

The history of the Gouverneur schools begins with the year 1809, when the first school was opened in a log house which stood near the present site of the Presbyterian church. To Silas Brooks of Antwerp, fell the honor of becoming the first schoolmaster. Evidently the responsibilities of the position were too great for him to bear for it is related that he resigned at the end of the first week and his place was taken by a young woman, Miss Betsy S. Sackett, who conducted the school for some time. Another of the teachers in this early school was Sylvester McMasters, but the names of the most of them have long been forgotten.

Early in 1826, the movement began for the establishment of a High School. A few years before, academies had been organized at Lowville and Belleville and there were some

First High School, Burned in 1839.

forty other schools of this grade in the state, but with the exception of the two mentioned above none were to be found in the northern part. Franklin Academy at Malone was not established until 1831, the Ogdensburg Academy came into existence in 1835, another was founded Watertown the next year, while the good citizens of Syracuse did not feel the need of an institution for higher learning until our own had been in operation for more than a quarter of a century.

The Gouverneur High School came into existence officially on April 5, 1828, when it was incorporated by the legislature. The school was made possible by the subscription of $540 with which a second story was added to the brick building that was being constructed at this time for the use of the public school. At first the High School met with considerable opposition from those who held that the common school was sufficient for the needs of the

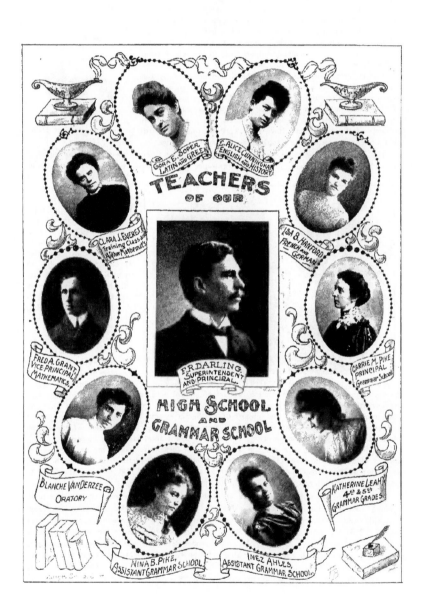

TEACHERS
OF OUR

CORA E. SOPER
LATIN AND GREEK

L. ALICE CUNNINGHAM
ENGLISH AND HISTORY

CLARA J. EVERET
Training Class
Math or Mathematics

ISA B. HANFORD
FRENCH AND GERMAN

FRED A. GRANT
VICE PRINCIPAL
MATHEMATICS

F. R. DARLING
SUPERINTENDENT
AND PRINCIPAL

CARRIE M. PIKE
PRINCIPAL
Grammar School

HIGH SCHOOL
AND
GRAMMAR SCHOOL

BLANCHE VAN DERZEE
ORATORY

KATHERINE LEAHY
4TH & 5TH
GRAMMAR GRADES

NINA B. PIKE,
ASSISTANT GRAMMAR SCHOOL

INEZ AHLES,
ASSISTANT GRAMMAR SCHOOL

people and thought that the new institution would be aristocratic in its tendencies. This opposition, however, soon died
out and the people became united in their support of the school.
Rev. Joseph Hopkins became the first principal and under his
leadership the number of students increased until in 1834 there
were 57 students and the money apportioned to the school from
the literature fund amounted to $205.95. Early in the same year
a two story brick building was completed and occupied by the
school. This structure stood on a lot which now forms the
eastern end of the public park. In 1837, Mr. Hopkins resigned
and the school passed under the control of the Black River Conference of the Methodist Episcopal Church, which assumed all

Prof. Joseph Hopkins.

the debts of the institution. Rev. Jesse T. Peck, who afterwards became President of Dickinson College, succeeded Mr. Hopkins as principal.

The first great crisis through which the school passed came in 1839, when the building
and all its contents burned. Most of the insurance proved worthless and the trustees found
themselves the guardians
of an institution practi-
cally bankrupt. The citi-
zens, however, promptly
rallied to its support and
subscribed $2,600. A loan
of $2,000 was obtained
from the State and this
enabled the authorities to
rebuild. The present site
of the High School was
purchased of Wolcott Griffin and a stone building
erected at a cost of $5,-
500. With its n a m e
changed to Gouverneur
Wesleyan Seminary, the
school occupied its new
quarters in 1840.

East Side, West Side and High School.

For nearly thirty years
the school prospered and little that is worthy of special note occurred. Then in 1868 came
the second crisis when the church transferred its support from Gouverneur to Antwerp.
Once more friends rallied to the support of the Seminary and by their energy turned what
had seemed a misfortune into a blessing. Those who had held aloof because of the church
affiliations of the school became strong supporters. The capital stock was increased to $50,-
000 and $4,000 was used to repair the buildings. The legislature passed an act allowing the
town of Gouverneur to levy a tax of $20,000 for building and repairs. This money, however,
was never raised. Instead a supplementary act was passed in 1871 allowing the town to
raise annually the interest on this sum for the support of the school.

In the meantime as the village grew, the number of pupils increased, until the old brick
building used as a public school became too small. A lot was purchased on Gordon Street,
East side, and a frame building with accommodations for a larger number of pupils was
erected. This was ready for use in 1873. With the advantage of a new building, ample
equipment and support by taxation, the public school flourished and soon began to encroach
upon the preserves of the Seminary. Able principals and teachers were employed and the
course was gradually extended until a year of high school work had been added. Everywhere
throughout the State similar conditions existed. In fact a new and powerful adversary was

arising which in a few short years was destined to overthrow the old line academy. This was
the public high school. One after another the old academies either passed out of existence or
were absorbed by their rivals. The movement began to be felt in Gouverneur in 1880. The
people gradually became restless under the burden of supporting two different systems and
here and there a citizen began to advocate consolidation.

TEACHERS, EAST SIDE SCHOOL.
Nellie Parsons, Principal;   Margaret Canfield,   Julia Regan,   Pearl Fletcher,   Mary S. Parks.
Margaret Cahill,   Blanche Hodgkins,   Iva I. Dodds,   Jennie McCloy, Principal South Side School

On the West Side of the river, there was another school district known as district No.
12, with its set of district officers, its school house and its teachers. This school also prospered
with the growth of the village, and as the marble industry flourished it became more and
more evident that it was to become a large school.

This was the situation when, early in the eighties, several of the prominent citizens on
both sides of the river began to urge the unification of the two public schools and the Semi-

John McCarty

nary. Prominent among the leaders of this movement were
John McCarty, Robert Markwick, J. S. Corbin, Fred H. Norton,
and B. F. Brown, who was at that time principal of the public
school on Gordon street. For several years the campaign was
carried on in the newspapers and on the street. The brunt of
the struggle was borne by John McCarty, to whom belongs in a
great measure, the credit for the final success of the movement.
Finally, March 29, 1887, a meeting called by Henry Sudds, John
McCarty, James W. Ormiston, trustees of District No. 1, and J.
B. Johnson, A. S. Whitney, Joseph Laberdee, trustees of District
No. 12, was held in Union hall. This meeting by a decisive vote
of 222 to 77 decided in favor of the Union Free School District.
It was also decided by this meeting that there should be nine

trustees of the new district and Henry Sudds, J. B. Johnson, L. M. Lee, J. W. Ormiston, Joseph Laberdee, B. L. Barney, John McCarty, A. S. Whitney and Fred H. Norton, were elected the first members of the Board of Education. Steps were immediately taken to complete the consolidation by securing control of the Seminary. There was no serious opposition and on May 23, 1887, the Seminary property was leased to the Union Free School District. Later

TEACHERS, WEST SIDE SCHOOL.

Harriet Marshall, Principal;   Mary Thayer,   Nora M. Palmer,   Mary Coulthart,   Jennie L. Wilson,
                    Winifred S. Palmer,   May L. Jeffers,   Agnes Hacket.

the title was transferred and the Gouverneur Wesleyan Seminary ceased to exist as a separate institution.

James F. Tuthill, A. B., was made the first superintendent of the new system of schools and principal of the High school, while B. F. Brown became vice-principal. The wisdom of the unification was immediately shown by the increased efficiency in all departments. The attendance rapidly increased and in 1889 it was found necessary to provide additional accommodations for the pupils. The question was settled for the time being by the building of an addition to the West Side School at a cost of $6,000 and the erection of a new building on Depot street just south of the railroad at a cost of $3,000. Mr. Brown's photograph reproduced appears in the Savings & Loan group.

The number of pupils attending the Seminary and at the East Side School continued to increase and it soon became evident that more room must be provided for these rapidly growing schools. Various plans were suggested and at the annual school meeting held Aug. 2, 1892, the first steps were taken toward providing for a new building by appointing a committee to report upon the matter at a later meeting. This committee reported September 13, and the special meeting voted unanimously in favor of a new building for the academic department of the schools. The real struggle came over the selection of the site. What was known as the Sheldon property on Church street was thought by some to be the proper place

South Side School.

for the new building while others urged the use of Dodge's grove. The matter was, however, finally decided in favor of the site of the old Seminary for the reason that the land where that building stood would revert to the original owner unless it continued to be used for school purposes. The Board of Education immediately secured plans and at a meeting of the voters held in Union Hall, February 23, 1893, submitted a proposition for the erection of a building at a cost of $47,500. This proposition was defeated by a vote of 449 to 432. The village had just been bonded for $60,000 to provide for water works and many of the tax payers, while not opposed to the idea of a new building, felt that action should be postponed until this debt had been reduced somewhat. The friends of the measure, however, did not allow the matter to drop, and at public meetings held March 4 and 11, in Preston's Hall, continued the campaign. The opposition was strong but at last at a meeting held in Union Hall, April 13, 1893, it was voted by 447 to 437 to appropriate $45,000 for the erection of a building. This amount did not prove sufficient and an additional $5,000 was spent in completing the structure. With this amount the present beautiful building was completed and occupied in 1895. At this time the name was changed from Gouverneur Seminary to Gouverneur High School, its original title. The pressure at the East Side School was relieved by the removal of some of the higher grades and the formation of a Grammar School in the new building.

Gouverneur Wesleyan Seminary, Demolished 1895.
Old Baptist Church   Old Presbyterian Church

Since the completion of the High School, the Board of Education has provided liberally for its equipment until at the present time it has a good physical laboratory with apparatus valued at $1,000. There is also a large natural history collection and an excellent working library of 1700 volumes. It is expected that a modern chemical laboratory will be fitted up in the near future. Three strong courses are offered at present, the academic, Latin-scientific and classical and gradu-

BOARD OF EDUCATION, 1905.

ation from these courses with a certificate from the Principal will admit to many colleges and schools which do no accept the diploma furnished by the State A teachers' training class has been instructed for some years and is now considered the strongest in the state The number that may be in the class at any one time is limited to twenty-five and there are so many applicants for places that it has become necessary to hold competitive examinations for admission

During the past year more than 1100 pupils have been in attendance in different departments of the school and twenty-nine teachers were employed The High School alone registered at one time 243 students, and more than 75 of these were non-residents This is the largest registration the High School has ever known Since the organization of the Union School system there have been 181 graduates A large proportion of these have gone to college and normal schools and it is hoped that the proportion will be still larger in the future

What the future holds in store for the schools of Gouverneur, we cannot tell For more than three-quarters of a century they have occupied a leading place among the schools of the state There will be no lagging behind In the future as in the past, there will be progress everywhere and they will continue to send forth men and women well fitted to win their way in life

PRESIDENTS OF THE BOARD OF EDUCATION

Henry Sudds, 1887-1888, F H Norton, 1888-1889; Robert Markwick, 1889-1895, A S Whitney, 1895-1897, M R Sackett, 1897-1903, C W Hewitt, 1903-Still serving

SECRETARIES OF THE BOARD OF EDUCATION

James Ormiston, 1887-1889 A I Johnson, 1889-1895 W R Dodge, 1895-1899, C W Hewitt, 1899-1903, S W Close, 1903-Still serving

CLERKS OF THE BOARD OF EDUCATION

Charles McCarty, 1887-1889 George F Pike, 1889-Still serving

MEMBERS OF THE BOARD OF EDUCATION

Henry Sudds, 1887-1888, J B Johnson, 1887-1888, L M Lee, 1887-1890 J W Ormiston, 1887-1889, Joseph Laberdee, 1887-1889, B I Barney, 1887-1889, John McCarty, 1887-1893, A S Whitney, 1887-1893, 1894-1897, F H Norton, 1887-1892 Robert Markwick, 1888-1897, B F Drury, 1888-1891, E H Neary, 1889-1890, George S Parsons, 1889-1895, A I Johnson, 1889-1895, J H Rutherford, 1890-1891, C W Hewitt, 1890-Still serving, Frank Starbuck, 1891-1897, B F Brown, 1891-1894, C H Graves, 1892-1898, W R Dodge, 1893-1899, A C Gates, 1893-1899, M R Sackett, 1895-1904, C P Laile, 1895-1901, G S Conger, 1897-Still serving, A J McDonald, 1897-1903, V P Abbott, 1897-Still serving, G D Hazelton 1898-1901 S W Close, 1899-Still serving, J C Callahan, 1899-Still serving, S H Davidson, 1901-Still serving, A A Potter, 1901-Still serving, H G Aldrich, 1903-Still serving, A J McCoy, 1904-Still serving

PRINCIPALS

———— Ruger and ———— Morgan (before incorporation), Rev Joseph Hopkins, 1830-1837, Principal, Rev Jesse T Peck, 1837 1840, Principal, Loren B Knox, 1840-1842, Principal, Rev A W Cummings, 1842-1844, Principal, Rev John W Armstrong, 1844-1850, Principal, William W Clark, A M, 1850-1852. Principal Rev E C Bruce, A M, 1853-1860, Principal, Rev Andrew Roe, A M, 1861-1863, Principal, Rev George G Dains, 1864-1870, Principal, M H Fitts, 1871-1876, Principal, H W Hunt, A M, 1877-1880, Principal, Martin R Sackett, A M, 1881-1887, Principal, James F Tuthill, A B, 1887-1891, Superintendent and Principal, Donaldson Bodine, Ph B, 1891-1898, Superintendent and Principal, John C Bliss, A B, 1898-1900, Superintendent and Principal, Harry DeW DeGroat, A B, 1900 1904, Superintendent and Principal, Frederick R Darling, A B, 1904-Still serving, Superintendent and Principal

THE SEMINARY AND SOME OF ITS TEACHERS AND ALUMNI.

By M. R. Sackett.

No rural county of New York can boast more or better educational facilities than St. Lawrence. A generous sprinkling of Scotch among its early settlers may be responsible for the high value placed upon sound learning in this northern county. A full fledged University of three colleges, a normal school second to none of the state, a fully equipped and endowed school of technology, together with numerous high schools, giving a full academic education and working under the general statute creating Union Free Schools, attest the large interest shown by the people of this section in the work of higher education. Gouverneur had hardly emerged from the stumps before her citizens took steps to secure educational facilities for their children in advance of the common school. In this movement lies the origin of the institution which was to become the Gouverneur Wesleyan Seminary. This was in the Spring of 1826. The school was to be controlled by the "subscribers," each ten dollars carrying one vote in the management of the school. The school was opened in 1827; the first teacher was named

Josiah Waid.

Ruger. The school was incorporated as the Gouverneur High School, April 25, 1828. The incorporators were Aaron Rowley, John Spencer, David Barrell, Harvey D. Smith, Josiah Waid, Alba Smith, Almond Z. Madison, Robert Conant, and Joel Keyes. Their working capital was made $20,000, in shares of ten dollars each. In 1830, a new school house was erected after wearying discouragements in a search for funds. It is said that the plans of this structure were drawn by Philip Kearney, a name to be remembered. The building consisted of a central portion two stories high with wings at each side. By the generosity of the community, with a subscription of $400, from Prof. Joseph Hopkins of Potsdam, who became its first principal, the building was finished and school opened in 1834. Hopkins resigned in 1837 and the trustees in March of the same year transferred the school to the Methodist Episcopal Church, under conditions set forth in written articles. Jesse T. Peck was the first principal of the school under the Methodist regime. The buildings and apparatus were burned in January, 1839.

The heroic struggles to rebuild, and to get the means for raising the money required need not here be told. With indomitable courage and energy, led by the principal, its friends rallied and the work was done .

The cost of the new structure was $5,500. April 25th, 1840, by act of the Legislature, the name of the institution was changed to the Gouverneur Wesleyan Seminary—the school which people now living remember, and which under the same corporate name, for forty-seven years, or until the establishment of the present school system of the village, exercised a powerful influence over the youth of the section and through them and their works upon subsequent time.

The building which all our adult population today recall, stood upon the site of the present high school building. It was demolished in 1894, and every stone of it hidden in the strong foundations of the present modern and handsome structure. This Seminary for many years, furnished the best academic education to be had in the county. It fitted for college and business life. It supported not only the usual literary courses but gave instruction in music and painting. Its students came from every town of the county, and its old catalogues show that "Upper Canada" contributed not a few students to the famous school. Jesse T. Peck was its first principal, a name famous in the annals of the Methodist Church. He became subsequently president of Dickinson College at Carlisle, Pa., and later was made a Bishop in his church, achieving its highest honor. He was the author of a number of books and a preacher of great eloquence and power He never lost his interest in educational work, which truth is abundantly attested by the benefactions of his will for Syracuse University, with the establishment of which great institution he had much to do He died full of years and honors some fifteen years since at his home, Syracuse, N Y

The Seminary was ever fortunate in its principal teachers They were successes in teaching and administration The principals in order were, Jesse T Peck, Loren B Knox, A W Cummings, Dr James W Armstrong (one of the ablest men and best teachers of his generation, a truly great man), W W Clark, Eli C Bruce, Andrew Roe, Geo G Dains, M H Fitts, Hiram W Hunt, and M R Sackett

Martin R Sackett, who was the last to hold the position, was elected in the Spring of 1880, before his graduation from college, and taught the Seminary successfully until the present system was inaugurated, 1887, the Seminary ceasing to exist as it had until that time been constituted

The institution sent out men who became eminent in many lines of activity over the nation This imperfect paper can note but in a cursory way, some of the men who have added fame to the old Seminary She furnished pioneers for the opening of the great West A number of her sons became justly eminent on the pacific coast In business, politics, the church, in literary and in scientific lines of activity—everywhere are to be found men who went out from the halls of the old sandstone building which faced the park for so many, many years We can mention only a few of them from a long list of equally worthy

Dr Erastus Wentworth went from the Seminary as a missionary to China at an early day before such sacrifices became common affairs He achieved success in his chosen avocation, but his work there broadened under his hand He possessed a mind wonderfully apt in linguistic research He was attracted by the study of the Chinese language and literature He studied it profoundly and became a leading authority, so recognized the world over, not only upon the language of that remote kingdom—far more remote then than now He was intrusted with important work by our government, which ultimately led to fair commercial intercourse and a friendly feeling We speak now of the "open door," it may not be generally known that a former Seminarian had much to do in achieving that mighty consummation in the Orient Clinton Hastings went from the Seminary in 1841 to Iowa, then way out west From there he migrated overland to California, was a 49er He became one of the first citizens of that great state both as a lawyer of the first rank on the coast and as a capitalist It was he who gave the funds to found the "Hastings Law School" at San Francisco, now the law department of the University of California His work in the organization of the new state of California and in various lines of activity was of an high order He wrote his name deeply upon the institutions of that rich land Another who made his mark in the great west was Ora S Easton He was also one of the Argonauts who sought gold on the Pacific coast He was the first city surveyor of San Francisco He mapped out the town which was destined to become a great city The Parsons family furnished a number of students all of whom amounted to something Charles S Parsons is at the present President of the State National Bank of St Louis, Mo, a leading bank of the west He was the president of the National Bankers Association from 1890-3 Another son, Lewis B Parsons, fitted for Yale at the Seminary, and was graduated from Yale College about 1846 He enlisted in the Civil War and arose to be a Brigadier General He was stationed at St Louis under Grant, and had charge of the quartermaster's department of the whole Mississippi valley His work was of such a character as to call forth compliments from the great commander in chief At the close of the war he became much interested in politics and achieved notoriety He was the candidate of the democracy of Illinois in 1884, for Governor, and although no democrat could have hoped to win in that state that year, General Parsons made a splendid run A relative of Gen Parsons was more fortunate in 1892 in the person of Adlai E Stephenson, who was elected Vice President with Grover Cleveland A third of the Parsons family, Philo P Parsons, was president of a large bank in Detroit Mich, from 1885 to 1895 This family surely has left its mark upon the civilization of our common country It should be a matter of pride to recall during the centennial days soon to be observed, the fact that the Parsons boys were started from Gouverneur Wesleyan Seminary

The school gave its full quota of boys to the War of the Rebellion She furnished five colonels and two generals at least and a multitude of minor officers Col Albert M Barney went from Gouverneur His command was the 142nd Regiment Col Abel Godard commanded the 60th Regiment which led the charge at Lookout Mountain To write the history of the gallant old sixtieth one would needs have to write the history of the Civil War The regiment was with McClellan on the peninsula, with Slocum at Gettysburg, then was sent west to Tennessee, then fought it out with Sherman in the Atlanta campaign Col William M Goodrich of Canton commanded the 60th when she went out He was shot at Antietam N Martin Curtis of Depeyster, a gallant soldier still living and hale and impressive in presence as ever, was a captain, then a colonel, then a general, remembered everywhere where the deeds of the sixties are recalled as the hero of Fort Fisher All these were Seminary students

The poet, Caleb, of Lewis County, not unknown to the literary world, was a student of the Seminary back in the forties

The Eustis family of Hammond sent two sons to the Seminary, both of whom have achieved prominent positions in the business and financial and political world John Eustis of New York City is a leading lawyer there, has been Park Commissioner, and is in every sense a strong man His brother, William H Eustis has made for himself a name in the west He went to Minneapolis in 1861 He finished at the Seminary in the class of '69, pursued his education at Wesleyan University and Columbia Law School He was associated in the practice of law with John R Putnam, subsequently Supreme Court Judge of this district He has won wealth at Minneapolis, has been mayor of that hustling city, ran for Governor on the Republican ticket, and was the first Republican in the history of the state to fail of an election, due we are sure, to no fault of his but to adverse conditions beyond his control He has had an influence in national politics The National Republican Convention of 1892 was held at Minneapolis largely through the efforts of Mr Eustis

Dr Clarence Waldo, professor of mathematics at Purdue University, is worthy of mention in any list of Gouverneurians who have made their mark He has devoted his abilities to the teaching profession and has accomplished a good work His brother, younger, Charles H Waldo, has achieved success in the railroad world, having worked all the way up from the telegraph key to the superintendency of the Cincinnati, Hamilton & Dayton Railroad, a large and growing line of the middle west

Judge James M Smith of Buffalo, got his start at the old Seminary He remembered the community with the gift of the site of our present village library He achieved great wealth and the respect of all

James M Madison also of Buffalo, who died but recently, was educated here He achieved wealth and position as a banker

J Lawrence Johnson of Heuvelton, attended the Seminary in the late sixties He is now a Chancery Judge in the courts of New Jersey

Walter C Noyes, one of the later time graduates, shortly before the Seminary was lost in the Union School, has made a success of himself and achieved a Judgeship in the Chancery Court of Connecticut

This list might be indefinitely extended were there space and time to look up the record fully No mention is here made of those living in this immediate vicinity who have been students of the old school It were only possible to give but a sketch of some of the more conspicuous names and this has been done with the idea of being just to all within the knowledge of the writer, and if any conspicuous omissions have been made they have been unintentional

THE EARLY PAPERS.

By Helen I. Parker.

Helen I. Parker.

It was mid-afternoon of an April day in 1849 when the first copy of the first newspaper to be published in Gouverneur was struck off from a hand press in a room on the ground floor of the building then standing on William street, known as the old church. Gathered about to witness the novel proceeding were as many persons as the small office would accommodate. and it was a cordial reception the new enterprise met with. A practical printer by the name of Wilson had brought into the town a hand press and sufficient type for printing a six-column folio, which he named "Northern New Yorker." As were other newspapers of the day, the "Northern New Yorker" was largely devoted to the publication of political debates and articles on questions of National policy. The news items were mostly upon events in distant cities, and the strictly local matter consisted almost entirely of advertising. Short stories. with a moral, and poetry, usually occupied the first page. The "Northern New Yorker" changed hands several times in the two years and three months of its existence. Besides its founder the names of Goodrich and Greenleaf appeared as editors and proprietors. Nelson Bruett & Co. owned the paper afterward.

In July, 1852, appeared "The Laborer," published at Gouverneur every Wednesday morning in Conklin's block, corner of Church and William streets, by Martin Mitchell. "The Laborer" was a temperance organ. The character of the reading matter was similar to the first mentioned. It was a five column folio and the typographical appearance excellent. At the beginning of 1853, Mr. Mitchell took a partner, Ira D. Brown, who continued his labors but a few weeks. The publication next appeared under the name of "St. Lawrence Free Press," Mr. Mitchell and A. M. Hurlbert, editors and publishers. It was enlarged to six columns to the page, and took an active part against slavery as well as intemperance. Local news items appeared more frequently. In its second volume the name was enlarged to "St. Lawrence Free Press and Maine Law Advocate," and Mitchell and Hurlbert were succeeded by Mitchell and Armstrong. Early in Vol. III, J. J. Emmes had become the editor. Emmes dropped the second part of the paper's title, but still continued to advocate temperance and anti-slavery. Early in the year 1855, the "St. Lawrence Free Press" was removed to Ogdensburg, and Gouverneur was without a newspaper for several years. Although the greater portion of news distinctively local was in the advertising columns, these early papers were a credit to the journalism of the day. No record of their circulation is within reach beyond the statement that there were seventy Smiths on the subscription list of the earliest paper.

THE GOUVERNEUR COMMERCIAL AND NORTHERN RECORDER.

In October, 1866, appeared the first number of "The Gouverneur Commercial," a six column folio, published monthly by Miss M. M. Smith, who was also the editor. It was largely devoted to local news, the Gouverneur Wesleyan Seminary among the principal topics, Miss Smith being much interested in that institution in which she was an instructor for some years. During the second year of its existence the publication was changed to a weekly and "Northern Recorder" added to the name. The paper continued under the same management until March, 1873, when the office was moved to Rome.

Several amateur papers have at different times been printed in Gouverneur. The earliest of these was "The People's Friend," printed by Alonzo Van Duzee, of Gouverneur, in 1869, but giving Watertown as the place of publication.

In 1872, B. G. Parker came into possession of the press and type used by Alonzo Van Duzee. He began printing a monthly, bearing the name of "The Nut Shell." It was a three column folio, and its existence reached into the second year. This was succeeded by "The Temperance Visitor", four columns, B. G. Parker, editor and proprietor, an outgrowth of enthusiastic temperance meetings held weekly in the old Seminary chapel. The first number appeared May 1, 1871, and the short lived venture lapsed during the summer. At the same time "The News," dated at Hailsboro, edited by Hurbie Clark, and printed by B. G. Parker, had a career of four months, its issues appearing semi-monthly from March 15, 1874, to the following July.

Robert W. Beardslee, twenty-eight years after the original 'Nut Shell' appeared started an amateur paper under the old name. It was entered at the post office as second class matter and existed for about two years.

The Grand Army Journal

The Grand Army Journal was established in Utica under the name of "The Campfire," in 1884. Both name and ownership were soon changed and Rev. George B. Fairhead became the editor and proprietor. On June 6th, 1894, B. G. Parker purchased the subscription list and good will of the paper, and published it from the office of the Gouverneur Free Press. Miss Helen I. Parker was the editor. In 1903, Miss Parker became also the owner of the paper. As the name indicates the paper is devoted to the Grand Army of the Republic, the Woman's Relief Corps, the Sons of Veterans and allied patriotic orders, and is the recognized official organ of these societies in New York State. It is a nine column folio, published every other Saturday, and its circulation is throughout New York and New England. Today the Grand Army Journal occupies the unique position of being the only publication in the United States devoted solely to the interests of the Orders above named.

The Northern Tribune

The Gouverneur Publishing Company was organized in the spring of 1887, for the purpose of publishing a newspaper for the town of Gouverneur and adjacent sections, and for conducting the business of printing and publishing generally. The stock of the company was fixed at $6,000, and was taken by citizens of the town, although the promoter of the company, M. R. Sackett, controlled a majority of the issue. An entirely new and complete outfit of newspaper and job type, presses, and other printing material and machinery was purchased and installed, the office being located in the second story of the Egert block. The publication of "The Northern Tribune," the name adopted for the paper, began June 11, 1887, when the first copy of the paper issued from the press. It's first "leader" announced that the new publication would be republican in politics, clean in tone, would stand for Gouverneur as against any other town, would print only wholesome matter as opposed to sensation disguised as news, would cater to those enterprises which make for good in the community. The people gave the new paper generous welcome. It added subscribers to its list rapidly and from the first did a large job printing business. In the fall of this year, the subscription list of the Ogdensburg Signal was purchased and added to the Tribune's, giving the paper a list as large as most similar papers achieve after years of effort. The history of the enterprise for some time following is not other nor different from that of the common experience of business ventures. Competition was sharp, there being at the time three weekly papers in the town. The newcomer had to sometimes battle hard for its share of trade, sometimes getting it, often taking a minor share. In the spring of 1892, Mr. Sackett purchased the plant entire, of the Gouverneur Herald-Times of its owner H. G. Reynolds, and consolidated its subscription list with that of the Tribune, selling the type, presses and other material to B. G. Parker, of the Gouverneur Free Press. The Tribune now removed its office to the larger and better adapted quarters in the Herald-Times block. A new and larger press was installed and the business greatly increased. The work of its editor had begun to attract the attention of the politicians of the county and in 1893, Mr. Sackett made a canvass of the county for the office of County Treasurer, achieving a unanimous nomination in the fall caucuses, equivalent in St. Lawrence County to an election. We believe it to be true that no weekly paper of the county ever had so large a circulation as this paper enjoyed during the years immediately following the purchase of the Herald-Times. Opportunity presented in 1897, for obtaining an office on the ground floor, and the present quarters in the Holmes block were leased.

Having been honored with an appointment to the consular service, the editor, Mr. Sackett found it impracticable to retain the active management of the business, at the same time serving the federal government, therefor the corporation leased its plant in February 1904 to Wm. F. Bowhall, who had been with the business in one capacity or another, with only two or three interruptions, from its inception, the editorial department of the paper

THE NORTHERN TRIBUNE STAFF.

remaining where it had been from the beginning, with Mr. Sackett. F. H. Lamon was installed as local editor, and under this arrangement the business has been conducted smoothly and successfully to date.

The paper has waged some notable battles for good government and local order. It has favored every enterprise looking to the upbuilding of the town of Gouverneur and believes that some share of the success the town has reaped has been due to its efforts. It has ever been outspoken in denunciation of what it believed wrong. While believing sincerely in the tenets of the republican party and upholding its policies, it has been willing to admit that democracy has her virtues, and with a great history behind it is entitled to the respect due to a real elemental force in the political life of the nation. In the exploitation of the great lumber, talc, marble, and other local enterprises the paper has done its full share. It was the first in print with the opening and advantages of the great lace plant now domiciled in town and doing so much to add wealth and population to Gouverneur. It was from the first an advocate of a proper celebration of Gouverneur's one hundredth anniversary of "Old Home Week." It has given large space and much attention to educational matters, believing that the school question and its collaterals furnish the biggest of problems with which a growing village has to deal.

The officers of the corporation at present are. President, Hon E W Abbott, Secretary, M R Sackett, Treasurer, B F Brown; Manager, Wm F Bowhall

THE HIGH SCHOOL ECHO

"The High School Echo," twelve two-column pages with cover, has from time to time been published monthly during the school year by the students of the High School It was devoted entirely to school news and printed at the office of the Gouverneur Publishing Company

The Methodist Sunday School has also at irregular intervals issued a paper for circulation among its members

"The Poultry Industry," owned and edited by John E Bennett, appeared September 23rd, 1899, and was issued monthly until January, 1901 It was in magazine form of sixteen pages and some of its issues reached a circulation of five thousand copies It was devoted to the poultry industry, and was printed at the office of the Gouverneur Free Press

The only daily newspaper excepting sheets temporarily issued for special occasions, published in Gouverneur up to this date was "The Gouverneur Record," of which the first number appeared Sept 17th, 1901, with Harold B Johnson, editor, and James D O'Brien, business manager The first numbers were of three short columns to the page A larger page, four columns wide soon appeared The paper was devoted to local news, general news and advertising, and sold at two cents per copy It was printed at the office of the Gouverneur Publishing Company With number 33 of the first volume, published October 24th, 1901, the publication ceased, for the reason that the owners could not make satisfactory arrangements with the printers

THE GOUVERNEUR TIMES

F E Merritt, a practical printer and experienced newspaper publisher, removed his printing office from Sandy Creek to Gouverneur during the summer of 1864, and on August 12th, 1864, issued Number 1, Volume 1, of the Gouverneur Times Typographically it was excellent for a country weekly The Times was started independent in politics, but in time became thoroughly republican It was in the last year of the Civil War that the career of the Times began Its salutatory, in referring to the war, expresses this sentiment We believe that in God's own time we shall be again united '

The Times was devoted to the usual local news and advertising, the dispatches from the scenes of war filling several columns of each issue until peace was declared It had no competitor for several years until the Northern Recorder, and later The Herald appeared It was enlarged from a seven column to an eight column folio and continued under the management of Mr Merritt until May 20th, 1879, when the outfit and good will passed to Messrs Ireland & Rich Changes in ownership were rapid for a few months until the proprietors of The Gouverneur Herald purchased it and consolidated it with that newspaper

The complete file of the Times is in the possession of B G Parker, and from its pages many facts have been gleaned by different writers in compiling this history Mr Merritt, its founder and owner for nearly fifteen years, is now a resident of Utica

THE GOUVERNEUR HERALD

With type and presses brought here from Watertown, James M Holmes and Frank M Redfield, under the firm name of Holmes & Redfield, launched The Gouverneur Herald The first issue appeared May 3, 1873 The office was established on the second floor of the wooden building on Main street corner of Park street Mr Holmes' connection with the paper was brief, and in July Mr Redfield took as a partner Horace G Reynolds to whom he sold his interest the following month H G Reynolds associated with him his elder half-brother, Jesse T Reynolds, who assumed the editorial work The Herald was Republican in politics and devoted to local and general news

At the big fire of Jan 13th, 1875, the Herald office was entirely consumed There was no insurance on the plant which was the property of Watertown parties In the stress for quarters by business concerns after the fire, Mr Reynolds secured a one-story wooden structure on Park street, then unused and formerly a barn. He converted it into suitable quarters, and installed another printing outfit, continuing there until the Reynolds marble front building was erected on Main street in which rooms suited for the various departments of newspaper work were especially provided for the Herald.

Two important additions were made to the efficiency and volume of the enterprise. Frank L. Cox entered the management soon afterward.

Under the firm name of Reynolds & Cox, and the purchase and consolidation of the Gouverneur Times increased the subscription list to an appreciable extent. Mr. Cox retired from the firm subsequently, and shortly afterwards the business was sold to The Gouverneur Publishing Company and B. G. Parker. The former took the list and good will, consolidating with the Northern Tribune, and Mr. Parker took the presses and type which were later removed to Potsdam to be used in publishing the Potsdam Recorder.

GOUVERNEUR FREE PRESS.

In March, 1882, Barnard G. Parker, a practical printer and newspaper man, sold the Norwood News which he had established and published for four years, and returned to Gouverneur, his native town, to engage in the newspaper business. Under his management

GOUVERNEUR FREE PRESS STAFF.

and ownership the Gouverneur Free Press was established, the first number appearing April 4th, 1882. The paper was a nine column folio, and has always retained that form. Capt. George Parker, father of the proprietor, was the editorial writer until his death the following year. The Free Press is Republican in politics and largely devoted to local news. Notwithstanding many and diversified business interests, B. G. Parker, the proprietor, has always maintained editorial command and business management of the paper. Miss Helen I. Parker was for some years local and then associate editor, retiring in February, 1903. Charles H. Clark, the present local editor, joined the staff in July, 1900. The Free Press has enjoyed an uninterrupted career under the one management for a longer term of years than any other Gouverneur newspaper, and in point of continual connection with the business Mr. Parker is the oldest newspaper man in St. Lawrence County.

THE HOTELS OF GOUVERNEUR.

By J. A. Spencer.

The first hotel in Gouverneur, 1808, was conducted by Israel Porter on the west side of the river. It was a small log structure but was later enlarged by the addition of a frame building, the boards being sawed by hand in the "saw-pits."

The old Porter Tavern was for many years the only hotel in the town of Cambray. In 1811, there were six licensed as Inn Keepers in the town, Israel Porter, Wm. Cleghorn, Rufus Washburn, Abraham Lewis, John Wilson, and Truman Bristol. These with the exception of the first were farm-houses and not rated as hotels or taverns.

Col. James Spencer

Dr. Spencer conducted a hotel on the present Johnstown road on what is now known as the McKean Hill, from 1812 to 1822. He then purchased the brick building occupied by John Brown, the first merchant in the town, as a residence. The building was erected in 1818. Dr. Spencer enlarged the building and conducted it as a hotel until he sold it to Moses Rowley, in 1824. It was sold on execution to Jas. Averill, who sold it to P. Van Buren, who conducted it until it was destroyed by fire in 1848. Mr. Van Buren rebuilt it as a private residence and it is still occupied by his daughter, Miss Emeline. Dr. Spencer was one of the three slave owners of the town. He had a man named "George" whom he brought from Connecticut. Dr. John Spencer, in 1828, built the Spencer House on Upper Main Street and conducted it until 1842, when he transferred it to his son, Col. James M. Spencer, who ran the Hotel until about 1884, selling it to Bogert & Morrison in 1884. In 1886 Bogert purchased Morrison's interest, selling in 1887 to E. Pierce of Macomb, who continued it until the house was burned in 1890.

The old Fosgate House was first opened in 1845 by Henry Hudson, who enlarged a dwelling formerly occupied by Caleb Morgan. He was succeeded by John Fosgate and his family who conducted it until 1857.

Van Buren House, 1860.

The Van Buren House on the North side of Main Street was built in 1849 by Peter Van Buren. The East end of the building was formerly a two-story dwelling purchased from Benj. H. Smith.

Mr. Van Buren was a Sergeant in the 248 Reg. of Inf.

Many parties and balls were held in this hotel. The following are the directors and floor managers of a ball held on Independence Day, 1850: Managers — John Bolton, Henry Gates, I. C. Stevens, Benj. Smith, T. B. Raymond, E. W. Cooper, Chas. Barnes, N. W. Howard. Floor Managers—E. McAllaster, Theo. Parker, C. P. Egert, B. N. Smith.

Peter Van Buren sold the house to his son, J. B. Van Buren, in 1808, who ran it until it burned in 1892. Jas. Van Buren rebuilt the Hotel which was again destroyed by fire in the winter of 1893.

A portion of the Van Buren Hotel lot was bought by A. L. McCrea, who erected the present St. Lawrence Inn. This was opened in 1899 by Robert Murphy who conducted it until 1898. Getman Bros. of Theresa succeeded him and conducted it until 1901, when the present proprietor, Everett Peck, took charge of this, the finest Hotel in Northern New York.

The Peck House was built in 1875 by C. T. Fuller and opened in 1876 by Capt. Daniel Peck, and was conducted by him until 1891.

Peter Van Buren.   John Foagate.   Daniel Peck.

The Kinney House was opened in October 1880, by Chas. M. Kinney, who conducted it until 1893. Mr. Kinney was a private of Battery D. 1st N. Y. Light Artillery. He was succeeded by his wife, Mrs. K. L. Kinney, who continued the Hotel until June, 1904, when it was purchased by P. Lavasseur of Massena, the present proprietor.

The Clinton House was built in 1804 by Robt. Webb, who kept it until 1896, when it was rented to J. Gillett. In 1897 it was leased by W. Kenyon who, with his sons ran it until 1901, when it was purchased by Wm. Smith. Mr. Smith conducted it till 1904 and sold it to its present proprietors, Randolph and Chase.

The Hinton House was built in 1896, on a portion of the site formerly occupied by the old Van Buren House. It was leased and is still conducted by Wm. Hinton.

The Gouverneur House was opened by Wm. Rice in 1896 and leased by him to Homer Kenyon in 1902, who is the present proprietor.

The Brooklyn House, on the West Side, was built in 1889 by Sidney Nash, who still conducts it.

The Grove House was built in 1890 by John Wainwright. He conducted it until his death in 1894. The House is now run by his widow, and son, Tunis.

For almost the entire history of the town, or nearly one hundred years, Gouverneur has had what may well be termed, first-class accommodations for the traveling public. It is true that Israel Porter began in a humble log cabin, but he afterward built the large two-story building now owned by Judge Neary on the West side, and conducted it as a hotel but for what time is not known. Dr. John Spencer was a man of conspicuous business ability and his various ventures in innkeeping could not have been less than efficient and satisfactory to his patrons. Col. James Spencer was a model manager, and Peter Van Buren has left a solid reputation as a host. Daniel Peck had long experience before coming to Gouverneur, and he and his son have kept the family reputation good. So, it will be seen that our village has never been without masterly management in its hotels. It boasts today, the finest hotel in appointments, table and service of any hotel north of the great cities.

THE DRY GOODS TRADE.

By E. D. Taitt.

In presenting this short sketch of the Dry Goods trade of Gouverneur, the writer has been given a very limited space. Such a history should contain a sketch of each Dry Goods house, its successes or failures, also a brief history of the lives of the merchants. The history of the numerous stores in the past sixty years is so interwoven, that it is with difficulty that such an article can be written in a few words. A brief statement of names, dates, and

Capt George Parker.   Capt. Geo. B. Winslow.   Charles S. Cone.

transfers is all that can be made. In the year 1857, the only so-called stores in town, commencing at the present Egert Block corner were as follows: The Tin Shop conducted by the late G. L. Van Namee and Capt. G. B. Winslow. The adjoining building east was the Tailoring department of A. S. Egert & Co. A gable roof building since moved to the corner of William and South Streets, now used as a residence by Mr. H. C. Smith. Adjoining this were the general stores of A. S. Egert & Co., Capt. Geo. Parker's grocery, Browne & Smith, and the Union Store Co. William E. Sterling and Chas. S. Cone conducted a general store on the present site of the Union Hall Block. The Cabinet Shop and Undertaking establishment of the late S. B. VanDuzee was the only other business place.

George F. Leak.   John N. Draper.   D. G. Wood.

The present Dry Goods houses of the town are: A. A. Potter & Co., Geo. F. Leak, J. E. McAllaster & Sons, J. H. Rutherford, and G. P. Taitt & Son. These are strictly Dry Goods houses. Messrs. H. H. Ryan, J. W. Ormiston and J. N. Draper carry quite extensive stocks of dry goods with other lines.

Mr. A. A. Potter commenced business in the Spring of 1879, the firm name being Potter & Sherwood. Mr. Sherwood died during the summer of 1887. Mr. Gregor was taken in as a partner and the firm name was changed to A. A. Potter & Co.

Geo. F. Leak is the successor to Leak & Snyder, young men from Utica, who came here in April 1904. Mr. Snyder retired in Feb. 1905.

The history of the dry goods houses of J. H. Rutherford, G. P. Taitt & Son, and J. E.

McAllaster & Sons, is a succession of changes from 1860 to about 1890. Mr. Rutherford, now of Main Street, commenced with Howard & Rutherford,— this business was bought two years later by Mr. G. P. Taitt. A few years later, Mr. Rutherford bought the interest of Mr. McAllaster,—of the firm of McAllaster & Wood. This partnership was dissolved about 1879, Mr. Rutherford moving to his present location.

Erwin S. Barnes   H. H. Ryan.   J. W. Ormiston.

The Dry Goods business of J. E. McAllaster & Sons is managed by one of the partners, Mr. R. T. Allen. This store was started in the early seventies by McAllaster & Wood, Mr. McAllaster selling to Mr. Rutherford. After Mr. Rutherford retired, Mr. Wood continued the business until his death in 1901. J. E. McAllaster & Sons purchased the business and have conducted it on its present site since that date.

George P. Taitt.

Mr. G. P. Taitt has been associated with the business street for a longer time than any other merchant. Coming to Gouverneur in 1858, he secured employment with the Union Store Co. He commenced business in his own name in 1860, then was associated for a short time with Capt. Parker. In the Spring of 1862, Mr. E. S. Barnes, Adam Killmer, and Mr. Taitt bought the old Union Store. Mr. Barnes soon retired. The firm of Killmer, Taitt and Jepson was then formed, this firm purchasing the business of A. S. Egert & Co. Mr. Taitt

Amos S. Egert

withdrew from this firm in two years, purchasing the business of Howard & Rutherford. Mr. J. H. Dickson was associated with Mr. Taitt for a few years but withdrew about 1875. Mr. Taitt continued in business alone until 1891, when his son Edward D. Taitt was admitted as a partner, the firm name being G. P. Taitt & Son.

In the good old days, general stocks were carried by all of the merchants; the change from general stocks to one regular line came during the years from 1875 to 1880. It is a well-known fact that the dry goods houses of Gouverneur carry larger stocks in proportion to the population than any other town in the country.

THE DAIRYING INDUSTRY.

By Walter W. Hall.

So far as the colonization of the white man is concerned, the history of New York State may be divided into two eras. The first extends from that autumnal day in 1608 when the "Half Moon" entered the bay at the mouth of the Hudson river, down to the close of the Revolution in 1783, and the second from that date when a free people took up that wonderful

career of advancement along all lines that make for national
greatness a career that even yet shows no signs of halting. The
first period was the time of the Dutch Colonists—first under the
Holland, later under the English flag, slowly pushing themselves
up the valleys of the Hudson and the Mohawk and their tributaries. Then as early as 1700, the Yankee, the man from New
England, filled with restless fever of that colonizing age, heard
of richer lands beyond the Hudson, and gathered his family and
household goods around him, and joined hands with the man from
the Rhine in carrying the ax and the plow into the wilderness.
Slowly the thin line of civilization crept westward through the
forest, halted and harrassed at every advance until the man
from Connecticut, and the man from the Hudson stood side

Walter W. Hall.

by side on the fields of Saratoga and Oriskany and proved in the stern argument of war the
right of a people to work out their own salvation in their own way. Note, that at the beginning of the Revolution, the advance guard of civilization rested on a line running from
Rome to Deposit at the Treaty of Fort Stanwix. Most of this was acknowledged Indian
lands. East of it was what we may now properly speak of as old New York. Then in 1783,
peace with honor came again and the men who had made freedom possible came back once
more to their homes, laid down the old flint-lock rifle, grasped the ax, set their faces toward
the setting sun and went forth an irresistable army of them to conquer the wilderness.

What a magnificent array it was flooding all around the bases of the Adirondacks,
sounding the ax through the rough mountains of the southern tier, clearing the giant forests
from the fertile lands of western New York, planting everywhere the school and the church,
carrying knowledge and law and justice into the wilderness until the state was won. We
never can pay enough reverence to those brave men and patient women who since the days
of New York Bay and Jamestown and Plymouth Rock have gone forth not knowing whither
they went to lay in the wilderness the foundations of American civilization.

Prior to 1851, cheese making and butter making were confined wholly to farm dairies.
When cheese were made, the milk of the herd was made into one cheese regardless of the
quantity or of the size of the herd. These cheeses were held in the farm dairy rooms, and if
butter was made it was also held in the farm house cellar, from the time the butter and
cheese making began in the spring until the dairy season closed in the fall, when the whole
season's output was sold. Up to this time, cheese making had been carried on in
England for centuries, and as the people came to this country, and engaged in agriculture,
farm dairy cheese making was continued. The size and quality of the cheese varied as the
quality of the milk and the skill of the maker varied. In nearly all cases the work was done by
women and the process was as simple as it could be made. The cream which came to the
surface of the milk during the night was carefully removed and made into butter for family
use. This was an act of economy, as they believed, if it was left on the milk it would all pass
off in the whey and be lost. The cheese were necessarily of a soft nature, and from the fact
that they had been made from milk of one dairy where conditions were under control, and
held in the dairy house until the casine was completely broken down and destroyed by
bacterial development and the natural cheese flavor had become fully developed, they were
considered very fine in quality. But, the system became expensive. The person who was
spending a large portion of her time in making one cheese each day, and in many cases one
in two days, could with proper equipment make the milk of several dairies with as little effort
as was given to the milk from the one herd. The first step toward a factory made cheese,
took place in Oneida county, New York, in 1851. Jesse Williams, a dairy farmer,
together with his sons living upon separate farms, pooled their milk and the father made
it into cheese, each receiving his share according to the number of pounds of milk he furnished.
The methods employed did not differ from that of the individual dairy, as the expense which
could be reduced by the pooling system, was the only inducement which offered itself at that

time But from this time on co-operation dairying, both butter and cheese making, began to
develop in New York State and was introduced into other states and Canada As time went
on and the demand for cheese increased, particularly from England, there was necessity for
changing the method employed in making The farm dairy cheese was nearly a sweet curd
product, and if not, it was due more to an accident than to any intention on the part of the
person in charge to improve the quality of the cheese But as the demand from England increased, the request for a more solid body accompanied the order, until after a few years,
the request came in the form of a demand The demand was such that it was necessary to
grant it, regardless of the tastes of American cheese consumers, and the result was a decrease
in consumption of cheese on this side of the Atlantic as it increased on the other From this
time on, the English "Cheddar" *system has been adopted in New York State for cheese making Among the first cheese factories which were built in this and adjoining towns, are the
old "Barber" at Richville, West Fowler, Little Bow, Schofield, in Dekalb, after which co-
operative butter factories and cheese factories have been increased in number until Gouverneur
has ten, Fowler has five, Hermon has eight, Hammond seven Edwards three, Depeyster five,
DeKalb twelve, and Rossie nine No sooner had we won the good opinion of English cheese
consumers the unscrupulous dairymen of our state, thinking that no one could tell the
difference, continued the pernicious habit of removing more or less cream from the milk
and making a "light skim" and branding it full cream American Cheese, when filling the orders from English exporters Not being satisfied with skimming alone, the "wise" ones introduced a system of "filled" cheese which were made from pure skimmed milk, with the addition of foreign fats, mixed by a force which, when made into cheese resembled full cream
quite well as far as texture was concerned, but after the cheese had reached the English shores,
the flavor became vile The Mercantile Exchange of London issued circular letters to the
manufacturers of this vile product, that if any more of it came to their country, it would
not be removed from the "docks "

    At this time, about 1878 to 1885, Canada and other British possessions had bent every effort
to make the very finest quality of full cream cheese, and to resemble those made in England
so closely that the difference could not be detected by the best judges on the English markets
They have already passed the English in the race and Canada has the proud distinction of
making the finest and best keeping quality of cheese of any made on earth, from an English
point of view Gouverneur and adjoining towns held the trade with England for both butter
and cheese, until the consumption in our own country increased to such an extent that the
foreign markets could not respond to the extreme high prices paid by our American dealers

    The industry has grown during the past fifty years to such an extent, that the little
shallow pan for raising cream by the "gravity" system, has given way to the Centrifugal
Separator, which has the capacity to separate 5,000 pounds of milk per hour and reduce the
amount of fat left in the skimmed milk to 5-100 of one per cent, and produce a cream that
contains 50% fat The little dash churn has given way to the mammoth combination churns,
with a capacity for churning 1,000 pounds of butter, and washing it at the same time without
removing it from the churn All of the many obstacles which stood in the way of the farm
dairy butter and cheese maker, have been removed, and the results of scientific research has
made the work comparatively easy With the assistance of all of the improved machinery,
such as the latest improved cream separator, combination churn, pasteurizers, and many other
less important improvements, one competent person can manufacture the butter from 10,000
pounds of milk in one day and prepare it for the refrigerator or for market

During the year of 1902

Gouverneur	produced	Butter, lbs	131,513
"	"	Cheese "	1 609 672
DeKalb	"	Butter "	99 230
"	"	Cheese "	1 646 936

---

* Named after a town in England where this system was discovered

Hermon	produced	Butter, lbs	232 854
"	"	Cheese "	941 945
Edwards	"	Butter "	11 281
"	"	Cheese "	501 416
Depeyster	"	Butter "	3 100
"	"	Cheese "	947 688
Rossie	"	Butter "	36 504
'	'	Cheese "	1 035 428
Macomb	"	Butter "	37 199
"	"	Cheese "	1 094 716
Fowler	'	Butter '	42 302
"	"	Cheese "	633 096
Hammond	"	Butter	6 688
"	"	Cheese "	677 518
	Total Product		9 691 085

The above is the product of the butter and cheese factories only, and in addition to this must be added the milk consumed in our villages, the butter and cheese made on the farms, and the milk shipped out of our county into the great consuming centers When we glance at the above figures, one cannot help but ask the question, What would become of the "Empire town" in the "Empire State," if the dairy cow should be taken from her support? It will also be seen, that Gouverneur and adjoining towns do their part toward making St Lawrence the banner dairy county of the United States, with her 93,500 cows, against Jefferson County, Wisconsin, with 33,500 cows as second highest, that we are doing our part toward making up the value of the dairy products of the United States which is $605,313,354 00 from 18,000,000 cows The improved machinery combines economy of labor and efficiency in the highest degree It makes it possible to handle the great flow of milk with comparatively slight cost, and when assisted by modern methods, as a result of scientific investigations, a uniformly fine quality of product follows The lack of uniformity in the methods, and of the quality of butter, when made on the farm, assist largely to bring about the co-operative system of today since the mysterious laws of nature have been solved to the extent that cream refining is made easy, and today a river of pure, well refined cream, is running from the cream vats into the churns every morning throughout our dairy community which has the appearance of glossy satin with a flavor developed that not only insures clean churning, but the high aroma and solid body which enables the dealers to carry it until June the following year, or until consumed The old tale that "the butter wont come" and the time when the dairy maid put a horse-shoe, or a silver dollar, or a clothespin in the churn 'for luck," has passed away and the scientific methods explain away all of the old troubles which once existed in the manufacture of butter and cheese

It was a century ago, that a little band of that innumerable company with their children and their goods, and their cattle came down the woodland trail to Gouverneur East of them was the great wilderness of Adirondacks West and North of them ran the vast mysterious river concerning whose wonders the French voyagers had been singing for generations So here where since has arisen so fair a civilization, these grand sires of ours made the rude beginnings of a home Measured by American standards of time, that was not long ago A hundred times have the deep St Lawrence snows whitened all the land A hundred times has been seen a miracle, for the south wind has breathed upon these old fields and they have been covered with living green

Those heroes of that heroic age have grown into a great, free, intelligent people Those forest clearings have broadened into leagues of fertile fields From these few cows driven down the woodland road, have come the herds that cover the hills of this great dairy county of St Lawrence As a people, our Coat of Arms might well be a cow at rest in a green field Of us it is true that where the dairy cow goes, she carries blessing May the lowing of herds, the mellow call of the cow boy, and the sleepy hum of the cream separator never cease to be heard in the land

Dairy statistics of the following towns during the year of 1844

	No Cows	Lbs Butter	Lbs Cheese
Gouverneur	1859	127,361	57,785
DeKalb	1199	81,885	236,195
Depeyester	876	78,250	21,122
Edwards	510	47,193	6,137
Fowler	1049	78,165	33,516
Macomb	448	37,915	2,734
Rossie	788	74,686	12,670
Hammond	1017	77,636	51,550
	8,076	609,421	424,059

PATRONS OF HUSBANDRY

By S F Hartley

On the 27th day of February, 1875, twenty-seven men and ten women met in what was called the Masonic Hall in the Egert Block, Town of Gouverneur, and organized what has passed into history as Gouverneur Grange No 303 of the Order of Patrons of Husbandry Officers elected were S J Hartley, Worthy Master, Geo S Parsons, Worthy Overseer, Thomas Miller, Worthy Lecturer A J Borland, Worthy Steward, O E Van Buren, Worthy Assistant Steward, Chas Henry Smith, Worthy Chaplain James Brown, 2nd, Worthy Treasurer, Lott Hall, Worthy Secretary, Mrs A B Billings, Worthy Ceres, Mrs Henry Brown Worthy Pomona, Mrs S F Hartley, Worthy Flora Mrs Charles Henry Smith, Worthy Lady Assistant Steward Gouverneur was the fourth Grange to organize in St Lawrence County, starting with twenty-seven charter members, but four of whom are now living and connected with the Order, viz Mr Frank H Smith, Mrs Chas Henry Smith, and Mr and Mrs S F Hartley

Our growth has kept pace with the demand of the farmers for organization and fraternal co-operation Our roll call shows 335 names in good standing, representing the substantial and progressive part of the agricultural community The objects of the Grange have been defined as co-operation for mutual benefit, and protection Education is inculcated, social relations fostered, and brotherly love cultivated Arbitration is also a prominent feature of our Order "Cultivate an observing mind It is delightful to acquire knowledge and much more so to diffuse it" is an injunction given every member of the Order and thus our discussion of topics pertaining to the farm and the home, are ever a source of pleasure and profit

Looking over results accomplished, probably no one act of the Grange has been of more benefit financially, or has done more to form a strong band of union between its members than the organization and successful operation of the Patrons Co-operative Fire Relief Association of St Lawrence County This company was organized Nov 6, 1876, in the early days of the Order, when there were but three active working Granges in the county, viz Potsdam, No 39, Crarys Mills No 51, and Gouverneur No 303

As soon as $100,000 in risks was secured, the first policies were issued Feb 8, 1879 The Association now has four thousand policies and carries something over eight million in risks

The first officers were: Noel O. Freeman, President, and Benj. Butterfield, Director, from Crarys Mills Grange. Charles F. Allen, Treasurer, and George W. Waldo, Director, from Potsdam Grange. Lott Hall, Secretary, and S. F. Hartley, Director, from Gouverneur Grange. Articles of Association and By-laws were adopted at the meeting of Nov. 8, 1878, and thus equipped the first purely mutual insurance company commenced business in St. Law-

rence County. For a time our annual reports were made and filed with County Clerk only, but soon after incorporation, the annual reports were filed with the department of insurance, Albany, N. Y. Our present Secretary, Mr. Harvey W. S. Knox, informs us that the cost of insurance on one thousand from this date of organization to the close of the last insurance year has been less than one dollar per year.

In matters of legislation in which our local grange has taken active interest, the so-called Bob Veal Law was first suggested in the discussions of our local grange. Mr. Frank H. Smith was delegated by Gouverneur Grange to visit Albany and confer with the Hon. Ira C. Miles, member of Assembly, from this district. Mr. Miles took the suggestion in hand and

after nearly two terms of hard work, succeeded in passing the act   Thus by his determined
efforts, marked ability and integrity of purpose, did our Hon Member of Assembly earn

PATRONS OF HUSBANDRY

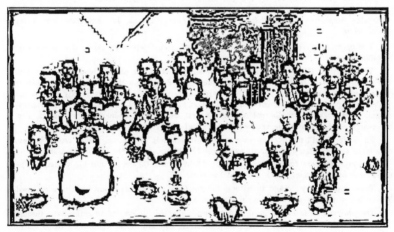

PATRONS OF HUSBANDRY

the grateful remembrance of the Patrons of this and adjoining counties   While the Grange organization looks carefully after the wants and welfare of its local members, it has come to
be a recognized power in maintaining the dignity and protecting the interests of Agriculture

The College of Agriculture at Cornell, The Experiment Station at Geneva, The Department of Agriculture at Albany, have no more hearty support, no higher appreciation of the work well done, than comes to them through the membership of the subordinate grange

> "And step by step since time began,
> We see the steady gain of man,
> That all the good the past has had,
> Remains to make our own time glad."

THE GOUVERNEUR AGRICULTURAL AND MECHANICAL SOCIETY.

By E W Duffie

The Gouverneur Agricultural and Mechanical Society was organized January 29, 1859, pursuant to an act of the State Legislature passed in 1855 "to facilitate the forming of Agricultural and Horticultural Societies.' A charter was granted to the following citizens of Gouverneur and surrounding towns Richard Parsons, George Lockie, Jr, Ossian L Barnum, F M Beardslee, George Rodgers, Milton Barney, Peleg Chamberlain, John Pooler, Jr, Lewis Loomis, David Hill, Henry H Haile

The officers for the year 1859 were. President, Henry H Haile, Fowler, 1st Vice Pres, George Rodgers, Gouverneur, 2nd Vice Pres, Milton Barney, Gouverneur, 3rd Vice Pres, David Day, 2nd, Macomb, 4th Vice Pres, Wm B Rich, Gouverneur, 5th Vice Pres, Benj F. Skinner, Gouverneur, 6th Vice Pres, Milton G Norton, Gouverneur, Secretary, George Parker; Treasurer, Augustus E Norton Directors, David Hill, Edward Hartley, F M Beardslee, Stephen Van Duzee, John Pooler, Jr, George Lockie, Jr Superintendent, Peleg Chamberlain

The organization of the Society being effected, steps were then taken toward securing suitable grounds for Fair purposes

From Messrs Egert & Averill, a lease was obtained of the plot of land included within the bounds of Main, Rock Island, Barnes, and Park Streets, no charges for the use thereof being made by the owners so far as the records show A race course was quickly constructed under the supervision of Edward Hartley, G L Van Namee and John Kenyon, and preparations went forward for the holding of the first annual fair upon this site which is now the center of the fashionable residential district of Gouverneur

For a floral hall, the St Lawrence Agricultural Society of Canton, kindly loaned the use of a large tent and temporary sheds were built for the housing of the live stock exhibit

The grounds were formally opened Sept 14, 1859, and the reader can easily imagine the excitement of expectancy which attended the event

Town and country flocked to witness the spectacle Sleek cattle and carefully groomed horses vied with each other for popular attention

The products of farm and garden in profusion greeted the eyes of an enthusiastic throng

The side-show barker and fakir, patent medicine and whip men, whose deep toned voices might plainly be heard above the general babble, all added gayety to the scene, likewise, shekels to their own pockets

Mr Thomas Clark of Jefferson County, N Y, delivered the address speaking upon agricultural topics The fair continued three days, and upwards of 2,000 admission tickets were sold besides the 200 family memberships issued

Light harness racing was the feature of the amusement programme, and most prominent among the local pioneers of this sport may be mentioned the names of Orin Partridge, A. S. Rhodes, Nate Garison, G. L. Van Namee, O. Judd, and W. Van Valkenburg. Subsequently

PRESENT OFFICERS, 1905.

Amasa Corbin, J. E. McAllaster, A. L. McCrea, J. H. Abbott, William Comstock, Judge Leslie W. Russell, and George Hossington, have been prominently identified with local racing interests.

Mr. Van Valkenburg, familiarly known as Van, holds the unique record of having driven the most winners and the largest number of heats in one afternooon of any teamster over the Gouverneur track, (sixteen), and he has participated in nearly every race meet during the history of the Society.

The Treasurer's report of the first meeting shows a surplus of $136.79, a matter of much satisfaction and encouragement to the promoters.

For seven successive years, fairs were held upon the original site.

In 1866, during the administration of Peleg Chamberlain, whose likeness appears else-where in this book, the society having become a permanent institution, it was decided that more commodious grounds should be secured to meet the growing demands, and twenty acres of land were purchased from B. Howard Smith, for the sum of $2,500.00. This plot was quickly transformed into the present Fair grounds, and the annual show held there, Sept. 12, 13, and 14, of the same year.

The receipts advanced from $820 in 1863 (the first available report), to $2,363 in 1866, when $256.50 was paid in premiums and the balance expended for permanent improvements, such as a grand stand, ticket office, sheds, fences, etc.

The present floral hall was erected in 1872 at a cost of $1,200, and notwithstanding its ample proportions a serious inconvenience occasioned by lack of space to properly display the exhibits has been experienced upon several occasions.

At this period of the Society's existence, of the 58 town fairs in New York State, only three exceeded ours in receipts and those were in the much more populous localities

Plowing matches and sale days were interesting features of the early fairs, and farmers derived much benefit therefrom

The first electric light (arc and incandescent) was one of the drawing attractions away back in the eighties, furnished free of charge to the Society, except for poles, by Mr C A Benton, representative of the large electrical company   Poles were set around the course and an evening racing program given in connection with the demonstration of the new light

Never but once prior to 1882, did the Society's gross income equal $3,000   In secretary's Winslow's report of 1881, he advised the abandonment of the fair, on the ground that it was badly incumbered and not self-sustaining

Amasa Corbin, Jr, became Secretary and began active work in 1882—with a debt on the Society of about $3,500   His first recorded official act was a resolution to borrow $225, with which to pay the interest on the debt   The following shows the growth of the fair for six succeeding years

In 1881, Geo Parker, Pres, Geo Winslow, Secretary, receipts, $3,154 35

In 1882, John Rogers, Pres, A Corbin, Jr, Secretary, receipts, $5,185 11

In 1883, John Rogers, Pres, A Corbin, Jr, Secretary, receipts, $5,821 61

In 1884, D G Wood, Pres, John Webb, Jr, Secretary, receipts, $6,112 72

In 1885, D G Wood, Pres, F H Norton, Secretary, receipts, $4,762 80

In 1886, A Corbin, Jr, Pres, F H Norton, Secretary, receipts, $8,470 36

During the entire existence of the Society, with the exception of the first two years, one of the present directors, Mr Frank H Smith, has been actively identified with the fair as one of its officers, and to his indefatigable efforts is due much praise for its successful career

Up to 1882, the grand stand consisted of fifty feet of seats without any roof over them It was deemed wild extravagance by many when the erection of the great grand stand was commenced in 1882   It more than paid for itself, however, the first year, from the rental of booths and the sale of seats, and has been a source of large revenue ever since

At the close of the fair in 1881, the receipts were sufficient to wipe out the entire debt and leave a large surplus   During the fall of 1881, however, the track was lengthened at a large expense and another indebtedness thereby incurred   In 1886 the affairs of the Society reached the high water mark, the receipts having exceeded $8,400   The well advertised attractions of that year consisting of the Great Sham Battle in which the 29th Separate Company of Ogdensburg, of which Mr Corbin was an honorary member, and the 35th Separate Company of Watertown, participated and went into the "field of carnage" side by side with the old veterans of the Civil War, the late Dr McFalls following the ambulance conveying the wounded from the battle field past the grand stand amid the tumultous applause of the largest mass of people ever assembled in the village of Gouverneur

During the early history of the organization and until recent years, annual addresses by men of prominence, constituted one of the principal attractions and among the list of men who have spoken at our fairs, we find the names of Horace Greeley, Geo W Bungay, Edward Everett, F E Spinner, Daniel Sickles, N M Curtis, and Roswell P Flower   It is a matter of general regret that this once popular feature of the program has been abandoned

That the fair is an institution deserving of the encouragement and patronage of our people is generally conceded, affording pecuniary benefits along with educational advantages

It has grown from an humble origin to its present proportions, keeping step with the progress of our thriving community under the guidance and direction of the loyal citizens upon whom from year to year, is placed by election, the burden of management   "Long live the Fair "

Maj. Henry H. Haile.　　　Edwin Dodge.　　　Peleg Chamberlain.

Andrew H. Turnbull.　　　George Lockie.　　　George M. Gleason.

John Rodger.　　　G. S. Conger.　　　Amasa Corbin.

Frederick J. Bolton.　　　E. D. Barry.　　　S. F. Hartley.

FORMER PRESIDENTS OF THE GOUVERNEUR AGRICULTURAL AND MECHANICAL SOCIETY.

List of Presidents of G. A. & M. Society.

Henry H. Haile,	1856-61	Amasa Corbin,	1886
Edwin Dodge,	1862-63	G. M. Gleason,	1887-88
John Porter,	1864	B. G. Parker,	1889-90
Peleg Chamberlain,	1865-71	F. H. Smith,	1891-92
George Parker,	1872-73	G. S. Conger,	1893
George Lockie,	1874-75	E. D. Barry,	1894-95
George M. Gleason,	1876-77	Fred J. Bolton,	1896
S. F. Hartley,	1878	J. H. Abbott,	1897-98
W. E. Bacon,	1879-80	Charles Fuller,	1899-01
George Parker,	1881	A. H. Turnbull,	1902-03
John Rodger,	1882-83	S. F. Hartley,	1904-05
D. G. Wood,	1884-85		

List of Secretaries of G. A. & M. Society.

George Parker,	1859-61	John Webb, Jr.	1885
C. F. Keyes,	1862	Fred Norton,	1886
A. B. Cutting,	1863-66	Frank H. Smith,	1887-88
W. H. Walling,	1867-68	W. W. Hall,	1889-90
George B. Winslow,	1869-70	J. B. Johnson,	1891
George Parker,	1871	D. A. Leggett,	1892
George B. Winslow,	1872-77	Frank H. Smith,	1893-99
George Parker,	1878	J. H. Abbott,	1900-01
George B. Winslow,	1879-81	D. A. Leggett,	1902-03
A. Corbin,	1882-83	Edw. W. Duffie,	1904-05
James R. Austin,	1884		

THE PAPER INDUSTRY.

By H. G. Aldrich.

Situated on the Oswegatchie river, two miles below Gouverneur village, is the principal plant of the Aldrich Paper Co. The corporation was organized in 1900 by Gouverneur and Watertown capitalists. The water power and saw mill property of Aldrich, Dean & Aldrich, at Natural Dam, together with thirty-two thousand acres of timber land, were purchased by that Company, and in the summer of that year the erection of the paper mill at that place

was begun. There was built a large and modern paper plant embracing ground and sulphite pulp mills. The paper mill has one 132 inch machine with an average capacity of 25 tons daily. The sulphite mill has two digesters and can turn out daily twenty tons of pulp. The wood pulp mill contains five grinders with a total daily capacity of twenty tons of ground wood. The Natural Dam affords a splendid water power for this plant, there being some two thousand horse-power available. The mill at Natural Dam gives steady employment to 125 men and women. The Company owns about forty houses in this hamlet. A branch of the N. Y. C. R. R. running direct to the mill, furnishes convenient shipping facilities.

H G. Aldrich.

In August, 1903, the Aldrich Paper Co. purchased of the Gouverneur Wood Pulp Company their pulp mill property at Emeryville. This mill situated on Edwards branch of the N. Y. C. R. R., is also located on one of the best water powers of the Oswegatchie river. There is a thirty-two feet head to furnish power for driving wheels of mill. There are eight grinders in this mill and its daily capacity is thirty tons. Fifty men find steady employment at this plant. The present officers of the Corporation (Aldrich Paper Co.) are: President, Charles R. Remington; Vice-President, Herbert G. Aldrich; Secretary, Samuel Child, and Treasurer, Nelson R. Caswell.

THE TALC INDUSTRY.

By A. J. McDonald.

Talc, which is a silicate of magnesia, is by no means a rare mineral, but the qualities which have made Gouverneur talc generally known and valuable in the manufacturing world, more especially in the business of paper-making, do not seem to be duplicated in any of the numerous deposits of the mineral which are known to exist at other localities in this country and Canada, as well as in several countries of Europe. This difference is in the physical qualities of the mineral rather than its chemical proportions which are almost identical with the talc of the various other deposits, of which mention has been made.

The local material has a fibrous character peculiarly its own, which, combined with a purely white color and a strong matting or felting tendency, in connection with paper pulp ingredients have made a wide field for its use in the paper-making trade, in which the major portion of the output is consumed. Its use in the manufacture of paint and rubber goods, while relatively small, is growing and in time will doubtless become an important factor in the business.

It might be well to say here that although no talc is mined in the town of Gouverneur, the fact that Gouverneur has always been the shipping point for the talc produced in the towns of Fowler and Edwards has given the name of Gouverneur Talc to the product, and as Gouverneur Talc it is known to almost all who have to do with it.

There are several versions of how talc happened to be discovered in this section and as to how it was first learned that it was valuable in the making of paper. The old geological surveys of the state mentioned the fact of talc being hereabouts, but this seems to have attracted no especial attention, and there seems to have been nothing done toward developing

S. C. Merritt.

the mineral until about 1873, when S. C. Merritt, a veterinary surgeon of Gouverneur, did some prospecting and called attention to the talc croppings and indications at various places in the town of Fowler. His work and the faith he had that the mineral was of value seems to have started an effort toward finding some use for which it was adapted. Within the next two or three years, Col. Henry Palmer, and G. A. Mendin of Gouverneur, and Daniel Minthorn of Watertown, N. Y., became interested in the attempt to utilize the talc deposits in a commercial way, and it seems to be conceded that to one of these three is due the credit of first suggesting its use in the manufacture of paper, for which as it proved, it was eminently adapted. In view of the conflicting claims as to who first suggested this use it is as well perhaps that the credit for the suggestion be shared equally by the three, and that they with S. C. Merritt, be accorded the honor and credit of originating and starting on its way the talc industry of Northern New York. During the years 1875-6, Palmer, Mendin and Minthorn, secured some mining leases in Fowler, and some crude grinding experiments were made of the talc found there. Attempts were made to interest capital for the business of mining and grinding the mineral, and developing a market for the product. As a result of these efforts, two talc mills were erected during the years 1876 and 1877, one of which was a steam mill on the farm of Abner Wight in Fowler, to grind the talc found on that property; the other being established in a water power mill on the Oswegatchie River below Natural Dam in the town of Gouverneur, which had been used to grind iron ore for paint and was known locally as the "Paint Mill." The talc for this mill was mined on the William Woodcock farm in Fowler.

The steam mill on the Wight property was owned by the Agalite Fibre Company, this company being organized and controlled by A. L. McCrea and Touro Robertson, both of New York, with some of their friends. With them were interested Col. Henry Palmer and G. A. Mendin. In July, 1877, A. L. McCrea, Jr., who had become interested in the company came to Gouverneur and assumed the management of the business. Grinding operations were conducted at this steam mill until the spring of 1878, when a portion of the Clark and Howard mill property at Hailesboro was leased and equipped for grinding talc, during the year 1879, the entire Clark and Howard mill property was purchased by the Agalite Fibre Co. and talc machinery installed. During the same year this company had also developed a mine of fibrous talc on the Nelson H. Freeman farm at Freemansburg, now Talcville, in Edwards, and thereafter their ore supply was obtained from that mine. The property and business of this company were purchased by the International Pulp Company in 1893, and are now operated by that corporation.

The mill property below Natural Dam was equipped as a talc mill during the years 1876-7 by the Mineral Attrition Mills Co., a corporation organized and controlled by Alfred C. Smith, Jr., and Thomas Girvan of New York, with some of their associates and Daniel Manthorn of Watertown, N. Y. During the years 1878-9, the property changed ownership and was owned successively by Henry C. Post of Paterson, N. J. Bennet P. Sharp of New York, and finally in February, 1879, acquired by Theodore W. Barnud of New York, who in 1884 organized the Natural Dam Pulp Co., to conduct the business, he retaining a controlling interest in the property. The Woodcock mine in Fowler supplied the ore ground in this mill until in 1879 when a mine was opened on a property owned by Edwin G. Dodge, near the Peabody Bridge in North Gouverneur. The ore from this mine was a variety of soapstone, and while the mine was worked for a year or two, the product was not satisfactory and almost constant prospecting was being done for a suitable material, resulting in the development of a mine in 1881 on the Anthony property at Freemansburg, in Edwards, from which the ore supply of this mill was thereafter taken. During the year 1891 a large new mill was built by the Natural Dam Pulp Co. on the Oswegatchie River, on a water power about half a mile above Hailesboro. Both of the mills of this Company were operated until 1893, when the properties were purchased by the International Pulp Co., and are now owned by that corporation.

During the year 1879, Col. Henry Palmer of Gouverneur who had then severed his relations with the Agalite Fibre Co., associated with Stephen B. Van Duzee and John S. Honeycomb, both of Gouverneur, organized the Gouverneur Pulp Co. to mine and grind talc. They developed a valuable talc mine on the Brayton property at Freemansburg, in Edwards, and built a mill on the Haile water power on the Oswegatchie River, a short distance below Hailesboro. A very successful business was conducted by this Company until 1882, when they disposed of their property to the Adirondack Pulp Co.

In 1880, the Gouverneur Talc Co. was organized by Amasa Corbin, Samuel Graves, Lawson M. Gardener and A. G. Gillet, all of Gouverneur. They bought a water power a mile above Hailesboro, in Fowler, of A. W. Brown, and built a mill, at the same time developing a mine on the Anthony lands at Freemansburg, in Edwards. The business of this Company was successfully conducted until 1882, when its properties were sold to the Adirondack Pulp Co.

The Adirondack Pulp Co. was organized during the winter of 1882-3 by Amasa Corbin, Jr., and some business associates, with the view of purchasing and consolidating the properties of the Gouverneur Talc Co. and the Gouverneur Pulp Co. This plan was carried out soon after the organization of the company and the properties were conducted by the Adirondack Pulp Co. until their sale to the International Pulp Co. in 1893.

The St. Lawrence Pulp Co. was organized during 1884 by M. M. Belding and associates of New York, and a mill built below Hailesboro, in Fowler, on a branch of the Oswegatchie River known as Mill Creek. The ore supply for this mill was procured from the Brayton farm in Edwards. The properties of this company were acquired by the International Pulp Co. in 1893.

Another talc corporation to enter the field in 1884 was the Northern New York Manufacturing Co., organized by William L. Palmer of Rochester, Leslie W. Russell, Milton D. Packard and William H. Kimball of Canton, N. Y., and some others. A stone building was erected on the Sayer lands in the village of Gouverneur, very near the present junction of the Gouverneur and Oswegatchie R. R. with the R. W. & O. R. R. tracks. Steam was used at this mill which so increased the cost of manufacturing, as to render the business unprofitable

The property changed hands several times and was finally destroyed by fire in 1893. What ore was ground at this mill was mined on the Woodcock property in Fowler.

In the latter part of the year 1888, Lawson M. Gardener of Gouverneur, who at that time had been out of the talc business for a number of years, purchased the Freeman or the old iron furnace water power at Freemansburg, and with some associates built a mill there and commenced the grinding of talc, the ore for this mill coming from a mine in the Gideon Freeman property a short distance from the mill and also from the Palmer mine on the Brayton land just across the Oswegatchie River from the mill, both of these mines being operated by power transmitted from this mill by wire cables. This mill and business were sold by Gardener and those interested with him to the Asbestos Pulp Co. in 1892.

Early in the year 1891, the Abbott Woolen Mill on the Oswegatchie River at Hailesboro, was leased to A. L. McCrea, Jr., who, in connection with James M. Sparks of Gouverneur, Fred W. Streeter and Frank H. Munson, of Watertown, equipped it as a talc mill, and commenced the grinding of ore obtained from the Palmer mine at Freemansburg. These parties continued the operation of this mill until the spring of 1892, when they disposed of the property to the Asbestos Pulp Co., a corporation organized largely through the efforts of A. L. McCrea, Jr., in the winter of 1891-2, to take over and consolidate the works of the Gardener mill at Freemansburg and those at the Abbott mill in Hailesboro, together with leases of the Palmer and Gideon Freeman mines at Freemansburg. The capital of the Asbestos Pulp Co. was principally furnished by Rochester men who controlled the company and operated its mines and mills until 1894, when the property was purchased by the International Pulp Co.

In the spring of 1891, the United States Talc Co. was organized with F. W. Emery of Boston, Mass., Newton Aldrich, W. R. Dodge and F. M. Burdick of Gouverneur, and Earl Bancroft of Edwards, as directors. This company had an excellent water power on the Oswegatchie River at Dodgeville, some seven miles up the river from Gouverneur on which they began the erection of a mill. This construction was not hurried, as there was every probability at this time of a railroad being built from Gouverneur to Edwards, and it was desired that the mill be so planned as to permit of the most economical connection with the railroad which was actually completed in 1893. The mill commenced grinding in 1894, obtaining its ore supply from a mine on the Anthony lands at Taleville, in Edwards, and later from the Nelson H. Freeman mine at the same place. The control of this business which is still in successful operation has not been materially changed since its organization. The present officers are F. W. Emery, Pres.; W. R. Jones, Treas.; F. M. Burdick, Sec.

During the years 1892-3, the steam mill on the Balmat farm near Sylvia Lake, in Fowler, was built by the American Talc Co., a corporation organized by Providence, R. I. people to engage in the talc business. The ore for this mill was taken from the Balmat mine on the same premises. The American Talc Co. continued in business until October 1901, when the property was purchased by the Union Talc Co.

The firm of Keller Bros., composed of Karl Keller and Ernest Keller, manufacturing wood pulp at Fullerville, in the town of Fowler, installed talc grinding machinery in a portion of their mill in 1895, and commenced the manufacture of talc. Their ore supply was obtained successively from mines on the Van Namee, Wilson and Arnold farms, all in the town of Fowler. In the latter part of 1901, Keller Bros. disposed of their plant to the Union Talc Co.

The Columbian Talc Co. was organized early in 1895 through the efforts of O. J. David of Gouverneur, and J. J. Wallace and William I. Clark of Fowler, and Earl Bancroft of Edwards, all of whom served on the first board of directors of the company. Considerable of the capital for this undertaking was provided by W. R. Candler and associates of Detroit, Michigan, and the company was controlled by them. The Columbian mill completed in the fall of 1895, was built on the "Island Branch" of the Oswegatchie River in Fowler, at a point some three miles from Gouverneur. The ore supply at this mill was the Arnold mine in Fowler. The Columbian Talc Co. disposed of its property to the Union Talc Co. in Oct., 1901.

The Ontario Talc Co., organized in November 1899, built their mill on the Oswegatchie very near Fullerville, in Fowler, and commenced the manufacture of talc early in 1900. The ore for the early operations of this mill was mined a few rods from their mill and on the same premises; later the mining operations of the company were transferred to the Van Namee mine about a mile from the mill, where their ore supply is still obtained. The directors of this company, unchanged since its organization, are L. M. Gardener and Anson A. Potter of Gouverneur, Edward B. Sterling, Gilbert B. Gregor and John Sterling of Watertown, N. Y.

The International Pulp Company incorporated early in 1893 with a capitalization of $5,-000,000.00, was organized on broad lines; the intention being to consolidate in this corporation the entire business of mining and grinding tale in this section. This plan and the formation of the International Company were largely due to the publicity and advertising given to the tale business in the efforts made during the years 1891-2 to bring about the building of a railroad from the various tale mines in Edwards to the mills in Fowler and on to the R. W. & O. R. R., at Gouverneur. This exploitation resulted in a very thorough investigation of the possibilities of the industry by H. Walter Webb, then prominently connected with the New York Central R. R. and W. J. Arkell, a well known publisher and capitalist, and their interesting the necessary capital to form the International Company. Its first board of directors included Agustus G. Paine, President; H. Walter Webb, Chauncey M. Depew, W. J. Arkell, Theodore W. Bayaud, John A. Manning, Touro Robertson and others. In April, 1893, this company purchased and took over the properties of the Natural Dam Pulp Co., Agalite Fibre Co., Adirondack Pulp Co., and St. Lawrence Pulp Co., and in April, 1894, purchased the properties of the Asbestos Pulp Co., thus securing all the properties that were manufacturing tale at that time. Efforts were made to acquire the properties of the United States Tale Co. and the American Tale Co., the mills of both these companies then being in course of construction, but it was found impossible to agree on terms for them and they were not purchased by the International Co. The properties and plants of this company have been consolidated to a considerable extent for convenience and economy in manufacturing, and many improvements introduced to perfect the quality of their product. The present officers of the corporation are Michael Doyle, President; M. M. Belding, Jr., Treasurer, and S. J. McCrimlisk, Secretary.

The Union Tale Co., organized late in 1901, was formed to purchase and consolidate the properties of Keller Bros., the Columbian Tale Co., and American Tale Co.; the transfer of these properties to the Union Co. was made very soon after its incorporation. The officers of the company are Charles E. Locke, Pres., and George Smallwood, Sec'y and Treas.

At this time, June 1905, the producers of Gouverneur Tale are the International Pulp Co., the Union Tale Co., the United States Tale Co., and the Ontario Tale Co., and the aggregate annual output is from 65,000 to 70,000 tons.

THE MARBLE INDUSTRY.
By D. J. Whitney.

The first retail marble business established in Gouverneur was in August, 1865, by N. E. Whitney and J. H. Sawyer, under the firm name of Whitney & Sawyer, which was succeeded in the Spring of 1866 by N. E. Whitney. In the Summer of 1867 D. J. Whitney was admitted

to partnership, it then becoming N. E. Whitney & Son. The senior member died in the Fall of 1868 and the son having purchased his interest continued it until he sold out to George Parker, early in the Spring of 1870, who continued it until December, 1871, when he sold to Whitney Bros., D. J. & T. J. They enlarged the business quite materially and furnished considerable cut stone work for buildings, the material used for several years being mostly sandstone or blue limestone, but in 1876 they commenced cutting Gouverneur stone for that purpose. The trimmings of the Presbyterian Church at Canton, N. Y. was the first building job to be done in what was later known as Gouverneur Marble. They first used some of this marble for monumental work during the

D. J. Whitney.

Winter of 1877-8 In the fall of 1877 their works were completely destroyed by fire and were rebuilt that fall, business being resumed in December In the fall of 1878 they sold their marble business to A S Whitney, a younger brother, and a couple of years later P R Whitney, the youngest brother of the family, joined as a partner They were together several years when they sold to Hulbut & Dunkelberg, this firm being composed of E B Hulbut and C C Dunkelberg The former retired after a couple of years and was succeeded by Dunkelberg Bros, and later by C C Dunkelberg, who conducted it until his death in 1903 In the settling of his estate the stock and business were sold to Crooks & McLean who were and are conducting a similar establishment at Carthage, N Y They still continue the business at the old stand on William Street, Mr McLean being the resident member This has grown from a small undertaking in 1865 until at the present time, and for several years past, it has become by far the largest retail marble business in Northern New York

From the first settlement of Gouverneur it had been the practice to blast out stone from ledges in nearby fields for foundation walls, road building and that class of work, but it was not until 1876 that quarry operations were conducted on any kind of a large scale In the early spring of that year, D J & T J Whitney and John S Honeycomb formed a co-partnership under the name of Whitneys & Honeycomb, and entered into a contract with the Town of Gouverneur to build the foundations of the present Main Street bridge, Honeycomb being only interested in the bridge contract and not the marble and cut stone business of the Whitneys They entered into a lease with James K Barney whereby they could quarry stone on his farm and selected a ledge back of his house as the place to make the opening, it now being the quarry of the Gouverneur Marble Co There were two derricks erected and a large number of men employed during the year and several hundred cords of stone removed The better class of this was utilized by the Whitneys for cut stone trimmings for buildings, bottom bases of monuments etc, the balance being used in the bridge piers and abutments The trimmings for the Presbyterian church at Canton came from this quarry With the completion of the bridge contract in December, Mr Honeycomb retired and Whitney Bros resumed operations at the quarry in the Spring of 1877 During this year the stone for the County Clerk's Office at Canton was got out as well as for several buildings in Gouverneur, among the latter were fronts for the Van Namee and Draper blocks With the close of work in the Fall this quarry was not worked for several years or until purchased by the Gouverneur Marble Co about 1886

In the late Fall of 1877, the Whitneys quarried some stock on the other part of the Barney farm southwest of the Lazenby lot and close to the Somerville road Some of this was worked up during the Winter and was the first that was made into monuments About this time dark marble had come into demand for monumental work and during 1878 some from this quarry was sold in the rough to marble dealers for that purpose, as well as being worked up locally During the Fall of that year, A S Whitney bought out the marble business of D J & T J Whitney and T J went to Vermont D J retained the quarries which were operated by him quite extensively in 1879 and a large quantity of it shipped for monumental purposes to Canada, Michigan, Indiana and Illinois, as well as being in good demand in our own state It was being put upon the market as Gouverneur Marble but during this year some of the western dealers nicknamed it "Whitney Granite," which term or "Whitney" is still applied by dealers to some considerable extent throughout the country when speaking about the products of the different quarries here

During the Spring of 1880 a misunderstanding arose between Whitney and Barney as to the terms of the lease and was followed by long litigation Work was therefore abandoned at this opening and another opening made across the road, an arrangement having been made by D J Whitney with F Bower Preston for a lease of part of the old Harvey D Smith farm Work was commenced on this lot July 1st, 1880 Up to this time quarrying had been done by taking advantage of the natural open seams and the use of plugs and feathers Powder was also used in natural breaking places to loosen up large masses so that it could be broken to required sizes but as the new quarry could not be worked in this way hand channelling was instituted About this time J F McAllaster became interested in the enterprise and the concern was called the Gouverneur Marble and Whitney Granite Co. An arrangement was made with a firm in Cleveland, Ohio, to saw the larger blocks while the smaller sizes were shipped to dealers as previously, either roughly broken or else pointed to size. A side track was put in during the Summer and followed in the Fall by a large steam power derrick. As hand channelling was a slow and expensive process it was replaced in the Spring of 1881 by a diamond drill channelling machine and this was the first modern quarrying machinery to be introduced here. Nov. 1st, 1883, an option was given on this property to New York capitalists and D. J. Whitney and his brother T. J., who had returned from Vermont ran this quarry for them under contract by the cubic foot until May 1st, 1884, when the option expired and they completed the purchase of the property and organized as the St. Lawrence Marble Co., retaining the services of both the Whitneys, D. J. staying in their employ until Aug. 1887, but T. J. has continued in the management up to the present time. A 16 gang mill was started in May and completed in the Fall and Winter. The Lazenby lot was also purchased about this time and about ten years later they acquired the fifty-five acre farm lot from the estate of J. K. Barney on which the first monumental marble was quarried. On account of insufficient capital being put in at the inception, coupled with some heavy business losses and a large falling off in their trade due to dull times, they went into receivers hands in Jan., 1896, and the plant was idle for several years but was bought in by M. M. Belding, one of the original stockholders, and a heavy creditor. He operated it successfully for about five years and was succeeded in the fall of 1904 by the St. Lawrence Marble Quarries who are its present owners.

The next quarry venture in chronological order was made by John N. Baxter and John A. Sanford of Rutland, Vt., in the Summer of 1881. They were assisted in the prospecting for a couple of months by T. J. Whitney, who had returned from Vermont, but he was not identified with them in developing the quarry which was situated on the old Hamlin farm now owned by Vasco P. Abbott. The opening was made about one hundred rods directly back of the lime kiln but, after working it until the summer of 1883, they were not satisfied with the quality of the marble they were getting and abandoned the undertaking and removed the machinery to Vermont.

In 1881, T. J. Whitney and others prospected with a diamond core drill on the McKean lot near the present site of the Gouverneur mill and later acquired this piece of land, organizing as the Whitney Marble Co., the incorporators being S. B. Van Duzee, Lewis Eckman, T. J. Whitney, Daniel Peck, J. W. Tracey, Abel Godard, F. H. Haile, H. E. Gates, G. P. Ormiston, and three others whose names have escaped the writer's memory. The quarry was developed during the first year and was under the management of T. J. Whitney, who retired after one year and was succeeded successively in the following years by most of the stockholders who at different times took an active hand in the management. In 1882 or 1883, they built a 4 gang mill which was partially destroyed by a boiler explosion May 1st, 1884, in which six men lost their lives. Boiler makers were repairing the boilers

and in testing them with steam caused the explosion, and as the Watertown Steam Engine Co. sent these men to make the repairs they assumed practically all the responsibility, rebuilt the mill and settled the death losses. In 1886 they purchased three acres of the J. K. Barney home lot from E. B. Hurlbut, this being where Whitney Bros. & Honeycomb took out marble for the bridge and other work and it has been in continuous operation to the present writing. Owing to insufficient capital at the outset, and their original quarry not producing a satisfactory quality of marble, they went into the hands of a receiver in 1887, and in the Fall of 1888 were reorganized into the Gouverneur Marble Co., the principal parties interested being S. B. Van Duzee, Lewis Eckman, Daniel Peck and G. P. Ormiston. The following spring

Lewis Eckman.

D. J. Whitney took the management and later became a stockholder and director. He had it in charge between 4 and 5 years during which time the mill was enlarged and other improvements made. He was followed in succession by Daniel Peck, A. Z. Turnbull and Maurice Eckman, who is in charge at present. In the morning of July 24th, 1904, the mill and other buildings were destroyed by fire and were rebuilt during the following Fall and Winter, sawing being resumed in March, 1905.

Davidson Bros., of Chicago, Ill., purchased about ten acres of J. B. Preston in 1888, it being part of the old Harvey D. Smith farm and opened up a quarry about sixty rods southwest of the St. Lawrence mill, E. B. Hurlbut being in charge. Several years later this was abandoned and a new opening made on the Milton Barney farm, formerly known as the Peter Van Buren farm, they in the meantime having purchased a portion large enough for their purpose. Their mill is at Watertown, N. Y., where the blocks are shipped for sawing. The concern is now known as the Watertown Marble Co., A. C. Davey being the general manager and Joseph Callahan in charge of the quarries.

The Empire State Marble Co., was organized in 1889 by D. G. Wood, J. W. Tracy, Gilbert Mollison and James Dowdle, the two latter being from Oswego, N. Y. They bought a part of the C. W. Overacker farm, opened a quarry and built a mill which was under the management of Mr. Tracy and later Mr. Esser, John Babcock and Mr.

W. R. Dodge.

Mitchell. The plant was sold to the Empire Marble Co. in July, 1895, the parties interested being W. R. Dodge, R. G. Dodge, L. S. Lansing, D. J. Whitney, and others, Mr. Whitney having charge of the business. This plant was leased to the Northern New York Marble Co. from Jan. 1st, 1901, to Jan. 1st, 1904, since which time it has been operated by the D. J. Whitney Co.

Some prospecting was done on the back part of the Wm. Kitts farm adjoining the Empire plant, which resulted in the forming of the Northern New York Marble Co., in 1890. W. A. Beach, Geo. B. Massey, and John Webb, were the parties principally interested. Mr. Webb was manager about eight years followed for a year by D. J. Whitney, who divided his time between that quarry and the Empire, and was succeeded by A. M. Jepson who is now secretary and manager. The Northern Crushed Stone Co. have a crushing plant on this property which is also in charge of Mr. Jepson. Their produce of crushed marble is used for road metal and concrete work.

A. M. Jepson.

In 1892 some preliminary work was done on part of the V. P. Abbott farm by the Oswegatchie Marble Co., those principally interested being V. P. Abbott, J. B. Abbott and a Mr. McGuire. They erected a derrick and put in some quarry machinery but discontinued after a few months, on account of the panic of 1893, and at present writing have not resumed.

Five or six years ago J. W. Tracy and H. P. Bingwanger, the latter of New York, commenced the development of a quarry of light colored marble on the farm of Samuel Graves on the Scotch Settlement road. It has been only partially developed and at present is not being worked.

The Gouverneur Cut Stone Co. started about six or seven years ago and was made up of five or six stone cutters part of whom retired after the first year or two leaving E. M. Hampton, Richard Mahon and O. B. Fisher interested. For the first two or three years they confined their efforts to building work, purchasing the sawed marble principally from the Gouverneur Marble Company, but later they branched out into finishing and wholesaling monumental marble. In 1902 they secured a lot from the Milton Barney farm owned by Mrs. G. B. Winslow and, after some preliminary work during that year, reorganized in 1903 into the

THE STONE CUTTERS.

Andrew Johnston, Joel Dahlquist, Robert Johnston, Lawrence Connell, Lee Collins, Robert McCaul, Edmond LaPointe, Edward Martin, Seymour Robinson, William Holden, John Jones, James McDonald, James Bodman.

Extra Dark Marble Co., when they further developed the quarry and built a mill. The management is in the hands of the above named parties.

The Rylstone Co. was organized in 1903 with Frank M. Norton as president, Fred H. Norton, vice-president, and R. C. Gooderman as manager. They are located on the back end of the Norton farm and have developed a quarry and built a mill, their first sawed product being turned out in the fall of 1904.

In 1901, D. W. C. Whitney and Edward Morrison secured part of the Clinton Hall farm about four or five miles from the village, near Peabody bridge, and opened a quarry of very white crystalline marble to be used for building purposes. From this beginning was organized in 1902 the White Crystal Marble Co., in which Chas. A. Lux, H. D. Brewster and others became interested with Whitney and Morrison. A mill was built that year and other improvements made so that they have been able to ship quite a large quantity of nice white building marble. D. E. Lux has been the manager since the retiring of Mr. Whitney and the death of Mr. Morrison.

O. B. Fisher

Hulburt & Scholton formed a partnership and started in the wholesale marble and finishing business in March 1898, handling marble from the different quarries here as well as from other localities. Their first place of business was on the Somerville road near the Gouverneur and St. Lawrence quarries but in the

Frank M. Norton.

course of about a year their quarters proved inadequate and they purchased what was known as the old tannery water power and lot on which there was a large building and removed to same making required improvements to meet the wants of their largely increasing trade. E. B. Hurlbut retired from the firm in 1903 leaving D. G. Scholton sole proprietor.

D. J. Whitney commenced a regular wholesale marble business in 1901. In addition to handling products from different quarries here and in Vermont, he has the entire output of monumental stock from a blue marble quarry in Pennsylvania to dispose of. Quite a considerable quantity of this latter marble is brought here to be finished. The name was changed in January, 1904, and incorporated as the D. J. Whitney Co. They are operating the Empire Marble Co. plant in connection with their wholesale business.

D. G. Scholton

The St. Lawrence Finishing Co. is composed of P. R. Whitney and W. B. Moran, who started in 1902. They are located at the St. Lawrence Marble Quarries and are doing marble finishing and a wholesale business.

The production of marble is one of the leading industries of Gouverneur and gives steady employment to more than two hundred men in quarrying, sawing, finishing and other work in connection with preparing it for market. The greater part of the product is used for monumental purposes but building work takes quite a large quantity of the lower grades.

As a marble producer, New York State ranks third, the bulk coming from Gouverneur. Vermont largely takes the lead in marble production and is followed by Georgia, which slightly exceeds our state.

THE MINERAL INDUSTRY.

By Amasa Corbin.

PYRITES.

The most recent mineral industry developed in Gouverneur is the mining and milling of Pyrites of Iron. Its principal use is in the manufacture of Sulphuric Acid. The mine is located five miles from the village of Gouverneur, and consists of several parallel veins dipping

Amasa Corbin.

to the northeast at an angle of about 50 degrees. Each vein is from fourteen to eighteen feet in thickness and the ore as mined carries about 70 per cent of iron sulphurets and 30 per cent of rock waste. Much of the ore is shipped and sold as it comes from the mine after being sorted. The residue is hoisted on an inclined railway, and delivered by a car over a 400 feet tramway to the concentrating plant where it is crushed, sized, dressed and washed over water-jigs such as are used in the great zinc and lead fields of Missouri. The concentrates from this mill are free from arsenic and yield about 48 per cent of sulphur. The capacity of the plant is about one hundred tons per day. The mine and mill are being operated by the Adirondack Pyrites Company, with a capital stock of $100,000, of which Amasa Corbin is President, O. J. David, Vice President, and R. G. Dodge, Secretary and Treasurer.

GARNET.

The cabinet of the late William D. Andrews contained several specimens of garnet from local sources, but the great deposit located on the farms of Frank Babcock and Elbert C. Pool, although within one mile of the village of Gouverneur, was unknown until located by J. S. and Amasa Corbin in 1902. The mineral occurs in a singular condition, consisting of masses of crystals, the largest being about the size of a marrowfat pea, embedded in a diorite matrix of extraordinary hardness. The crystals are so plentiful that they compose about twenty per cent of the whole mass. No similar formation is known to exist elsewhere. The matrix has well developed flowage lines wherever exposed to weathering action, showing the undoubted volcanic origin of both matrix and crystal. The mine was not an accidental discovery however. Becoming cognizant of Amasa Corbin's activity in promoting large corporations for mining lead and zinc in Joplin, Mr. A. Hill of Pettis County in the same state, Missouri, a brother of Mrs. Byron Billings of this village, wrote Mr. Corbin as follows:

Hughesville, Mo., (no date).

Mr. A. Corbin, Jr.,

Dear Sir:—

I take the liberty to write you in reference to mining as you seem to be lucky in finding mines. There is, about one mile north of Gouverneur on the road that goes over to Little Bow, past the Ros. Streeter place, across the flat beyond, up the rise to where William Walling used to live, go a little east along the side-hill not far, there is a perpendicular rock eight or ten feet high, of granite. Sixty-five years ago my father, Nathan Hill, built a fire by the rock. The fire shelled the rock and in the shells, there was some kind of mineral I know not. The mineral came out of the shells in particles the size of wheat and they were hard and sharp. Perhaps you may examine it. Your father, if alive, will know me. I am 84 years old.   A. HILL.

O. J. David.

Just prior to the receipt of the foregoing letter Mr. O. J. David had interested Mr. Corbin in the commercial uses of garnet, especially as an abrasive, and they had visited the garnet mines in the vicinity of North Creek, N. Y. Mr. Hill's description of his discovery as being of the "size of wheat" and "hard and sharp," led to investigation which resulted in the location of an extensive ledge of garnet covering several acres. The mineral rights were obtained of the heirs of the late Judge Dodge, a lease procured and a company formed for working the mine. A concentrating plant was erected and several hundred tons of the material was milled at a profitable margin.

Meantime, carborundum, an abrasive manufactured at Niagara Falls, was found to be harder and sharper and better adapted to buffing leather which was the principal use for garnet and corundum theretofore, and in less than one year it superceded both in the market. The plant of one of the most extensive users of garnet was also destroyed by fire in 1903 and the mining of Gouverneur garnet ceased. A recent order for $700 worth of garnet concentrates indicates that the industry may again be revived. Carborundum is not well adapted to wood polishing, being too brittle from its crystalized edges being thin.

THE IRON INDUSTRY.

By J. B. Johnson.

Iron was discovered in Gouverneur about the year 1812 at a point near the present boundary line of the towns of Gouverneur and Rossie, one and one-fourth miles from Sommerville. It was first mined about one year later at the point of original discovery, the mine being then and since known as the "Kearney."

J. B. Johnson.

The ore was in this early history of the mine hauled to the Rossie Furnaces where it together with similar ores, was made into foundry pig iron.

The Kearney mine has been operated at intervals since. Prior to 1886, the product was used in nearby charcoal furnaces, much going to Rossie, Fullerville and Sterlingbush, and the writer is informed that a considerable quantity was at one time hauled by teams to Utica. This, however, is without substantial verification. About 2,000 tons were sold to the Fullerville furnace as late as the year 1882.

The first shipments to more remote points by rail were about the year 1873, when Messrs. Lott Frost and George F. Paddock of Watertown having leased the mine from Messrs. Pope, Wheelock and Co., of Ogdensburg, the then owners, formed the Northern N. Y. Iron and Mining Co., and operated to the capacity of the mine for about two years, then getting into financial difficulties, abandoned it allowing the lease to terminate. It then remained idle until 1880, when John Webb, Jr., leased it and equipping it with modern machinery, operated it with great success for about two years, when a question arising regarding the Southern boundary, i. e. the boundary between the Kearney and Rossie Iron Co.'s property, a prolonged suit at law occurred, finally decided in favor of the latter Co., and the property came into their possession, and was operated by them until about 1894, when they discontinued operations dismantling all of their mines in that vicinity.

Messrs. Wells and Westbrook next became the owners of the property and operated it from about Jan. 1900 until Aug. 1901, when they sold to the Rossie Iron Ore Co., who have operated it since.

In 1882, John Webb, Jr., and W. R. Dodge, comprising the firm of John Webb, Jr. & Co., leased from the heirs of Philip Kearney, the mineral rights upon the farm of Bardine Clark, lying northeast of and adjoining the Kearney Ore Bed property, and developed thereon what was subsequently known as the Clark mine. This property was operated as a mine until 1896 when the low price of iron rendered operation unprofitable and it was closed down. The ore of these mines is recognized by consumers as excellent in quality, although not high in percentage of metallic iron, averaging about 45 per cent. and being rather high in silica. The formation is sedimentary and occurs at the conjunction of Potsdam Sandstone, and Limestone. The quantity is apparently limitless and the mines referred to have unquestionably a bright future when the desirable qualities of their ores are better known. In the Northern part of the town, near Elmdale, are numerous out-croppings none of which, however, have been worked.

AN EXTINCT INDUSTRY.

By Frank Starbuck.

Frank Starbuck.

The lumber industry of Gouverneur was at one time of great magnitude and importance. The old "sash" saw of Israel Porter had gone through successive transformations, under John Fosgate to the "muley," under Bidwell & Waldwin to the "gang" and under Starbuck & McCarty to the "circular" and the "slabber." The Morris mill at Natural Dam under Rockwell Barnes and his descendants, followed at a slower pace, the bulk of the sawing of lumber being done in this village from about 1820 to the close of the Civil War. In these years there was no floating of logs down the Oswegatchie, its bosom was unvexed by boom and pier, and the supply for the reciprocating teeth of the insatiable saws was hauled by teams into the mill-yards to be again loaded upon the "log-boat" and delivered at the mill upon the "log-way." No lumber was sent away for there was no means of freighting it. All this was changed upon the advent of the railway. The Oswegatchie for a hundred miles above the town, traversed a dense and primeval wilderness, untrodden save by the feet of the hunter and soon the reduction of this vast storehouse of material was being wrought into forms adapted to the uses of the builder.

In September, 1866, came Abijah Weston, already an extensive mill owner in all the Northern States and Canada, having large forest tracts, and associated with him Newton Aldrich and Orison Dean, also experienced lumbermen from the eastern side of the Adirondack mountains, "to operate in the lumber business at the Natural Dam." The firm was amply equipped with means and experience and had a trade already established co-extensive with the demands of the whole country. The fall was spent in digging stone for piers, and the winter in lumbering, the logs aggregating one million feet. At the same time timber was obtained for the mill which was erected the following spring. A branch railroad was built to the main line about one mile in length and a railway bridge was thrown across the river leading to the mill. A shingle mill was also built that year. In 1870 a planing mill was added and dressed lumber was thereafter shipped largely. In 1886 a kindling-wood plant was built and in 1888 a box factory which two latter enterprises were destroyed by fire in 1894. Four years later the saw mill averaged 16,000,000 to 17,000,000 feet annually, almost wholly of pine, spruce and hemlock. The shingle mill produced 600,000,000 shingles annually during this time. The company early acquired a large tract of forest land, aggregating about 50,000 acres at the headwaters of the Oswegatchie and its tributaries. In 1898 Abijah Weston's estate was retired from the firm by the purchase of that interest by Herbert G. Aldrich, and the firm name was changed to Aldrich, Dean & Aldrich. Two years after this in 1900, the business and remaining forest lands were sold to the Aldrich Paper Co., reserving the stock of sawed lumber and logs in the river. Of these there were about 40,000,000 feet which were soon marketed and the lumber yard, covering about 100 acres, was stripped of its valuable contents and became a barren waste of sand. This mill in the heyday of its existence was one of the largest in the country.

Meantime the industry in the village boundaries was not languishing. Isaac Starbuck who had been a lumberman and tan-

Newton Aldrich.

nery proprietor in Starbuckville and Horicon near lake George, came in 1869 in April, and with John McCarty and John P Matteson, bought the old Fosgate-Porter mill of its then owners, Bidwell & Baldwin, and after improving the property, continued it as a manufactory of lumber. The natural accompaniments of lath and shingles and a planing mill were carried on. This mill being possessed of a limited water power, was unequal to the demands of the trade of Starbuck, McCarty & Co., and a steam mill of a capacity of 10,000,000 feet annually was erected and equipped with a modern system of handling the lumber and by-products. This mill burned in July 1887, and was rebuilt the same year. In 1887, Mr. Matteson died and the two remaining members of the firm continued the business. They had a considerable tract of forest land on the river above, which they supplemented by the purchase of logs from land-owners adjacent to the stream. Their shipping yard was convenient to the main line of the railroad, and being about three feet above the track facilitated the handling of their product expeditiously. March 24, 1892, Mr. Starbuck died and was succeeded by his son, the contributor of this article. The business was discontinued in the fall of 1895 and the mill was thereafter dismantled and sold. The lumber business here and at the Natural Dam gave employment to a large number of men and when it was discontinued, much hardship was experienced by them. Continuing for about forty years, it added greatly to the wealth and prosperity of the town and many were the regrets at its discontinuance.

John McCarty.

The place of these two important industries has been taken by the Aldrich Paper Co., the successor at Natural Dam of the lumber business there. In point of numbers, there are less men employed but in output, the value is increased. The Oswegatchie now bears from the remote wilderness, logs of smaller size than once floated to the booms, and these are reduced to pulp and paper and daily shipped to the consumers, the great daily press of the country.

THE BAR OF GOUVERNEUR.

By H. Walter Lee and Robert E. McLear.

The writing of a brief history of the Bar of Gouverneur, having been assigned to two of the younger Attorneys, it has been necessary for the writers to gather their information largely from histories, public records and from personal conversations with some of the older members of the Bar, who have practised their profession in this town for many years.

It appears that in early times, it was the custom for nearly all persons between whom questions of difference would arise, to submit their cases to a Justice of the Peace, without the aid or assistance of an attorney on either side. The Justice acting as sole arbitrator and from his decision an appeal was seldom taken. The Courts of the Justices of the Peace were created prior to the year 1829, and Mr. Isaac Austin was the first Justice. The office at that time, and for many years afterward, carried more weight than it does now, and matters public and private were passed upon by the learned Court.

Robert E. McLear

Perhaps no Justice who ever served in the Town wielded the influence of Harvey D. Smith, who located here in 1824. He held the office for about thirty years and passed his judgment upon a multitude of matters that were brought before him by all sorts and conditions of men. Although never admitted to the Bar, he served as

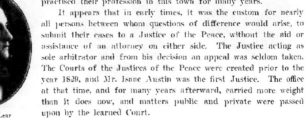

A. T. JOHNSON

G. S. CONGER

THE BAR OF GOUVERNEUR

J. F. COOK.

F. H. NORTON.

E. H. NEARY.

A. H. ABBOTT.

J. C. DOLAN

V. P. ABBOTT.

CHAS. BODMAN

Special County Judge from January 1, 1859, to December 31, 1859, when he was elected Surrogate which office he held for three years.

The first attorney to locate in Gouverneur who became identified with the history of the town, was Edwin Dodge who came here as agent of the Morris estate in the year 1829. Mr. Dodge was County Judge of St. Lawrence County for two terms and as such was one of the Judges of the Court of Oyer and Terminer, which was a Court of Criminal Jurisdiction composed of the Justice of the Supreme Court, County Judge and Justice of Sessions.

Edwin Dodge.

The office of Surrogate, one of the most important in the County, has been held by two Gouverneur Attorneys since the death of Harvey D. Smith,—Dexter A. Johnson who served from January 1, 1878, to the time of his death in July, 1880, and Vasco P. Abbott who succeeded Mr. Johnson and held the office until December 31, 1892.

The office of Special County Judge has been held by Gouverneur attorneys for the past forty-five years, commencing with E. H. Neary who served from 1860 to 1876; V. P. Abbott from 1876 to 1880; G. S. Conger from 1880 to 1896, and Arthur T. Johnson from 1896 to the present time. E. H. Neary also held the office of United States Commissioner for the Northern District of New York, for a period of about 25 years and until the repeal of the act creating Commissioners.

G. S. Conger.

E. H. Neary.

Forty years ago the legal profession had but a small number of representatives. Edwin Dodge, Charles Anthony, Cornelius A. Parker, William H. Andrews and Edwin H. Neary were the principal practitioners.

Two Gouverneur attorneys have held legislative office, Edwin Dodge, who was a Member of Assembly, for the year 1832 and George M. Gleason who served as Member from 1866 to 1871. Mr. Gleason also held the important position of Collector of the Port of Oswegatchie.

Among the attorneys who practiced for a long period of years in Gouverneur was J. Bower Preston who, a short time after the war, came from Buffalo and remained until the time of his death in 1898.

George M. Gleason.

Maj. J. B. Preston.

The first woman to be admitted to the Bar in St. Lawrence County and one of the first in the State was Miss Grace E. Robinson of Gouverneur, who was admitted as an Attorney and Counselor at Law on December 2, 1892. Miss Robinson formed a legal and matrimonial partnership with Chas. M. Hale, on June 26, 1895, and for several years the husband and wife practiced law at Gouverneur under the firm name of Hale & Hale. For the last five years they have resided at Canton, Mr. Hale being Clerk of the Surrogate Court and Clerk of the Board of Supervisors.

There are now fifteen attorneys in Gouverneur actively engaged in practice, namely: Vasco P. Abbott, Arthur H. Abbott, Herbert G. Aldrich, Gerrit S. Conger, John F. Cook,

James C Dolan, Joseph George, Dallas M Hazelton, Arthur T Johnson, H Walter Lee, Robert E McLean, Edwin H Neary, Arthur W Orvis, George W Parker, C Arthur Parker

Attorneys residing in Gouverneur but not in practice Cyrus W Hewitt, Archie F Mc-Allaster, Fred H Norton

Attorneys who have practiced in Gouverneur, but who now reside elsewhere William S Carmer, Charles N Reynolds, Charles M Hale, Grace Robinson Hale, William Neary, Edward H Neary, Jr

THE MEDICAL PROFESSION.

By Dr S W Close

The story of the Medical profession in the early settlement of a community is the story of the lights and shadows of human life Of all classes of men the physician pre-eminently has a genuine experience of life He surely sees down into the depths of it The rich man does not attempt to deceive his doctor, or put the best face on his character as he does with a priest On the other hand the doctor knows the joys and pleasures of his little community and always is invited to be a sharer therein So it comes about that he is relatively and actually the most important man in the settlement, always the one sought out in sickness and trouble and not infrequently the only one to perform the last rites, when some loved one is committed to the dust

In the settlement of Gouverneur, a physician, Richard Townsend, a young man of about 26, was the pioneer Acting as the agent of Gouverneur Morris he brought a party of settlers to the town in the summer of 1804 He seems to have had more love for adventure, political, and business life, and farming than for his profession, as it is recorded that he never practiced the healing art except for a brief time about 1813 when an epidemic of typhus fever prevailed

For a time 1811-1814, he held the office of supervisor, and in 1816 he was postmaster Very little is known of his personal life, beyond the fact that late in life he became a Quaker, was much esteemed in the settlement and died in 1826

It is recorded by one of our historians that Gouverneur has ever been known as one of the healthiest localities upon record,' and on this account, no doubt, all of our earlier physicians have been forced to engage in other callings to enable them to secure a living So when Dr John Spencer came to Gouverneur in the spring of 1807, bringing his family from Windsor, Conn , he came not to secure a lucrative field of work but to establish a practice in his chosen profession and build a home for his later years

Like the country practitioner in all fields, Dr Spencer was resourceful, practical, and willing to work Very often he must make long trips through the primitive forest in all kinds of wintry weather, and on foot with nothing to break the monotony save the inquisitive note of a blue jay, the glimpse of a startled deer, the slow trot of a bear, the sharp bark of a fox, or the fiercer cry of a hungry wolf But it was during these long walks that he did much of his hard thinking, and smoothed out seeming difficulties to the common sense level of practical experience

Dr Spencer was an eminently practical and successful physician, but as he grew older the exigencies of professional work caused him to relinquish it to others In 1822 Dr Spencer bought the "Brick Hotel," which was located near the east end of the Main street bridge and from this time did little professional work

By reference to a day book of Dr Spencer s, we learn that the fee for a visit varied from $ 50 to $3 00—that he was able to lend money to a man with a sick wife—that he received in pay all sorts of produce—e g 3 bush oats—75, 37¼ lbs honey, with the pot $3 50, 5 bush wheat $5 00, 19 lbs sugar $1 17, 18 lbs veal $ 54, 10 pumpkins $ 20, 1 bush peas $ 63, 3½ days work on the highways $2 62, 111 lbs beef $3 42, 27 lbs 12 ozs butter $1 72,

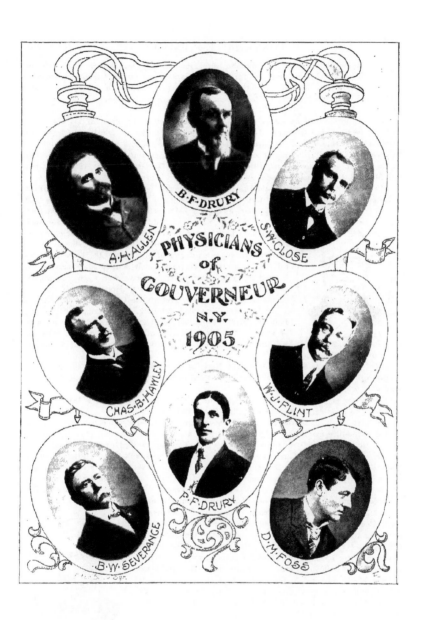

PHYSICIANS of GOUVERNEUR N.Y. 1905

B·F·DRURY

A·H·ALLEN

S·W·CLOSE

CHAS·B·HAWLEY

W·J·FLINT

B·W·SEVERANGE

P·F·DRURY

D·M·FOSS

20¾ lbs. cheese $1.36, and so on. We also learn from this day book that he had a yoke of oxen which he rented to his neighbors for 25 cents per day, and that he sometimes went with the oxen and worked himself. One charge reads, Raymond Austin, Dr To ½ days work, myself and oxen drawing logs, $ .75. Evidently the kind of work determined the amount of pay.

Of the professional associates of Dr. Spencer during the later years of his work very little can be learned at this time. Drs. Murdock, Orvis and Griffin are said to have "exercised their art with caution," and "to have paid equal attention to the rich and the poor," and left the field of labor with the respect and love of their fellow citizens. All of these passed out of the history of Gouverneur more than fifty years ago. Dr. Griffin died in 1847, and Orvis and Murdock had previously moved away.

In the year 1835, about the time that Dr. Orvis moved away, there came to Gouverneur a young physician who was for about forty years prominent among his professional associates and

Dr. S. C. Wait.

in the affairs of the town—Dr. Samuel Clark Wait. He was born in Mayfield, New York, June 1st, 1807, and began his life work as a public school teacher and a teacher of music. These occupations were not suited to his taste, and he began the study of medicine, receiving his degree of M. D. from the Fairfield Medical School, in 1833. He immediately located in Somerville, N. Y., and two years later moved to Gouverneur, where he soon became the leading physician of the town. He was actively interested in the schools and the Presbyterian Church, of which he was a member. Dr. Wait died Oct. 30th, 1875, leaving a widow and four daughters. Three daughters are still living, Mary J., wife of Chas. C. Oakes of Colorado; Katherine A., wife of Welcome A. Farnsworth of Colorado; and Sarah E., wife of Byron N. Scott of Black River, N. Y.

Mrs. Oaks is the daughter of Electa Keyes the second wife of Dr. Wait; and Mrs. Farnsworth and Mrs. Scott of Polly Thrall his third wife. The sixth wife, Jane E. Merriman died July 9th, 1893.

Dr. Peter O. Williams came to Gouverneur in 1847 and remained until 1854, when he removed to Coxsackie, N. Y., where he died March 19th, 1887.

In 1854, Dr. S. L. Parmelee came to Gouverneur. He enjoyed a lucrative practice, was a man of positive moral and religious convictions, and one of the leading physicians of the town until 1876 when he removed to Watertown, N. Y., where he died April 17th, 1881.

Dr. Edgar H. Merrick practiced here for about five years 1864-1869. He later went to Gananoque, Ont., and then to Toronto, where he died in May 1890. He left a widow formerly Sarah E. Carpenter, a son Edgar, now residents of this town, and a daughter Mrs. Snell of Potsdam, N. Y. Dr. Merrick was educated in Gouverneur Wesleyan Seminary, and McGill University, and was prominently identified with the building of Trinity Episcopal Church.

Dr. James B. Carpenter located in Gouverneur in 1867 coming from Theresa, N. Y., where he had been in practice for 20 years, excepting the years of his service as surgeon of the 35th N. Y. Volunteers. For many years Dr. Carpenter was the leading physician of the town. During his later years he spent his winters in Florida and relinquished the active practice of his profession. He was highly esteemed in the town, served as president of the village, and was a very generous contributor to many worthy causes. His death occured Oct. 28th, 1895. His only child, Mrs. Andrew Irving is a resident of the village.

Dr. J. B. Carpenter.

Another physician very prominently identified with the professional, political, and business life of the community was Dr. David McFalls. He was born in the town of Morristown, N. Y.,

Dr David McFalls

spent his early boyhood in Rossie, and on the 30th of June, 1848, received his degree of M. D. from the college of Medicine, Castleton, Vt. After practicing his profession in his boyhood town for a number of years, he enlisted as a soldier, and on Aug. 25th, 1862, was commissioned surgeon of the 142d Regiment, N. Y. Vol., and served in that capacity until the close of the war. Returning to Rossie he resumed his professional work. In 1873 he came to Gouverneur, where, with the exception of four years in Park City, Utah, he remained until his death April 6th, 1891. Dr. McFalls was an active, public spirited man, a leader among men. He represented the 1st St. Lawrence County Assembly District in Albany for two terms, 1877-8, was for a number of years one of the Coroners of the County and held many offices within the gift of his professional brethren.

Dr. McFalls married Miss Cornelia Pierce of Rossie, May 10, 1854. The widow and two children, David McFalls of Buffalo, N. Y., and Mrs. Stanley C. Reynolds of Corning, N. Y., survive.

Dr. Chas. M. Wilson began the practice of medicine in Gouverneur in 1871, and took a prominent place until 1888 when he removed to Park City, Utah, where he now resides, and is engaged in active practice.

Dr. Thomas R. Hossie was for a number of years engaged in the drug business in this town, but later engaged actively in medical practice until his death in 1900. He was very actively interested in Masonry.

Several other physicians have been located here for a longer or shorter time, among them Dr. A. J. Spencer, a relative of Dr. John Spencer, now in New York City; Dr. G. E. Baldwin, now in Syracuse; Dr. E. J. Guyette, now in Mendon, N. Y.; Drs. S. Dandurand and B. C. Cheeseman, now in Watertown, N. Y.; Dr. P. Monakey, now in Burke, N. Y., and Dr. Grosvenor Swan, now deceased.

Dr. Grosvenor Swan.

At the present time the following physicians are actively engaged in medical practice in Gouverneur: Dr. B. F. Drury, who came in 1876; Dr. A. H. Allen, in 1881; Dr. S. W. Close, in 1886; Dr. Charles B. Hawley, in 1888; Dr. Wm. J. Flint, in 1890; Dr. Fred F. Drury, in 1891; Dr. J. A. Rega, in 1895; Dr. B. W. Severance, in 1898, and Dr. David M. Foss, in 1900.

For sketches of the resident physicians the reader is referred to the biographical part of this history.

DENTISTS.

By Dr. Jas. Spencer.

Dr. James Spencer, son of Col. J. M. Spencer, was Capt. of Co. H. 20th N. Y. Cavalry, served in the Rebellion to the close of the War, commenced the study of Dentistry in 1870, and graduated from Philadelphia Dental College in 1872, commencing the practice of dentistry in Gouverneur in 1876 and still continues at the present time.

George B. Barnes, graduate of the Pennsylvania College of Dentistry in 1878, and commenced practicing in Gouverneur in 1877 and continued until 1905.

Dr. Connor, graduate of the Philadelphia Dental College in 1897. Commenced the practice of Dentistry in Gouverneur in 1898 and has continued until the present time.

Dr. A. H. Van Allen, graduate of the Pennsylvania College of Dental Surgery in 1897. Commenced practice of his profession in Gouverneur in 1898 and still continues.

Drs. McNulty, Brasie, Connor, Spencer, Van Allen.

Dr. I. G. Brasie, graduate of the Pennsylvania Dental College of Surgery in 1903. Commenced practice in Gouverneur in 1904, having purchased from Dr. Barnes his dental business.

Dr. A. M. Myers.

Dr. Thomas P. McNulty, graduate of The University of Pennsylvania in 1904. Dr. McNulty came to Gouverneur Jan. 1, 1905, and is associated in practice with Dr. Jas. M. Spencer.

Dr. Dan Waid practiced dentistry in Gouverneur from 1854 to the time of his death in 1860. He was succeeded by his brother, Dr. Andrew J. Waid, who practiced dentistry in this town from 1860 to 1870 and was succeeded by Dr. Stevens who practiced till 1875, then leaving this profession for the purpose of studying medicine.

Dr. Myers, graduate of Pennsylvania Dental College, practiced from 1868 until the time of his death which occurred in 1876. He was a man of engaging personality and made friendships that have survived the more than quarter of a century since his death.

THE POSTMASTERS OF GOUVERNEUR.

By J. B. Abbott.

The postal service was established in the town of Gouverneur Oct. 28th, 1818, and Richard Townsend was appointed postmaster. There was a small increase of business for the first few years but for many years past there has been a steady increase, as the

J. Brayton Abbott

town expanded in population and large business interests have grown up. Since the present postmaster has held the office the business has increased more than fifty per cent. The Rural Free Delivery System has been established whereby the farmers of the surrounding country are accommodated by their mail being delivered to them daily at their homes—bringing them into close touch with the business of the village and all sections of our country. There are five delivery routes from this office, all of which have been established in the past five years. This large increase represents to some extent the great prosperity of this beautiful village. Below are the names of postmasters that have held the office since the organization of the town of Gouverneur: Richard Townsend, October 28, 1818; Moses Rowley, August 3, 1824; Edwin Dodge, June 14, 1830; Chauncey Dodge, March 26, 1849; Charles Anthony, April 9, 1853; William H. Bowne, June 15th, 1855; Stephen B. Van Duzee, April 20, 1861; George B. Winslow, May 27, 1865; Horace G. Reynolds, March 3, 1883; William R. Dodge, May 18, 1886; Abram C. Gates, April 22, 1890; C. Pliny Earle, May 4, 1894; Justus B. Abbott, Feb. 10, 1899.

THE FIRE DEPARTMENT.

By A. W. Orvis.

The Fire Department of Gouverneur Village at present consists of three organizations: Gouverneur Fire Company, No. 1, Marble City Hose Company No. 1, and Rescue Hook and Ladder Company. Each of these has its separate officers, but all are included in one central organization, having general authority over the separate companies, and all the members join in an annual election of officers for the department.

The officers of the Gouverneur Fire Department at the present are: Chief Engineer, Thomas R. White; Assistant Chief, William A. Green; Secretary, Frank H. Farmer; Treasurer, Gilbert E. Hutton.

Ezekiel F. Beardslee.

The first fire company in Gouverneur was "The Fire Bucket Brigade" which was organized about 1859. It included as members Charles Anthony, George Parker, W. R. Fosgate, Gilbert L. VanNamee, Charles Clark, Henry Rogers and other business men. Charles Clarke was the first foreman, and Charles Anthony, drill master. Well water and pails were the principal equipment for fighting fire, but with these the fire company was very successful in subduing several fires, though no very large conflagration ever visited Gouverneur until considerably later than this date.

About the year 1867, the Gouverneur Water Works Company was incorporated and a water main was laid from the Main St. bridge to the Spencer Hotel, at the corner of Main and Depot streets. The water was forced by pumps from the water power at the island, by a method known as the "Holley System." This was a great improvement in fire protection for the business part of the village.

In 1868, The Gouverneur Hose Company, No. 1, was organized. Its first officers were: Foreman, J. Bower Preston; Asst. Foreman, Albert M. Barney; Sec'y., Ezekiel F. Beardslee; Treasurer, Wm. P. Fosgate. A constitution and by-laws were made and applied as far as was practical in a volunteer fire company. A hose cart and regulation cotton hose were purchased by the village, a fund for the same having been voted and a small sum of money was turned over to the Treasurer of the Fire Company for its use. Uniforms of red shirts, hats

GOUVERNEUR FIRE DEPARTMENT NO. 1.

R. Rutherford, F. Chisholm, G. H. Robinson, W. Trewey, C. Casseleman, G. R. Thompson, Eng'r. H. O. Johnson, W. Hayden, L. Lewis, E. J. Farber, 1st F.,
E. C. Mosher, fireman. S. M. David, Sec'y.

and belts were purchased and the new fire company presented a very respectable appearance. Many a hard battle with the fire fiend was fought by this company during the ten years of its existence, as will be seen by referring to the dates of principal fires given below. Some dissatisfaction arose, and on account of friction between the Village President and the Fire Company the members withdrew in a body.

This Company having thus disbanded, the village Board of Trustees selected a number of citizens to form a new company. A meeting was held January 29, 1878, and a fire company

was re-organized under the name of "Gouverneur Fire Company No. 1", by which name it is still known. The first officers of this fire company were: Foreman, John Webb, Jr.; Asst. Foreman, Albert N. Barnes; Sec'y., Frank L. Cox; Treasurer, Charles A. Ormiston. The company had about forty members among whom were Edward H. Drake, John P. Matteson, Geo. P. Ormiston, Orin H. Beardslee, Wallace H. Foster, Thomas H. Chisholm, Bradley L. Barney.

In this year, 1878, the brick Hose House was built on Clinton Street, which is still occupied by the fire company, and the basement of which is used as a village lockup.

In 1880, the LaFrance Steam Fire Engine was purchased and was used at all fires requiring it up to the year 1900. The purchase of the fire engine was largely due to the efforts of

Frank L. Cox.

Edgar H. Drake, the first Chief Engineer of the Fire Department, whose death March 10th, 1882, was the first death occurring in the present Gouverneur Fire Company No. 1, and his name engrossed on nickle plate was placed upon the steamer in commemoration of his services.

In 1900 Gouverneur village established a system of municipal water works, building a pumping station with a stand pipe on the hill southeast of the village, and a system of ten inch and smaller water mains extending on all the principal streets of the village. The cost was about $60,000—and the work was accepted Jan. 2, 1891. The stand pipe is at such a height that the water pressure on Main street is about 80 pounds to the square inch, and is sufficient to throw water over the highest buildings in the village without the use of the steamer.

Wallace H. Foster.

Until 1895 the water was pumped by steam power, but since that time electric power is used to run the pumps. In 1903, another stand pipe was erected within a few feet of the old one, and the pump house was enlarged, and new pumps installed, and the following year an additional 10 inch main was laid from the pump house to the main street, so that Gouverneur Village now has the best system of water works that can be found and the most adequate fire protection enjoyed by any village with a volunteer fire department.

Marble City Hose Company No. 2, was organized in 1891, with about twenty-five members, Alexis S. Whitney being the first foreman. This Company occupies the brick and marble hose house which was built in 1894 on Main St., Brooklyn side.

In 1894, the "Rescue Hook and Ladder Company" was organized with twenty members. A wagon, truck, and ladders were purchased by the village, and this company was installed in the hose house on Clinton street with Hose Co. No. 1.

About this time, 1894, the membership of each of the three companies was reduced to twenty members, a total of 60 active firemen.

In 1904, Gouverneur Village purchased a team of horses for the use of the fire department and general village work. The hose house on Clinton street was remodelled to accommodate this team and apparatus, with dwelling above for driver and family. A new hose wagon with pole, alarm bell and extension ladder was purchased, the hook and ladder truck to be drawn by the horses to fires. These changes necessitated other quarters for the assembly room, which is now located in the third story of E. W. Gaddis block on Main street.

The village can well feel proud of its fire department, of its standing at home and abroad, in duty performed at fires, and in the high character of its members. All the organization are members of the "New York State Fire Association" and are represented by delegates at each yearly convention. Two of the members are now holding appointments on committees of the State organization, George H. Robinson on committee of Topics, and Dexter A. Leggett on Legislature Committee.

The three companies are each provided with good dress uniforms, and each has silk banners of appropriate design which were presented to the respective companies by the ladies of the village.

Dexter A. Leggett.

It is impossible in the space allowed to give proper tribute to the many brave men who have served as volunteer firemen in Gouverneur's fire department. Many of them have passed away, but their memory is cherished not only by the remaining firemen, but by the community in which they did their work, and which they served so well, risking their very lives without fee or reward other than the consciousness of work well done. The village can afford to deal generously with its firemen, and among those who have held the position of Chief Engineer of the Fire Department for one year or more are: Edgar H. Drake, Henry C. Rogers, Frank Levasseur, Frank L. Cox, Geo. P. Ormiston, John McCarty, Bradley L. Barney, Cyrenus Vail, Albert W. Hill, Alexis S. Whitney, Dexter A. Leggett, Thomas R. White.

Albert W. Hill.

Henry C. Rogers.

A partial list of the Foremen of Gouverneur Fire Company No. 1, is as follows: Aaron B. Cutting, J. Bower Preston, H. J. Warren, A. M. Burt, Jr., Bradley L. Barney, Frank Levasseur, Alexis S. Whitney, John Webb, Jr., Frank L. Cox, John McCarty, Thomas H. Chisholm, Edward W. Gaddis, Homer Hurlbut, Stephen A. Ackerman, George H. Robinson, Dexter A. Leggett, John G. Gilmore, Geo. H. Whittaker, Arthur T. Newell, Geo. A. Palmer, Lewis E. Beardslee, Eli C. Mosher.

Cyrenus Vail.

Those who have held the office of Foreman in Marble City Hose Co.,

Aaron B. Cutting.

No. 2, are: Alexis S. Whitney, Thomas Anderson, Samuel Taylor, Samuel H. Davidson, Wm. McCullough, George Cottrell, O. L. Simons, Thomas Brown, Fred Ierlan, William Cassaw, William A. Green, George E. Bracey.

The Foremen of Rescue Hook and Ladder Company have been: Gilbert E. Hutton, Thomas R. White, Ellis H. Ethridge, John Farley, Lawrence W. Bennett, Claude Gates.

PRINCIPAL FIRES.

G. E. Hutton.

The fires resulting in the largest losses to manufacturing plants and business houses in Gouverneur Village are given in the following list which is generally correct.

It is recorded in past history that a flour and grist mill of Israel Porter burned in 1825, located on the west side of the river.

Brick Hotel owned by Peter Van Varen, burned in 1848, located at corner of Main and Wall streets.

Flour and grist mill, with part of bridge, burned in 1853.

Two-story tenement block on Clinton street, burned Dec., 1864, owned by Erwin S. Barnes, estimated loss, $3,000.

Large wooden row of buildings from Park street to Potter Block on North side of Main street, burned Jan. 15, 1875. The principal owners of the property were: Herald Office, Evan Mosher, W. F. Sudds, A. Kinney, W. A. Short, James M. Sparks, James Brodie and Killner & Morris. Estimated loss $50,000.

Three story frame hotel and store building, burned April 18, 1881. Owners, Peter Van Buren and Wm. Whitney. Located on North side of Main street. Estimated loss $20,000.

Frame Factory, doors, sash and blinds, Corbin Machine Shop and Foundry. Located North side of Main street near the bridge. Burned Aug. 5, 1882. Owners S. B. Van Duzee Mfg. Co., and J. S. & A. Corbin. Estimated loss $30,000.

Frame building of Stephen Burtis and Post Office, occupied by Horace G. Reynolds. Located on Main street, north side. Burned July 16, 1884. Estimated loss $10,000.

Large steam saw mill owned by Starbuck & McCarty, located on Hailesboro street near river. Burned July 9, 1887. Estimated loss $30,000.

Frame and brick hotel and barns (Spencer Hotel,) owned by Everett D. Pierce. Located corner of Main and Depot streets. Burned Nov. 23, 1889. Estimated loss $10,000.

Three-story brick veneered hotel, Van Buren House, North side of Main street. Burned Jan. 8, 1893. Principal owners, James B. Van Buren. Stocks—Isaac I. Block, Max Tumpousky, James W. Ormiston. Estimated loss $50,000.

The store of J. W. Ormiston contained the Town Clerk's office, and all the Town records were burned in this fire.

Frame carriage and paint shop with one dwelling, located on South side of Brooklyn street (West Main), owned by Turnbull & Gardner. Burned July 23, 1887. Estimated loss $5,000.

Gouverneur Marble Company's mill located on Somerville street just West of Village. Burned July 23, 1901. Estimated loss $30,000.

THE READING ROOM AND LIBRARY.

By Mary I. Beardslee.

One of the institutions of which Gouverneur is justly proud, and which belongs to the last quarter century of its history, is the Reading Room and Library. In 1885, a few brave hearted women realizing the need of something that would not only attract, but also be a benefit to the youth of our town, in the face of many discouragements and seeming impossibilities, decided to furnish a room with a limited number of magazines and books, which would be open to all who might wish to avail themselves of its privileges.

The project of a free Reading Room had its origin in the Woman's Christian Temperance Union and the first money contributed, $30, was by that organization, and used in purchasing furniture. A meeting was called, an organization formed the name, "Gouverneur" Free

Reading Room Association" adopted, officers elected, with Mrs. C. E. Hotchkiss as President and committees appointed to solicit subscriptions and membership. A "New England" dinner was served, an "Old Folks Concert" given, which was liberally patronized so that in December the same year, $291 were in the treasury. Rooms in the Reynolds' building were secured and Jan. 14, 1886, were opened to the public with a "book reception" and 40 vols. were contributed by those present, which with a number of magazines subscribed for the donation of local and county papers, and Miss Mary Fowler installed as Librarian, the Reading Room in the minds of the most interested, at least, was an assured success.

Reading Room and Library.

Judge James M. Smith of Buffalo sent, through Mrs. Anthony, two checks of $50 each, one from himself and the other from Mr. Robert Wilson to be used in the purchase of books. The daily attendance increased so much that before the close of the first year, it was found desirable to secure larger rooms in the St. Lawrence block, which were better suited to the purpose for which they were opened, that of providing good reading and harmless amusement for many boys and girls whose homes were destitute of both. These rooms were leased for two years, a loan exhibition was held Oct. 20, 1886, which added $91.59 to the treasury. There now being over 300 books in the library, it was made a circulating library. Tickets were sold at $1.50 per year, or books loaned at 1 cent per day, the money accruing to be known as a "book fund" and used only in the purchase of books. At the close of the year, an inventory showed 365 books, $50 worth of magazines and $200 in the hands of the Treasurer.

In October, 1888, through the efforts of Mr. Newton Aldrich, President of the Town Board, a lease of what was known as the Seminary house was obtained (by the payment, as rent, of taxes and making needed repairs) and occupied until early in 1894, when the space which it covered was needed for the new High School building, then to be erected. Rooms were again taken in the St. Lawrence block. During this time the constitution and by-laws were revised, the Association was incorporated, giving its legal standing and making it possible to receive $200 from the State yearly, provided an equal amount should be expended for books, over and above the current expenses. May 10, 1895, Judge Smith who from the first was a loyal friend of the undertaking, purchased the Sheldon property, located on Main street near the High School building at a cost of $3,500 and gave

Newton Aldrich.

it to the Association as a permanent location for the library. On October 31st, of the same
year, through the generosity of Mr B. G. Parker in giving the members the privilege of
publishing one edition of his paper, the "Woman's Edition of the Free Press" was issued.

Judge Smith received the first completed copy which came from the press, for which
he sent the Treasurer his check for $50. Others paid liberally for their copies and the project
proved a financial success. The money realized was used in making repairs and fitting the
building which had been donated, to receive the library which now numbered 1200 vols. This
was the Library home for several years, when it again became evident that more room was
required to meet the constant growth in attendance and number of books to be loaned. Mr
Aldrich, ever a friend to whatever makes for the betterment of the community, placed $5,000
in the hands of a committee to be used for a new building on the site given by Judge Smith.
This was completed and the keys given to the Board of Trustees, Sept. 28, 1900. A reception was held on that evening by the members which was well attended by three or four
hundred friends of the Library, all expressing great pleasure in the commodious rooms
which will serve as a home for the Library for many years to come. For several years the
town has voted an appropriation of $200 to $300 toward the support of the Library.

Those who have served as President during the twenty years are as follows: Mrs C. E.
Hotchkiss, Mrs Wm H. Whitney, Mrs J. T. Reynolds, Mrs E. H. Neary, Mrs I. M.
Gardner, Miss Jennie Dean, Miss Helen Parker, Mrs Andrew Irving, Miss Jennie Dean,
Mrs E. H. Neary.

The Librarians have been: Miss Mary Fowler, Miss Mary B. Brodie, Miss Hattie Church
Mrs Jessie E. Paul, Mrs N. F. Ellsworth.

The Library today contains 1040 vols. Average daily attendance 50. Books loaned during last year 5295.

THE ROUND TABLE

By Arthur T. Johnson

The Round Table Club of Gouverneur, was organized November 2nd, 1899, at the Unitarian Church, where its meetings have all been held.

Its object is fully stated in the preamble to its constitution, which reads as follows:

The purpose of this Society is to bring its members into pleasant social relations with one
another, and to afford opportunity to discuss, on a perfectly free platform, without sectarian
or other limitations, and without restriction in the range of subjects, questions (especially
living ones) of importance or interest to any thoughtful mind. It is to deal with the earnest
things of philosophy and life, and it is understood that any question whether in science, religion or philosophy, in literature or education, in history politics, economics or social
science, shall be eligible for discussion.

The following named gentlemen were charter members: Charles McCarty, H. D. Catlin,
George G. Royce, James F. Sayer John F. Cook, Arthur W. Orvis, Charles B. Hawley, Ger-
ritt S. Conger, S. F. Hartley, J. S. Corbin, Arthur I. Johnson, T. M. Robinson and C. Lellan
Allen.

And the following have since been duly elected: H. H. Noble, T. R. Hessie, George N.
Gleason, H. Walter Lee T. D. C. Ormiston, O. J. David Seward A. Conger, H. H. Herring
F. H. Norton, B. W. Severance George W. Parker, Harold B. Johnson, Joseph George,
Harry W. Forbes, Lloyd J. Corbin, Allen Wight, E. J. Noble, C. A. Livingston, Robert E.
McLear, Robert A. Irving, Amasa Corbin, W. L. Beers, R. M. York, and F. H. Lamon.

Any gentleman, a resident of Gouverneur, of good moral character is eligible to membership, which is limited to forty.

Meetings of great interest have been held each year every two weeks on Wednesday
evening, from October to May, at which live questions of every nature have been discussed,
after thorough investigation with much profit to the members.

At least one meeting each year has been addressed by a gentleman not a member of the Club upon some subject with which he was particularly familiar

The club is believed to be the best of its kind in Northern New York

---

BROTHERHOOD OF ST PAUL, CHAPTER NO 55

By George H Robinson

On Dec 21, 1898, Chapter No 55 of the Brotherhood of St Paul, an auxiliary of the Methodist Church, was organized in Gouverneur with about ten charter members It is composed entirely of men, banded together for mutual aid in church work, who hold their regular meetings on the second Tuesday evening of each month They have a roll call at present of fifty active members A venison supper is served annually under the auspices of the Brotherhood, whose proceeds go directly into the channels of Christian work The Brotherhood officers at present are as follows Geo H Robinson, President, Frank Wood, Vice President, George Frazier, Sec'y, William A Miller, Treas Appointed officers Chairman Christian Work Committee, Wm Whitney, Chairman Social Committee, F C Mosher, Chairman Membership Committee, H Beach

In March, 1903, they organized the "Cozy Branch" Sunday School on the West side and have since maintained it and are now preparing to build a neat and commodious chapel at the corner of West Main and Reade Streets The membership of the School is at present about 180

The Brotherhood of St Paul originated in Little Falls nearly nine years ago, is the oldest Methodist men's society and has become the largest Protestant denominational fraternity It has made great strides in growth and has accomplished a marvelous amount of good

---

MARBLE CITY CHAPTER, NO. 92, ORDER OF THE EASTERN STAR.

By Anna F Rogers

This Chapter was organized March 24, 1893. in the Masonic Hall, Gouverneur, N Y Mr Geo H Gilmour, Worthy Patron of Empire Chapter No 68, being deputised by Most Worthy Grand Matron of Grand Chapter, State of N Y, to organize a Chapter of O E S at Gouverneur duly obligated the following qualified ladies and gentlemen

Charter members Ida E Harrigan, Harriet Sparks, Hattie C Smith, Sophie Tumpowsky, Florence Payne, Lydia Woodworth, Kathleen McCarty, Mary I Chandler, Anna Tumpowsky, Cornelia M Sparks, Augusta Whitney, John McCarty D J Whitney, Nannie L McCarty, Martha Fuller, Marion J Sackett, Frank H Smith, Mary E Bowne, W H Hall, Mabel W Foster, Helen M Jepson, Julia S Nears, Martha C Reynolds, A L Fuller, Lizzie B Hall, A G Smith

The work of the degree was then exemplified with Mrs Florence Ackerman as candidate

At the first regular meeting in April, twenty petitions were received and so our beautiful Order has continued to grow, 205 persons having been admitted up to the present time The following named persons having held the highest offices safely guiding our ship of State into this prosperous year of 1905 Florence Payne, Worthy Matron, 1 yr, Ida Harrigan, Worthy Matron, 2 yrs, Hattie Hulbut, Worthy Matron, 1yr, Ida L Wright, Worthy Matron, 2 yrs Mary C Loveland, Worthy Matron, 1 yr, Zelma Henderson, Worthy Matron, 1 yr, Sarah Starbuck, Worthy Matron, 2 yrs Worthy Patrons, Frank H Smith, 2 yrs, Chas McCarty, 1 yr, Daniel J Whitney, 1 yr, Alexis S Whitney, 4 yrs

The present officers, for year 1905, are Ida Loveless, Worthy Matron, B W Severance, Worthy Patron, (5th year), Philena Severance, Asso Matron, Clara W Legate, Secretary,

Anna Harvey, Treasurer; Elma Gaddis, Conductress; Adaline Earle, Asso. Conductress; Sarah Bockus, Marshal; T. T. Soper, Sentinel; Rhoda F. Graves, Adah; Onie J. Gorman, Ruth; Venetia Wright, Esther; Gertrude Leak, Martha; Geruah Dodds, Electa; Nellie F. Holt, Organist; Anna G. Flint, Chaplain.

The Eastern Star is the basis of the Degrees of the Order. Its lessons are Scriptural, its teachings moral, and its purposes are beneficent.

We trust that when we are called hence by the Grand Patron on high, He "whose Star we have seen in the East," may give us each a fraternal welcome.

ERWIN H. BARNES POST, G. A. R., NO. 156, DEPT. OF NEW YORK.

By G. S. Conger.

This Post was organized May 5th, 1880, with 36 charter members. Gerrit S. Conger served as its first Commander, with D. J. Whitney as Adjutant.

Its subsequent commanders have been as follows: James M. Spencer, William H. Whitney, Fred H. Norton, George M. Gleason, Silas W. Payne, George S. Parsons, Jay F. Hodgkins, Elmer W. Grey and Warren B. Pike.

For a name it selected that of the first soldier from Gouverneur to fall in battle mortally wounded. Erwin H. Barnes, son of Erwin S. Barnes and Lucretia Allen Barnes, was born November 22, 1843, and answered Lincoln's first call for volunteers, in April 1861, at the first Recruiting Meeting held in Gouverneur. He volunteered as a private in Company D, 16, N. Y. Vol. Inf., Commanded by Capt. George Parker, and he fell mortally wounded at the battle of Gaines Mill, June 27th, 1862.

George S. Parsons.

The Post has always had the confidence and loyal support of the people of Gouverneur and its membership comes from all the towns represented in this "Old Home Week." Its special purpose has been the rendering of assistance to destitute and needy soldiers and the families of those deceased and the proper observance of "Memorial Day."

It has sought to inculcate true patriotism and love of country and its influence will long be felt in this community. It has been represented in all the Department Encampments and nearly all of the National Encampments since its organization and with its famous "Steel's Drum Corps," attended the National Encampments at Washington and Buffalo in a body.

The "Woman's Relief Corps Auxiliary to Barnes Post" was organized February 15th, 1892, and is composed not only of the wives and relatives of soldiers, but of many prominent and patriotic ladies of the town.

It has been of great service to the Post in its charitable and patriotic work. In 1900, the Post and Corps by joint effort erected a granite monument in Riverside Cemetery in Gouverneur, on a lot presented to the Post by Comrade Lorenzo Smith, and the same was with impressive ceremony dedicated to the soldiers of 1861-5.

To this lot have been removed the bodies of several Revolutionary soldiers and soldiers of 1812, and in it lie buried many Union soldiers.

The Post has also been materially assisted in its work by the "Ladies of the Grand Army of the Republic", an organization composed entirely of the wives and descendants of Union soldiers and the beautiful flag now carried by the Post was a present from the Ladies of the G. A. R.

A camp of the Sons of Veterans has recently been formed with E. H. Cole as Captain, and on their strong arms the old veterans now lean for support.

ERWIN H. BARNES POST, G. A. R.

The following is the Roster of the Post Those marked (*) appear in the group picture of the G A R

CHARTER MEMBERS	RANK	COM'Y	REG'T	STATE	SERVICE	DATE OF DEATH
Gerrit S Conger	Private	Co D	1st	N Y	Light Art	
B M Miller	Corporal	" H	20th	"	Cavalry	
*Lorenzo Smith	{ Pri'e	" I	92d	"	Infantry and	
	Private	" H	20th	"	Cavalry	
*Malon H Maxner	Private	" H	186th	"	Infantry	
J M Reynolds	Captain	" H	186th	"	Infantry	Deceased
*Thomas Prittie	Private	H	193d	"	Infantry	
D J Whitney	{ Sergeant	" C	24th	"	Cavalry and	
	Private	" C	1st	"	Vet Cavalry	
Henry Rogers	Corporal	" D	16th	"	Infantry	
James I Sayer	Private	" H	1st	"	Artillery	
*Levi N Smith	Private	" D	18th	"	Cavalry	
James B Carpenter	Surgeon	35th N Y	Infantry			Deceased
*Stephen M Thayer	Sergeant	" D	1st	N Y	Light Art	
Joseph Clifton	Corporal	D	1st	"	Light Art	Deceased
W H Whitney	Lieut	" B	50th Engineers			
George M Gleason	Lieut	D	60th	N Y	Infantry	Deceased
A N Barnes	Private	" L	193d	"	Infantry	
J P Richardson	Corporal	" H	20th	"	Cavalry	
*William Bero	Private	" D	1st	"	Light Art	
Joseph Laberdee	Corporal	" B	142d	"	Infantry	
J T Reynolds	Captain	" A	93th	"	Infantry	Deceased
John P Conger	Lieut	B	106th		Infantry	
Lucius J Ayers	{ Private	B	16th	"	Infantry and	
	Private	" D	1st	"	Light Art	Deceased
Samuel Masters	Private	" A	142d	"	Infantry	
Thomas Hayden	Private	" B	142d	"	Infantry	January 9, 1888
George Parker	Captain	" D	16th	"	Infantry	May 11, 1883
George B Winslow	Captain Bat D	1st	"	Light Art	September 30, 1893
James T Smith	Private Co I	92d	"	Infantry	January 17, 1885
William Woods	Private	" D	106th	"	Infantry	March 28, 1887
MEMBERS MUSTERED IN						
Charles R Allen	Private	" D	1st	"	Light Art	Deceased
Joseph Amond	Private	" F	16th	"	Heavy Art	Deceased
Hiram Apple	Private	" K	14th	"	Heavy Art	
J R Austin	Private	" A	39th	Wis	Infantry	
*Leander Austin	Private	" I	11th	N Y	Cavalry	
Silas A Ackerman	{ Private	" C	10th	"	Heavy Art	
	Private	" E	10th	Mich	Infantry	
Orville E Ayers	Private	" H	20th	N Y	Cavalry	Deceased
C B Austin	Private	" B	5th	"	Artillery	
*Alonzo H Bishop	Private Co K	14th	N Y	Heavy Artillery	
William Boscoe	Private	" F	9th	"	Heavy Art	Deceased
Julius C Bishop	Sergeant	" G	16th	"	Infantry	Deceased
John Bassett	Private	" F	20th	"	Cavalry	
Isaac I Beardslee	Private	" D	1st	"	Light Art	Deceased
J B Blodgett	Private	" M	11th	"	Cavalry	
John Boshaine	Private	" E	1st	"	Light Artillery	
Nathan Brotherton	Private	C	10th	"	Heavy Art	Deceased
*George A Bush	Private	" B	142d	"	Infantry	

Members Mustered In	Rank	Comp'y	Reg't	State	Service	Date of Death
A M Barnes	1st Lieut	" D	16th	"	and Col and	
	Brev BrigGen		112d	"	Infantry	August 23, 1886
Milburn C Butcher	Private	" D	1st	"	Light Artillery	
W Beckers	Private Co C		10th	"	Cavalry	
George Bishop			106th	"	Infantry	
*J H Barker	Private	L	92d	'	Infantry	
Peter Bean	Private	" C	3d	"	Artillery	Deceased
J K Bolton	Lieut	" B	106th	"	Infantry	
*H H Brown		" C	10th	"	Heavy Artillery	
James A Bennett	Private	" H	39th	Wis	Infantry	
Geo Bacon		" B	142d	N Y	Infantry	
+Peter Boscoe	Private	" B	112d	N Y	Infantry	
*Fred Charter	Sergeant	" C	106th	"	Infantry	
Abner Cross	Private	' C	106th	"	Infantry	
+Charles Clark	Private	" C	90th	"	Infantry and	
	Private	" A	6th	U S	Cavalry	
Joseph Clifton	Private	" M	19th	N Y	Cavalry	
*James Crowder	Private	" C	20th	"	Cavalry	
J V Clark	Private	" I	14th	"	Cavalry	
Chas A Cunningham	Private	" D	1st	"	Cavalry	
Rodney L Conant	Lieut	" I	11th	"	Cavalry	
J C Clifford	Private	" B	18th	"	Cavalry	Deceased
Alex Carbinaw	Private	C	92d	"	Infantry	
*Wm D Cleveland	Corporal	' D	1st	"	Artillery	
Lewis Chevalley	Private	" D	4th	U S	Artillery and	
	Private	" I	92d	N Y	Infantry	
Colvin Conger	Sergeant	" I	92d	N Y	Infantry	Deceased
*Aaron Cooper	Corporal	" D	1st	"	Light Artillery	
*George Cooper	Private	" A	14th	"	Heavy Artillery	
M B Comov	Private	" H	1st	"	Light Artillery	
W H Cunningham	Corporal	" D	1st	"	Artillery	Deceased
+Brainard Cross	Corporal	" D	1st	"	Artillery	
J P Cronker	Private	" C	35th	"	Infantry	
*S C Conger	Private	" D	186th	"	Infantry	
James W Crawford	Private	" G	142d	"	Infantry	
Perry Cross	Private	" D	1st	Wisconsin	Cavalry	
Milo B Collins	Private	" I	14th	N Y	Heavy Artillery	
Edward Cutting	Private	" I	11th	"	Cavalry	Deceased
Darius Chapin	Lieut	" M	1st	"	Artillery	
John Dusharm	Private	Co I	1st	N Y	Artillery	
Thomas Downing	Private	" B	60th	"	Infantry	
David E Downing	Private	" D	16th	"	Infantry	
*Amasa S Davis	Private	" M	14th	"	Cavalry	
John B Day	1st Sergeant	" I	11th	"	Cavalry	Deceased
M F Dimmock	Private	" D	16th	"	Infantry	November 14, 1885
David Doran	Private	" H	15th	"	Cavalry	Deceased
Patrick Dolan	Private	" C	106th	"	Infantry	Deceased
Edward G Derby	Surgeon	94th	N Y		Infantry	Deceased
James Davenport	Lieut	Co E	32d	N Y	Infantry	
Samuel Dunkelberg	Private	" B	96th	"	Infantry	
*James Dion	Private	" K	10th	N Y	Heavy Artillery	

MEMBERS MUSTERED IN	RANK	COMP'Y	REG'T	STATE	SERVICE	DATE OF DEATH
Philip Donolly	Private	" M	5th	N Y	Heavy Art	July 14, 1903
Wm Dougharty	Private	" B	5th	Iowa	Cavalry	
Gilson Downs	Private	' F	193d	N Y	Infantry	
John C Eager	Private	" D	16th	"	Infantry	Deceased
Jonathan Ellsworth	Private	" I	11th	"	Heavy Artillery	
Lewis Fuller	Private	Co B	142d	N Y	Infantry	
Milton W Fowler	Private	C	60th	"	Infantry	
Matthew Fletcher	Private	G	13th	'	Cavalry	
*E F Fishback	Sergeant	B	60th	"	Infantry	
*Charles Field	Private	" K	6th	"	Heavy Artillery	
*Ephriam Forbes	Private	' C	15th	"	Engineers	
George W Fox	Private	" C	60th	"	Infantry	November 24, 1888
James Fulry	Private	" G	11th	"	Heavy Artillery	
Hugh Foy	Private	" K	11th	"	Heavy Artillery	
*Simeon Fishback	Private	' B	60th	'	Infantry	
H S Fox	Private	" D	10th	"	Light Artillery	
Walter Fleming	Private	' F	20th	"	Cavalry	
*Norman Fuller	Seaman	U S N gunboat Susquehanna				
*E W Gleason	Private	Co L	1st	N Y	Light Artillery	
Elmer W Gray	Private	" A	14th	"	Heavy Artillery	
Asa Green	Private	" G	14th	"	Heavy Artillery	
Ward Glazier	Private	' I	92d	'	Infantry	
*W A Goodnough	Private	" M	11th	"	Cavalry	
W H Goodnough	Private	" H	20th	"	Cavalry	
John H Graves	Private	' B	112d	"	Infantry	Deceased
James Gaddis	Private	" C	106th	"	Infantry	Deceased
Frank W Gillette	Private	" C	20th	"	Infantry	
Geo Gillett	Private	' C	20th	"	Cavalry	
R L Goodrich	Private	musician—16th		"	Infantry band	
James J Green	Private	Co G	14th	"	Heavy Artillery	
J V Goodrich	Private	" D	106th	"	Infantry	
Daniel Graves	Private	" B	60th	"	Infantry	
Abel Godard	Colonel	60th N Y Volunteer Infantry				Deceased
Enoch P Griffith	Private	Co K	60th	N Y	Infantry	
James W Harmon	Private	Co B	92d	N Y	Infantry	
*W H Hazelton	Lieut	" A	142d	"	Infantry	
*Henry Harland	Private	" C	106th	"	Infantry	
James Hurst	Lieut	" B	60th	"	Infantry	
James Hutton	Private	" B	112d	"	Infantry	
George Hill	Private	" D	16th	"	Infantry	
Joseph B Huntley	Private	" D	13th	'	Light Artillery	
J T Hodgkin	Private	— K	18th	"	Cavalry	Deceased
Thomas Huftle	Private	" F	10th	"	Heavy Art	Deceased
A V Hyde		" C	50th	"	Engineers	
Charles M Howe	Private	— —	10th	"	Heavy Artillery	
Norman House	Private	— —	60th	"	Infantry	
A J Holbrook	Lieut	" E	5th	Mass Vol	Infantry	
David Ingerson	Private	Co I	92d	N Y	Infantry	April 23, 1886
Thomas Ierlan	Private	" H	10th	'	Heavy Art	November 16, 1886
Vilas Ingram	Private	' K	6th	"	Heavy Artillery	

Members Mustered In	Rank	Comp'y		Reg't	State	Service	Date of Death
Geo W Jones	Private	Co	I	193d	N. Y.	Infantry	
James Johnson	Private	"	I	11th	"	Cavalry	
Ephraim Johnson	Private	"	D	106th	"	Infantry	
H W Johnson	Private	"	H	20th	"	Cavalry	
*Proctor Jewett	Private	"	K	11th	'	Heavy Artillery	
*Ashel C Johnson	Private	"	A	106th	"	Infantry	
Wm A Johnson	Private	"	I	11th	'	Cavalry	Deceased
Gilas Johnson	Private	"	D	106th	"	Infantry	
Epaphroditus Johnson	Private	"	C	10th	"	Cavalry	May 17, 1901
Rob W Jones	Private	"	D	1st	"	Light Artillery	
S B Johnson	Private	'	I	11th	"	Cavalry	
*H S Jones		'	A	20th	"	Cavalry	
*Wm Jones							
Lewis E Knowlton	Private	Co	B	142d	N Y	Infantry	Deceased
John L Krake	Private	"	B	142d	"	Infantry	Deceased
Henry Kenyon	Private	"	B	142d	"	Infantry	Deceased
Luther O Klock	Private	"	D	186th	"	Infantry	Deceased
Minton Keene	Private	"	D	1st	"	Light Artillery	
Milton Keech	Lieut	"	L	37th	Ill	Infantry	
Charles Kinney	Private	"	D	1st	N Y	Light Artillery	
*Wm Knowlton	Private	"	K	16th	"	Heavy Artillery	
Jonas Krake	Private	"	D	20th	"	Cavalry	
C M Kinney	Private	"	D	1st	"	Light Art	Deceased
Andrew Lachine	Private	Co	D	1st	N Y	Light Artillery	
Andrew M Leach	Private	'	C	1st	"	Light Art	Deceased
John Leary	Private	"	E	2d	"	Cavalry	Deceased
Moses Ludrick	Private	"	K	142d	"	Infantry	Deceased
James Larock	Private	"	I	11th	"	Cavalry	
+H P Legate	Private	"	H	20th	"	Cavalry	
Jas R Livingston	Sergeant	"	D	16th	'	Infantry and	
	Private	"	H	20th	"	Cavalry	Deceased
*Wallace Lyons	Private	'	B	142d	"	Infantry	
Morris Lee	Private	"	B	142d	"	Infantry	Deceased
Allen C Leigh	Private	"	G	20th	"	Cavalry	
Wm Lachine	Private	"	L	14th	"	Heavy Artillery	
Geo W Lenst	Private	"	D	1st	"	Artillery	
Wm E Lamb	Private	"	K	2d	'	Cavalry	Deceased
E C Loucks	Private	"	L	5th	"	Light Artillery	
Orrin Lesure	Private	"	F	193d	"	Infantry	
Edward A Legate	Private	"	H	20th	"	Cavalry	Deceased
*Geo F Locke	Private	"	L	1st	'	Light Artillery	
*C B Minnick	Private	Co	D	14th	N Y	Heavy Artillery	
William Martin	Private	"	M	19th	"	Cavalry	
Lewis H Mitchel	Private	'	I	6th	"	Cavalry	
Wm McKean	Captain		I	92d	"	Infantry	Deceased
John Maddock	Private	"	K	99th	"	Infantry	Deceased
David McFalls	Surgeon		112d	N Y	Infantry	Deceased
*Wm McIntyre	Corporal	Co	C	10th	N Y	Heavy Artillery	
Wm Martin	Private	"	D	1st	"	Heavy Artillery	
Wallace McKean	Private	"	D	1st	"	Light Artillery	

Members Mustered In	Rank	Comp'y	Reg't	State	Service	Date of Death
Henry W Miller	Private	C	16th	"	Infantry	
Samuel E Magaw	Private	" M	35th	"	Infantry	
Lyan Mosher	Private	" C	10th	'	Heavy Artillery	
Geo D Morrison	Private	" B	92d	"	Infantry	Deceased
David A McIntosh	Private	" A	142d	"	Infantry	
Charles A Millett	Commissary		11th	"	Cavalry	Deceased
Henry McIntosh	Private	" D	1st	"	Infantry	
William T Miller	Sergeant	" H	20th	"	Cavalry	May 3, 1881
J T McCombs	Private	" D	16th	"	Infantry	
Patrick McKail	Private	" M	2d	'	Cavalry	
Aaron Marsales	Private	" C	11th	'	Heavy Artillery	
W R McKean	Private	" D	1st	'	Light Art	Deceased
James K Merrithew	Private	" D	1st	'	Light Artillery	
G L Merrithew	Private	" D	106th	"	Infantry	
James Maybee	Private	" C	1st	"	Light Art	Deceased
*W M Moore	Private	" H	1st	"	Light Artillery	
John W Marcellus	Private	" H	13th	"	Cavalry	
Geo Matice	Private	" H	20th	"	Cavalry	
*James Murphy	Private	" G	142d	'	Infantry	
Wm I Miller	Sergeant	" H	1st	"	Cavalry	
Fred H Norton	Ass't Eng'r U S Steamship Colorado					
Henry Ncener	Private	— —		Penn	Cavalry	
James F Noyce	Private	Co I'	6th	Vt	Infantry	
John O'Brien	Private	Co C	2d	N Y	Light Artillery	
H E Orford	Private	" I	1st	"	Light Artillery	
Frances Oakley	Private	' E	10th	"	Light Art	Deceased
S W Payne	Private	Co E	20th	N Y	Cavalry	
Isaac W Payne	Private	" D	1st	"	Light Artillery	
*Warren B Pike	Private	C	11th	"	Cavalry	
Stephen Porter	Private	I	20th	'	Cavalry	
G W Parker	Private	H	10th	"	Heavy Artillery	
Nelson O Phelps	Corporal	" I	50th	"	Engineers	Deceased
*George S Parsons	Private	' I	11th	"	Cavalry	
George Porter	Private	D	1st	"	Light Artillery	
J N Patterson	Private	' H	92d	"	Infantry	Deceased
J B Preston	Major		20th		Cavalry	Deceased
Daniel Peck	Captain	" K	106th		Infantry	Deceased
F H Partridge	Sergeant	" B	60th	'	Infantry	
Thomas Patton	Private	" B	112d	'	Infantry	Deceased
F H Payne	Private	" I	11th	"	Cavalry	
Nelson Pike	Private	" I	106th	"	Infantry	
*George B Pike		" D	1st	"	Light Artillery	
Richard Peck	Private	" I	106th	"	Infantry	
Samuel W Phelps	Private	" D	106th	"	Infantry	
N F Pratt	Private	" H	93d		Infantry	
Timothy Quill	Private	Co H	20th	N Y	Cavalry	Deceased
Thomas Quinn	Private	" G	3d	"	Infantry	Deceased
L R Quinn			60th	"	Infantry	

MEMBERS MUSTERED IN	RANK	COMP'Y	REG'T	STATE	SERVICE	DATE OF DEATH
Andrew J Rounds	Private	Co A	142d	N Y	Infantry	
Chas W Rickerson	Private	" C	10th	"	Heavy Artillery	
Geo W Rowley	Private	" D	14th	"	Heavy Artillery	
Thomas Ritchie	Private	" A	142d	"	Infantry	Deceased
S D Rich	Sergeant	" I	11th	"	Cavalry	Deceased
*George E Radigan	Private	" F	60th	"	Infantry	
John Rowe	Private	" C	106th	"	Infantry	March 7, 1889
L J Richardson	Lieut	" D	1st	"	Light Artillery	
*Moses Rising	Private	" E	123d	"	Infantry	
Roswell Reed	Private	" E	1st	"	Light Artillery	
John H Rivers	Private	" G	20th	"	Cavalry	
E A Rich	Lieut	" K	60th	"	Infantry	
Martin Riverside	Corporal	" B	60th	"	Infantry	
Rob Ray	Private	" I	93th	"	Infantry	Sept 23, 1903
*Walter Robb	Private	" C	20th	"	Cavalry	
W F Sudds	Private	Co I	11th	"	Cavalry	
Wm W. Siver	Private	" A	106th	"	Infantry	
Daniel W Smith	Private	" C	10th	Vt	Infantry	
Orrin Shippee	Private	" A	106th	N Y	Infantry	
Charles Swem	Private	" B	16th	"	Infantry	Deceased
Webster N Smith	Private	" I	11th	"	Cavalry	
+Jas M Spencer {	Captain	" H	20th	"	Cavalry	
	Private	" F	16th	"	Infantry	
John M Sterling	Private	" F	193d	"	Infantry	
*Samuel Smith	Corporal	" I	92d	"	Infantry	
*Lucius J Smith	Private	" D	106th	"	Infantry	
Braxton N Smith	Private	" D	1st	"	Light Art	Deceased
Fred D Steele	Private	" H	186th	"	Infantry	Deceased
H S Schwartz	Private	" F	60th	Penn	Infantry	
Edward Sayer	Private	" C	106th	N Y	Infantry	
James Stone	Sergeant	" C	14th	Penn	Cavalry	
Thos H Soper	Private	" B	60th	N Y	Infantry	
W H Smith	Private	" —	92d	"	Infantry	
Charles H Smith	Private	" D	106th	"	Infantry	July 16, 1885
Alexander Savage	Private	" A	142d	"	Infantry	March 17, 1887
Willard Stowell	Private	" A	20th	"	Cavalry	Dec 30, 1897
James F Sayer	Private	" H	1st	"	Light Artillery	
Samuel Shaw	Private	" A	106th	"	Artillery	
Patrick Shay	Private	" H	94th	"	Infantry	
John J. Stevens	Corporal	" K	60th	"	Infantry	
*Amos Streeter	Private	" M	10th	"	Infantry	
Theodore Shepard	Private	" B	97th	"	Volunteers	
*Charles D Shaw	Private	" H	7th	"	Light Artillery	
Geo B Sheldon	Private	" I	92d	"	Infantry	
Daniel Stanton	Private	Co B	13th	Wis	Regt	
Thomas Schampine	Private	" H		N Y	Battery	
James B Stearns	Private	" C	1st	"	Light Artillery	
Charles Snow	Private	" I	115th	"	Infantry	
*Jesse Streeter	Private	" I	11th	"	Cavalry	
*Wm Scott .						
George P Taitt	Lieut	Co B	—	N Y	Infantry	

Members Mustered In	Rank	Comp'y		Reg't	State	Service	Date of Death
*Alva J Trude	Private	"	D	1st	"	Light Artillery	
M J Thias	Private	"	A	142d	"	Infantry	
Jacob Thomas	Private			142d	"	Infantry	
Willard Thayer	Private	"	C	1st	"	Light Artillery	Deceased
Ansel W Tompkins	Private	"	D	16th	"	Infantry	
Russell Tripp	Private	"	—	31th		Infantry	
Jacob Thomas	Private	"	A	11th	'	Artillery	
Geo A Tann	Private	"	C	59th	"	Infantry	
Chas B VanNamee	Private	Co	H	142d	N Y	Infantry	
Spencer S VanPelt	Private	"	H	186th	"	Infantry	Deceased
Nelson VanPatton	Private	"	B	186th	"	Infantry	
J E VanOrnum	Private	"	K	106th	"	Infantry	
Seth VanOrnum	Private	"	B	142d	"	Infantry	
Andrew J VanDuzee	Private	'	D	1st	"	Light Artillery	
A H VanNorman	Private	"	B	142d	"	Infantry	
Lorenzo Woodard	Private	Co	E	1st	N Y	Light Artillery	
*Osman Welch	Sergeant	"	C	20th	"	Cavalry	
*John Washburn	Private	"	A	112d	"	Infantry	
*Richard Woodard	Private	"	D	186th	"	Infantry	
Edwin Walker	Private	"	D	106th	"	Infantry	
Simon Washburn	Private	"	B	60th	"	Infantry	Feb 25, 1885
Braxton A Woodcock	Private	"	H	24th	"	Cavalry	
Lyman Weed	Private	"	E	117th	"	Infantry	
*Charles E Wright	Private	"	D	1st	"	Light Artillery	
*Jonn Wall	Marine					with U S Navy	
David Webster				68th	Ohio	Infantry	
James Wall	Private	"	I	5th	Iowa	Cavalry	
Hiram Walrath	Private	"	H	14th	N Y	Heavy Artillery	
R H Wood	Private	'	I	100th	"	Infantry	
M B Warren	Sergeant	"	I	146th	"	Infantry	

ERWIN H. BARNES WOMAN'S RELIEF CORPS.

Erwin H Barnes Woman's Relief Corps, No 200, Department of New York, was organized Feb 15th, 1892, with forty charter members

This society is auxiliary to the Grand Army of the Republic, and its objects are to assist that Order in its work, to aid the Union soldiers of the Civil War and dependent members of their families who may be in sickness or distress, to promote patriotism in the community and especially to inculcate lessons of patriotism among the children, to aid in the proper observance of Memorial Day and to enjoy the benefits of social and fraternal intercourse with the membership of the Order The Order numbers over one hundred and forty thousand, of which there are ten thousand in the State of New York

The first President of Barnes Corps was Mrs Florence E Payne, who served until January, 1893, when she was succeeded by Miss Helen I Parker, who served two years Mrs Anne F Turner, Mrs Martha A Reynolds, Mrs Harriett Barnes, and Mrs Elizabeth Smith were the successive presiding officers Miss Parker was again elected, serving in 1902 and 1903 Mrs Anna E Rogers was the President in 1904 The present principal officers are: Mrs Dell A Hodgkins, President, Mrs Agnes Hartley, Senior Vice President, Mrs Cornelia Legate, Junior Vice President, Mrs Pearl A Turnbull, Secretary, Miss Helen I Parker, Treasurer

GLEASON CIRCLE, No. 32—LADIES OF G. A. R

Georgia Brooks   Eliz. Rondiette   Julia Ray   Laura Butcher
(Ass't Cond'r)   (Secretary)   (Sen. V. P.)   (Treas.)   Bertha Chaddic
Mary Jordan   Phoebe Jones   Eva Johnson   Cordelia Keech   (Organist)
(Guard)   (Chaplain)   (Priest)   Jun. V. P.)
Clara Smith   Hazel Dodds
(Cond'r)   (Ass't Guard)

The ritualistic and floor work, adorned with four silk parade flags carried by color bearers who are regular officers of the Corps, is impressive and attractive.

Barnes Corps now numbers sixty-four members, nineteen of whom are on the charter list. That the local Corps is held in esteem in the Order is evidenced from the fact that honors of officers, both elective and appointive, on the staff of the Department President, have been repeatedly bestowed upon members of Barnes Corps.

Regular meetings are held the second and fourth Tuesday evenings of each month, at Maccabee Hall, third floor of Egert building.

St Lawrence county has six societies of the W R C, located at Potsdam, Gouverneur, Canton, Norwood, DeKalb Junction and Hermon.

GLEASON CIRCLE No 32, LADIES OF G A. R

Gleason Circle No 32, Ladies of G A R, was organized by Mrs Eva Call Johnson, on Feb 13, 1903, with eighteen charter members as follows Mis Nellie Holt, Mis Mary Heselwood, Mrs Maria Butcher Mrs Alice Call, Mis Clara Smith, Mrs Maggie Fordham, Mis Susan Smith, Mrs Minnie Magee, Mrs Elizabeth Woodward, Mrs Phoeby Jones, Mrs Malinda Maxim Mrs Sarah Bracey, Mrs Laura Butcher, Mrs Bessie Lytle, Mrs Ella Thayer, Mrs Julia Ray, Mis Cordelia Keech, Mrs Eva Johnson

Comrade G S Conger of Barnes Post 156, instituted the lodge and installed the following officers President, Mrs Nellie Holt, Senior Vice President, Mis Clara Smith, Junior Vice President, Mrs Mary Heselwood, Secretary, Mrs Eva Johnson, Treasurer, Mrs Laura Butcher, Chaplain, Mrs Maggie Fordham, Conductor, Mrs Alice Call, Assistant Conductor, Mrs Bessie Lytle, Guard, Mrs Ella Thayer, Assistant Guard, Mis Susan Smith

On January, 1904, Comrade G S Conger, again installed the officers with Mrs Clara Smith as President

The present officers were installed by Comrade Warren Pike in January, 1905, and are as follows President, Mrs Eva Johnson, Senior Vice Pres, Mis Julia Ray, Junior Vice Pres, Mrs Cordelia Keech, Secretary, Mrs Elizabeth Bouchette, Treasurer, Mrs Laura Butcher, Chaplain, Mis Phoeby Jones, Conductor Mrs Clara Smith, Asst Conductor, Mis Georgia Brooks, Guard, Mis Mary Jordan, Asst Guard, Miss Hazel Doads

The objects of this Order as laid down in the constitution are to assist the Grand Army of the Republic in its high and holy mission and encourage and sympathize with them in their noble work of charity, to extend needful aid to members in sickness and distress, to aid sick soldiers, sailors or marines, and especially to look after the Soldiers Homes, Soldiers Widows Homes and Soldiers Orphans Homes

To be eligible to membership in this Order, one must be either a mother, wife, sister, daughter, or blood kin niece of an honorably discharged soldier, sailor or marine, of the war of 1861 to 1865

All soldiers, sailors and marines who can produce an honorable discharge are entitled to membership as honorary members, but have no vote and are not subject to assessments or dues

The organization was named after the Hon G M Gleason of Gouverneur It has a membership of 82 active and 107 honorary members, and has in its treasury $180 00

BATTERY "D"

By H O Johnson

To Mr Thomas W Osborn, a young law student in the office of Starbuck & Sawyer, Watertown, N Y, belongs the honor of initiating the movement which resulted in the organization of one of the most famous light batteries that took part in the war of 1861-1865, Battery D 1st N Y Light Artillery After the first battle of Bull Run, Mr Osborn decided to form a company of light artillery After his plans were well matured, he consulted Mr

Sawyer, who fortunately was a personal friend of Colonel Guilford D. Bailey of the regular army, who was authorized to organize a regiment of light batteries. Mr. Sawyer wrote Col. Bailey, asking if Mr. Osborn's proposed company would be received in his regiment, a favorable reply being received, Mr. Osborn at once commenced recruiting. In Mr. George B. Winslow of Gouverneur, was found an able assistant and together they secured the necessary one hundred men, reporting to Col. Bailey on Aug. 20, that the company was complete. All the

Herbert O. Johnson.

men recruited by Mr. Winslow, nearly half of the company were from Gouverneur and its immediate vicinity. August 25th the men reported at Watertown, and on the 28th left there for Elmira, where they arrived Sept. 4th. Col. Osborn says, "not a man who signed the roll was missing," being the fourth company to reach Elmira, they were designated Company D.

Sept. 6th, 1861, the Company was mustered into United States service. The officers elected were: Captain, Luther Kieffer, who had been in the regular army; 1st Lieutenant, Thos. W. Osborn; 2nd Lieutenant, Geo. B. Winslow. The first commissions received, however, were Kieffer, Major; Osborn, Captain; and Winslow, 1st Lieut. Oct. 29th, the Company left Elmira for Washington, reaching there on the evening of the 31st. That night they were quartered in a large frame building called the "Soldier's Rest," where they slept on the bare floor with knap sacks for pillows. Nov. 6th, they were transferred to Camp Barry, where a school of instruction for light artillery had been established. The battery remained there until March 2nd, 1862, under the instruction and drill and there they were equipped with four three-inch rifled guns, horses and other supplies.

Sunday morning, March 22, 1862, Battery D started for the front, it being the second battery deemed fit for service; battery B being the first to go. They were loaded on transports and taken down the Potomac as far as the Confederate blockade would permit, reaching Liverpool point in the afternoon and camping about a mile from the river. While there the battery had its first little brush with the enemy. A section of the battery was detailed to do duty opposite the blockade batteries. They got permission of Capt. Osborn to open fire on the enemy—twelve shells were fired by Battery D, and about twenty-three by the enemy. No one was hurt and Mr. Hilts says, "The boys were considerably amused by their first experience."

Capt. Geo. B. Winslow.

On April 9th, they started in transports for Fortress Monroe to join the Army of the Potomac. Mr. Brainard Cross says of this trip that after reaching Chesapeake Bay, a terrific storm came up; they were separated from the steamer that had them in tow, and for a time there was a very poor show of their ever reaching land and he confessed that he was very much "scared." They got a glimpse of the Confederate gunboats, Yorktown, and the famous Merrimac, while landing. The battery reported to Gen. Hooker, then commanding the second division of the third corps, and engaged in the seige of Yorktown. Three days after the evacuation of Yorktown by the enemy, they started in pursuit of the retiring Confederates. May 5th, 1862, at the Battle of Williamsburg, Battery D took part in its first real fight, and here as Col. Osborn says, "The battery acquired the reputation of discipline, endurance and reckless bravery which remained with it during the war, and which, too, from the beginning to the end it maintained."

The Battery did not fight with its own pieces, but manned those of a battery of regulars who could not stand the hot fire and abandoned their guns. Major Wainwright called for volunteers from Battery D and the officers and men served the guns of the regulars through the battle. Here "Young Garrison" of Gouverneur was killed, the first man of the battery killed. Lieut. Stopler, was wounded and Mr. Hilts lost an arm. Here, too, Mr. Geo. Westcott, a gunner, captured three stalwart confederates alone, and with an empty gun. Mr. Westcott was killed at Chancellorsville. Like all men of the battery, he was a good soldier.

May 31st and June 1st, the battery was engaged at the Battle of Seven Rivers, doing good service. In this battle, Battery A was captured and Col. Bailey was killed, while spiking the guns after all of Battery A's horses had been killed. Upon the re-occupation of the Field of Seven Rivers by the Federals, Battery D occupied the redoubt at the Twin Rivers where Battery A had been captured, remaining there with an occasional part in some skirmish, until June 25th, when it moved to the front and was engaged in the Battle of Oak Grove.

Monument to Battery D at Gettysburg.

After the battle, it returned to the redoubt. On June 29th the Battery was engaged in the battle of Peach Orchard, after which they were ordered to report to the commanding officer at Savage Station, and at five o'clock in the afternoon, June 29th, they opened the fight of Savage Station, for General Sumner by firing the first shot, which the Richmond papers said killed Gen. Griffith of the Confederate Army. They knocked out the moving battery that the enemy had named the "Railroad Merrimac" before it had fired more than two shots. Mr. Ed. W. Anderson in a letter to Colonel Osborn says, "Do not fail to mention how our little rifle guns knocked out that Railroad Battery, the enemy ran out on a car—How we just swept that four gun battery—clean off the face of the earth. It only took a half dozen shots to do it. We cleaned up that job and finished them before the other batteries on our left got to work."

Here Col. Osborn, then a Captain, had the novel experience of having a full battery open fire on him. He says, "I had often been a target for infantry sharp shooters, but to be a target for sharp shooting by a whole battery was new to me."

At the close of the battle, Gen. Sumner ordered the battery to report its own command. It reported to Gen. Hooker just as the battle of Glendale opened. He considering that the battery was being overworked, ordered it to move on to Malvern Hill. It had gone but half a mile, when the battle was so fierce, that without orders, Capt. Osborn ordered the battery into position and it did effective service.

On the morning of July 2nd, during the temporary absence of Capt. Osborn, the enemy made a dash from the woods in front of the battery. Gen. Griffith refused to give Lieut. Winslow orders to open fire, so Winslow opened without orders. Capt. Bramhill, who was a quarter of a mile to the right, also opened fire without orders. Winslow and Bramhill secured a good cross fire and broke up the enemy's lines, driving them back to the woods.

Battery D went into position with Hooker's division on the brow of a hill and was a very busy company until the battle of Malvern Hill was fought and won. An incident of this battle was the cleaning out of a lot of sharp-shooters who had taken cover in a house and out building about three-quarters of a mile from the battery. Corporal Sterling, a gunner, and chack shot of the battery at that time, was ordered to put a few shots in a barn that was sheltering sharp shooters. The first shell fired went through the barn, and the second exploded in the barn, setting it on fire. A general officer on learning what battery had driven out the sharp shooters, said of it, "I never saw such deadly work done by a battery as I witnessed at Savage Station and now, here today."

After Malvern Hill, the army went into camp and entrenched at Harrison's Landing. Lieut Winslow whose health was badly broken, was ordered North to enlist men for the battery. While here the equipment of the battery was changed from the three inch rifled guns to light brass twelve-pounders, and it was notified that it was selected as the best battery in the division.

The battery took part in Gen. Pope's campaign in Northern Virginia after which the 3rd army corps was detailed to garrison the defences of Washington. This was to give it a chance to recuperate from the suffering in previous campaigns.

While at Washington the battery received ninety-eight recruits enlisted by Lieut Winslow, among whom were S. M. Thayer, H. W. Freeman, and many others from Gouverneur.

The 3rd corps rejoined the army at Falmouth. At Fredericksburg on Dec 13th, Battery D lost one man killed and one man wounded.

Feb 6th, 1863, Capt. Osborn was detailed to duty on the staff of Gen Berry, Chief of Artillery, commanding the 2nd division of the 3rd corps. Lieut Geo B Winslow took command of the battery.

The battery was actively engaged in the Battle of Chancellorsville. On the evening of May 2nd, Stonewall Jackson received the wound from which he died, and at the time he was directly in front of Battery D, not more than 300 yards away. On the morning of May 3rd, the hottest fighting was directly in front of the battery. It put up a fierce fight while its ammunition lasted and until the enemy was within 100 feet of the line where it withdrew in perfect order. Shortly after Chancellorsville, Capt Osborn was promoted and assigned to another corps and Winslow was promoted to Captain.

At the battle of Gettysburg, Battery D was engaged on the 2nd day of July only, but was in the fiercest of the fight, it was in the famous Wheat Field when it fought until the position became untenable. When by command of Gen Birney, Capt Winslow withdrew piece by piece losing heavily during the movement. The battery lost eighteen men wounded and missing.

Two days after the battle of Gettysburg the 3rd army corps, including Battery D, started after Lee, where at battle of Wapping Heights July 23, and on Aug 1st, reached Brandy Station where it remained until Sept 16th. While at Brandy Station the term of enlistment of the first 100 men expired. There had been many deaths, many more were disabled. The service had been most severe, yet every man able to perform the duties of a soldier re-enlisted.

The Battery was at Mine Run on Nov 27-28 but took no active part in the battle and on Dec 3rd, returned to Brandy Station where it remained until April 30th, 1864.

May 5th, at the Battle of Wilderness, Capt Winslow was wounded from the effect of which he finally died in 1883. Capt Winslow did not again command the battery, the command devolving upon Lieut Richardson.

'   May 10, 11 and 12th, was fought the Battle of Laurel Hill, Battery D was in the hotest of the fight, firing over 600 pounds of ammunition. The batteries of Spottsylvania Court House, North Anna, and Tolopotomoy Creek were all fought in May and in the last, D was the only battery engaged. June 3rd, G. S. Conger was wounded at Bethsada Church. Lieut DeMott and one man were killed, and Capt Richardson says, "How any one escaped is beyond comprehension". June 18th occurred the battle of Norfolk Railroad and Jerusalem Plank Road on the 20th.

There was but little more fighting for the battery until Sept 29th when occurred the short struggle at Poplar Grove Church and on the 30th the battle of Piebles Farm where Lieut Richardson was wounded, and his connection with the battery ceased.

Oct 1st the battle of Chapple House was fought and here Capt Hazelton took command of the battery.

The political campaign that resulted in the second election of Lincoln was at its height.

at this time. An interesting souvenir of that election deserves copying here, especially as it
is signed by two of the bravest of

Aaron Cooper.

Battery D's brave men, one of whom
is the moving force in the annual re-
union of that famous battery. It is
a "Soldiers Power of Attorney."
After reciting an Act of Legislature
to enable electors absent from the
State on military duty to vote; it
reads: "I, Aaron Cooper, a member
of Co. D, of the first Regiment of
Light Artillery, N. Y., State Volunteers, now at or near Petersburg,
in the State of Virginia, and being

Stephen M. Thayer.

a resident of the Town of Gouverneur, County of St. Lawrence, do hereby enpower Edward
Hall, of the town of Gouverneur, County of St. Lawrence, to cast for me and in my name
or stead—my vote or ballot the same as if I were personally present at the polls at the
election to be held on the eighth day of November, 1864.   Signed,

                                                                AARON COOPER.

Witness:

         S. M. THAYER.

Then comes the affidavit beginning: On this 8th day of October, 1864, personally appeared before me, etc., and signed James B. Hazelton, 1st Lieut. 1st N. Y. Light Artillery,
Commanding Battery D.

Edward Hall.

The document was enclosed in an envelope and sealed; that was
enclosed in another envelope which was addressed to Edward
Hall, Esq. On the outer envelope are instructions in which the
recipient is cautioned but to open the inner envelope but to deliver it to the inspectors of election on election day—they were to
open it, and if found correct, were to permit Mr. Hall to cast a
vote for Mr. Cooper.

The day before the election, Nov. 7th, occurred the "affair"
of Hatcher's Run, and in Feb. 1865, a reconnoissance of six days
in the severe cold with no fires. The rest of the time from the
1st of Oct., 1864, to March 11, 1865, the battery remained in camp.
March 29th, it started in the final campaign of the war, Lieut.
Johnson in command. On the 31st of March, the battle of Butler
House or Gravelly Run was fought; Lieut. Johnson was knocked

off his horse by a spent ball and for half an hour Lieut. Babcock was the only commissioned
officer on duty.

Sergeant Stephen M. Thayer, in his diary says, "Batteries D and H are the ones that
must go to the extreme front at every alarm, just as they always have done in this campaign
under Gen. Grant."

At Five Forks, April 1st, it had it easy and on that day for the first time it guarded
prisoners—one section with Sergeant Thayer as Sergeant of the Guard, was trained on the
prisoners with orders to open fire if they tried to escape.

Then came the morning of April 9th, and Appomattox. The fighting was over, after
being in active service from Sept. 6, 1861, to April 9th, 1865, taking its part in the thirty-six
recognized battles.

The men were mustered out and discharged June 18, 1865. Thus ending the war of record
of as brave a company as ever "went forth to do battle," in all the world's history.

GOUVERNEUR MORRIS CHAPTER, DAUGHTERS OF THE AMERICAN REVOLUTION.

By Mrs Zelma Burt Henderson

On June twenty-fifth, eighteen hundred and ninety-eight, invitations were issued by Mrs Annabelle Andrews Wolfe to attend a meeting at her home to consider the organization of a Chapter of Daughters of the American Revolution Three years before this Mrs Wolfe had joined Leray de Chaumont Chapter of Watertown and Mrs G S Conger was a member of Swekatsi Chapter of Ogdensburg The pleasant associations thus formed made them anxious that their friends here should be interested in kindred topics At this meeting there were present, Mesdames E H Neary, C T Moffett, S W Payne, T S Whitney, R T Allen, B F Severance, Emelia Crane Anthony, J W Henderson, Wm Neary, June Dodge, George Pike, Ann Rushton, L M Gardner, G E Baldwin, G S Conger, Misses Dean, Helen Parker, Sarah Parker and Daisy Barnum

At our request that a Chapter be formed here the State Regent, Mrs Belding, appointed Mrs Wolfe, Regent

As evidence of the dilligent efforts of Mrs Wolf, on January 10, 1899, a meeting was held at her home for the purpose of perfecting the organization with nineteen charter members Officers were then elected and the first official act was a courtesy extended in recognition of the patriotism of a young soldier (Wm Canfield), who laid down his life in the struggle to free Cuba

Contributions were given to the funds for the monument to Lafayette, a statue of Washington to be given to France, also for a monument to a nurse of the Cuban Army, Rubena Hyde Walworth A fund has also been set aside to procure suitable markers for the graves of Revolutionary and 1812 soldiers, in this vicinity With the hearty approval of the State Regent, our Chapter was named for one whom we all unite in honoring in this our Centennial birthday—Gouv Morris Communicating with Mrs Henrietta B Morris, we learned that the colors of the Morris livery and coat of arms were scarlet and gold, which were adopted as our Chapter colors Scarlet and yellow carnations were adopted as the Chapter flower

Our gavel was made from the historical Washington elm which still stands in Malden, Mass owned by Mr Dexter and sometimes known as the Dexter elm This was presented by Mr Whittemore through Miss Sarah Parker

Hon I C Miles presented us with a Revolutionary roll for New York and Vermont

Mr W H Andrews gave us a magnificent lap-stone, formed, dressed and polished by his own hand The stone was made from a piece of one of the pillars of the old National Capitol which was burned in 1814

Among other objects of historic value which have been given us by interested friends, is a copy of the last will of Gouverneur Morris

Believing that our first and chief efforts should be in our home town we have striven to keep burning the fires of patriotism kindled by our ancestors and to that end have offered a prize of $5 in gold for the best essay, written on American history by a student of the High School, the subject being selected by the "Daughters," and announced at the Annual Commencement Exercises

A feature in the celebration of Independence Day, which has met with the approval of the patriotic portion of the community is the public service annually held in one of the churches under the auspices of Gouv Morris Chapter

A corner in the public library has been loaned by the Association for present use, in exhibiting some articles which could be appropriately shown there, including the lineage books, Revolutionary roll, a fac-simile of the Declaration of Independence, etc

Our membership is forty Our study has been most interesting, extending from pre-Revolutionary periods through Colonial History with something of local history

DAUGHTERS
OF THE
AMERICAN
REVOLUTION

Mrs. Louise H. Case
Mrs. Edith Reusswig
Miss Mary Couser
Mrs. Arthur Orvis.
Miss Blanche Hodgkins
Mrs. Geo. Dodds.
Mrs. York.
Mrs. Lucy C. Hawley.
Miss Emma Sheldon.
Mrs. E. H. Neary.

Daughters of the American Revolution

Only once has death entered our circle to diminish our number On March seventeenth, 190{, one of our charter members, Mrs Emelia Crane Anthony, was called to join the great majority in her Father's home

"It is God's will that whoever is born a subject, should not reason but obey "

The objects of this society according to Article II of our National Constitution are

(1) To perpetuate the memory of the spirit of the men and women who achieved American Independence, by the acquisition and protection of historical spots, and the erection of monuments, by the encouragement of historical research in relation to the Revolution and the publication of its results, by the preservation of documents and relics, and of the records of the individual services of Revolutionary soldiers and patriots, and by the promotion of celebrations of all patriotic anniversaries

(2) To carry out the injunction of Washington in his farewell address to the American people, "To promote, as an object of primary importance, institutions for the general diffusion of knowledge," thus developing and enlightening public opinion, and affording to young and old such advantages as shall develop in them the largest capacity for performing the duties of American citizens

(3) To cherish, maintain, and extend the institutions of American freedom, to foster true patriotism and love of country, and to aid in securing for mankind all the blessings of liberty

GOUVERNEUR MORRIS CHAPTER D A R

CHARTER MEMBERS

Mrs Martha Church Conger
Mrs Anna Belle Andrews Wolfe
Mrs Emilia Crane Anthony
Mrs Adelaide McAllaster Allen
Miss Sarah Helen Adams Parker
Mrs Julia Sheldon Neary
Miss Emma Jane Sheldon
Mrs Gertrude Alcott Neary
Mrs Florence Earle Payne
Mrs Caroline McCarty Williams

Mrs Mary Whitney Bowne
Mrs Lucy Chapin Hawley
Mrs Zelma Burt Henderson
Mrs Eva Drake Peck
Mrs Eleanor Cooper Pike
Mrs Delia Cleveland Hoogkin
Miss Blanche Adeen Hodgkin
Mrs Nettie Cleveland Royce
Mrs Philena Woodruff Severance

IN MEMORIAM

Emilia Crane Anthony

ELECTED MEMBERS

Mrs Nina Carpenter Irving
Mrs Nettie Sternburg Whitney
Mrs Harriett Church Orvis
Mrs Millicent Pope Sheldon
Mrs Emily Hagar York
Mrs Louise Haile Case
Mrs Isadore Waite Foster
Mrs Lena Cook McAllaster
Mrs Catherine J Griffing Aldrich
Mrs Zeruah Johnson Dodds
Mrs Clara Whitney Legate
Mrs Ella McKean Whitney

Miss Jennie Winifred Hudson
Mrs Eleanor Terwilliger Lamon
Mrs Julia Foster Drury
Mrs Edith Norton Reusswig
Mrs Evangeline Norton Foster
Mrs Anna Bowne Dodge
Miss Mary Church Conger
Miss Ruth Burt Henderson
Miss Elizabeth Carpenter Ormiston
Miss Jennie Dean
Miss Cora Dean

CHAPTER REGENTS

Mrs Anna Belle Andrews Wolfe
Mrs Edward H Neary

Mrs George Elton Pike

PRESENT OFFICERS

Regent, Mrs George Elton Pike

Vice-Regent, Mrs Andrew Irving

Secretary, Mrs. J. Wesley Henderson Chaplain, Mrs. Richard M. York.
Treasurer, Mrs. Robert Dodge Historian, Mrs. Charles B. Hawley
Registrar, Mrs. Everett J. Peck

WINNERS OF PRIZE ESSAY.

Subject 1900—New York in the Revolution—Won by George V. Webster.
Subject 1901—Our Navy in the Revolution—Won by Wm. Lee Soper.
Subject 1902—The Women of the Revolution—Won by Glenn W. Severance.
Subject 1903—What the Fourth of July means to us—Won by Wm. G. Smith.
Subject 1904—Colonial Schools—Won by Miss Hazel Clifton.
Subject 1905—The social and domestic conditions in the North American Colonies—Won by Miss Helen P. White.

GOUVERNEUR LODGE No. 217, FREE AND ACCEPTED MASONS.

By H. H. Gerner.

During the year 1850 several Master Masons residing in Gouverneur desiring to establish a lodge of that ancient Order united in a petition to W. H. Milnor, Grand Master of the Grand Lodge of the State of New York, asking for authority.

Sylvanus Cone.

This was granted and their first meeting "under dispensation" was held in what was known as "Lady's Hall" in the old Seminary building, Jan. 24, 1851, with Sylvanus Cone as Master, Josiah Waid, Senior Warden; William Holmes, Junior Warden; there were also present, Wm. H. Bowne, Newell Havens, Myron Cushman, O. L. Barnum, B. H. Smith, Edward Easton, Wm. Barnet, Wm. H. Andrews and Wm. R. Fosgate.

At the session of the Grand Lodge on June 5, 1851, the committee on warrants being satisfied with the progress made, recommended that a charter be issued to Gouverneur Lodge. The Grand Lodge approved of their recommendation and a charter was issued on June 9, 1851, signed by Most Worshipful, Oscar Cole; Grand Master; Right Worshipful, Nelson Randall, Deputy Grand Master; Right Worshipful Dan S. Wright, Grand Senior Warden; Right Worshipful Wm. Holmes, Grand Junior Warden.

On July 8th, 1851, Worshipful Brother, A. Kingsbury, of Canton, acting under authority of the Grand Master, constituted Gouverneur Lodge, No. 217, installing Benjamin F. Skinner, Master; Josiah Waid, Senior Warden; William Holmes, Junior Warden; and the lodge began

Myron Cushman.

Ossian L. Barnum.

its existence as a permanent body with seventeen members, sixteen Master Masons and one Fellowcraft.

Interwoven with its history since that date are the names of men who have been most prominent in the upbuilding of the town; although it encountered the opposition which the prejudices of those days prompted, there were always faithful brethren to maintain its ex-

OFFICERS OF MASONIC BLUE LODGE.

J. G. Clutterbuck John Carroll Wm. Draper Thos. Draper Wm. Palmer
    Albert Rowley H. H. Geener J. B. Abbott

istence and through steady growth it stands today the largest and strongest lodge in the twenty-third Masonic District of the State, having a membership at the beginning of the present year of 318.

The following is a list of the brethern who have served as its Master: B. F. Skinner, Sylvanus Cone, H. L. Conklin, Isaac A. Waid, C. A. Parker, A. E. Norton, Geo. B. Winslow, A. M. Barney, A K. Jepson, J. M. Reynolds, John McCarty, Geo. W. Carpenter, Geo. H. Clark, Frank H. Smith, S. A. Ackerman, T. R. Hossie, W. J. Donaldson, John Webb, A. S. Whitney, W. F. Bowhall, Jno. E. McFerran, Chas. McCarty, J. V. Baker, D. G. Scholton, H. H. Gerner.

William H. Bowne.

EDWARDS LODGE, NO. 833, I. O. O. F.

By Wm. Gardner.

Instituted at Edwards, N. Y., April 19th, 1901, with 45 charter members, the officers being N. G., M. H. Holbrook; V. G., E. C. Locke; Sec., Mott. Meldwin; Treas., Volney A. Miller. The following brothers withdrawing from their own lodges and signing petition

William Gardner.

for charter: M. H. Holbrook of Gouverneur Lodge No. 325; E. C. Locke of Gouverneur Lodge No. 325; R. P. Peterson, of Gouverneur Lodge No. 325; S. J. Darrah of Gouverneur Lodge No. 325; Joseph Dulack of Antwerp Lodge No. 477; Fay N. Gontremont of Mountain View Lodge No. 280.

We as a lodge feel indebted to our Sister Lodges for their aid in assisting us in the establishement of an Odd Fellows' Lodge at this place, and this locality has proven to be a favor-

W. S. Woodcock.

able place for the advancement of Odd Fellowship. There are now 115 members and since the time of organization there has been no member suspended or expelled.

At the time of institution the second floor in what is known as the Andrews block was leased for use as a lodge room, but as the membership increased it was found that there was

Milo E. Woodcock.

not sufficient room in which to properly exemplify the work. An action was taken for the erection of a building where the lodge might have a home of their own, and with that point in view a building committee was appointed consisting of Bros. E. A. Merkley, Wm. Gardner, W. S. Woodcock, W. B. Newton and Milo E. Woodcock, with authority to purchase a site and erect a suitable building. This committee met with remarkable success, having purchased the lot

L. D. Raymond.

known as the Haile lot, and erected thereon, a solid brick building 32x74, with basement, banquet room, and lodge room above, at an expense of about $6,000, which is an ornament to

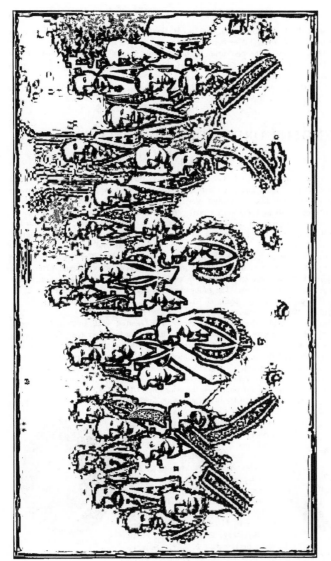

INDEPENDENT ORDER ODD FELLOWS, No. 325

Top Row, left to right—C I Mosher, P. G., W A VanDuree P G, Geo W Parker, P G, Geo H Robinson, P. G, John G Gilmour, P G, N E Brown,
P G., C E Bowman P. G.
Second Row—C N Holt, P G, Van C Borkus, P. G., R M Perival, Secretary, J V Baker, P G, C F Bancroft, P G, E H Neary P ',
Third Row—F Farrington, I G, W McRobbie, War, Herbert Clapp, R S S, F C Downey, L S, Jas Corson Chap, R McCall Cond, E Tracey, O G
Fourth Row—J V Porter, J S N C, G A Allen, R S N G, F R Butters N G, M W Randall, V G, E J Loveless, P G, Jno I McEathren

the place and a credit to the fraternity, and proof that the Order has been founded on a solid basis not only in this town but in the world at large.

Feb. 3rd, 1905, witnessed the dedication of our Temple, and it was the pleasure of this Lodge at that time to entertain the grand Master of this State, Arthur S. Tompkins, who performed the dedicatory ceremony.

The officers at the present time are: N. G., Eddie Beach; V. G., W. O. Cleland; Sec., Wm. Gardner; Treas., L. D. Raymond.

INDEPENDENT ORDER OF ODD FELLOWS No. 325.

By G. E. Bancroft and G. H. Robinson.

Amongst the many organizations in Gouverneur we feel that when special mention is made none more truly merits a more honored place in "Old Home History", than the Gouverneur Lodge of Odd Fellows No. 325. Instituted April 4th, 1888, with ten charter members they sprung into existence, receiving their State charter they began the struggle of life. Although like most all societies its youthful days were beset by many discouragements, still it sturdily pushed forward, supported and surrounded by the elements that unite in the one great cause, to "do good," especially in succoring and relieving the wants and needs of the widows and orphans, sacredly pledging their honor that no member should suffer from neglect or after death sleep in the "Potters field." It has never faltered or wavered, and after these years of struggles and triumphs, enters the 20th century with a glowing past record and a working lodge of 325 active members. The following are a list of the charter members: T. B. Mackey, Allen Murdock, Wm. H. Hall, G. A. Palmer, P. Fleming, Jacob Green, L. A. Moore, Wm. Culver, Wm. J. Perrin.

The past history of Odd Fellowship is bright with its exalted work and unselfish deeds performed. In public or private, in the home where destitution or want too often reigns— where the unfortunate too frequently find a narrow home and a meagre existence—to the polished drawing rooms of the palace and the gilded home of the millionaire, or in contrast in the happy domestic home of the farmer to the unknown home of the wanderer on the plains, or tossed on the changing tide of old ocean. Anywhere, everywhere, no exclusion, no matter what the environments or surroundings, the same "heart touch" is there. Here the God inspired elements of this unselfish Order bloom and give forth its mellowed fragrance of love.

F. W. Sprague.

"One with God is a majority", and everything founded on this heavenly principle must and will succeed and bear grand fruits for eternal life. Out of the ten charter members only one Geo. A. Palmer, remains in good standing and still continues a resident of Gouverneur. The present officers of the lodge are: Fred R. Butters, Noble Grand; M. W. Randall, Vice Grand; G. H. Summerfeldt, Recording Secretary; R. M. Percival, Financial Secretary; F. W. Sprague,

George W. Parker.

Treasurer; G. W. Parker, H. Walter Lee, G. A. Palmer, Trustees.

The thirty Past Grands who served as Noble Grands of this Lodge are as follows: T. B. Mackey, Allen Murdock, Geo. A. Palmer, J. V. Baker, Geo. H. Robinson, G. H. Summerfeldt, Geo. E. Bancroft, C. F. Smith, John A. Jones, L. B. Murray, E. H. Neary, C. E. Bowman, W. A. VanDuzee, Chester M. Hale, E. J. Loveless, C. L. Mosher, O. L. Sutherland, S. S. Dunkelberg, Alfred Smith, N. E. Brown, C. N. Holt, Geo. A. Parker, V. C. Bockus, H.

Walter Lee, Geo. B. Barnes, H. O. Johnson, T. R. Rutherford, G. A. Allen, J. G. Gilmour, Charles L. Brown.

The names of four Past Grands who joined the lodge by card are R. M. Percival, A. L. Storie, Myron Gates, and J. E. Bosworth.

During the history of this lodge 496 have been admitted to full membership, 19 of whom have passed through death's dark valley to the Grand Lodge in the eternal world, over whose names we let fall the mourning drapery of death. Since the lodge was instituted it has paid in sick benefits to the members $3,594.50, $500 of which was paid out during the past year. The furniture and furnishings are conservatively estimated at $3,000, a large percentage of which is new, having been purchased during the year of 1904.

The financial condition of the lodge is excellent, the cash on hand amounting to $2,600.

Two of the Past Grands, Geo. A. Palmer and R. M. Percival, are the two oldest Odd Fellows in the lodge as far as years of service are concerned. The former joined the Briar Hill Lodge, No. 470, Oct. 6th, 1879. The latter becoming a member of Brockville Lodge No. 9, Aug. 22, 1882. Both were admitted to Gouverneur Lodge by card.

THE TEMPLE CLUB.

By Chas. McCarty.

Among the popular social organizations of Gouverneur is Temple Club, located in a pleasant suite of rooms on the second floor of the Masonic Temple.

This Club was organized in 1897 with a membership of about sixty which has increased steadily, numbering at the present time nearly one hundred, made up from among the best class of the Town's citizens.

While its name and location might imply that its membership is restricted to the Masonic Order, such is not the case. Although its qualifications for membership have been fixed at a high standard, it is cosmopolitan, depending not upon wealth or influence, but entirely upon the standing and character of the applicant. The membership is restricted to men over twenty-one years of age, residents of the town of Gouverneur. Non-residents are admitted to limited membership under a special provision of its Constitution.

For the purpose of making a better working organization, the Club was incorporated in 1902.

On its tables are to be found the best periodicals of the day for the instruction and entertainment of its members. Innocent amusements furnish diversion; games of chance of every character being prohibited by its constitution.

John A Lockie.

The entire absence of discord or contention has been a noticeable feature of the existence of this organization; harmony, goodfeeling, and a spirit of fellowship always pervading.

Its public receptions are remembered as among the most successful and enjoyable social events.

The following gentlemen have served the Club as its Presidents: M. R. Sackett, A. J. McDonald, C. C. Dunkelberg, and James C. Dolan.

Its official list at present is made

D. G. Scholton.

up as follows: President, James C. Dolan; Vice-President, D. G. Scholton; Secretary, M. W. Bigarel; Treasurer, John E. McFerran; Directors, D. G. Scholton, M. W. Bigarel, S. A. Easton, Chas. R. Rodger, and Alfred Smith.

OFFICERS OF COURT GOUVERNEUR, NO 621, I. O. F.

Wm. Cassaw,   Wilbur Davis,   James Catson,   Peter Finnecan,   Louis Boulett,   Ed Fredenburg,

A. Kellough,   A. J. McCoy,   R. L. Kinney,   T. R. White,   James Bulger,   Henry Bucklin.

From its roll of membership, death has stricken the names of Dr T R Hossie, John McCarty, Chas C Dunkelberg, John A Lockie, Edward Morrison, William Rutherford and George W Walker, a loss felt by the community wherein they were well and favorably known, as well as by the Club

In providing a place where men can spend an hour in amusement and social converse when the cares and burdens of the day are left behind, this Club is doing its share, through promotion of friendship and increase of confidence among men to build up the standard and ideals of life

THE FORESTERS.

By R L Kinney

Court Gouverneur, No 620, was instituted Dec 14th, 1893, by Geo L Faichney, D D S C R, assisted by G S Philips, A D S C R, and held its first meeting Dec 21, 1893, with the following officers James M Spencer, Jr C D H C R, John McBride, C R ; A E Smith, P C R, John A Jones, V C R, J R Richardson, R Sec'y, F M Peterson, I S, W L Mix, Treas, Wm A Smith, S W, T R White, J W, Earl S Rickerson, S B, Edward Locke, J B, T B Mackey, Chap, Dr Fred Drury, Phy

The Order is for fraternal insurance of its members on the assessment plan, at as low rates as are possible to provide funds to promptly pay all losses and, so successfully has it been managed by the Supreme Court that it has accumulated nine millions of dollars in its Treasury, and is today, one of the strongest if not the strongest fraternal insurance order in the world The Order in Gouverneur numbers among its members some of the most substantial business men, doctors, lawyers, and men from every walk in life, and is constantly increasing in membership and influence, and is one of the most progressive orders in the village Meets every Monday night at Foresters Hall, Union Hall block Numbers one hundred and ninety members in good standing Visiting brothers are always warmly welcome

OSWEGATCHIE TENT No 244, K O. T. M.

By Gottlub Lohr

This group are the officers for 1905 of Oswegatchie Tent No 244, a subordinate branch of the Order known by the title Knights of the Maccabees of the World " Oswegatchie Tent's creation dates from November 6th, 1893, and was instituted by Deputy Spencer, with seventeen charter members, some of whom are yet living, as, A F Thayer, A E Eager, G W Briggs, W H Draper, Sam Taylor, and Clinton O Burch The object of this organization is to provide sick, accident and death benefits to the members and their families and to assist one another in time of danger, need and sorrow, for (practically speaking) a very small sum of money annually, which may be paid monthly, quarterly or annually, according to the members ability or inclination

Oswegatchie Tent had its adverse conditions to contend with like most new creations, its first important battle occurred in 1897-98, equal to the battle fought by its valiant hero "Judas Maccabeus" at Mizpah and the second one in 1901 and 1902 also equal to the one fought at Bethsur, only these battles fought by this tent were for fraternal achievements and the financial protection of the widows and orphans of its departed members

It being the smallest fraternal insurance society up to six years ago, has since then outgrown all others as regards timber, numbers and members, and lodge quarters which are one of the

OSWEGATCHIE TENT NO. 244.

First Row—Left to Right— G. Lohr, A. K.; T. R. White, P. C.; J. A Spencer, L. C.; T. A. Wells, Trustee
Second Row—W. H. Booth, M. a. A.; J. G. Gilmour, C.; A. Patterson, Chap.; A. J. Taylor, Sergt.; Jos. Gardner, Pick.;—A. Simpson, Sent.
Third Row—W. F. Clark, 1st M. o. G.; ¼ P. O. Sprague, Trustee; S. W. Close, Phys.; Geo. Forbes, 2d M. o. G.

finest in town with all home comforts. Its present membership is three hundred and thirty-two, ont of which thirteen are social members. Oswegatchie Tent had nine deaths in its history for which it paid nine thousand five hundred dollars to the beneficiaries and over three thousand dollars in sick and accident benefits, the sick benefit being five dollars a week. The accident benefits are according to the occupation a member works in and the hazardous nature of the work governs the amount of benefits received.

Its blessings are manifold and the moral standard of the member is raised, because the Order is continually trying to inculcate manly principles, integrity and veracity, all of which raise the standard of citizenship, therefore it should at all times receive the respect and support of every community where such a branch is located, especially the tax payer, on account of the fraternal support toward one other, which lowers the poor account. Oswegatchie Tent's quarters are located in the Egert block and occupy the entire upper floor, formerly occupied by the Odd Fellows.

The present officers are a bright looking lot of men and represent as a whole the most progressive element in the organization, which the members acknowledged by electing them, and it is to their efforts as well as some of their predecessors and Deputy Bacon that this Tent has no equal in this part of the State numerically or financially.

GOUVERNEUR COUNCIL No 1190 ROYAL ARCANUM.

By R M York

Gouverneur Council No 1190 Royal Arcanum, was organized October 1, 1889, with the following charter members: J B Johnson, W H West, C C Cunningham, J H Coats, J J Rutherford, W E Brodie, H F Marsh, H G Reynolds, J D Harrigan, George R Thomson, Robert Marwick, W J Barr, Frank L Cox, A A Hildreth, R M York.

The Council has now a membership of seventy-five, and is in a sound and healthy condition. There have been four deaths among the members since its organization, and beneficiaries have received $10 000.

The present officers are: R M York, Regent, Lynn Sprague, Vice Regent, W E Lynde Orator, J J Rutherford, Past Regent, W F Leonard, Secretary, A K Dillabaugh, Collector, H I Marsh, Treasurer, E C Mosher, Chaplain, J A Cummings, Guide, W Perran, Warden, F W Sprague Sentry, E H Cole Trustee, I I Block, Trustee, A A Potter Trustee, Dr S W Close, Medical Examiner.

THE CITIZENS CLUB.

By Clarence L Stinson

Organized Dec 14th, 1892. Pres, J B Carpenter, V P, Chas McCarty, Rec Sec'y, Wm Neary, Fin Sec'y, J C Woodworth, Treas A I Woodworth.

Incorporated June 27th, 1898. Pres Andrew Irving, V Pres, M L Loveland, Rec Sec'y, J A Spencer, Fin Sec'y, R G Dodge, Treas, H Sudds.

1905—Pres Charles H Anthony, V Pres Jas C Dolan, Rec Sec'y, T J Whitney; Fin Sec'y J P Killmer, Treas P A Graves.

THE WOMAN'S CHRISTIAN TEMPERANCE UNION.

By Mrs J L Duffie

Our local W C T U dates back properly to the evening of Jan 1st, 1884, when Mrs Mary I Hunt of Boston, Mass, State Superintendent of Scientific Instruction, delivered a lecture in Union Hall, subject "Waiting for the Verdict". At the close of her temperance talk she called upon the ladies present for an expression of their attitude upon the question

GOUVERNEUR COUNCIL No 1192, ROYAL ARCANUM

Walter Leonard, Flt Mosher, Frank Sprague I H Cole, Dr S W Close, J J Rutherford, R M Vonk, Lynn Sprague, J A Cummings, H F Marsh, H A Dillahaugh

of forming a local union and by a vote it was decided to go ahead with the work The week following, Miss Blanche Hazelet State Officer, met the ladies in the parlors of the Baptist Church, and then organized our society consisting of eleven charter members Officers elected President Mrs J E Duffic, Vice President, Mrs H S Eddy, Rec Secretary, Miss Lillian Tautt, Treasurer, Mrs Elmina Dods, Cor Secretary, Mrs H L Rugg, Superintendent of Scientific Instruction, Miss Grace Van Duzee, Supt Junior Work Miss F Nicols Thirty-one members were enrolled the first year

In the autumn of 1884, we served our first supper, the net receipts were $30, which we put by towards starting a Reading Room for our young people At a business meeting Oct 20, 1885, Mrs J R Crane proposed a joint conference of committees of ladies from the several churches, with the officers of the Union, relative to the raising of funds for the erection of a Public Library They decided upon and gave a New England supper which netted $129 and this sum with $30 subsequently voted by the W C T U from their treasury was in reality the nucleus of the Ladies' Reading Room fund In 1891, the Union purchased and caused to be erected at the lower end of the Park a handsome drinking fountain with ice refrigerator at a cost of $185 We have striven as a society to create public sentiment for the abolition of the drink traffic by scattering temperance literature at our annual fair and at public meetings As a society we have tried to relieve poverty and suffering in our midst, and the good accomplished during its existence is incalculable At the second annual business meeting held in 1886 Mrs H S Randall was chosen President, and served twelve years Under her leadership the Union did some grand work Next President, Mrs Mary L Beardslee who served only one year, but was an inspiration to the society The present incumbent, Miss Mary Sayer, has held the office for six years and has been an indefatigable worker

Two business and one social meetings are held every month The membership at present date, numbers 116 June 14th, 1905

THE MOTHER'S CLUB

By Mrs C B Austin

On account of certain conditions then existing in the W C T U it was thought best by several of the members to organize a Mother's Club, which was done Dec 3, 1898 Mrs C B Austin was elected President The Club continued to affiliate with the W C T U until Feb 22nd, 1902, at which time it was organized independent of the W C T U, believing that more good could be accomplished as a separate organization, which has been verified by results The object of this society is to sympathize with and assist Mothers in the duties of the home Subjects of interest to the home are considered in their meetings which are held monthly in the various homes, endeavoring to reach all parts of the town in their work

Sewing schools have been held and much philanthropic work accomplished

Present officers are Mrs C B Austin, President, Mis Barr, Mason, Hart Lang, Vice Presidents Mrs S Gamble, Sec, Mrs Willard Thayer, Treasurer

THE ST LAWRENCE COUNTY SOCIETY FOR THE PREVENTION OF CRUELTY TO CHILDREN.

Was incorporated in January, 1899 with the following trustees Robert Markwick, A W Orvis, James A Dickson, M F Gallivan, William Dodds, A W Rogers, Miss Helen I Parker, Miss Mary A Sayer and Miss Alida McFalls

The first officers of the society were: President, Rev. A. W. Rogers; Vice President, Rev. James A. Dickson; Secretary, Miss Helen I. Parker; Treasurer, Rev. M. F. Gallivan; Agent, Mr. William Dodds.

The objects of the society are to rescue children who are in a condition of suffering and want, or without proper guardianship, or living under evil influences. The society aids in enforcing the laws for the protection of children, and assists the various courts in prosecuting worthy cases. As many as fifty children have come under its jurisdiction and care in a single year.

Rev. J A. Dickson.

The officers last elected were: President, Robert Markwick; Vice President and Secretary, Miss Helen I. Parker; Treasurer, Miss Mary A. Sayer; Agent, John G. Gilmour; Attorney, H. W. Lee.

The death of Mr. Markwick, May 15, 1905, leaves a vacancy at present in the office of President.

BUSINESS DIRECTORY OF GOUVERNEUR.

By J. C. Dolan.

AGRICULTURAL IMPLEMENTS.

Barry E. D..............................Clinton Street.
Collins, Harlow D.........................Rock Island Street.
Easton, E. C.............................Clinton Street.
Fuller Fred B............................Clinton Street.
Roulston Bros. ....Main Street.

ATTORNEYS AND COUNSELORS.

Abbott, Arthur H.........................147 Main Street.
Abbott & Dolan, Vasco P. Abbott, James C. Dolan, 175 Main Street.
Aldrich, Herbert G:.......................127 Main Street.
Conger, Orvis & McLear.—G. S. Conger, A. W. Orvis, Robt. E. McLear, Corner Church and John Streets.
Cook, John F.............................93 Main Street.
George, Joseph ....147 Main Street.
Hazelton, Dallas M.......................127 Main Street.
Johnson, Arthur T. (Special County Judge), 119 Main Street.
Lee, H. Walter...........................Corner Church and John Streets.
Neary, Edward H..........................57 Main Street.
Parker, C. Arthur........................93 Main Street.
Parker, George W.........................Corner Main and Park Streets.

BAKERS.

Eager, A. E..............................55 Main Street.
Smith, Henry C...........................119 Main Street.
Geo. Bartholomew ....73 Trinity Ave.

BANKS.

Bank of Gouverneur.......................Corner Park and Main Streets.
President, Newton Aldrich; Vice President and Cashier, Henry F. Sudds; Ass't. Cashier, Jas. O. Sheldon. Directors, Newton Aldrich, Henry F. Sudds, C. H. Anthony, E. D. Barry, J. H. Rutherford.

First National Bank   117 Main Street
    President, Frank M Burdick, Vice President, Fred H Haile, Cashier, A L Wood-
worth Directors, Frank M Burdick, Fred H Haile, A L Woodworth, Lorenzo Smith,
Arthur T Johnson

BARBERS

Bowman, Chas E   St Lawrence Inn
Briggs, Frank G   81 Main Street
Call, Arthur L   Cor Main and Park Streets
Corbin, W H   75 Main Street
Fredenberg, Edw S   75 Main Street
Gillett, Ernest   Main Street
Leonard, Walter   145 Main Street
Cohi, G   131 Main Street
Mallett, John   193 Main Street
Massaw   West Main Street

BICYCLES AND REPAIRS

Freeman, L N & Co   Clinton Street
Lytle, Walter E   Clinton Street

BLACKSMITHS

Allen, G A   Clinton Street
Bouck, John M   Cor Main and Wall Streets
Doane, J H   Austin Street
Fortune, w J   Clinton Street
Holt, Capt   Clinton Street
Hutt, Benj   Clinton Street
Laberdee, Martin   Clinton Street
Merritt, W H   Park Street
Merritt, C B   .   Water Street
McKean, Wm   Park Street
Webster, J A   Clinton Street
Williams, D A   West Main Street

BROKER

R M Brown   99 Main Street

BOOKS AND STATIONERY

Donald, Chis C   51 Main Street
Draper, Wm H   153 Main Street
Kinney, B O   83 Main Street
Merid Bros   37 Main Street

BOOTS AND SHOES

Block, I I   99 Main Street
Edgar, F J   101 Main Street
Kinney, A & Son   79 Main Street
Marsh, H I   73 Main Street
Ormiston, Jas W   Cor Park and Main Streets
Schwartzman, J   133 Main Street

BOTTLING WORKS

Brooks, R J   191 Main Street
Scalzo, Fred   Depot Street

BROODER AND INCUBATOR MANUFACTURERS

Bennett, J A & Sons   West Main Street
Pettis, Fh   ⁄   Mill Street

CARRIAGE DEALERS

Barry, E D   Clinton Street
Freeman, F N & Co   Clinton Street
Henderson, J W   Clinton Street

CIGAR MANUFACTORIES

Laval, Andrew   West Main Street
Seaman, B H   51 Main Street

CLOTHING AND FURNISHINGS

Block, I I   99 Main Street
Elliott Bros   145 Main Street
Gerner, H H   133 Main Street
Kinney A & Son   79 Main Street
Tait, Geo L   Church Street
Schwartzman, J   133 Main Street

COAL DEALERS

Corbin, W S   Near Depot
Jenne & Laidlaw—E A Jenne, W A Laidlaw, Rear of Depot
Noble, H H   Rear of Depot

CARPENTERS

Barnes, A N	Lynde, W E	Rogers, Henry
Backus, David	McRobbie, William	Robinson, Geo
Clapp, Al	Miller, Jerry	Stacy, Geo
Ethridge, Ellis	Palmer, Geo	Stone, F J
Johnson, J H	Puttie, Thos	Turnbull, Frank
Jerden, Frank	Pickit, Alonzo	Wilson, John
Love, Fred	Quill, Thos	West, J W
Lytle, Henry		

CONTRACTORS AND BUILDERS

Carpenter, J H	Ethridge, Ellis	Post, Henry H
Corbin, W S	Johnson J H	

CLUBS

Citizens' Club   153 Main Street
Masonic Temple Club   Masonic Temple

DENTISTS

Brasie, Ivan   Cor Main and Park Streets
Connor, Wm R   107 Main Street
McNulty, T P   121 Main Street
Spencer, Jas A   121 Main Street
Spencer, Jas M   121 Main Street
Van Allen, W C   103 Main Street

DRAYMEN

Conkey, Chas	Leach, Walter	Rickerson, Chas
Goodale, Earl	Hutton, John	Whalen, Wm
Harper, Henry	Martin, I H	Whalen, Jas
Hayden, Henry		

DRESSMAKERS

Ayers, Mrs Lucy   Somerville Street
Ferguson & Jamieson   Park Street
Henderson, Mrs J W   Clinton Street
Lytle, Mrs Walter E   Gleason Street
Love, Mrs Fred   Gleason Street
Lytle, Mrs Elmer   Peck Block

McGillis, Mrs J H   147 Main Street
McNally, Mrs Kate   Babcock Street
Prouts, Mrs Hiram   Somerville Street
Rawson Mrs E C   Cor Barnes and Gordon Streets
Scott, Bessie   Barnes Street
Storie, Carrie   Main Street
Stinson, Susan B   Sterling Street
Wilson, Nellie   Gordon Street
Williard Mrs A   103 Main Street
Whitney, Mrs P R   Somerville Street

DRUGGISTS

Donald, C C   51 Main Street
Draper, Wm H   153 Main Street
Kinney, B O   83 Main Street
Mead Bros   97 Main Street
Nicholson, J J   West Main Street
Payne Chemical Company   191 Main Street

DRY GOODS

Leak, Geo F   79 Main Street
McAllaster, J E & Sons   95 Main Street
Taitt, Geo P & Son   81 Main Street
Potter, A A & Co   131 Main Street
Rutherford, J H   149 Main Street

EXPRESS COMPANY

American Express Company   173 Main Street

FARMERS' SHEDS

Clinton Street Sheds   Clinton Street
Fuller, Fred B   Clinton Street
Van Norman, Albert   Rear of Bank of Gouverneur
Roulston Bros   Main Street

FLOUR AND FEED

Frazier, P A   Clinton Street
McAllaster, J E & Sons   Clinton Street—West Main Street
Noble, H H   Near Depot

FLORISTS

Brainard, I M   Rock Island Street
Rogers, H C   .   Cor Church and John Streets

FURNITURE

Markwick & Cushman   177 Main Street
Mosher & Sprague   169 Main Street
Van Duzee, S B Mfg Co   Church Street

GROCERS

Brown, N E   Clinton Street
Cole, E H   57 Main Street
Davis & Sprague—W A Davis, B W Sprague—137 Main Street
Frazier, A P   Clinton Street
Fuller, A L   Clinton Street
Hazelton, G D   West Main Street
Harvey & Newell—Warren W Harvey, Arthur Newell—129 Main Street
Hutton, G E   167 Main Street
McFerran & Sprague—John E McFerran, Lewis Sprague—195 Main Street

Moxley, Sam	Grove Street
Randall, Rella J	West Main Street
Swett, Lotus A	179 Main Street
St Louis, Adolph	Grove Street

HARDWARE

Bowne & Co	.Church Street
Cutting & Perrin	91 Main Street
Williams, D H	185 Main Street

HOTELS

St Lawrence Inn	Main Street
The Hinton	Main Street
Clinton House	Clinton Street
Marble City Hotel	Depot Street
Brooklyn House	West Main Street
Grove Hotel	West Main Street
Gouverneur Hotel	Clinton Street

ICE DEALERS

Freeman, Henry H

INSURANCE

Baker, J V & Co—J V Baker, Frank B Harris—143 Main Street	
Brown, B F	Cor Church and John Streets
Larle, C P	81 Main Street
Leggett, D A	55 Main Street

JEWELERS

Hall, F K	101 Main Street
Laberdee, E S	51 Main Street
York & Goodnough—R M York, R E Goodnough—173 Main Street	

LAUNDRY

Gouverneur Steam Laundry	John Street

LIVERIES

Bickford, John G	Rear of St Lawrence Inn
Campbell, C E	Trinity Avenue
Dickson, A A	William Street
Holt, Marvin	John Street
Overacker, Albert W	Trinity Avenue
Smith, A. C	. Clinton Street

LUMBER

Gouverneur Lumber Company	Hailesboro Street
Parker, B G	West Main Street
Van Duzee, S B Mfg Co	Main Street

MACHINE SHOPS

Gouverneur Machine Works

MEAT MARKETS

Jackson, E W	57 Main Street
Hall, W H	137 Main Street
Munger & Quinn	West Main Street
Swett, Lotus A	179 Main Street

MILLINERY

Clark & Boudiette	177 Main Street
Carpenter, Mrs B J	William Street
Easton, Mrs A N	Trinity Avenue

McIntyre, Miss E J   133 Main Street
Mosher, Mrs L C   John Street
Tautt. Geo P & Son   81 Main Street
Ryan, H H   Masonic Temple

MUSICAL INSTRUMENTS

Marsh, J M   143 Main Street
Union Hall Music Store   Church Street

NEWS STANDS

Draper, Wm H   133 Main Street
Kinney, B O   83 Main Street

MANUFACTURERS

Aldrich Paper Co   Natural Dam
Adirondack Pyrites Co
Bennett, J A & Sons, Brooders and Incubators, West Main Street
Ontario Talc Company, offices 131 Main Stret, Mill at Fullerville
International Pulp Co, offices Union Hall Bldg, General Offices New York City   Seven Talc Mills
Union Talc Company's Offices, offices 167 Main Street, Three Mills
U S Talc Co Offices 19 Main Street Mill Dodgeville
Pettis, Eli, Brooders and Incubators, Mill Street
McAllaster, J F & Sons, Flour and Feed, Main Street

MARBLE QUARRIES

St Lawrence   Gouverneur   Davidson
Northern New York   White Crystal   Ralstone
Empire   Extra Dark

MARBLE DEALERS

Crooks & McLean   William Street
Scholton, D G   West Main Street
Whitney, D J   Main Street

OPTICIANS

Cummings, J Arthur   133 Main Street
Hall E K   101 Main Street
Severance, B W   37 Main Street
York, R M   173 Main Street

PAINTERS AND PAPER HANGERS

Bignall, Harvey D   Laston, Sermour   Shepard, L H
Beach, Henry   Kenyon, Chas   Woodman, Fred
Barbary, Murray   Porter, M A   Wooster, Jos
Booth, Wesley   Raymond, Chas

PLASTERERS

Barbary George   Barbary, Walter   West, Ed

PHOTOGRAPHERS

Cunningham, C C   Main Street
Rumons, C L   Park Street
Shepard, L W   John Street

PHYSICIANS

Allen, A H   William Street
Close, S W   Cor Church and Grove Streets
Drury, B F   Cor Howard and Park Streets
Drury, F F   Park Street
Ebnt, Wm J   Main Street

Foss, D M — John Street
Hawley, Chas B — Main Street
Rega, John A — Barnes Street
Severance, B W — 53 Main Street

PRINTERS AND PUBLISHERS

Cox, Frank — 55 Main Street
Gouv Free Press — Cor Main and Park Streets
Grand Army Journal
Northern Tribune — 179 Main Street

STONE MASONS

Bush, George	Desharm, Jas	Summons, Edw
Compo, John	Gardner, Jos	Snow, Chas
Countryman, Wm	McCarthy, Wm	Watson, Zachary
Castleman, Chester	rost, Henry H	Watson, Owen

STENOGRAPHERS

Broeffle, Eunice —Conger, Orvis & McLean Law Office, Cor Church and John Streets
Bogart, Roy D—U S Tale Co Office, 119 Main Street
Fulton, Mrs Etta E—D J Whitney Marble Co Office, Main Street
Hodgkin, Harry D—Gouv Machine Co Office, Main Street
Graham, John N—D J Whitney Marble Co Office, Main Street
O'Brien, Bertha F —Abbott & Dolan's Law Offices
Spotten, Mary —J A Bennett & Sons Office, West Main Street

REAL ESTATE

Brown, B F — Cor Church and John Streets
Baker, J V & Co—J V Baker, Frank B Harris—143 Main Street
Pattison, John — Cor Park and Main Streets
Rogers, H C — Cor Church and John Streets
Sheen, D H — 177 Main Street

RESTAURANTS

Eager, A E — 53 Main Street
Johnson, G B — Under Post Office
Smith, H C — 119 Main Street
Turnbull, J C — Clinton Street

SHOE MAKERS

Boudrette, E D — West Main Street
Gardner, Alfred — Clinton Street
Leahy, James — Marsh Shoe Store
McGee, R A — Ormiston Shoe Store
O'Brien, Peter — 55 Main Street

TELEPHONE AND TELEGRAPH COMPANIES

Central New York Telephone and Telegraph Company
Great Northwestern Telegraph Company
Western Union Telegraph Company
North Western Telephone Company

UNDERTAKERS

Markwick & Cushman — 177 Main Street
Mosher & Sprague — 169 Main Street

VARIETY STORES

Draper, John N — 75 Main Street
Ormiston, Jas W — Cor Park and Main Streets
Ryan, H H — Masonic Temple

VETERINARIES.

Merritt, S. C..............................Water Street.
Summerfeldt, Geo. H.......................Park Street.

WOOD YARDS.

Corbin, W. S..............................Rear of Depot.
Jenne & Laidlaw—E. A. Jenne, Wm. A. Laidlaw—Rear of Depot.
Noble. H. H...............................Rear of Depot.

THE LACE INDUSTRY.

By Chas. H. Clark.

The pride of Gouverneur is the splendid plant of the International Lace Manufacturing Company erected in 1892 principally through the brains, energy and capital of its citizens and the Lesser brothers. It stands on the Brooklyn side of the river on a site the most advantageous from a health and shipping standpoint that could have been chosen. By its location in Gouverneur a page is added to the history of the village of which every citizen is now proud.

In the early part of June, 1902, the Messrs. J. S. and Morris Lesser of 511 Broadway, New York City, sent out a prospectus of the International Lace Manufacturing Company to

Morris Lesser.

their customers in the various towns in different states of this country. One of these prospectuses came to A. A. Potter. who immediately called the attention of the Lessers to Gouverneur's advantages and invited them to pay it a visit. Later the Lessers sent Robert A. Irving up to look over the ground and report to them. A meeting of the business men of the town was called at which Mr. Irving unfolded the particulars of the enterprise and at a public meeting subsequently held, a committee was appointed consisting of F. M. Burdick, G. S. Conger, H. G. Aldrich and V. P. Abbott who visited New York, investigated the financial and general character standing of the Lessers and reported that everything was more than satisfactory and recommended their proposition to Gouverneur citizens.

An agreement was formulated and subscriptions amounting to $85,000 obtained and nego-

Anson A. Potter.

tiations were opened in earnest with the Lessers. J. S. Lesser came to Gouverneur and satisfying himself as to the conditions, such as water, freight rates, etc., he decided to locate the mammoth plant here.

After reaching this decision he objected to the one-sided agreement. A meeting of the subscribers was called and it was deemed best to modify the agreement so that instead of Gouver-

G. S. Conger.

neur's subscriptions being payable when the plant was in operation it should be paid in installments of equal amounts, in the same ratio as the Lessers paid theirs and as the money was required. This necessitated the agreement to be re-signed which caused a hitch in the progress of the enterprise and for a time it looked exceedingly doubtful as to whether Gouverneur after all was going to capture the magnificent industry. Other towns in New York

INTERNATIONAL LACE MANUFACTURING COMPANY'S MILL

State were making desperate efforts to induce the Lessers to locate in their respective towns, offering them fully as good inducements

It was now that B G Parker was induced by the citizens to take the matter up and from that moment there was something doing until the last hitch had been swept away, and the location of the plant in Gouverneur was settled in its favor Everybody recognized the fact that Mr Parker is a man of splendid business training, excellent executive ability and fully conversant with the intricacies involved in a proposition of the kind that confronted them After his determination to do what he could to land the industry in Gouverneur, he went to New York had an interview with the Lessers and obtained their promise that if Gouverneur would agree to raise the stipulated amount under the modified agreement they would sign to erect the plant Armed with this promise, Mr Parker returned home and at once set the wheels of progressiveness in motion A meeting of the subscribers was called, the situation explained, enthusiasm aroused, and the lace mill for Gouverneur assured

Directly after the location of the plant was decided upon and sufficient money had been raised to assure the success of the project, Architects Williams & Johnson of Ogdensburg were selected to draw plans and specifications of the buildings The design of the plant was drawn up after the most modern and latest improved style of buildings under the plans as laid out by J S Lesser

There is not a lace plant in the United States or any other country where everything has been so judiciously modelled to facilitate at the least expense the manufacture of its products

The contract for constructing the buildings above the foundations was let to the H P Cummings Company, of Ware, Mass

Work was commenced for the foundations of the buildings under B G Parker's supervision at noon September 8, 1902 The first stone was laid in the early part of October, the roofs on the buildings were finished January 1, 1903 the mill completed the following June and the first loom started October 15, 1903

A brief description of the buildings follows The entire group forms a horse shoe or a three sided parallelogram, the open end being toward the east with a court running in between the buildings fifty feet in width

The dimensions of the buildings are 171 feet from north to south and 561 from east to west The two story building is in the form of a capital letter T with the cross part toward the south From the easterly end of the cross of the T a building one story high extends 365 feet toward the east ending at the chimney stack and the power house This is the finishing plant Fifty feet north of this building at the other end of the T is another building running easterly and parallel to the finishing plant which is the manufacturing building 400 feet in length

The automatic devices for protecting the building from fire are of such a superb nature that it costs the company only six cents on each one hundred dollars of insurance carried

Ten looms are operated and 250 to 300 people employed, entailing a pay roll of $2,500 a week, adding greatly to the prosperity of the town The massive plant requires about 150 h p to make its big looms and other machinery hum and has a capacity of 250 h p The mill has a capacity for an output of $500,000 worth of lace curtains a year The market for the sale of the company's goods is principally throughout the United States

The International Lace Manufacturing Company is incorporated under the laws of New York State The product of the mill was formerly manufactured solely at Nottingham, England, and it is practically a new industry in this country There are now about $25,000,000 invested in the lace business in this country, which was brought to the United States by the McKinley law and which protects the manufacturer by a 70 per cent tariff against England's manufactured article

The machines used are a very complicated affair each weighing five tons and consisting of thirty thousand pieces These machines are made in Nottingham and until within the past ten years Nottingham supplied the world with its lace goods

The firm of J. S. Lesser & Co., who are the leaders in Gouverneur's lace industry have been established in the lace trade since 1876 and are experts in the business. The citizens of Gouverneur have done a great work for the town in securing for it this magnificient industry and they are now ever ready to give it a helping hand.

To A. A. Potter is due the credit for first moving to secure this industry, and to those named who followed up his beginnings, must be awarded the credit for securing it.

RIVERSIDE CEMETERY.

By H. Sudds.

Previous to 1857, the only burial place available to residents of Gouverneur Village and vicinity, was a small graveyard, which the records show was owned by the town, situated directly in the rear of the present Presbyterian Church, of which not a trace now remains, and which was subsequently sold and the proceeds used to apply on the expenses of the removal of bodies therefrom, but it becoming more and more apparent that both on account of its crowded condition and for sanitary reasons, larger grounds, away from the center of the village, were needed, a preliminary meeting was held on the 22nd day of June, 1857, and Gouverneur Cemetery Association was duly organized under the laws of the State, the management being vested in a board of twelve Trustees, the original members of which were: William E. Sterling, B. B. Beckwith, Edwin Dodge, S. B. VanDuzee, Chas. Anthony, Cornelius A. Parker, Thomas M. Thayer, John Robertson, Milton Barney, William H. Bowne, Harvey D. Smith and Richard Parsons, who elected as the first officers, B. B. Beckwith, President; Charles Anthony, Vice President; C. A. Parker, Secretary, and S. B. Van Duzee, Treasurer.

Rev. B. B. Beckwith.

This board, with highly commendable judgment and foresight, at once purchased of the Babcock Estate the grounds now occupied as a cemetery, containing about thirty-five acres, lying between the left bank of the Oswegatchie River and William Street, at a cost of $1,500, naming it Riverside Cemetery, and the present beautiful condition and appearance of the grounds, bear convincing testimony that no better selection could possibly have been made. B. F. Hathaway of Flushing, Long Island,

Milton Barney.

an accomplished landscape gardener and surveyor was engaged to lay out the grounds and about $1,000 was expended for this and other improvements, the removal of the bodies from the old graveyard was undertaken by the Cemetery Association and the work performed in the year 1860.

The presidents of the Association have been successively, B. B. Beckwith, Edwin Dodge, Charles Anthony, William R. Dodge and Newton Aldrich. The Vice Presidents, Charles Anthony, Edwin G. Dodge, William R. Dodge, James B. Carpenter and A. B. Cutting; and the Treasurers, S. B. Van Duzee, William H. Bowne, and Henry Sudds. William Miller was Superintendent from 1857 to 1893, when he was succeeded by William H. Hazelton, the present incumbent.

The present Board of Trustees consists of Newton Aldrich, A. B. Cutting, E. D. Barry, G. S. Conger, F. M. Burdick, J. E. McFerran, J. H. Rutherford, Henry Sudds, James D. Easton, E. H. Neary and C. W. Hewitt, and the officers, Newton Aldrich President; A. B.

Cutting, Vice President, Henry Sudds, Secretary and Treasurer, and W H Hazelton, Superintendent

Effort has been made to select Trustees who would take a personal interest in the cemetery, and the great improvement of the last few years, bears witness to their care and attention, want of funds alone preventing their still greater improvement

The Association now has about $8,000 in good investments, and the interest on this, and the receipts from the sale of lots, are used for running expenses   Lots were originally sold at a uniform price of $25 but during the past few years many choice lots have been sold at from $50 to $200   Meanwhile there is an ample supply of free burial lots for the poor

A small receiving vault was provided about 1864, but its size and condition is not now all that could be desired, and a new one, in connection with a small chapel, is perhaps the greatest present need

The Association undertakes the perpetual care of lots, on payment of a sum of $100 or more, about twenty lot owners having already made this arrangement, and the Trustees strongly recommend this as a very fitting and appropriate provision for the permanent care of those gone before, besides assisting in providing a fund for the general care of the grounds

PERSONAL SKETCHES.

By J. B. Johnson.

Post office addresses are Gouverneur, N. Y., unless otherwise given.

The Publishers arranged the order in which the sketches appear, (other than alphabetical) varying same to accommodate cuts and appearance of pages typographically.

Acknowledgements are due Hon. C. R. Walker and Mrs. Ida R. Hendricks of Richville, for assistance in preparing DeKalb sketches.

Dr. Frank Allen, physician and surgeon, Richville, N. Y., was born at Antwerp in 1860. After a course of study in the Gouverneur Academy, he took a medical course in the University of the City of New York. He also took a course of study at Burlington, Vt. He came to Richville in September, 1888, succeeding Dr. Chas. B. Hawley. He was married to Miss Anna J. Todd of Edwards in 1887. Out of this union, two sons were born, Roy T. and F. Don. Mrs. Allen died in 1892. In 1893 he was again married to Miss Mary L. Hurd of Richville. He is a Mason of high standing. His parents were Lonzo D. and Mary (Cummings) Allen.

Emory W. Abbott, born in Hopkinton, 1819. Parents were J. B. Abbott, born in Connecticut, 1789, and Daraxa Russell Abbott, born in Vermont, 1794. Was educated in the common schools of Hopkinton and Edwards and married in 1839 to Hannah S. Pickett. There are three children living, J. Henry, J. B., and Vasco P., all of the town of Gouverneur. Mr. Abbott was prominently engaged in farming and manufacturing and was a merchant of Fowler for many years. Was member of Assembly, First District, St. Lawrence County, 1856-57. Supervisor of Fowler from Feb. 1860 to 1865, during Civil War period. Was active in filling quotas of soldiers for the county. Has been a magistrate in the towns of Fowler and Gouverneur almost continuously from 1847 to the present time.

Emory W. Abbott.

Justus B. Abbott, born in Fowler, 1842. His parents were Emery W. Abbott, born in Hopkinton, 1819, and Hannah S. Pickett Abbott, born in Fowler, 1819. Was Educated in G. W. Seminary and married in 1864 to Francis A. Wight. Has three children, Sherman A., Lester H., and Wight V. Mr. Abbott taught school in the years 1859-60. Was from 1866 to 1872 a merchant in Minnesota. Was engaged in the same capacity at Spragueville, this county, for several years, at the same time was also engaged in farming. He now holds his second term as postmaster of Gouverneur. His portrait will be found in the group picture of the Masonic Blue Lodge.

J. E. Abbott.

Dr. Andrew H. Allen, whose portrait appears with the group of physicians, was born in Antwerp in 1855. His parents were Lorenzo D. Allen, born in Massachusetts in 1818, and Mary Cummings, born in Massachusetts, 1820. He was educated in Ives Seminary and L. I. College Hospital, from which institution he graduated in 1879. Was married in 1880 to Libbie A. Cheney. Has four children, E. Blanche, Grace M., Maude B., and Hazel Belle. Dr. Allen studied medicine with the late Dr. H. Abel of Antwerp, first practiced in Spragueville, N. Y., where he remained until August, 1881, then locating in Gouverneur. Member of St. Lawrence Medical Society, Northern N. Y. Medical Society and American Electro Therapeutic Association

Chester B. Austin, born in Harrisburg, Lewis Co., 1838. His parents were Lacey Benson Austin, born near Utica in 1810, and Abigal (Myers) Austin, born near Utica, 1813. He was

educated in the common schools and at Fairfield Seminary. In 1861 married to Frances M. Terry. Mr. and Mrs. Austin are the parents of Eva F. (Austin) Ackerman. Mr. Austin was first employed as a clerk in the store of W. & J. Johnson, Depauville, in 1856, continuing in their employ until Aug. 7, 1862, when he enlisted in the 10th N. Y. Heavy Artillery. Was disabled on account of sickness and discharged Nov. 29, 1862. Attempted to re-enlist but was not accepted. In 1863 entered the employ of Alexander Campbell of Watertown. Was later with Davis and Bartlett as traveling salesman. Was in business with N. E. Douglas in Theresa, was again employed as traveling salesman continuing until failure of health. Supplied the pulpit in the Methodist Church at DeKalb, from Nov. 15, 1904 to April 9, 1905.

Chester B. Austin.

Daniel Austin, born in Argyle, Washington County, March 8, 1806. His parents were Daniel Austin and Mary Elizabeth Davis. He was educated in Gouverneur and in May, 1833 married to Amanda Hurlbut. Mr. and Mrs. Austin are the parents of Daniel Isaac, John Henry, Layfayette Francis and Mary. His death occurred in 1888 and that of Mrs. Austin in 1880. He lived for a time on land now occupied by the River-

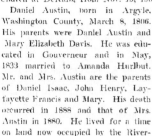

Daniel Austin.

Mrs. Daniel Austin.

side Cemetery and helped at clearing the forest away in that section of the village. He was an excellent citizen and did his part in the making of the town after his arrival in the early 30's.

Stephen Aldous, born in Wilby, England, in 1793. He was educated with horse and wagon selling Yankee notions and dry goods. Was married Oct. 26, 1818, to Margaret Crawford. Mr. and Mrs. Aldous are the parents of William, James, Louis, Charles and Esther. Came to Gouverneur in 1817 after having served eight years in the English Army. Cleared the farm known as the Overacker farm at North Gouverneur. Was one of the early members of the first Baptist Church. A man of industry and integrity. He died at the home of his grandson, James O. Sheldon, aged 95 years, 26 days. Was the father of six sons and six daughters.

Stephen Aldous.

Vasco Pickett Abbott, born in Fowler, N. Y., May 20, 1847. His parents were Emery W. Abbott (see biographical sketch), born in Hopkinton, July 26, 1819, and Hannah Pickett Abbott, born in Fowler in 1819. He was educated in Gouverneur Wesleyan Seminary, St. Lawrence University, and Union University. He was married in 1872 to Anna E. Farmer. Mr. and Mrs. Abbott are the parents of two children, Worth P., and Hugh. Mr. Abbott was graduated from St. Lawrence University in 1867, A. B. Albany Law School, Union University in 1868, LL. B. Admitted to practice May 20, 1868, settling in Gouverneur in 1871. Was Special County Judge from 1876 to 1881; Surrogate of St. Lawrence County in 1881-93. Delegate to the Constitutional Convention in 1894. Has been Trustee of Canton University for twenty years. Trustee of Gouverneur Wesleyan Seminary and High School, fifteen years. His portrait appears in the group of Attorneys and Board of Education.

Levi Aldous, born in Babcock neighborhood, Gouverneur, Nov. 5. 1837. His parents were Stephen Aldous, born March 10, 1793 and Margaret Crawford, born Nov. 1, 1798.

Educated in Gouverneur and March 10, 1863, married Margaret Kichner. Mr. and Mrs. Aldous are the parents of George Stephen, Charles Eddy, D. D. S., Robert Henry, Mrs. Julia Aldous Corbin, and Marion L. A member of I. O. O. F. since 1864, Member of Baptist Church since 1866. Member Royal Arcanum since 1891. Member of Improved Order of Heptosophs since 1893. Treasurer Master Plumber's Association of Passaic, N. J. Member Passaic Encampment No. 62 and Daughters of Rebecca No. 36. William Levi Aldous, eldest son of the subject of this sketch, born June 28, 1864, died July 30, 1904, leaving a widow, nee Mary Van Riper and three children, Florence Edna, Edith Marie and Marion Louise.

Levi Aldous.

A. L. Althouse, born in Edwards, N. Y., Oct. 1, 1861. His parents were Peter Althouse, born at Beverly, Canada, 1810, and Eliza Ann Leach Althouse, born in Fowler, 1821. Mr. Althouse was educated in public schools of Gouverneur. Has been Supt. of Water Works since 1891 with the exception of two years, 1903-04, being re-appointed in the Spring of 1905. Mr. Althouse owns the house first occupied by Peter Althouse which was the third frame building in Gouverneur. Peter Althouse ran a blacksmith shop still known as Althouse shop on Austin Street until about a year before his death, 1890.

A. L. Althouse.

Herbert G. Aldrich, was born in Luzerne, Warren Co., N. Y., Dec. 3, 1860. Early in life his father, Newton Aldrich, moved to Gouverneur. Mr. Aldrich attended school at G. W.

Seminary from which he was graduated in 1880 being valedictorian of his class. He then took a classical course at Hamilton College, graduating in the class of 1884 with honors. After reading law a year in the office of Nelson L. Robinson of Canton, he entered the Law Department of Harvard University and was graduated from the Law School of that University in 1888. He was admitted to the bar in 1889.

On account of the protracted illness of his father beginning in 1896, Mr. Aldrich gave much of his attention to the business affairs of Weston, Dean & Aldrich, and in 1898 purchased the interest of the late Abijah Weston in the co-partnership. When the saw mill property was converted into a paper manufacturing

H. G. Aldrich.

plant by the Aldrich Paper Co. he became a large stockholder and was subsequently elected a director and vice-president. He is director of the U. S. Talc Co. and of Bank of Gouverneur. Being greatly interested in the location of the plant of the International Lace Mfg. Co. in Gouverneur, he subscribed liberally to the stock of that corporation, and was chosen one of its resident directors, a trust which he has held until he interposed his positive declination to further serve in that capacity at the last annual election of the Co. He is a member of the Board of Education of Gouverneur schools. In politics he is a Republican. Has been married twice, Sept. 3, 1890 to Jennie A. Loucks, deceased, and April 20, 1905 to Mrs. Anne C. Fish of New York City. He has one child by his first marriage, Ruth K. His portrait appears in the Board of Education group, also that of Bank of Gouverneur and O. H. W. Ex. Com.

Peter Absalom.

Peter Absalom, of Fowler, born in Loraine, France, June 20, 1815. His parents were Sebastain Absalom, born Nov. 27, 1778, in France, died in Fowler, Dec. 30, 1858, and Margaret A. Tiserand, born in Loraine, Sept. 13, 1788, died in Fowler, May 25, 1872. Mr. Absalom sailed from France in 1831 in one of M. DePeau's ships, and resided in New York City during the winter, removing to the farm in Fowler, May 25, 1832, where he continued to live until his death, Aug. 26, 1890. Mr. Absalom was a natural mechanic and did much of the construction of the buildings upon his farm. A loom is still in existence built by his hands. Mr. Absalom died respected by his neighbors. He sought no worldly honors, he courted no public favors.

Elijah Bailey, born at New Fame, Vt., 1824. Parents were David Bailey, born at New Fame, Vt., 1785, and Sarah Goodell Bailey, born at New Fame, 1792. Educated at New Fame, and married July 6, 1847 to Maria Miller. Two children are living, Mrs. J. E. Bass and Wilbur Bailey.

Mr. Bailey came to Gouverneur at the age of eight years. He started in the then common vocation of cutting and piling green timber for the manufacture of black salts. Purchased a farm and built thereon, of logs, his first residence. Worked for a time at Richville, N. Y. at the cooper's trade, then came to Gouverneur where he was employed as a mason. Mr. Bailey on his eightieth birthday built a chimney.

Elijah Bailey.

Almon Barrel came to Gouverneur in the fall of 1827, with his father, David Barrel. He bought 100 acres of land where Bower Morris now lives, subsequently building the brick house still in excellent preservation. He afterward added to his original purchase and at the time of his death still owned the one hundred acres first bought. He is remembered well as a man of staunch character, unyielding in his spirit of fairness and honesty toward everybody with whom he had business relations. He had a ready command of language and could make one disposed toward crooked ways wince under his sharp sarcasm. Astride of a good bay mare, he often went to the "snowshoe" in DeKalb, where his son-in-law, Volney Morris, lived, to hunt deer, his rifle (always the best then obtainable, for he was a skillful marksman) swung across the pommel of his saddle. This was about 1850, the region about the snowshoe (an island in the Oswegatchie) being at that time still a dense wilderness with an occasional clearing. "Aunt Fanny Dewey" previously spoken of, was his sister and the wife of Jesse Dewey. Another sister, Prudence, married Israel R. Parsons and lived on the farm now occupied by Andrew C. Dodds on the Richville road. Parsons built the house still standing, but left it about 1850 to live with his daughter in the village, Mrs. Marcus Chamberlain, then a widow. A daughter of Almon Barrel still lives near the old homestead, Mrs. Giles Haywood, born April 13, 1830. Mr. Barrel was born in Washington County in 1806.

Cornelius F. Brown.

Cornelius Franklin Brown, born in Gouverneur, 1851. His parents were Robert Comb Brown, born on mid ocean 1828, and Margaret R. Dodds, born in Rossie, 1828. He was educated in G. W. Seminary and married 1878 to Elizabeth M. Collins of Rossie. Mr. and Mrs. Brown are the parents of two children, Royal C., and Hazel M. Mr. Brown is a prosperous farmer in Rossie, well and favorably known in Gouverneur.

Robert C. Brown.

Robert M. Brown, born in Rossie, 1854. Parents were James Brown, born in Scotland, and Margaret Comb, born in Scotland. Mr. Brown was educated in Gouverneur Wesleyan Seminary, and has been thrice married; to Jennie Morrison, in 1875; Philinda Babcock, in 1877, and Sarah J. Laclare, in 1887. Mr. Brown is the father of six children, two by his second wife, Winnifred M. and Floyd S., and four by his third wife, Ethel S., Robert R., Ella and Guy. Mr. Brown went to Dakota in 1882 where he engaged in farming and stock raising, returning to Gouverneur in 1895, since when he has occupied the farm of the late James Brown on the Johnstown Road.

Benjamin F. Brown, born in Gouverneur 1856. His parents were Christopher Brown, born in Rossie, 1819, and Roxana Drake Brown, born in Gouverneur, 1817. He was educated

in G. W. Seminary and Antwerp Seminary, Potsdam Normal, Brockport Normal and Rochester University. Was first married in 1886 to Jean F. Paul who died April 11, 1889, and to whom were born Hazel Jean and Marion Ruth. Was married in 1892 to Anna S. Backus, to whom were born Gertrude S., Malcolm C., and Caroline Delight. Mr. Brown's maternal grand-parents were among the early settlers of Gouverneur. Mr. Brown commenced teaching school at 16 years of age, continuing teaching except when a pupil, until his 36th year. Assisted in the organizing of Richville Union Free School in 1883, compiling the first printed graded course of study for common schools in St. Law. Co. Taught at Hammond,

James Gilbert Brown.

Morristown and Gouverneur. Had charge of public school 3 years prior to organization of Union Free School. Was among the important advocates of that system. Was first vice-principal of Gouverneur High School. Since 1891 has been in the insurance, loan and real estate business. Assisted in organizing Gouverneur Savings and Loan Association, with which he has been identified since. His portrait appears in the group of the officers of that association, and in that of the O. H. W. Executive Com. The portrait appearing here is of James Gilbert, a brother who died about twenty-five years ago .

Albert B. Brown, born in Gouverneur, 1875. His parents were Henry Brown, born in Rossie, 1839, and Charlotte Becksted, born in Williamsburg, Ont., in 1844. He was educated in the High School at Gouverneur and married in 1892 to Amy Sprague. Mr. and Mrs. Brown are the parents of Helen May and Ralph Ernest.

David H. Balmat, of Fowler, born in Champion, N. Y., May 16, 1822. His parents were John D. Balmat, born in Paris, France, Jan. 3, 1785, and Mancy, daughter of Major Goodar, born near Utica. John D. Balmat died in Fowler Jan. 30, 1862. Major Goodar, maternal grand father of the subject of this sketch, came to this country with Lafayette and was wounded in the battle of Brandywine. Mr. David H. Balmat was married to Saphrona Wight, deceased. Four children are living. Mr. Balmat was the owner of extensive farming lands in Fowler, underlaid with talc and pyrites. One of the talc mines is now being operated by the Union Talc Company.

David H. Balmat.

Edwin C. Babcock was born in Gouverneur in 1867. His parents were Byron Babcock, born in Gouverneur in 1841 and Emily Overacker, born in Gouverneur. He was educated in G. W. Seminary and married in 1893 to Mary L. Morris. Mr. and Mrs. Babcock are the parents of Earl B., Carrie and Kate. Mr. Babcock is a prosperous farmer residing upon the farm formerly owned by his grand-father.

Albert Frederick Billings, born in Gouverneur in 1860. His parents were Byron Billings, born in Vermont in 1825, and Ann Hills, born in Gouverneur, 1823. He was educated in the public schools and in 1881 married to Addie Tyler. Mr. and Mrs. Billings are the parents of Vera Ann, Mary Louise, Byron Tyler, Dorris Olive, and Beatrice Blanche.

Colbert Austin Bennett, born in Cornwall, Ont., Jan. 17, 1876. His parents were James A. Bennett, born in Montreal in 1842 and Elizabeth O'Grady born in Ireland in 1849. Mr. Bennett was educated in Gouverneur High School and April 24, 1899, married to Bertha H. Draper. Mr. Bennett is the father of Colbert Ralph Bennett. Mr. Bennett, together with his brother, began the manufacture of brooders and incubators in 1896 and in 1900 purchased the Starbuck & McCarthy planing mill where they are now manufacturing mission furniture.

John Emerson Bennett, born in Montreal 1872. His parents were James Austin Bennett, born in Cornwall, Ont., 1842, and Elizabeth O'Grady Bennett, born in Ireland. She

John E. Bennett.

died Oct. 31, 1904, at the age of 55 years. Mr. Bennett came to Gouverneur in 1889 with his parents. His father was a veteran of the Civil War, having joined the army in Oconto, Wis., Co. H, 39th Reg. Wisconsin Volunteers. After Mr. Bennett senior married he resided in Chicago, Ill., and St. Louis, Mo., and Montreal, P. Q., pursuing his trade as carriage maker. Subject of the sketch has living three brothers, Colbert, Lawrence and Winafred and three sisters, Mae, Nettie and Ella. Mr. Bennett is an inventor of some note, having produced Pioneer Clover Meal Poultry Food, the Champion Brooders and Champion Incubators. He is the founder of the Bennett & Millett Co., which firm introduced the Champion Brooder, now extensively sold by the successors of this firm.

John H. Berry, of Rossie, was born in Ontario, 1862. His parents were John Berry, born in Ireland in 1831 and Betsy McAvoy Berry, born in Ireland in 1835. He was educated in Ives Seminary, Antwerp, and married in 1891 to Isabelle Tenney. Mr. Berry is an expert cheese maker and owns a cheese factory at Spragueville. He was appointed by Gov. Flower as expert and agent in the department of agriculture, which position he held for two years. He was elected supervisor of Rossie in 1887 and re-elected in 1888, serving 2 years. He was again elected supervisor in March of the present year. Mr. and Mrs. Berry are the parents of Bessie L., Maybel I. and Dorris H.

John H. Berry.

Isaac M. Brainard.

Isaac Milton Brainard, born in Lairdville, N. Y., 1827. His parents were Landon Brainard, born in Haddon, Ct., 1791 and Ella Hunt Brainard, born in Hinsdale, N. Y., 1797. He was educated in Clinton Academy and in 1862 married H. R. Caulkin. Mr. Brainard has two children, William and Emily E. Brainard Johnston. Mr. Brainard's ancestor, David Brainard, was a missionary to the Indians. Was born in 1718. Mr. Brainard came to Gouverneur to educate his children in the old G. W. Seminary. Mr. Brainard in company with his son have, for many years, been engaged in market gardening. They also have a large green house.

George J. Bowman, of Fowler, was born in Adams, 1868. His parents were J. A. Bowman, born in Jefferson County and Adell Bowman, born in Oswego County. Mr. Bowman is a cheese maker by profession, having followed that avocation for thirteen years. He has sold butter and cheese in Gouverneur and on the Canton board for nine years of the thirteen. He built the Hailesboro butter and cheese factory in 1890, selling it in 1898. In 1890 he bought the Leahy farm in Fowler and in the fall of 1903 sold it to John Babcock and moved on the John Day farm, near Hailesboro.

George D. Burnett, born in Canada, 1866. His parents were Edwin Burnett, born in De-Kalb and Caroline Dorn Burnett. He was educated in DeKalb and married to Ella Lafelle. Mr. and Mrs. Burnett are the parents of James and Hazel. Mr. Burnett is an extensive farmer, operating 600 acres of land in DeKalb, 160 of which was the original farm settled upon by James Burnett, his grand-father, in the early history of DeKalb. Mr. Burnett moved to Gouverneur several years ago, conducting here and in DeKalb a large breeding farm.

Ezekiel F. Beardslee.

Ezekiel F. Beardslee, born in Gouverneur, 1843. His parents were Ebenezer L. Beardslee, born in Johnstown, 1793, and Nancy Murphy, born in 1806. He was educated in G. w. Seminary and Eastern Business College and married in 1874 to Mary L. Winslow. They are the parents of Robert Winslow Beardslee. Mr. Beardslee was for some years in the grocery business here, later he became a member of the firm of Beardslee & Dodge, millers, in which business he continued until his death. He was a member of the Masonic Order, a Republican in politics and active and honorable in all of his business relations.

William H. Bowne, born in Gouverneur in 1824. His parents were of Quaker origin, coming from Flushing, L. I. At the age of twenty he entered the dry goods store of Winslow as clerk, continuing in the dry goods business until about 1880. During the time he was associated as a partner with Henry Smith. D. G. Wood and Milton Barney. He was agent for the Am. Express Co. until that office was transferred to Mr. McCarthy. He served as postmaster under Pres. Buchanan and was president of Gouverneur village. His father was Jas. Bowne, born at Flushing, L. I., and his mother was Eliza Wilson, born at New Providence, Bahamas.

William H. Bowne.

Lalius D. Brown, born in DeRuyter, N. Y., 1849. His parents were Samuel E. Brown, born in Unadilla Forks, 1825 and M. A. (Wheeler) Brown, born in Binghamton, 1830. Mr. Brown is a woolen mill overseer and was married in 1901 to Mrs. Stella Bolton McKean. Mr. and Mrs. Brown are the parents of Edith M. Brown, Lillian M. McKean and Robert M. McKean. Mr. Brown has had charge of the weaving department of the Woolen Mills at Wegatchie. Has been employed at different times at Providence, R. I., Philadelphia, Pa., and throughout the west and on the Pacific coast. He is at present employed with the International Lace Mfg. Co. He is a member of the Masonic Lodge, 217, F. & A. M.

Lalius D. Brown.

Sidney Brown of Fullerville, was born in Edwards, April 21, 1863. His parents were Robert Brown, born in Edwards, Feb. 12, 1821 and Elizabeth Webb Brown, born in Edwards, April 25, 1837. He was educated in Edwards and Nov. 19, 1885, married to Julia A. Wight. They are the parents of Sayle A., Nora L., and Sidney C. Brown. Mr. Brown is by profession a cheese maker having worked at the trade fifteen years. In 1880 he learned the barbers trade which he still follows on occasions. He is the present proprietor of the Franklin House, Fullerville. He is a grandson of Robert Brown, one of the first settlers of the town of Edwards.

Sidney Brown.

William F. Bowhall, born in Stockholm, N. Y., 1861. Educated in Canton High School and in 1881 married to Jeanette Myers. Mr. Bowhall is by profession a printer. Served his apprenticeship in the St. Lawrence Plain Dealer office at Canton. Was foreman in the Northern Tribune office for nearly 12 years, leasing the same office in 1904. Is now conducting the business. His portrait appears among the Tribune staff.

Alfred Bush.

Alfred Bush, Richville, N. Y., was born in Canada in the year 1853. His father's name was Archie Bush and his mother's maiden name was Elizabeth Prasser, a native of England. He received his early education in the public schools at Rensselaer Falls, N. Y. Was married in 1886 to Miss Ruby Barnum of Hermon township. One child was born unto them, Mary B. Bush. Mr. Bush as always been a staunch Democrat in politics, refusing all offers of high position in his party, preferring to serve them in his quiet modest way. About ten years ago he purchased the Daniel Gardner farm on the Gouverneur road, where he has very successfully followed his chosen occupation as farmer and apiarist.

James Brown, born in Ancram, Scotland, 1821. Parents were Archibald Brown, born

James Brown.

in Scotland and Margaret Comb born in Scotland. He was educated in Rossie and in 1845 married to Jeanette Turnbull. They are the parents of Margaret C., Robert M., Elizabeth E., and James A. Brown. Mr. Brown came to America in 1829, landing in Ogdensburg and settled in Rossie. Moved to the town of Gouverneur in 1855, locating on the farm on Johnstown Street. Moved to the village of Gouverneur in 1877, where he died in 1900.

Mrs. James Brown.

Charles H. Bowne, born in Gouverneur in 1848. Married in 1874 to Mary Eliza Whitney.

Charles H. Bowne

To Mr. and Mrs. Bowne were born two children, William C., and Anna. Parents of Mr. Bowne came to Gouverneur from Flushing, L. I., taking up farms in Northeast of the town. Mr. Bowne went to California in 1849, remaining there for three years, returning was a farmer in Gouverneur for some time. Coming to Gouverneur in 1868, entering in the hardware business with Bradley L. Barney, whom he subsequently

William C. Bowne.

succeeded. Mr. Bowne's father, Jas. Bowne, born at Flushing, L. I., 1787, and mother, Eliza Wilson, born in New Providence, Bahamas, 1793.

Mary Eliza (Whitney) Bowne, born in Mexico, Oswego Co., April 21, 1845. Her parents were Oliver Cady Whitney, born in Granville, Washington County, Jan. 31, 1806, and Lois Crossman Whitney, born in Mexico, Jan. 8, 1808. Mrs. Bowne received her education in Mexico Academy and was married April 9, 1874 to Charles Hicks Bowne, of Gouverneur. Mrs. Bowne is a Daughter of the Revolution, a member of the Episcopal Church, and Library Association.

Frank B. Beaman, Richville, N. Y., born at Philadelphia, N. Y., in 1855. Educated in public schools at Antwerp and took a course of study at Oberlin, O. He is a licensed Pharmacist and has conducted a store here since 1877. He is President of the Board of Education. He is serving his second term as postmaster. Politically, he is a strong Republican and is very fond of debating on the issues of the day. He was married to Ruth Walker in 1880 and has one son, Daniel W. His father's name was Ezra B. Beaman and was born in Westmoreland County, Mass., in 1804. His mother's maiden name was Lydia M. Jones, born at Philadelphia, in 1824.

Frederick John Bolton, born in Gouverneur, Oct. 13, 1852. His parents were John Bolton, born in Frankfort, Pa., 1805, and Prudence Foster Bolton, born in Gouverneur, June

28, 1811. He was educated in the G. W. Seminary and in Ogdensburg. Was married Sept. 12, 1868, to Jennie Chisholm. Mr. and Mrs. Bolton are the parents of Maria Benton Bolton. Mr. Bolton is a member of the Grange, Masons, and a prominent farmer, residing on the homestead farm, Kearney Road. Everard Bolton, great, great, great grand-father, came from Rosshere-fordshire, England, 1682, with William Penn in the ship Welcome, settling in Byberry, Bucks Co. Pa. He belonged to the Society of Friends. Mr. Bolton's great, great grand-father was born in 1697 and died 1795. The grand-father of Joseph Bolton, Frederick Bolton, was born in 1769 and died in 1862. Came to Gouverneur from Frankfort, Pa., in 1808, living for many years

Frederick J. Bolton.

in the old Morris Mansion at Natural Dam. He was a stone mason by trade and laid the walls of the old Morris Mansion about 1808, Rockwell Barnes doing the carpenter work thereon. Maria Benton Bolton is the seventh generation from Edward Bolton who came to this country with Penn.

Charles S. Bodman, Jr., born in Gouverneur in 1882. His parents were Charles S. Bodman, born in Theresa in 1852 and Anna Leary Bodman, born in Wexford, Ireland. Mr. Bodman received his preliminary education in the Gouverneur High School, graduating in classics and also graduated from the Law division of Union University at Albany in 1905. Now a practicing attorney. His portrait appears in the group of Attorneys.

Ossian L. Barnum was born in Bangor, Franklin County, in 1816. He came to Gouverneur when in boyhood years, and as he grew to manhood took up a farm on the Johnstown road about three miles from the village. He married about that time and reared a large family, subsequently removing to the A. I. Shattuck farm in Hermon, where he died in 1880. Ordinarily he was known among his fellow-townsmen as "LaCarva" and was esteemed for his probity and good citizenship. He was a man who kept in touch through the newspapers, with all that the world was doing and was able to comment judiciously upon affairs at home and abroad. There was a debating society formed in the school district where he lived on the Johnstown road, which is remembered for its membership of farmers who were able to discuss intelligently the national crisis then approaching, any member of which could mount the rostrum and talk interestingly

Ossian L. Barnum.

to a crowd of listeners. This society was a single instance of the educative effect of public discussions. LaCarva Barnum was a member of this club and was usually equipped for the forensic contests occurring fortnightly. He was progressive in his business, early tried and purchased improved farm machinery and in politics was clear-visioned and prophetic. The old stock, composed of such as he, seems to have gone with the passing years.

Lucretia Allen Barnes, born in Westfield, Vt., No. 26, 1823. Her parents were Erastus Allen, born in Shelburne, Mass., and Paulina Wilder Allen, born in Shelburne, Mass. She was educated in the G. W. Seminary and married in 1842 to Edwin S. Barnes. Has one child living, Celia E. Barnes Smith. Mrs. Barnes came to Gouverneur in 1835 at the age of twelve years. Married at the age of nineteen. Was the mother of four children. After marriage she resided at Evans Mills for five years, then at Orwell, Oswego County, finally settling in Gouverneur where her husband died. (See biographical sketch of Erwin S. Barnes.) Her portrait appears with the "Matrons of the Early Days."

Nathan E. Brown, born in Vermont, in 1855. His parents were Aldis A. Brown, born in Vermont, and Phyla A. Tenney, born in Vermont. Educated in the public schools of Vermont and New York. Was married in 1878 to Mrs. L. J. Crawford. Mr. Brown has been successfully engaged in the grocery business in Gouverneur for the past twenty-five years. He is prominent as an official in the Baptist Church, and a member of the Masonic and Odd Fellows' lodges and his portrait appears in the group picture of the latter organization. At the present time Mr. Brown conducts one of the largest grocery stores in the village, being located in the new Freeman building on Clinton street.

Nathan E. Brown.

Frank M. Babcock, born in Gouverneur in 1855. His parents being Sheldon Babcock, born in Fabius, Jan. 27, 1817, and Lydia Mason Babcock, born at Plattsburg, Sept. 2, 1819. He was married to Jennie Brown in 1876. They have four children, Leon, Ethel, Ione, and Luava. Mr. Babcock was educated in the Gouverneur Wesleyan Seminary and has been a farmer and breeder of thoroughbred stock for some years. He is a member of the New York Protective Legion. Owns and operates 250 acres of land, part of which is in the village of Gouverneur. Sheldon Babcock, the father of the subject of this sketch was among the early settlers.

William Francis Burlingame, born in Russell in 1873. His parents were William Ira Burlingame, born in Russell, in 1837, and Harriet M. McKinsey Burlingame, born in Essex County, N. Y. Mr. Burlingame was educated in Russell and is by profession a cheese and butter maker, having received his instruction in the Dairy School at Ithaca.

William F. Burlingame.

Isaac I. Block, born in Germany, May 15, 1867. His parents were Samuel Block, born in Seidargan, Poland, and Sarah D. Isaacs, born in Neustadt, Poland. Mr. Block was educated in Germany, and married Feb. 5, 1896, to Rachel Solomon, who was born in Syracuse, N. Y., June 20, 1873. Has one child, Ruth Dorothy. Mr. Block came to the United States at the age of 16, landing in New York, May 5, 1883. June first, following, went to Syracuse and soon after commenced selling notions and jewelry, continuing in this line until 1887, when he bought a team and started a traveling store, selling dry-goods, clothing and jewelry in Jefferson, St. Lawrence and Oswego Counties. In 1892 he bought the good will and business of Farmer Bros., of Gouverneur. He has continued in the clothing business until the present time. He is a member of the Gouverneur Lodge, F. & A.

Isaac I. Block.

M., 32nd degree Mason; member of Syracuse Consistory, Mystic Shriners; member of Media Temple, Watertown; member of Gouverneur Council R. A. M.; Oswegatchie Tent, No. 244, K. O. T. M., and of the Temple Club.

Bradley L. Barney of Hanford, Cal., born in Gouverneur in 1849. His parents were

Milton Barney, born in Henderson, N. Y., 1804, and Catherine Starr Van Vuren, born in Mayfield, N. Y. Mr. Barney was educated in Gouverneur and in 1873 married to Mary E. Herring. Mr. Barney was for some time engaged with C. H. Bowne in the hardware business. Was one of the organizers of the Gouverneur Machine Co., of which institution he was for some time President. He moved to California about 1886.

William H. Bell.

William Henry Bell, born in Williamsburg, Ont., 1854. He was a son of James Wellington Bell, born in County Antrim, Ireland, in 1823. He was educated in Williamsburg, Ont. and married in 1888 to Eva J. Boss. Mr. and Mrs. Bell are the parents of Hazel, Ireel and Merton Bell. Mr. Bell is at the present time hotel keeper at Edwards. Previous to entering the hotel business, he was a brick layer and plasterer. For many years conducting billiard parlors in Gouverneur, thence moving to Talcville, where he ran the hotel for thirteen years. Now proprietor of the American House in Edwards.

Wayland Lewis Beers, born in Montana, N. J., in 1867. His parents were William Beers, born in Montana, N. J., Oct. 1828, and Lydia A. Miller, born in Harmony, N. J. in 1831. Educated at Peddie Institute, 1890; Brown University, 1895; Union Seminary and Columbia College. Married in 1890 to Elizabeth Beardsley. Mr. and Mrs. Beers are the parents of Howard Wayland. Mr. Beers has been a clergyman since 1896. Accepted a call of the First Unitarian Church at Gouverneur, June, 1904. Previous settlements were in Northern New York and St. John, N. B., Canada. His portrait appears in the group of clergymen.

Marvin W. Babcock was born in Gouverneur in 1867. His parents were Jacob Babcock, born in Gouverneur and Martha Streeter Babcock, born in Gouverneur, 1835. Mr. Babcock was educated in Gouverneur and married in 1888 to Addie Austin. Mr. and Mrs. Babcock are the parents of two children, Pearl and Harold. Mr. Babcock is a prosperous farmer on the Somerville road. Mr. Babcock is an enterprising farmer and a breeder and lover of good horses. He has developed many desirable matched pairs and is a persistent advocate of good roads.

Marvin W. Babcock.

Joseph Vinton Baker was born in the town of Antwerp, N. Y., Oct. 24th, 1849, the son of John W. Baker and Susan Williams. He came to Gouverneur in 1877 and has engaged in

Joseph V. Baker.

the insurance business continuously ever since. He is superintendent of the Methodist Episcopal Sunday School and Treasurer of the Church. He is also a member and past presiding officer of Gouverneur Lodge No. 217, F. & A. M., Gouverneur Chapter No. 233, R. A. M., and Marble City Commandry No. 63, K. T. He was married to Louisa E. Harris in 1871. Mrs. Joseph Vinton Baker was born at Fowler, N. Y.,

Mrs. J. V. Baker.

April 21st, 1852, the daughter of Alvin O. Harris and Mary D. Hodgkin. She is a member of the Methodist Episcopal Church, Woman's Christian Temperance Union and Order of the Eastern Star. Mr. and Mrs. Baker have three children, Coralyn E., Leslie W., and Josie Viva. His portrait also appears in the Odd Fellows' group.

Frederick Henry Brown of Rossie, born in Rossie, June 29, 1869. His parents were John Henry Brown, born in Gouverneur May 10, 1842, and Edith Wilson Brown, born in Rossie. He was educated in Rossie and married July 17, 1873, to Hattie Ann Taylor. Mr. and Mrs. Brown have one child, Leon Raymond. Mr. Brown learned the cheesemaker's trade early in life, working at Elmdale, River Road, and Wegatchie factories. Purchased the farm and commenced farming at his present home on the Campbell road in the town of Rossie in 1892.

Wm. Baird was born in Brockville, Ont., 1850. His parents were Joseph Baird, born in Canada, and Amanda Pulman, born in Lisbon, N. Y. Occupation, gardener. He was married in 1868 to Adeline Blair. He has one child, Lillian Baird Ware.

William Baird.

J. W. Barbary was born in Oswego in 1855. His parents were Joseph Barbary, born in Canada, and Maria Sparback, born in Canada. Mr. Barbary came to Gouverneur in 1874. Is by occupation a painter and carpenter.

Eli P. Bacon, born in Rossie in 1865. His parents were Wilfred Bacon, born in Rossie in 1829 and Charity Jepson Bacon, born in Rossie in 1830. He was educated in Rossie and in Gouverneur. He lived on the home farm in Rossie until 18 years of age, then learning the carpenter's trade, which he followed until 1879, then went to Park City, Utah, and was employed in a silver mine. Returned to Gouverneur in 1882, going into the boot and shoe business. He served as policeman in 1884. Member of the Masonic order, K. O. T. M. and Foresters. Deputy great commander of K. O. T. M.

Eli P. Bacon.

John Alfred Beach was born in DeKalb, Aug. 20, 1862. His parents were John Beach, born in Canada and Paulina Rowley, born in DeKalb. Educated in DeKalb and married in 1880 to Ida Alvora Todd. He has one child, Nettie Blanche, born in DeKalb. Mr. Beach is a dairy farmer and now located in the Town of Gouverneur, where he has won the respect and esteem of his neighbors. John Beach, the father of the subject of this sketch, died in the army.

John A. Beach.

Mr. G. B. Barnes, born in Fowler in 1854. His parents were Franklin Barnes, born in Fowler, and Melinda Pickett Barnes born in Fowler. Mr. Barnes was educated in the Gouverneur Wesleyan Seminary, Potsdam Normal Institute, and Pennsylvania College of Dental Surgery. He was married in 1880 to Anna M. Cushman. Mr. Barnes practiced dentistry in Gouverneur for about twenty-seven years. He is a prominent member of the I. O. O. F. Is now occupied as a commercial traveller.

Edward D. Barry, born in Canada in 1855. His parents were Edward Barry, born in Canada in 1802, and Eliza Swarts Barry, born in Canada in 1812. Mr. Barry's mother was a descendent of the early New England settlers, having removed from Vermont to Canada. Mr. Barry was educated in Canada and in 1886 married to Emogene Payne. Mr. Barry came to this country in early life and became prominent in manufacturing circles. Commencing the manufacture of wagons, carriages, etc., in Richville, soon after removing to Gouverneur where he has since conducted the Barry Emporium. He is a director of the Gouverneur Bank and has been President of the Excise Board, President of the Board of Health, member of County Republican Committee and Delegate to State Republican Committee in 1904. Director of International Lace Manufacturing Co. His portrait is in the group of officials of the Bank of Gouverneur.

Frank L. Cox, born in Culpepper Court House, Va., Feb. 7, 1850. His parents were Robert A. Cox, born at Port Tobaco, Md., and Maria Ward Lane Cox, born in Virginia. His paternal grand-father was Capt. Jesse Cox of Maryland. His maternal grand-father was Benedict Middleton Lane of Virginia. He was educated in Virginia and Washington, D. C. Married June 10, 1875 to Louisa A. Barnes of Gouverneur. Mr. Cox is the father of four children, of which but one lives, Frank Erwin Cox, of Gouverneur, N. Y. Louisa A. Barnes Cox died in 1885. Mr. Cox was again married in January, 1894, to Mary Newell. He has been engaged in the printing business in Gouverneur continuously since 1873.

Frank L. Cox.

J. Arthur Cummings, born in Wheeling, W. Va., Dec. 3, 1857. His parents were James Davidson Cummings, born in Paisley, Scotland and Eliza J. Passenger, born in Fowler 1832. Mr. Cummings was educated in Watertown and in 1874 married to Mary E. Youngs. Mr. Cummings was engaged for many years in Gouverneur in the undertaking business. He is now by profession an optician. His portrait is in the Arcanum group. Mr. Cummings is an expert with the drum and his services are often contributed when the Drum Corps of Gouverneur heads the military organizations of these parts.

J. A. Cummings.

James Clark, born in Gouverneur, July 4, 1832. His parents were James Clark, born in Bucklyn, Mass., 1796, and Lydia Woodward Clark born in Bucklyn Mass. 1796. Mr. Clark was educated in Gouverneur Wesleyan Seminary in 1853-54-55. He has been married three times, his first wife being Mrs. Ives; his second Orcelia J. Sartwell, and the third was Mrs. S. J. Horton. No children are living. The elder James Clark, in 1831, settled upon and cleared up the farm now owned and occupied by the subject of this sketch. Mr. Clark has held numerous important positions and town offices. He is a member of the Gouverneur Grange, and is and has been his entire life a prominent member of the Methodist Church. Since the above sketch was written the death of Mr. Clark occurred Aug. 10, 1905.

James Clark.

John Proctor Crary of Rossie, born in Carthage, Aug. 6, 1831. His parents were A. K. Crary, born in Lewis County Feb. 24, 1792, and Clarisa Wright, born in Oneida County in 1795. He was educated in Carthage and in 1852 married to Margaret Furnier, deceased.

In 1883 married to Mary Doughin. Mr. Crary is the father of John H., Joseph F., Margaret, Mary Allen, Daniel and Elizabeth M. Mr. Crary settled in Rossie when about 16 years of age. Entered the employ of George Parish with whom he continued in various capacities until operations were discontinued in the furnaces, then became a contractor in which line he continued until the furnace was put in operation by the Rossie Iron Works. Was employed by that firm until the furnace closed down in 1867. In 1873 purchased a saw mill of Mr. Parish in Rossie village and carried on business of lumbering and shingle manufacturing until 1880, then selling the mill to W. W. Leonard and William Allen. In 1895, together with Otis Brooks, he bought the Rossie furnace property, subsequently Mr. Crary bought out Mr. Brooks' interest in the property which he now owns and occupies. Mr. Crary's grandfather was one of the first settlers of Lewis Co. Was by profession a surveyor.

Amasa Corbin, born in Gouverneur, Dec. 31, 1843. His parents were Amasa Corbin, born in Champlain, N. Y., Dec. 12, 1802, and Phoebe Maria Foster Corbin, born in Han-

cock, Mass., Sept. 5, 1809. He is the father of Arthur F., Grace H. and Ralph H. Mr. Corbin was educated in the Gouverneur Wesleyan Seminary. Was a teacher at eighteen, president of business college under the firm name of Bryant, Stratton & Corbin, at Bridgeport, Conn., in 1864-5, also at Poughkeepsie in 1866. General agent and superintendent of Insurance Co. for several years. President of the St. Law. Manufacturing Co. and of the Adirondack Pulp Co. of Gouverneur, both of which businesses he organized. Pres. of the Gouverneur A. & M. Society. President and director in several zinc industries in Missouri, which he promoted and organized. These Zinc Companies involved the investment of nearly two millions of dollars. Mr. Corbin is the

Amasa Corbin.

president of the Adirondack Pyrites Co., now operating near Gouverneur.

Walter Spencer Corbin, born in Philadelphia, Pa., 1870. His parents are Jay S. Corbin, born in Gouverneur and C. Anna Hill Corbin, born in Gouverneur. He was educated in the graded schools and married in 1897 to Lulu May Haymen. Mr. Corbin is the father of Jay S. Corbin Jr., and is a coal dealer, which occupation he has pursued since 1894. Aside from his business as coal dealer, he is a contractor for sewer and water works construction, being well equipped and posted for that business. Mr. Corbin pretends to no social or political aspirations but has the respect of the business community.

Walter S. Corbin.

Benjamin Collins was born in New Hampshire, 1806, and married to Betsy Foster. Mr. Collins was one of the early settlers of the town of Fowler and the father of Harlow, Louis, Calista and Fremont.

Benj. Collins.

Daniel Hurlbut Cutting, born in Colwell's Manor, 1808, and married in 1834 to Jane Barrows. Of this union two children are living, A. B. Cutting of Gouverneur, N. Y., and H. G. Cutting of Bradford, Pa. Mr. Cutting learned the carriage maker's trade in Vermont and moved to Crary's Mills in 1833, where he married and continued to live at Potsdam and Crary's Mills, now known as Hannawa Falls, until his wife died in 1842. He was married the second time to Catherine Church in 1844, moving soon after to Norfolk. He returned again to Crary's Mills where he lived until 1863, when he came to Gouverneur, residing here with his son. His death occurred in 1902. Mr. Cutting's ancestors were among the early New England settlers of the United States.

George F. Carpenter.

George Fletcher Carpenter, of Fowler, N. Y., was born in Johnstown, N. Y., 1823. His parents were Stephen Carpenter, born in Johnstown, Sept. 26, 1799, and Ann Eliza Olmstead Carpenter, born in Johnstown, Nov. 17, 1795. Mr. Carpenter was educated in Hailesboro, N. Y., and married in 1854 to Louisa D. Hoard. Four children are living, Lilla, Jennie, Minnie and Arthur. Mr. Carpenter came to Fowler when fourteen years of age and worked for some time in a saw mill at Antwerp. Next engaged in the grocery business at Shingle Creek, now known as Spragueville. Mr. Carpenter's wife died in 1898. He is now and has been for some time engaged in the care of bees, devoting much time to their study.

Ralph Corbin, born at Gouverneur, 1879. His parents are Amasa Corbin, born in Gouverneur, 1843, and Alice Thorp Corbin, born in Bridgeport, Conn., 1842. He was educated in Gouverneur High School and in 1904 married to Jessie Onstott. Mr. Corbin is by profession a mine operator, which he has followed since 1900.

Ralph Corbin.

Arthur F. Corbin.

Arthur F. Corbin, born in Bridgeport, Conn., 1867. His parents are Amasa Corbin, born in Gouverneur, Dec. 31, 1843, and Alice Thorp, born in Bridgeport, Conn., 1842. He was educated in Gouverneur Wesleyan Seminary and is now in the hotel business. Has been operator in mines and real estate since 1903.

Joseph C. Callahan, born in Danbury, Vt., May 5, 1855. His parents were Robert Callahan, born in County Cork, Ireland, and Elizabeth Lennahan Callahan, also born in County Cork, Ireland. He was educated in Rutland, Vt., and married to Mary Tennicu, to whom were born five children, Elizabeth, Joseph Henry, Leo Augustine, Robert Emmett, and Thomas J. Mr. Callahan is by profession a superintendent of quarries. He is now the Supt. of the Watertown Marble Co's. plants at Gouverneur and Canton. Previous to accepting his present position, he was for eight years in charge of the machinery of the Gouverneur quarries. Has been a member of the board of education since 1899. His portrait appears in the group of the board of education.

Aaron Cooper was born in Jefferson County, N. Y., March 13, 1834. He married Laura

A. Hunt in 1855, was educated at Farm Ridge, Ill., and took up the calling of a carpenter, when 16 years old. He has diversified with lumbering, running saw-mill and farming. August 22, 1862, he enlisted to serve in Battery D., 1st N. Y. Light Artillery for "three years or during the war." He was discharged June 16th, 1865. His father was Haskill Cooper who was born in Leray, N. Y., in 1800, married Louisa Sweet, who was born at Alexandria, N. Y., Dec. 22, 1808. Aaron Cooper first came from Leray to Gouverneur in 1816 and settled on a farm about one mile from Richville toward Gouverneur but a little distance off the direct road. The land he took up is still the property of his descendants. He was a soldier in the war of 1812 and served at Sackett's Harbor and Goose Bay. The subject of our sketch came from fighting blood. To the

Aaron Cooper.

present generation the fact of service in the Civil War carries the evidence of valor, of deprivation in the service of the nation and of personal danger beyond estimate. But the enlisted man, while knowing these things to be true in general, has a different estimate of those he knew in the field. There were degrees of courage, of suffering, of faithful service never spoken outside the circle of comradeship but nevertheless real, and vivid in the memories of those who wore the blue. Tried by this judgment, the record of Aaron Cooper stands out among the best. These qualities rarely shine upon the page of history, for those who hear them are not given to the recital of their own deeds. How many reputations in and out of the army would change had not some one in the past held the key which unlocked the mystic and enduring resources of the printed page! No man knowing Aaron Cooper could doubt that any trust given him would be fulfilled if in his power to fulfill it. He will be remembered as a man of sterling good sense, an accurate memory, a peculiar and uncommon faculty for clear statement and a stalwart honesty that no allurement could sway. There were thousands of as good soldiers as he, but there were none better. And that is an achievement than which none can be more worthy. His portrait also appears in the contributed article "Battery D".

E. C. Curtis, born in Virginia in 1868. His parents were Henry Curtis, born in Jefferson County, N. Y., 1825, and Thankful Babcock Curtis, born in Jefferson Co., 1830. He was educated in Alexandria, and married in 1890 to Maggie McLellan. He has two children, Emma and Velma. Mr. Curtis is an extensive manufacturer of cheese and butter, owning and controlling several factories in Gouverneur and vicinity, five in all. During the year 1904 he manufactured 663,165 pounds of cheese and 142,032 pounds of butter. He has devoted himself to the manufacture of cheese for American consumption at which he has been very successful. He is also owner of about 385 acres of land in Macomb. He resides in the village of Gouverneur.

E. C. Curtis.

Wm. L. Collins.

William Lester Collins, born in Fowler, in 1875. His parents were Harlow Collins, born in Fowler and Ora Sweet Collins, born in Fowler. Mr. Collins was educated in the public schools of Fowler and the Gouverneur Wesleyan Seminary and in 1873 married to Ida May Fullington. They have two children, Jessie L., and Douglas H.

Benjamin Franklin Chandler, born in Richville, 1832. His parents were Arza V. Chandler, born in Camillus, N. Y., 1794, and Esther Babcock, born in Orwell, Vt., 1796. He was

educated in Richville and in 1857 married to Ellen Holland. He was again married to Catherine Spooner in 1883. Mr. Chandler is the father of Carrie Belle, and Edwin Spooner Chandler. Arza B. Chandler, father of the subject of this sketch, was one of the early settlers of the town of DeKalb, coming here with his wife from Orwell, about 1823 and clearing a farm about one-half a mile north of Richville, which is now owned by the subject of this sketch. At the time when the farm was on the stage route from Watertown to Ogdensburg, Mr. Chandler, Sr., kept a hotel. After moving here he made a visiting trip to Vermont in a lumber wagon. Mr. Chandler is the owner of about one mile square of land. He is a Prohibitionist and takes great interest in bee culture.

Benj. F. Chandler.

Benjamin F. Churchill, of Macomb, was born in Oswegatchie, in 1829. His parents were Bartholomew Churchill, born in Dutchess Co., 1798, and Sarah W. Taylor Churchill, born in Canada, 1811. Mr. Churchill was educated in Oswegatchie and Macomb and in 1853 married to Emily Parker. They are the parents of Sarah, VanBuren, John, Hubbard, Jennie and Stella. Mr. Churchill is a descendent of John Churchill, who came to America in the Mayflower. He came to Ogdensburg in a cart drawn by oxen through the wilderness, then inhabited by wolves, bears, panthers and deer, the latter were quite common. Mr. Churchill settled near Brasie Corners where he has always lived.

Benj. F. Churchill.

Garrett S. Conger, born in Canandaigua, Sept. 25, 1847. His parents were Calvin Conger, born in Malone, Aug. 7, 1807, died Feb. 6, 1902, and Rosanna Parker, born in Morristown, Jan. 31, 1812. She died March 30, 1889. Mr. Conger was educated in G. W. Seminary and in 1873 married Martha Adams Church, who was born Jan. 10, 1850, daughter of the late Daniel Church. Mr. and Mrs. Conger are the parents of Alger A. and Mary H. C. Conger. Mr. Conger was a private in Battery D, 1st N. Y. Light Artillery, (Winslow's Battery) and participated in the battles of Wilderness, Laurel Hill, Spottsylvania, N. Anna River, Totopotomy Creek, Bethsada Church, Cold Harbor, Weldon R. R., Five Forks, Appomatox and several others. He received a shell

G. S. Conger.

wound in the left knee at Bethel Church. His father and three brothers were also in the service; together they took part in fifty battles. Mr. Conger is a member of the G. A. R. and was repeatedly elected commander of Barnes Post. He was junior vice commandant of the department of New York in 1884. Was attorney for the legislative committee that investigated expenditures of armories and arsenals of the state. Is a graduate of the law department of the University of Michigan. Studied law in the offices of Chas. Anthony and E. H. Neary. Is now a member of the firm of Conger, Orvis & McLear. Was special county judge from 1880 to 1897. His portrait also appears in the group, board of education, attorneys and the G. A. R.

Charles H. Clark, born in Hailesboro, May 16, 1862. His parents were Charles A. Clark and Jane Hurlbut Clark. His mother died when he was a child. Mr. Clark's primary education was secured in the G. W. Seminary from which he graduated with the class of 1881. In the fall of that year he entered Hamilton College from which he graduated in class of 1885. After leaving college he studied law in the office of Judge Rollin H. Smith and was admitted to the bar in 1888. He then entered the newspaper business. Four years ago he joined the staff of the Gouverneur Free Press. He was promoted to local editorship upon that paper. His portrait is in the Free Press staff group picture.

E. L. Cunningham.

Elbert L. Cunningham was born in Gouverneur in 1868. His parents were William H. Cunningham, born in Gouverneur, April 15, 1835, and Julia Crawford Cunningham, born in Gouverneur, Nov. 13, 1837. He was married in 1889 to Eva Herrick. They have two children, Lena J. and Edith. Mr. Cunningham is filling his second term as Highway Commissioner of the town of Gouverneur. He is a member of Gouverneur Lodge, F. & A. M. and I. O. O. F.

Mr. Arthur E. Cushman was born in Gouverneur, June 21, 1863, the son of Talcott H. Cushman, born at Ellisburg, Jefferson County, N. Y., and Anna Conner Cushman, born at Ottawa. He was educated in the Gouverneur Wesleyan Seminary; is and has been engaged in the furniture business since 1887.

Arthur E. Cushman.

George Henry Carswell was born in England, at Dover on the English Channel, in 1837. He came to Gouverneur in 1849 and after arriving at his majority, took up a farm within that

George H. Carswell.

fertile strip of clays running through the town in North Gouverneur, parallel with the trend of the rocky ridges of the town. He was named George for his father, his mother's maiden name being Hannah Mummery, both being English born and bred. Our subject was one of the students at the old Gouverneur Wesleyan Seminary in its palmy days, and is remembered for his bright, alert mentality and his readiness at absorbing knowledge. He was a keen disputant in the debating clubs of the institution, which at that time were well known for their membership of young men of unusual promise. His gift of argument was carried into practical life later and his determined questionings at the annual town-meetings then carried out on the New England system so that any taxpayer could be heard, are well remembered. The division of the town into districts has destroyed this privilege. Physically, he was never strong and he contracted consumption when 48 years old, dying in 1880 of that disease. He was a loyal American citizen, never allowing his ancestry or birthplace to influence him in his obligations to the country of his adoption. In politics he was a Democrat of the staunch, Jeffersonian sort and continued such while so many of his party associates lost their bearings during the commotion of the early 60's. He was never a waverer then because he had opinions based on intelligent and broad views, nor did he cover his opinions by silence or evasion. Few men were better trusted than he by those knowing him intimately and his death was a distinct loss to the community as is that of every man willing to stand for something openly and without dissimulation. It is fitting that the memories of such men as George Carswell should be preserved.

William R. Conner, born in Gananoque in 1874. His parents were Wm. Conner, born in Canada and Catherine Scott Conner, born in Ireland. Mr. Conner is by profession a dentist. Was educated in Philadelphia, Pa. He has practiced his profession in Gouverneur for several years. His portrait appears in the group of dentists.

Christialana Estelle Cushman, born in Gouverneur in 1842. Her father was Myron Cushman, born in Bennington, Vt., 1812, and her mother was Susan Wade Cushman, born in a log house on the Wade farm in Gouverneur in 1818. She was educated in Gouverneur, and is occupied as a house keeper. Myron Cushman, father of the subject of this sketch, and whose portrait appears in this history, enlisted in the 92nd Reg. U. S. A., War of the 60s.

Aaron B. Cutting was born in Pierrepont, N. Y., in 1836, his parents are Daniel H. Cutting, born near Rouses Point, in Canada, in 1808, and Jane Barrows, born in Canton, N. Y., in 1810. Mr. Cutting commenced the hardware business in Gouverneur in 1861 and excepting for an interval of about two years, has continued in that business since. He is a Scottish Rite Mason, has been village trustee, Secretary of Gouverneur Agricultural and Mechanical Society and held many other important positions in the village. He is one of the oldest merchants in Gouverneur and has won an enviable reputation.

Aaron B. Cutting.

Dr. Samuel W. Close, whose portrait appears in group of physicians, was born in Toronto, Canada, May 2, 1857. His parents were John R. Close and Sarah A. McCarty. Dr. Close received his preliminary education in Potsdam State Normal School. His medical education in the University of New York. He was married June 16, 1886 to Clara A. Smith. Mr. and Mrs. Close are the parents of three children, Alison J., Dorothy L., and Catherine C. Dr. Close is secretary of the Medical Society of the County of St. Lawrence, which position he has held for the past 17 years. He is a member of the Northern N. Y. and N. Y. State Medical Societies. Mrs. Clara Smith Close is a great grand-daughter of Eleaser Nichols, one of the first settlers of Gouverneur. His portrait is also in the group of Maccabees and also in the Arcanum group.

Arthur F. Coates, born in Olcott, N. Y., 1857. His parents were Luman B. Coates, born in Olcott, Oct. 15, 1832 and Emily R. Cooper Coates, born in Olcott, Feb. 21, 1835. He was educated in Olcott and Lockport, N. Y., and married in 1884 to Nellie W. Kilmer. Was station agent at Gouverneur from 1882 to 1888. Traveling freight agent for the R. W. & O. R. R. from 1888 to 1891. He is now sales manager for the D. & H. Coal Co's. Utica office. He has recently organized a stock company at Utica, N. Y., for dealing in coal, wood and lumber.

Arthur F. Coates.

Rev. James Greenly Clutterbuck, see portrait in group of clergymen, was born in Hamilton, Ont., 1872. His parents were William Clutterbuck, born in Anapolis, Novia Scotia, 1841, and Mary Greenly Clutterbuck, born in Perth, Ont., 1845. Mr. Clutterbuck was educated at Northwestern University, Ill., and Colgate University, Hamilton, N. Y. He was married in

1893 to Myrtle Dean. He is the father of Paul Dean and Dorris Clutterbuck. Mr. Clutterbuck's father's family occupied conspicuous places in the British Army and served in a number of historic battles. His portrait is also in the Blue Lodge group.

George W. Cameron.

George W. Cameron, born in Hermon, N. Y. His parents were Hugh Cameron, born on the Atlantic Ocean and Martha Holmes Cameron, born in Canada. He was married in 1890 to Lillian E. Wood. Mr. and Mrs. Cameron are the parents of two children, L. Douglas and Donald. He has been engaged in the manufacture of butter and cheese, learning the business in Laconia, Wis. He owned and operated the Breese, Little Bow, Rock Island and Cottage Grove Creameries. In each of the above factories he acted as salesman.

Chas. C Cunningham.

Charles C. Cunningham, born in Macomb, 1857. His parents were John Cunningham, born in Edinburg, Scotland, 1820, and Isabelle Story Cunningham, born in Roxburyshire, Scotland, 1823. He was educated in the public schools of Macomb and married in 1891 to Mary F. Beardslee. Mr. and Mrs. Cunningham are the parents of two children, Worth B. and Isabelle. Mr. Cunningham is a photographer, operating the Cunningham Studio, and resides on Beckwith St., Gouverneur.

Harlow W. Collins, born in Fowler, 1848. His parents were Benjamin Collins, born in New Hampshire and Betsy Foster born in Gouverneur. Mr. Collins was educated in Hailesboro and about 1874 married to Anna M. Sweet. Was a farmer in the town of Fowler until about 1898, when he moved to Gouverneur where he has since resided.

Jay S. Corbin. Inventor. Born 1840.

Watson F. Carpenter.

Watson F. Carpenter, born in Brownville, 1862. His parents were Jeremiah Carpenter, born in Brownville, and Elizabeth Underwood Carpenter, born in Hermon, N. Y. Mr. Carpenter is by occupation a commercial traveler. He was educated in Ives Seminary at Antwerp, and Perkins Academy, Copenhagen. He finished his education in 1883 and commenced the manufacture of butter and cheese in Jefferson County in 1884. Continuing in Frankfort and McNitt, N. Y., until 1889, when he moved to OxBow where he remained until 1901. Since that he has been engaged in the sale of dairy and agricultural implements. He is now employed by D. H. Burrell Co., of Little Falls, N. Y. Mr. Carpenter was married in 1889 to Laura McNitt. They have two children, Bertha Laura and Gladys Elizabeth.

Edson H. Cole was born in Gouverneur, 1876. His parents were Seth Cole, born in Gouverneur, and Ellen Reed born in Hermon. He was educated in the Gouverneur Seminary and in Rochester. Was married in 1896 to Grace L. Phillips. They have two children, E. Harold and Willabel. Mr. Cole is engaged in the grocery business on Main street. He is a member of the lodges of Odd Fellows, Royal Arcanum, National Protective League, and Sons of Veterans. His picture is in the Arcanum group.

Mrs. A. S. Carpenter born April 4, 1833. Was the adopted daughter of Mr. and Mrs. Raymond Austin of Gouverneur. Was married Sept. 15, 1855 to Alfred S. Carpenter, who was born Feb. 15, 1823 in Haileshoro, N. Y. They were the parents of two daughters, one of whom still lives, Miss Josephine Carpenter, residing with the subject of this sketch. Mr. Alfred Carpenter's parents were Jonathan Carpenter and Lucy Johnson Carpenter, who came to the town of Fowler from Johnstown, N. Y.

Griffith E. Davis, Richville, N. Y., was born in Wales in the year 1849. He received his education in the district school. Always followed his chosen occupation as dairy farmer. He has been twice married. His first wife was Emma Murtor Macomb, by whom he had two daughters, Mabel and Myrtle. His second wife, Miss Minnie Hill of Rensselaer Falls, by whom he had one daughter, Ethel E. He is a very active worker in all matters religious, a member of the first Congregational Church. In politics he has helped to gain victory always on the Republican side. Very conscientious in all his doings. Five years ago he sold his farm on the Welsh road and moved into the village. Not content without any land to work, he has purchased a number of acres adjoining his village property.

Griffith E. Davis.

John Davis, Jr., born in Wales, in 1844. His parents were John Davis, born in Wales and Jane Davis, also born in Wales. He was educated in Gouverneur and married in 1873 to Eliza Stammer. Mr. Davis is a successful farmer and the father of Glena J. Davis and Lulu B. Davis. He lives in Gouverneur.

James H. Dickson, born in Rossie, 1844. His parents were John Dickson, born in Gouverneur and Catherine McGregor. He was educated in G. W. Seminary and married in 1846 to M. J. Taitt. Mr. and Mrs. Dickson are the parents of Cyrus J. Dickson. Mr. Dickson moved to Adams, Mass., in 1875, living there two years, thence moving to Scotland, S. D., where he now resides. He is engaged in the mercantile business and the handling of grain, live stock and coal.

Asa Davis, born in Fowler, Nov. 9, 1834. His parents were Edward O. Davis, born in Ohio, 1801, and Julia Brown Davis, born in Vermont, 1802 He was educated in Fowler and in 1865 married to Mary J. Clark Mr. Davis is by occupation a farmer, having followed farming his entire life, residing always in Fowler and Gouverneur, excepting one year, which was spent in Fayette County, Ia. Their children are Florence L. and Wilbur A.

Asa Davis.

Samuel H. Davidson, born in Granville County, Canada, 1861. His parents were John Davidson, born in Antrim County, Ireland, 1816, and Anna Edwards, born in Marlboro, Canada. He was educated in the common schools of Rossie and 1890 married to Mary E. Metcalf. They are the parents of Lena E. and Dorothy R. Mr. Davidson is by profession a stationary engineer in which capacity he has been in the employ of the St. Lawrence Marble Works for many years. He was a member of the Board of Trustees of Gouverneur village for two years; member of the Board of Health one year and the Board of Education four years. One of the organizers of the Gouverneur Assn., No. 20 of the National Association of Stationary Engineers, of which he is now president. He has been a resident of Gouverneur for twenty years and of St. Lawrence County for forty-one years. His portrait appears in the group pictures, Board of Education and Fire Co., No. 1.

Anna Caroline Dodds, born in Gouverneur, 1854. Her parents were Alexander Dodds, born in Kelso, Scotland, and Elmira L. Leavitt, born in Gouverneur, N. Y., June 5, 1825. She was educated in G. W. Seminary. They were married Sept. 15, 1848, settling on a farm in Scotch Settlement. Moved into the village in 1875. Mr. Dodds died in 1894 and Mrs. Dodds in 1898. They were the parents of Emma L., Anna C., Albert W., and Isabelle J. Emma married L. L. Clark and died in 1888, leaving one daughter, Edna B.

Owen E. Davis, born in Troedyrhinfergam, South Wales in 1863. His parents were Evan Davis, born in Troedyrhinfergam, in 1832 and Frances Davis, born in Slwynbedw, So. Wales, in 1832. Mr. Davis was educated in Druen, New Castle, England. His post office is Richville.

Owen E. Davis.

Andrew Dodds, born in Roxburyshire, Scotland, 1785. His father was John Dodds, born in Scotland. He was educated in Scotland and in 1815 married to Margaret Rutherford. Andrew Dodds came to America in 1818, settling on a farm in Rossie. In 1836 he came to Gouverneur, bought a farm, removing the timber from the same. He lived upon the farm until the death of his wife in 1855. He died in 1867.

John B. Day, born in Worcester, N. Y., Oct. 15, 1833. His parents were Benjamin Day, born in Swansey, N. H., May 27, 1787 and Elmira Fuller Day, born in Schenectady, March 28, 1792. He was married March 4, 1858, to Ann Baxter. Mr. and Mrs. Day are the parents of Marvin H., Ida Sweet, Ella A. Bowman, Bertha E. Clark, Will Bettie Howe, and Eva J. Robinson. Mr. Day was a prominent farmer in Fowler, holding important town offices.

John B. Day.   Mrs. John B. Day.

Frederick F. Drury, whose portrait appears in group of physicians, was born in Edwards, 1868. His parents were Benjamin F. Drury, M. D., born in Canton, N. Y., 1836, and Mary A. (Ritchie) Drury, born in DeKalb, N. Y., 1838. He was educated primarily in the Gouverneur Wesleyan Seminary and married in 1896 to Julia E. Foster. Dr. Drury graduated in the Gouverneur Wesleyan Seminary in 1887. His medical education was obtained in the University of Vt., and Bellevue Hospital College, New York, from which college he graduated in 1891. He is a practicing physician and surgeon in Gouverneur and at present one of the coroners of St. Lawrence Co. Mr. and Mrs. Drury are the parents of Frederick F., Jr., Mabel Foster and Foster Taitt Drury.

Homer W. Dailey was born in Gouverneur, N. Y., March 28th, 1861. His parents were Henry Dailey, born in Franconia, N. H., March 13th, 1822, and Alma Hall Dailey born in Lockport, N. Y., in 1828. Mr. Dailey was educated in G. W. Seminary and in 1888 married to Mary E. Sprague. Mr. and Mrs. Dailey are the parents of Raymond E. They reside on the Tuthill road where Mr. Dailey was born.

Alexander A. Dickson, born in Rossie. His parents were John Dickson, born in Roxburyshire, Scotland, 1808 and Catherine McGregor Dickson, born in Perthshire, 1810. Mr. Dickson was educated in G. W. Seminary and in 1878 married to Helen McGregor. They are the parents of one child, John E. Dickson. He resides in Gouverneur.

O. J. David.

Orin J. David, born in Wayne County, Mich., in 1855. His parents were James R. A. David, born at Troy, N. Y., and Elmira Meff, born at Amsterdam, N. Y. He was educated at Detroit, Mich., and was married in 1882 to Cora M. J. Sterne. He has six children, Blanche C., Grace, Sydney M., Auberey, Earl and Pearle. His present occupation is miner and promoter. Mr. David commenced lumbering in Michigan in 1874, after which he managed mines in Lake Superior, Wyoming, and Iowa. He came to Gouverneur in 1892 and assisted in organizing the U. S. Talc Co. and the Union Talc Co. Was president of the last company for three years. He is at present engaged in mining in Joplin, Mo. Mr. David's father distinguished himself in the war of the rebellion, rising from the ranks to the command of a regiment.

Robert Dodds, born in Rossie, 1823. His parents were Andrew Dodds, born in Scotland, 1785, and Margaret Rutherford Dodds, born in Scotland in 1797. He was educated in the common schools of Rossie and married in 1849 to Susan Deans. Mr. and Mrs. Dodds are the parents of Jennie, Frank, Clark and John. Robert Dodds managed his father's farm until his death which was in 1872. His wife died in 1890.

David E. Davis, born in Wales, 1844, and married to Sarah Jones in 1867. Mr. and Mrs. Davis are the parents of Jennie C. Thomas. Mr. Davis came to the United States in 1856 with his parents, settled in Richville and lived in Gouverneur for forty years.

David E. Davis.

Frank Andrew Dodds, born in Gouverneur, Dec. 26, 1851. His parents were Robert Dodds, born in Rossie in 1824 and died in Gouverneur in 1871, and Susan H. Deans Dodds, born in OxBow, in 1826. Died in 1891.

Frank A. Dodds.

He was educated in the Gouverneur Wesleyan Seminary and married Nov. 26, 1872, to Matilda Althouse, who was born in Gouverneur, Nov. 25, 1855. Mr. and Mrs. Dodds are the parents of seven children, Alberta Dodds Overacker, Maude S., Robert D. S., Francis E., A. Murray, Claud K. and Stanley C. Mr. Dodds is by occupation a farmer and resides near Elmdale. His paternal grand-father was Andrew Dodds, see biographical sketch, who came from Scotland to Rossie in 1818 and settled in what is now known as the Scotch Settlement near OxBow.

Mrs. Frank A. Dodds

Anna Laura Bowne Dodge, born in Gouverneur, Nov. 28, 1878. Her parents were Charles Hicks Bowne, born in Gouverneur, July 23, 1828, and Mary E. Whitney Bowne, born in Mexico, Oswego County, N. Y., 1845. She was educated in Gouverneur, Tarrytown and New York. Married Nov. 9, 1899, to Robert Griffin Dodge. Mr. and Mrs. Dodge are the parents of one child, Dorothy Bowne Dodge. Mrs. Dodge is a Daughter of the Revolution and member of the Episcopal Church. Her daughter, Dorothy Bowne Dodge, is the sixth generation from Charles Hicks.

Mrs. Abby Lynde Dickson, born in Richville, Aug. 12, 1835. Her parents were Alfred S. Phelps, born in Sterling, Mass., Nov. 18, 1806 and Jerusha Bosworth Phelps, born in Bethle-

Rev J. A. Dickson.

hem, Mass., May 12, 1801. Mrs. Dickson was educated in Richville and married in 1856 to Carlos W. Lynde. She is the mother of Anna M. Lynde Clark, deceased, and Mary Lynde Watson, children of Carlos W. Lynde. Mrs. Dickson was married the second time to Rev. James A. Dickson in 1879. Her father, Alfred S. Phelps, came to Richville with his parents at the age of two years. The mother,

Mrs. Jerusha Bosworth Phelps.

Jerusha Bosworth, came to Richville cary in life with her brother, Jabez Bosworth. There was no bridge when they came to Richville at Gouverneur nor was there any highway between Gouverneur and Richville. Her father Samuel W. Phelps was in the war of 1812 at Sacketts Harbor as Captain. Her great grand-father, Elijah Phelps, was in the Revolutionary War. An uncle, Edward Herrick Phelps, was killed at Lookout Mountain, Civil War. A brother, Samuel W. Phelps, was in the 106th Reg. N. Y. Vol. for three years and participated in the battle of the Wilderness and six other engagements. Was twice wounded.

Henry S. Day.

Henry Simeon Day, born in Hermon, 1874. His parents were Simeon P. Day, born in 1832 and Susan Weeks Day, born in Jefferson County, in 1842. Was educated in Hermon school and married in 1903 to Lottie May Hill. Mr. Day was a student of Cornell University Dairy School class of 1899. Is a successful farmer in Hermon. Has dairy of 30 cows. His post office is Simpson, N. Y.

William Henry Draper, born in Champion, Sept. 9, 1864. His parents were George Draper, born in Champion, May 29, 1835 and Helen M. Newell Draper, born in Gouverneur, Dec. 28, 1841. He was educated in G. W. Seminary and first married June 24, 1891, to Stella Matteson, who died June 28, 1895. December 17, 1895, he married Grace Keech. Mr. and Mrs. Draper are the parents of Dorothy Helen, Herbert G. and Marion B. Mr. Draper is the proprietor of the Draper Drug store on Main street. His portrait is also in the Blue Lodge group.

William H. Draper.

Robert Griffin Dodge, born at Harrisville, 1870. His parents were William Robert Dodge and Jane Noyes. Mr. Dodge was educated in the G. W. Seminary and Andover College. He was married Nov. 9, 1899 to Anna Laura Bowne. Mr. and Mrs. Dodge are the parents of one child, Dorothy Bowne Dodge. The subject of this sketch has been since leaving school, employed in the post-office, with U. S. Talc Co., in the store of C. H. Bowne & Co., Secretary and treasurer of the Empire Marble Co., and is at present secretary, treasurer and manager of the Adirondack Pyrites Co.

Benjamin Franklin Drury, whose portrait appears in group of physicians, was born in

Canton, N. Y., in 1836. His parents were Isaac Drury, born in Vermont and Elizabeth Van-Allen Drury, born in Vermont. He was educated in the common and select schools and married in 1859 to Mary A. Ritchie. They have three children, Julia L., Frederick F., and Albert N. Dr. Drury spent his early life on a farm. At the age of 20 he commenced the study of medicine, graduating at Burlington, Vt., in June, 1854. He has been continually engaged in the practice of his profession since, for the last 28 years in Gouverneur and vicinity.

Charles Clement Dunkleburg, born at Fort Covington, Feb. 25, 1863. His parents were Samuel Dunkleburg, born in Lockport, May 9, 1831, and Maria White Dunkleburg, born in Russell, in 1829. He was educated at Canton, N. Y., and Oct. 26, 1886, married Hana May Sabin. Mr. Dunkleburg was the father of Charles, Stanley, Florence and Frances Dunkleburg. Mr. Dunkleburg came to Gouverneur in 1889, buying out the Whitney Bros. marble finishing business, then conducted by Alexas and P. R. Whitney. He was one of the trustees of the Baptist Church and a prominent member of the building committee in the construction of the new church. He was a prominent Mason, Odd Fellow, and member of the Temple Club. He was trustee of the village

Charles C. Dunkleburg.

and one of Gouverneur's most highly honored and respected citizens. Mr. Dunkleburg died suddenly at Syracuse where he had been taken from Star Lake to undergo an operation for appendicitis.

Byron W. Dewey, born in Gouverneur, 1843. His parents were Warren Dewey, born in Hartford, N. Y., 1815, and Altha Leavett, born in Gouverneur on the old Leavett farm in 1818. Mr. Dewey is by occupation a farmer. Was educated in Gouverneur Wesleyan Seminary, and married 1870 to Anna C. Howe, who was born in Grand Haven, Mich. Mr. and Mrs. Dewey are the parents of five children, Altha, Claud, Harriett, Warren, Jr., and Jay Leavett. Mr. Dewey has been occupied as a farmer since 1875, prior to which time he was a tanner and currier. He was a soldier in the war of the 60's.

Byron W. Dewey.

William Robert Dodge, born in Gouverneur June 16, 1834. His parents were Edwin Dodge, born in Kent, Conn., Dec. 13, 1801, and Jerusha Lay Sterling Dodge, born

in Lime, Conn., May 25, 1803. Mr. Dodge was educated in Gouverneur and in 1866 married to Jane Noyes. Mr. and Mrs. Dodge are the parents of Edwin, Robert G., Richard P., Gertrude L., and Mrs. Catherine N. Dodge Gill. Mr. Dodge held the office of President of the village in the year 1881, was appointed post-master in 1885 and held this office one term. Commenced his business career as clerk for Wm. E. Sterling in this village, a little later established in connection with C. H. Russell, an express line from Watertown to Ogdensburg; the first system of pony express in Northern New York. He later engaged in railroading and located in Cincinnatti and St. Louis, returned to St. Lawrence Co.

W. R. Dodge

and engaged in the tanning business under firm name of Beach & Dodge, operating a large tannery in Harrisville. About 1873 he sold out his business in Harrisville, returning to Gouverneur. Soon after coming to Gouverneur he formed a partnership with John Webb under the firm name of John Webb, Jr. & Co., and engaged in mining iron ore at the Kearney mine. He was Vice President, and one of the originators of the Gouverneur Wood Pulp Co., also the U. S. Talc Co., and the Empire Marble Co. He was director of the Bank of Gouverneur.

George M. Dodds, born in Gouverneur, 1854. His parents were Andrew Dodds, born in Scotland, 1813 (see biographical sketch) and Sally Smith Dodds, born in Gouverneur, 1810. He was educated in G. W. Seminary and married in 1878 to Ruie J. Johnson. Mr. and Mrs. Dodds are the parents of Bertha A., G. Wilson, Bly A., and Vincent. Mrs. Sally Smith Dodds, mother of the subject of this sketch, was the daughter of Willard Smith, one of the first settlers (see history). Mr. Dodds served the town as Commissioner of Highway from 1891 to 1903. Has been director and superintendent of the Gouverneur Agricultural and Mechanical Society from 1894 to the present time. He is a prominent and prosperous farmer on the Richville road. His portrait

George M. Dodds.

also appears in the group of officers of the Gouverneur Agricultural and Mechanical Society.

Wilbur A. Davis.

Wilbur A. Davis, born in Fowler, 1877. His parents were Asa Davis, born in Fowler, 1834, and Mary J. Clark Davis, born in Gouverneur, 1839. Educated in Gouverneur High School, and married in 1899 to Clara Belle Sprague. Mr. and Mrs. Davis have one child, Robert L. Davis. Subject of sketch was born on a farm and followed that occupation until 1900, working about a year after that as a mill wright. In 1903 he became connected as a partner with the firm of Davis & Sprague. Is an Odd Fellow, member of Royal Arcanum Lodge and I. O. O. F., of which body he is Financial Secretary. His portrait also appears in the Foresters' group.

Amasa Stephen Davis, born in Fowler, 1830. His parents were Edwin O. Davis, born in Ohio, 1801 and Julia A. Davis, born in Conn., 1805. Educated in the common schools of Fowler and married 1851 to Adaline L. Newton. Mr. and Mrs. Davis are the parents of four children, Mrs. Davis Lamb, Eugene L. Davis, Stephen A., and Arthur. Mr. Edwin O. Davis, father of the subject of this sketch, moved into the town of Fowler in 1825, where he lived continuously until his death, 1884. Amasa S. Davis served in the War of the Rebellion, 1864-5, in the 14th N. Y. Heavy Artillery.

Amasa S. Davis.

Edwin G. Dodge.

Edwin Gardner Dodge, born in Gouverneur, Aug. 10, 1839. His parents were Edwin Dodge, born in Kent, Conn., Dec. 13, 1801, and Jerusha Lee Sterling, born in Lime, Conn., May 25, 1803. Mr. Dodge was educated in Gouverneur and Auburn, N. Y. Was never married. He was by occupation a mill and land owner. Was president of the village of Gouverneur from 1872 to '76. He was prominent in Democratic politics of the state. Was for many years member of the Democratic State committee.

Frederick Raymond Darling, born in Andover, N. Y., Nov. 7, 1873. His parents were Edwin B. Darling, born in Elkland, Pa., August 2, 1850, and Hattie A. Chase Darling, born in Andover, N. Y., Nov. 14, 1855. He was educated in Hornellsville High School and Cornell

University. Received degree of A. B. in the University of Chicago. Is by occupation a teacher, having held the following positions: Prin. Woodhull Union School, 1896-98; Prin. Limestone Union School, 1898-1901; Prin. Portville Union School, 1901-04. Supt. of schools in Gouverneur 1904 to the present time. He is of New England descent, his ancestors having come to this country prior to 1700. He is a descendant of Rodger Williams. He was married to Emma A. Sehn, Aug. 26, 1896. Mr. and Mrs. Darling are the parents of Carl Egbert, born Aug. 20, 1903. His portrait appears in the group of High School teachers.

Alexander Dodds.

Alexander Dodds with his wife and five children, three boys and two girls, came to this country from Scotland in 1833, and settled three miles east of Gouverneur on a farm that was named Mount Hillie, in what became the Scottish settlement. One of the daughters, Catherine, married David Hill, and settled on a farm near Ravenwood. The other daughter, Marguarette, married John Thompson, both settling within a half mile of the old homestead. Andrew, the elder son settled on a farm within one and one-half miles, and Alexander on a farm across the road from the old homestead. John, remaining on the old farm where three children were born; Jane Elizabeth, now Hodgkins, and Alexander Dodds now of Grand Rapids, Mich., and Wm. A. Dodds. For 25 years death did not enter the Scottish settlement, but after that it came often, and all of the family that came from Scotland have passed away. W. A. Dodds died in Sept. 1876. G. H. and Elizabeth Hodgkins are now enjoying the old homestead, Mount Hillie, of the days gone by. The farm is now known as Highland Home. Alexander Dodds 3d, whose portrait appears, is now a manufacturer of wood-working machinery at Grand Rapids, Mich. He learned the trade of machinist in Gouverneur where he spent the years up to his majority, and after going west, made and patented several inventions which he now manufactures.

John N. Draper.

John Newell Draper, born in Gouverneur, Nov. 21, 1870. His parents were George Draper, born in the town of Champion, May 29, 1835 and Helen M. Newell Draper, born in Gouverneur, Dec. 28, 1841. Mr. Draper was educated in G. W. Seminary and married Feb. 24, 1897, to Nellie C. Hibbard. He has conducted a store in Gouverneur since 1898, previous to which he was a book-keeper.

Helen Maria Draper, born in Gouverneur, Dec. 28, 1841. Her parents were John D. Newell, born in Saratoga County, N. Y., July 19, 1811, and Olive Smith Newell, born in Edinburg, Saratoga Co., Oct. 1, 1812. Mrs. Draper was educated in the G. W. Seminary and married Sept. 23, 1863, to George Draper. She is the mother of William H., Dora M. Draper Palmer, John W., Bertha H. Draper Bennett, Kathleen G. Draper Kinney and Bessie P. deceased. Mrs. Draper after the death of her husband in 1885, carried on the business inaugurated by him to financial success. Mrs. Draper has been an enterprising towns-woman, always living to the progress of the community.

Helen M. Draper.

Elmer Wentworth Estes, born in Lexington, Maine, Dec. 25th, 1852. His parents were Richard Estes, born in New Hampshire in 1792, and Jane Cook, born in Embden, Maine. Richard served in the war of 1812, and died in 1862 at the age of seventy. The subject of this sketch was educated in Farmingham, Maine, has been twice married, his first wife was Jane Perkins, deceased. His second wife, to whom he was married Sept. 10th, 1894, was Mary Lathrop. Mr. Estes is the father of Maud, Sumner, Alvin, Wentworth Hayden and Jane Mary. Mr. Estes is an expert manufacturer of wood pulp and is in charge of the Aldrich Paper Company's mill at Emeryville.

James D. Easton.

James Dunham Easton, born in Brockville, Ont., 1828. His parents were Solomon Easton, born in Hartford, Conn., and Aurilla Galuchia Easton, born in Shaftsbury, Vt. Mr. Easton was educated in Brockville, Ont. Came to Gouverneur in March, 1850, and engaged in the occupation of Blacksmith. He was president of the village in the sixties. Was married to Lydia L. Hoover in 1852, and has two children living, Seymour A. and Eva Caroline. Seymour A. married Sarah Drake and has one child, Ruth, born April 2, 1892. Eva Caroline is now the wife of C. F. Kennon. Has one daughter, Frances E., born Nov. 14, 1897.

Lewis E. Eckman born in Bavaria, Germany, 1838. His parents were Bernard Eckman, born in Bavaria 1789 and Getta Sigbart Eckman, born in Bavaria, Jan. 1794. He was educated in Bavaria and married in 1867 to Babette L. _____

Lewis Eckman.

Mr. and Mrs. Eckman are the parents of Bernhard, Morris and Clara Eckman. Mr. Eckman came to this country in 1853, learning upholstery business in New York. Came to Gouverneur in 1858, entering the employ of S. B. VanDuzee. This position he held until 1864, then entered co-partnership under the firm name of Vanduzee & Eckman. This co-partnership was incorporated in 1882, under the name of S. B. VanDuzee Mfg. Co., with which concern he has been actively interested until the present time. He was one of the pioneers of the marble business in Gouverneur, being interested in the Whitney Marble Co., now the Gouverneur Marble Co., which has been steadily in operation since 1888. Mr. Eckman is the only survivor of the original corporation, viz: Whitney Marble Co., and has held the position of treasurer continuously since the organization of that company.

William A. Freeman, born at Athens, Ont., 1865. His parents were William Freeman, born in England and Lucy Jackson Freeman. Mr. Freeman was educated in Athens Ont., and married in 1891 to Augusta McArthur. He is by occupation a manufacturer of butter and dairy products. Mr. Freeman came to Gouverneur in 1899, engaging in the manufacture of dairy products. First employed in East Gouverneur factory, then became owner and manager of that factory. Has kept pace with the progress of his profession and is now an expert. Was the recipient of a silver pitcher at the annual convention of the N. Y. S. D. Assn. in Watertown in December, 1900, competing with the entire state for best cheese for American consumption, for highest two years scoring. Won gold medal same year at Paris Exposition for highest scoring American cheese. He is an active member of the Board of Trade and salesman for his factory on Johnstown street, this town.

William A. Freeman.

Herbert G. Farmer, born in Fowler, 1858. His parents were Francis Farmer, born in Herkimer and Louisa Homer, born in Fowler. Mr. Farmer was educated in Gouverneur and in Canton University. He was married Dec. 16, 1888, to Hariet Elizabeth Packard, who was born July 31, 1858. Mr. and Mrs. Farmer are the parents of three children, Glenn, Ruth and Milton. Mr. Farmer was for many years in the clothing business in Gouverneur, selling out to I. I. Block, who still continues the business. He is now a commerical traveler. He is a member of the Masonic and Odd Fellows lodges and the Royal Arcanum.

Oscar P. Fuller, deceased. Born at Fullerville in 1843. His parents were Leman Fuller, born in Vermont, and Abigal Parker Fuller, born in Fowler. He was educated at Fullerville and in the Gouverneur Wesleyan Seminary. Married to Martha A. Rolph in 1860. Three children are now living, Fred B., Helena M. and Ainsworth L. Mr. Fuller was engaged for many years at Gouverneur in the sale of agricultural implements.

Oscar P. Fuller.

Ole B. Fischer, born in Chaumont, Jefferson County, N. Y., in 1869. His parents are Daniel W. Fischer and Emily Marks Fischer. He was educated in Chaumont and married in 1890 to Laura VanDewalker. Mr. Fischer is by occupation a stone cutter. He was instrumental in the organization of the Gouverneur Cut Stone Co. and later the Extra Dark Marble Co., of which Mr. Fischer is Treasurer. The Extra Dark Marble Co. are the contractors for a memorial arch. Mr. Fischer is a member of Gouverneur Lodge, 325, I. O. O. F. Mr. and Mrs. Fischer are the parents of Carl Fischer. Mr. Fischer was leader of Gouverneur Citizens band for seven years. Member of Prof. Sudds' Union Hall orchestra for fifteen years.

O. B. Fischer

Ichabod Gardner Farmer, born in Fowler, Dec. 9, 1832. His parents were Jos. Farmer, born in Cambridge, Washington County, Aug. 29, 1797, and Ruth Brown Farmer, born in Herkimer, N. Y., April 10, 1807. Educated in the town of Fowler and married in 1856 to Clarisa Rhodes. Mr. and Mrs. Farmer are the parents of Frank H., of Gouverneur, and Myron G., of Buffalo. Mr. Farmer occupied his own farm between Hailesboro and Gouverneur until 1884, removing to Gouverneur Village where he resided until his death in 1904. Was an active member of the Grange since 1875 of which he was for some time the master. Was prominent and influential member of the Unitarian Church. Energetic, honest and progressive citizen.

Ichabod G. Farmer.

Mrs. Clarisa Rhodes Farmer, born in Fowler, Dec. 21, 1836. Her parents were Beloved Rhodes, born in Brownville, Jeff. County, May 15, 1809, and Hannah Sweet, born in Adams, Jefferson County, Sept. 22, 1816. She was educated in the town of Fowler and married in 1856 to Ichabod G. Farmer. Mrs. Farmer is the mother of two children, Frank H., of Gouverneur, and Myron G. of Buffalo. She has been an active member of the Grange since 1876; member of the Unitarian Church and an efficient worker of that society. Was treasurer of the Womans' Alliance. Mrs. Farmer's grandfather, Aaron Rhodes, was one of the pioneers of the town of Fowler as was also her maternal grandfather, Orin Sweet.

Mrs. I. G. Farmer.

Dr. Daniel Montefiore Foss, whose portrait appears in the group of physicians, was born in Lawrence. in 1860. His parents were Daniel Foss, born in Fairfield, Vt., 1829, and Charlotte V. Montefiore Foss, born in New York City, 1833. He was educated in Lawrenceville Academy, University of Minnesota and University of Vermont. He was a member of the United States army in 1879. Assigned to hospital corps under Surgeon Gen. Morgan and was stationed at Fort Thompson, Crow Creek Reservation. Was present at the surrender of Sitting Bull and his band. Resigned from the army in 1881 and began the practice of medicine in DeKalb in 1886, removing from there to Depeyster in 1888, coming to Gouverneur in 1900. He took post graduate course in 1899.

Fred B. Fuller, born in Fowler, July 18, 1861. His parents were O. P. Fuller, born in Fullerville in 1840, and Martha A. Rolph Fuller, born in Fowler in 1840. Mr. Fuller was educated in Gouverneur Wesleyan Seminary and married October 13, 1902 to L. S. Marselles. Mr. Fuller is engaged in the sale of farming implements and dairy supplies. He is proprietor of the Farmer's Sheds on Clinton Street.

Fred B. Fuller.

Grant W. Fuller, born in Fullerville, in 1869. His parents were Daniel Webster Fuller, born in Fullerville in 1834 and Irene Woodcock Fuller, born in Fowler, 1838. He was educated in the public schools of Fullerville and Albany Business College. Was married in 1895 to Mary A. Towne, of Potsdam, N. Y. Has one child, Louise Towne Fuller. Mr. Fuller has served two years as village trustee.

Nelson Horatio Freeman, born in Edwards, Sept. 2, 1844. His parents were Thomas Freeman, born in Biddenden, Eng., Jan. 7, 1804, and Phoebe Carr Freeman, born in Steventown, Rensselaer County, in 1807. Died April 14, 1890. Mr. Freeman went to California in 1863, returning settled on his farm in Talcville in 1868. Talc was discovered upon his farm in 1875. He moved to Gouverneur in 1892 and settled upon the corner of Beckwith and Sterling streets, where he now resides. Together with his son Frank, he constructed what is known as the Freeman Block on Clinton street in 1902. Mr. Freeman is an enterprising gentleman, prominent in matters that enter into the welfare of the community. Mr. Freeman's father came to America in 1826, settling in Edwards, on what is known as the Thomas Freeman farm. Had ten children all of whom grew up.

Nelson H. Freeman.

Mrs. Eliza J. Noble Freeman, born in Edwards, June 18, 1847. Her parents were John Noble, born in Edinburgh, Scotland in 1817, and Mary Rushton Noble, born in New York City in 1824, and died Sept. 1, 1900. Mrs. Freeman's father was one of the early pioneers of Edwards, settling where the village of Edwards now stands. He bought considerable land, was also a dealer in cattle, driving them to Montreal and Quebec markets. Accompanied by a dog, they would start with their drove through what was then a comparative wilderness. Mrs. Freeman's grandfather came to this country when her father was two and one-half years old, settling near Edwards on what is known as the William Brown farm.

Mrs. N. H. Freeman.

Jane Wright Ferguson, born Aug. 25, 1819, at Ormskirk, England, married Thomas Ferguson in 1837, graduated from a medical college in Edinburg, Scotland, in 1843 after studying medicine under Dr. Laughton of Southport, England; such is the history of one of the excellent women who made Gouverneur her home. She practiced her profession of obstetrics over forty years here and elsewhere, with credit to herself and the gratitude of her patients. Left alone with eight children to provide for at the death of her husband, the moral fibre interwoven in her character became known to her friends as she successfully battled with adverse circumstances, and all her children were brought to maturity, a credit to her wise direction and untiring industry. Her vigorous common sense, her winning personality and her assuring presence made her welcome in numberless homes. Mrs. Ferguson was related through her marriage with the royal house of Stuart, long reigning upon the English throne.

Clarence Henry Fuller, born in Antwerp in 1851. His parents were William Fuller, born in Jefferson County in 1825, and Elizabeth Martin Fuller. He was educated in Antwerp and in 1882 married to Alice Smith. Mr. and Mrs. Fuller are the parents of Edith, Pearl, Morris Albert, Etta Alice and Clarence Henry Jr. Mr. Fuller has hauled tale for twenty years.

Clarence H. Fuller.

William Samuel Griffith, born in Gouverneur, N. Y., 1853. His parents were William Griffith, born in N. Y. City, August 1, 1806 and Elizabeth Herriman Griffith, born in New Hampshire, August 2, 1820. Educated at Griffith School House and Gouverneur Wesleyan Seminary. Married in 1882 to Nora J. Wight. Mr. Griffith, the father of the subject of this sketch, and brother Samuel, came to Gouverneur from Oneida in 1840. Bought a farm near Griffith Bridge, still in the family. They were among the first to make dairy cheese in the town. This cheese was sold in Ogdensburg at a price of three to four and one-half cents. Subject of the sketch made cheese for about twelve years. Exhibited cheese at Columbian Exhibition at Chicago in 1893, receiving diploma and medal for high scoring. Mr. Griffith now resides upon his farm about two miles from Griffith Bridge adjoining that of Lott Hall.

William S. Griffith.

Hannibal S. Fox, born in Indian River, Lewis County, in 1840. Parents were Abraham Fox, born near Ft. Plain and Eleanor Putnam, born near Fort Plain. Mr. Fox came to Gouverneur in 1876 from the west to take charge of the Gouverneur Flouring Mills to bring up the standard of the flour. Entered the employ of Dodge & Beardslee and remained in their employ and that of their successors for 28 years. He now resides at 25 Washington Street, Ogdensburg, N. Y.

Hannibal S. Fox.

Frank N. Freeman.

Frank Nelson Freeman, born in Edwards in 1877. His parents were Nelson H. Freeman, born in Edwards in 1844, and Eliza Jane Noble, born in Edwards in 1848. Educated in Gouverneur and Poughkeepsie, and married in 1901 to Grace E. Mosher. Mr. Freeman's early life was spent on the homestead farm in Edwards. At the age of 13, moved with his people to Gouverneur, where he pursued a course in the High School. In 1898 took a business course at Eastman College, Poughkeepsie, soon after entered the harness, carriage and implement business, together with his father. The growth of business compelled the erection in 1902 of what is now the Freeman block on Clinton street. Mr. Freeman is a prominent member of the Masonic, Odd Fellow and Encampment orders.

Grace E. Mosher Freeman, born in Philadelphia, N. Y., in 1878. Her parents were Charles L. Mosher, (see biographical sketch), and Addie A. Scram, born in Antwerp in 1856. She was educated in Gouverneur and in 1901 married to F. N. Freeman, (see biographical sketch).

Mrs. F. N. Freeman.

Dr. William J. Flint, whose portrait appears in the group of physicians, was born in Oneida County in 1867. His parents were Robert Flint, born in New York and Mary A. LeClare Flint, born in New York. Dr. Flint is a practicing physician and surgeon having practiced his profession in Gouverneur since 1890. He received his preliminary education in Cazenovia Seminary, graduated from the N. Y. Homeopathic Medical College and Hospital. He was married in 1892 to Anna D. Goodfellow. Has one child, Mildred Irene. Rev. Robert Flint is a Methodist Clergyman now upon the retired list. Dr. Flint's maternal grandfather came from France to America with the Lafayette Expedition.

Wallace H. Foster.

Mrs. Isadore LeWaite Foster, born in Hammond, May 30, 1847. Her parents were Sydney S. Waite, born in Herkimer, June 6, 1807, and Julia A. Pond Waite, born in Addison, Vt., June 9, 1873. Subject of the sketch was educated in Herkimer, Hammond and Addison, Vt. Was married March 19, 1868 to Wallace H. Foster, who died Jan. 25, 1890. Mrs. Foster has two children living, Julia E. Foster Drury, wife of Dr. Fred Drury, of Gouverneur, and James Bowne Foster, of Hanford, California. Her portrait appears in the D. A. R. Group.

Of Wallace H. Foster, one who knew him intimately says: "He was the soul of honor, a steadfast and reliable friend, a man of good business ability and a citizen whom to know was to esteem."

Enoch P. Griffith, Richville, N. Y., was born in South Wales, in the year 1842. Emigrated to this country with his parents, the late Ebenezer and Esther (Jones) Griffith in the year 1856. When the Civil War broke out, he enlisted in Co. K, 60th N. Y. Infantry and served four years. At the close of the war, he bought the blacksmith shop conducted at the time by J. L. Nash. He built the shop now owned by A. F. Owens. For upwards of ten years he conducted a first-class hardware store. He was married in 1866 to Miss Jane Jones and have three children, Maria, wife of A. W. Overacker, Walter O., and Webster L. Mr. Griffith is a member of Richville Lodge, No. 633 F. & A. M., a staunch Republican and is well posted on all topics of the day.

Webster Everett Griffith, born in Richville, March 17, 1876. His parents were E. P. Griffith, born in Wales, 1842, and Jane Jones Griffith, born in Lewis Co. Mr. Griffith received his preliminary education at Richville, graduating at Gouverneur High School and married June 1, 1898, Bessie Walch. They are the parents of one child, Margaret. After graduating at Gouverneur High School, Mr. Griffith entered Cornell University Dairy School in 1895, from which institution he graduated with honor. First accepted a position as manager of a Creamery at Bangor, Franklin County. This factory was the first factory to distribute the proceeds from average of butter fats rather than the weight of milk. This sampling and computing falling upon Mr. Griffith as well as the keeping of books and accounts for the association. He returned to Cornell in 1896 where he pursued an advanced course. After completion of the course,

Webster E. Griffith.

accepted a position with W. R. Boynton & Co., Madrid. He remained with Messrs. Boynton two years, then passed civil service examination and was appointed expert by Commissioner of Agriculture. In 1889 was made butter inspector at Cornell University which position he now holds. In 1902 took post graduate course in Ohio State University.

William Gardner.

William Gardner, born in Edwards in 1860. His parents were Alvin L. Gardner, born in Sacketts Harbor in 1834, and Christiana Gier Gardner, born in Edwards in 1838. Mr. Gardner was educated in Edwards and in 1881 married Teresa Murty. Mr. Gardner is a retired farmer. Was elected supervisor of Edwards which office he now holds. Has been president of the village and trustee, which position he now holds. Has been Superintendent of the Ontario Talc Co., which position he held from the organization for five years, during which time the company constructed their talc mill at Fullerville and did much of their development work. Mr. Gardner is now engaged in extensive lumber operations in Edwards.

Hermon H. Gerner, born in Lowville, 1871. His parents were Joseph Gerner, born in Germany, 1830 and Johanna Frick Gerner, born in Germany. Mr. Gerner was educated in Lowville and married in 1904 to Nina Thayer. Mr. Gerner is a tailor by profession, conducting a shop in Gouverneur. He is a prominent Mason, member of the various Masonic bodies in Gouverneur and master of the lodge. Member of the Masonic Temple Club. His portrait appears in the Blue Lodge group.

Edward W. Gaddis, born in DeKalb in 1860. His parents were James Gaddis, born in Ireland in 1830, and Mary McLornen Gaddis, born in Ireland in 1832. Was educated in the common schools of DeKalb and married in 1886 to Elma M. Seaver. Mr. and Mrs. Gaddis are the parents of five children, Raymond, Ruth, Fred, Edith and Esther. He has been in the grocery business since 1882. Served as village trustee, 1904-5. Member of Gouverneur Lodge No. 217, F. & A. M. Since retiring from mercantile business Mr. Gaddis has engaged in extensive building operations.

Edward W. Gaddis.

A. A. Gates, Richville, N. Y., was born in Fowler in 1850. Educated in the Gouverneur Wesleyan Seminary. He has been twice married. His first wife was Miss Frances Bacon who died in 1889. In June 1896 he was married to Miss Hattie Andrew of Antwerp, by whom he has two sons, A. Morris and Merrill A. He was in the feed and lumber business at Antwerp for a number of years. Last autumn, he sold out his interest there and took possession of the Richville Mills. His method of doing business is "on the square" which has gained him a reputation as an honest and upright business man. He is a Mason. In politics a Democrat. His parents were A. F. Gates who was born in Champion in 1825 and his mother's maiden name was Jane Nicholson of Lewis County, N. Y.

Louisa A. Griffin Cornwall, born in Redwood, 1862, her parents were Nicholas Bush, born in Metz, France, 1824 and Elizabeth Dollinger, born in Lerayville, Jefferson County, 1824. She was educated in Redwood and married in 1881 to Florence D. Griffin. She has one son, James Driscoll Griffin. Mrs. Cornwall's mother, Elizabeth Dollinger, was a niece of Ignatius Von Dollinger, who started the reform Church at Munich. (See encyclopedia).

Louisa A. Griffin Cornwall.

Driscoll Griffin.

Ross E. Goodenough, born in Fowler, 1877. His parents were Wm. Henry Goodnough, born in Gouverneur, 1830 and Ellen Kitts Goodnough, born in Fowler, 1832. He was educated in Gouverneur High School and married in 1901 to Anna Gene Parsons. Has one child, Dorothy Hope Goodnough. Mr. Goodnough is a partner in the Jewelry firm of York & Goodnough.

Horace Elon Gardner, born in Gouverneur in 1855. His parents were Nelson Gardner, born in Rodman, Jefferson County, N. Y., in 1826, and Harriet White, born in DeKalb in 1826. He was educated in Gouverneur Wesleyan Seminary and married in 1884 to Edith R. Hildreth. Mr. and Mrs. Gardner are the parents of Grover, Cecil, Vernon, Clyde, Earl, Herbert, Stella and Ernest. Spent his early life as a farmer and resides near Richville.

Horace E. Gardner.

Joseph George, born in Madrid, Feb. 7, 1850. His parents were Henry George, born in Waterford, Ireland, 1796, died 1869, and Elizabeth Green, born in Cork, Ireland, 1804, died 1902. He was married in 1877 to Cornelia Graves. Mr. George came here from Richville several years ago and entered the practice of law which he has continued until the present time.

Ward Glazier, born in Oak Lane, Mass., in 1818. His parents were Jabez Glazier, born in West Boylston, Mass., and Sarah Tucker Glazier, born in Shrewsbury, Mass. Mr. Glazier was educated in Fowler and G. W. Seminary and married in 1840 to Mahitable Bolton, to whom were born three children, George H., Arthur W., and Lena J. Mr. Glazier's life is more fully set forth in the Monograph on Gouverneur.

Ward Glazier.

Abram Caleb Gates, born in Gouverneur, 1840. His parents were Caleb Gates, born in Vermont, Jan. 26, 1811, and Harriet Miller Gates. He was educated in the district schools and G. W. Seminary and married in 1881 to Fannie Johnson. Mr. and Mrs. Gates have one child, Nellie Harriet, born Sept. 27, 1882. Mr. Gates lived on the farm until about 23 years of age, removing to the village of Gouverneur and engaging in business with J. M. Sparks. Later worked for W. P. Herring five years, buying stock in Canada. Was a keeper in Dannemora prison four years. Postmaster in Gouverneur during President Harrison's administration. Is the present Superintendent of Poor of St. Law. Co., and resides at Canton.

Abram C. Gates.

Rev. W. E. Gale.

Rev. Watson E. Gale, born in Moirah, Franklin County, 1862. His parents were Ezra Gale born in New Fame, and Soloma Pierce, born in Connecticut. Mr. Gale was educated in Franklin Academy and in 1886 married to Fannie M. Anderson. They are the parents of F. Bethel, L. Bernice and C. Beatrice. Mr. Gale is a Methodist minister, and has been for two years pastor of the Hailesboro and Natural Dam Churches.

Benjamin Cross Goodnough, born in Fowler, July 19, 1876. His parents were Eugene Herbert Goodnough, born in Spragueville, and Amelia Jane Cross Goodnough, born in Fowler. He was educated in Gouverneur Wesleyan Seminary and married Oct. 22, 1896 to Rose Lawrence. He is the father of four children, Howard Benjamin, Everett Lyle, Murray Lee, and Donald Lawrence. Mr. Goodnough is a prominent farmer residing on the Spragueville road, this town.

Benj. C. Goodnough.

Arthur J. Gilson.

Arthur Judson Gilson, born in DeKalb in 1872. His parents are Edwin M. Gilson, born in DeKalb in 1836 and Angeline Wilson Gilson, born in Depeyster in 1853. He was educated in DeKalb and in 1891 married to Mary A. Weatherup. They are the parents of Ray, Ralph, Harry and Belle. Mr. Gilson is a successful cheese and butter maker in the town of Hermon. Is now repairing the Elm Grove factory which he intends to make his home and permanent place of business.

Fred Spencer Hill, born in Gouverneur, 1868. His parents were David Hill, born in St. Boswells, Roxburyshire, Scotland, and Chloe Kennan Burnett, born in DeKalb, 1831. He was educated in G. W. Seminary and 1905 married to Helen E. Graves. Mr. Hill is a farmer residing on what is known as the Scotch Settlement Road. Mrs. Hill is a relative of the famous litterateur, George Kennan.

Stephen V. R. Hendrick, Richville, N. Y. (the portrait is of his son, W. L. Hendrick), born at Easthampton, Mass., in 1831. Educated at Easthampton, Mass. He was married to Miss Helen E. Lynde of Richville in 1856. They have one son living, Rev. W. L. Hendrick of Norwich, Mass. Mr. Hendrick has been actively engaged as contractor nearly all his life. In politics he is a staunch Democrat of the old school. A member of the Congregational Church. He is a man of good judgment and is fearless in his convictions. He is the son of Stephen and Nancy (Phelps) Hendrick, both residents of Massachusetts. Few men living have so intimate a knowledge of the early history of the old Potsdam & Watertown R. R. as Mr. Hendrick. Geo. B. Phelps, a relative and a contractor from Springfield, Mass., from which state Hendrick also came, gave him many contracts at grading as was also true on the Watertown & Rome portion

W. L. Hendrick.

of the road. He tells of the struggles of Judge Dodge, Hiram B. Keene and others to get the road completed. When ready for the rails there was no money to buy them. There were none rolled in this country then, and the first laid on the road came from England. The directors, including Dodge and Keene became personally responsible for them, signing notes as collateral security. They were obliged to meet these obligations when they became due. Each of the directors named paid $10,000 from his private fortune and this was true of the others on the board. How much of this, if any, was returned to them when the road was transferred, is not known, but doubtless they re-

Col. H. B. Keene.

covered the full amount when this portion of the road was merged into the R. W. & O. System. He tells of a trip of the directors to Canton when the rails were first laid. The engineer, not having been paid his wages for several months, "opened the throttle" and the road being rough, soon had the occupants of the car in a state of nervous prostration. Being expostulated with on stopping, he told the terrified officials to "pay me up then—you" and that concluded the interview. The writer has a vivid remembrance of riding over the Ogdensburg branch with Mr. Hendrick about twenty-five years ago, and being told of the struggles to get the grading done with little money to pay the men and an insufficient supply of teams and equipment. There was a trifling rock-cut pointed out which gave him infinite trouble

Judge Dodge.

with the resources he had at command. Probably the necessity for the personal endorsements spoken of above, was only a part of the Wall street end of the affair, it being the settled plan there to make residents along the line put up every dollar possible so that when the inevitable foreclosure of the bondholders came, there would be more in the "pot" for them.

Willis P. Hendrick, one of twin sons of Stephen V. R. and Helen Lynde Hendrick, was born at Richville, Dec. 2, 1856. He was educated in the public schools of his native town with about three years in Oberlin College, O. His health incapacitated him for further study. For one year he engaged in business with his brother at Easthampton, Mass. He was married Oct. 9, 1881, to Miss Ida R. Hendrick of Springfield, Mass. Seven children were born unto them, Helen, Isabel, Stephen, Carl, Joel, Rachel and Lois, the younger born two days after her father's death. Mr. Hendrick joined Richville Lodge, I. O. G. T., No. 85 when 12 years old and became a Good Templar of International repute. At 14 years of age he became a member of the 1st Congregational Church and for a number of years held the office of clerk.

He was closely associated with all the auxiliaries of the church. He was also a faithful member of Richville Lodge, No. 633, F. & A. M., and was also associated with the Foresters and Maccabees. For a number of years he was editor of the St. Lawrence Templar. In 1897 he established the Richville Recorder and DeKalb Township Telegram; but was called away before he realized the fruits of his labors. For two terms he held the position of postmaster and was justice of the peace three terms. He died Feb. 2, 1900, loved and respected by all.

William H. Haile, Richville, N. Y., was born in DeKalb, in 1840. He had the usual experience of farmers' sons. When 26 years old he married Viola M. Scripture, of Herman, and to them have been born Lulu M., Welby W., and Melvin H. He has 250 acres well equipped with buildings and modern machinery for all agricultural purposes and his farm is in a high state of cultivation as a result of his personal supervision. He has, in addition to managing his farm, held the position as salesman of butter and cheese for nearly all of the factories of his and adjoining towns, numbering no less than sixteen the present year. He has held the position as President of the Canton Board of Trade for several years. His ability, together with his honesty and diplomacy, have given him a wide reputation as salesman of dairy products. He is a member of Richville Lodge No. 633 F. & A. M., and Richville Chapter No. 291, O. E. S.

William H. Haile.

Mr. Haile is held in the highest esteem by all persons that he has come in contact with either in a friendly or business way.

Gilbert H. Hodgkins, born in Fowler, 1838. His parents were Phineas Hodgkins, born in Fowler in 1806, and Esther Hawkin Hodgkins, born in Vermont. Mr. Hodgkins was educated in Gouverneur Wesleyan Seminary and married in 1875 to Jane Elizabeth Dodds. Mr. and Mrs. Hodgkins are the parents of two children, Grace J., and Harry H. The subject of this sketch taught school in the brick school house now occupied by the Gouverneur Steam Laundry in 1864-5. Was in the insurance business in Canton representing the Agricultural Insurance Co. of Watertown, for several years, beginning such occupation in 1866. Now a retired farmer on Rowley street, Gouverneur.

Jay Fuller Hodgkins, born in Fowler in 1845, his parents were Phineas Hodgkins and Esther Hawkins Hodgkins. When not yet eighteen years old he enlisted in the 18th N. Y. Cavalry serving until the close of the war. Participated in the Red River expedition under Gen. Banks. Remained in Texas until discharged. Returning home pursued a course in the Gouverneur Wesleyan Seminary and in 1871 was married to Della Cleveland, who together with one daughter, Blanch A., survive him. Mr. Hodgkins was a well known dairy operator having manufactured and dealt in cheese here and in this vicinity for many years. For several years he had owned and operated the Hodgkin or Gouverneur factory near this village. His death occurred June 3, 1903. Mrs. Hodgkins' portrait appears in group 2, D. A. R.

Jay F. Hodgkins.

Westel Hildreth, born in Fowler, 1829. Died in Gouverneur, 1904. His parents were Amos Hildreth, born in Chesterfield, N. H., 1789, and Eunice Johnson Hildreth, born in Lancaster, Mass., 1792. He was the father of Albert, Elmer, Eugene, Evlyn, Frank and Inez Hildreth, all of whom were educated in the G. W. Seminary and Gouverneur High School. The sons are successful business men in the East. The oldest daughter, Miss Evlyn, lives with her mother in Gouverneur. The other daughter, Inez, is the wife of Mr. G. W. Edwards, a slate manufacturer of Granville. Mr. Hildreth, prior to his death, lived for some years on Barney St., moving there from the farm on Rock Island road.

Edwin K. Hall, born in Potsdam, Oct. 30, 1868. His parents were Theodore A. Hall, born in Malone, July 24, 1834, and Mary M. West Hall, born in Broadalbin, N. Y., July 12, 1843. Mr. Hall was married Oct. 7, 1892 to Ella M. Cook. Mr. and Mrs. Hall are the parents of three children, Claud M., Theodore F., and Maria M. Mr. Hall gained his education in Potsdam, working his way through school by the sale of papers, pop corn, etc. After finishing school worked for some time with carpenters and masons, then as clerk in a store. Learned the jewelry trade with Fred Hall. His first business venture was in the jewelry business in W. Va. Was nine years in the jewelry business in Watertown, coming to Gouverneur from there. Now conducts a successful jewelry establishment on Main street.

Edwin K. Hall.

Amos Hildreth, born in Chesterfield, N. H., 1789. Married to Eunice Johnson. Amos Hildreth, founder of the Hildreth family in this section was an early pioneer, coming here from Herkimer in 1818. He bought 112 acres of land two miles from Gouverneur, returned to Herkimer for his family, moving here in April, 1819. Six of his children were born here of whom only one is now living, Mrs. Susan Hilts, wife of William J. Hilts. Mr. Hildreth died in 1876.

Sylvester Fobes Hartley, born in Gouverneur, 1838. His parents were Edward Hartley, born near Perth, in 1807, and Jeanette Sophia Thomas Hartley, born in Perth, Canada, 1806.

Mr. Hartley was educated in the district schools and G. W. Seminary and married in 1871 to Agnes Wilson. Mr. and Mrs. Hartley are the parents of Winifred Laura, Seward Wilson, Chester Arthur, and Ernest Sylvester. Mr. Hartley spent his early life upon his farm in North Gouverneur, moving to Gouverneur about 1883. Was for five years after coming to this village treasurer of the St. Lawrence Manufacturing Co. Has always been identified with the Gouverneur Agricultural Society of which he is now President. Mr. Hartley is an enthusiastic agriculturalist and is identified with all institutions for its advancement. Mr. Hartley's portrait appears also in the group of charter members of Patrons of Industry and in the officers

S. F. Hartley.

of the Gouverneur Agricultural and Mechanical Society.

Agnes (Wilson) Hartley, born in Maitland, Ont., 1848. Her parents were Andrew Wilson, born at Glasgow, Scotland in 1808, and Jane Bolton, born near Perth, Canada, in 1818. She was educated in the common schools of Canada and in 1871 married to Sylvester F. Hartley. (See biographical sketch). She is the mother of Winifred Laura, Seward Wilson, Chester Arthur, and Ernest Sylvester Hartley. Andrew E., father of the subject of this sketch, came to Canada in 1815, was self educated. Was justice of the peace in the place for fifteen years. Member of the County Council for several years. Mrs. Hartley is a prominent member of Gouverneur Grange. Her portrait is also in the group of charter members of the P. of I.

Mrs. S. F. Hartley.

William J. Hilts, born in Boonville, 1828. His wife's father, Amos Hildreth, was born in Chesterfield, N. H., 1789, and his wife's mother, Eunice Johnson, was born in Lancaster, Mass., 1792. He was married in 1854 to Susan Hildreth. Mr. and Mrs. Hilts are the parents of Sumner, Alice, Hattie, Annette, Helen, and Grace. Mr. and Mrs. Hilts' children were born and educated in Gouverneur. All but two are now in the West. Mrs. William Thompson now resides in this town, and Miss Grace is a teacher in Garden City, L. I.

Martin VanBuren Hazelton, born in Fowler, March 2, 1838. His parents were Joseph H. Hazelton, born in Poultney, Vt., Feb. 21, 1809, and Elmira Wight Hazelton, born in Fairfield, Herkimer County, June 20, 1814. Mr. Hazelton is by occupation a farmer, was educated in the common schools of St. Lawrence and Jefferson Counties. Married April 8, 1863 to Clarinda Rhodes. Mr. and Mrs. Hazelton are the parents of Lydia I. Hazelton Kelley of Fowler, and Annette E. Hazelton Bancroft of Edwards. Mr. Hazelton assisted his father in the clearing up of a farm on what is now known as the Russell Turnpike in Fowler, and experienced the usual trials incident to such occupation. Left home in 1863 and purchased a farm in Jefferson County, between Antwerp and Philadelphia. Paid for the same from the proceeds of the farm in six years. Returned to Fowler in 1869, buying the Chas. Hale farm. In 1875 moved

M. V. B. Hazelton

to the Simeon Hazelton farm at Little York. Mr. and Mrs. Hazelton are members of the New York State Grange and Gouverneur Grange No. 303, Pomona Grange of St. Lawrence Co.

Cyrus W. Hewitt, born in Dickinson, N. Y., 1846. His parents were Henry Hewitt, born in Shelburne, Vt., 1810, and Emily Prentiss Hewitt, born in Charlotte, Vt., 1814. He was educated at Potsdam Normal School and Albany Law School. Was married in 1880 to Mary A. Thompson. Mr. and Mrs. Hewitt are the parents of four children, Florence, Harry, Carl, and Ryland. Mr. Hewitt taught school on various occasions from 1869 to 1875, after which he took up the study of law which profession he practiced two years prior to 1880 Representatives of the Hewitt family have taken active part in all the wars of this country from Bunker Hill to Manilla. Mr. Hewitt is President of the Board of Education in this village and his

Cyrus W. Hewett.

portrait appears in the group of that body.

Dr. Charles Barzilla Hawley, whose portrait appears in group of physicians, was born in Millroches, Canada, in 1847. His parents were Jesse Barnum Hawley, born in Seneca Falls, N. Y., in 1797, and Rebecca L. Hitchcock Hawley, born at Fort Covington, N. Y. Dr. Hawley completed his education in Michigan University and Cincinnatti College of Medicine and Surgery. He was married in 1871 to Lucy Chapin. Dr. and Mrs. Hawley are the parents of Henry Bartlett and Jesse Benson of New York and Cincinnatti. Dr. Hawley has practiced his profession in Gouverneur since Dec. 13, 1888. Mrs. Hawley's portrait will be found in D. A. R. group No. 1.

John Wesley Henderson, born in South Mountain, Ont., Jan. 4, 1859. His parents were Isaac Chauncy Henderson, and Melinda Guernsey Henderson. He was educated at South Mountain and Jan. 18, 1884, married to Zelma Burt. Mr. and Mrs. Henderson are the parents of Ruth Burt and Kate Morse Henderson. Mr. Henderson came to Gouverneur in 1881, entering the employ of O. H. Waldo as telegraph operator and harness maker. In 1882 started business for himself. In 1895 adding to his business the handling of carriages, etc., which he still continues.

John W. Henderson.

Louis J. Haile, born Nov. 3, 1823. His parents were James Haile born in Putney, Vt., and Tabitha Johnson Haile, born in Putney, Vt. Was educated in Gouverneur Wesleyan Seminary and married in 1849 to Lucy A. Leach. Four children of this union are now living—

Edith C., J. Lewis, Elmer L. and Lucy E. Mr. Haile's parents were among the first settlers of Gouverneur, coming into the town in 1808. Drove from Antwerp to Gouverneur with an ox team through the forest where just sufficient trees were cut to mark the road. Settled in Scotch Settlement where he continued to live until his death, as did also the subject of this sketch. Mr. Haile, the subject of this sketch, was assessor of the town, road commissioner and one of the prominent and influential habitants. Died April 15, 1880.

Joseph F. Hawkey, born in Glenvale, Ont., in 1879. His parents were Thomas Hawkey, born in Cornwall, Eng., and Sarah Toland Hawkey, born in Gananoque, Ont. Educated at Glenvale, Ont. Mr. Hawkey is an athlete and professional wrestler. Has won eleven out of twelve wrestling matches. Defeated W. R. Holmes, April 1, 1905, and Capt. Duncan C. Ross at Gouverneur, May 6, 1905. He is the champion middle weight of Ontario.

Joseph F. Hawkey.

Alva B. Hargrave, born in Lisbon, May 13, 1863. His parents were Henry W. Hargrave, born in Madrid, April 23, 1829, and Sarah W. Lylle, born in Lisbon, Aug. 6, 1830. He was educated in the common schools of Lisbon and married in 1882 to Deborah C. Morgan. Mr. and Mrs. Hargrave are the parents of three children, Myra L. Dollar, Maude and Lena M. He has been engaged in the manufacture of butter and cheese 26 years until 1889 in the town of Lisbon, removing to Heuvelton. In 1899, purchased the Stone Creamery and Cheese Factory of that place, operating the same until the present time. Was a successful candidate for position of cheese inspector in 1900, receiving highest score in competitive Civil Service examination, receiving his first appointment in 1901. He received numerous prizes in New York State Dairymen's Association, New York State Fair and Pan-American Exhibition. A few of these prizes

Alva B. Hargrave.

were as follows: Solid silver medal given by Jeff. County Agricultural Society. $10 cash prize and silver loving cup, won after three competitions. Received a score of 100 on cheese exhibited at Pan-American Exhibition for cheese made for American consumption, and 99½ per cent. at State Fair for cheese for consumption in England.

Erwin B. Hurlbut, born in DeKalb in 1856. His parents were Andrew J. Hurlbut, born in Depeyster, Oct. 25, 1829, and Clarisa Barney Hurlbut, born in Gouverneur. He was educated in Gouverneur and in 1880 married to Hattie R. Marsales. Mr. Hurlbut has been prominently interested in the Marble business for 25 years, as superintendent of the Davidson Quarries and later as a partner in the firm of Hurlbut & Scholton, marble finishers. Retired in 1903. Is now one of the town assessors.

Erwin B. Hurlbut.

Mrs. Eliza Bowne Foster Hall, born in Gouverneur, July 22, 1850. Her parents were Isaac Foster born in Gouverneur, Feb. 16, 1815, and Eliza Bowne Foster born in Sautucket, L. 1., 1813. Mrs. Hall was married to William Henry Hall Nov. 17, 1886. She was educated in G. W. Seminary and has one daughter, Susie Mary. Mrs. Hall's great great grandfather, William Foster, was in the Revolutionary war.

Joseph Howes, deceased, born in Ashfield, Mass., Sept. 3, 1809. His parents were Joshua Howes, born in Cape Cod, Mass., and Hepzibah Hall Howes, born in Mass. He was educated in the public schools of Massachusetts and married Oct. 26, 1837, to Margaret Stevens. Emigrated to New York State at the age of 21. Engaged in manufacturing in St. Johnsville. Joined State Militia in which he was appointed ensign, 6th Reg. N. Y. Light Infantry by Enos Thorp, Governor. Was promoted to Lieutenant by W. L. Marcy, served until his discharge. Discharge being as captain after eight years service. Discharge was signed by Brigadier Lewis Averill. He was married Oct. 26, 1837, soon after moving to Gouverneur. Purchased a farm on North Side. Was an active member of the Presbyterian Church, held position of elder for thirty years. His wife, Margaret, died Sept. 9, 1864. Sept. 21, 1865, married to Hannah Saunders and

Joseph Howes.

moved from the farm into the village, March, 1874, building a house on the corner of Rock Island and Rowley Sts., where he died Sept. 8, 1884.

Captain N. Holt, born in DeKalb, 1859. His parents were Cortland C. Holt, born in DeKalb, 1819, and Helen A. Thornhill Holt, born in DeKalb, 1836. Mr. Holt is by occupation a blacksmith and has conducted a blacksmith shop in Gouverneur since 1883.

Captain N. Holt.

Eaton W. Hurst, born in Macomb in 1870. His parents were James Hurst, born in Ireland in 1830, and Patience Wilson Hurst, born in Macomb. He was educated in Macomb and Gouverneur and married in 1892 to Carrie A. Truax. They have one child, Marion L. Hurst. Mr. Hurst is the proprietor of the Cold Spring cheese factory at Macomb. He is one of Macomb's leading cheese manufacturers and citizens. The factory is operated as a butter factory during the winter months.

Eaton W. Hurst.

William H. Hazelton, born in Hammond, 1842. His parents were John Hazelton, born in Boston, 1801, and Elizabeth Yerdon, born in Herkimer County, 1807. Educated in Gouverneur and married in 1867 to Mariette E. Carpenter. They were the parents of Everett, Earl, Leta and Cecil Hazelton. Mr. Hazelton enlisted in 1862 and served three years in 142 Reg. Infantry. Carried flag of that regiment for two years. Was promoted to Second Lieutenant Nov. 17, 1864, and discharged June 5, 1865. Mr. Hazelton's first wife died Sept. 27, 1887. He married for his second wife Hattie Campbell. She is the mother of one child, Vivian Pearl. Mr. Hazelton was for three years quartermaster of the Barnes Post 156. Is employed as Superintendent of the Riverside Cemetery.

William H. Hazelton

James F. Hill, born in Hammond in 1891. His parents were James Hill, born in St. Boswell, Scotland, and Jeanette Shields Hill, born in Melrose, Scotland. He was educated in Gouverneur and in 1834 married Jane Storie. They are the parents of two children—Mary and Edwin, with whom Mr. Hill resides. Mr. Hill's parents came to this country in 1818 settling in Hammond. In 1828 they moved to Gouverneur on what is known as the Scotch Settlement road. The descendants of James Hill, Sr., and Jeannette Shields Hill now residing in this vicinity number about forty.

James F. Hill.   James Hill.

Alvin Orville Harris born in Fowler March 1, 1824. His parents were Ebenezer Harris, born in Vermont Oct. 30, 1796, and Turpenia Streeter born in Vermont Nov. 23, 1796. He was educated in Fowler and G. W. Seminary and married Jan. 6, 1848, to Mary D. Hodgkins. Her parents were Phineas Hodgkins, born in Fowler 1806, and Esther Hawkins, born in Vermont. Mr. and Mrs. Harris are the parents of Julia M., Louisa E. Hodgkins Baker, Ella M. Hodgkins Parlow and Frank B. Mr. Harris was a farmer in Fowler until 1878, then moved into the town of Gouverneur on what is known as the Little Bow road. Came to Gouverneur in 1882 and for a number of years conducted farmers' sheds on Park street.

William Henry Holt, born in DeKalb in 1861. His parents were Cortland C. Holt, born in DeKalb in 1819, and Helen Frances Thornhill Holt, born in DeKalb in 1836. Mr. Holt was educated in the common schools of DeKalb and married in 1904 to Clara E. Townsley. Mr. Holt has been a resident of Gouverneur for several years conducting a livery and sale stable.

William H. Holt.

Walter W. Hall was born near Gouverneur, in 1849. His father, Edward Hall, was a thrifty farmer of New England ancestry, and his mother's maiden name was Catherine McChesney. He was educated at the Gouverneur Wesleyan Seminary. In his early business career he acquired an enviable reputation as a cheesemaker, and at one time owned one of the largest factories in Northern New York. Being a careful investigator and an earnest student, the product of his factory was in quick demand at the top price. In 1891, his services were sought by the state, and he was tendered and accepted the position of Dairy Instructor at Cornell University, where he has been actively engaged for a period of fourteen years. Mr. Hall married Emma Holt of Carthage, N. Y., in 1878, and they have three children, Clarence L., Ruth M. and Jean L. His portrait also appears in the group of O. H. W. Executive committee.

Walter W. Hall.

Albert M. Hilts was born in Fowler, N. Y., in 1879, his parents were Fred S. Hilts, born in Fowler March 27th, 1859, and Luella A. Rhodes Hilts, born in Fowler, Nov., 1858. Mr. Hilts has been occupied as a railroad brakeman since 1901, and resides in Carthage, N. Y.

Lucy A. Rutherford Jewett, born in Gouverneur June 19, 1842. Her parents were William Rutherford, born in Scotland, Oct. 23, 1813, and Jane Smith Rutherford, born July 16, 1817, in

Gouverneur. Jane Smith Rutherford was the daughter of Willard Smith (whose biographical sketch is in this history). Mrs. Jewett is by occupation a house wife—was educated in Gouverneur, where she has always resided. Allen Smith, brother of our subject was the first white child born in the town of Gouverneur.

Albert W. Hill.

Albert W. Hill, born in Gouverneur in 1858. His parents were Andrew Hill, born in Hammond in 1828, and Margaret Thompson, born in Gouverneur in 1833. He was educated in Gouverneur and in 1885 married to Jennie M. Sartwell. Mr. and Mrs. Hill are the parents of Clara E. and Edith L. Mr. Hill is a machinist by trade, was for some years superintendent of he Gouverneur Machine Co. Is now employed in the New York Air Brake Works, Watertown.

Mr. Fred Henry Haile was born in Hailesboro, N. Y., March 8, 1843. His parents were Henry H. Haile, born in Fairfield, Herkimer County, N. Y., in 1802, and Eliza Goodell Haile. Mr. Haile served with honor and distinction in the war of the 60's. Was Sergeant in Co. D 16th New York Infantry; Captain Co. F 18th New York Cavalry. His portrait appears in the group of officials connected with the First National Bank. He has been prominent in the organization and management of several pulp mills and has been identified with both the Talc and Marble interests in this vicinity, and is now a director in the First National Bank. The portrait is of Maj. Henry H. Haile, father of the subject of the sketch.

Maj. Henry H. Haile.

Edward Hall.

Edward Hall, born in Ashfield, Mass., in 1821. His parents were Lott Hall, born in Cape Cod, Mass., in 1792, and Achsah Paddock Hall, born in Holden, Mass., 1796. He was married to Catherine McChesney in 1843. Is the father of Lott, Ella M., and Walter W. Hall, all of whom are living. Spent his early years upon a farm at Ashfield, Mass., after which he served an apprenticeship as a Yankee peddler, traveling mostly through New York State. At the age of twenty-two years, married and settled upon a wild farm where he now resides.

Gilbert E. Hutton, born in Macomb, 1865. His parents were William Hutton, born in England, and Mary Bristow Hutton, born in Morristown, N. Y. He was educated in Gouverneur, and married in 1893 to Anna D. Fox. Mr. Hutton is a grocery merchant in Gouverneur, also a breeder of fast horses. He is a member of the Masons, Odd Fellows and K. O. T. M. Has been for some years a Vice-President of the Gouverneur A. & M. Society. Was two years a member of the Board of Trustees. Mr. and Mrs. Hutton have three children living, Donald, Ralph and Anna F.

G. E. Hutton.

William Henry Hall, born in Ft. Jackson, Feb. 20, 1859. His parents were Theodore Alonozo Hall and Mary M. West Hall. Mr. Hall was educated at Norwood and Nov. 17, 1886, married Eliza Bowne Foster. Mr. and Mrs. Hall are the parents of one child, Susie Mary. William H. Hall was news agent on the railroad, and shipping clerk in a commission house in Toledo. Is a charter member of the Odd Fellows lodge of Gouverneur; Free Mason; member of the Eastern Star; Citizens' Club and Masonic Temple Club. Has been a resident of Gouverneur for 20 years.

Dallas M. Hazelton, born in Fowler, 1878. His parents were George D. Hazelton, born in 1849, and Ellen A. Carr, born in Antwerp, 1850. Mr. Hazelton was educated in Gouverneur High School and Albany Law School and married in 1903 to Ethel B. Taitt. He graduated from law school in 1901 and was admitted to the bar. Is a Democrat in politics. Was trustee of Gouverneur village in 1902.

Dallas M. Hazelton.

George D. Hazelton.

Levi Hurlbut, born in DeKalb in 1851. His parents were Thomas Hurlbut, born in Depeyster and Jane Giffin Hurlbut, born in Morristown. Mr. Hurlbut was educated in DeKalb and married in 1873 to Elmira J. Stevenson. Six children are living, Fred E., Orla B., Clyde S., Bertie E., Howard S., and Ethel P.

Levi Hurlbut.

Charles P. Holmes, born in Carthage, 1827. His parents were Elijah Holmes, born in Fairfield, Herkimer County, N. Y., and Eliza Pitman Holmes, born in New London, Ct. Mr. Holmes was by occupation a commercial traveler. He was educated in Carthage and was married in 1854 to Amelia Hurlbert. He died April 5, 1888, at Hailesboro, N. Y.

Charles P. Holmes.

William M. Hinton, born in Syracuse, N. Y., 1866. His parents were T. Harry Hinton, born in England, and Olive Barton Hinton, born in Syracuse. Mr. Hinton was educated in Syracuse, N. Y., and was married in 1887 to Isabelle Frisbie. Mr. and Mrs. Hinton are the parents of William B. and Harry.

He was engaged in manufacturing in Weedsport prior to 1891, whence he moved to Canton, N. Y., remaining there until 1896, when he came to Gouverneur, and engaged in the hotel business.

He has during the past year erected an Opera House in Muskogee, I. T., known as the Hinton Opera House.

His father was until his death a prominent musician of Syracuse, N. Y.

Lott Hall, born in Gouverneur, April 7, 1844. His parents were Edward Hall, born at Ashfield, Mass., July 1, 1821, and Catherine McChesney Hall, born in Danube, Herkimer Co., N. Y. Was educated in Gouverneur Wesleyan Seminary. Is a prominent farmer and breeder. Charter member of Gouverneur Grange; former Secretary of the Grange Insurance Co.; President of the St. Lawrence Farmers Insurance Co., and has the honor of having written the first Mutual Insurance policy upon farm property ever issued in St. Lawrence Co.

Mr. Hall has been for many years prominently identified with Gouverneur's interests and has held various positions of honor in connection with the Gouverneur Agricultural and Mechanical Society, of which he is yet an active director.

John Brayton Johnson, born in Gouverneur Oct. 14, 1850. His parents were John Johnson, born at Johnstown, N. Y., 1804, and Sally Freeman, born in Somerville, N. Y., 1817. Was educated at public schools at Somerville, G. W. Seminary and Poughkeepsie. Married Dec. 29, 1875, to Elizabeth J. Bowtell. Mr. and Mrs. Johnson are the parents of John B., Jr., born Sept. 16, 1878; died Sept. 16, 1899; Harold Bowtell, Martha Deliza, and Herbert Douglas Johnson. Came to Gouverneur in 1883, and entered the employ of the St. Law. Manufacturing Co. Bought interest in the Gouverneur Machine Co. 1885, was Secretary and Manager of that institution until 1895. Conducted the machine shop and foundry until 1902, then organized the Johnson Iron Co., of which he has been president since. Was a member of the first Board of Trustees of the Gouverneur Free School; member of the Board of Trustees of Gouverneur Village, during

J. B. Johnson.

the inception and construction of the water works system; President of the village 1901-2. His portrait also appears in the group of Old Home Week Executive Committee.

Mrs. J. B. Johnson.

Elizabeth J. (Bowtell) Johnson, born in Richville Sept. 8, 1851. Her parents were Henry Seymour Bowtell, born in Boston, Mass., in 1824, and Deliza Prudence Kendal born in Lewis Co. in 1826. Mrs. Johnson was educated in the public schools of Lewis and St. Lawrence counties and Dec. 24, 1876, married to J. B. Johnson. Is the mother of J. B. Johnson, Jr., who died in 1899, Harold Bowtell, Martha D. and Douglas H. Johnson.

Harold Bowtell Johnson born in Somerville, Aug. 9, 1880. His parents are John B. Johnson, born in Gouverneur Oct. 14, 1850, and Elizabeth J. Bowtell Johnson, born in Richville Sept. 8, 1851. Mr. Johnson was educated in the Gouverneur High School and married March 4, 1903, to Jessie Roslinn Parsons, who was born Jan. 9, 1882. After graduating Mr. Johnson was occupied for some time as correspondent of Watertown Times and other papers. In 1901 was employed as reporter on the Helena, Mont., Record. In 1903 was local editor for Northern Tribune. July 1, 1904, entered the employ of the Watertown Times, which position he still continues to hold.

Harold B. Johnson.

Mr. William Owen Jones now of N. Y. city, was born in Wales. His parents were Rev. David Jones, born in Wales, and Elizabeth Davis Jones, also born in Wales. He was educated in Oberlin College, Ohio, from which he graduated in the class of 1881. Was married to Jessie F. Pound. They have one child. Mr. Jones was private secretary to the general management of the Northern Pacific R. R. from 1881 to 1887. Private Secretary to the President and Assistant Cashier of the Chase National Bank of New York City from 1887 to 1903. He is at present First Assistant Cashier of the National Park Bank in New York City.

Herbert O. Johnson.

Herbert O. Johnson born in Somerville, 1856. His parents were John Johnson, born in Johnstown, N. Y., May, 1801, (see biographical sketch), and Sally Freeman Johnson, born in Somerville, 1816. Mr. Johnson was educated in G. W. Seminary and in 1895 married to Eva F. Call. They are the parents of Lloyd Herbert and Calvin Wilson Johnson. Mr. Johnson is by trade a machinist and has been for some time Superintendent of the Johnson Iron Co.'s Works. Member of the I. O. O. F. and was in 1904 appointed village clerk, holding this position until March, 1905. His portrait will be found also in group of Fire Co. No. 1.

Mr. George B Johnston was born at Ottawa, Canada, in the year 1845. His parents were William Johnston, born in Ireland, and Catherine Johnston, born in Ireland. Mr. Johnston was educated in Ottawa. He has been married twice, his first wife being M. E. Fairborn. His second, Emma Brainard. His children are Helena C. and Lila L. L. He is at present occupied as shipper for the Aldrich Paper Co. Was for several years manager for the Aldrich, Dean & Aldrich Lumber Mills. He is a member of the Potsdam Lodge, 303, F. & A. M.

George B. Johnson.

Abner H. Johnson.

Abner Henry Johnson, born in Wilna, 1831. His parents were John Johnson, born at Hartford, Ct., 1784, and Zeruah Bligh Johnson. Mr. Johnson was educated in the common schools of Fowler and married first in 1853 to Lydia S. Glazier to whom were born Dewitt Clinton and Eloyenen. Married second time to Paulina Collins in 1870 to whom were born Leslie A. and Grace B. Mr. Johnson for many years conducted an establishment for the sale of general merchandise in Spragueville. Retired several years ago, moving to Gouverneur where he has since resided.

William R. Jones, born in Remsen, N. Y. His parents were Robert W. Jones, born in England, and Elizabeth Jones, born in Remsen. He was educated in the common schools of Oneida County and Whitestown Seminary. Married 1878 to Henrietta L. Hatch. Mr. and Mrs. Jones are the parents of Robert H. and Emery H. Jones. Mr. Jones spent his early life in Oneida county in farming and mercantile business, entering the employ of the U. & B. R. R. R. and American Express Co. in 1871, remaining in their employ until 1881. Then removed to Fine, N. Y., as Superintendent for the Sole Leather Tannery Co., remaining in their employ until 1893, when he came to Gouverneur to accept the Superintendence and Treasurership of the United States Talc Co., which position he still holds.

William R. Jones.

Rev. David Jones, born in Llanpumsent, Carmarthanshire, South Wales, July 9, 1821. His parents were William and Elizabeth Jones. Graduated at Carmontur College 1834 and from Theological Seminary 1847. Was pastor at Horeb and Breaciafa 1847-50. He was ordained July 25, 1850, at Talsarn, North Wales. Dismissed 1853. Pastor at Drewen and Bethesda, South Wales, in 1853 and 1865. Installed at Richville, N. Y., became pastor of the Welsh Congregational Church of that place. Performed his duty at that church for 21 years. He was married Feb. 26, 1854, to Elizabeth Davies of Drewen, Cardiganshire, South Wales, who survives him. Four of his eight children are living—William O. Jones, New York, (see biographical sketch), Dr. John D. Jones, Utica, N. Y., Miss Margaret Jones, Richville, and Miss Carbett Jones, of New York City. Mr. Jones died of Bright's Disease June 3, 1886, aged 64 years.

Rev. David Jones.

Ezra A. Jenne.

Ezra A. Jenne, born in Fullerville, N. Y., Aug. 20, 1842. His parents were Joseph C. Jenne, born in Fowler April 28, 1812, and Sarah Jane Johnson, born in Westmoreland, Aug. 18, 1818. Educated in Rossie and Oct. 22, 1874, married Lavilla E. Moody. Mr. and Mrs. Jenne are the parents of Mabel Reita, deceased, and Hazel Preston. From 1866 to 1892, Mr. Jenne traveled for a wholesale boot and shoe firm in New York. In 1887 he, together with S. H. Austin, Charles Fuller and Fred H. Haile, established a wood pulp mill at Fullerville, N. Y. In 1893 built Standard Pulp Mill at Jenne's Falls, which he superintended for 12 years. 1905 bought out the coal business of A. S. Whitney in Gouverneur. Resides on Rowley St.

Acil C. Johnson, born in Fowler, 1838. His parents were Henry Johnson, born in Vermont, 1793, and Hannah Brown Johnson born in Fowler, 1807. Was married in 1860 to Nancy Johnson and in 1873 to Mary Beerman. Has one child—Cora Truelove. Mr. Johnson was educated in Fowler and has been a merchant in that town since 1903.

Jason Jeffers, born in Theresa, N. Y., Feb. 12, 1840. His parents were Frederic Jeffers, born in Snellsbush, Herkimer Co., in 1821, and Lovina Pierce Jeffers, born in Pamelia, Jeff Co., N. Y., 1824. He was married to Margaret C. Brown, who was born in Gouverneur Oct. 10, 1843. Miss Brown was a daughter of the late James Brown, born in Glasgow, Scotland, May 11, 1821, and Jeanette Turnbull Brown, born in Glasgow, Oct. 29, 1821. Mr. Jeffers is by occupation a farmer. Received his education in the public schools of Theresa. Mr. and Mrs. Jeffers are the parents of five children—Fred J., Della, Carrie C., Blanche A., and Nina E. Jeffers.

Jason Jeffers.

Arthur T. Johnson, born near Burlington, Vt., March 12, 1859. His parents were Thomas P. Johnson and Harriet L. Newton, natives of Vermont, the family moving to St. Lawrence county in 1863. Mr. Johnson was educated in the common schools and Eastman Business college. He taught school several terms and commenced the study of law in 1882 in the office of Conger & Gleason. Admitted to practice in 1886, then entered into co-partnership with George M. Gleason under firm name of Gleason & Johnson, which co-partnership was continued until 1900, since when Mr. Johnson has been practicing alone, giving his entire attention to his profession. Has held various local offices. Is director of the First National Bank, has been Special County Judge for nine years, and at the recent convention was nominated for the fourth term. His portrait appears in the group of attorneys and in the Old Home Week Executive Committee.

Rodger Daniel Jones, born in South Trenton, N. Y., 1853. Parents were Daniel Jones, born in Steuben, N. Y., 1812, and Margaret Davenport Jones, born in Sharon, N. Y., 1816.

Mr. Jones has been a contractor and merchant in Gouverneur for many years. Was educated at South Trenton and Holland Patent, N. Y. Was first married to Abbie E. Crane, in 1875. By this union two children were born—Mrs. Lulu M. Rhodes, now of Austin, Pa., and Mrs. Hattie A. Oakes of New York, N. Y. Mr. Jones married for his second wife Lucy A. Robinson in 1880 to whom were born William R., Susie C., Daniel R. and Charles E. Mr. Jones came to Gouverneur from Utica, N. Y., in 1875, pursuing his occupation as contracting painter and sign writer. In 1896 he built a store and flat on West Main St., which he has since occupied. He is a Master Mason, belonging to Lodge 217, F. & A. M. served on the board of village trustees and water board during the years 1903-4. Was elected financial secretary of the Painter's Union No. 340, in which capacity he has served for three years. Was president of the Trades Assembly in 1904.

Rodger D. Jones.

Edmund D. Johnson born in Fowler, 1857. His parents were Homer Johnson born in Fowler and Nancy E. Brewster Johnson, born in Fowler. He was educated in Fowler and in 1884 married to Mary Sprague. Mr. and Mrs. Johnson have one child, Morris. His postoffice is Fowler.

Edmund D. Johnson.

John Kilmer, born at Fort Ann, N. Y., August 5, 1824. His parents were Wm. Kilmer, born at Arguyle, October 18, 1791, and Esther Porter. Was married Jan. 7, 1852, to Sarah McKean. Two children are living—John P. Kilmer of Gouverneur, N. Y. and Ellen W. Kilmer Coats.

Mr. Kilmer died in Gouverneur May 18, 1902. He was for many years engaged in the business of retail grocer, and various manufacturing enterprises. Was seven years trustee of Gouverneur village and for five years Commissioner of excise.

John Kilmer.

William Arthur Jones born near New Quay, South Wales, 1869. His parents were John Jones, born in Rhydlewis, 1836, and Hannah (Harris) Jones, born in New Castle, 1841. Mr. Jones was educated in the common schools and married in 1893 to Anna M. Davis. They are the parents of Thomas and Mildred Hannah. Mr. Jones came to this country in August, 1889, and worked upon a farm until October, 1892, then entered the employ of the railroad company as brakeman. Became freight conductor in 1895 and passenger conductor in 1899. Is a member of Gouverneur Lodge 217 F. & A. M., Gouverneur Chapter and Gouverneur Commandery.

William A. Jones.

Albert Morris Jepson born in Gouverneur 1870. His parents were Alfred K. Jepson, born in Hammond, 1841, and Helen M. Kilmer Jepson, born in Gouverneur in 1845. He was

A. M. Jepson.

Mrs. A. M. Jepson.

educated in the public schools of Gouverneur and G. W. Seminary and married in 1893 to Nellie M. Pierce. Mr. Jepson was 4½ years in the employ of the First National Bank, ten years in the employ of the Northern New York Marble Co., as director of which company he is now secretary and superintendent. Mr. Jepson's father, Alfred K. Jepson, was for several years supervisor of the town of Gouverneur and also served as town clerk. Was president of Gouverneur village.

Lewis I. Jones, Richville, N. Y., was born at Richville in 1876, and is the son of Henry and Hannah (Davis) Jones. Received his education in the Richville Union Free school. In 1895 he was united in marriage to Miss Fannie M. Southwell. Being a natural born machinist, he went to work in his father's shop. Not contented with what little machine work that was done here, he went to Massachusetts and remained there until his fathers health gave out, when he came here and took possession of the blacksmith and machine shop. He is a member of Richville Lodge No. 633, F. & A. M. and very successful in business.

Clarence M. Johnson.

Clarence Murrell Johnson, born in Somerville, N. Y., 1870. His parents were Wilbur Wright Johnson, born in Gouverneur, in 1847, and Melvina S. Atwood, born in Depeyster. Mr. Johnson is by occupation a musical instructor. Was educated in Gouverneur Wesleyan Seminary and Boston Conservatory of Music. Was married in 1898 to Paulina Seaman of Gouverneur. Has two children—Dorothy Louise and Clarence Wilbur.

Hiram Bannister Keene, born in Pompey, Onondaga Co., N. Y., June 17, 1810. His parents were Joh Keene of Scotch descent and Nancy Keene also of Scotch descent. He was educated in Pompey and was for many years a farmer and real estate dealer in Southern St. Lawrence County and in Antwerp, Jefferson County. Col. Keene attended school but fifteen months prior to his marriage, nine months after. Was a man of great energy and good judgment. Was interested in the construction of Watertown and Potsdam railroad. Was for many years Justice of the Peace. Keene's Station was named after Mr. Keene. He was captain of a company belonging to the 84th Reg. N. Y. State Militia and later promoted to Colonel, same regiment, which position he held until the regiment was abandoned. Was for many years President of the Union Agricultural Society of Antwerp. Was a discoverer of iron ore on his farm near Keene's

Col. H. B. Keene.

Station. Was station agent at Keenes for eleven years. President of the Board of Trade of Gouverneur 12 years. Died Feb. 18, 1902.

Alexander Kellough, born in Dundas County, Ontario, 1872. Came to Gouverneur 1898 and conducted a hardware store on Clinton St. for several years, selling out in 1904. Since selling out, he has been occupied as a contractor. Has been successful in constructing several water mains and sewer jobs. Made a petition to the Board of Trustees during the past winter for gas light franchise, this proposition not being accepted. Is a member of Gouverneur Lodge, 217 F. & A. M., 325 I. O. O. F., Oswegatchie Tent, K. O. T. M.; Court Gouverneur, Foresters, an active member of Young Men's Republican League. In religion a Methodist. His portrait is found in the group of Foresters.

Bert Orrin Kinney, born in Gouverneur, 1873. His parents were Orrin Kinney, born in Fowler Jan. 10, 1834, and Electa A. Bignall Kinney born in Clintonville, 1838. He was educated in Gouverneur Wesleyan Seminary and married in 1896 to Kathleen G. Draper. They have one child—Harold D. Mr. Kinney served several years in Gouverneur as a druggist clerk and in 1896 became proprietor of a drug store which he has since conducted.

Abraham L. Katzman, born in Minsk, Russia, Aug. 20, 1863. His father was Jacob Katzman, born in Russia about 1841. Educated in Russia and married April 1, 1883 to Slava Rachael. Has five children—Fannie, Max, Samuel, James, and Esther.

Mr. Katzman came to this country, arriving in Philadelphia in 1888. Was employed some time in Pennsylvania and came from there to Glens Falls, N. Y., thence to Watertown. Located in Gouverneur in 1902. Is engaged in the occupation of buying and selling merchandise in Gouverneur and vicinity. Is a member of Oswegatchie Tent No. 244 K. O. T. M.

Abraham L. Katzman.

Mrs. Thankful J. Shippee Keyes, born at Catamount Hill, Coleraine, Franklin Co., Mass., May 20, 1823. Her parents were Amasa Shippee, born July 26, 1774, at Charlemont, Franklin Co., Mass., and Rhoda Androus Shippee, born Jan. 9, 1786 at Charlemont, Mass. Educated in the common schools of Coleraine, and married May 16, 1850, to Levi Hillman Keyes, who died Aug. 16, 1896. Has one child, Henry May Keyes. Mrs. Keyes was employed in early life in a cotton mill. Her mother carded, spun and wove the linen for the first flag ever raised over a school house in the United States. The loom upon which this work was done is still in existence. Mrs. Keyes' father made the poles used for the flag staff. Levi Hillman Keyes enlisted with Scotts 900 in 1862.

Walter Lytle, born in Rensselaer Falls, N. Y., May 13, 1867. His parents were Joseph Lytle, born in Canada and Sarah Gillespie Lytle, born in Ireland. He was educated in Rensselaer Falls, and married in 1895 to Sarah Love. Mr. Lytle came to Gouverneur in 1892 and pursued his trade as carpenter and joiner, which he followed until 1901, when he engaged in the business of selling and repairing bicycles, which business he now conducts. Mr. Lytle is an enthusiastic sportsman and regarded as an expert rifle shot.

Walter Lytle.

Ella S. B. Lockie, born in Gouverneur, 1854. Her parents were John C. Brown, born in Ancrum, Scotland, 1808, and Betsey Wilson Brown, born near Lillies Leaf, Scotland, 1811. Was educated at Gouverneur Wesleyan Seminary and married 1878 to John A. Lockie. Has one son, Weldon G. Lockie. John C. Brown, the father of Mrs. Lockie, came from Scotland in 1829, settling with his parents in Rossie. Had a fair education, was a stone cutter by trade, at which he found ready employment. Was employed in the construction of the furnace and other buildings connected with the iron works. In 1840 took up and commenced clearing a forest farm in the northwest of the town, now owned by Weldon Lockie. He was upright, generous and public spirited. Died 1870, the wife dying 1893.

Benjamin Leavitt, born Aug. 18, 1785, in Poultney, Vt. Came to Gouverneur in 1808 or 9. Bought and cleared a farm on the Richville road 2½ miles from Gouverneur now known as the Dewey farm. After clearing a small piece and building a house, he started for Vermont on foot, Feb. 18, 1811. Married Cynthia Ashley, who was born Nov. 17, 1787. Bought an ox team and brought what goods they had on a sled drawn by oxen, his wife coming on horse back, riding a horse given her by her father. Mr. Leavitt remained on the farm all his life, dying in 1875. His wife died in 1877. They were the parents of eight children, Benjamin F., William A., Asaph W., Altha Y., John A., Harold W., Elmira L. and Halsey C. The children were widely scattered, all being now dead except John A. who resides in Bloomingdale, Mich.

Benjamin F. Leavitt.

Chas. C. Laidlaw.

Chas. C. Laidlaw, born in South Edwards, N. Y., January 27, 1844. His parents were Thomas Laidlaw, born in Edinburgh, Scotland, 1801, and Eliza Blood Laidlaw, born in Temple, N. H., 1803. He was educated at South Edwards and married Dec. 29, 1869, to Viola D. Shaw. He has one son, Chas. Dean, of Canton, N. Y. Mr. Laidlaw came to Gouverneur May 22, 1864 and was employed as clerk and book-keeper for ten years, after which he entered the grocery and crockery business, which business he pursued here for many years, finally returning to Edwards and engaging in farming. His postoffice is at the last named place.

Francis H. Lamon, born in Macomb, Ill., Jan. 20, 1879. His parents were Pliny E. Lamon, deceased, born in Watertown, and Mary E. Carpenter, born in Watertown. He was educated in Watertown and New York City and married Dec. 24, 1902 to Eleanor M. Terwilliger. Attended Watertown Schools and Art Students League, the latter during the winter of 1897-8. In 1898-9 attended Northern Business College in Watertown. In March 1899 took position with the St. Law. Mills, Dexter, N. Y. Came to Gouverneur in 1900 and entered the employ of Gouverneur Wood Pulp Co. and U. S. Talc Co. April 1, 1904, took the local editorship of the Northern Tribune. Is Gouverneur correspondent for the Watertown Times and Syracuse Post Standard. Mr. Lamon's portrait will also be found in the group of "Old Home Week" Executive Committee and also in the Tribune staff.

I. H. Lamon.

Eleanor Terwilliger Lamon, born in Owego, N. Y., 1877. Her parents were Jesse E. Terwilliger, deceased, born in Kingston, N. Y., 1847, and Marcella E. Evans, born in 1849. Teacher of English in 1898 to 1902, the last two years in Gouverneur High School. Member of St. Lawrence Travelers Club and Gouverneur Morris Chapter D. A. R. Ancestor Jan (John) VanAken, founded city of Aix La Chapelle, Germany. Ancestor Gideon VanAken built first stone house at Rondout, N. Y. Abram VanAken great, great grand-father, famous Indian fighter at Kingston and Captain in Revolution. Ancestor Christian Deyo, Huguenot refugee to Holland from France, thence to New Platz, N. Y. Mrs. Lamon's portrait also appears in D. A. R. group 2.

Mrs. I. H. Lamon

Lyndon Holt Landon, born in Pierpont, N. Y., in 1886, his parents being Frank Landon and Cora A. Holt Landon. He is at present a student in the Gouverneur High School and is President of the Athenean Society of that school and President of the class of 1905; Secretary of the Gouverneur High School Athletic Counsel.

John A. Lockie, born in Gouverneur, 1849. Parents were George Lockie born in Maxton, Scotland, 1810, of whom see biographical sketch in body of history, and Catherine McLaren,

John A. Lockie.

born in Perth, Scotland in 1815. Educated in Gouverneur Wesleyan Seminary and married in 1878 to Ella S. Brown. Died in Nov., 1900. Survived by his wife and one son, Weldon G. Lockie. Mr. Lockie removed from his farm to Gouverneur village in 1894 and resided here until his death, gaining the respect, confidence and warm friendship of a wide circle of friends. Mr. Lockie was conspicuous for his integrity of character, firm and unflinching adherence to right and manly deportment. Was a director of the Savings and Loan Association and for many years Treasurer of the First Presbyterian Church Society. At his death the following was placed upon the records of the church: "A man of modest bearing, unusual integrity, unflinching in the acts of right and justice, the friend of rich and poor alike, he won the confidence and esteem of all our citizens."

Colin J. Lockie, born in Gouverneur, 1845. His parents were George Lockie, born in Scotland, 1810 (see sketch in history) and Catherine McLaren Lockie, born in Perth, Scotland, 1815. Mr. Lockie was educated in the common schools of Gouverneur and in the G. W. Seminary and was married in 1878 to Jennie Dodds. Mr. and Mrs. Lockie are the parents of George and Catherine. Mr. Lockie is a prominent farmer near Elmdale. Is successful breeder of sheep and has for many years been prominent in politics in Gouverneur, holding many town offices.

Colin J Lockie.

Walter E. Leach.

Walter Earl Leach, born in Gouverneur in 1877. His parents were John Spicer Leach, born in Vermont, in 1838, and Sarah C. Barrell Leach, born in Gouverneur in 1841. He was educated in Gouverneur High School and married in 1900, to Eva E. Fox Has one son, John Robert Leach. Mr. Leach's occupation since 1901, has been that of a drayman. He is a member of the K. O. T. M. and Young Men's Republican League. Mrs. Leach is the daughter of the late George Washington Fox, veteran of the Civil War, having served in Co. C., 60th N. Y. State Vols. during the war. Her mother was Sarah Jane Shippee Fox, granddaughter of Rhoda Androus and Amasa Shippee, who made and raised the U. S. Flag in 1812, the first flag ever raised over a school house in the U. S. (See biographical sketch of Mrs. Keyes.)

Gottfried Lohr, whose portrait appears in the group of Maccabees, came to America from Bavaria in 1887, arriving in Canton May 9th, where his father already resided. He conducted a barber shop in Canton until 1894 when he came to Gouverneur and bought out William Robar. Has continued to operate the shop in Gouverneur since. Mr. Lohr is a member of the Maccabees of which institution he has been Secretary since 1899. Mrs. Lohr was born in Weurtemberg. They have four children. Mr. Lohr is one of Gouverneur's substantial and successful citizens.

Dexter A. Leggett, born in Fowler Dec. 20, 1847. His parents were Apollos Legate, born in Massachusetts, 1805, and Eunice Parsons Legate, born in Massachusetts, 1810. He is by profession an insurance and real estate operator. Was educated in Gouverneur Wesleyan Seminary. Apollos Legate and wife came from Massachusetts in 1836, settling in Fowler. He pursuing the occupation of farmer and mason. Moved to Gouverneur in 1876. Died May 30, 1882. Eunice Parsons Legate died in 1888. The subject of this sketch was married on Sept. 1, 1879, to Lilla D. Howe. Mr. and Mrs. Leggett are the parents of the following children: Halsted Howe, born June 24, 1880, died May 6, 1899; Marion Harland Leggett, born Dec. 3, 1887, and Harold Dexter Leggett, born June 6, 1889. Mr. Leggett has held various town offices in Fowler and Gouverneur. Was deputy sheriff three years, village trustee two years, Chief of Gouverneur Fire Department for several years, and member

Dexter A. Leggett.

of the department for twenty-three years. He is at the present time a member of the Board of Directors of Gouverneur A. & M. Society, of which association he was secretary for several years.

John S. Leach.

John S. Leach, born in Whitesfield, Vt., in 1836. His parents were John Leach, born in New Berlin, N. H., and Lucy Hawley Leach, born in Windsor, Vt. Mr. Leach was educated in Gouverneur and married Sarah Barrell. Mr. and Mrs. Leach are the parents of Bertha, Julius, Mae and Walter. Is a prominent farmer and stock breeder, residing on the Scotch Settlement road near Gouverneur.

C. A. Livingston, born in Coventry, Vt., 1864. His parents were John Livingston, Jr., born in Sorell, Canada, in 1858, and Esther deGarlaneau, born in Paris, France, in 1828. Was married in 1901 to Alice R. Corbin of Gouverneur. Mr. Livingston is a clergyman. Was educated in Vermont Seminary, and pursued elective courses in institutes of America, Germany and Berkeley. Mr. Livingston is a descendent on the paternal side of the Livingstons prominent in the early history of New York State. He is now located in Morristown, N. Y.

Alice Corbin Livingston, born in Gouverneur in 1867. Her parents were J. S. Corbin and Christia Ann Hill Corbin. Was educated in Gouverneur Wesleyan Seminary and Pratt Institute of Brooklyn. Married in 1901 to Rev. C. A. Livingston. Mrs. Livingston several years ago made an extensive tour of European countries, an account of which appeared in the local papers at that time in twelve letters written by her while enroute. Her portrait appears in the contributed article for this history, "Picturesque Gouverneur."

Alice Corbin Livingston.

Jennie Dodds Lockie, born in Gouverneur, 1850. Her parents were Robert Dodds, born in Rossie in 1823, and Susan Deans Dodds, born in OxBow, 1825. Was educated in Gouverneur Wesleyan Seminary and married in 1878 to Colin J. Lockie. Mr. and Mrs. Lockie have two children—George and Catherine. Mrs. Lockie was a teacher in the common schools in the vicinity of Gouverneur.

George F. Lockie, born in Elmdale, Dec. 13, 1842. His parents were George Lockie, Jr. (see biographical skeich) and Cathrine McLaren. He was educated in Gouverneur and in 1897 married to Emma Campbell. Mr. Lockie enlisted Sept. 1, 1864, in the famous Battery D. He was assigned to Battery L. Served in front of Petersburg about ten months until the close of the war and was in grand review in Washingon May 23, 1865, where he was discharged. He subsequently lived in Tennessee about ten years, being occupied as a railroad contractor. Here he met with an accident which disabled him and he returned home and engaged in farming. He is a successful business man and one of Gouverneur's prominent farmers.

George F. Lockie.

William A. Laidlaw.

William Andrew Laidlaw, born in Macomb, 1879. His parents were Alexander Laidlaw. born in Macomb, 1840, and Sarah P. Mills Laidlaw, born in Macomb, 1845. He was educated at Richfield Springs and married in 1902 to Adelaide Hartman. Mr. and Mrs. Laidlaw are the parents of one child, Frances Alyce. Mr. Laidlaw's occupation is that of a teacher. He was employed on the farm until 21, then entered school and graduated in 1894, has since been a teacher. Was principal of Redwood schools for six years. Mr. Laidlaw's grand-father came from Jedburg, Scotland, in 1832. The name of Laidlaw is supposed to have been deriven from Lydesdale.

George F. Leak, born in Chatham, Ont., 1859. His parents were Henry B. Leak, born in Chatham, Ont., and Jane A. Flooter, born in Amesbury, Ont. He was educated in Canada and in 1896 married Gertrude B. Cater, of Watertown. Mr. Leak came to Watertown in 1889, and was employed by A. Bushnell & Co. He was naturalized in 1888. Was for seven years window dresser in the employ of John A. Roberts & Co., of Utica. Opened drygoods emporium in the Duffie Block under the firm name of Leak & Snyder in 1904. Mr. Leak bought out his partner's interest Feb. 1, 1905, and continues to conduct the business.

George F. Leak.

Thomas Lavack.

Thomas Lavack, born in Canada in 1830. In 1856 married to Mary Force. Mr. and Mrs. Lavack are the parents of Frank, Able, Judson, Fred and Annice. He resides on the Kearney road, on what was at one time the Bowne farm.

George E. Legate, born in Shelburne Falls, Mass., in 1863. His parents were Edwin Legate born in Fowler, and Sophrona Colwell.

Mr. Legate was educated in Gouverneur and married in 1890 to Lillian Pierce. They have four children, Murray, Gladys, Alza and Odell. Mr. Legate resides on the Rock Island road.

John W. Laidlaw.

John W. Laidlaw, born in Rossie, Aug. 4, 1856. He was the second son of James Laidlaw. Was married in 1881 to Iantha Story, who was born in Rossie. Mr. and Mrs. Laidlaw are the parents of Earl E., Andrew K., and Arthur J., and one daughter, Jennie I. Soon after marriage, Mr. and Mrs. Laidlaw moved to Gouverneur, he being the first Laidlaw to become a resident of this town. Located on the Pooler farm just east of the village, the farm being at the time owned by Frank M. Holbrook. Mr. Laidlaw bought the farm in 1887 and resided there until his death, May 28, 1900. Mrs. Laidlaw and her four children still reside upon the farm.

Judson H. Lalone, Richville, N. Y., born in Lisbon, N. Y., in 1864. Was married to Miss Esther A. Brown in 1886. Four children are the result of that union, Marion, Mildred, Marie and Merrill. Mr. Lalone is a first class butter and cheese maker, having had the experience of about twenty-six years of almost continual service. No one in his employ works as hard as he, always taking the butt end. He belongs to the Masons, Odd Fellows and several other secret societies. He is a Republican in politics and is a man upright in all his dealings.

Judson H. Lalone.

Edward S. Labardee.

Edward S. Labardee, born in Gouverneur in 1866. His parents were Joseph Labardee, born in Canada and Amelia Rehor, born in Canada. He was educated in Gouverneur Wesleyan Seminary and was married in 1903 to Fannie F. Johnson of Phœnix, N. Y. Mr. Labardee has been engaged in the jewelry business in Gouverneur for the past twenty years, commencing business with John Reynolds in 1885, continuing until October when he engaged with J. C. Lee, for whom he worked until 894, when he engaged in the same line for himself, continuing until the present.

Morris Lesser was born in Germany, March 17th, 1858. At the age of twelve he left school and entered mercantile life, learning the lace trade in this country, having come here at the age of seven. He has continued in the same line since. In 1876 he became associated with the firm of J. S. Lesser and Company in which company he is still interested. Mr. Lesser was instrumental in organizing the International Lace Manufacturing Co., of which he is general manager. His residence is on Beckwith Street.

Morris Lesser.

Norman J. Lang, born in Canada, 1864. His parents were Henry Lang, born in Canada, and Catherine Dool Lang. He was educated in Gouverneur. Was formerly employed in Whitney's drug store. Is now by occupation a commercial traveler. Resides when in Gouverneur with his father.

Carlos Webster Lynde, of Richville, was born in Antwerp in 1834 and was the only son of A. Barnard and Mary Bishop Lynde. When a young man he was clerk in the general

store of the late Moses Barber for a number of years and soon after opened what was called the Union Store. He also dealt considerably in real estate, and was justice of the peace for a number of years. Mr. Lynde was a charter member of Richville Lodge, F. & A. M., No. 633, the first meeting of which was held in a room over the Union Store. He was greatly beloved by old and young and was everybody's friend. His death occurred in 1868 at the age of 34.

C. W. Lynde.

A. B. Lynde.

Eddis Nelson Miller, residence at 414 Fifth Avenue, New York City. Born in Gouverneur, Feb. 1, 1872. His parents were Jeremiah Fairbanks Miller, born at Kingsbury, N. Y., in 1836, and Harriett Melvina Nelson Miller, born at Fort Ann, Oct. 16, 1839. Mr. Miller was educated in Gouverneur High School at which institution he graduated in class of 1890. Mr. Miller's maternal ancestors came to this country, settling in Massachusetts in 1630. He has been a resident of New York City since 1896.

James W. Marshall, born in Spragueville, Nov. 24, 1846. His parents were Samuel Marshall, born in England and Mary Jane Murray, born in Ireland. Mr. Marshall was educated in the G. W. Seminary and public schools and April 13, 1870, married to Delia Isabelle Freeman, daughter of Chauncey Freeman, born in Herkimer, March 4, 1807, and Harriet Smith, born in DeKalb in 1810. Mr. Marshall was the father of Harriet M., Frank M., Clark H., Cecil Clare, and Roy J. Marshall. Mr. Marshall commenced his business career in the drug store of Dr. Spencer in Gouverneur. Later taught school for several seasons. Learned the business of cheese manufacturing which he followed in Spragueville and Somerville. His later years were occupied upon the farm formerly owned by Chauncey Freeman. He held many public offices in Rossie (see history of that town). He died April 11, 1905, well known and highly respected throughout the town of his nativity, as well as the entire county of St. Lawrence.

James W. Marshall.

John McCarty, born in Hartford, Washington County, N. Y., April 30, 1837. His parents were Patrick McCarty, born in Ireland, and Mary Murray, born in Ireland. They were farmers. Mr. McCarty was educated in the common schools of Washington County and married April 3, 1866, to Nannie Lane Cox, of Warrenton, Vt. They are the parents of Virginia, Kathleen, Maria C., Mary M., Nannie L., Sadie and Charles R. Mr. McCarty came to Gouverneur in 1868 and engaged in the lumber business in the firm of Starbuck & McCarty. Was President of Gouverneur Village two terms, Commissioner of Highways 12 years, member of the Board of Education, member of all the Masonic Orders. Was prominent in the building of the Masonic Temple. He died Dec. 16, 1902.

John McCarty

James A. Mills, born in Antwerp, N. Y., 1866. Parents were Thomas Mills, born in Rossie, and Euphemia Laidlaw Mills, born in Macomb. He was educated in Oxbow, and married in 1891 to Jessie E. Smith, of Gouverneur. He was engaged for several years in this vicinity in the manufacture of cheese. Now occupied as a traveling salesman.

M. Duane Morris, deceased. Occupation, farmer, grocer and dealer in farm produce. Born in Depeyster in 1830. His parents were Harolin Morris, and Clarissa Bullard. He

M. Duane Morris.

was married in 1856 to Maria Sheldon. (See Timothy Sheldon). One child survives Mr. Morris, Grace Morris Babcock. Mr. Morris was during his early life a prosperous farmer on the Rock Island Road; later in the grocery business in co-partnership with John Kilmer under the firm name of Kilmer & Morris. As a firm they built two stores. Upon the dissolution of the co-partnership, each of the partners took one store, Mr.

Mrs. Morris.

Morris taking what is now known as the Morris store. Jonathan Morris, Mr. Morris' grandfather, was a descendant of Gouverneur Morris from whom the town of Gouverneur is named. While in the grocery business and later, he dealt largely in butter, cheese, and country produce. He was for many years commissioner of highways. The farm owned by Mr. Morris was bought in 1856 and consisted of 320 acres, of which but ten acres were cleared. He built the farm house now standing upon the farm. He died in 1890, leaving a widow who still survives him.

Chester David Merriman, born at Somerville, Dec. 11, 1863. His parents were Lyman Merriman, born at Somerville in 1822, and Caroline Hannah Freeman Merriman, born at Somerville in 1829. Mrs. Merriman's mother was a direct descendant of David Freeman, one of the first settlers of Rossie. Mr. Merriman was married on October 1, 1884, to Minnie May Carpenter, who was born in July, 1865, and was the daughter of George F. Carpenter whose biography appears. Mr. Merriman is an influential farmer residing near the Rossie line on what is known as the Ore Bed Road. Mr. and Mrs. Merriman are the parents of Harold Arthur, Louise, Allen, Chester, Carleton, Pauline and Isabelle.

Chester D. Merriman.

Wayne O. Munger.

Wayne O. Munger, born in Copenhagen in 1850. His parents were Sylvanus Munger, born in Massachusetts in 1806, and Anna Rich, born in Copenhagen in 1816. He was educated in Copenhagen and in 1879 married Martha S. Fletcher. Mr. and Mrs. Munger are the parents of two children, Ethel, (Mrs. Earl G. Graves) and Lloyd. Mr. Munger is a member of the firm of Munger & Quinn and conducts a meat market in West Gouverneur. He came to Gouverneur in 1900 and has been in business here since. He is a member of the Orient Lodge No. 238 F. & A. M., of Copenhagen; Gouverneur Chapter No. 233 R. A. M.; Court Gouverneur Foresters No. 630.

Ebin Willis Mack, born in Antwerp, August 8, 1856. His parents were Lyman Mack, born in Antwerp, Nov. 6, 1806, and Murinda Witherell, born in Antwerp, Oct. 12, 1813. He was educated in Antwerp and married in 1885 to Josephine Austin. He is the father of three children, Willis Earl, Helen Josephine, and Jessie Irene. His present occupation is that of a farmer, which has been his calling for about eighteen years. Prior to that, he was a manufacturer of cheese. Mrs. Mack's father, James Austin, was born in Scotland, 1830. Her mother was Jeanette Johnson Austin, born in Antwerp, in 1835.

J. Walter McLean, born in Winchester, Ont., Oct. 3, 1873. His parents were John McLean, born in Dunfries, Scotland, Nov. 1835, and Caroline Hammell McLean, born in Chesterville, Ont., May, 1840. He was educated in Dunbar, Ont., and married Dec. 4, 1894, to Cora M. Morrow. They have one child living, Mildred E. Mr. McLean was one of a family of six brothers and four sisters, of whom five brothers and three sisters are living as are also his parents. Has had 17 years experience in granite and marble business and is at present one of the proprietors of Gouverneur, Carthage and Brownville Granite and Marble Works, employing about twenty-five men. Mr. Mc-

J. Walter McLean.   Lean is a member of Gouverneur Lodges No. 217 F. & A. M., No. 325, I. O. O. F., Oswegatchie Tent, 244, K. O. T. M., and of the Temple Club.

Albert M. Myers, born in Theresa, Jefferson County, in 1846. His parents were Miles Myers, born in Herkimer County, in 1805, and Caroline Spaulsberry Myers, born in Jefferson County in 1820. Mr. Myers was educated in Gouverneur and in the College of Dentistry. Was married in 1872 to Olive A. Graves. Mr. and Mrs. Myers have one child, Mrs. Clark S. Northrup. Dr. Myers practiced his profession in Gouverneur for several years. He died in 1876.

Dr. A. M. Myers.

Andrew Murray, born in Scotland, Jan. 21, 1830. Married in 1856 to Susan Gates. Mr. and Mrs. Murray are the parents of Andrew A., Mrs. V. C. Eddy, and Leon B. Murray. Mr. Murray conducted a general blacksmith shop in Fowler from 1849 to 1857, purchasing in 1857 the Gates farm in Hermon. In 1870 he purchased the Goodman Carpenter farm near Gouverneur. Followed farming until 1890 when he retired, moving to his present home on Park street.

Andrew Murray.

Robert E. McLear, born in Rossie, 1877. His parents were George McLear, born in Morristown in 1833, died March 19, 1893, and Hannah E. Ranney, born in East Williamsburg, Ont., Sept. 26, 1842. Mr. McLear was educated in Gouverneur High School, Packard Commercial School of New York and New York Law School, and was married in 1905 to Edna M. Sayers. Mr. McLear is a lawyer in Gouverneur.

Robert E. McLear

Harrison C. Maine, born in Hermon, 1844. His parents were Clark Maine, born in Albany, 1812, and Lucinda Mather Maine, born in Vt. He was educated in Hermon and in 1870 married Christiana Cousins. They are the parents of four children, Brayton, Pliny, Myrtle and Arthur. Mr. Maine has been supervisor of Hermon for nine years. President of Canton Board of Trade, five years. Justice of peace 26 years still continuing in that office. Commissioner of Highways, 5 years. Was member of Co. D., Capt. Parker's Reg., 16 N. Y. Vols., enlisting in 1861. Past Master of Masonic Lodge of Hermon. Director of P. F. R. Association and Master of the Grange. His address is Hermon, N. Y.

Charles J. Maxiner.

Charles Julius Maxiner, born in DeKalb, April 16, 1861. His parents were Julius Maxiner, born in Germany, and Ruth Angeline Cole, born in DeKalb. Educated in G. W. Seminary and married in 1883 to Luella Storrin to whom was born three children, Mildred, Zada and Ira. His second wife was Cora Dailey, to whom he was married in 1899. Mr. Maxiner was for some time a farmer but for the past five years has been a manufacturer of lime near Gouverneur. Julius Maxiner, the father of Charles Maxiner, was a member of Scotts 900. He died in New Orleans in 1865.

Eli C. Mosher, born in Antwerp, October 6, 1863. His parents were Norman Mosher, born in Philadelphia, Nov. 29, 1829 and Julia A. Snow Mosher, born in Wilna, N. Y., Aug.

Eli C. Mosher.

19, 1836. He was educated in G. W. Seminary and married Jan. 24, 1894, to Florence L. Henderson. Mr. and Mrs. Mosher are the parents of L. Evadel and Helen A. Mr. Mosher was a farmer until a few years ago when he took up the carpenters' trade. He is a charter member of the Parker Camp, S. of V., past presiding officer of the Royal Arcanum and member of the Brotherhood of St. Paul. Mrs. Mosher was born at Wegatchie, Aug. 14, 1872. She was the

Florence L. Mosher

daughter of E. E. Henderson and Mary Wilcox Henderson. Is a member of the Methodist Church, and Supt. of the Junior League. She has conducted a millinery business here for five years. His portrait also appears in the Arcanum group and also in Fire Co., No. 1 group.

Dr. Ellis Albert Merkley, born in Winchester, Ont., in 1870, the son of Richard Merkley. He married in 1893 to May Stiles. They are the parents of one child, Leona. Dr. Merkeley was educated in McGills Medical College, Montreal, and is now a practicing physician and surgeon in Edwards. He was a direct descendant of Col. Merkeley who figured prominently in Canadian history.

Dr. Ellis A. Merkley.

H. Frank Marsh, born in Antwerp, April 4, 1844. His parents were Hiram Marsh, born in Trenton, N. Y., April 4, 1811, and Lucinda Seaver, born in Wallsfield, Vt., 1816. He was married Jan. 26, 1868, to Mary E. Eggleston. Mr. and Mrs. Marsh are the parents of Norris E. and Roy D. Mr. Marsh is by trade a shoe maker which trade he followed for about ten years. Was about three years in Odell, Ill., in the boot and shoe business, then returned to Antwerp where he conducted the same line until 1873, when he came to Gouverneur, establishing a business there which he still conducts. He is a member of Royal Arcanum, and resides on Austin Street.

George F. Mosher.

George Freman Mosher, born in Wilna, Jeff. Co., 1854. His parents were Norman Mosher, born in Sterlingville, Jeff. Co., N. Y., 1829, and Julia A. Snow Mosher, born in Wilna, 1837. He was educated in Antwerp and in 1878 married to Eva P. Miller. Mr. and Mrs. Mosher are the parents of four children, Lyndon, Archie, Norman and Claud. His occupation has been that of a farmer his entire life.

Mrs. Eva P. Mosher.

Charles McCarty, born in Hartford, N. Y., 1852. Parents were Patrick McCarty, born in Ireland, and Mary Murray, born in Ireland. Was educated in the public schools of Hartford and Hartford Academy. He was reared and spent his youth upon a farm, then learned the machinist's trade. He came to Gouverneur April 16, 1875, working for two years for Starbuck & McCarty, then entered the office of W. H. Bowne as book-keeper, where he was occupied for 5 years. Then express agent which business he has continued since, with brief intervals. He was president of the village in 1897. Mr. McCarty has always been prominent in affairs social and political in Gouverneur.

Julia A. Snow Mosher, born in Wilna, Jeff. Co., N. Y., Aug. 19, 1836. Her parents were Jonas Snow, born in Putney, Vt., April, 1790, and Mary Davy Snow, born in Springfield, N. Y., Dec. 1792. Mrs. Mosher was married in 1853 to Norman Mosher and is the mother of George F., Eugene H. and Eli C. Mosher. She was post-mistress at Homestead, N. Y., 12 years. Member of the Methodist Church, Gouverneur, and member of the Gouverneur Grange, No. 303. Her late husband, Norman Mosher, enlisted in Co. D, 186 Reg. N. Y. State Vols., Civil War. Her father was a veteran of the war of 1812, and her grand-father, James Snow, died in the Revolutionary Army.

Charles L. Mosher, born in Philadelphia, N. Y., Jan. 15, 1852. His parents were Leonard W. Mosher, born in Mohawk, Feb. 10, 1811, and Margaret S. Strickland Mosher, born in Philadelphia, May 18, 1816. He was educated in Philadelphia and married in 1875 to Addie A. Scram. They are the parents of one child, Mrs. F. N. Freeman. Mr. Mosher is in the furniture and undertaking business as partner of Mosher & Sprague establishment. His portrait will be found also in the group of Odd Fellows.

Charles L. Mosher

James Murphy, born in Rossie, Oct. 22, 1836. His parents were Thomas Murphy, born in Ireland and Mary Hans Murphy, born in Ireland. Mr. Murphy was educated in Rossie and Sept. 22, 1869, married to Rose Mullen. He is the father of three children, James C., Catherine and Mary. Mr. Murphy is a miner by profession, having pursued his vocation in Western mining camps, the lead mines of Rossie, ore mines near Keenes Station, Talc mines of Fowler, Pyrites Mines of DeKalb and in prospecting for minerals throughout northern New York.

Isaac N. Morrison, born in Gouverneur, in 1851. His parents were George Morrison, born in England in 1811 and Elizabeth Hodge Morrison, born in Scotland in 1818. He was educated in Gouverneur Wesleyan Seminary and in 1888 married Louise Peterkin. They have one child, Jessie Zoe. Mr. Morrison is a speculator and dealer in live stock.

Albin S. McBrier, born in Rodman, Jeff. Co., 1839. His parents were Henry McBrier, born in Ireland, 1805, and Kaziah Stone, born in Ireland, 1805. He was educated in G. W. Seminary and in 1863 married to Calista C. Brown. Mr. and Mrs. McBrier are the parents of E. Morton, and Mildred. Mr. McBrier is a capitalist and is engaged in the real estate business.

Albin S. McBrier.

J. M. Marsh.

J. M. Marsh, born in Antwerp, in 1851. His parents were Harvey S. Marsh and Lucinda Seaver. He was educated in Antwerp and came to Gouverneur in 1886. Mr. Marsh was the first to introduce music in the public schools in Gouverneur.

Lewis H. Mitchell, born in Gouverneur in 1833. His parents were Hiram H. Mitchell, born in Holland Purchase, N. Y., in 1810, and Sally M. Sears Mitchell, born in Vermont in 1810. Mr. Mitchell was educated in the common schools of Gouverneur and first married to Sarah J. Marshall in 1860. Again married in 1888 to Cora E. Hewlett. Mr. Mitchell enlisted in the U. S. Volunteer service, 6th Reg. N. Y. Vol. Cavalry, Nov. 12, 1861. He re-enlisted in the field and was discharged June 9, 1865. At the organization of his company it consisted of 112 men. At the close of the war, it consisted of 18 men. Of the original volunteers present to receive their discharge at the close of the war, but one remained. Mr. Mitchell was slightly wounded and had two horses shot from under him. Since the close of the war he has been occupied mainly as a carriage painter until failure of health recently.

Lewis H. Mitchell

Harvey H. Noble, born in Verona, N. Y., 1847. His parents were Edward Noble, born at Westfield, Mass., 1814, and Maria Little, born in Vienna, N. Y., 1820. He was educated

at Whitestown Seminary and in 1876 married Edna L. Wood. He has three children, Kathleen Noble Conger, Robert and Edward. Mr. Noble moved from Rome to Potsdam in 1870 coming to Gouverneur in 1873, where he acted as station agent until the fall of 1879 when he went to St. Louis remaining there until the spring of 1880. He returned to Gouverneur in 1880 and entered the employ of the Bank of Gouverneur as book-

Mrs. E. L. Noble.

Harvey H. Noble.

keeper where he remained until 1883, then went to Adams, Mass., for a few months, returning to Gouverneur, he entered the coal business, which he has pursued until the present time. Mrs. E. L. Noble's portrait is attached.

Edwin H. Neary, born in Elphin, Ireland, 1834. His parents were William Neary and Bridget Bradagan. He was married in 1861 to Margaret Cochrane, deceased, to whom were born two sons, William and Edward H., both practicing lawyers. Mr. Neary was again married in 1893 to Julia Sheldon. He came to the United States in 1848 and graduated at the Ogdensburg Academy in 1853. Studied law and was admitted to practice in 1856. Opened an office and began practicing law in Gouverneur in 1859. Was made Judge in 1860, which office he continued to hold until 1876. Served as U. S. Commissioner 22 years, prior to 1900. His portrait also appears in the group of Attorneys and among the Odd Fellows.

E. H. Neary.

Frank M. Norton.

Frank M. Norton, born in Oswego in 1873. His parents were Fred H. Norton, born in Gouverneur and Matilda Gray Norton, born in Pittsburg, Pa. Mr. Norton was educated in Gouverneur High School and married in 1902 to Mabel Rae. Is by occupation a traveling salesman. Is now Treasurer of the Rylstone Marble Co.

Edna Lois Wood Noble, born in Westport, N. Y., in 1855. Her parents were Eli Wood, born in Springfield, Vt., in 1804, and Mary F. Smith Wood, born in Lewis, Essex County, in 1816. She was married in 1876 to Harvey H. Noble. Mr. and Mrs. Noble are the parents of Kathleen Louis Noble Conger, Robert and Edward Noble. Mrs. Noble's portrait appears on preceding page.

Edward Henry Neary, Jr., born in Gouverneur Sept. 16, 1875. His parents were Edward Henry Neary, born in Elphin, Ireland, in 1831, and Margaret Cochrane, born in Ogdensburg in 1832. Mr. Neary is a lawyer. Was educated in Gouverneur High School and St. Lawrence University. Studied law with his father and was admitted to practice about the year 1899. Now resides at 31 Nassau Street, New York City. Is assistant secretary of the Tallulah Falls R. R. Co.

E. H. Neary, Jr.

Fred H. Norton, born in Gouverneur, 1842. His parents were Milton G. Norton, born in Lanesboro, Mass., Dec. 7, 1804, and Marilla E. Foster, born in Hancock, Mass., Sept. 3, 1807. Mr. Norton was educated in G. W. Seminary and married Feb. 3, 1871, to Matilda Gray. Mr. and Mrs. Norton are the parents of Edith H. Norton Reisswig, Frank M., and Evangeline H. Norton Foster. Mr. Norton is a veteran of the Civil War and served in the U. S. Navy in the engineers corps in 1863-5. He was attached to the Board of U. S. Naval Prize Commissioners at Washington, D. C. He was admitted to the bar in 1863. Was in active practice in Washington at the time of his appointment in the U. S. Navy. His portrait will be found in the group of attorneys.

Julia Sheldon Neary, born in Gouverneur, 1851. Her parents were Henry Sheldon, born in Gouverneur, July 2, 1814, and Martha (Aldous) Sheldon, born in Gouverneur, April 16, 1824. Mrs. Neary was by occupation a graduate trained nurse in New York City prior to her marriage with Edward H. Neary, which occurred in 1890. Her portrait is in group I, D. A. R.

Henry Sheldon, father of the subject of this sketch, was the son of Timothy Sheldon (see biographical sketch), and for many years kept the only book store in Gouverneur. Mrs. Neary is a member of the Baptist Church, and a prominent member of the D. A. R.

Adelbert A. Newton, born in Fowler, in 1858. His parents were Lorenzo C. Newton, born in Champion, May 10, 1824, and Julia A. Davis Newton, born in Fowler, May 5, 1832. He was educated in Fowler and married in 1887 to Laurena H. Kellogg. He is by occupation a superintendent of Talc mills. Mr. and Mrs. Newton are the parents of one child, Mabel P.

James Walker Ormiston, born Feb. 1, 1842, on a farm near the village of OxBow. Mr. Ormiston is of Scotch descent, his ancestors having been land owners near Hawick, Scotland. His great grandfather, James Ormiston, settled in the town of Rossie in 1818. Mr. Ormiston's parents were James Ormiston and Isabelle Story Ormiston. He was educated in the common schools near Little Bow, the Gouverneur Wesleyan Seminary and in College at Rochester, N. Y. In early life was occupied as bookkeeper in Cedar Rapids, Ia., and Fon Dulac, Wis., returning to Gouverneur, he was for many years employed as bookkeeper for Messrs. Kilmer & Jepson. In 1876 entered business for himself, in the sale of boots and shoes, which he still continues. Was for 19 years town clerk of Gouverneur and for several years trustee of schools. He was married October 14, 1874, to Winifred M. Carpenter, daughter of Hon. T. D. Carpenter. Mr. and Mrs. Ormiston are the parents of three children, Thomas, Elizabeth and Winafred. Mrs. Ormiston died in 1903.

J. W. Ormiston.

Joseph Howes Overacker, born in North Gouverneur, Jan. 29, 1851. His parents were John W. Overacker, born in Herkimer Co., Aug. 27, 1810, and Susanna Howes, born in Ashfield, Mass., Sept. 13, 1813. He was educated in Gouverneur and married Sept. 10, 1885, to Ella M. Morse. They are the parents of Hazel May. Mr. Overacker removed to Gouverneur village in 1902, to a home on West Main St. Mr. Overacker's father came to Gouverneur in 1844, and died May 14, 1885. Buried at North Gouverneur. His grand-father John Overacker, born Feb. 26, 1797, and died Jan. 30, 1817. His grand-mother, Phebe Overacker, was born May 23, 1780, and died Jan. 16, 1850.

Charles Wesley Overacker, born in Gouverneur, August 2, 1818. His parents were John W. Overacker, born in Valley Danube, Herkimer County, August 10, 1810, and Susan Howes Overacker. He was educated in Gouverneur, and married Jan. 1, 1872, to Levina A. Hodges. Mr. Overacker was among the first manufacturers of cheese in the town of Gouverneur, commencing in 1871.

Charles W. Overacker.

Arthur W. Orvis was born in Champion, Jefferson County, N. Y., February 18, 1859, the third son of Chester Orvis and Esther A. (Ware) Orvis. Besides common and select schools he attended the Watertown High School, and afterward taught school five years. He began the study of law with G. S. Conger at Gouverneur in 1883, graduated at Albany Law School

In May, 1886, and was admitted to the bar the same month, and with the exception of three years, 1889-1891, during which he was Deputy County Clerk at Canton, he has ever since resided at Gouverneur village. In June, 1889, he married Harriet Church, daughter of Daniel Church, of Wegatchie. He has been president of Gouverneur village twice, 1894 and 1903, having been elected each time on non-partisan tickets, while he has been defeated for the same position on both regular republican and democratic tickets. He is inclined to be independent in his views, and has been trustee of the Unitarian Church ever since its organization in 1896.

His father, Chester Orvis, was born at Gowanda, Erie Co., N. Y., September 11, 1823, being a son of Chester Orvis one of the first settlers of Forestville, Chautauqua Co., N. Y., and a soldier of the War of 1812, in which he was taken prisoner at the battle of Queenstown Heights. The first Chester was a son of Gershom Orvis of Brattleboro, Vermont, who was a soldier in the Second Line Regiment under Gen. Washington in the Revolutionary War, an early settler of Paris, Oneida County, N. Y., from where he emigrated in 1802, and settled in LeRay, Jefferson County. One of his sons, Dr. Horatio Orvis, was the first doctor at LeRaysville and was the family physician of James LeRay de Chaumont, during the latter's residence at the LeRay mansion at that village. Another son, Dr. Charles Orvis, was a physician at OxBow several years about 1830, from where he removed to Gouverneur and practiced medicine for some years, living in a house which stood on the northeast part of the present High School grounds.

William W. Ormiston (son of Rob. Ormiston and Jeanette Hill) was born at OxBow, N. Y., in 1859. His father was born at Jedburg, Scotland, in 1807, and his mother at Hammond,

William W. Ormiston.

Mrs. W. W. Ormiston.

N. Y., in 1823. Robert Ormiston reached America in 1818 and at once located on the farm now owned by Alexander Dickson in the town of Rossie. William W. Ormiston was educated at Gouverneur and subsequently became a tailor, the calling which he now follows.

Mrs. William W. Ormiston (formerly Grace M. Cook) was born at Antwerp, N. Y., in 1876, the daughter of Judge John F. Cook and Jane Copeland. Mr. and Mrs. Ormiston were married October 3, 1901. Her portrait also appears in group 2 of the D. A. R.

James Bryant Olds, born in Macomb in 1871. His parents were Philemon Olds, born in Macomb in 1848, and Sarah Ann Wheeler, born October 15, 1853. He was educated in Gouverneur and in 1902 married to Belle Bright. Mr. and Mrs. Olds are the parents of Dorris, Harold and Philemon Olds. Mr. Olds is superintendent for the Robinson Clay Product Co., of New York, and resides at 124 Bulls Ferry Road, Hoboken, N. J. Until consumed by fire, on July 25, 1904, Mr. Olds ran the Elmdale Mills at Elmdale, N. Y., which place was named by his mother. These mills were built by Mr. Olds' father as was also the present dam.

James B. Olds.

Charles Walker Ormiston, born in OxBow, Oct. 24, 1849. His parents were Hugh Ormiston, born in Scotland and Nannie Barnes, born in New England. He was educated in OxBow and married June 8, 1871, to Esther Backus. They are the parents of George H., Charles L. and Carrie M. Ormiston Storie. Moved from OxBow to Ogdensburg and lived there three years, then moving to Rossie in 1884, and has resided there since. He has been justice of the peace in Rossie, for eight years which office he still holds. He was post master for twelve years, prior to December, 1904. He is a Mason, belonging to Gouverneur Lodge, No. 117.

Albert Wendall Overacker, born in Gouverneur March 3, 1864. His parents were John W. Overacker, born in Mohawk Valley, Aug. 27, 1810, and Deborah Augsbury born in Springfield, Otsego Co., Nov. 23, 1823. They were married January 19, 1856. Mr. Overacker was educated in G. W. Seminary and married March 3, 1886 to Margaret Maria Griffith. They are the parents of Jennie Deborah Overacker. Mr. Overacker was a cheese maker for 21 years. He came to Gouverneur in 1903 and resides on Rowley St. He is conducting a livery business on the corner of Park St. and Trinity Ave. He is a member of the I. O. O. F.

Anson A. Potter, merchant and manufacturer, was born at OxBow, N. Y., about 1855. He is the son of S. C. Potter and Christie Ann Dodd, and was educated at the Gouverneur Wesleyan Seminary. He entered the employ of Taitt & Dickson in 1872, and from 1879 to 1887 was senior member of the dry goods firm of Potter & Sherwood. A. A. Potter & Co. succeeded Potter & Sherwood upon the death of the latter. Although active in mercantile pursuits, Mr. Potter is the moving spirit in many other undertakings for the betterment of Gouverneur. He is Secretary and Treasurer of the Ontario Talc Company and was actively instrumental in the organization of the Lace Mill industry. Janet Gregor of Hammond, N. Y., became his wife in 1872, and they have two children, Helen M., and Howard J. Mr. Potter instituted the movement which led to the locating of the International Lace Manufacturing Company in Gouverneur and but

Anson A. Potter.

for his persistance the project would have failed. His portrait will also be found in the Board of Education group.

John W. O'Brien, born in Ireland in 1842. Is the son of James O'Brien. Educated in Gouverneur and in 1862 married to Mary Waters. Mr. and Mrs. O'Brien are the parents of Anna McAvoy, William S., Elizabeth Riley, Jerome, John and James S. Mr. O'Brien in 1848 moved to this country with his parents, settling in the town of Gouverneur, near Elmdale. After completing school work, commenced farming and the manufacture of lime. Was a miner in Colorado from 1863 to 64. Served in the U. S. Army Transportation Department. In 1900 moved to Gouverneur village. Is now member of the Village Board of Assessors and Gouverneur Grange.

John W O'Brien

George S. Parsons, born in Gouverneur, June 29, 1843. His parents were Myron Parsons, born in Johnstown, August 1, 1807, died October 27, 1891, and Amanda Barnes Parsons, born in Simsbury, Ct., Jan. 22, 1810. Died April 16, 1893. Educated in G. W. Seminary and married Sept. 17, 1872, to Martha S. Dodds, to whom were born five children, now Mrs. H. Douglass Smith, Mrs. Hal A. Wilbur, Mrs. Burton L. Snyder, Mrs. Harold B. Johnson, and J. Otis Parsons. Mr. Parsons spent his boyhood on his father's farm on Johnstown Road. Taught four terms of school. Enlisted August 18, 1862, Co. 1, 11th Cavalry, serving until the close of the war. Returned to Gouverneur and became a farmer on the Parsons home tead until 1886, then moving to Gouverneur village. Mr. Parsons has always been prominent in public affairs holding the office of Assessor for several terms. Is a prominent G. A. R. man, has been several times commander of the Post. Was member of the Board of Education during the

George S. Parsons.

construction of the present high school building. His portrait is among the charter members of the P. of I.

James Parker.

M. Sabin Parker, born in Gouverneur in 1830. His parents were James Parker, born in Canterbury, Ct., April 1, 1782, and Erminia Sackett Parker, born in Greenville, Washington County, Dec. 11, 1796. Educated in Gouverneur Wesleyan Seminary. James and John Parker, the first who was the father of the subject of this sketch, came to Gouverneur April 19, 1808, and cleared up the farm now occupied by Mr. Parker. In 1814, the father of Mr. Parker with two yoke of oxen and a wide sled with two chairs carried Gouverneur Morris and wife to Russell Turnpike near Fullerville. The chairs are now in the possession of Mr. Parker. The portrait is of James Parker.

Everett John Peck, born in Fullerville, Jan. 11, 1860. His parents were Daniel Peck, born in Clarendon, Vt., and Martha C. Fuller Peck. He was educated in Gouverneur and Poughkeepsie, and was married Feb. 1884 to Eva Cassen Drake. Mr. and Mrs. Peck are the parents of 1 child, Donald Allen Peck. Mr. Peck for many years, in connection with his father, the late Daniel Peck, conducted a hotel known as the Fuller House in Gouverneur. Removing into Missouri, conducted a hotel there for about two years, returning here, he leased the St. Lawrence Inn, which he has conducted since. Is a member of the Masonic and Macabee Lodges. Donald Allen Peck, Mr. Peck's son, is the fifth generation from Willard Smith and the sixth from Aholiab Smith. Allen Smith, whose portrait appears, was the first white child born in the town of Gouverneur, May 8, 1806, on the farm now owned and occupied by G. M. Dodds. He was the grand-father of Mrs. Eva C. D. Peck.

Allen Smith.

George W. Parker.

Geo. W. Parker, born in Macomb near Brasie Corners, May 9, 1865. His parents were William Louis Parker, born in Morristown, Sept. 12, 1832, and Deborah J. Lee, born in Antwerp, June 11, 1836. Mr. Parker was educated in G. W. Seminary and Utica Business College. Was married Dec. 25, 1890, to Leonora A. Chase. Mr. and Mrs. Parker are the parents of Hazel Viola, and Deborah A. Mr. Parker taught school for several years. Has been Police Justice of Gouverneur for five years, and has been practicing law since 1895. Both of Mr. Parker's grandfathers were in the Revolutionary War. Mr. Parker's grandfather, John Parker, was hetcheling flax in a barn, and when informed by the minute men, shouldered his musket and left immediately. The Odd Fellows' group also contains his portrait.

Silas Wright Payne, born in Antwerp, 1847. His parents were Welcome Payne, born in Herkimer County, 1800, and Martha B. Lynde, born in Vermont, 1808. Mr. Payne was educated in Antwerp Liberal Institute and married in 1875 to Florence Earl. Mr. and Mrs. Payne are the parents of one child, Florence Belle Payne.

Welcome Payne settled in Rossie, St. Law. Co., near Sommerville. Enlisted in the War of the Rebellion in 1862 in Co. C., 10th N. Y. Heavy Artillery. The subject of this sketch served in the War of the Rebellion, Co. E., 20th N. Y. Cavalry. He moved to Gouverneur in 1882 from Antwerp, going into the drug business which he continued for several years, selling out to C. C. Donald. Is now proprietor of Payne's Drug Store on Main St.

B. G. Parker, born in Gouverneur, May 13, 1858. His parents were Capt. George Parker, and Helen R. Barnard Parker. Mr. Parker was educated in G. W. Seminary. Soon after completing his education, he entered into journalism; the founder of the Norwood News and later of the Gouverneur Free Press, of which he is the present proprietor. Mr. Parker has been prominent in the development of Gouverneur and was largely instrumental in bringing the International Lace Co. here. His portrait is in the group picture of the Free Press staff and also among the officers of the Savings & Loan Association.

James H. Parker.

James H. Parker, born in Watertown, 1862. His parents were John G. Parker, born in Napanee, Ont., and Sarah Butterfield, born in Watertown, N. Y. He was educated in Watertown, and in 1884 married to Anna McCargar. Mr. and Mrs. Parker are the parents of Lena, Ruth, Grace and Mollie. Mr. Parker is the present proprietor of the Gouverneur cheese factory built by Abner G. Gillett in 1869. At this factory Mr. Gillett in his early days received the milk from 1000 cows. Mr. Gillett sold the factory to W. W. Hall in 1873, and it ultimately passed into the hands of J. F. Hodgkins, from whom Mr. Parker purchased it.

Walter R. Perrin, born in Potsdam, Nov. 22, 1864. His parents were Philanda W. Perrin, born in Pierpont in 1823, and Louisa Fay Perrin, born in Potsdam in 1828. He was educated in the Potsdam Normal School. Mr. Perrin taught school for three years, from 1882 to 1885. Entered the employ of H. D. Thatcher & Co. drug store where he was employed until about 1889. Came to Gouverneur in 1889 and together with A. W. Dewey, bought what was known as the Whitney Drug Store. Mr. Perrin bought Dewey's interest in 1896 and continued the drug business until 1902, selling out to Mead Bros. Formed a co-partnership with A. B. Cutting in 1892 under the firm name of Cutting & Perrin, dealers in hardware. They bought out M. E.

Walter R. Perrin.

Loveland in 1903, which business they still conduct. Mr. Perrin was elected supervisor in 1903 and re-elected in 1905. Member of the Masonic bodies in Gouverneur, Odd Fellows, Royal Arcanum and Foresters.

Florence Belle Earle Payne, born in Antwerp, N. Y., 1883. Her parents were Silas Wright Payne, born in Antwerp, 1847 and Florence Earle Payne, born in Edwards. She

Florence B E Payne.

moved to Gouverneur when six months of age. When of school age, she attended Union Free School and subsequently the High School. Was a student of St. Lawrence University, graduated from Cornell University in 1905. She became an Episcopalian at Ithaca in 1904. Albert Rickman, relative on the mother's side, was a member of the early council of the city of Albany. Her great, great, grandfather, Elisha Smith, was a Revolutionary pensioner. Her great, great grand-father, Thomas Tanner, served in the French and Indian War and later in the War of Revolution. He participated in the Battle of Long Island, where he was taken prisoner. She is a descendent of Roger Williams. Her grand-father and father served in the War of the Rebellion and a great, great uncle in the War of Mexico. The Earls, Miss Payne's relatives on the maternal side are related to Lord Lytton, author of Owen Meridith.

George E. Pike, born in the town of Antwerp in 1865, his parents were George Pike, born at Pike's Corners, town of Rossie, in 1838, and Helena Olive Newell, born in Saratoga County. N. Y., in 1837. Mr. Pike was educated in the G. W. Seminary and in 1894 married to Eleanor Couper. After graduating from the old Seminary, in 1884, with class honors, he entered the employ of Laidlaw & Kinney, continuing in their employ until Nov. 1st, 1886, when he was employed by the First National Bank as book-keeper, continued in this capacity for seventeen years.   In 1894 he entered the employ of the International Lace Manufacturing Company as office manager, which position he now holds. In 1888 he was elected School district clerk and clerk of the Board of Education, which position he has held since.   His portrait will be found in the group picture of the Board.   In 1898 he was appointed district treasurer of the Union Free School, which position he still holds.   Mr. Pike was one of the initial members of the Gouverneur Savings and Loan Association, and has served upon its board of directors for the past ten years. He is a successful breeder of Ayrshire cattle, and a member of the Ayrshire breeders' association of America. He is the owner of the Clover Home Farm near Gouverneur, and manager of the Birch Creek farm in Macomb. Upon the latter farm are kept about 100 head of cattle.

Helen I. Parker, born in Gouverneur, the daughter of George and Helen R. Parker. She was educated in G. W. Seminary and in early life became identified with the newspaper business in Gouverneur. She was for many years local editor of the Gouverneur Free Press. Is now editor of the Grand Army Journal. Is prominent in the local societies especially those devoted to patriotic, educational or philanthropic work. She is now an officer of the Reading Room Association, St. Lawrence County Society for the Prevention of Cruelty to Children, Barnes Woman's Relief Corps, St. Lawrence Co. Ass., Woman's Relief Corps, and member of the New York Press Association and American Academy of Political and Social Science.

Helen I. Parker.

There is still to be seen, adorning an old shed on the road to the station, a large white sign board bearing this curious inscription, "Uncle Jim's Establishment." To those who remember the quaint, kindly old man whom everyone called Uncle Jim, it means much. James Phelps, of Richville, was born in Mass., March 27, 1788, and came to Richville, from the vicinity of Worcester, Mass, about 1810. He began the manufacture of potash and pearlash in the old ashery that still stands back of the present gristmill, and did a considerable business in the days when it was necessary to ship the manufactured product to New York via the St. Lawrence, Lake Ontario and the Erie Canal, it first being hauled by team to Ogdensburg. Failing in this business he opened a grocery or general store, the first to be built at the settlement, on what is now Main St., which he called, "Uncle Jim's Establishment," and worked at his trade, that of shoemaker,

James Phelps.

when opportunity offered. His goods were all shipped to "Uncle Jim," Richville, and his books were marked in a similar manner. Earnest, honest and friendly, he was the confidant of all the small boys and he enjoyed the respect and esteem of their elders. His death occurred at the home of his daughter in Hermon, in 1868.

Samuel Coy Potter, born in Antwerp, 1831. His parents were Anson Potter, born in Oneida County, 1805, and Betsy Kellogg Potter, born in Oneida Co., 1811. He was educated at Antwerp and Felts Mills. Was first married in 1852, to Christy A. Dodds. He has one son living, Anson A. Potter. Mr. Potter was married a second time to Nancy Fife in 1886. His first business enterprise was in Watertown, in 1849, from whence he moved to OxBow in 1853, continuing business there until 1875, when he came to Gouverneur. He was interested with Mr. Minthorn in prospecting for talc and iron. First leased the mine now operated by the Ontario Talc Co., of which mine and mill he and his son are the present owners of one-third interest.

Samuel Coy Potter.

Cassius A. Parks, born in North Hero, Vt., in 1833. His parents were Nathan Parks, and Susan Sawyer Parks. Mr. Parks received his education in the common schools of Brasier. Was married to Adeline Pooler, to whom was born one child, Harry N. Parks, residing in Watertown. Mr. Parks was one of the pioneer machinists of Gouverneur and was employed at that trade as journeyman and proprietor for over forty years. He now resides at No. 44 Academy street, Watertown, N. Y.

Cassius A. Parks.

John Pattison, born in Macomb, Feb. 7, 1869. His parents were William Pattison, born in Ireland, 1828, and Jane McConnell Pattison, born in Ireland, 1822. He was educated in Gouverneur High School and married in 1903 to Adelia I. Kneissel. Mr. Pattison was engaged as a farmer in the town of Macomb for ten years. Since residing in Gouverneur he has conducted a real estate and loan business. Is a member of Oswegatchie Tent No. 244, K. O. T. M.

John Pattison.

A. E. Payne, born in Fowler, Dec. 19, 1859. His parents were W. Kendall Payne, born in the town of Rossie, and Sophrona Belle Payne, born in the town of Rossie. Mr. Payne was educated in the public schools of Spragueville and the Gouverneur Wesleyan Seminary. He is at present a wholesale and retail lumber, cement and charcoal dealer in Salt Lake City, Utah.

A. E. Payne.

Cornelius Arthur Parker, born in Gouverneur, 1851. His parents were Cornelius Adam Parker, born in Gouverneur, 1821, died 1899, and Jane A. (Williams), born in Onondaga Co. He was educated in G. W. Seminary and commenced practice of law in 1874.

Frederick W. Peterson, born in Hermon, N. Y., 1857. His parents were Danford Peterson, born in Hounsfield, 1817, and Elizabeth Peterson, born in Coleran, Mass., 1811. He was educated in the common schools of St. Lawrence County. Married in 1882 to M. Sophia Eddy. Mr. Peterson has resided in Gouverneur since 1882, he came here from Richville, N. Y., and engaged as a clerk in a dry goods store. Is now occupied as bank clerk in the Bank of Gouverneur. He has one son, Eddy Wright Peterson.

Lyman Quinn, born in Gouverneur, May 4, 1871. His parents were Thomas Quinn, born in Ireland, Oct. 11, 1835, and Sophia Norton Quinn, born in Canada, Aug. 27, 1834. He was educated in Gouverneur and married in 1903 to Matilda Rogers. He is by occupation a paper hanger and painter, has conducted a meat market since 1900, a member of the firm of Munger & Quinn.

Lyman Quinn.

Henry C. Rogers was born in Rossie in 1869. His parents were Henry Rogers, born in Rossie March 20, 1841, and Anna E. Parsons Rogers, born in Gouverneur, Jan. 3, 1848. He was educated in G. W. Seminary and married in 1899 to Elizabeth Williams. Mr. Rogers is a telegraph operator and manager of the W. U. Telegraph Co., of Gouverneur, and one of the directors of the Gouverneur Loan Association. His portrait will be found in the group of officers of that organization.

Henry Clinton Rogers.

Mrs. Elizabeth Williams Rogers, born in Hermon, 1871. Her parents were John B. Williams, born in Richville, 1834, and Julia N. Ellis Williams, born in Gouverneur, 1842. Mrs. Rogers was educated at Fairfield Seminary and Crane Institute at Potsdam. She was married in 1899 to Harry C. Rogers. Mrs. Rogers is a vocal musician of note.

Mrs. H. C. Rogers.

Marvin W. Randall, born in Antwerp, 1851. His parents were Hezekiah Randall, born in Antwerp, and Diana Eggleston Randall, born in Antwerp. He was educated in the Gouverneur Wesleyan Seminary and married in 1872 to Eudocie Babcock. He has three children, Carl, Albert and Grace. He is a prosperous farmer in Gouverneur. His portrait will be found in the group of Odd Fellows.

Charles N. Reynolds, born in Watertown, N. Y., 1865. His parents were Jesse T. Reynolds, born in Jefferson County, 1834, and Martha C. Hunt Reynolds, born in Jefferson Co., 1835. Mr. Reynolds is by occupation a lawyer. He was educated in Gouverneur Wesleyan Seminary. Held the position of Village clerk for some time in Gouverneur. He was appointed Search Clerk of St. Lawrence County clerk's office in 1892. Appointed Deputy Clerk of St. Lawrence Co., January 1, 1895, which office he has held to the present time, serving under three clerks. Mr. Reynold's father, Jesse T. Reynolds, was 1st Lieut. in Co. A, 35 N. Y. Vol. Infantry, War of the Rebellion, and was for many years a prominent newspaper man in Gouverneur. His postoffice address is Canton.

Charles E. Runions.

Charles Edgar Runions, born in Lisbon, in 1870. His parents were John Norman Runions, born in Canada, and Mary Harper Runions, born in Ireland. He was educated in Lisbon and married in 1903 to Eva May Chase of Theresa. He is by occupation a photographer. Is a member of the Gouverneur Lodge F. & A. M. and the St. Lawrence Chapter, 172, R. A. M., also I. O. O. F.

Henry Herbert Ryan, born in Croghan, Lewis Co., 1866. His parents were Hugh Ryan, born in Oneida Co., 1839, and Mary Bradstein, born in Lewis Co., 1844. He was educated in Watertown and in 1890 married to Eliza McCormick. They are the parents of Hubert, Derwood and Leo Ryan. Upon leaving school Mr. Ryan learned the miller's trade which profession he followed for six years. Entered the employ of Sherwood Bullard & Co. as manager of their general store which position he held for seven years. Moved to Talcville, buying out N. A. Gardner & Co. in 1890, operated this store for six years. Removed to Potsdam and engaged in the grocery business. Came to Gouverneur in 1900 and purchased one-half interest in the World's Branch which was conducted under the firm name of N. A. Gardner & Co. Bought Miss Gardner's interest in 1904 and has conducted the business since.

H. H. Ryan.

H. M. Ray.

H. M. Ray, born in Lisbon, 1843. His parents were William Ray, born in Ireland, 1790, and Jane Miller Ray, born in Ireland, 1802. He was educated in Ogdensburg and in 1863 married to Elizabeth E. Service. Mr. Ray enlisted in 1861 and served two years in the 6th N. Y. Cavalry under Capt. Riley Johnson of Ogdensburg.

Was contractor and builder for fifteen years in the city of Chicago.

Elmer John Robinson, born in Fowler, Jan. 3, 1874. His parents were Jasper Robinson, born in Antwerp, Feb. 15, 1846 and Martha R. Newton, born in Edwards, Sept. 11, 1848. Mr. Robinson was educated in the public schools, Gouverneur High School and Potsdam Normal School, class of '99. He was married June 23, 1900, to Nellie C. Quill, who was born Aug. 24, 1879. Mr. Robinson taught school until the spring of 1900, then entered the employ of M. E. Loveland, hardware merchant in Gouverneur. He remained with Mr. Loveland until the sale of the store in 1903 to Cutting & Perrin, with whom he is still employed. He has a home on Rowley Street.

Stanley Clifford Roulston, born in Russell, N. Y., 1876. His parents were Charles D. Roulston, born in Russell, April 17, 1840, and Emma Burlingame, born in Russell, March

20, 1845. He was educated in Hermon and Cornell Dairy School. Married in 1898 to Agnes Bericol. Mr. and Mrs. Roulston are the parents of Charles A., Douglas A., and Marion E. Mr. Roulston's mother was a distant relative of Silas Wright. His father served in the War of the 60's, Co. D, 128 Light Artillery.

John Rodgers.

John Rodgers, born in Gouverneur Aug. 6, 1838. His parents were George Rodgers, born in Scotland, Oct. 21, 1806, and Jeanette Thomson, born in Scotland Jan. 21, 1809. He was educated in G. W. Seminary and May 1, 1840, married to Mary A. Rutherford. They are the parents of Jennie H., Rodgers Hill, William Herbert, Bertha M. Rodgers Storie, deceased, and Charles Rutherford Rodgers. Mr. and Mrs. Rodgers resided until 1900 on their farm on the Scotch Settlement road and then moved to their home corner of Rock Island and Rowley Sts., Gouverneur village. Mr. Rodgers was identified with the G. & A. M. Society of which he was at one time president.

Robert E. Rastley, born in Drimalague, Ireland, 1842. His parents were John Rastley, born in Ireland, 1808, and Catherine Hurley, born 1812. He was educated in Jerusalem Corners and St. Lawrence University. Married in 1876 to Catherine Long. They are parents of Robert Charles, Elizabeth M., John H., Ella K. and George W. Went to England when a boy and at the age of 13 came to America with his parents, settling at Jerusalem Corners, afterwards removed to Canton and later to Macomb, where he lived until about 11 years ago, then retiring and moving to Gouverneur.

Robert E. Rastley.

Henry C. Rogers

Henry C. Rogers was born in Rossie in 1841. His parents were Henry Rogers, born in Cornwall, Eng., in 1818, and Mary Blight Rogers, born in Cornwall, England, 1816. Mr. Rogers was educated at G. W. Seminary, and in 1866 married to Anna E. Parsons. Mr. and Mrs. Rogers are the parents of Harry C. Rogers. Mr. Rogers is a carpenter by trade and has been a resident of Gouverneur for many years. He has been prominent in the Fire Department, of which he was at one time Chief.

Mrs. L. F. G. Robinson.

Luella J. Gates Robinson, born in Fowler, 1852. Her parents were Abram F. Gates, born in Chaumont, Jeff. Co., N. Y., and Jane Nickelson Gates, born in Lewis Co. She was educated in the common schools and G. W. Seminary and March 27, 1878, married to George H. Robinson. Has one son living, William Abram. At the age of 19 Mrs. Robinson began teaching school and continued this profession until 1878. The portraits are Mrs. L. F. G. Robinson and Abram F. Gates.

Abram F. Gates.

James J. Rutherford, born in Gouverneur, 1842. His parents were Andrew H. Rutherford, born in Scotland, 1801, and Betsy Brodie Rutherford, born in Scotland, 1810. He was

educated in G. W. Seminary and in 1872 married to Jane J. Ormiston. They are the parents of Robert O., William A., Nettie E. and Harvey J. Mr. Rutherford's great grandfather, James Rutherford, born in Scotland, 1768, emigrated to America in 1832, with a part of his family of ten sons and two daughters. Before reaching their destination, James Rutherford's wife died of cholera. Arriving at Gouverneur he purchased farm upon which he lived until his death, in 1846. This farm became the future home of the father and mother of the subject of this sketch, upon which they lived until their death, which occurred, the father in 1890, and mother in 1880. The old farm is now owned by Mr. Rutherford. The Rutherford family, first and last have done their share in maintaining the reputation of the settlers of Scotch Settlement for trustworthiness and reliability among their fellowmen.

James J. Rutherford.

George H. Robinson, born in Macomb, Aug. 18, 1851. His parents were William Robinson, born in Yetholm, Scotland, and Margaret Hardy Robinson, born in Edinburgh, Scotland. Mr. Robinson was educated in the district schools of Macomb and G. W. Seminary and was married March 27, 1878, to Luella J. Gates of Hermon. They have one child living—William Abram. Mr. Robinson is by occupation a carpenter and millwright. Spent his early life upon a farm in the town of Macomb. Mr. Robinson's father served an apprenticeship as a carpenter in Scotland, and from him, Mr. George H. Robinson received his early instruction in the trade he now follows. For the last 15 years, Mr. Robinson has been occupied principally in the building of mills. Is the owner of a farm on Johnstown Street, but now resides in the village of Gouverneur. Is a member of I. O. O. F. and Masonic lodges. Member of Brotherhood of St. Paul. Of the last he has been President since its origin. His portrait will also be seen in the group of Odd Fellows and Fire Co. No. 1.

George H. Robinson.

William Robinson, born in Yetholm, 1810. He was educated in Scotland, and December, 1833, married to Margaret Hardy. Mr. Robinson was the father of John, Margaret Catherine and George. Left Scotland May 24,1863,landing in Quebec July 16, 1863. They came from Quebec to Prescott, requiring two weeks for the journey. From Prescott they came to Antwerp where they remained one year then purchased a farm in the town of Macomb upon which they remained until Mr. Robinson died Nov. 28, 1874. Mrs. Robinson died Aug. 24, 1887, at the age of 75 years. The portrait is hers. They were the parents of 12 children, the above mentioned four of which only survive. Mr. Robinson was noted as a man of great integrity. Was a member of the Presbyterian Church.

Mrs. M. H. Robinson.

Emery W. Rowley, born in Antwerp, in 1842. His parents were Lewis Rowley, born in Taberg, N. Y., and Sarah Ann Briggs Rowley, born in Antwerp. Mr. Rowley was educated in Gouverneur and married in 1868 to Florence N. Myers. They are the parents of four children, Nellie, Altha, Albert M., and William H. Mr. Rowley occupies, together with his sons, the farm known as the Morris Farm on the Rock Island road. A portrait of Albert M. appears in the Blue Lodge group.

Catherine Robinson, born in Macomb in 1848. Her parents were William Robinson, born in Yetholn, Scotland, 1810, and Margaret Hardy Robinson, born in Edinburgh, Scotland, 1811. She was educated in Gouverneur Wesleyan Seminary.

Hezekiah S. Randall.

Hezekiah S. Randall, born in Antwerp, 1824. His parents were William Randall, born in Herkimer County, 1788, and Amanda Ross Randall, born in Herkimer County, 1788. Mr. William Randall, father of the subject of this sketch, came to this county in 1808 and assisted in building the first grist mill ever built in the county at Heuvelton. In 1809, moved to Antwerp and built a grist mill at Wegatchie. Served in the war of 1812. Subject of this sketch was educated in Antwerp and Gouverneur, and married 1818 to Diana Eggleston. Has one son, Marvin R.

Henry Rushton, born in Lancashire, Eng., July 16, 1815. His parents were John Rushton and Ann Norris Rushton. He came to New York with his parents when about two years of age, removing to Edwards in 1828 and married, 1865, Ann J. Armsbury. Mr. and Mrs. Rushton were the parents of one child, who died in infancy. Mr. Rushton was engaged in manufacturing in Edwards for many years and was highly esteemed. He died Dec. 16, 1892, a short time after moving here. Was buried at Edwards in the family lot in the cemetery at that place.

Henry Rushton.

L. B. Raymond.

Leverett B. Raymond, born in Edwards, 1844. His parents were James Raymond, born in Mount Holly, Mass., and Sarah Chollister Raymond, born in Russell. Mr. Raymond was educated in Edwards and in 1867 married Virginia Richie, to whom were born three children—Minnie, Effie and Etta. Mr. Raymond was a member of the 20th N. Y. Volunteer Cavalry, Capt. Ellsworth's Co.; he enlisted in 1864. For many years operated the stage route between Gouverneur and Edwards and is now a merchant in Edwards.

Harlow Rhodes, born in Fowler, 1849. His parents were Beloved Rhodes, born in Washington Co., N. Y., in 1809 and Hannah Sweet Rhodes, born in Washington Co., 1816. Was educated in the public schools of Fowler and married in 1870 to Mary L. Hitchcock. Mr. and Mrs. Rhodes are the parents of one child—Carrie L. Mr. Rhodes is a prominent farmer in Fowler.

Harlow Rhodes.

Alfred William Rogers, born in Brantford, Ont., 1868. His parents were Rev. W. G. Rogers, born in Newbury, Eng., and Emily Poole Rogers, born in Abbington, Eng. Mr. Rogers is by profession a clergyman. Was educated at Colgate University and Rochester Theological Seminary. Was married 1897 to Daisy C. Laing and was for several years pastor of the First Baptist Church of Gouverneur.

Rev. A. W. Rogers.

Samuel Smith was born in Gouverneur in 1834. His parents were Jason Smith, born in Washington County, and Jane Crawford Smith, also born in Washington County. He was educated in Gouverneur, and was married in 1854 to Elizabeth Markwick. Has one son living, Elmer W. Smith, one of the faculty of Hamilton College. Mr. Smith was born and still lives in one of the oldest houses in town, built in 1822. The house is of brick and was built for a hotel, but was never used for that purpose. Mr. Smith's parents were among the first settlers of this town. He was a member of Co. I, 92 N. Y. Infantry, served one year and three months.

William F. Sudds, composer, was born in London, England, March 5, 1843. When seven years of age, his parents came to the United States, and located on a farm in Gouverneur. His musical inclination was manifested at an early period and at fifteen he was a self-taught player upon a violin, guitar, cornet and violincello. A year or two later he was permitted by a friend to practice upon her piano, and eagerly availed himself of the opportunity, although it necessitated his walking three miles after his day's work. In the Civil War he enlisted as a private, and when he joined his regiment had a much battered cornet. His performance upon this being heard by the band-master, he was ordered to report for duty as a musician. While connected with the band he composed and arranged many pieces for it, some of

W. F. Sudds.

which became very popular with the regiment. During the latter part of the war, Mr. Sudds was a "convalescent" in a hospital at New Orleans, and here he took his first regular piano lessons from a French lady. At the close of the war he returned to the farm, but many applications convinced him that a remunerative vocation awaited him as a teacher. He became a pupil in the Boston Conservatory, studying organ-playing under Eugene Thayer, and the violin and composition under Julius Eichberg, who gave him much encouragement, and predicted the success that he soon realized. His compositions for orchestra include four overtures, viz: "From Ocean to Ocean," "A Night in June," "The Merry Chanter," "The Viking's Daughter," and many marches, waltzes, gavottes, etc. Among the choicest of his works are, "Five Tone Pictures," for violin solo with piano accompaniment. Of his vocal compositions, "Whatever is the Best," "Across the Sands O'Dee," "As a Tale That is Told," "Romance of a Hammock," "The Way of the World," the duet, "O That We Two Were Maying," and the charming "Fairy Song," a trio of female voices, are considered his best. In church music his works include "Anthem Gems," 3 vols.; "Graded Anthems," 1 vol.; "Sacred Trios," 1 vol.; "Sacred Duets," 1 vol.; "Y. M. C. A. Praise Book," for male voices, 1 vol.; The Star of Bethlehem," a Christmas Cantata; and several anthems, Te Deums, etc., issued in sheet form only. A volume of "Organ Gems" and "Fifty Organ Voluntaries," comprise his work in this line of composition. The success of his instruction books resulted in compiling the following: "The National School for Piano," "National Guide for Reed Organ Playing," "Preliminary Method for Piano," (1897.) "Easy Method for Parlor Organ," "Progressive Studies for Reed Organ," (8 books), "Modern Guide to Violin Playing," "Modern Reed Organ Method," (1897). Since 1899 some 50 more of his works have been published. The music publishers, Oliver Ditson & Co., were the first to recognize the merits of his compositions, as is evinced by the following:

Boston, February 22, 1881.

Friend Sudds:— Any piano pieces of yours will always be acceptable, for you have shown more ability in this line of composition than any man in America, except Gottschalk.

Yours very truly,

OLIVER DITSON.

Notwithstanding the labor involved in the composition and editing of, in all, upwards of 400 works, Mr. Sudds has meantime conducted a successful business as music dealer as well as manager of the opera house. For several years, however, the details of his business has been, to a great extent, consigned to the management of Mr. Chas. M. Taitt, thus permitting him to spend his summers at his summer-home, at Chippewa Bay, N. Y.

Dr. Grosvenor Swan, born March 27, 1819. His parents were Abel Swan, born in Ashfield, Mass., 1790, and Betsy Bond Swan, born in Heath, Mass., 1793. Dr. Swan received his preliminary education in the public schools of his native town. He was by profession a physician and surgeon. His children are Charles A., Jennie A., Helen M., Mary M., and William R. Dr. Swan practiced medicine in Richville and Gouverneur for many years. He removed from here to Hartford, Conn., in the early 70's and died at the latter place.

Dr. Grosvenor Swan.

Benjamin W. Severance, whose portrait appears in group of physicians, was born in Willsboro, N. Y., July 31, 1855. His parents were William Severance, born in Essex, N. Y., and Eunice M. Hayes Severance, born in Willsboro, N. Y. He was married to Philena S. Woodruff of Moriah. Dr. Severance is a graduate of the Homeopathic Hospital College of Cleveland, Ohio, 1882. A graduate of the Eye and Ear Dept. of the post graduate Hospital of New York City, class of 1897. Practiced his profession for 16 years in Moriah, Essex Co., and came to Gouverneur March, 1898, purchasing the Dr. Baldwin property on John St., where he has since resided. Has been in active practice in Gouverneur since that time. Has three sons, Glenn, Spencer and Carl. Dr. Severance is at present a member of the Board of Trustees of Gouverneur Village.

Isaac Warren Stacy, born in DeKalb, Aug. 25, 1830. His parents were Peletiah Stacy, born in Cooperstown, N. Y., 1792, and Jerusha Tanner Stacy, born in Cooperstown, 1800. He was educated in G. W. Seminary and in 1856, married Sarah A. Johnson. Mr. and Mrs. Stacy are the parents of May G. Stacy Murray, Elmer A., William P., and Atta E. Mr. Stacy was for some time in the lumber business in Fowler prior to 1860. Conducted a store in Somerville for several years, then removing to a farm in Gouverneur where he remained until his death. Mrs. Sarah A. Johnson Stacy was a grand daughter of Caleb Johnson. (See biographical sketch in body of history.)

Isaac Warren Stacy.

G. H. Summerfeldt, born in Pennsylvania in 1855. His parents were W. H. Summerfeldt, born in Germany and Sarah Bowman Summerfeldt. He was educated in the public schools of Canada and Ontario Veterinary College. Married in 1878 to Margaret Brooks. He is prominent in the lodge of Odd Fellows of Gouverneur and is a successful veterinary surgeon.

Henry Conklin Smith, born in Gouverneur, 1864. His parents were Frank H. Smith, born in Moira, Franklin Co., 1836, and Martha Parsons Smith, born in Gouverneur. Mr. Smith was educated in Gouverneur Wesleyan Seminary and married in 1894 to Kathleen McCarty, daughter of the late John McCarty. Mr. Smith has been identified with various manufacturing interests in Gouverneur. He is now the proprietor of Smith's Restaurant and Confectionery. He has one daughter, Virginia Middleton.

David J. Sholton, born in Holland, 1865. His parents were John W. Sholton, born in Holland in 1827, and Hannah A. Stemerdink Sholton, born in Holland, 1848. Mr. Sholton was educated at Muscatine, Ia., and married in 1890, to Emma Barger. They have two children, Gertrude A. and Helen A. Mr. Sholton is engaged in the manufacture of monuments, building stone, etc., in Gouverneur. He is president of the village and the designer of the memorial arch.

D. J. Sholton.

Mr. Frank H. Smith was born in Franklin County, N. Y., in 1836. His parents being Daniel D. Smith, born in New Hampshire in 1814, and Eliza Salls Smith, born in Northfield, Vt., in 1816. Mr. Smith is a prominent and well known farmer of the town, and has served the Gouverneur Agricultural Society as president, secretary, superintendent and director since 1875. His portrait appears in the group of officers of that society.

James E. Seavey, born in Gouverneur, in 1837. His parents were Samuel Seavey, born in Maine in 1799 and Thankful Poole Seavey, born in Antwerp, 1801. He was educated in the common schools of Gouverneur and married in 1860 to Laura J. Spink. The children of Mr. and Mrs. Seavey are Elmer E., and Otie M. McLain. Samuel Seavey, father of the subject of this sketch, came into the town of Gouverneur in 1834, at which time there was no bridge across the river leading to North Gouverneur and he had to swim his cattle across. Two of his sons served in the War of the Rebellion, Samuel L. and Norman D.

James E. Seavey.

Mrs. Lovina A. Poole Smith, born in Hermon, Feb. 12, 1835. Her parents were Ezra Poole, born Dec. 11, 1792, and Roxana Seavey. Ezra Poole was one of the pioneers of the town of Hermon. He was one of the first justices of the peace. He was a mill-wright and mechanic, employed in the building of the first mills in Hermon. He built Goddard saw-mill in Richville. Died June 21, 1882. One of the first school houses in Hermon was constructed by Mr. Poole from a small building upon his premises. Mrs. Lovina Poole Smith came to Gouverneur in 1885 and built the small house in the rear of her present residence, on Clinton St. Was a charter member of Gouverneur Grange Patrons of Husbandry. Her portrait appears in the group of charter members of that organization. The portrait accompanying is of Ezra Poole.

Ezra Poole.

Charles A. Staplin, born in Gouverneur, 1870. His parents were Monroe Staplin, born in Turin and Lucy Borland Staplin. He was educated in Gouverneur and 1896 married to Stella Foster. Mr. and Mrs. Staplin were the parents of Beulah, deceased.

Charles Henry Smith.

Charles Henry Smith, born in Gouverneur, July 29, 1834. His parents were William Smith and Hulda Clark Smith. He is by occupation a farmer. Was educated in Gouverneur and married on Dec. 24, 1855, to Lovina Poole.   Mr. Smith enlisted in August, 1862, Co. D, 106 Reg. N. Y. Vol. He was promoted successively to Corporal and Sergeant, acting as Drill Sergeant. He was in 16 general engagements, participating in the entire battle of the Wilderness. He was once wounded at which time he received a short furlough. Discharged in 1865.   He was a charter member of the Gouverneur Grange Patrons of Husbandry.   Died July 16, 1885.

Lorenzo Smith, born in the town of Gouverneur, at Little Bow, in 1846. His parents were Jason Smith, born in Hartford, Conn., 1802, the son of Capt. Benj. Smith, and Jane Crawford Smith, born in Hartford, Conn. For more particular details regarding Mr. Smith's ancestors see body of history. Mr. Smith was educated in the common schools of Gouverneur. He was married to Dulana D. Waldo, who died Nov. 3, 1890, leaving one son, Roy W. Smith. Mr. Smith has always been prominent in public affairs in Gouverneur and St. Lawrence County of which he was sheriff. He is at present one of the directors of the First National Bank. His portrait will be found in the group of First National Bank officials.

Lorenzo Smith.

Mrs. Lorenzo Smith, formerly Clara C. Crane, born in Watertown, 1860. Her parents were Jesse Crane and Mary Jane Cory Crane. She was educated in Watertown High School and July 13, 1898, married to Lorenzo Smith. Mrs. Smith was previously married in 1883 to Elisha W. Chaddie, who died May 7, 1896. Mr. and Mrs. Chaddie were the parents of Bertha May. Mrs. Smith came to Gouverneur in 1880 and has, since resided here. She is secretary of Rebecca Lodge, Past President of the Gleason Circle and member of the Baptist Church. Her portrait appears in the group of Gleason Circle.

Frank Wellington Sprague, born in Antwerp, June 29, 1853. His parents were Oliver P. Sprague, born Nov. 15, 1823, died April, 1887, and Ruth Fosgate, born in Gouverneur,

F. W. Sprague.

Oct., 1826, died Feb., 1879. Mr. Sprague was educated in G. W. Seminary and married March 22, 1872, to Emogene R. Cross. They are the parents of Clarabel S. Davis and Lyman A. Sprague. Mr. Sprague commenced his business life upon what is known as the Temple farm in Gouverneur. In 1880 he moved his family to Odebolt, Ia. In 1882 he returned to Hailesboro, where he built a cheese factory. In 1886 he bought out A. A. Potter & Co's. stock of general merchandise in Hailesboro, continuing the business until 1900, then selling out to G. M. Holmes. He came to Gouverneur, buying out Isaac Burr, of the firm of Mosher & Burr, furniture dealers. He resides on Barnes St. Mr. Sprague held several offices in the town of Fowler, among them, justice of peace. Was village president in 1904-5. Mr. Sprague's father, Oliver P. Sprague, was an extensive real estate operator in this vicinity. Mr. Sprague's grand-father, Ichabod Sprague, was born in Vermont, 1797; died at Sandy Creek, 1873. His grand-mother, Hulda Lynn, was born near Ogdensburg, 1803; died at Little York, 1883.

Homer E. Smith, born in Gouverneur, in 1863. His parents were Joseph Smith, born in Coleraine, Mass., and Margaret Borland Smith, born in DeKalb, N. Y. He was educated in Richville and married in 1885 to Della Hamilton. They have one child, Emerson. They reside upon what is known as the Smith farm on the Richville road. Postoffice, Richville.

Irving Smith was born in Gouverneur, in 1865. His parents were Joseph Smith, born in Massachusetts and Margaret B. Borland Smith, born in DeKalb. He was educated in Heuvelton, and married in 1892 to Luella Cobb. They have one child, Bernice L. Smith. Mr. Smith is a progressive farmer, and an active Prohibitionist. His postoffice address is Richville.

Alonzo Smith, was born in Gouverneur, Sept. 12th, 1824, his parents were Jason Smith, born in Hartford, Conn., April 12, 1802, and Jane Crawford, born in Hartford, Conn., July 10th, 1802. He was twice married, May 18th, 1848, to Cynthia Stoddard, and Feb. 23, 1859, to Caroline M. Gates. Mr. Smith was the father of Don Clayton Smith, deceased. Mrs. Caroline Gates Smith, was born in Edwards, March 26th, 1838. Her parents were Nelson Gates, born in Smyrna, N. Y., Sept. 16th, 1780, died in Gouverneur, Nov. 20, 1875, and Hannah A. Payne, born in Edwards, Sept. 6, 1815, died July 4th, 1870.

Alonzo Smith.

Archibald Frederick Spooner, born in DeKalb, 1858. His parents were Edwin J. Spooner, born in Heuvelton, 1829, and Agnes Miller, born in Morristown, 1831. He was educated in DeKalb and married in 1892 to Lettie Chandler. They are the parents of Alice Chandler Spooner. Mr. Spooner's father was one of the first settlers in the town of DeKalb coming into that part of the town called Over the River, about 1830. He helped to build what is known as the River road. He cleared up a farm from the forest upon which he lived until his death. His wife died in 1890. They were of Scotch descent, moving to Morristown from Glasgow, Scotland, about 1825. Was member of Battery D, First N. Y. Light Artillery, serving one year during the war, discharged June 17, 1865. Mr. Spooner is a dealer in carriages and implements and an extensive farmer.

Archibald F. Spooner.

Monroe Staplin, born in Turin, N. Y., in 1843. His parents were Alva Staplin, born in Rutland, Jefferson County, N. Y., and Angeline Woolworth Staplin, born in Turin, N. Y. He was educated in Gouverneur and in 1865 married Lucy Borland. They are the parents of two children, Cora and Charles. Mr. Staplin is a farmer and resides on the Rock Island road.

A. B. Stevens, born in Nottingham, England, 1870. His parents were Charles E. Stevens, born in Milverton, Eng., 1837, and Lucy Forteseue Stevens, born in London, 1839. Mr. Stevens was educated in Nottingham, England, and married in 1901, to Eliza Robinson. Mr. and Mrs. Stevens are the parents of Charles Ernest. Mr. Stevens is a lace machinist, and came here with the International Lace Co., taking charge of the machinery in that institution. He resides on Rowley St.

A. B Stevens.

Samuel Smith was born in Putney, Vt., Jan. 22, 1798, was married to Cynthia Willard, Dec. 31, 1823, came to Gouverneur in the year 1824, first settling on the Somerville road, took up a farm on which he made several payments, but finding the title was not good he vacated and took up another farm one mile from the village on the Rock Island road, where they lived until declining years. He purchased a house and lot in Gouverneur village, the lot extended from the corner where the Peck hotel was erected to Trinity Avenue. They were known as "Uncle Sam" and "Aunt Cynthia," living there until the spring of 1866, when they removed to Canton. Samuel Smith died August 12, 1866, Cynthia, Sept. 13, 1866, only one month apart. They were brought back to Gouverneur for interment in Riverside cemetery. Cynthia Willard was born in Charlestown, N. H., March 22, 1800 and was a direct descendant of Maj. Simon Willard, who was one of the founders of Concord, Mass., and commander-in-chief of the forces of Mass., during King Philip's war. She had eight children by Samuel Smith.

Harvey L. Smith, third son of B. Howard and Caroline Smith, born in Gouverneur, March 7, 1837. He was educated in G. W. Seminary and 1870 married to Harriet L. Thrall. Mr. and Mrs. Smith are the parents of H. Douglass Smith, teacher in Joliet, Ill. Mr. and Mrs. Smith retired from the farm in 1887, moving into the village, where they have since resided.

Harvey L. Smith.

William Franklin Skinner, (see portrait in group of clergymen,) was born in Cambridge, N. Y., 1856, and married in 1895, to Catherine J. Markwick. Mr. and Mrs. Skinner are the parents of George Dickson, and Robert Markwick Skinner. Mr. Skinner is the pastor of the Presbyterian Church and came to Gouverneur in 1897.

Isaac Starbuck, born in Chestertown, N. Y., 1819. His parents were Charles Starbuck, born in Nantucket and Sarah Starbuck born in Nantucket. Mr. Starbuck was educated in Chestertown and married in 1842, to Ann Mead. Mr. Starbuck came to Gouverneur in the 70's, engaging in the lumber business, being the senior partner in the firm of Starbuck, McCarty & Co., which business he continued until his death, leaving one son, Franklin Starbuck.

Isaac Starbuck.

Franklin Starbuck, born in Starbuckville, N. Y., 1860. His parents were Isaac Starbuck, born in Chestertown and Ann Maria Mead Starbuck, born in Chestertown. Mr. Starbuck was educated in G. W. Seminary and married in 1881, to Sarah Sparks. Four children are living, Harold, Gregory, Donald and Catherine. Mr. Starbuck commenced his business career as book-keeper for Starbuck, McCarty & Co., in 1878. Later on he took charge of the marketing of their stock of lumber. In 1892 he succeeded Mr. Isaac Starbuck in the business. In 1902 he inaugurated the Gouverneur Lumber Co., of which he is the general manager.

Frank Starbuck.

James Otis Sheldon, born in Gouverneur, 1863. His parents were Henry Sheldon, born in Gouverneur, 1814, and Martha Aldous Sheldon, born in Gouverneur, 1824. Mr. Sheldon was educated in public schools of Gouverneur and G. W. Seminary and married in 1888 to Lillian A. Taitt. Two children are living, Marion Lou, and Gertrude A. Mr. Sheldon entered the employ of the Bank of Gouverneur in 1883 as collection clerk, becoming teller in 1888. He was appointed assistant cashier in 1900. Is now village treasurer and trustee of the Gouverneur Savings and Loan Association. His portrait will be found in the group of officers of the Bank of Gouverneur.

Lotus A. Swett.

Lotus A. Swett, born in Gouverneur, N. Y., 1869. His parents were Bion Swett, born in Clayton, Jefferson Co., N. Y., and Catherine Beardslee Swett, born in Gouverneur. He was educated in G. W. Seminary and at Poughkeepsie, N. Y. Was married April 29, 1896 to Catherine McCloy. Has one child, Catherine McCloy Swett. Mr. Swett is engaged in the grocery business in Gouverneur.

Catherine McCloy Swett, born in Prescott, Ont., July 11, 1864. Her parents were William McCloy, born in Ayrshire, Scotland, and Sarah Chisholm, born in Beanley, Scotland. She was by occupation a music teacher. Was educated in Gouverneur Wesleyan Seminary and married April 29, 1896 to Lotus Swett. She died May 17, 1898, leaving a husband, Lotus A. Swett and one child, Catherine McCloy Swett.

Catherine M. Swett.

Rev. M. G. Seymour (see portrait among clergymen) was appointed pastor of the Methodist Church, April 17, 1905. Served in Ilion, N. Y., before coming to Gouverneur.

Benson W. Sprague.

Benson W. Sprague, born in Gouverneur, 1870. His parents were Wellington Sprague, born in Fowler in 1852, and Helen Chapin Sprague, born in Russell. He was educated in Gouverneur and Odebolt, Ia. Married in 1891 to May E. McKean. Mr. and Mrs. Sprague are the parents of Jessie, Dean H., and Helen Sprague.

D. H. Sheen, born in Brasher, March 17, 1858. His parents were Thomas Sheen, born in Dublin, Ireland, and Anna Burns, born in Dublin, Ireland. Mr. Sheen was married in 1888 to Line LaVack, who died April 19, 1893, leaving two children, Morris and Mabel. He married the second time Tilda M. LaVack, to whom were born Howard, Jennings and Marion. Mr. Sheen received his early education in Brasher, pursued farming and teaching several years. In 1883 he came to Gouverneur and entered the employ of the Free Press as collector. Has been engaged in the real estate business for the past 12 years and is a successful operator.

D. H. Sheen.

Mary E. Sprague, born in Fowler, 1869. Her parents were Robert McKean, born in

Gouverneur, Nov. 22, 1847, and Ellen Mack McKean, born in Antwerp. Mrs. Sprague was educated in Gouverneur and in 1891 married Benson W. Sprague. She is the mother of Jessie, Dean and Helen Sprague. Mrs. Sprague's father served in the war of the Rebellion, was a member of Battery D. 1st Reg., N. Y. Light Artillery.

Ira Sheldon Seaman, born in Gouverneur, January 25, 1857. His parents were Alfred Seaman, born in Somerville, and Sarah Sheldon Seaman, born in Lewis Co. He was educated in Gouverneur, and married Helena Washburn, Nov. 12, 1890. Has one son, Lester Harold, born in Gouverneur, Nov. 24, 1896. Mr. Seaman's paternal grand-father, Ambrose Seaman, was one of the first settlers of the town of Rossie. The subject of this sketch is at present Master of the Gouverneur Grange, Patrons of Husbandry.

Ira S. Seaman.

Jacob Swartzman, was born in Poland in 1866. His parents were Meyer Swartzman, born in Poland, 1845, and Rachell Aronsohn, born in Poland, 1843. Mr. Swartzman was educated in Poland and in 1893 married to Etta Jacobs. They are the parents of Lenore, Eva and Roslin. Mr. Swartzman came to America in 1884. He traveled on the road in St. Lawrence County for eight years, at the end of which time he settled in Gouverneur, engaging in the clothing business.

Jacob Swartzman.

Jesse Streeter, born in Fowler, 1832. His parents were Rhodes Streeter, born in Barnestable, N. H., 1788, and Abigal Koyl, born in 1790. He was educated in the common schools and married to Clarisa D. Thomson, in 1861. They have two children, Inez and Wallace. Mr. Streeter's father came to this country in early life. Subject of sketch was three years in Civil War. After discharge he remained on farm until past 70 when he came to this village where he has since resided, his home being on Caroline St. He is a member of Barnes Post G. A. R. and various Masonic bodies of this and other towns.

Stephen M. Thayer, born in Prescott. Ont., 1838. His parents were Thomas M. Thayer, born in Chateaugay, July 31, 1812, and Melinda M. Moore, born in Burlington. Vt., Aug. 11, 1811. Mr. Thayer was educated in Gouverneur and on Dec. 31, 1868, married Abbie M. Day. He enlisted in the late Civil War, Aug. 26, 1862, in Battery D., 1st N. Y. Light Artillery, and served until the close of the war in 1865. His brother George D. Thayer, enlisted Jan. 4, 1864, in Co. F., 14th Reg. N. Y. Heavy Artillery, was wounded in the battle of Weldon R. R., Va., Aug. 18th, 1864. Discharged June, 1865, from Lincoln General Hospital, D. C., and died at home in Gouverneur, Oct. 1865, from the wounds. He was born in Gouverneur April 17, 1842. Mr. Stephen M. Thayer

Stephen M. Thayer.

is by occupation a salesman. His portrait shows him as he appeared in 1863 when home on a furlough.

Maitland H. Streeter, born in Gouverneur in 1871. His parents were H. D. Streeter, born in Gouverneur, and Mary Mott Streeter. He was educated in the common schools of Gouverneur and in 1891, married to Ottie M. Babcock. Their children are Glenn S. and Mary M.

Frederick Gaeteno Scalzo, born in Catanzaro, Italy. October 3, 1877. Parents were Gabriel Scalzo, born in Catanzaro, 1851, and Maria Stella Cambrome, born in the same place. Mr. Scalzo was educated in New York City and is at present a hotel keeper, merchant and contractor.

Willard Thayer was born in Gouverneur, 1832. His parents were Horace Thayer, born in Washington County, 1802, and Betsy Parker Thayer, born in Washington Co., 1808. He

was educated in Gouverneur and in 1859, married to Miss A. E. Chase. They are the parents of Mrs. H. A. Newell, and W. B. Thayer. Mr. Thayer served in the Civil War. Mrs. Thayer has the unique distinction of having saved four lives during the fifteen years since her arrival at young womanhood. Being a woman of retiring nature she has never made a boast of life saving, but it seems that a medal should be given. Since the foregoing was written, Mr. Thayer's death has taken place, July 17, 1905. His whole life, dating from his young manhood, is well remembered. His first venture in business was to lease (in connection with Edward Mix, now living at Newfane, Niagara Co., N. Y.) the farm of Amasa Corbin, Sr., and his total assets at this

Willard Thayer.

time were a horse and harness. He was always a prudent man, a good farmer, and he accumulated a fine fortune by constant work and intelligent husbandry.

George Peter Taitt, born in Rossie, March 9, 1839. His parents were James Taitt, born in Scotland, 1803, and Allison Douglas Taitt, born in Douglas City, Isle of Man, 1809. Mr. Taitt was educated in the common schools of Rossie and G.

W. Seminary and was married Sept. 20, 1864, to Lucretia M. Barnes. By this union three children were born, Lillian, Allison, now Mrs. J. O. Sheldon, Edward Douglas, of the firm of G. P. Taitt & Son, and Mildred Louisa, a teacher of science. Mrs. Lucretia M. Taitt died Aug. 17, 1887 and in 1889 Mr. Taitt married Helen C. Mosher Schram. Mr. Taitt's grand-mother was a descendent of John Knox. Mr. John Taitt, grand-father of G. P. Taitt, came to Rossie, settling in the wilderness in 1819, on what is now known as the McDougal farm. Mr. Taitt came to Gouverneur March, 1850, as a clerk in the Union Store. He entered the mercantile business for himself in 1860 and has con-

George P. Taitt.

tinued in business here since with the exception of one year when he was in Kansas. He was a member of Co. B, 142 N. Y. Vol. of which he was Lieut. Mr. Taitt purchased the first N. Y. draft issued by the banking firm of Chas. Anthony & Co., in 1850.

Dr. Daniel M. Taylor, born in Canton, 1861. His parents were James Taylor, born in Waddington, 1827, and Mary McCrosty, born in Waddington, in 1826. The elder Taylor and wife were of Scotch parentage. Dr. Taylor taught school in Kansas when 19 and 20 years of age. He was educated in Canton University and Medical School. He is now a practicing physician and surgeon of Edwards.

Dr. D. M. Taylor.

George Roger Thomson, born in Gouverneur, N. Y., May 1, 1851. His parents were James Thomson, born in Scotland, 1814, died 1859, and Matilda Middlemarsh Thomson, born in Scotland and died in 1863. Mr. Thomson was married to Agnes Matilda Hill. Has three children, Harry, Flora M., and Fannie, all are living. He was educated in Gouverneur, and by trade is a machinist. In connection with Andrew Hill, he operated the machine shop and foundry where the Johnson Iron Works now is in the years of 1878-9. He has been engaged wtih machine shops in various capacities as proprietor, superintendent and machinist for thirty years. Has been a member of Gouverneur fire company for twenty-four years. He is a member of Gouverneur F. & A. M. and of the Royal Arcanum. His portrait will be found in the group of Fire Co. No. 1.

James M. Thrall.

James Murdock Thrall, born in Gouverneur, 1841. His parents were Melville H. Thrall, born in Johnstown, N. Y., 1814, and Esther M. Smith Thrall, born in Poultney, Vt., 1813. He was educated in G. W. Seminary and married first in 1871 to Alice Gleason, and again in 1894, to Ella Rodger. His children are Henry G., Helena A., Melville H., and Alice R. Mr. Thrall is a farmer. He has been an elder of the Presbyterian Church since 1885. His grand-father was a soldier of the war of 1812. Another ancestor, John Thrall, was a soldier of the Revolutionary War. Mr. Thrall's mother was a daughter of Harvey D. Smith, whose biography appears in the body of this work.

James W. Thraves, born in Depeyster, 1872. His parents were Joseph Thraves, born in Nottinghamshire, 1822, and Anna Hooper, born in Nottinghamshire in 1826. He was educated in Depeyster and in 1895 married to Lottie M. Taylor. They are the parents of one child, Mildred. Thomas Thraves has been actively engaged in the cheese business for 15 years, operating at DeKalb for the past 9 years. The business has grown 100 per cent. since taken on by Mr. Thraves. His post office address is Richville.

James W. Thraves.

Max Tumpson, born in Poland, 1847. He was married in 1871, to Sophie Leiser. Mr. and Mrs. Tumpson have living five children, Anna, Louis, Martha, George and Rae. Mr.

Max Tumpson.

Tumpson emigrated to America in 1883, his family following in 1884. Became a citizen of the United States in 1888. First came to Ogdensburg, removing from there to Richville in 1887. He came to Gouverneur in 1889. Conducted a clothing business here for several years. His children, Anna, Martha, Geo., and Rae are graduates of Gouverneur High School. Anna was a graduate of Schamvenka Conservatory of Music of Berlin. Martha was a graduate of Albany Normal College and George of the University of Michigan. Admitted to the bar in 1904. Louis is engaged in the mercantile business in Des Moines, Ia. Mr. Tumpson and family moved to Connellsville, Pa., in 1900, where they now reside.

Albert James Tyner, DeKalb Junction, N. Y., born in De-Kalb, 1862. His parents were James Tyner, born in Brasher, 1830, and Cynthia Weymouth Tyner, born in DeKalb, 1836. He was educated in the common schools of DeKalb. Albert James Tyner's grand-father emigrated from Ireland, 1825, and located at Brasher, later moved to DeKalb where James Tyner was born. He has lived in DeKalb continuously since. Mr. Tyner is serving his second term as Highway Commissioner for the town of DeKalb. In politics he is a Republican and a strong advocate of temperance and reform.

Albert J. Tyner.

Andrew H. Turnbull.

Andrew Hunter Turnbull, born in Fowler, 1857. His parents were Andrew Turnbull, born in Leith, Scotland, 1813, and Ann H. Dodds Turnbull, born in Scotland, May 9, 1812. Mr. Turnbull was educated in Gouverneur Wesleyan Seminary and married in 1882 to Jennie L. Carpenter, daughter of George F. Carpenter (see biographical sketch). Has one child, Guy Andrew Turnbull. Andrew Turnbull, father of the subject of this sketch, came to this country at the age of six years and was fourteen weeks upon the voyage. Mr. Turnbull has been assessor of the town of Gouverneur, which position he still holds. He was President of the Gouverneur A. & M. Society in 1903. He is now one of its directors.

George Lockie Tait, born in Gouverneur, July 9, 1868. His parents were John B. Tait, born in Rossie, May 21, 1837, and Jane Ormiston Lockie Tait, born July 21, 1842. Mr. Tait's grand-parents, John Tait, Robert Ormiston, and George Lockie were among the early settlers of the town of Rossie. The two former settling in Rossie in 1815 and the latter in 1819. John Tait and Robert Ormiston were among the founders of the First Presbyterian Church of Rossie. Mr. Tait is by occupation a tailor and is at present time proprietor and manager of the Tait Tailoring establishment. He was married in 1894 to Amelia Fuller Hodgkins. He has one son, Sterling Lockie Tait.

George L. Tait.

S. B. VanDuzee.

Stephen Brown VanDuzee, born in Hartford, Washington County, N. Y., 1809. His parents were James VanDuzee and Abigal Brown VanDuzee. He was educated in the common schools of Gouverneur, and married in 1837 to Ruby Hobart. Mr. VanDuzee came to Gouverneur in 1817 or 18 and resided here until his death in 1893. He was an active, enterprising business man, greatly interested in the growth of the town. Was one of the founders of the S. B. VanDuzee Manufacturing Co. Influential in the promotion of the talc industry in this vicinity. One of the founders of the Gouverneur Marble Co., of which he was at one time president. Held many prominent offices in town and was President of the village and also postmaster.

Harry C. VanAllen, born at Mountain, Ont., 1873. His parents were Wm. S. VanAllen, born in Mountain, Ont., 1834, and Jerusha Cassleman VanAllen, born in Morrisburg, Ont., 1839. Dr. VanAllen was educated at Morrisburg, Ont., and Penn. College of Dental Surgery, and was married in 1898 to Lottie B. Smyth. He has been a resident of Gouverneur for the past seven years, practicing his profession of Dental Surgeon. He is a member of Gouverneur Lodge, 325, I. O. O. F.

Harry C VanAllen.

Gilbert L. Van Namee.

Gilbert L. VanNamee, born Dec. 17, 1832. His parents were John VanNamee and Betsy Seaman, early settlers of the town. He was educated in Gouverneur Wesleyan Seminary. His first wife was Miss Freeman to whom were born two children, Rose and Winafred, both of whom live in Syracuse, N. Y. He again married May 15, 1866, to Miss Adella E. Spencer, daughter of Col. James M. Spencer and Carbadana Bullard, the latter now living. Mr. VanNamee taught school in this vicinity. In early life clerked in the store of Sterling & Cone. Was in 1861 in the hardware business where the Egbert Block now stands. Was in the Drug business from 1870 for many years. In 1877 he built the store in Main St. now occupied by the Kinney Drug Store. The last years of his life he was engaged in manufacturing. His death occurred Nov. 20, '02.

Cyrenus Vail, born in Chateaugay, Franklin Co., N. Y., Nov. 4, 1838. Mr. Vail came to Gouverneur when six years of age and lived upon a farm in North Gouverneur until 48 years of age. When a boy he helped to clear up a farm and planted corn among the stumps with an old ax. Cut wheat and rye with a sickle using the utmost care that not a head of grain should be lost. He remembers that the farmers drove through Main St. with their ox teams with the sand rolling up in a beautiful cloud. Mr. Vail, although a Democrat in the Republican town of Gouverneur, served for two terms as town assessor; two terms as commissioner of highways and was for nineteen years street commissioner of the village.

Cyrenus Vail.

William Whitney

William Whitney, born in Antwerp, 1838. His parents were Nathaniel Whitney, born in New Hampshire, 1786 and Clarisa Hurr Whitney, born in New Hampshire 1792. He was educated in the G. W. Seminary and married in 1861 to Rosetta A. Cushman. Mr. and Mrs. Whitney are the parents of Addis Merrill, now residing in Boston and Wilbur Burton, residing in Williamsport, Pa. Mr. Whitney was for 30 years a druggist in Gouverneur, having purchased the drug store of H. K. Spencer, pioneer druggist. He is now in the life insurance business. He resides on Gordon street. Mr. Whitney's father served in the War of 1812 under General Brown.

Orange Gersham Waldo, born in Sacketts Harbor, Nov. 6, 1823. His parents were Abithar Waldo born in Shaftsbury, Vt., Dec. 16, 1780, and Hannah Homan, born in L. I. Mr. Waldo was educated in South Champion, Jeff. Co., and married May 6, 1848, to Barbara Zoller. Mr. Waldo moved to Hammond when a young man, established himself in the harness business. Was post master, justice of the peace, and manager of telegraph office. In 1866 he moved to Gouverneur to educate his family, finding employment as agent on the R. W. & O. R. R. Three of his sons are following railroading at the present time. Later he entered into business for himself. For several years previous to his death, he was telegraph operator. In politics he was a

Orange G. Waldo.

Republican until some years before his death when he joined the Prohibition party. He was a man of clear and vigorous thought and respected by the entire community.

William Walker.

William Walker, Richville, N. Y., first saw the light of day in the year 1843. His father, Horatio Walker, who came from Massachusetts, was one of the early settlers of DeKalb. He married Miss Ruth Smith of DeKalb. The subject of our sketch followed farming until 1873. Since that time he has been in the mercantile business continuously. He served as postmaster for twelve years. In 1869, he was united in marriage to Miss Amelia E. Lynde and they have one adopted daughter, Miss Ada Lynde Walker. Mr. Walker is a Republican in politics and has always stood by his party. He is a member of Richville Lodge No. 633, F. & A. M. Through his upright and honorable method, he has gained the respect of the entire community.

Mrs. Ella Mae Parsons Wilbur, born in Gouverneur, 1875. Her parents were George S. Parsons, born in Gouverneur, 1843, and Martha S. Dodds Parsons, born in Gouverneur, 1851. She was educated in Gouverneur High School and graduated from Potsdam Normal School. She was married in 1895 to Hal A. Wilbur. Mr. and Mrs. Wilbur are the parents of Jessie, May and Exton Parsons Wilbur.

Mrs. E. M. P. Wilbur.

Allen Wight was born Nov. 14th, 1824. His father, John Wight, was born in Mass., in 1796. His mother, Laura Hodgkins, was born in Washington County, N. Y., in 1802. He

Allen Wight.

was first married to Lucy Geer in 1853. Second married to Mrs. Lucy Johnson Wight, 1859. He was sent to district school at Little York when six years old, having learned to spell words of one syllable and to make figures on a piece of red slate picked up in the fields. He attended summer school until 12 years old and only winter terms afterward until 17. He taught the winter school near the West Fowler Church when

Mrs. Lucy J. Wight.

19. He worked making friction matches two seasons. Taught the Island Branch School when 21 and the Little York summer school in 1847. In the fall of that year he packed his homespun clothes in a bundle and went on foot to Albany and entered the Normal School. A three years' course at that time consisted of eight classes. He entered the fifth class and kept ahead of his class during the half years' term. He came home as he went. He purchased Davies' text book on surveying and after spending three weeks reading it, purchased Asa L. Hazelton's compass and went to work. He has surveyed the larger share of Fowler and many lots and farms in 13 other towns. After teaching 9 more terms of district and select school, never receiving more than $26 per month and board himself, in 1856 he received the appointment to the office of school commissioner. He served four years and a half at a salary of $600 a year. At eighty-one years, Mr. Wight still carries the compass and field-book when called upon. His work as a surveyor was always characterized by careful accuracy in which every detail that might lead to errors was eliminated. He has followed a life of activity and usefulness, and early became a

disciple of vegetarianism which he has persisted in with almost constant regularity and to this he ascribes his present well-preserved vigor and health.

Esther A. Ware was born near Felts Mills, N. Y., July 31, 1831, the only daughter of Samuel and Mary Ware, natives of Franklin Co., Mass. Her great grand-father, Michael Ware, was a soldier under Gen. Lincoln in the Revolutionary War. She died April 14, 1896, soon after her husband, who died March 19, 1896, and their oldest son Frank C., died May 1 of the same year.

Richard Woodward, born in England, 1832. His parents were Joseph Woodward, born in England, 1780, and Ann Irvin Woodward, born in England in 1785. He was educated in the common schools or rather the Sunday schools which were all the schools that were free in England. He was married in 1856 to Caroline Coleman. They are the parents of Charles M., Ellen M. Love, Jane A. Burch, and Caroline A. Turner. Mr. Woodward landed in New York Nov. 1853. He enlisted in 1864 for the Civil War, Co. D., 186 N. Y. Infantry. Discharged June 1865. Has been overseer of the poor, assessor and supervisor of the town of Macomb, his post office address being at the latter place.

Richard Woodward.

Daniel J. Whitney, born in Canton, Feb. 15, 1848. In 1858 he moved to Ogdensburg with his parents, finishing his education at the Ogdensburg Academy. Commenced his business career as clerk in a wholesale and retail grocery store, devoting only part of his time to the duties, the balance he spent at school. In Oct., 1863, enlisted in Co. C., 24th N. Y. Vol. Cavalry. Was promoted to corporal, second and first sergeant of the company and later quartermaster sergeant of the regiment. Participated in nearly every battle of the Army of the Potomac, fought during 1864-5. He was wounded at Poplar Spring Church, Sept. 30, 1864; taken prisoner in the battle of Five Forks, March 1, 1865, being one of the prisoners turned over to Gen. Lee. Was mustered out and returned to Ogdensburg in August, 1865. Three or four weeks later, came to Gouverneur and commenced learning the trade of marble and stone cutting in his

Daniel J. Whitney.

father's works. Two years later became partner with his father and at the father's death in 1868, became sole proprietor. In 1870 he sold out to George Parker, acting as his foreman. In 1871 he was foreman of the stone cutters on the new capitol at Albany. He repurchased the Marble Works of Mr. Parker, in partnership with his brother Thomas J. Whitney. In 1876, Whitney Bros., together with Mr. Honeycomb, commenced first quarrying of Gouverneur Stone. Sold out retail business in 1878. Mr. Whitney has always been actively identified with some of the leading marble interests (see history of marble business). In 1897-8 he was in Canada developing marble quarries there. He is president of the Empire Marble Co. and D. J. Whitney Co., and has interest in other marble quarries. Mr. Whitney was married Dec. 2, 1866, to Augusta D. Ayres and they have four children, DeWitt C., Bertha A., Everett A., and Mildred E.

John J. Wallace, born in Halifax, N. S., April 20, 1866. His parents were Samuel James Wallace, born in Halifax, March 17, 1836, and Mary Brenen, born in Kilkenney, Ireland. He was educated in Halifax, N. S., and Nov. 15, 1893, married to Florence M. Howe. Mr. and Mrs. Wallace are the parents of Fay Marguritte. Mr. Wallace came to Fowler in 1883 and was employed by the Agalite Fiber Co. In 1885 he was employed by the St. Law. Pulp Co. and in 1889 became foreman of the St. Law. Pulp Co. and in 1892 superintendent. In 1893 he was foreman of the U. S. Talc Co. In 1895 became connected with the Columbian Talc Co. as superintendent. Had charge of the construction of their mill. He continued with the

Columbian Talc Co. until it was sold to the Union Talc Co. Of the latter company he was assistant superintendent until 1903, when he became superintendent. His post office is Fowler.

D. G. Wood.

Duncan G. Wood was born in Lower Canada, 1838. He was educated in Canada and married to Catherine r. Skinner. He was the father of Dorothea and Charles D. G. Came to Gouverneur in about 1861 and entered the employ of W. H. Bowne. Later he purchased an interest with Mr. Bowne, continuing the co-partnership for several years. Dissolved partnership with Mr. Bowne and bought one-half interest with J. E. McAllister. Mr. McAllister retired at the end of three years, selling out to J. A. Rutherford. The firm of Wood & Rutherford continued about six years. Mr. Wood then buying Mr. Rutherford's interest, and continuing the business alone until his death in 1891.

W. S. Woodcock, born in Edwards, in 1865. His parents were Jason Woodcock, born in Edwards and Margaret Cleland Woodcock born in Edwards. Mr. Woodcock was educated at Edwards and in 1887 married to Carrie Harmon. They are the parents of two children, Glenn and Lawrence. He is one of the firm of Woodcock Bros., lumber merchants and speculators at Edwards.

W. S. Woodcock.

Charles Williams, born in Franklin County, Mass., 1833. His parents were Henry Newton Williams, who came to St. Lawrence Co. in 1834. His mother was the daughter of Caleb

Charles Williams

Totman, who died in 1905, aged 94 years. Mr. Williams received his education in the public schools and G. W. Seminary. Taught school in Michigan, Wisconsin and New York in early life. He married Bethel Leonard in 1857. Spent his early married life on a farm in Hermon. Came to DeKalb in 1865 and in Nov., 1870, he purchased the lime works near Richville, which business he has continued until the present time. He sold one-half interest in the lime business in 1893 to the son of the late Manley E. Johnson. This partnership continued until the present time. Mr. Williams has been at the head of the lime business in this vicinity for thirty-four years, using from 1000 to 3000 cords of wood annually and employed from ten to fifteen men. Has never had a written contract nor law suit. Mr .Williams was a free soiler, voting for John C. Fremont in 1856. He was a Republican until 1884, since then he has voted the Prohibition ticket. He is identified with the Congregational Church, holding that every citizen should be identified with some religious works. His post office is Bigelow, N. Y.

Ellis Woodworth, born in Gouverneur, May 9, 1869. His parents were A. L. Woodworth, and Lydia E. Conger Woodworth. He was educated in G. W. Seminary and in 1899 was married to Bessie Haynes Smith, of Syracuse. Mr. and Mrs. Woodworth are the parents of Frances Woodworth, who was born Jan. 24, 1901. Mr. Woodworth was engaged in active newspaper work for a number of years in Gouverneur. For the past five years he has been in the wholesale paper business.

Chapman V. White, Richville, N. Y., son of Horace and Clarissa P. (Lake) White, was born at Richville in the year 1867. Was married to Miss Anna Shipper in 1888. They have two daughters, Carrie M. and Irene H. Mr. White takes great pride in his farm and everything pertaining to agriculture. He is a Mason of high standing, an Odd Fellow, Royal Forester, and a Maccabee. He was reared in the Democratic fold; but the gates were not high enough to hold him. He is a staunch believer in the Republican principle. His post office is Richville.

Donald H. Williams, born in Belleville, Jeff. Co., N. Y., 1863. His parents were Alexander H. Williams, born in Ontario and Mary A. McDonald Williams, born in Ontario. Mr. Williams was educated at Pulaski Academy, Pulaski, N. Y., and married in 1890 to Caroline McCarty. Mr. and Mrs. Williams are the parents of two children, Hazel E., and Donald A. Mr. Williams came to Gouverneur in 1893 and entered the employ of J. H. Carpenter in his hardware store. He continued with Mr. Carpenter for five years, then purchased the store and has continued its operation since.

Donald H. Williams.

Fred S. Walker, Richville, N. Y., was born in the year 1867. He is the son of Isaac and Emmeline (Spencer) Walker. He received his education in the Richville school. Was married to Miss Minnie B. Woodcock in 1893 and has one son Isaac. After leaving his father's farm he learned the tinsmith trade and conducted a shop here for a number of years. Nearly 2 years ago he started a hardware store in connection with his shop. He has the best equipped general hardware store in Northern New York. He is a member of the Masonic fraternity.

Fred S. Walker.

Milo E. Woodcock, born in Edwards in 1861. His parents are Jason Woodcock, born in Edwards and Margaret Cleland Woodcock, born in Edwards. He was married in 1882 to Cora Johnson. They are the parents of two children, Vane and Grace. Mr. Woodcock is a member of the firm of Woodcock Bros., lumber dealers. The firm of Woodcock Bros. is among the most prominent business institutions of Southern St. Law. Co., and have done much toward the development of the lumber industry in and about Edwards.

Milo E. Woodcock.

Byron U. Wight, born in Fowler, 1861. His parents were Andrew Wight, born in Fowler, 1833, and Agnes B. Whithead Wight, born in Edwards in 1838. He was educated in the public schools of Fowler and married in 1886 to Edna A. Barnes. Mr. and Mrs. Wight are the parents of Glen J., Daniel G., Hugh B., Ernest B. and Earl M.

Byron U. Wight.

James Harvey Winshoro, born in Edwards, 1834. His parents were Ormul Winshoro, born in Vermont, 1800, and Rhoda Banister Winsboro, born in Vermont, 1801. He was educated in Edwards and married in 1859 to Cornelia Rushton, to whom were born three children, Anna J., Nellie Betsy and Mary. Mr. Winsboro enlisted in 1861 at the first call for troops in the 16th Reg. N. Y. Infantry, in Capt. Parker's Co., for two years. Since receiving his discharge he has resided in Edwards where he is now a Justice of the Peace.

John Nelson Wainwright, born in Macomb, Jan. 5, 1848. His parents were Nathan Wainwright, born in England and Adeline Thornton Wainwright, born in Depeyster. He was ed-

ucated in Macomb and married Oct. 16, 1868, to Olive Haskins. Mr. Wainwright came to Gouverneur at the age of 18, working in the lumber mill at Natural Dam. Lived three years in Hailesboro, removed to Theresa, buying a farm. He was proprietor of a store in Philadelphia. Later ran a grocery store on Main St., in Gouverneur. In 1885 he bought the Somerville house which he ran for three years. He then bought the Norton place, West Main street, which he rebuilt into a hotel and operated until his death which occurred Aug. 20, 1904. Mr. Wainwright was the father of Luella May Barker, Louis Judson and Elmer John Wainwright.

John N. Wainwright.

Joseph A. Wooster, born in Redwig, 1852. His parents were Lawrence B. Wooster, born in Hammond, Dec. 13, 1827, and Sylvia Cowan, born in Hammond, 1830. Mr. Wooster was educated in Hammond and in 1885 married to Ella Millett, who was born in Gouverneur, 1862. Mr. Wooster learned the trade of painter and decorator. Served in the shops of the Union Pacific R. R. Co., at Omaha, Neb. Came to Gouverneur in 1882, where he has resided since.

Joseph A. Wooster.

Charles E. Webb, born in Edwards, 1866. His parents were R. Webb, born in Edwards, 1848 and Hattie Buck, born in Hermon, 1853. He was educated in Edwards and 1897 married to Carrie Masters. Mr. and Mrs. Webb are the parents of Gladdis Beulla.

John D. Ward, born in Ireland, 1853. His parents were Nathan Ward, born in Ireland, and Bridget Doyle, born in Ireland. He was educated in the common schools and married to Alice Cramer. Mr. Ward is a prosperous farmer, owning the farm and residence formerly owned and occupied by Philip and Archibald Kearney.

John D. Ward.

Joseph Warren West, born in Gouverneur in 1866. His parents were William West, born in Peterboro, near London, Eng., 1842, and Caroline Windborne West, born on Wolfe Island, Canada, 1841. He was educated in Gouverneur, and married in 1891 to Agnes L. Hall. They have three children, Helen C., Elva M. and Lyall F. Mr. West is a contractor and dealer in lumber and building material.

Edgar Howard Woodward, born in North Lawrence, 1858. His parents were Amasa Clark Woodward, born in Rutland, N. Y., Sept. 9, 1820, and Francina Howard Woodward, born in Bethel, Me., Aug. 8, 1824. The father of the subject of this sketch, Rev. A. C. Woodward, joined the Black River Methodist Conference in 1854, subsequently preaching in nearly every town in St. Lawrence Co. He was superannuated in 1844. He died in 1888. Edgar Howard Woodward married in 1884 Mrs. Amelia L. Kills. They are the parents of Jennie H., Clark B. and G. J. Woodward. His post office is Gouverneur.

James Harvey Winslow, of Edwards, was born in that town in 1834. In 1859 he married Cornelia Rushton, and the children of this union are named Anna J., Nellie Betsy, and Mary. Mr. Winslow comes of Vermont stock, his father, Oramel Winslow, being from that state as well as his mother, Rhoda Banister. He enlisted in 1861 under the first call for troops in the 16th Infantry and was a member of Capt. Parker's company. He was in the service two years. Has served his town as Justice of the Peace and is a man of character and excellent standing in his native town.

John Henry Wood was born in Rossie, N. Y., Sept. 12, 1852. His parents were Andrew Wood, born

James H. Winslow.

near Glasgow, Scotland, and Matilda Markwick, born in England. Both came to this country when quite young. Mr. Wood was married March 9, 1881, to Martha Eliza Comstock. He is a successful farmer residing in Gouverneur on the Johnstown road. Was in the War of the Rebellion, having enlisted from Hermon.

Nathan Hale was one of the early and desirable settlers in Gouverneur. He came from Herkimer, N. Y., in 1821, and located in the Scotch Settlement in 1833, taking a deed on the farm now occupied by Jesse Hill. His father was born in Rhode Island and came with Nathan from Herkimer. The family were closely

John H. Wood.

related to Capt. Bronson of the Revolution. He married Sarah Ann Sheppard of Herkimer. He left a family of six children as follows: Walter, Ruth Ann, Henry W., Isabel Jane, Louisa Elizabeth, and Sarah. A complete and very interesting history of Nathan Hale was supplied by his daughter Louisa, now Louisa Hale Parry, of Hunt, Livingston County, N. Y., but it was accidentally mislaid and destroyed, greatly to the regret of the author. He died in 1892, aged 85. He was a man of sterling character.

George D. Hazelton, was born in Fowler, N. Y., Dec. 1st, 1849. His parents were Thomas J. Hazelton, born in Fowler, Dec. 8, 1816, and Fanny Wight Hazelton, born in Fowler, Dec. 26, 1819. He was educated in the public schools of Fowler, at the Gouverneur Wesleyan Seminary, and Potsdam Normal School. Was married Nov. 6th, 1873, to Ellen H. Carr, who was born in Antwerp, Nov. 8th, 1850, and died Feb. 13, 1904. Mr. and Mrs. Hazelton were the parents of Dallas M., whose portrait appears among the attorneys of Gouverneur. Mr. Hazelton after marriage resided upon a farm in Fowler until 1893 when he removed to Gouverneur

Nathan Hale.

Thomas J Hazelton.

and engaged in the mercantile busi-

George D. Hazelton.

ness on West Main St., which he still continues. Was a member of the Board of Education 1898-9 and 1900. Was Village President 1900 and 1901. Mr. Hazelton is a staunch Democrat and has the respect of the entire community.

CONTENTS.

INDEX.

Lightning Source UK Ltd.
Milton Keynes UK
UKHW020029100223
416723UK00004B/82